HEBREW BIBLE: HISTORY OF INTERPRETATION

Foreword by
Walter Harrelson

Edited by
John H. Hayes

HEBREW BIBLE: HISTORY OF INTERPRETATION

Foreword by
Walter Harrelson

Excerpted from the
DICTIONARY OF BIBLICAL INTERPRETATION
Edited by John H. Hayes

ABINGDON PRESS
Nashville

HEBREW BIBLE: HISTORY OF INTERPRETATION

Copyright © 2004 by Abingdon Press.

Excerpted from the *Dictionary of Biblical Interpretation*,
edited by John H. Hayes, Abingdon Press, 1999.

This book is printed on acid-free paper

ISBN 0-687-036666

Cataloging-in-Publication Data is available from the Library of Congress.

Scripture quotations, unless otherwise indicated, are from the New Revised Standard
Version of the Bible, copyright © 1989 by the Division of Christian Education of the
National Council of the Churches of Christ in the United States of America.

The Hebraica® and Graeca® fonts used to print this work are available from
Linguist's Software, Inc., PO Box 580, Edmonds, WA 98020-0580
Tel (206) 775-1130.

04 05 06 07 08 09 10 11 12 13 — 10 9 8 7 6 5 4 3 2 1

MANUFACTURED IN THE UNITED STATES OF AMERICA

CONTENTS

General Articles

FOREWORD

One of the great strengths of the ground-breaking *Dictionary of Biblical Interpretation*, published by Abingdon Press in 1999, was its bringing together the fruits of both Jewish and Christian interpretation of the Bible. The *Dictionary* did so in three ways: by including biographical sketches of a large number of Jewish and Christian biblical scholars, by treating themes and movements important to both communities, and by tracing the history of both Jewish and Christian readings of each book of the Jewish and Christian Bibles. The Abingdon Press editors present here the history of how the thirty-nine books of the Old Testament have been interpreted. They add, for good measure, essays treating topics of particular importance in the history of interpretation: on the Pentateuch, or Torah (the first five books of the Bible), the Ten Commandments, Poetry, and the Prophets.

The two-volume work is bulky and expensive. This collection is designed for classroom use and as a supplement to introductions and handbooks on the Old Testament. Like its predecessors, *Methods of Biblical Interpretation* and *New Testament: History of Interpretation* (Abingdon, 2004), it should serve that purpose admirably. Serious students of the Bible have excellent guides for understanding the biblical books in their historical, social, and cultural contexts. They also have fresh studies of the Bible's literary structure and qualities and the impact of these upon contemporary ways of human and religious understanding. What is lacking is an extended and imaginative treatment of the ways in which the Bible has been read and understood from biblical times to today. This collection goes far toward providing just that need. Students in college and seminary classes will be able to place their own study of the Bible alongside the history of the Bible's interpretation for well over two millennia. Advanced biblical students and their professors will also find the volume of great help, I predict. Many of the greatest of biblical interpreters through the centuries gave scant attention to the insights and approaches of their early predecessors. Nineteenth century scholars dealt well with the eighteenth century and with aspects of Reformation and Counter-Reformation studies. Twentieth century scholars rarely gave major attention to research earlier than the nineteenth century. The widespread assumption was, one fears, that little was to be learned from earlier, "pre-critical" days.

The greatest strength of the essays presented here, in my judgment, is their inclusion of the history of Jewish exegesis. Some Christian scholars through the centuries knew and made significant use of Jewish studies of particular books of the Bible and Jewish methods of study and liturgical use of Scripture. The majority did not. Not until the twentieth century did widespread collaboration among Jewish and Christian scholars begin to flourish. Even in recent times, the (growing) number of Christian scholars who in their research have regularly drawn upon the history of Jewish interpretation of the Bible has been small indeed.

Biblical scholars have tended to leave the history of interpretation of the Bible to historians. The situation is changing, however, due in part to the recognition that the Bible itself contains a history of interpretation: later writers use and transform the events and themes of earlier traditions and writings. See, for example, how each of the essays that close the volume provides an extended history of intrabiblical interpretation ("intertextuality," as it has been called). That same process, of course, has continued throughout Jewish and Christian history.

The history of biblical interpretation today confronts an urgent challenge: is it possible for scholars to offer concrete and practical guidance to those members of religious communities who draw extraordinary and dangerous inferences and conclusions from their sacred texts? When biblical interpretations threaten the health, safety, and very life of human beings today, all possible resources need to be marshaled to combat such interpretations. One resource, surely, is better knowledge and understanding of the long history of how the Bible has been read, claimed for the life of faith, and interpreted by and for the intellectual leadership of a community and an age.

Another great advantage of the essays presented here is that they are done by specialists in the science and art of biblical study who also have a considerable mastery of the history of interpretation. No doubt, many of the essays required special studies in new fields on the part of the writers. As single entries in the Dictionary, they may not have received quite the attention of biblical specialists that they surely will receive in the present format. Here is a history of the interpretation of the entire Hebrew Bible, a history marked by controversy, conflict, and all too frequent violence. The biblical text is still treated in many religious communities as a divine gift that is exempt from critical study. This history of interpretation may not be able to loosen and enlarge that perspective, but who can say?

Today's interpreters continue to disagree on many points, but it is noteworthy that there is major agreement on many aspects of biblical interpretation by those who approach the Bible from quite different standpoints. This collection offers a rich insight into the varieties of biblical interpretation that have developed over the centuries. From earliest days, as these essays show, both Jewish and Christian interpretation of the Hebrew Scriptures has displayed that variety.

The collection presented here will, I predict, spur scholars and their graduate students to follow up many of the topics with their own research. As they do so, they will find much to help and guide them in other essays in the Dictionary from which the essays were taken. Of very great assistance in that connection will be the hundreds of biographical essays on biblical interpreters through the ages. Both historians and biblical scholars owe John Hayes and his colleagues a huge debt of gratitude for their fine work. Is another volume planned that will single out the major figures in biblical interpretation through the centuries?

Walter Harrelson
Vanderbilt University Divinity School, emeritus
Wake Forest University Divinity School, adjunct
May 2004

PUBLISHER'S FOREWORD

This volume collects the articles on the history of critical research for the individual books of the Hebrew Bible and some broad areas of Hebrew Bible study (The Decalogue, Deuteronomistic History, Pentateuchal Criticism, Poetry, Prophecy and Prophets) that originally appeared in the two-volume *Dictionary of Biblical Interpretation* (ed. J. Hayes, 1999) and is intended as a supplemental text for seminary and university classes on the Hebrew Bible or the history of biblical exegesis. It is also suitable for introductory level courses on biblical interpretation and for graduate students preparing for exams.

The emphasis throughout has been on the questions and issues posed by critical scholarship, from early Christian and medieval exegesis to Reformation interpretations, and into modern critical studies. The essays have not been altered except to correct misprints, correct and update the bibliographies, make minor grammatical corrections, and to adapt the abbreviations and other style matters to the *SBL Handbook of Style*.

ABBREVIATIONS

General

abr.	abridged	HB	Hebrew Bible
approx.	approximately	Heb.	Hebrew
Aram.	Aramaic	HT	Hebrew Translation
art(s).	article(s)	i.e.	*id est*, that is
aug.	augmented	ibid.	*ibidem*, in the same place
b.	born	ill.	illustration
B.C.E.	Before the Common Era	inc.	incomplete
bib.	biblical	into.	introduction
bk(s).	book(s)	J	Jahwist or Yahwist source (of the Pentateuch)
C.E.	Common Era		
c.	circa	Lat.	Latin
cent(s).	century(ies)	lit.	literally
cf.	compare	LT	Latin Translation
chap(s)	chapter(s)	LXX	Septuagint
comb.	combined	MS(S)	manuscript(s)
contr.	contributor	MT	Masoretic Text
corr.	corrected	NT	New Testament
D	Deuteronomist source (of the Pentateuch)	OG	Old Greek
		OL	Old Latin
d.	died	OT	Old Testament
dept.	department	P	Priestly source (of the Pentateuch)
dir.	director		
diss.	dissertation	par.	paragraph
Dtr	Deuteronomistic (history; writer)	pl.	plural
E	Elohist source (of the Pentateuch)	posth.	posthumous
ed(s).	editor(s)	pt(s).	part(s)
e.g.	*exempli gratia*, for example	pub.	published
Eng.	English	repr.	reprint
enl.	enlarged	repub.	republished
esp.	especially	rev. ed.	revised edition
est.	established	RGS	*Religionsgeschichtliche Schule*
et al.	*et alii*, and others	sec(s).	section(s)
etc.	*et cetera*, and the rest	supp.	Supplement
ET	English Translation	tr.	translator/translation
frg(s).	fragment(s)	trans.	transcribed
Ger.	German	Vg.	Vulgate
Gr.	Greek	v(v).	verse(s)
GT	German Translation	vol(s).	volume(s)

English Biblical Translations

ASV American Standard Version
CEV Contemporary English Version
KJV King James Version
NEB New English Bible
NIV New International Version
NJB New Jerusalem Bible
NRSV New Revised Standard Version
REB Revised English Bible
RSV Revised Standard Version
TEV Today's English Version (Good News Bible)

Books of the Bible
Hebrew Bible

Gen	Genesis	Song (Cant)	Song of Songs (Song of
Exod	Exodus		Solomon or Canticles)
Lev	Leviticus	Isa	Isaiah
Num	Numbers	Jer	Jeremiah
Deut	Deuteronomy	Lam	Lamentations
Josh	Joshua	Ezek	Ezekiel
Judg	Judges	Dan	Daniel
Ruth	Ruth	Hos	Hosea
1–2 Sam	1–2 Samuel	Joel	Joel
1–2 Kgdms	1–2 Kingdoms (LXX)	Amos	Amos
1–2 Kgs	1–2 Kings	Obad	Obadiah
3–4 Kgdms	3–4 Kingdoms (LXX)	Jonah	Jonah
1–2 Chr	1–2 Chronicles	Mic	Micah
Ezra	Ezra	Nah	Nahum
Neh	Nehemiah	Hab	Habakkuk
Esth	Esther	Zeph	Zephaniah
Job	Job	Hag	Haggai
Ps/Pss	Psalms	Zech	Zechariah
Prov	Proverbs	Mal	Malachi
Eccl (or Qoh)	Ecclesiastes (or Qoheleth)		

New Testament

Matt	Matthew	1–2 Thess	1–2 Thessalonians
Mark	Mark	1–2 Tim	1–2 Timothy
Luke	Luke	Titus	Titus
John	John	Phlm	Philemon
Acts	Acts	Heb	Hebrews
Rom	Romans	Jas	James
1–2 Cor	1–2 Corinthians	1–2 Pet	1–2 Peter
Gal	Galatians	1–2–3 John	1–2–3 John
Eph	Ephesians	Jude	Jude
Phil	Philippians	Rev	Revelation
Col	Colossians		

Apocrypha and Septuagint

Bar	Baruch		Jdt	Judith
Add Dan	Additions to Daniel		1–2 Macc	1–2 Maccabees
Pr Azar	Prayer of Azariah		3–4 Macc	3–4 Maccabees
Bel	Bel and the Dragon		Pr Man	Prayer of Manasseh
Sg Three	Song of the Three Young Men		Ps 151	Psalm 151
Sus	Susanna		Sir	Sirach/Ecclesiasticus
1–2 Esd	1–2 Esdras		Tob	Tobit
Add Esth	Additions to Esther		Wis	Wisdom of Solomon
Ep Jer	Epistle of Jeremiah			

Rabbinic Texts

Tractates are identified by the following abbreviations:

b.	Babyonian Talmud
bar.	baraita
m.	Mishnah
t.	Tosefta
y.	Jerusalem Talmud

ʿAbod. Zar.	ʿAbodah Zarah		Meg.	Megillah
ʾAbot	ʾAbot		Meʿil.	Meʿilah
ʿArak.	ʿArakin		Menaḥ.	Menaḥot
B. Bat.	Baba Batra		Mid.	Middot
B. Meṣiʿa	Baba Meṣiʿa		Miqw.	Miqwaʾot
B. Qam.	Baba Qamma		Moʿed	Moʿed
Bek.	Bekorot		Moʿed Qaṭ	Moʿed Qaṭan
Ber.	Berakot		Nas.	Našim
Beṣah	Beṣah (=Yom Tob)		Naz.	Nazir
Bik.	Bikkurim		Ned.	Nedarim
Demai	Demai		Neg.	Negaʿim
ʿErub.	ʿErubin		Nez.	Neziqin
ʿEd.	ʿEduyyot		Nid.	Niddah
Giṭ.	Giṭṭin		ʾOhal.	ʾOhalot
Ḥag.	Ḥagigah		ʾOr.	ʾOrlah
Ḥal.	Ḥallah		Parah	Parah
Hor.	Horayot		Peʾah	Peʾah
Ḥul.	Ḥullin		Pesaḥ.	Pesaḥim
Kelim	Kelim		Qinnim	Qinnim
Ker.	Kerithot		Qidd.	Qiddušin
Ketub.	Ketubbot		Qod.	Qodašim
Kil.	Kilʾayim		Ros Has.	Ros Haššanah
Maʿaś. Š	Maʿaśer Šeni		Sanh.	Sanhedrin
Maʿaś.	Maʿaśerot		Šabb.	Šabbat
Mak.	Makkot		Šeb.	Šebiʿit
Makš.	Makširin		Šebu.	Šebuʿot

Seder	Seder		T. Yom	Ṭebul Yom
Seqal	Seqalim		ʿUq.	ʿUqṣin
Soṭah	Soṭah		Yad.	Yadayim
Sukkah	Sukkah		Yeban.	Yebamot
Taʿan.	Tanʿanit		Yoma	Yoma (= Kippurim)
Tamid	Tamid		Zabim	Zabim
Tem.	Temusah		Zebah	Zebahim
Ter.	Terumot		Zera.	Zeraʿim
Ṭehar.	Ṭeharot			

Additional Rabbinic Works

ʾAbot R. Nat.	ʾAbot de Rabbi Nathan
ʾAg. Ber	ʾAggadat Berešit
Bab.	Babylonian
Der. Er. Rab.	Derek Ereṣ Rabba
Der Er Zuṭ.	Derek Ereṣ Zuṭa
Gem.	Gemara
Mek.	Mekilta
MHG Shem.	Midrash HaGadol Shemot
Midr.	Midraš (cited with abbreviation for biblical book)
Pal.	Palestinian
Pesiq. R.	Pesiqta Rabbati
Pesiq. Rab Kah.	Pesiqta de Rab Kahana
Pirqe R. El	Pirqe Rabbi Eliezer
Rab.	Rabbah (following abbreviation for biblical book)
Ṣem.	Ṣemahot
Sipra	Sipra
Sipre	Sipre
Sop.	Soperim
S. ʿOlam Rab.	Seder ʿOlam Rabbah
Tan. Shem.	Tanchuma Shemot
Talm.	Talmud
Yal.	Yalquṭ

Periodicals, Reference Works, and Serials
(in alphabetical order, by abbr.)

AASF	Annales Academiae Scientiarum Fennicae
ACEBT	*Amsterdamse Cahiers voor Exegese en Bijbelse Theologie*
ACEBTSup	Amsterdamse Cahiers voor Exegese en Bijbelse Theologie Supplement Series
ASOR	American Schools of Oriental Research
ASSOR	Annual of the American Schools of Oriental Research
AB	Anchor Bible
ABAW	Abhandlungen der Bayrischen Akademie der Wissenschaften
AbB	*Altbaylonische Briefe in Umschrift und Übersetzung. Edited* by F.R. Kraus. Leiden, 1964—
ABD	*Anchor Bible Dictionary.* Edited by D.N. Freedman. 6 vols. New York, 1992.
AbenR	*American Benedictine Review*

ABRL	Anchor Bible Reference Library
ACEBT	Amsterdamse cahiers voor exegese en bijbelse theologie
ACW	Ancient Christian Writers, 1946-
AES	*Archives européenes de sociologie*
AGJU	Arbeiten zur Geschichte des antiken Judentums und des Urchristentums
AJSL	*American Journal of Semitic Languages and Literature*
AJT	*Asian Journal of Theology*
AnBib	Analecta biblica
ANCL	Ante-Nicene Christian Library
ANF	Ante-Nicene Fathers
ANGr	
ANRW	*Aufstieg und Niedergang der römischen Welt*
AOAT	Alter Orient und Altes Testament
APOT	R.H. Charles (ed.), *Apocrypha and Pseudepigrapha of the OT* (2 vols., 1913)
ArBib	Aramaic Bible
ASNU	Acta seminarii neotestamentici upsaliensis
ASTI	*Annual of the Swedish Theological Institute*
ATANT	Abhandlungen zur Theologie des Alten und Neuen Testaments
ATA	Alttestamentliche Abhandlungen
ATD	Das Alte Testament Deutsch
ATLA	American Theological Library Association
ATR	*Australasian Theological Review*
ATSAT	Arbeiten zu Text und Sprache im Alten Testament
BA	*Biblical Archaeologist*
BASOR	*Bulletin of the American Schools for Oriental Research*
BBB	Bulletin de bibliographie biblique
BBB	Bonner biblische Beiträge
BBET	Beiträge zur biblischen Exegese und Theologie
BEATAJ	Beiträge zur Erforschung des Alten Testaments und des antiken Judentum
BeO	*Bibbia e oriente*
BETL	Bibliotheca ephemeridum theologicarum lovaniensium
BEvT	Beiträge zur evangelischen Theologie
BFCT	Beiträge zur Förderung chrislicher Theologic
BGBE	Beiträge zur Geschichte der biblischen Exegese
BGPTM	Beiträge zur Geschichte der Philosophie (und Theologie) des Mittelalters
BHS	*Biblica hebraica stuttgartensia*
BHT	Beiträge zur historischen Theologie
Bib	*Biblica*
BiBh	*Bible Bhashyam*
BibInt	*Biblical Interpretation*
BibOr	Biblica et orientalia
Bijdr	*Bijdragen: Tijdschrift voor filosofie theologie*
BiSe	The Biblical Seminar
BIS	Biblical Interpretation Series
BJRL	*Bulletin of the John Rylands University Library of Manchester*
BJS	Brown Judaic Studies
BJuS	Biblical and Judaic Studies
BK	*Bibel und Kirche*
BKAT	Biblischer Kommentar, Altes Testament. Edited by M. Noth and H. W. Wolff

BN	Biblische Notizen
BNB	Biblische Notizen Beiheft
BO	*Bibliotheca orientalis*
BOT	Boeken van het Oude Testament
BPC	*Biblical Perspectives on Current Issues*
BR	*Biblical Research*
BSac	*Bibliotheca sacra*
BSNA	Biblical Scholarship in North America
BT	*Bible Translator*
BTAVO	Beihefte zum Tübinger Atlas des Vorderen Orients
BTB	*Biblical Theology Bulletin*
BTZ	*Berliner Theologische Zeitschrift*
BWANT	Beiträge zur Wissenschaft vom Alten (und Neuen) Testament
BZ	*Biblische Zeitschrift*
BZAW	Beihefte zur Zeitschrift für die alttestamentliche Wissenschaft
BZNW	Beihefte zur Zeitschrift für die neutestamentliche Wissenschaft
CAT	Commentaire de l'Ancien Testament
CBC	Cambridege Bible Commentary
CBET	Contributions to Biblical Exegesis and Theology
CBQ	*Catholic Biblical Quarterly*
CBQMS	Catholic Biblical Quarterly Monograph Series
CBSC	Cambridge Bible for School and Colleges
CCARJ	*Central Conference of American Rabbis. Journal*
CCCM	Corpus Christianiorum, Continuatio Mediaevalis
CCSL	Corpus Christianiorum, Series Latina
CH	*Cahiers d'histoire*
CHB	P. R. Ackroyd et al. (eds.), *Cambridge History of the Bible* (3 vols., 1985-87)
Ching Feng	*Ching Feng*
ChrCent	*Christian Century*
ChW	*Cristliche Welt*
CJT	*Canadian Journal of Theology*
ConBOT	Coniectanea biblica: Old Testament Series
ConJ	*Concordia Journal*
ConNT	Coniectanea neotestamentica
COT	Commentaar op het Oude Testament
CRB	Cahiers de la Revue biblique
CurBS	*Currents in Research : Biblical Studies*
CRSS	Classics in Religious Studies
CSEL	Corpus scriptorum ecclesiasticorum latinorum
CTP	Cadernos de teologia e pastoral
CTM	*Concordia Theological Monthly*
CWS	Classics of Western Spirituality. New York, 1978-
DACL	*Dictionnaire d'archéologie chrétienne et de liturgie*
DB	*Dictionnaire de la Bible.* Edited by F. Vigouroux. 5 vols. 1895-1912
DBSup	*Dictionnaire de la Bible: Supplément.* Edited by L. Pirot and A. Robert. Paris, 1907-1953
DJD	Discoveries in the Judean Desert
DMA	J. R. Strayer (ed.), *Dictionary of the Middle Ages* (13 vols. 1982-89)
DS	Dictionare de Spiritualité

EAJJ	*East Asia Journal of Theology*
EB	Echter Bibel
EBib	*Etudes bibliques*
EdF	Erträge und Forschung
EHAT	Exegetisches Handbuch zum Alten Testament
EHPhR	Études d'histoire et de philosophie religieuses
EHS.T	Europäische Hochschulschriften. Reihe 23. Theologie
EM	Emerita. Madrid
EMMÖ	Erlanger Monographien aus Mission und Ökumene
EncBrit	*Encyclopedia Brittanica*
EncJud	*Encyclopaedia Judaica*
EncReal	M. Eliade (ed.), *The Encyclopedia of Religion* (16 vols. 1987)
EQ	Evangelical Quarterly
EstBib	Estudios bíblicos
EncBrit	Encyclopedia Britannica
ErFor	Erträge der Forschung
ErIsr	Eretz-Israel: Archaeological, Historical, and Geographical Studies
EstTeo	Estudios teológicos
ETL	Ephemerides theologicae lovanieses
EvErz	Der evangelischer Erzieher
EvT	Evangelische Theologie
ExpB	Expositor's Bible
Exp Tim	Expository Times
FAT	Forshungen zum Alten Testament
FBBS	Facet Books, Biblical Series
FC	Fathers of the Church
FCB	Feminist Companion to the Bible
FOTL	Forms of the Old Testament Literature
FRLANT	Forschungen zur Religion und Literatur des Alten und Neuen Testaments
GBS	Guides to Biblical Scholarship
GCS	Griechischen christlichen Schriftsteller
GOTR	Greek Orthodox Theological Review
GRLH	Garland Reference Library of the Humanities
GTA	Göttinger theologische Arbeiten
GTS	Gettysburg Theological Studies
HAT	Handbuch zum Alten Testament
HBC	J.L. Mays et al. (eds.), *Harper's Bible Commentary* (1988)
HBT	Horizons in Biblical Theology
HJPAJC	*E. Schürer,* History of the Jewish People in the Age of Jesus Christ *(3 vols., rev. G. Vermes et al., 1973-87).*
HKAT	*Handkommentar zum Alten Testament*
HKNT	*Handkommentar zum Neuen Testament*
HNT	Handbuch zum Neuen Testament
HRWG	Handbuch religionswissenschaftlicher Grundbegriffe
HS	Historische Studien
HSAT	Die Heilige Schrift des Alten Testaments (ed. H. Herkenne and F. Feldmann)
HSAT (K)	Die Heilige Schrift des Alten Testaments (ed. E. Kautzsch)
HSM	Harvard Semitic Monographs
HTR	Harvard Theological Review

HUCA	*Hebrew Union College Annual*
HUCM	Monographs of the Hebrew Union College
HvTSt	*Hervormde teologiese studies*
IB	*Interpreter's Bible*
IBC	Interpretation: A Bible Commentary for Teaching and Preaching
ICC	International Critical Commentary
IDB	*The Interpreter's Dictionary of the Bible*. Edited by G. A. Buttrick. 4 vols. Nashville, 1962
IDBSup	*Interpreter's Dictionary of the Bible: Supplementary Volume*. Edited by K. Crim. Nashville, 1976
Int	Interpretation
IRT	Issues in Religion and Theology
IRM	*International Review of Missions*
ISBL	Indiana Studies in Biblical Literature
ITC	International Theological Commentary
IThS	Innsbrücker Theologische Studien
JAAR	*Journal of the American Academy of Religion*
JAF	*Journal of American Folklore*
JANESCU	*Journal of the Ancient Near Eastern Society of Columbia University*
JAOS	*Journal of the American Oriental Society*
JBL	*Journal of Biblical Literature*
JBLMS	Journal of Biblical Literature Monograph Series
JBQ	*Jewish Biblical Quarterly*
JBR	*Journal of Bible and Religion*
JBS	*Journal of British Studies*
JDTh	*Jahrbücher der biblischen Wissenschaft*
JE	*The Jewish Encyclopedia*
JECS	*Journal of Early Christian Studies*
Jeev	*Jeevadhara*
JFSR	*Journal of Feminist Studies in Religion*
JH/LT	*Journal of Hispanic/Latino Theology*
Jian Dao	Jian Dao
JITC	*Journal of the Interdenominational Theological Center*
JJS	*Journal of Jewish Studies*
JNSL	*Journal of Northwest Semitic Languages*
JOTT	Journal of Translation and Textlinguistices
JPS	Jewish Publication Society
JPT	*Jahrbücher für protestantische Theologie*
JQR	*Jewish Quarterly Review*
JR	*Journal of Religion*
JRAS	*Journal of the Royal Asiatic Society*
JRT	*Journal of Religious Thought*
JSJ	*Journal for the Study of Judaism in the Persian, Hellenistic, and Roman Period*
JSJSup	Journal for the Study of Judaism in the Persian, Hellenistic, and Roman Period, Supplment.
JSNTSup	Journal for the Study of the New Testament: Supplement Series
JSOT	*Journal for the Study of the Old Testament*
JSOTSup	Journal for the Study of the Old Testament. Supplement Series
JSP	*Journal for the Study of the Pseudepigrapha*

JSPSup	Journal for the Study of the Pseudepigrapha. Supplement
JSS	*Journal of Semitic Studies*
JTC	*Journal for Theology and the Church*
JTL	*Journal für theologische Literatur*
JTS	*Journal of Theological Studies*
JTSA	*Journal of Theology for Southern Africa*
JZWL	*Jüdische Zeitschrift für Wissenschaft und Leben*
KAT	Kommentar zum Alten Testament
KD	Kerygma und Dogma
KEH	Kurzfasstes exegetisches Handbuch zum Alten Testament
KHC	Kurzer Hand-Kommentar zum Alten Testament
KK	Kurzgefasster Kommentar zu den heiligen Schriften Alten und Neuen Testaments
LCC	Library of Christian Classics
LCL	Loeb Classical Library
LD	Lectio divina
LEC	Library of Early Christianity
LTK	*Lexicon für Theologie und Kirche*
LW	J. Pelikan and H.T. Lehman (eds.), *Luther's Works*
MDB	*Mercer Dictionary of the Bible*
MGWJ	*Monatsschrift für Geschichte und Wissenschaft des Judentums*
MPIL	Monographs of the Peshitta Institute Leiden
MSU	Mitteilungen des Septuaginta-Unternehmens
MThZ	*Münchener theologische Zeitschrift*
MTZ	*Münchener theologische Zeitschrift*
NBf	*New Blackfrairs*
NCB	New Century Bible
NCBC	New Century Bible Commentary
NCE	*New Catholic Encyclopedia*
NDIEC	*New Documents Illustrating Early Christianity*
NEB	Die Neue Echter Bibel
NEB.AT	Neue Echter Bibel. Kommentar zum AT
NIB	New Interpreter's Bible
NICOT	New International Commentary on the Old Testament
NISB	*New Interpreter's Study Bible*
NJBC	*The New Jerome Bible Commentary.* Edited by R. E. Brown et al. Englewood Cliffs, 1990
NKZ	Neue kirchliche Zeitschrift
NPNF	*Nicene and Post-Nicene Fathers*
NovT	*Novum Testamentum*
NovTSup	Novum Testamentum Supplements
NovTSup	Supplements to Novum Testamentum
NRTh	La nouvelle revue théologique
NTAbh	Neutestamentliche Abhandlungen
NTAbhNF	Neutestamentliche Abhandlungen Neue Forschung
NTOA	Novum Testamentum et Orbis Antiquus
NTS	*New Testament Studies*
NTTS	New Testament Tools and Studies
NZM	*Neue Zeitschrift für Missionswissenschaft*
OBO	Orbis biblicus et orientalis

ÖBS	Österreichische biblische Studien
OBT	Overtures to Biblical Theology
OLA	*Orientalia lovaniensia anelecta*
OLZ	*Orientalistische Literaturzeitung*
OTG	Old Testament Guides
OTL	Old Testament Library
OTM	Oxford Theological Monographs
OTP	J.H. Charlesworth (ed.), *The Old Testament Pseudepigrapha* (2 vols. 1983)
OTS	Old Testament Studies
PAAJR	Proceedings of the American Academy of Jewish Research
PEQ	*Palestine Exploration Quarterly*
PerTeol	*Perspectiva teológica*
PIBA	*Proceedings of the Irish Biblical Association*
PJ	*Palästina-Jahrbuch*
PL	J. Migne, Patrologia latina (21 vols.; 1844-64)
PMS	Publications in Medieval Studies
ProEccl	Pro Ecclesia
Proof	*Prooftexts: A Journal of Jewish Literary History*
PRSt	*Perspectives in Religious Studies*
PTS	Patristische Texte und Studien
PW	Pauly, A. F. *Paulys Realencyclopädie der classischen Altertumswissenschaft.* New Edition G. Wissowa. 49 vols. Munich, 1980.
QD	Quaestiones disputatae
RAC	*Reallexikon für Antike und Christentum*
RB	*Revue biblique*
RCB	*Revista de cultura bíblica*
REB	*Revista eclesiástica brasileira*
RelLife	*Religion in Life*
RelSoc	*Religion and Society*
RelSRev	*Religious Studies Review*
RevistB	*Revista bíblica*
RevQ	*Revue de Qumran*
RGG	*Religion in Geschichte und Gegenwart*
RHA	*Revue hittite et asianique*
RHPR	*Revue d'historie et de philosophie religieuses*
RivB	*Rivista biblica*
RMT	Readings in Moral Theology
RSR	*Recherches de science religieuse*
RStR	*Religious Studies Review*
RTAM	*Recherches de théologie ancienne et médievale*
SAC	Studies in Antiquity and Christianity
SBAW	*Sitzungsberichte der bayerischen Akademie der Wissenschaften*
SBS	Stuttgarter Bibelstudien
SBL	Society of Biblical Literature
SBLDS	SBL Dissertation Series
SBLBMI	SBL Bible and its Modern Interpreters
SBLBSNA	SBL Biblical Scholarship in North America
SBLMS	SBL Monograph Series
SBLSBS	*SBL Sources for Biblical Study*

SBLSP	*SBL Seminar Papers*
SBLSCS	SBL Septuagint and Cognate Studies
SBLSP	SBL Seminar Papers
SBLSS	SBL Semeia Studies
SBLSymS	SBL Symposium Series
SBM	Stuttgarter biblische Monographien
SBS	Stuttgarter Bibelstudien
SBT	Studies in Biblical Theology
SC	Sources chrétiennes. Paris: Cerf, 1943-
ScEs	*Science et esprit*
SCJ	Sixteenth –century Journal
Scr	*Scripture*
ScrTh	*Scripta theologica*
ScrHier	Scripta hierosolymitana
SCS	Studies of Church and State
SEAJT	*South-east Asia Journal of Theology*
Semeia	*Semeia*
SemSup	Semeia Supplements
SemeiaSt	Semeia Studies
SFSHJ	South Florida Studies in the History of Judaism
SHANE	Studies in the History of the Ancient Near East
SJCA	Studies in Judaism and Christianity in Antiquity
SJLA	Studies in Judaism in Late Antiquity
SJOT	*Scandinavian Journal of the Old Testament*
SJT	*Scottish Journal of Theology*
SMRT	Studies in Medieval and Reformation Thought
SNTSMS	Society for New Testament Studies Monograph Series
Sobornost	*Sobornost*
SOTI	Studies in Old Testament Interpretation
SPAW	Singungsberichte der preussischen Akademie der Wissenschaften
SPB	Studia postbiblica
SR	*Studie in Religion/Sciences religieuses*
SSN	Studia semitica neerlandica
StPhilo	*Studia Philonica*
STDJ	Studies on the Texts of the Desert of Judah
StPtr	*Studia patristica*
StTh	*Studie theologica*
SubBib	*Subsidia biblica*
SUVK	Videnskapsselskapets skrifter
SVTQ	*St. Vladimir's Theological Quarterly*
SWBA	Social World of Biblical Antiquity
TB	Theologische Bücherei: Neudrucke und Beritche aus dem 20. Jahrhundert
TH	Theologie historique
ThBer	*Theologische Berichte*
TBl	*Theologische Blätter*
TBT	*The Bible Today*
TDNT	*Theological Dictionary of the New Testament*
TEH	Theologische Existenz heute
Text	*Textus*

ThA	Theologische Arbeiten
ThSt	Theologische Studiën
ThT	*Theologisiche tidschrift*
TJ	*Trinity Journal*
TLZ	*Theologische Literaturzeitung*
TOTC	Tyndale Old Testament Commentaries
TQ	*Theologische Quartalschrift*
TRE	*Theologische Reakenzyklopädie*. Edited by G. Krause and G. Müller. Berlin, 1977–
TRu	Theologische Rundschau
Tru NF	Theologische Rundshau, Neue Folge
TSJTSA	*Texts and Studies of the Jewish Theological Seminary of America*
TSAJ	*Texte und Studien zum antiken Judentum*
TSK	*Theologische Studien und Kritiken*
TU	Texte und Untersuchungen
TUGAL	Texte und Untersuchungen zur Geschichte der altchristlichen Literatur
TUMSR	Trinity University Monograph Series in Religion
TynBul	Tyndale Bulletin
TynNTL	Tyndale New Testament Lecture
UBL	Ugaritisch-biblische Literatur
UF	*Ugarit-Forschungen*
UCOP	University of Cambridge. Oriental Publications
USQR	*Union Seminary Quarterly Review*
VF	*Verkündigung und Forschung*
Vid	*Vidyajyoti*
VSAT	Verbum Salutis, Ancien Testament
VT	*Vetus Testamentum*
VTSup	Supplements to Vetus Testamentum
WA	M. Luther, Kritische Gesamtausgabe (= "Weimar" edition)
WBC	Word Biblical Commentary
WdF	Wege der Forschung
WMANT	Wissenschaftliche Monographien zum Alten und Neuen
WUNT	Wissenschaftliche Untersuchungen zum Neuen Testament Testament
WiWei	*Wissenschaft und Weisheit*
YJS	Yale Judaica Series
YNER	Yale Near Eastern Researches
ZAW	*Zeitschrift für die alttestamentliche Wissenschaft*
ZDPV	*Zeitschrift des deutschen Pälastina-Vereins*
ZNW	*Zeitschrift für die neutestamentliche Wissenschaft*
ZRGG	*Zeitschrift für Religions- und Geistesgeschichte*
ZS	*Zeitschrift für Semetistik und verwandte Gebiete*
ZTK	*Zeitschrift für Theologie und Kirche*
ZWT (NF?)	*Zeitschrift für wissenschaftliche Theologie*

CONTRIBUTORS

A. G. Auld
University of Edinburgh
Edinburgh, Scotland

T. K. Beal
Eckerd College
St. Petersburg, Florida

D. R. G. Beattie
The Queen's University of Belfast
Belfast, Northern Ireland

C. T. Begg
The Catholic University of America
Washington, DC

E. Ben Zvi
University of Alberta
Edmonton, Alberta
Canada

A. Berlin
University of Maryland
College Park, Maryland

D. L. Christenson
William Carey International University
Pasadena, California

J. H. Eaton
University of Birmingham
Birmingham, England

M. V. Fox
University of Wisconsin
Madison, Wisconsin

J. G. Galambush
College of William and Mary
Williamsburg, Virginia

R. E. Gane
Seventh-Day Adventist Theological
   Seminary
Andrews College
Berrien Springs, Michigan

M. P. Graham
Pitts Theological Library
Emory University
Atlanta, Georgia

D. M. Gunn
Texas Christian University
Fort Worth, Texas

W. C. Gwaltney, Jr.
Milligan College
Johnson City, Tennessee

J. Hahn
Plochingen, Germany

J. H. Hayes
Candler School of Theology
Emory University
Atlanta, Georgia

C. Houtman
Vrije Universiteit Amsterdam
Amsterdam, Netherlands

S. Japhet
Hebrew University
Jerusalem, israel

R. W. Klein
Lutheran School of Theology
Chicago, Illinois

P. G. Kuntz
Emory University
Atlanta, Georgia

S. D. McBride
Union Theological Seminary and
  Presbyterian School of Christian
  Education
Richmond, Virginia

W. McKane
St. Mary's College
St. Andrew's, Fife, Scotland

J. Magonet
Leo Baeck College
Sternberg Center for Judaism
London, England

R. R. Marrs
Pepperdine University
Malibu, California

E. A. Matter
University of Pennsylvania
Philadelphia, Pennsylvania

A. D. H. Mayes
Trinity College
University of Dublin
Dublin, Ireland

C. A. Moore
Gettysburg College
Gettysburg, Pennsylvania

H. D. Neef
Eberhard-Karls-Universität Tübingen
Tübingen, Germany

C. A. Newsom
Candler School of Theology
Emory University
Atlanta, Georgia

J. M. O'Brien
Lancaster Theological Seminary
Lancaster, Pennsylvania

W. G. Plaut
Holy Blossom Temple
Toronto, Ontario
Canada

S. N. Rosenbaum
Dickenson College
Carlisle, Pennsylvania

M. Saebø
Norway Lutheran School of Theology
Sandvika, Norway

J. F. A. Sawyer
The University of Newcastle upon Tyne
Newcastle upon Tyne, England

S. E. Schreiner
The Divinity School
University of Chicago
Chicago, Illinois

M. E. Shields
Drury College
Springfield, Missouri

A. Siedlecki
Glaslyn, Saskatchewan
Canada

W. S. Towner
Union Theological Seminary and
  Presbyterian School of Christian
  Education
Richmond, Virginia

R. W. Whybray (deceased)
University of Hull
Hull, England

H. G. M. Williamson
Christ Church
University of Oxford
Oxford, England

J. T. Willis
Abilene Christian University
Abilene, Texas

THE PENTATEUCH

Genesis

1. *Poetry, Drama, Novels.* The earliest interpretations of Genesis are found in the biblical Canon itself. Thus Psalms 33 and 136 are poetic retellings of the story of creation; Job 40:15 begins a long paean that serves as a poetic homily on Gen 1:21; and Isa 54:9-10 evokes the image of the rainbow covenant (Gen 8:21-22). This tradition had its successors in Jewish as well as Christian liturgies and has inspired poetry across the centuries, of which J. Milton's *Paradise Lost* (1667) has become the most widely read. In the twentieth century biblical poetry was spurred by A. Klein and flowered in Hebrew writing. It has had echoes in medieval miracle plays and such modern dramas as Beer-Hoffmann's Jacob, reaching its apex in T. Mann's Jacob-and-Joseph cycle (*Joseph und seine Brüder* = *Joseph and His* Brothers, 1934), which has been called "the most profound treatment of this biblical theme in literature" (S. Liptzin, *EncJud* 11 [1971] 883).

While all of these are interpretations of Genesis themes and evoke them vividly, they develop them independently in their own modes. This is the function of fiction, poetry, and liturgy; but this very function also removes them from our specific focus, which is the elucidation of the sacred text, its history and setting.

2. Translations. This exclusion applies also to the translations of Genesis that have appeared over the past two millennia and more. To be sure, every Translation is a form of commentary; and more often than not it has been through the medium of translation that the text has had its greatest impact. But intelligibility rather than interpretation is the primary purpose of most translations. Thus the Septuagint holds comment to a minimum, as does the Aramaic version of *Tg. Onkelos*, although the latter eschews all anthropomorphisms and uses euphemisms when a sense of propriety calls for them. The Palestinian Targumim indulge frequently in homiletical expansions of the text and for this purpose freely employ midrashic materials. Tg. Jonathan, for instance, explains the plural verb form describing God's activity in Gen 1:26 (*wayyō 'mer 'elō hîm na 'ăseh 'ādām*, literally, "And God said 'Let *us* make *'ādām*' ") *by* expanding it into: "God said *to the angels who ministered to him*, 'Let us make *'ādām*.' " In rendering the next verse it adds that God created *'ādām* with 248 members and 365 nerves, then overlaid them with skin, which God filled with flesh and blood. *Tg. Yerušalmi* also takes liberties with the biblical text and enlarges Gen 1:27 philosophically by saying that it was the Word of God that created *'ādām*.

Other translations, especially the Vulgate, the Douay, the KJV, and the Luther Bibles, have by their very impact on language shaped the understanding of the text. A small example: Genesis 3 leaves the nature of the fruit that Adam and Eve ate unspecified, and the rabbis speculated that it might have been the grape. But because the Latin *malum* can mean either "apple" or "evil," the notion arose that the fatal fruit had been an apple.

3. *Quran.* Islam, although using many Genesis tales and images, did not incorporate the Torah as such into its faith structure and, therefore, did not claim to interpret the biblical text, as did Jewish and Christian traditions. Rather, the biblical text was reshaped in the Quran (see Quranic and Islamic Interpretation) and supplanted by it, thereby removing it from our purview of biblical interpretations.

4. Early Interpretations. Along with the written text went an oral tradition that preceded the written collections found in Mishnah, Talmud, and the many midrashic compendia. While there were relatively few occasions for halakhic starting points in Genesis (among the exceptions were Gen 1:28 [see *m. Yebam.* 6:6] and 32:33) the book engendered an enormous amount of aggadic comment.

a. *'Aggadah*. This *'ăggādâ* is distinguished by a unique approach to the Torah text that stretches the basic principles of Hermeneutics by a free-flowing, imaginative approach to religious questions in the widest sense. It makes its points by treating God at the same time in the most respectful and yet familiar way; it takes the text seriously but not literally; and it freely invents divine and human discourses and actions—all for the purpose of finding deeper meaning in the Word of God. This led later on to the habit of exploring the text in four different ways: through *pĕšaṭ*, plain meaning; *remez*, allusive meaning; *dĕraš*, homily; and *ṣôd*, hidden meaning. The first letters of these four methods spell *pardes,* which in the oral tradition stood for the garden containing the tree of knowledge from which Adam and Eve were removed and to which human beings no longer have access. If there was a way back it could only be, this tradition held, through a thorough and many-sided knowledge of the biblical text. It is possible that this fourfold interpretation was assimilated from medieval Christianity through the *Zohar,* the fountainhead of Jewish mysticism. (For a large sampling of this vast material see L. Ginzberg [1921–38].) A few examples must suffice.

On Gen 3:9, in asking, "Where are you?" did God not know where Adam was? God asked in order to open the way to repentance (*Tanhuma, Tazri'a* 1:9). On Adam's answer, "I was afraid because I was naked" (Gen 3:10), not physical, but religious nakedness is meant. Adam was afraid because by his transgression he was stripped of the one commandment (*mitzvah*) he had received. A human being without a mitzvah is truly naked (*Pirqe R. El.* 14). What was the real sin of Sodom and Gomorrah? The cities were so rich that their streets were paved with gold, but instead of sharing their wealth with others the inhabitants closed the access roads to keep unwanted strangers away (ibid., 25). On the deception of Isaac, when the blind patriarch said, "The voice is the voice of Jacob, yet the hands are the hands of Esau" (Gen 27:22), he spoke prophetically. "The voice of Jacob" means learning and truth; "the hands of Esau" denotes force and violence. As long as the voice of Jacob is heard in the houses of prayer and learning, the hands of Esau will not prevail (*Bereshit Rabbah* 65:20). Of Joseph facing the entreaties of Potiphar's wife: The text says "he refused" (Gen 39:8). The rarely used *shalshelet* sign is placed over the word to indicate delay, for the woman insisted again and again and Joseph refused again and again (ibid., 98:20). Jewish preaching until today has leaned heavily on such ancient *'ăggādâ*.

b. *Philo*. The first individual writer to comment broadly on Genesis was Philo Judaeus of Alexandria, who saw the text through the lens of *remez*. For him the sacred Word hinted at allegorical and philosophical rather than "plain" meanings, and it is this deeper understanding that reveals the real intent of Scripture. In Philo's view abstractions are the highest level of reality and must therefore be discovered in the text. Thus the story of primal humanity is a symbol of the moral development of the soul; the ancestors are the impersonations of the active law of virtue; and Joseph is a study in how the wise must live. Philo calls the serpent in the garden of Eden the symbol of pleasure. It is said to have uttered a human voice because pleasure employs innumerable champions and defenders who take care to advocate its interests and who dare to assert that it should exercise power over everything.

c. *Ishmael and Akiba*. While Philo's direct influence on Jewish tradition was small, in part because he wrote in Greek, his basic concept had its parallel in the rabbinic mainstream. Two rabbis of the second century who exerted great influence on the interpretation of the biblical text argued (not unlike Philo) the basic question: How was one to approach God's Word—through its plain meaning or through extended understanding? R. Ishmael (the principal purveyor of hermeneutical principles) held that Torah "speaks in human language"—that is, plainly. R. Akiba, on the other hand, taught that Torah was unlike any other book and had to be read with attention to every stroke and letter (see *b. Ber.* 31b; for an example of Akiba's attention to the smallest detail, see *b. Menaḥ.* 29b on the meaning of the untranslatable *'et*. In subsequent Jewish tradition both Ishmael's and Akiba's approaches found their place in the *'ăggādâ*, which often blurred their disagreement, for it became the nature of this tradition not to claim that one had arrived at the only authoritative understanding of the divine Word. It was different with the determination of what constituted *hălākhâ*, but it was always clear that this was the result of a human decision, arrived at by majority vote or consensus.

5. *Medieval Jewish Commentaries.* a. *Saadia.* Systematic comment on Genesis (as on Torah in general) begins with the Babylonian scholar and communal leader Saadia ibn Joseph, who wrote a word-by-word commentary on the Torah as well as philosophical considerations on its major themes, especially creation (defending the notion of *creatio ex nihilo*). He was also the first to treat of biblical *hapax legomena*, and his contribution to the understanding of difficult words was considerable. Saadia's commentary was made possible by the work of the Masoretes, who arrived at a standard text.

b. *Rashi.* The most celebrated Jewish commentator of all time was the French scholar Solomon ben Isaac, commonly known as Rashi. To him, the text was to be understood by way of *pĕšaṭ*, by which he meant "common sense approved by tradition." Thus on Gen 3:8 he wrote: "I am concerned only with the literal meaning of Torah and with such *'ăggādōt* which explain the biblical passages in a suitable manner." A full three quarters of his explanations incorporate midrashic explanations, and the rest rely on his far-reaching mastery of all Jewish sources as well as on his keen linguistic sense. He paid close attention to the Masoretic accents, often followed *Onkelos*, occasionally explained him (Gen 49:24; 43:15), and sometimes rejected him (15:11). The terseness of his style, his lucidity, and his unquestioned authority made his commentary in turn the subject of intensive study among Jews and even some Christian scholars, especially Nicholas of Lyra. Two examples: Genesis 2:2 relates that God created Adam from the dust of the earth, which according to Rashi God took from the four corners of the earth so that human beings might be at rest everywhere. Genesis 32:8 says that on meeting Esau, Jacob was beset by both fright and anxiety. Comments Rashi (based on *Bereshit Rabbah* 76:2): "Fright—that he might be killed [by Esau]; anxiety—that he might be led to kill the others."

c. *Abraham ibn Ezra.* Next in importance to Rashi ranks A. Ibn Ezra, who was not inclined to follow Rashi's basic reliance on the use of Midrash for the purpose of explaining the plain meaning of the text. Of independent mind, he was the first to cast doubts on Mosaic authorship of the Torah, although he merely hinted at it. Thus Gen 12:6 ("The Canaanites were then in the land"—clearly a post-Mosaic phrase) drew his observation that "the informed will understand."

d. *Others.* Of the many successors to Rashi and ibn Ezra few exerted a greater influence than M. ben Nachman ("Ramban" or Nachmanides). His wider perspective of the book's spiritual context has had continued appeal and brought him increased attention in the twentieth century. He was also convinced that the text contained hidden meanings, and thus he became an important link in the spread of medieval mysticism.

D. Kimhi ("Radak") brought to the text his great knowledge of grammar and syntax; and I. Abravanel was the first to approach the text, not so much on a word-by-word basis, but by raising questions that he thought needed answers. O. ben Jacob Sforno achieved wide popularity by his trenchant observations; in commenting on the Babel story he called attention to "the real crime" of the builders: They tried to impose one religion on humankind. God prevented this and by dispersing the nations kept alive a variety of idolatries, for God knew that out of this adversity would eventually come a recognition of the supreme ruler.

e. *Hasidism.* The hasidic movement (see Hasidism) arose in the middle of the eighteenth century in Eastern Europe. Among its characteristics was renewed attention to the spiritual life of the individual, and frequently the interpretation of the biblical text served as a vehicle for this purpose. Two examples: God's command to Abraham in Gen 12:1, *lek-lĕkā* (lit., "get on with it!" [so Nachmanides]) was interpreted to mean "Go to yourself," i.e., God asks Abraham to discover his own spiritual core (see *'Iṭṭurēy Tōrâ* 1:83). Similarly, the words *wayyiggaš yĕhûdâ* (Gen 44:18) are usually rendered, "Then Judah drew near." The hasidic teacher asks, "To whom did Judah draw near?" and answers, "To himself, for only when Judah became himself at his best was he able to speak as he did" (ibid., 1:389).

f. *In the wake of emancipation.* Three commentaries of the emancipation and post-emancipation era signify the tensions in which Jews found themselves. (1) M. Mendelssohn's German rendering of the Torah text was a work of revolutionary impact, which was to be counterbalanced by the *Bî 'ur,* a Hebrew commentary that aimed to preserve traditional views. (2) This latter task was undertaken with greater success by S. Hirsch in his thoroughly orthodox commentary, which was written in German and laid the spiritual foundation for the emergence of Jewish neo-orthodoxy. Hirsch looked to the text for contemporary relevance and was at all times a homiletician par excellence. Two examples: Why, in Gen 10:9 is Nimrod's name linked to that of God? Because he oppressed people in God's name. Nimrod was the prototype of all tyrants who pretend that their crown is "by God's grace," and thus their power politics and hypocrisy are characterized by the expression "like Nimrod." Hirsch interpreted *lek-lĕkā* (Gen 12:1) as "go by yourself." "This is one journey which must be made alone. One must become a stranger in the world to view it clearly." (3) Me'ir Loeb ben Yehi'el Michael was the last great link to medieval tradition in the midst of emancipation. He followed Abravanel's method of asking questions arising from the text and ibn Ezra's close attention to words and meanings. Thus, on the story of the tower of Babel he commented on the words "All the earth had . . . the same words" (Gen 11:1). This expression, *dĕbārîm 'ahadîm,* could also mean "few words," i.e., that humans had a small vocabulary. Since both the learned and the unlearned spoke "the same words" there was no technical or philosophic jargon to separate people from each other.

6. Modern Jewish Commentaries. One of the greatest single contributions to the study of Genesis was made by B. Jacob, a German rabbi whose massive commentary was published during the early days of the Nazi regime and must be considered a masterpiece of careful scholarship and wide erudition. Jacob gave special attention to the weaknesses of the documentary hypothesis and insisted on the basic unity of the book (though he did not see Moses as its author).

His intellectual successor, U. Cassuto, also upheld the unitary nature of the Genesis text and expanded on Jacob's explication of the numbers system, which he showed underlies all of Genesis. Most important, he gave special attention to the literary structure of the book, to its nuances of language, and to its relationship to Ugaritic sources.

The most popular Jewish commentary of the twentieth century came out of England. Edited by J. Hertz (1929–36), it tried to fortify traditional values through a vigorous rejection of all higher criticism. While it does mention non-Jewish writers, it does so only when they praise the ethical and literary values of Genesis. This apologia attempted to combat the rise of anti-Semitic sentiment and at the same time give the Jewish reader a renewed sense of pride and worth.

Y. Kaufmann (1937–57), in his large history of Israel's faith, disputed some of the basic tenets of the then regnant critical school without rejecting its methods outright. He denied that Israel's monotheism was the result of a gradual development away from the pagan worldview, seeing it rather as a sudden spiritual eruption. He saw Moses rather than Abraham as the progenitor of the new faith.

A generation later W. Plaut's *[Bereshit] Genesis* (1974) set out to enlarge the insights of Jewish tradition with those from Christian, Muslim, and secular sources as well as to take full cognizance of the findings of Literary, archaeological, cognate, and linguistic inquiries. It distinguishes between three levels of commentary: The first, historical-antiquarian, accepts the basic insights of critical scholarship and explains the text as it was understood in its own day;

the second, traditional, shows how the text was interpreted across the millennia by exegesis or eisegesis; and the third level is represented by considerations of what the text might mean in our day, regardless of what it meant yesterday. (Later editions of Plaut's Genesis commentary appeared as part of *The Torah: A Modern Commentary* [1981, 1995, 10th ed].)

7. Between Jew and Christian. On the whole the rich work of Jewish commentary rarely reached students outside the Jewish realm, just as Jews paid little attention to Christian savants. Even after the advent of emancipation Jewish and Christian Bible scholars often remained largely ignorant of each other. Thus, in the Christian camp *The Interpreter's Bible* and *The Jerome Biblical Commentary*, to name but two, contain few references to the two millennia of Jewish scholarship. Both these works, oriented toward the Protestant and Roman Catholic communities respectively, support critical scholarship but generally do not look across the demarcations of faith communities to widen their appreciation of the text. This is so in part because each tradition has been concerned with firming up its own foundations and, therefore, has been inhospitable to independent inquiry that might weaken it.

8. Christian Interpretations. a. *Foundations.* There is a fundamental difference in the approach Jewish and Christian interpreters have taken when dealing with Genesis. Both saw God's work rehearsed in its pages, but its goal was viewed differently. To the former the book was essentially a prolegomenon to the creation of God's chosen people: God had created the world and crowned it with the human species, which, however, disappointed God, who subsequently turned to Abraham and made him the progenitor of Israel to whom the Torah would be entrusted and thereby the task of *tiqqûn ʾōlām,* the perfection of the world. To Christians, in contrast, Genesis is a double *prolegomenon*: to history in general (including Israel) and thence to Christ. Thus the focus shifted; the forward thrust of the book was not salvation through Sinai but through the Savior.

Christian commentary has tended to view Genesis (like all of the HB) as pointing toward Jesus and his mission. Words and passages have been seen to hint at his coming and at the theology of the developing *ecclesia*. Thus the sweeping *rûaḥ* in Gen 1:2 has been understood not as "wind" but as "Spirit," a hint at the Holy Spirit of the Trinity. The expulsion from Eden became a special focus of Christian teaching. While in normative Judaism the myth found no resonance whatsoever, it became central to Christian teaching: "By the offense of one, judgment came upon all men to condemnation" (Rom 5:12, 18; see also 2 Esdras 7:18). This basic human flaw was to be redeemed through Jesus Christ. In this fashion Genesis became a theological starting point for the church.

It is interesting to note that Origen (d. c. 254) fell into disfavor in part because he was thought to be too close to the Jewish view and that his allegorizing followed Philo more than the emerging Christian consensus, which was firmed up by Jerome (d. 420), who was also well acquainted with rabbinic sources. Augustine (d. 430) influenced subsequent commentary on Genesis, not only through the application of hermeneutical rules, but by his emphasis on the Christian view necessary to employ them properly. For instance, he understood Jacob's supplanting of Esau to hint at Jesus, whose ministry helped the Gentiles to supplant the Jews; hence Jacob's acts were not deception but divine mystery. Thereafter, all Christian commentary on Genesis remained Christ-centered.

The same is true even for some moderns who have fully accepted the results of modern scholarship and have themselves contributed greatly to it. A prime example is G. von Rad. In his commentary he comments on F. Rosenzweig's discussion of the redactional process. Rosenzweig had called the final arranger of the text "R," to stand for *rabbēnû,* "our teacher" or "master" (see M. Buber and Rosenzweig [1939] 322). Von Rad responded, "From the standpoint of Judaism that is consistent. But for us, in respect to hermeneutics, the redactor is not our master... We receive the OT from the hands of Jesus Christ, and therefore all exegesis of the OT depends on whom one thinks Jesus Christ to be" (1956, 41). To him and many others Genesis is essentially *Heilsgeschichte* in the Christian perspective. Much of what will appear below under the heading of "higher criticism" qualifies as Christian interpretation as well.

b. *Literalism.* A literal reading of Genesis by the church resulted in the seventeenth-century trial of Galileo, who was forced to recant his teaching that the earth revolves around the sun and is therefore not the center of the universe. The latter part of the nineteenth century saw the bitter controversy over Darwinism in which the "biblicists" were headed by S. Wilberforce and the "rationalists" by T. Huxley. In the United States the conflict was played out in the Scopes trial of 1925. For the time being it ended the hold on public education the literal understanding of the creation process had previously exercised. But in the latter part of the century the conflict once more came to the fore. American and Canadian "creationists" have claimed that the biblical account in Genesis 1–2 is as scientific as the theory of evolution and, therefore, deserves equal treatment in schools and textbooks and is to be presented to the student as a viable alternative.

This battle has been waged by Protestant fundamentalists, who see "secular" approaches to the creation of the world as a threat to their faith. The Roman Catholic Church, on the other hand, not unlike Jewish tradition, has taken a more relaxed "analogous" view of the biblical creation stories. "They relate in simple and figurative language . . . the fundamental truths presupposed for the economy of salvation, as well as the popular description of the origin of the human race and of the Chosen People" (*JBC*, 8).

9. Higher Criticism. a. *Beginnings.* It needs to be stated again that the study of the Bible has come primarily from scholars belonging to one or another faith community. The majority have been academics teaching in seminaries or university departments of theology whose function it was to strengthen their religion by enlarging the scope of its intellectual underpinnings. In works on Genesis one finds, therefore, scholarly agendas that are sometimes clear and at other times unspoken. When an independent writer like Spinoza (d. 1677) set out to explore the text "in a spirit of entire freedom and without prejudice" (*Tractatus theologico-politicus* [1670] chaps. 7–10) the Amsterdam Jewish community punished him with the ban. Generally, however, scholars have made their contributions from within the bounds of their own communities. In addition, one must keep in mind that the study of Genesis—because of its material a crucial book—has frequently borne the stamp of particular perceptions of history.

This is demonstrable in the case of the founders of Pentateuchal Criticism—K. Graf and J. Wellhausen—who attempted to reconstruct the development of the Genesis document. Building on the work of their predecessors, they separated three main literary streams and assigned them to the J, E, and P documents, dated them, judged their historical value, and viewed them from the perspective of Israel's spiritual development. Graf and Wellhausen began with the assumption that history started from primitive beginnings and slowly, but inexorably, moved in an upward fashion. Applying this view to Genesis (and to biblical history in general), they saw its concepts of God and ethics grow from simple and crude perceptions to more exalted levels, pointing ultimately to the advent of Christianity.

They proceeded to deny Genesis an intrinsic historical value. The tales, they said, were largely etiological. One could not gather from them "any historical knowledge of the Patriarchs, but only about the time when the narratives which concern them took shape in the people of Israel" (Wellhausen, *Prolegomena to the History of Israel* [1883] 331).

b. *Gunkel.* The debate over historicity was shifted to another arena with H. Gunkel's pathbreaking commentary in 1901. He concentrated on what became known as form-critical analysis (see Form Criticism) and viewed the book as a repository of sagas, which he described as ancient forms of poetic stories dealing with events and personalities of the distant past. They were at first passed along by oral transmission and contained much etiological material.

Genesis, he wrote, dealt primarily with individual sagas, and he proceeded to set them into their proper framework. His incisive exploration had a profound influence on biblical scholarship, which now focused on the literary character of the text.

Unfortunately, Gunkel was also infected with a sense of personal animus against Judaism, which colored his writings. The biblical figure of Jacob was the special target of his disdain; he described him as the archetypical Jew, whose deception delighted his "happy heirs." A similar animus was exhibited by Friedrich Delitzsch, who tried to show that Genesis was unoriginal in that most of its tales were borrowed from the Babylonians (*Babel und Bibel* [1902–1905; ET 1906];). Because of such judgments many Jewish scholars viewed higher biblical criticism as "a form of subtle anti-Judaism, if not anti-Semitism . . . often present in much of the 'critical' literature" (H. Hummel, *EncJud* 4 [1971] 907).

c. *Radicals and conservatives.* The understanding of the literary and theological nature of Genesis was developed in a new direction by a cadre of German scholars. Building on Gunkel, von Rad attempted to show that biblical saga was not merely poetic fantasy but the sum total of living historical recollection. "No stage in this work's long period of growth is really obsolete, something of each phase has been conserved and passed on as enduring" (1956, 31, 27). Primeval history was seen as a period of alienation from God, with Abraham the key to the *Heilsgeschichte* and Israel's journey the key to the world's history. This view has been contested by C. Westermann (1966–82) in his extensive commentary. He does not see chaps. 1–11 as subservient to salvational history but as providing a perspective of their own—a universal canvas that attempts to describe the world as it was and does not at all focus on Israel. Its overriding theme, as that of all of Genesis, is the praise of God's majesty.

While von Rad related the Genesis sagas to traditions of the exodus, M. Noth (1950) saw them stemming from the league of tribes, each of which had specific traditions concerning its own ancestors prior to settlement in Canaan. Thus the sagas were largely etiological; therefore, nothing could be said about the time and place of the patriarchs. Noth's views, built on his highly conjectural theory of an Israelite amphictyony, attracted a great deal of critical attention; and some of his successors expanded it radically.

G. Mendenhall (1962) conjectured that the whole idea of Israel's peoplehood came after the league of tribes had been instituted and that the conjoint Genesis and Exodus traditions reflect nothing of the tribes' true history. According to Mendenhall, there was no "patriarchal history," since Israel did not have ancestors different from those of the Canaanites. J. Van Seters (1975) went one step further and saw the entire Abraham saga to be a late, perhaps postexilic, theological invention.

Alongside this radical school has been a more conservative wing that sharply criticized the views of Noth as "nihilistic" and instead asserted that much of Genesis was indeed rooted in historical events (see J. Bright [1956] 52, 54). "As a whole the picture in Genesis is historical, and there is no reason to doubt the general accuracy of the biographical details and sketches of personality which bring the Patriarchs to life with a vividness unknown to a single extrabiblical character in the whole literature of the Ancient Near East" (W. F. Albright [1963] 5). Others taking a somewhat similar point of view were R. de Vaux, who adduced supporting evidence from the research of N. Glueck and the occurrence of Genesis names in Mari and Nuzi sources. To these have been added the Ebla finds, but their meaning has been the subject of much debate, especially since many of the extant texts remain unpublished.

The moderate wing includes I. Engnell, whose Uppsala school has stressed the long line of oral traditions that were said to have been committed to writing only at a late date. E. Speiser saw the accepted J/E/P schools themselves to have derived from a common tradition (which he calls T). To him Abraham is the father of biblical monotheism, and the history of the biblical process is the story of the monotheistic ideal (1964, XLIX). The motive power of this process was spiritual rather than economic or political, and this gave it its particular character. In his assessment of Abraham's role he departed from the view proposed by Y. Kaufmann, who ascribed this distinction to Moses.

d. *New Vistas.* The writings of B. Childs (1979) have made an important new contribution to our understanding of Genesis. In his analysis of chaps. 1–11 he strikes a middle ground between von Rad and Westermann in that he emphasizes the unifying theme of *tōlĕdōt*, which makes Genesis into a perceptual whole, while at the same time giving the primeval stories a distinct place of their own. "The Genesis material is unique because of an understanding of reality which has subordinated common mythopoetic tradition to a theology of absolute divine sovereignty" (1979, 158). Childs also takes up Kaufmann's view and stresses the role of Moses in the formation of the tradition, a role earlier critical commentators had played down. Last but not least, he sees oral and literary traditions, on the one hand, and cultic traditions, on the other hand, as shaping each other in a process of dynamic tension and in an attempt to separate modern perceptions from the text as it is, stresses the importance of looking at it through the eyes of ancient Jewish comment as well. N. Sarna (1989) and *Olam ha-Tanakh* combine close attention to traditional Jewish interpretation with insights derived from cognate languages and cultures as well as recent archaeological studies that have shed new light on prominent places mentioned in Genesis, like Shechem and Ber Sheba.

Another stage of interpretation may be termed literary and has been pioneered by E. Auerbach, Z. Adar (1967), and R. Alter (1981). It goes beyond Gunkel in its attention to the nuances of Hebrew words and phrases and of key terms and images and thus reveals a new dimension of comprehension. Its interest lies less in how the text came into being than in what it says in its present form. Finally, Feminist criticism has entered the field and has explored aspects of understanding and thereby significantly added to the exploration of the biblical text (see P. Trible [1978] and the surveys by A. Brenner [1993] and P. Bird [1994]).

In fact, there has been a turning away from the preoccupation with historiography and documentary analysis and to a concern with the completed surface of the text (Sarna, XVIII). "Literary criticism has often been paralyzed by a too minute distinction of sources which pulverizes the texts and makes them unintelligible" (de Vaux [1951] 23). The holistic approach developing in many disciplines must also find its way into the appreciation of the text, and nowhere is this more urgent than in our view of Genesis. Although there are elements of etiology, the text overwhelmingly conveys a sense of authenticity. Genesis primarily retells; it does not originate (E. Speiser [1957] 201–16; similarly de Vaux [1951] 24). We must be cautious not to superimpose our own modern ideas on an ancient text that arose in a mind-set very different from our own. And finally, the long-standing separation between Jewish and Christian scholarship is being bridged by such scholars as Childs and Plaut, and the enlarged view thus made possible will contribute to further fruitful exploration of the book. Recent commentaries on Gen include the critical English edition of Bonhoeffer's 1937 theological commentary (1997), Brodie (2001), Capon's imaginative commentary on Gen if the book were produced as a film (2003), Kass (2003), and Turner (2000).

Bibliography: Z. Adar, *Sefer bĕrešît, mābhō᾽ lĕ ʿalām hammiqrā ᾽î* (1967). **W. F. Albright**, *The Biblical Period from Abraham to Ezra* (1963). **R. Alter**, *The Art of Biblical Narrative (1981); Genesis/Translation and Commentary* (1996). **G. A. Anderson**, *The Genesis of Perfection: Adam and Eve in Jewish and Christian Imagination* (2001). **G. T. Armstrong**, *Die Genesis in der alten Kirche* (BGBH 4, 1962). **K. Armstrong**, *In the Beginning: A New Interpretation of Genesis* (1996). **E. Auerbach**, *Mimesis* (1953; ET 1954). **B. W. Bacon**, *The Genesis of Genesis: A Study of the Documentary Sources of the First Book of Moses in Accordance with the Results of Critical Science Illustrating the Presence of Bibles Within the*

Bible (1892). **P. Bird,** *Feminism and the Bible: A Critical and Constructive Encounter* (1994). **D. Bonhoeffer,** *Creation and Fall: A Theological Exposition of Genesis 1-3* (Dietrich Bonhoeffer Works 3, 1997). **A. Brenner** (ed.), *A Feminist Companion to Genesis* (1993; second series 1998). **J. Bright,** *Early Israel in Recent Biblical Writing* (SBT 19, 1956). **T. L. Brodie,** *Genesis as Dialogue: A Literary, Historical, and Theological Commenatry* (2001). **M. Buber and F. Rosenzweig,** *Die Schrift und ihre Verdeutschung* (1939). **R. F. Capon,** *Genesis: The Movie* (2003). **U. Cassuto,** *A Commentary on the Book of Genesis* (2 vols., 1944-49; ET 1961–64). **B. S. Childs,** *Introduction to the OT as Scripture* (1979). **P. R. Davies and D. J. A. Clines** (eds.), *The World of Genesis: Persons, Places, Perspectives* (JSOTSup 1998). **O. Eissfeldt,** *Die Genesis der Genesis: Vom Werdegang des ersten Buches der Bibel* (1958, 1961). **J. M. Evans,** *Paradise Lost and the Genesis Tradition* (1968). **D. N. Fewell and D. M. Gunn,** *Gender, Power, and Promise: The Subject of the Bible's First Story* (1993). **W. W. Fields,** *Sodom and Gomorrah: History and Motif in Biblical Narrative* (JSOTSup 231, 1997). **T. W. Flanxman,** *Genesis and the "Jewish Antiquities" of Flavius Josephus* (BibOr 35, 1979). **J. P. Fokkelman,** *Narrative Art in Genesis* (SSN 17, 1975). **T. Fretheim,** "Genesis," *NIB* (1994) 1:319-675. **J. Gable,** *The Bible as Literature: An Introduction* (1986). **L. Ginzberg,** *The Legends of the Jews* (7 vols., 1921-38). **W. H. Green,** *The Unity of the Book of Genesis* (1895). **A. J. Greenberg** (ed.), *'Ittûrêy Tôrâ* (5 vols., 1965-). **H. Gunkel,** *Genesis* (HKAT I, 1, 1901, 1910³; ET 1997). **B. Halpern,** *The First Historians: The HB and History* (1988). **R. P. C. Hanson,** *Allegory and Event: A Study of the Sources and Significance of Origen's Interpretation of Scripture* (1959). **M. Harl,** 1, *La Genèse Les Bibles d'Alexandrie,* (1986). **J. H. Hertz** (ed.), *The Pentateuch and Haftorahs: Hebrew Text, English Translation, and Commentary* (1929-36). **P. Humbert,** "Die neuere Genesis-forschung," *TRu 6* (1934) 147-60, 207-28. "Israel, History of," *ABD* 3:526-76. **L. R. Kass,** *The Beginning of Wisdom: Reading Genesis* (2003). **Y. Kaufmann,** *The Religion of Israel: From Its Beginnings to the Babylonian Exile* (8 vols., 1937-57; abridged ET 1960). **K. E. Kvam, L. S. Schearing, and V. H. Ziegler** (eds.), *Genesis and Gender* (1999). **N. Leibowitz,** *Studies in the Book of Genesis: In the Context of Ancient and Modern Jewish Bible Commentary* (1972). **N. Lemche,** *Ancient Israel: A New History of Israelite Society* (Biblical Seminar 5, 1988). **A. Levene,** *Early Syrian Fathers on Genesis* (1951). **G. P. Luttikhuizen** (ed.), *The Creation of Man and Woman: Interpretations of the Biblical Narratives in Jewish and Christian Traditions* (2000). **T. Mann,** *Joseph und seine Brüder = Joseph and His Brothers series* (4 vols.; 1934-44). **F. García Martínez and G. P. Luttikhuizen** (eds.), *Interpretations of the Flood* (Themes in Biblical Narrative 1, 1998). **E. G. Mendenhall,** "The Hebrew Conquest of Palestine," *BA* 25 (1962) 66-87. **J. Neusner,** *Judaism's Story of Creation: Scripture, Halakhah, Aggadah* (2000). **S. Niditch,** "Genesis," *Women's Bible Commentary* (ed. C. A. Newsom and S. H. Ringe, 1992) 10-25; *Folklore and the Hebrew Bible* (1993); *Oral World and Written Word: Ancient Israelite Literature* (Library of Ancient Israel, 1996). **M. Noth,** *The History of Israel* (1950; ET 1960). **A. Pagolu,** *The Religion of the Patriarchs* (JSOTSup 277, 1998). **W. G. Plaut,** [Bereshit] *Genesis* (1974); *Torah: A Modern Commentary* (1981, 1995). **G. von Rad,** *Genesis* (ATD, 1956; ET 1961). **I. N. Rashkow,** *The Phallacy of Genesis: A Feminist-psychoanalytic Approach* (Literary Currents in Biblical Interpretation, 1993). **D. Redford,** *Egypt, Israel, and Canaan in Ancient Times* (1992). **G. A. Rendsburg,** *The Redaction of Genesis* (1986). **F. E. Robbins,** *The Hexaemeral Literature: A Study of the Greek and Latin Commentaries on Genesis* (1912). **G. A. Robbins** (ed.), **Genesis 1-3 in the History of Exegesis: Intrigue in the Garden** (SWR 27, 1988). **N. M. Sarna,** *Genesis: The Traditional Hebrew with the New JPS Translation* (JPSTC, 1989). **J. Skinner,** *Genesis* (ICC, 1910). **E. A. Speiser,** "The Biblical Idea of History in Its Common Near Eastern Setting," *IEJ* 7 (1957) 201-16; *Genesis* (AB 1, 1964). **T. Thompson,** *The Origin Tradition of Ancient Israel* (JSOTSup 55, 1987). **P. Trible,** "A Love Story Gone Awry," *God and the*

Rhetoric of Sexuality (1978) 72-143. **L.A. Turner,** *Genesis* (Readings, 2000). **J. Van Seters,** *Abraham in History and Tradition* (1975); *Prologue to History: The Yahwist as Historian in Genesis* (1992). **J. D. Thompson,** *Critical Concordance to the Septuagint: Genesis* (Computer Bible Series 53, 1998). **R. de Vaux, Genèse (1951);** "Method in the Study of Early Hebrew History," *The Bible in Modern Scholarship* (ed. J. P. Hyatt, 1965) 15-29. **G. J. Wenham,** *Story as Torah: Reading the Old Testament Ethically* (Edinburgh, 2000). **A. Wénin (ed.),** *Studies in the Book of Genesis: Persons, Places, Perspectives* (JSOTSup 1998). **C. Westermann,** *Genesis* (BKAT 1, 3 vols., 1966–82; ET 1984–86). **J. Wilcoxen,** "Narrative," *OT Form Criticism* (TUMSR 2, ed. J. H. Hayes, 1974) 57-98. **A. Williams,** *The Common Expositor: An Account of the Commentaries on Genesis, 1527-1633* (1948). **P. R. Williamson,** *Abraham, Israel, and the Nations: The Patriarchal Promise and Its Covenantal Development in Genesis* (JSOTSup 315, 2000). **E. van Wolde,** *Stories of the Beginning: Genesis 1–11 and other Creation Stories* (1997). **F. Zimmer,** *Der Elohist als weisheitlich-prophetische Redaktionsschicht: eine literarische und theologiegeschichtliche Untersuchung der sogenannten elohistischen Texte im Pentateuch* (Herders biblische Studien 22, 1999).

W.G. PLAUT

THE PENTATEUCH

Exodus

The forty chapters of the book of Exodus report on the liberation of the Israelites from slavery in Egypt, their trek to Sinai, and the revelation of the law that took place there.

1. *The HB*. The events portrayed in the book are partially reinterpreted and theologically deepened in the remainder of the HB. Speeches and sermons refer to the exodus traditions (Moses in Deut 29:1-5; Joshua in Josh 24:5-7, with the people's answer in 24:16-17; Samuel in 1 Sam 10:18; Nehemiah in Neh 9:9-21). Altogether, Deuteronomy borrows from Exodus numerous traditional materials (e.g., texts from the book of the covenant, Exod 21:22-23:33; cf. Exod 21:1-11 with Deut 15:12-18, etc.) Among the preexilic prophets, Hosea saw in the period of desert wanderings the bridal period of the people with their God (in this, Jeremiah is dependent on Hosea: Jer 2:2; Hos 2:15; 11:1-2). At the same time Hosea announced the judgment of God as a return to Egypt (Hos 8:13; 9:3, 6; 11:5). According to Amos, Israel could derive no special status from the exodus, since even the Philistines had been called out of Kaphtor and the Aramaeans out of Kir (Amos 3:1-2; 9:7). Ezekiel viewed the early history of Israel in the desert as a history of sin, insofar as Israel held fast to the idols of Egypt and broke the law (Ezek 20:6-26). Exilic and postexilic salvation Prophecy looked forward to a new exodus out of the exile: The old exodus would be completed when Israel was led home in healing (Ezek 20:32-38). Deutero-Isaiah calls the people to forget the early history of Israel in order to understand the time to come (Isa 43:16-21; cf. Jer 23:7-8). Many exodus events are mentioned in the psalms (see Pss 78:12-53; 105:23-45; 106:7-33; 114; 136:10-16); e.g., the wonder at the Red Sea and the revelation at Sinai are described in cosmic terms as well as with the application of mythic elements (e.g., Ps 77:17-21), and Israel is allegorically and poetically transfigured as the vine Yahweh brought out of Egypt (Ps 80:9).

2. *Extra-canonical Writings of the HB and Contemporary Literature*. In Hellenistic-Roman Judaism the memory of the exodus acquired a central significance (see 1 Macc 4:9). The conflict between Yahweh and Nebuchadnezzar/Holofernes in Judith has the same structure of events as that between Yahweh and Pharaoh in Exodus. The hymn in Judith 16 was inspired by the Song of Miriam in Exodus 15. Exodus also lends to the book of Judith the terminological means of its theological exposition.

A presentation of the oppression of Israel in Egypt until the exodus is found in the book of Jubilees (chaps. 46–49), where the Mosaic traditions in Exodus 3–14 are depicted as the struggle between Satan (Mastema) and the angel of God. *Jubilees* presents itself as a revelation of the angel of God to Moses on Sinai (*Jubilees* 1), during which Moses received the contents of the books of Genesis through Leviticus.

The dream-visions of the Ethiopian book of Enoch interpret the exodus from Egypt as the flight of sheep from wolves (*1 Enoch* 89:10-27) and Moses as the shepherd who leads the flock into the promised land (*1 Enoch* 89:28-40). The tragedian Ezekiel attempted to edit dramatically the material of Exodus 1–15 in his drama "Exagoge" and in this way created a counterpart to profane Greek tragedy. In the Wisdom of Solomon the Theology of Exodus and wisdom theology are united in an imposing symbiosis. In an artful literary composition the wisdom of Israel is celebrated as having already proved itself superior to the wisdom of Egypt, the land of wisdom, during the exodus (Wis 11:2-19, 21).

The exodus events were turned completely around by several non-Jewish historians (Manetho [3rd cent. B.C.E.], Chaeremon [1st cent. C.E.], Lysimachos [c. 361–281 B.C.E.], Apion [1st cent. C.E.], Tacitus [b. 55 C.E.]), according to whom the exodus was a case of the flight of lepers who had earlier oppressed the Egyptians with the help of the Hyksos. In contrast, the Jewish historian

Artapanus (fl. 2nd cent. B.C.E.), describing the life of Moses with considerable haggadic expansions and in a novelistic style, maintained that Moses had provided the Egyptians with a variety of cultural institutions.

Josephus offered an exhaustive version of the exodus traditions (*A.J.* 2.9-3.15), though one that has been embellished with various legends. Moses appears as, among other things, the victorious leader of the army of the Egyptians against the Ethiopians (*A.J.* 2.10). The miraculous nature of the event at the Red Sea is weakened (2.16.5), while the story of the golden calf (Exodus 32) is consciously left out. Philo of Alexandria composed two books on the life of Moses (*Mos.* 1, 2) and an Exodus commentary (*Quaestiones in Exodum*). Understanding the exodus as a philosophical allegory, he depicted the Sinai event as a supra-dimensional mystery: The wanderings of the Israelites in the Sinai desert became a transposition into a divine locale, a growing of the soul out of and beyond the world of materiality, the senses, and suffering.

3. The NT. Christological, ecclesiological, sacramental, paraenetic, and anti-Jewish polemical interpretations of various exodus traditions are found in the NT.

a. *Christological interpretations.* The way of the child Jesus leads to Egypt and back, according to Matthew. As was once true of Israel, so also it is now true of Jesus: "Out of Egypt I have called my son" (Hos 11:1 in Matt 2:15). The story of "the massacre of the innocents" in Bethlehem (Matt 2:16-18) corresponds to the return of Moses from Midian (Exod 4:19-20). Even at the end of Matthew features of the exodus tradition become clear: The Last Supper of Jesus with his disciples is a passover meal (Matt 26:17; cf. Exod 12:14-20). The entire NT tradition sees in Jesus the passover lamb (John 19:36; 1 Cor 5:7; cf. Exod 12:36). Hebrews 12:18-24 compares the revelation on Sinai in its entirety with the revelation manifested in Jesus Christ.

b. *Ecclesiological interpretation.* What is ascribed to the Israelites in Exod 19:16 now applies to the Christians, who, according to 1 Pet 2:9, are now "the royal priesthood and the holy people."

c. *Sacramental and paraenetic modes.* Paul uses a haggadic Midrash on the exodus and wilderness wanderings to demonstrate to the Corinthians that one's salvation is never ultimately secured. In this treatment he sets the march through the sea in parallel with baptism, manna with the communion bread, and Christ with the rock of Exod 17:6. Hebrews 3:7-19 juxtaposes the behavior of the Christians with that of the Israelites in the wilderness. Hebrews 11:23-29 lists as paradigmatic for faith the behavior of the midwives (Exod 2:2), of Moses (Exod 2:11-15; 12:11, 22-23), and of the people during the crossing of the sea (Exod 14:22, 27).

d. *Anti-Jewish polemic.* In the sermon of Stephen parts of the exodus story (particularly Exodus 1–3; 32) are taken up in order to show that the Israelites are "stiff-necked" and that they have broken the law (Acts 7:51-53). Moses is depicted as a "type" of Christ, who is rejected by the people even though God has sent him as a liberator (Acts 7:35). At numerous other places in the NT individual verses from Exodus are cited or expounded (e.g., in the "antitheses" of the Sermon on the Mount; cf. Matt 5:21 with Exod 20:13; Matt 5:27 with Exod 20:14; in Jesus' discourse on the resurrection, Matt 22:32; cf. Exod 3:6; in the Pauline epistles, cf. Rom 9:15 with Exod 33:19, etc.). In addition, one finds legendary expansions stemming from contemporary literature (e.g., 2 Tim 3:8, legends of Jannes and Jambres).

4. *The Early Church.* During this period, Exodus was usually expounded in Pentateuchal commentaries or in sermons. Important contributions in the third to the sixth centuries were composed by Origen (*Selecta et Homiliae in Exodus*), Diodore of Tarsus (*Fragmenta in Exodum*), Jerome (*Liber Exodi*), Augustine (*Quaestiones et locutiones in Exodum*), Cyril of Alexandria (*Glaphyri in Exodum*), Theodoret of Cyrrhus (*Quaestiones in Exodum*), Procopius of Gaza (*Commentarii in Exodum*), Gregory the Great (*Expositio sup. Exodum*), and Isidore of Seville (*Quaestiones in Exodum*). In these works the modes of interpretation applied in NT

times are carried farther. The typological interpretation of people, events, and instructions from Exodus took on considerable significance, and these features expressed the events of the Christian truth and Heilsgeschichte (salvation history).

a. *Christological interpretations.* Several features were taken to signify the incarnation of God: Exod 3:14-15, with the designation of the God who is unchanging and unchangeable, "the God of Abraham, Isaac and Jacob" (Augustine *Serm.* 6.84-87); the transformation of Moses' staff into a serpent (Exod 4:3; Augustine *Serm.* 6.104-108), and the miracle of the manna (Exod 16; Origen *Homily on Exod* 7:5). According to other interpretations, the manna and quails point to the coming of Christ for the last judgment (Hilary *Tract. myst.* 1.40).

The christological interpretation of Exodus 12 achieved great significance: The description of the paschal lamb (v. 5) became a *locus classicus* for the sinlessness of Christ, the virgin birth, and the single year of his effective ministry. In the dating of the paschal feast to the 14th of Nisan (vv. 3, 6) the church fathers found a prophecy of the crucifixion. That the paschal lamb was slaughtered in the evening (v. 6) announced Christ's crucifixion at the end of the world (for exhaustive interpretations of Exodus 12 see Zeno of Verona [*Tractate on Exodus* 12] and Gaudentius of Brescia [*Tractate on Exodus* 12]).

Moses was frequently compared with Christ, e.g., the threatening situations at their respective births and the correspondence between Pharaoh and Herod (e.g., Hilary Tract. myst. 1.28). Moreover events from the life of Moses were interpreted christologically: Moses' slaying of the Egyptian signified Christ, who slays the devil (Hilary *Tract. myst.* 1.29; Cyril of Alexandria *Glaphyr. on Exod* 1:7; Augustine *Faust.* 22.90).

b. *Ecclesiological and sacramental interpretations.* Jerome interpreted the wandering of the people of Israel through the desert as the wandering of the church through history (*Epist.* 78), in which the church was not destroyed in spite of persecution. Receiving the law on Sinai foreshadowed the reception of the Holy Spirit at Pentecost (Exodus 19, cf. Acts 2; Jerome *Epist.* 78). Some argued that the bush that burned without being consumed (Exodus 3) referred to the constant renewal of the church after times of persecution (Jerome *Epist.* 78; Theodoret of Cyrrhus *Graec. affect. curatio,* 9.27).

The sacramental interpretation of the exodus received its firm place in the catechism partially because baptism was administered at Easter, the Christian Passover. According to the prescriptions laid down by Paul (1 Corinthians 10), the wonder of the manna was transformed into the model of the Eucharist—that is, of the spiritual feeding of the church during its own exodus here on earth (repeatedly attested by Cyprian, Ambrose, Augustine, J. Chrysostom, and Theodoret of Cyrrhus). Just as the blood of the Passover lamb was smeared on the doorposts and lintels, so also should Christians receive the *sacramentum passionis* with the mouth unto salvation. Exodus 15:1-19 won liturgical significance as the first of the "cantica" only after the time of the early church.

c. *Paraenetic interpretations.* Paraenetic (homiletic) texts from Exodus, above all the Decalogue (Exod 20:1-21), were frequently used and had a long, effective history, although details and events from other Exodus pericopes were interpreted paraenetically as well. Paraenetic texts are exhortatory texts used as homiletical vehicles to impart values and wisdom for the contemporary audience; thus, e.g., the manna stories become precursors to the Eucharist and a preparation for Christian martyrdom (see B. Childs [1974] 297). Additionally, exegetes, beginning with Augustine (and through the late Middle Ages), suggested that since the Israelites were told to request objects of silver and gold from the Egyptians (Exod 3:22; similarly, Exod 11:2; 12:35), Christians were required to make use of the ancient arts (and secular literature and philosophy) and further that a synthesis between ancient philosophy and Christian theology was possible. Exodus 3:22 served as a *locus classicus* for this interpretation.

d. *Monastic and spiritual-mystical interpretations.* From quite early times the liberation of the Israelites was interpreted as an example for the call to the monastic life (J. Cassian [c. 360–after 430]). The ever-recurring wish to return to Egypt (Exod 16:3, etc.) recalled the monk who, pulled by the old passions, returned to the old proclivities (Cassian *Conl.* 21.28). The elders (Exod 18:21) recalled the senior monk who was installed over ten monks (Cassian *Inst.* 4.7), and the fasting of Moses (Exod 34:28) was seen in connection with monastic asceticism (Cassian Conl. 21.28).

Gregory of Nyssa, in his Life of Moses (De vita Moysis), took the path already trod by Philo when he interpreted the exodus as a progression toward God. He tied this theme together with a rich variety of individual typological interpretations and explained the details of the exodus as symbols of a timeless philosophical truth and as prefigurations of Christ. The monastic writers often depicted the events of the exodus as symbols of the path of the soul, especially Cassian (*Conl.* 3.7; 5.14-16), Philoxenus of Mabbug (*Hom.* 9), and John Climacus (*Lib. ad. Past.* 15).

e. *Anti-Jewish interpretations.* Although the church fathers frequently appropriated rabbinic traditions (e.g., Origen's *Hom.* 5:5 on Exod 14, and the haggadic perspective that each of the twelve tribes had made its own way through the Red Sea; cf. *Deut Rab.* 11:10), in other instances their interpretations ignited strife between Jewish and Christian theologians. The exegesis of Exodus 12 and 32 makes clear that something substantial was at stake; e.g., after the church fathers aligned the paschal lamb with Christ, they stressed that the Jewish Passover had no further value (e.g., Aphrahat [early 4th cent.], Chrysostom, Zeno of Verona [d c. 375]). The smelting of the golden calf (Exodus 32) marked, according to some church fathers, the dissolution of the Sinaitic covenant (Ephraem the Syrian Comm. in *Diatessaron* 20.35; Augustine, *Serm.* 88.21, 24); and the ceremonial law was treated as a divine penalty for this sin (Justin, *Dial.* 20.3). Rabbinic exegesis developed a converse tendency to defend the Israelites and to ameliorate their guilt. According to one extreme perspective, God had to share in the guilt, since God gave the people so much gold when they left Egypt (*b. Ber.* 32a).

5. Rabbinic Interpretations. In the rabbinic literature the individual aspects of the exodus events and the revelation on Mt. Sinai were frequently treated in halakhic and haggadic texts. Important interpretations outside the Talmud and Mishnah are found in the Mekhilta of Rabbi Ishmael (*Mek.*) and in the Mekhilta of Rabbi Shim'on ben Yohai (*Mek. R. Shim.*). From a later time (though with earlier components) stem the Exodus Rabbah, with an exegetical Midrash on Exodus 1–10 (*Exod. Rab.* 1) and a homiletical Midrash on Exodus 12–40 (*Exod. Rab.* 2), the homily-Midrash Tanhuma Semahot (Tanḥ. Sem.), the *Pirqe Rabbi Eliezer* (*Pirqe R. El.*), with the Mosiac history down to the revelation after the sin with the golden calf (*Pirqe R. El.* 40-48), as well as the collection found in the *Midrash HaGadol* (*MHG. Shem.*) and other works.

Besides the reference to individual verses as *dicta probantia* of halakhic reflections, several legends have been woven into haggadic texts (a typical example: b. Soṭah 11a-12b on Exod 1:18-2:7), including the stories of Jannes and Jambres, the wise men of Pharaoh's court, and the report of an initial abortive exodus of the tribe of Ephraim under the leadership of Jagons thirty years before the actual exodus (*Sem. Rab.* 2:11; *Pirqe R. El.* 48, etc.). Individual episodes, moreover, were given novel interpretations, e.g., the sojourn of Moses in Midian (Exodus 2) became his time of testing; the burning bush (Exodus 3) symbolized Israel's need and God's compassion (*Tanḥ. Sem.* 14; *MHG. Sem.* 3:2).

The exodus, the revelation at Sinai, and the acceptance of the obligations that grew out of those experiences remained of central significance for Judaism. According to the Babylonian Talmud, every Jew in every age was obligated to imagine that he or she personally had come up out of Egypt (*b. Pesaḥ* 10:5; *b. Pesaḥ* 116b). The relevant events were brought together and interpreted in the Passover Haggadah, where the hope in the eschatological liberation of Israel stood next to the remembrance of the deliverance from Egypt (*b. Ber.* 12b; *Exod. Rab.* 3:12; *Shir. Rab.* 2:8).

6. *The Quran*. The *Quran* (see Quranic and Islamic Interpretation) allots extensive space to the events reported in Exodus; reports of this kind are found above all in *Suras* 2:49-75; 4:153-54; 7:103-71; 10:75-92; 11:96-99; 17:101-3; 20:9-98; 23:45-49; 26:10-68; 27:7-14; 28:3-51; 40:23-47; 43:46-56; 44:17-33; 51:38-40; 79:15-26. The exodus traditions are here presented exhaustively, with partial repetitions and considerable divergences (cf. the report of the golden calf in *Suras* 7 and 20). Thus Moses, as a typical representative of God, begins with the task of converting unbelievers (Pharaoh and his people). The Israelites comprise a minority who are finally saved along with Moses, while the great mass of the people (Egyptians) fall victim to divine judgment (e.g., *Sura* 51:38-40; 79:15-26). In addition to HB traditions, rabbinic traditions are enumerated (twelve streams from the rock [Sura 7:160]; the elevation of Sinai over the people [Sura 4:154]).

7. *The Middle Ages (Christian Interpretations)*. a. *The early Middle Ages*. Among the learned Irish of the seventh century, scholars strove to explain the wonders of the exodus reports rationally: The dry seabed (Exod 14:16, 22) was explained through freezing; the miracle of the manna (Exod 16:14-15) through clouds, which could hold manna seeds just as they could contain hail (Pseudo-Augustine *De mirabilibus Sacrae Scripturae*). The commentaries of the Carolingian period show little originality and largely take over exegetical traditions from the early church. Bede, besides his commentaries *Comm. in Exodum* and *Quaestiones super Exodum*, composed *De tabernaculo et vasis eius ac vestibus sacerdotum* on Exod 24:12–30:21, in which he delineated the origin, midpoint, and goal of the church and the ideal forms of the Christian life. Walafrid Strabo (*Glossa ordinaria lib. Exod.*) borrowed numerous interpretations from Josephus to explain strange phenomena and geographical details. Rabanus Maurus (*Comm. in Exodum*) ascribed to the book of Exodus the central place in the Pentateuch since nearly all the sacraments of the church are prefigured there.

b. *The High and Late Middle Ages*. In the eleventh century P. Damian wrote an investigation *De decalogo et decem Aegypti plagis* in addition to his Exodus commentaries (*Collectanea in librum Exodi; Testimonia Exodi*). From the twelfth century a number of Exodus commentaries by theologians of the various orders are extant, particularly from the Benedictines, Bruno of Segni (*Expositio in Exodum*), Rupert of Deutz (*In Exodum*), Georgius Brituliensis (*Explanatio Exod*), Richard of Préaux (*Comm. in Exodum*), and from the Augustian canon, Andrew of St. Victor (*Expositio historica super Exodum*). Relevant meditations on partial pericopes, individual cult objects, and legal provisions in the book come from these and other authors. In many individual cases the exegetes followed the typological-allegorical, the *heilsgeschichtlich*-ecclesiological, and the moral interpretations of the earlier exegetical tradition but at the same time often provided some characteristic, novel interpretations.

Bruno of Segni considered the instructions of Exodus primarily as instructions for the contemporary church, particularly with respect to bishops and priests. Thus the purple in the curtain (Exod 26:31) recalled the obligation of the pope to practice justice. The secret of Jesus Christ and the stations of his passion were also brought forth to the reader (e.g., in Exod 29:10-14). Rupert of Deutz emphasized the christocentric character of Exodus as well, while Andrew of St. Victor's love of interpreting the Scriptures in vernacular language and interest in philological questions stamped his commentary with rational explanations.

During this period the ascetic-mystic perception became of particular concern and gripped, e.g., Richard of Préaux, especially in texts dealing with the theophany on Mt. Sinai. The natural phenomena that accompanied the theophany (Exod 19:16) made plain the path leading from the fear of God to the person's conversion, although even at its conclusion the fear of God remained (Exod 20:18-19). Richard of St. Victor (*Expositio difficultatum suborientium in expositione tabernaculi foederis*) chose the form of the ark of the covenant as the starting point for a consideration of the six stages of contemplation, with the two cherubim symbolizing the two highest steps. For Georgius Brituliensis, the fire and the thornbush designated the whole person with whom God became one, the fleshly essence becoming thereby spiritual. The tent shrine played an important role in this mystical mode of interpretation (Exodus 26) and from the time of Gregory I was seen as a model of the *ecclesia universalis*. Petrus of Celle (*De tabernaculi Moys*) carried out a mystical and moral interpretation. In contrast, Adam of Dryburgh (*De tripartitu tabernaculo*) attempted to illustrate and concretize the tent's individual components by creating great cycles in which the saints of the Bible and early church history as well as personalities of contemporary history corresponded to its parts.

In the fourteenth century, partially under the influence of Jewish exegesis, the first commentaries began to appear in which a determination of the literal and/or historical sense of the text was the central consideration. This was particularly the case with the commentary of Nicholas of Lyra (*Postillae perpetuae in Exodum*), which was heavily dependent on Rashi. Even M. Eckhart had laid special emphasis on an interpretation of individual verses through comparative biblical citations in his commentary (*Expositio libri Exodi*). For the interpretation of individual laws he drew on Maimonides, while for allegorical interpretations he generally referred to other authors.

8. *Medieval Jewish Exegesis*. In the Babylonian talmudic schools of the ninth and tenth centuries, interpretations by Saadia Ibn Joseph (Tafsir) and by Samuel of Chofni, among others, were added to the Torah commentaries. Numerous commentaries were composed in the High and Late Middle Ages, including works by R. Abraham Ibn Ezra, who wrote a long and a short commentary on Exodus; R. Shelomo ben Isaac (Rashi, 12th cent.); R. Hisquia bar Manoach (13th cent.); R. Moses ben Nachman (see Nachmanides); and R. Nissim Gerondii (14th cent.). These commentaries focused primarily on the literary sense and were concerned with a synoptic presentation in light of later biblical-exegetical traditions. Thus, on the basis of Exod 20:5-9, Ibn Ezra assumed that before Moses the Israelites had generally worshiped other gods. He interpreted the forty years of wandering in the wilderness as a time for a free and independent generation able to liberate Canaan to arise (in opposition to the Christian explanation of the wilderness wanderings as the penalty for the sins of the people).

9. *The Reformation Era*. In his "Sermons on the Second Book of Moses" (composed 1524–27; *WA 16*), Luther maintained that Exodus was an example of how God held faithfully to God's promise, how the grace and goodness of God were still valid for distressed, afflicted, and frightened Christians, and how God's wrath was directed toward stiff-necked, unrepentant people. There are sermons on every chapter, including allegorical interpretations of chaps. 1–4, 12, 14–15, 17, 23, and 25–30. Yet Luther avoided the overdrawn allegorizing of others; e.g., the explanation of the burning bush (Exodus 3) as Mary the mother of God. For him the bush represented Christ, while in chap. 1 he saw not only Israel under Pharaoh but also Christians living in affliction under the pope. Yet in chap. 12 he maintained the traditional allegorical interpretations and considered Christ to be the paschal lamb; the waters of Marah (Exod 15:22-26) to refer to the law of God; and the wandering in the wilderness to signify the melancholy of life.

Calvin gave a strictly historical interpretation of the exodus traditions (*Comm. in quatuor reliquos Mosis libros in formam harmoniae digestus* [1563]), avoiding the allegorical wherever possible. The burning bush (Exodus 3) was for him, as in Jewish exegesis, an image of oppressed Israel, who nonetheless suffered no damage, since God was with them. The Passover (Exodus 12) prefigured the death of Jesus. The manna (Exodus 16) represented Christ's flesh, on which the Christian soul fed in hope of eternal life. The ark of the covenant (Exodus 25) was the focal point for the collection of the legal and historical records of Israel and thus the locus for the formation of the HB.

An interpretation of Exodus 1–24 by Zwingli survives (*Annotationes zu Exodus* [1527]). He placed a historic-grammatical approach in the foreground of his exegesis (under the influence

16

of Josephus and D. Kimhi, among many others), which nonetheless gave ample space to typological references to Christ; e.g., Christ the paschal lamb (Exodus 12) and the container in which the manna was kept (Exod 16:33-4), which reflected the humanity of Christ in which lay the deity—the actual bread of life.

10. *Early Period of Biblical Criticism.* In the early history of criticism, from the sixteenth to the beginning of the nineteenth centuries, numerous Exodus commentaries were composed, overwhelmingly in Pentateuchal or biblical commentaries, with the main issues being the philological clarification of difficult passages. Ancient translations, Christian and Jewish exegesis of earlier centuries, ancient authors, and other sources were assembled in a rich mass and compared and evaluated in order to interpret individual verses. Of particular note were the commentaries, usually written in Latin, listed here by author and year of publication: A. Tostado (1528); C. Pellican (1532); D. Carthusianus (1534); J. Brenz (1539); R. Stephanus (1541); L. Lippomann (1550); N. des Gallars (1560); C. Spangenberg (1563); J. Ferus (1571); L. Osiander (1573); H. Oleaster (1586); B. Pereira (1601); L. Ystella (1609); E. Sa (1610); J. Drusius (1617); J. de Mariana (1620); L. Marius (1621); J. Bonfrère (1625); H. Ainsworth (Eng. [1627]); C. à Lapide (1630); J. Menochius (1630); A. Rivet (1633); T. Cajetan (1639); C. Jansen (1639); H. GROTIUS (1644); J. Piscator (1646); L. de Dieu (1648); J. Tirinus (1656); A. Varenius (1659); J. Trappe (Eng., 1662); G. Estius (1667); J. Osiander (1676); M. Polo (1678); C. Frassen (1705); J. Clericus (1733); C. Starke (1763); C. Houbigant (1777); W. Hezel (1780); A. Calmet (1789); E. Rosenmüller (1828).

11. *Modern Exegesis in the Nineteenth and Twentieth Centuries.* a. *Historical-critical exegesis.* Modern historical-critical research began in the first half of the nineteenth century. Previously an inestimable number of monographs, commentaries, and individual contributions had been concerned with questions pertaining to the book's interpretation. Historical, Literary-critical, tradition-historical, and religion-historical lines of inquiry stood in the foreground of these works. Among these commentaries are those of G. Bush (Eng., 1841); M. Kalisch (Eng., 1855); A. Knobel (KEH, Ger., 1857); C. Keil (BC, Ger., 1861); J. Murphy (Eng., 1868); J. Lange (THBW, Ger., 1874); A. Dillmann (KEH, Ger., 1880); G. Chadwick (Eng., 1890); S. Hirsch (Ger., 1893); B. BACON (Eng., 1894); R. Moulton (Eng., 1896); H. Strack (KK, Ger., 1894); A. Dillmann/V. RYSSEL (KEH, Ger., 1897); F. von Hummelauer (CSS, Lat. 1897); J. Macgregor (Eng., 1898); H. Holzinger (KHC, Ger., 1900); (HSAT[K], Ger., 1909); B. Baentsch (HK, Ger., 1903); W. Benneth (CeB, Eng., 1906); A. McNeile (WC, Eng., 1908); B. Eerdmans (Ger., 1910); J. Weiss (Ger., 1911); S. Driver (Eng., 1911); J. Conell (NBC, Eng., 1912); G. Harford (PCB, Eng., 1919); H. Gressmann (SAT, Ger., 1921); H. Grimmelsmann (Eng., 1927); F. Böhl (TeU, Dutch, 1928); P. Heinisch (HSAT, Ger., 1934); J. H. Hertz (Ger., 1937); B. Beer and K. Galling (HAT, Ger., 1939); E. Kalt (HBK, Ger., 1948); U. Cassuto (Heb., 1951; ET 1967); W. Gispen (Dutch, 1951); J. Rylaarsdam (IntB, Eng., 1952); H. Frey (BAT, Ger., 1953); H. Schneider (EB, Ger., 1955); A. Clamer (Fr., 1956); H. Junker (EB, Ger., 1958); M. Noth (ATD, Ger., 1959); R. Murphy (PBiS, Eng., 1960–62); G. Auzou (Fr., 1961); D. Stalker (PCB, Eng., 1962); B. Napier (LCB, Eng., 1965); G. te Stroete (BOT, Dutch, 1966); G. Davies (TBC, Eng., 1967); B. Couroyer (SB, Fr., 1968); M. Greenberg (HB I, Eng., 1969); F. Fensham (Dutch, 1970); J. P. Hyatt (NCeB, Eng., 1971); R. Clements (CBC, Eng., 1972); E. Munk (Fr., 1972); R. Cole (TOTC, Eng., 1973); F. Michaeli (CAT, Fr., 1974); B. Childs (OTL, Eng., 1974); W. Schmidt (BK, Ger., 1974); G. Knight (Eng., 1976); W. Fields (Eng., 1976); N. Leibowitz (Heb./Eng., 1976); B. Boschi (Ital., 1978); E. Zenger (Ger., 1978); F. Huey (Eng., 1980); H. Ellison (Eng., 1982); L. Meyer (Eng., 1983); N. Sarna (Eng., 1986, 991).

a. Literary-critical approaches. The history of modern interpretation of the exodus traditions begins in the middle of the eighteenth century with the literary-critical study of the Pentateuch. In 1753 Exod 6:3 gave J. Astruc the key to Pentateuchal Criticism: On the basis of this text he separated the texts in Genesis and Exodus according to their respective uses of the divine names Yahweh and Elohim. In the course of the nineteenth century, literary-critical lines of investigation stood in the forefront of Pentateuchal research, and with regard to Exodus these reached their high point toward the end of the century. Important in addition to the numerous treatments of the entire Pentateuch were A. Jülicher's 1880 dissertation, "Die Quellen von Ex I-VII"; his "Die Quellen von Ex VII, 8-XXIV," 11 in JPT 8 (1882) 79-127, 272-315; and B. Bacon's *The Triple Tradition of the Exodus* (1894). The priestly pericopes in Exodus were separated with relative ease, especially in Exod 6:2-12; 7:1-7, 12, 16; and in 25:1-31:17 and chaps. 35–40. However, the literary-critical isolation of the J and E materials was developed with much greater difficulty in Exodus than in Genesis (according to the various theories as well as the further identification of sources and differentiations within J and E), since after Exodus 3 the divine name criterion could no longer be applied reliably. Generally, sufficient arguments are now lacking to ascribe a particular pericope to any source with certainty. For example, it can now be established on the basis of a synthesis of forty-eight analyses of Exodus 32 in the period between 1857 and 1978 that five scholars ascribed Exod 32:1-6 to J and nineteen to E; six scholars found parts of both J and E, while eighteen were unable to prefer any assignment to one of these sources. More recent research rejects an indentification of texts with one of the older sources (J or E) and places high value on differentiating between earlier and later passages. In this process, literary layers have also been discovered that belong in the realm of the proto-deuteronomic (Exod 4:21-23; 19:3b-9; 24:3-8, 18-21; 32:7-14).

   b. Tradition-historical approaches. The results of investigations starting from a tradition-historical perspective began to have a decisive influence on the historical interpretation of the book of Exodus no later than the work of G. von Rad (*Das formgeschichtliche Problem des Hexateuchs* [1938] = *The Problem of Hexateuch* [1966]). J. Wellhausen (*Die Composition des Hexateuch* [1899]) had already recognized the isolation of the Sinai tradition, and Galling had elaborated the exodus tradition as the primary tradition, in contrast to the Sinai tradition (*Die Erwählungstradition Israels* [1928]). Von Rad referred to the absence of the Sinai tradition in the confession in Deut 26:5-10 and localized the exodus and Sinai traditions at two distinct cultic sites in Israel. Even Noth regarded the exodus and Sinai as two variant themes that in the history of the traditions had gone their own separate ways before being bound together in the Pentateuch (*Überlieferungsgeschichte des Pentateuch* [1948] = *A History of Pentateuchal Traditions* [1972]). Others rejected this separation of the two traditions (J. Bright, *A History of Israel* [1960]), and assured results were not forthcoming in spite of numerous further studies in the following years. In all probability different groups of the Israelites' ancestors had taken part in either the exodus or Sinai events, although this hypothesis can at present be neither proved nor refuted. It is at the same time unclear in which relationship Yahweh and Moses originally stood to the exodus and Sinai traditions, although Moses plays the most important role in the Sinai tradition as the recipient of the revelation of Yahweh (see H. Gese [1974]).

   Since literary-critical and tradition-historical investigations ceased to take into account the book's present unity, certain approaches have established new emphases in research, including stylistic-structural and linguistic studies conducted on the basis of a "canonical approach" (see Canonical Criticism) and "stylistic criticism." Here the composition of the book's various parts is emphatically considered in terms of each part's final literary form (see Childs, *Exodus* [1974, 1979]). Stimulated by these perspectives, R. Moberly has interpreted Exodus 32–34 as a "coherent and clearly defined unit" (*At the Mount of God* [JSOTSup 22, 1983]).

   c. Religion-historical approaches. The study of ancient and modern Near Eastern cultures and religions resulted in new sources of knowledge for the derivation of numerous exodus traditions. In the nineteenth century the study of Canaanite religion resulted in a new understanding of calf images (the golden calf, Exodus 32). A complete consensus had existed as late as the first decades of the nineteenth century that these images derived from the Egyptian gods Apis and Mnevis. However, the investigations in the following decades led to the conclusion that they derived from the territory of Canaan, where the originally nomadic Israelites had found a new homeland.

With research into Babylonian culture and religion at the end of the nineteenth century, the obvious relationship between the book of the covenant (Exod 20:22–23:33) and the code of Hammurabi was recognized. The connections as well as the peculiarities of Israelite religion in relation to its environment became clear through further religion-historical studies.

d. Historical approaches. It had been recognized already in the nineteenth century that the events of the exodus, the deliverance at the Red Sea, the revelation on the mountain of God, and the wandering in the wilderness had been rewoven into the genre of *Sage* and illuminated by the light of *Heilsgeschichte*. This transformation led to numerous uncertainties in the clarification of the historical circumstances of the book. Nevertheless, there were repeated attempts to tie the exodus events to historical developments drawn from other sources. The thesis that the exodus of the Israelites could be connected to the expulsion of the Hyksos was represented until about 1900 (see Steindorff, RE 3 1:211) and had been maintained as early as Josephus (*C. Ap.* I. 14.25). In the course of the twentieth century, historical research could discover no traces in Egyptian texts of the migration to and emigration from Egypt of the people who would become the Israelites. It was still accepted, however, that the events behind Exodus 1 occurred in the first half of the thirteenth century B.C.E. With the Israelites it was a question of Semitic nomads who had settled in the eastern delta and who had fallen into forced labor there. The "Pharaoh of the Liberation" was, presumably, Rameses II (1290–1224); the "Pharaoh of the Exodus" was Merneptah (1224–1204) or even Seti II (1200–1194).

Attempts to localize the geographical sites named in Exodus are connected with lines of historical inquiry concerning the exodus from Egypt and the wilderness wanderings. Such attempts go back to the time of the early church (e.g., the pilgrimages of the nun Etheria in the 4th cent., *Peregrinatio Etheriae*, and of the pilgrim of Placenza in the 6th cent., *Antonini Placentini Itinerarium*). Exact knowledge of these geographical relationships was not acquired, however, until the numerous expeditions of the nineteenth century, which occasioned many provisional localizations. Nevertheless, none of the places of the exodus events has been unequivocally identified, despite intensive efforts. The same is true of the "mountain of God" in the wilderness: While most scholars identify this site with the massive range in the southern part of the Sinai peninsula, others seek it, with good reason, in the district southeast of the Gulf of Aqaba.

e. Systematic-theological and philosophical exegesis. No special role was ascribed to the exodus traditions (apart from the ethical interpretation of the Decalogue) in the systematic theology of the twentieth century. K. Barth saw the exodus as the history of God's covenant of grace and the realization and completion of God's love (*Church Dogmatics*, 2:2, 673ff.). With W. Vischer (*Das Christuszeugnis des ATs* [1936]) the traditional allegorical interpretations of the historical church reemerged: The child Moses in his little ark of reeds prefigures the child in the stall in Bethlehem; the Passover is set aside and fulfilled by the consecration of the Last Supper of Jesus; the trek through the Red Sea symbolizes Christian baptism, etc. D. Bonhoeffer ("Opposition and Surrender," Letter of June 27, 1944) emphasized that the exodus represents historical salvation this side of the boundary of death, in contrast to the salvation myths of the ancient Near East.

New impulses came into theology through the Marxist philosopher E. Bloch (*The Principle of Hope* [1959; ET 1986]), who interpreted Israel's exodus in the sense of emancipation, rebellion, change, transformation, and expectation. The exodus became a symbol for the program of a permanent exodus of socio-historical hope. Bloch was criticized from various sides, above all for tracing the salvation events back to a revolutionary people's movement and not to the initiative of Yahweh (see H. Kraus [1972]). Conversely, J. Moltmann took up Bloch's suggestion in his *Theology of Hope* (1964; ET 1967) and thereby gave strong impulse to a stream of thought that became important in Latin American Liberation Theologies, where present experiences and hopes are placed in parallel with the biblical events of the exodus (see TRE 10 [1982] 746-47). For Latin American interpreters G. Pixley and C. Boff (1991), the liberation of the Hebrew people has significance for the entire oppressed world. Accordingly, C. Moon (1991) aligns the history of Korean *minjung* with the history of the Hebrews in Exodus, while J.-M. Ela (1991) suggests an African reading of this text requiring the interpreter to enter into solidarity with the marginalized.

Liberation theologies based on the exodus, however, have been challenged due to the rise of Post-Colonial and Feminist interpretations of the Bible. While recognizing the potential for liberation inherent in the exodus, I. Mosala (1989; 1993) and R. Weems (1992) notice that this same liberating message has been used to exploit and dominate other groups. For this reason they suggest that interpreters take into account issues of gender, class, and racial struggles when reading Exodus in order to expose possible underlying ideologies. This is further demonstrated by Palestinian scholar N. Atteek (1991), who argues that liberation for the Hebrew people creates hostility for the Egyptians and the Canaanites as the Hebrew God displaces these indigenous people; this "liberating" story is used by some to justify the displacment of the indigenous Palestinians in modern Israel. Similarly, Native American scholar R. Warrier (1991) parallels the displaced Native Americans with the Canaanites and argues that the exodus fails to be a liberating model for all people.

Meanwhile, feminist interpreters have noticed the prominent roles played by women in the exodus story (*An Asian Group Work* [1991]; D. Setel [1992]). Were it not for women (Miriam, the midwives, Moses' mother, Pharoah's daughter), the exodus would not have happened. In addition, feminists (see N. Steinberg [1993]) are beginning to examine biblical law (e.g. the book of the covenant [Exodus 21–23]), searching for clues that may shed light on the status and role of women in ancient Israel.

Bibliography: C. S. Anderson, "Divine Governance, Miracles, and Laws of Nature in the Early Middle Ages: The De mirabilibus Sacrae Scripturae" (diss., UCLA, 1982). **G. W. Ashby,** *Go Out and Meet God: A Commentary on the Book of Exodus* (ITC, 1998). **An Asian Group Work,** "An Asian Feminist Perspective: The Exodus Story (Ex. 1:8-22; 2:1-10)," *Voices from the Margin* (ed. R. S. Sugirtharajah, 1991) 255-66. **N. S. Ateek,** "A Palestinian Perspective: Biblical Perspectives on the Land," ibid., 267-76. **A. O. Bellis and J. S. Kaminsky** (eds.), *Jews, Christians, and the Theology of Hebrew Scriptures* (SBLSymS 8, 2000). **W. Brueggemann,** "The Book of Exodus," *NIB* (1994) 1:675-982. **G.W. Coats,** *Exodus* 1-18 (Forms of Old Testament Literature 2A, 1999). **R. J. Coggins,** *The Book of Exodus* (2000). **J. Daniélou,** *RAC* 7 (1969) 22-44. **D. Daube,** *The Exodus Pattern in the Bible* (All Souls Studies 2, 1963). **J. J. Davis,** *Moses and the Gods of Egypt: Studies in the Book of Exodus* (1986). **H. Donner,** *Pilgerfahrt ins Heilige Land* (1979). **T. B. Dozeman,** *God at War: A Study of Power in the Exodus Tradition* (1996). **J. M. Ela,** "A Black African Perspective: An African Reading of Exodus," *Voices from the Margin* (ed., R. S. Sugirtharajah, 1991) 244-54. **T. Fretheim,** *Exodus* (IBC, 1995). **A. H. Friedlander,** "Die Exodus-Tradition: Geschichte und Heilsgeschichte aus jüdischer Sicht," *Exodus und Kreuz im "kumenischen Dialog zwischen Juden und Christen* (Aachener Beiträge 8, 1978) 30-44. **H. Gese,** *Vom Sinai zum Zion* (BEvT 64, 1974). **E.S. Glaude,** *Exodus! Religion, Race, and Nation in Early Nineteenth-century Black America (2000).* **F. H. Gorman,** *Exodus, Leviticus, and Numbers* (2003). **N. K. Gottwald and R. A. Horsley** (eds.), *The Bible and Liberation: Political and Social Hermeneutics* (1993). **R. Gradwohl,** *Bibelauslegungen* *aus jüdischen Quellen* (1986). **J. Hahn,** Das "Goldene Kalb" (EHS.T 154, 1981). **R. S. Hendel,** "The Exodus in Biblical Memory," *JBL* 120 (2001), 601-622. **S. Herrmann et al.,** "Exodusmotiv," *TRE 10* (1982) 732-47. **J. K. Hoffmeier,** *Israel in Egypt : the Evidence for the Authenticity of the Exodus Tradition* (1999). **J. G. Janzen,** *Exodus* (1997). **W. Janzen,** *Exodus* (2000). **R. B. Kenney,** "Ante-Nicene Greek and Latin Patristic Uses of the Biblical Manna Motif" (diss., Yale University, 1968). **K. Kiesow,** *Exodustexte im Jesajabuch: Literarkritische und motivgeschichte Analysen* (OBO 24, 1979). **H. J. Kraus,** "Das Thema 'Exodus': Kritische Anmerkungen zur Usurpation eines biblischen Begriffs," *Biblisch-theologische Aufsätze* (1972) 102-19. **W. Langewellpott,** "Untersuchungen zur Geschichte der lateinischen Exodusauslegung" (diss., Zürich, 1979). **G. Larsson,** *Bound for Freedom: The Book of Exodus in Jewish and Christian Traditions* (1999). **N. Leibowitz,** *Studies in Shemot in the Context of Ancient and Modern Jewish Bible Commentary* (2 vols., 1976). **F. Maschkowski,** "Raschis Einfluss auf Nikolaus von Lyra in der Auslegung des Exodus," *ZAW 11* (1891) 268-90. **C. H. S. Moon,** "A Korean *Minjung* Perspective: The Hebrews and the Exodus," *Voices from the Margin* (ed. R. S. Sugirtharajah, 1991) 228-44. **I. J. Mosala,** *Biblical Hermeneutics and Black Theology in South Africa* (1989); "Biblical Hermeneutics and Black Theology in South Africa: The Use of the Bible," *The Bible and Liberation* (ed. N. K. Gottwald, 1993). **J. D. Newsome,** *Exodus* (1998). **E. W. Nicholson,** *Exodus and Sinai in History and Tradition* (Growing Points in Theology, 1973). **S. Niditch,** *Folklore in the Hebrew Bible* (1993). **R. E. Nixon,** *The Exodus in the NT* (TynNTL, 1962). **R. North,** 'Perspective of the Exodus Author(s),' *ZAW* 113 (2001) 481-504. **R. J. Owens,** *The Genesis and Exodus Citations of Afrahat the Persian Sage* (MPIL 3, 1983). R. Paret, *Der Koran: Übersetzung, Kommentar, und Konkordanz* (2 vols., 1980–81. **G. V. Pixley,** *On Exodus: A Liberation Perspective* (1983; ET 1987); G. V. Pixley and **C. Boff,** "A Latin American Perspective: The Option for the Poor in the OT," *Voices from the Margin* (ed. R. S. Sugirtharajah, 1991) 215-27. **D. U. Rotzoll,** *Abraham Ibn Esras langer Kommentar zum Buch Exodus* (2000). **H. P. Schlosser,** "Quellengeschichtliche Studie zur Interpretation des Leben-Mose Zyklus bei den Vätern des 4. Jahrhunderts" (diss., Freiburg i. Br., 1972). H. Schmid, *Die Gestalt des Mose* (EdF 237, 1986). **R. Schmidt,** *Exodus und Passa* (OBO 7, 1982). **W. H. Schmidt,** *Exodus, Sinai, und Mose* (EdF 191, 1983). **D. Setel,** "Exodus" *Women's Bible Commentary* (ed. C. A. Newsom and S. H. Ringe, 1992) 26-35. *J. Siebert-Hommes, Let the Daughters Live! The Literary Architecture of Exodus 1–2 as Key for Interpretation (1998).* **M. S. Smith,** "Remembering God: Collective Memory in Israelite Religion," *CBQ* 64 (2002), 631-651. **N. Steinberg,** "The Deuteronomic Law Code and the Politics of State Centralization," *The Bible and Liberation* (N. K. Gottwald, 1993). *A. Stock, The Way in the Wilderness: Exodus, Wilderness, and Moses Themes in OT and NT (1968).* **S. S. Stuart,** "The Exodus Tradition in Late Jewish and Early Christian Literature" (diss., Vanderbilt University, 1973). **R. S. Sugirtharajah,** *Voices from the Margin: Interpreting the Bible in the Third World* (1995). **J. D. Thompson,** *A Critical Concordance to the Septuagint: Exodus* (Computer Bible Series 54, 1998). **P. Trible,** "Bringing Miriam Out of the Shadows," *BR 5* (1989) 14-25. **J. Van Seters,** The Life of Moses: the Yahwist as Historian in Exodus-Numbers (1994). **R. A. Warrior,** "A Native American Perspective: Canaanites, Cowboys, and Indians," *Voices from the Margin* (ed. R. S. Sugirtharjah, 1991) 277-88. **R. J. Weems,** "The Hebrew Women are Not Like the Egyptian Women," *Semeia 59* (1992) 25-34. **P. Weimar and E. Zenger,** *Exodus: Geschichten und Geschichte der Befreiung Israels* (SBS 75, 1975, 1979).

J. HAHN

THE PENTATEUCH

Leviticus

Before the modern era interpreters of Leviticus mainly sought to find relevance in its message in order to apply it within living religious traditions that were distanced to varying degrees from the ancient Israelite community originally addressed by the book. Modern critical scholarship has shifted the primary focus to reconstruction of the book's origin(s) and the ancient historical reality reflected in it.

The destruction of the Second Temple in 70 C.E. and the rise of modern biblical criticism in the eighteenth and nineteenth centuries divide the interpretation history of Leviticus into three periods, which can be called Temple Period, Pre-Modern Period, and Modern Period.

1. *Temple Period.* As long as the Temple and the institutions connected with it remained, the ritual and ethical prescriptions of Leviticus could be carried out within a fully functioning cultic and legal system. At this stage, which probably began before the HB had been completed, interpreters applied and adapted those laws with reference to the developing tradition of the Temple (Hag 2:11-12; cf. Lev 6:20 [Eng. 27]) and attempted to communicate them in an acceptable manner (e.g., Septuagint) to the dispersed Jewish community.

In the Second Temple period differing views regarding the manner in which the instructions of Leviticus should be carried out created disputes between Jewish groups. For example, rabbinic sources report a disagreement between the Sadducees and the Pharisees regarding the manner in which the high priest should bring incense into the Holy of Holies on the Day of Atonement (Lev 16:12-13; J. Lauterbach [1927] 173-205). Texts found at Qumran reflect dissatisfaction with the Jerusalem priesthood and its practices, including its application of Leviticus. For example, the Temple Scroll (11QTemple) presents a rewritten Torah as a program for reforming the Temple and its institutions in accordance with Pentateuchal laws and extra-canonical prescriptions, which were viewed as coming from God at Mt. Sinai.

Besides literal meaning, other modes of interpretation were employed during the Second Temple period. The book of *Jubilees* (2nd cent. B.C.E.) treats the laws of Leviticus as though they were in force during the patriarchal era. The *Letter of Aristeas* includes a combination of tropology and allegory (145-48): Birds forbidden to be eaten (Lev 11:13-19) are identified as carnivorous and dominating by force, which teaches humans to avoid lording it over others by brute strength. Philo of Alexandria (1st cent. B.C.E.–1st cent. C.E.) sought to harmonize Torah and philosophy through allegory, explaining, e.g., that the required physical perfection of priests (Lev 21:17-21; 22:4) symbolized the perfection of the soul (*The Special Laws*, 1:80). The NT found ongoing meaning in the sacrifices of Leviticus by viewing them as typological prefigurations of Christ's sacrificial death on the cross and subsequent priestly mediation in the heavenly temple (Hebrews 7–10). This typology has served as a framework for subsequent Christian interpretation of Leviticus.

2. *Pre-Modern Period.* After 70 C.E. Jewish interpretation of Leviticus turned to the question of how the Jewish community could continue to maintain its identity as God's holy people in spite of the loss of the Second Temple. In the Mishnah, Tosefta, and Palestinian and Babylonian Talmuds, the rabbis compiled traditional legal materials explaining and supplementing biblical prescriptions, including those of Leviticus. These works sought to maintain continuity with the Temple through discussion of its form, procedures, and principles of holiness.

To provide an acceptable understanding of the biblical text, the Aramaic Targumim included expansions and interpretive renderings. For example, the Targumim avoid anthropomorphic language, like the idea that Yahweh smelled sacrifices (e.g., Lev 1:9; A. Hurvitz [1982] 55).

Jewish interpretation developed midrashic literature, which relates the biblical text to rabbinic traditions. *Sipra* is a halakhic Midrash to Leviticus that provides legal commentary on the Hebrew text. *Leviticus Rabbah* (probably 5th cent.) is a homiletical Midrash that presents homilies on topics related to portions of Leviticus.

During late antiquity, Christians developed spiritualizing modes of interpretation. Origen (3rd cent.) believed that proper exposition must go from literal sense to moral and spiritual meaning. For example, he allegorically interpreted the priest who removes the animal's hide (Lev 1:6) as "one who removes the veil of the letter from the word of God and uncovers its interior parts which are members of spiritual understanding" (Origen [1990] 35). Augustine and Cyril (5th cent.) also presented spiritual meaning along with plain sense. Other fifth- to seventh-century Christian expositors and collectors of interpretation included Hesychius, Theodoret, Procopius, and Isidore of Seville (see W. Yarchin in J. Hartley [1992] xlv-xlvii).

From medieval times through the dawn of the modern era, Jewish scholars working in the rabbinic tradition focused on the literal meaning of the Hebrew text of Leviticus (see J. Milgrom [1991] 63-66). To varying degrees, these exegetes also employed some other modes of interpretation, including Midrash and mysticism.

Saadia Gaon (10th cent.) sought the plain sense even though his Arabic translation is not literal. Ibn Janah (11th cent.) presented exegetical excurses along with his Dictionary of biblical Hebrew. The influential verse-by-verse commentary of Rashi (11th cent.) blends literal and midrashic interpretation, consulting earlier rabbinic opinions to give multiple explanations of texts.

In the twelfth century, Samuel Ben Meir (Rashbam) concentrated on literal meaning even more than did Rashi, while A. Ibn Ezra stressed etymology and grammar, often arriving at original interpretations. Bekhor Shor emphasized the rational basis of the commandments and parried Christian allegorical interpretations. Maimonides (Rambam) demonstrated the value of Pentateuchal law. D. Kimhi (Radak, 12th to 13th cents.) used philology, but also presented homiletical interpretations based on rabbinic literature.

In the thirteenth century, Nachmanides (Ramban) developed literal interpretation and used the Talmud, midrashic literature, and the Zohar to give reasons for commandments. Hezekiah ben Manoah based much of his work on that of earlier Jewish exegetes, and Bahya ben Asher placed mystical interpretations alongside the plain sense.

In the fourteenth century, Aaron ben Joseph Ha-rofe "the elder," a Karaite, provided strictly literal exegesis with occasional Midrash. Ralbag presented philosophical and theological discourses and hermeneutical principles (see Hermeneutics). Aaron ben Elijah, another Karaite, concentrated on the plain sense, but also produced some allegorical and metaphysical interpretations, while Jacob ben Asher emphasized the views of Rashi and Ramban.

Abravanel (15th cent.) focused on the moral rationale for the commandments. Isaac ben Moses wrote philosophical homilies based on Leviticus, and O. Sforno (15th–16th cents.) concentrated on literal meaning. E. Lunshitz (17th cent.) made extensive use of earlier Jewish exegesis.

In the eighteenth century, Hayyim ibn Attar used mystical, kabbalistic interpretation. Naphtali Herz Wessely addressed historical and philological concerns. Malbim referred to non-Jewish modern thinkers as well as to Jewish exegetes.

Through medieval and Renaissance-Reformation times, Christian expositors regarded the literal meaning of the so-called old law, including Leviticus, as a source for various kinds of spiritual meaning in addition to typology, e.g., allegory, tropology, and anagogy. In the twelfth century, Rupert of Deutz used allegorically derived moral meaning to aid the monastic struggle against carnal temptation (see Yarchin in Hartley, xlviii). Ralph of Flaix carried spiritual interpretation to the extreme, regarding the Mosaic laws as a cryptogram in which the inner spiritual meaning was hidden from most Jewish people by the letter of the text. On the other hand, Hugh of St. Victor and Andrew of St. Victor and an anonymous contemporary commentator concentrated on the literal meaning of the Hebrew text and utilized rabbinic sources (see B. Smalley [1974] 13-15).

In the thirteenth century, William of Auvergne reacted against allegorization, using Maimonides' *Guide of the Perplexed* to insist that the ancient Israelites could understand and gain value from the literal meaning of the law. John of La Rochelle countered by emphasizing that the law did have a spiritual sense as a prefiguration of the new Christian law. Thomas Aquinas sought to clarify the relationship between literal and spiritual meaning (see Smalley, 25-68).

In the fourteenth century, Nicholas of Lyra cited rabbinic exegesis and concentrated on the plain sense of the Hebrew text more than previous interpreters had. From the sixteenth to eighteenth centuries this focus on the literal meaning of the Hebrew became the trend among such Christian scholars as Dionysius de Ryckel, T. Cajetan, Calvin F. Vatablus, C. Jansen, J. Leclerc, A. Calmet, and E. Rosenmuller (see Yarchin in Hartley, xlix-li).

3. *Modern Period*. Modern interpretation of Leviticus has abandoned midrashic and spiritualizing modes of interpretation in favor of the literal meaning of the text. However, some Christian scholars have continued to refer to the concept that the sacrifices typified Christ.

Pentateuchal Criticism, which arose in the eighteenth and nineteenth centuries, seeks to understand the plain sense in light of historical-critical theory, which differentiates between hypothetical literary sources on the basis of distinctive linguistic and conceptual characteristics. This approach was embraced by both Christian and Jewish scholars, and by the second half of the nineteenth century a number of scholars had come to regard Leviticus as comprising part of a priestly narrative source that was also woven through the narratives of Genesis, Exodus, and Numbers along with Jahwistic (J) and Elohistic (E) sources. Deuteronomy was taken to represent another source (D).

K. Graf, A. Kuenen, and J. Wellhausen developed the idea that the priestly source (subsequently known as P) was the latest of the Pentateuchal sources and should be dated after the fall of the monarchy, thus eliminating Mosaic authorship of the final form of Leviticus. Wellhausen interpreted the fact that P does not require worship at a central sanctuary, as does D, to mean that after the exile P simply assumed centralization (1885, 34-38). The basic profile of the JEDP documentary hypothesis is still accepted by many scholars today.

Another influential theory was Graf's identification of legal material belonging to Leviticus 18–26 as a discrete literary entity (1886, 75-83). A. Kayser (1874, 64-79) included Leviticus 17 in the corpus, which A. Klostermann (1893, 385) referred to as *Heiligkeitsgesetz*, "Holiness Code," subsequently known as "H." Wellhausen argued that an originally independent H corpus was incorporated into P by a priestly revision (376-79). Subsequently, L. Paton, A. Bertholet, and B. Baentsch sought to reconstruct the redactional process by which the H chapters reached their present form.

A number of commentaries that applied a critical approach to Leviticus appeared in the late nineteenth century. M. Kalisch dealt extensively with comparative religion. A. Dillmann wrote a revision of A. Krobel's 1857 commentary on Exodus and Leviticus and subsequently updated this work with V. Ryssel S. Driver and H. White provided brief historical and philological notes along with an English translation that differentiated between literary sources (P, H, later additions) by means of colors.

Some nineteenth-century commentaries were not controlled by the critical approach. S. Luzzato (Shadal) pursued the plain sense of the text in the tradition of the medieval Jewish exegetes. Christian exegetes who accepted Mosaic authorship of Leviticus include C. Keil, A. Bonar, F. Gardiner, G. Bush, and S. Kellogg. While Kellogg asserted the basic Mosaic origin of the legislation contained in Leviticus in accordance with the claims of the book, he allowed for the possibility that later persons could have written and edited the Mosaic law (1900, 4-5).

In his OT introduction Driver gathered a number of the strongest late nineteenth-century arguments for a late dating of P (1897, 136-57). Points like these have set the agenda for much of the twentieth-century debate regarding the dating of P relative to that of other Pentateuchal sources: (a) The elaborate legislation of P was not in operation during the preexilic period; (b) Deuteronomy does not presuppose the stricter, more complex legislation of P; (c) at least in some respects, such as the prohibition of priestly officiation for Levites, P appears to be later than Ezekiel; (d) in its religious conceptions, such as emphasis on divine transcendence and focus on statistical and chronological data, P bears the marks of a later age; and (e) P incorporated H at a late date. While the laws of H preceded Ezekiel, the paraenetic framework of H cannot be much earlier than Ezekiel because Leviticus 26 has the exile in view.

Driver did not regard these conclusions as incompatible with the idea that "Moses was the ultimate founder of both the national and the religious life of Israel" (152). While Moses began the ancient traditional basis upon which Leviticus rests, the book reflects a long development leading to its final shape in the age subsequent to Ezekiel (153-57). Other critical scholars have been less ready to affirm a Mosaic origin for Leviticus, but they generally accept the view that the composition of Leviticus was a complex process of accretion involving several stages. Such interpreters have made numerous attempts to reconstruct the composition history of Leviticus in order to shed light on the development of the Israelite religion.

Critical commentaries of the first half of the twentieth century include those of A. Bertholet; B. Baentsch; A. Ehrlich, who was concerned with textual criticism and suggested many emendations of the Hebrew text; A. Kennedy; A. Chapman and A. Streane; P. Heinisch; and A. Clamer.

Y. Kaufmann accepted the existence of documentary sources but argued that P was older than D, thus the order JEPD. His reasons include the idea that written Torah, which includes P, is the product of the earliest phase of Israelite religion; it was not an outgrowth of literary Prophecy, as claimed by Wellhausen (Kaufmann [1960] 157-66). The antiquity of P is shown by such factors as its anthropomorphisms, the fact that it presupposes the existence of local altars, its characterization of the prophets as civil and military leaders, and its ignorance of Jerusalem's significance (206).

B. Eerdmans and S. Küchler denied an originally independent existence of H for such reasons as the absence of clear structural and conceptual unity (Eerdmans [1912] 83-87; Küchler [1929] 61-62). Most scholars have not been persuaded by their arguments. The introduction of form and tradition-historical criticism by G. von Rad and K. Rabast has brought attention to the formation of individual units within H. Von Rad saw H as containing teaching for the community based on older laws and presented in sermonic form (1953, 35).

D. Hoffmann's commentary is Jewish in the traditional sense. Along with original exegesis, he made extensive use of rabbinic sources; and although he was aware of critical theory, he argued for Mosaic authorship. His reasons for attributing Leviticus to Moses include the wilderness setting of the laws concerning the offering and the argument that Leviticus 8–10 could hardly come from a later priestly writer to benefit priestly interests because it has Moses, a non-priest, officiating at the consecration of the tabernacle, followed by the story of Nadab and Abihu (Hoffmann [1905–6] 1:13-14).

A. Noordtzij, a conservative Protestant, also attributed the contents of Leviticus to the Mosaic period. However, he accepted the idea that the Mosaic legislation would have been adapted and supplemented during subsequent centuries.

In the second half of the twentieth century, scholars were divided into three main groups with regard to the composition of Leviticus: those who held to the former consensus that Leviticus was produced after the fall of the First Temple in 586 B.C.E., whether during or soon after the exile or as late as Ezra's reform; those who followed Kaufmann in arguing for a preexilic dating of P; and those who maintained a basic Mosaic origin in accordance with the assertions of Leviticus that its laws were transmitted through Moses during the wilderness period.

Although the dates for Leviticus postulated by scholars range over a millennium, their views are not as mutually exclusive as they may appear. Those who believe that the book was completed for the benefit of the postexilic Second Temple community acknowledge the inclusion of early materials; and those who emphasize a Mosaic background allow in varying degrees for later developments in the recording, transmission, supplementation, and adaptation of the legislation.

Critical commentaries with a late date for P include those of H. Schneider; H. Cazelles; M. Noth; K. Elliger (1966), who presents a detailed analysis of literary strata within Leviticus; J. Mays; N. Snaith; J. Porter; W. Kornfeld; B. Levine; E. Gerstenberger; and P. Budd (1996). According to Noth, the history of the traditions behind Leviticus begins with the story of the first great sacrifices in Leviticus 9, which belongs to the original P narrative. Later additions resulted in chaps. 8–10, to which chap. 16 was connected. Chapters 1–7, detailing sacrificial procedure, were added before chap. 8 because the sacrifices of chaps. 8–10 required knowledge of the procedure. The purity laws of chaps. 11–15 were added before chap. 16 to introduce this aspect of cleansing before the great cleansing ritual of the Day of Atonement. The independent Holiness Code book was added as chaps. 17–26, and chap. 27 was appended (Noth [1965] 12-15). R. Rendtorff, however, follows F. M. Cross in viewing the priestly writer(s) as editing earlier tradition rather than producing an originally independent work to which subsequent redactors added (Rendtorff [1985] 138, 146, 162).

Scholars who have supported Kaufmann's view that Leviticus was essentially a preexilic document include J. Milgrom (1991), A. Hurvitz (1982), and M. Paran, whose philological studies have reached the conclusion that the language of P belongs to the preexilic era (see Zevit and J. Blenkinsopp [1996]). M. Weinfeld has pointed out that deuteronomic literature quotes Leviticus but not the reverse, which is understandable only if P precedes D (1972, 180-82). I. Knohl argues that a "Holiness School" (HS) was the redactor of P, which he calls "Priestly Torah" (PT), the opposite of Wellhausen's hypothesis that H was incorporated into P by a priestly redactor. "Since HS originated in the period from the rule of Ahaz to that of Hezekiah, the PT material in the Pentateuch must have been composed earlier" (1995, 220).

Scholars who argue that the basic material in Leviticus originated with Yahweh's revelation to Moses include W. Gispen, M. Segal, R. Harrison, and J. Hartley (1992). G. Wenham, who does not commit himself to a particular composition theory but has difficulty accepting a postexilic date, summarizes the main arguments for the Mosaic view (1979, 8-9): (a) statements that Yahweh spoke these words to Moses are supported by the fact that the material assumes a setting in the wilderness; (b) comparison with non-Israelite cultic practices shows that the cultic system of Leviticus is not anachronistic for the wilderness period; (c) the laws of Leviticus do not adequately address the setting of the postexilic community, which faced such problems as intermarriage; (d) Ezekiel knew and quoted Leviticus. Investigation of the composition history of H has continued with literary-critical, form-critical, and tradition-critical studies by such scholars as W. Kornfeld; L. Elliott-Binns; H. G. Reventlow, who saw the H material developing in a covenant festival setting (1961, 162-67); R. Kilian; C. Feucht; and W. Thiel (1990).

In the last half of the twentieth century, the consensus that H was an originally independent, self-contained corpus has fallen apart. K. Elliger and A. Cholewinski (1976) see H as a redactional supplement to P (Elliger, 16; Cholewinski, 138-40). H. Sun finds no evidence of a pre-P compositional layer running through the entire H corpus and thereby attesting to its unity (1990, 560-61). V. Wagner argues that H is part of the larger unit comprising Exodus 25–Leviticus 26

(1974, 307-16). I. Knohl regards H as the product of a "Holiness School," which had a distinct theological and liturgical perspective and whose work is found elsewhere in Exodus–Numbers, to the extent that this school should be regarded as the redactor of P (see above).

Other trends in Leviticus scholarship include the following: (a) scholars are becoming more cautious in their reconstructions of the composition history of Leviticus (see Budd, 8); (b) there is renewed interest in viewing the text of Leviticus synchronically in order to deal with its theological message and relevance for modern readers; e.g., Milgrom has found fresh perspectives by viewing the cultic legislation of Leviticus as a coherent system that reflects priestly theology and values. G. Wenham, R. Harrison, and G. Knight connect commentary with relevance for Christian readers; (c) tools and data available to exegetes are expanding. In addition to close reading of the text, textual criticism, higher critical methodologies, and comparative linguistics, scholars are making increasing use of anthropological and sociological approaches and sources, e.g. the work of M. Douglas (1966) and D. Wright (1987). At the same time, discoveries of ancient Near Eastern material culture and texts continue to shed light on ancient religious history, language, and culture relevant to study of Leviticus.

Bibliography: H. L. Apothaker, *Sifra, Dibbura de Sinai: Rhetorical Formulae, Literary Structures, and Legal Traditions* (Monographs of the Hebrew Union College 28, 2003). **S. E. Balentine,** *Leviticus* (Interpretation, 2002). **W. H. Bellinger,** *Leviticus and Numbers* (NIB, OT Series 3, 2001). **J. Blenkinsopp,** "An Assessment of the Alleged Pre-Exilic Date of the Priestly Material in the Pentateuch," *ZAW 108* (1996) 495-518. **P. J. Budd,** *Leviticus* (NCB, 1996). **C. M. Carmichael,** *Law, Legend, and Incest in the Bible: Leviticus 18–20* (1997). **A. Cholewinski,** *Heiligkeitsgesetz und Deuteronomium: Eine vergleichende Studie* (AnBib 66, 1976). **M. Douglas,** *Purity and Danger: An Analysis of the Concepts of Pollution and Taboo* (1966); *Leviticus as Literature* (1999). **S. R. Driver,** *An Introduction to the Literature of the OT* (International Theological Library, 1897). **B. D. Eerdmans,** *Das Buch Leviticus* (Alttestamentliche Studien 4, 1912). **K. Elliger,** *Leviticus* (HAT, Erste Reihe 4, 1966). **F. H. Gorman,** *Divine Presence and Community: A Commentary on the Book of Leviticus* (ITC, 1997). **H.-J. Fabry and H.-W. Jüngling** (eds.), *Levitkus als Buch* (BBB 119, 1999). **M. Ginsberg,** *Sifra, with Translation and Commentary: Dibura Denedabah* (South Florida Studies in the History of Judaism 194, 1999). **L. L. Grabbe,** *Leviticus* (OTGu, 1993). **K. Graf,** *Die geschichtlichen Bücher des Alten Testaments: Zwei historisch-kritische Untersuchungen* (1866). **J. Hartley,** *Leviticus* (WBC 4, 1992). **R. Hecht,** "Patterns of Exegesis in Philo's Interpretation of Leviticus," *StPhilo 6* (1979– 80) 77-155. **D. Z. Hoffmann,** *Das Buch Leviticus* (1905–1906). **A. Hurvitz,** *A Linguistic Study of the Relationship Between the Priestly Source and the Book of Ezekiel* (CRB 20, 1982). **W. C. Kaiser, Jr.,** "The Book of Leviticus," *NIB* (1994) 1:983-1191. **Y. Kaufmann,** *The Religion of Israel* (tr. and abr. M. Greenberg, 1960). **A. Kayser,** *Das vorexilische Buch der Urgeschichte Israels und seine Erweiterungen: Ein Beitrag zur Pentateuch-kritik* (1874). **G. Klaus,** *Das Heligkeitsgesetz Leviticus 17–26: Ursprüngliche Gestalt, Tradition und Theologie* (BZAW 271, 1999). **S. H. Kellogg,** *The Book of Leviticus* (ExpB, 1900). **A. Klostermann,** *Der Pentateuch: Beiträge zu seinem Verständnis und seiner Entstehungsgeschichte* (1893). **I. Knohl,** *The Sanctuary of Silence: The Priestly Torah and the Holiness School* (1995). **D. Krochmalnik,** *Schriftauslegung: die Bücher Levitikus, Numeri, Deuteronomium im Judentum* (Neuer Stuttgarter Kommentar, AT 33, 2003). **S. Küchler,** *Das Heiligkeitsgesetz Leviticus 17–26: Eine literar-kritische Untersuchung* (1929). **J. Z. Lauterbach,** "A Significant Controversy Between the Sadducees and the Pharisees," *HUCA 4* (1927) 173-205. **H. Maccoby,** *Ritual and Morality: The Ritual Purity System and Its Place in Judaism* (1999). **J. Milgrom,** *Leviticus 1–16* (AB 3, 1991). **R. North,** *The Biblical Jubilee, after Fifty Years* (Analecta biblica 145, 2000). **M. Noth,** *Leviticus: A Commentary* (OTL,

1965). **Origen,** *Homilies on Leviticus 1–16* (FC 83, 1990). G. von Rad, *Studies in Deuteronomy* (SBT, 1953). **R. Rendtorff,** *The OT: An Introduction* (1985). **H. G. Reventlow,** *Das Heiligkeitsgesetz: Formgeschichtlich Untersucht* (WMANT 6, 1961). **A. P. Ross,** *Holiness to the Lord: A Guide to the Exposition of the Book of Leviticus* (2002). **J. F. A. Sawyer** (ed.), *Reading Leviticus: A Conversation with Mary Douglas* (JSOTSup 227, 1996). **S. K. Sherwood** (ed.), *Leviticus, Numbers, Deuteronomy* (Berit Olam series, 2002). **B. Smalley,** "William of Auvergne, John of La Rochelle and St. Thomas Aquinas on the Old Law," *St. Thomas Aquinas, 1274-1974* (ed. A. Maurer, 1974) 11-71. **H. T. C. Sun,** "An Investigation into the Compositional Integrity of the So-Called Holiness Code (Leviticus 17–26)" (diss., Claremont Graduate School, 1990). **J. D. Thompason,** *A Critical Concordance to the Septuagint: Leviticus* (The Computer Bible 55, 1998). **B. L. Visotzky,** *Golden Bells and Pomegranates: Studies in Midrash Leviticus Rabbah* (Texts and Studies in Ancient Judaism, 2003). V. Wagner, "Zur Existenz des sogenannten 'Heiligkeitsgesetzes,'" *ZAW 86* (1974) 307-316. **W. Warning,** *Literary Artistry in Leviticus* (BibInt series, 1999). **M. Weinfeld,** *Deuteronomy and the Deuteronomic School* (1972). **J. Wellhausen,** *Prolegomena to the History of Israel* (1885). **G. J. Wenham,** *The Book of Leviticus* (NICOT 3, 1979). **J. W. Wevers,** *Notes on the Greek Text of Leviticus* (Septuagint and Cognate Studies 44, 1997). **D. P. Wright,** *The Disposal of Impurity: Elimination Rites in the Bible and in Hittite and Mesopotamian Literatures* (SBLDS 101, 1987). **Z. Zevit,** "Converging Lines of Evidence Bearing on the Date of P," *ZAW 94* (1982) 481-511.

R. E. GANE

THE PENTATEUCH

Numbers

1. *The Foundational Period.* a. *Numbers.* The earliest interpretation of Numbers occurs within the book itself. Commentary on legal judgments clarifies, extends, and even qualifies existing law. Numbers 18:20 clarifies law concerning compensation for priests (18:8-19) and Levites (18:21-24) by stating that priests forfeit land ownership as a consequence of their office. Numbers 19:10b-13 extends the law of corpse contamination from native Israelites to include resident aliens. Numbers 36:1-12 qualifies the inheritance rights of daughters (27:1-11) who marry outside of their tribe. Narrative literature is also reinterpreted through commentary. The positive portrayal of Balaam as a foreign seer (Numbers 22–24), for example, is qualified by the story of his ass (22:22-35) when this donkey becomes more clairvoyant than the seer. The negative portrayal of Balaam is extended further with the addition of 31:8, when the seer is killed along with the Midianites for having led Israel into idolatry with the Baal of Peor.

b. *HB.* Interpretation of Numbers is scattered throughout the HB. First Chronicles 30:2-3, 25 applies the law proscribing a second Passover from Num 9:6, 9-11, 14 in order to add priestly along with lay defilement as a reason for postponing observance of the feast one month. The language of the priestly blessing (Num 6:24-27) is reinterpreted for liturgical use (Psalms 4; 67:2), and the negative interpretation of Balaam continues to be developed. Deuteronomy 23:5-6 states that Balaam wanted to curse Israel but was restrained by God. Joshua 13:22 adds that he was killed for practicing divination.

c. *Translations.* Interpretation continues in ancient recensions and translations of the Hebrew text. The Samaritan Pentateuch interpolates passages from Deuteronomy into Numbers (e.g., the incorporation of Deut 3:1-3 into Num 21:33-35 in the account of the defeat of Og). The Septuagint often interprets the Hebrew in rendering the text into Greek. The protective role of Levites in the campsite (1:53), for example, changes from warding off divine "wrath" in the Hebrew to warding off "sin" in the Greek translation. The Greek translation also replaces all references to God as Yahweh with Elohim in the story of Balaam and his ass (22:22-35). Interpretation continues in the Aramaic Targumim. Anthropomorphisms in the Hebrew are avoided in *Targum Onkelos.* Reference to "before your face" in the Hebrew version of the song of the ark (10:35-36) is changed to the phrase "before you" (*Tg. Onq.* 10:35). More extensive interpretation is also evident. Moses' allusion to himself as giving birth to Israel in Num 11:12 is replaced with a paraphrase utilizing masculine imagery: "Am I the father of this whole people...?" (*Tg. Onq.* Num 11:12). Targum Pseudo-Jonathan exhibits even more extensive interpretation. The final oracles of Balaam, for instance, provide the occasion for messianic speculation along with an apocalyptic interpretation of world history including Rome and even Constantinople (*Tg. Ps.-J.* 24:19-25).

2. *Formative Jewish and Christian Interpretation.* a. *Rabbinic interpretation.* Rabbinic interpretation is rooted in the teaching of the dual Torah that emerged in the Second Temple period well before the common era. Moses received two forms of revelation on Mount Sinai. The written Torah was the complete revelation from God available for all to read, consisting of the biblical books Genesis, Exodus, Leviticus, Numbers, and Deuteronomy. Moses also received an oral Torah passed on only to rabbinic teachers. Oral Torah provided continuity with the fixed, written Torah, clarifying ambiguities and problems of interpretation for later generations. As such, the oral Torah provided a deeper meaning (*derash*), while also clarifying the plain sense (*peshat*) of the written Torah. The rabbinic tradition of oral Torah is codified in Mishnah, Talmud, and other midrashic writings. Rabbinic interpretation of Numbers distinguishes between legal (*halakhic*) and non-legal (*aggadic*) texts.

i. Halakhah. The law concerning a wife suspected of adultery illustrates halakhic interpretation (Num 5:11-31). Such a woman was required to undergo an ordeal of drinking a potion to determine guilt or innocence. Numbers 5:14 notes a condition of jealousy in the husband as an essential part of the procedure, but the circumstances and process of expressing jealousy are not stated. Early rabbinic interpretation explored how the husband was to express his jealousy: "R. Josua says, 'He expresses jealousy before two witnesses' " (*m. Soṭah* 1:1). The topic of jealousy returns in *Sipre Numbers*, where the emphasis changes from communication to the conditions of jealousy: "The purpose of Scripture [Num 5:14]...is solely to teach you that under no circumstances do people impose the rite of drinking the bitter water unless there is a genuine doubt about the matter "(*Sipre Numbers* 7:14).

ii. Aggadah. Aggadic interpretation of non-legal lore was a more free-flowing and speculative reflection on Scripture, exploring allusive (*remez*) and even hidden (*sod*) meanings in the text. Already in the Mishnah details of the story of Balaam are expanded. The mouth of his donkey was one of ten acts of creation on midnight eve of sabbath (*m. ʾAbot* 5:6). Balaam and his disciples are compared to Abraham (*m. ʿAbot* 5:19): they possess a grudging spirit, arrogant demeanor, and a proud soul, which leads them to Gehenna. Reflection on Balaam is expanded further in the Babylonian Talmud. He is unable to enter the world to come, represents hatred, had a crippled foot and a blind eye (*b. Sanh.* 103b), advised Pharaoh on how to destroy Israel in Egypt, returned to Baal of Peor out of greed for payment, and was killed at age thirty-three (*b. Sanh.* 106a, b).

b. *Philo.* Philo Judaeus of Alexandria introduced Greek allegorical method into the interpretation of Numbers. Ambiguities in the Torah are no longer resolved through plain meanings but in the application of non-literal, symbolic readings arising from Greek conceptions of natural law, virtue, and the centrality of the divine soul in humans as the source of wisdom. Philo's interpretation of the ashes of the red heifer (Numbers 19) provides an illustration of legal interpretation (*Spec.* 1. 257-79). The purpose of the law is to purify a person's body, but more important, to purify the soul of passion and distemper. The ashes of the red heifer aid in the purification process when mixed with cedar wood, hyssop, and scarlet wool, which are symbols requiring an allegorical interpretation; they purge the soul, allowing the mind to contemplate the universe. When Philo recounted Hebrew lore, he tended to rationalize the stories as is evident in his interpretation of Balaam. He continued the tradition of interpreting Balaam negatively; but the divine oracles become fictions, the donkey loses its ability to speak, and Israel's superiority arises from the fact that the people's souls spring forth from divine seed (*Mos.* 1. 263-304).

c. *NT.* NT literature blends rabbinic and Hellenistic methods of exegesis to interpret the teaching and life of John the Baptist and Jesus in relationship to Torah. For example, the annunciation of the birth of John the Baptist in Luke (1:15) links John with the Nazirites and conforms him to their vows (Num 6:3). Yet in Matthew (5:33-37) Jesus has authority to change Torah law on vowing (Num 30:2). The dual quest of relating the new teachings of Jesus to the Torah and the life of the church to the history of Israel gives rise to typology. "Typological exegesis is the search for linkages between events, persons or things within the historical framework of revelation" (G. Lampe and K. Woolcombe [1957] 40). It emphasizes continuity and unity between Torah, the teachings of Jesus, and the life of the church. Paul forged the method in 1 Cor 10:1-10 in interpreting the story of water from the rock (Num 20:7-11). He identified Jesus with the rock and Christian sacraments with the water from the rock (baptism) and the manna in the wilderness (Eucharist). Typological reading allowed the church at Corinth to become the wilderness community for Paul. The method was extended in Hebrews where Jesus is not simply identified with Moses but judged to be superior (Heb 3:3; Num 12:7 [LXX]).

3. *Patristic and Medieval Interpretation.* a. *Patristic interpretation.* Debate ensued in early

Christian interpretation of Numbers over the limits of typology. Two examples illustrate the difference between the Alexandrian and the Antiochene methods of interpretion.

i. Origen. Origen illustrates the Alexandrian school's tendency to infuse typology with allegory. In *Homilies on Numbers* IX, he stated that some written laws should be avoided, others read literally, and still others interpreted allegorically; e.g., in his interpretation of Numbers in the *Commentary on the Gospel According to John*, he noted geographical locations from Israel's wilderness journey in Num 33:6, where names indicate "facts useful for the interpretation of passages" (*Com. Jo.* 6.216). But there is also a science (*logos*) to the study of names that is important for interpreting HB locations. The river Jordan, for example, indicates "the word of God which became flesh and dwelt among us" (*Com. Jo.* 6.220). The five animals used for sacrifice on the altar (7:77-88) are carefully described according to their type and means of mobility, but there is also a spiritual (*logos*) significance to the animals as a shadow of heavenly things revealed through Jesus Christ (*Com. Jo.* 6.263-67).

ii. J. Chrysostom. Allegory was more restricted in the Antiochene tradition of interpretation. Chrysostom favored the plain sense of Numbers as a source for moral teaching over allegorical significance. The humble character of Moses (Num 12:3) provides an example for all Christians (*Homilies on Genesis* 34) and priests (*Treatise Concerning the Christian Priesthood* 4). Moses' acceptance of prophetic activity in Eldad and Medad (11:29) teaches that ministry must not be pursued for personal gain. The suffering of Israel in the wilderness (11:5; 14:4) is part of God's larger design, teaching Christians that a laborious life is meant to encourage longing for a future life rather than satisfaction with the present age (*The Homilies on the Statues* 6).

b. *Jewish medieval commentaries.* Rabbinic interpretation extended throughout the patristic period. A rich tradition of Jewish interpretation continued to flourish in the medieval period, ranging geographically from communities in the Middle East to Europe.

i. Saadia Ibn Joseph. Saadia is considered the preeminent exegete of the gaonic period. Born in Egypt, he rose to become the Gaonate of Sura (head of the academy of Sura) in Babylonia. He wrote a commentary on the Torah as well as the first systematization of Jewish belief, entitled *The Book of Belief and Opinions*. Interpretation of Numbers is scattered throughout this treatise, e.g., the book's opening words, "The Lord spoke..." indicate that God created speech. Anthropomorphisms (face [6:25], divine ear [11:18], and mouth [16:32]) are interpreted nonliterally. Contradictions suggesting the abrogation of law are resolved. Thus, for instance, the two commands to Balaam that he first stay and then go to Balak (Num 22:12, 20) enhance his exalted station—Baalam goes only when Balak sends higher-ranking officials.

ii. Shelomo ben Isaac. Known by his acronym, Rashi, he wrote commentaries on the HB and on the Babylonian Talmud in Provence, France, and is noted for emphasizing the plain or simple meaning of Torah (*peshat*) as opposed to a deeper or homiletical meaning (*derash*). His commentary on the home of Balaam in Pethos (Num 22:5) illustrates his method: "The Aramaic word *pethor* means 'a table,' the same as the Hebrew word *šûlḥān,* which gives us the word *šûlḥānî,* 'a money-changer.' So "Balaam was like a money-changer...the plain meaning, however, is that it is the name of a place."

4. *Modern Interpretation.* a. *Reformation and Renaissance.* i. *Calvin.* The Reformer's claim of *sola scriptura* in opposition to the Roman Catholic Church, the rebirth of classical studies during the Renaissance, and the discovery of Jewish medieval interpreters fueled a renewed quest for the literal sense of Scripture in Protestant biblical interpretation. Calvin's interpretation of Numbers in his *Harmony of the Last Four Books of Moses* reflects the new hermeneutical situation. The law is central in his interpretation of Torah, requiring knowledge of the original language and historical context for proper interpretation. He explored historical background to interpret the account of the consecration of the Levites in Numbers 8 (*Harmony* 2:214-19), and the text is further clarified through careful grammatical and linguistic study of

Hebrew. He concluded that the permission granted the Levites to eat a portion of the tithe outside the Temple (Num 18:31) is clarified if the particle *kî* is read adversatively (*Harmony* 2:287). He also noted that the Hebrew word for "tabernacle" (*mô ʿēd*), translated as "assembly," "appointment," "church," and "testimony," is better translated "convention," since the verb *yā ʿad* means "to contract or agree with another, or at least to meet for the transaction of mutual business" (2:297-98).

Historical study served polemical purposes, lending authority to the Protestant claim of *sola scriptura*. Study of the Aaronide priesthood and Levites, for example, refuted the claim of papal authority. According to Calvin, Christ (not the pope) represented Aaron (*Harmony* 2:221). Focus on the literal meaning of the text also brought contradictions into clearer focus (e.g., accounts of Moses' father-in-law in Exodus 18 [Jethro] and in Numbers 10 [Hobab]). Calvin resolved such literary problems through harmonizing different accounts rather than exploring the possibility of distinctive authorship; thus Hobab was actually the son of Jethro. But repetitions, differences in style, and the death report of Moses led other Reformers, like A. Bodenstein von Karlstadt, to raise questions concerning the Mosaic authorship of the Torah (*De canonicis scripturis Libellus*, G1b-3b, G4b-H1b).

ii. B. de Spinoza. Spinoza solidified modern historical-critical interpretation of the Pentateuch in *Tractatus theologico-politicus*. His quest to free politics from religion required a reevaluation of scriptural authority. He wrote that "the universal rule in interpreting Scripture is to accept nothing as an authoritative Scriptural statement which we do not perceive very clearly when we examine it in the light of its history" (*Treatise* 7). History for Spinoza meant original language, analysis of the content of each book, and authorship. Such a method requires no special revelation from God, only natural reason. Building on the earlier work of A. Ibn Ezra (1089-1164), Spinoza concluded that Moses was not the author of the Pentateuch. Third-person references to Moses throughout Numbers constituted strong evidence for him, e.g., " 'Moses talked with God'; 'The Lord spoke with Moses face to face'; 'Moses was the meekest of men' (12:3)" (*Treatise* 8). However, he believed that portions of the Pentateuch were authored by Moses, concluding from Num 21:14, for example, that Moses wrote "The Book of the Wars of the Lord." Nevertheless, the application of a rational, historical-critical method led to the conclusion that the book of Numbers, as well as the Pentateuch as a whole, was a compilation by later writers.

b. *Advocates and Opponents of Historical Criticism.* The rejection of Mosaic authorship called into question the presupposition of past Christian and Jewish interpreters that there was a unity of revelation from Moses to the present time that made Scripture reliable and authoritative. Spinoza stated the new problem: "The history of the Bible is not so much imperfect as untrustworthy: the foundations are not only too scanty for building upon, but are also unsound" (*Treatise* 8). The ensuing debate over Mosaic authorship of the Pentateuch changed the nature of interpretation. Thus the literal sense of Scripture was redefined to mean the historical reliability of Numbers as a book authored by Moses rather than the plain or simple meaning of the text as had been the case in past Jewish and Christian interpretation. Two commentaries, one from the late nineteenth century and the other from the early twentieth century, illustrate the impact of historical criticism of Numbers.

i. C. F. Keil. Keil's introduction to Numbers, written in 1870, consists of polemical arguments for Mosaic authorship. The influence of Egyptian history (the building of Hebron before Zoan in Egypt [Num 13:22]) and culture (reference to food [11:5]) indicates close contact between the writing of Numbers and the Egyptian life of Moses. The literary style of Numbers and the childlike naiveté of the literature, with its immediate contemplation of nature, also signify the book's early origin (11:12; 22:5, 11; 27:17). Numbers 33:2 even states that Moses wrote an account of the different wilderness campsites (repr., 1981, 17-32). The desire to confirm the historical authenticity of the literature also takes over the commentary, thus great care is given to account for the seemingly large figures in the census of Numbers 1 and the need to harmonize these figures with the number of firstborn males (1:1-15). And since the story of the fiery snakes (21:4-9) must also be anchored in history, Keil refuted interpretations that identify the copper snakes as a symbol like the imagery of St. George and the dragon or other ancient imagery of snakes as symbols of healing. The reliability of Numbers requires a literal interpretation of the snakes, and literal means that the event really happened.

ii. G. B. Gray. Gray's commentary on Numbers, published in 1903, represents the flowering of historical-critical research within the framework of the documentary hypothesis. Mosaic authorship no longer plays a role in interpreting the book; instead portraits of Moses and Israel in the wilderness reflect later periods of Israelite history and religious customs. Gray concluded that Numbers was composed of J, E, and P. The J (Yahwist) source is a tenth- or ninth-century B.C.E. history reflecting the life and customs of the Davidic monarchical period. Examples of J include Israel's departure from Sinai (10:29-32), request for meat (11:4-15, 18-24a, 31-35), and a portion of the Balaam narrative (22:22-35). The story of the seventy elders (11:16, 17a, 24b-30), the vindication of Moses (12:1-15), the embassies to Edom and to the Amorites (20:14-21; 21:21-24a), and most of the Balaam narrative (chaps. 22–24) derive from E (the Elohist), an eighth-century B.C.E. history written for the northern kingdom of Israel and advocating a more prophetic view of religion. J and E are separate histories spanning the books of Genesis, Exodus, Numbers, and possibly also Joshua. Gray also concluded that the greatest portion of Numbers (1:1-10:10; 15:17-21, 22-31; 16:8-11; 17:1-7; 19; 26-36) derives from P (Priestly history), which represents a body of literature from the exilic period and later consisting of law and narrative. The result of locating the book's different literary sources within their appropriate historical setting is a history of Israelite religion from the monarchical period into the late Second Temple period.

c. *Twentieth-century interpretation.* Two effects of historical-critical research on Numbers endure in contemporary research. The first is the conclusion that the book was not written by Moses in the late Bronze Age but instead manifests a history of composition spanning the religious development of Israel. Second, priestly tradition and theology dominate the book. Most twentieth-century interpreters build on these two foundations, although the methods of interpretation vary widely.

i. J. Milgrom. The Jewish Publication Society Torah Commentary is written to reflect advances in Jewish biblical scholarship in the fields of archaeology, history, language, and religion and to bring this "new world of knowledge" into conversation with "the great tradition of Jewish Bible commentary" (preface). Milgrom's commentary on Numbers (1990) reflects the best of this effort, focusing on the plain sense of the text while weaving in past rabbinic and medieval interpretations. While a history of composition is acknowledged, an early date for the priestly tradition is the central focus. The incorporation of anthropological research on holiness and religious purity is perhaps the most significant advance in contemporary research. Insight into gradations of holiness (chap. 2; 3:5-43), the rationale for biblical impurity (5:1-4), and the danger of encroachment (chaps. 3 and 18), for instance, clarify the danger of pollution and the power of purgation in priestly religion.

ii. B. Levine. The Anchor Bible commentary is a non-ecclesiastical series aimed at "reconstructing the ancient setting of the biblical story, as well as the circumstances of [the text's] transcription and the characteristics of its transcribers." Levine's commentary on Numbers reflects a growing lack of confidence by biblical scholars in source criticism while also demonstrating linguistic advances in comparative Semitic languages. Levine acknowledges the source criticism of Gray's commentary but limits his study of the transmission of Numbers primarily to nonpriestly (JE) and priestly (P) literature. JE designates a composite Torah document fashioned in the seventh century B.C.E. P is chronologically later. The challenge in interpreting Numbers, according to Levine, is "to explain how priestly writers recast the JE traditions and expanded upon them, thereby reconstructing the record of the wilderness period so as to focus on their central concerns" (Numbers [1993] 49). The morphology of Hebrew words, along with comparison to other Semitic parallels, frequently informs the interpretation of specific texts. Thus analysis of the verbal root *nqh* in the interpretation of the ritual ordeal of the wife suspected of adultery (5:11-31) leads to the conclusion that "purification is integral to the magical dimension of judicial ordeals" (192-212, esp. 207-8).

iii. Current interpretation. The close of the twentieth century and beginning of the twenty-first century has witnessed a renaissance in the interpretation of Numbers. Jewish commentaries blend traditional and modern forms of interpretation for religious and cultic use (N. Leibowitz [1980]; W. Plaut [1979]). Christian commentaries span the political, confessional, and methodological spectrum. Some are aimed specifically at evangelicals (T. Ashley [1993]), while others target broader audiences for lectionary preaching (D. Olson [1996]; G.J. Wenham [1997]; W.H. Bellinger [2001]; S.K. Sherwood [2002]) or theological reflection (T. Dozeman [1998]). Methodology ranges from historical-critical (P. Budd [1984]), to theological and literary (K. Sakenfeld [1995]; J.T.K. Lin [1997]; D. Frankel [2002]), to anthropological (G. Wenham [1981]; M. Douglas [1996]) forms of interpretation.

Bibliography: T. R. Ashley, *The Book of Numbers* (1993). **M. J. de Azcárraga Servet,** *Las Masoras del Libro de Números : Códice M1 de la Universidad Complutense de Madrid* (Textos y Estudios Cardenal Cisneros 66, 2001). J. R. Baskin, *Pharaoh's Counsellors: Job, Jethro, and Balaam in Rabbinic and Patristic Tradition* (1983). **W. H. Bellinger, Jr.,** *Leviticus and Numbers* (NIB, OT series 3, 2001). **R. Brown,** *The Message of Numbers: Journey to the Promised Land* (The Bible Speaks Today, 2002). **P. J. Budd,** *Numbers* (1984). **E. G. Clarke,** *The Aramaic Bible: Targum Pseudo-Jonathan: Numbers* (1995). **E. W. Davies,** *Numbers* (1995). **M. Douglas,** *In the Wilderness: The Doctrine of Defilement in the Book of Numbers* (JSOTSup 158, 1996). **T. B. Dozeman,** "The Book of Numbers," *NIB* (1998) 2:1-268. **I. Drazin,** *Targum Onkelos to Numbers: An English Translation of the Text with Analysis and Commentary* (1998). **M. Fishbane,** *Biblical Interpretation in Ancient Israel* (1985). **D. Frankel,** *The Murmering Stories of the Priestly School: A Retrieval of Ancient Sacerdotal Lore* (VTSup 89, 2002). **E. Gass,** *"Ein Stern geht auf aus Jakob" : sprach- und literaturwissenschaftliche Analyse der Bileampoesie* (Arbeiten zu Text und Sprache im Alten Testament 69, 2001). **G. B. Gray,** *Numbers* (1903). **B. Grossfeld,** *The Aramaic Bible: The Targum Onqelos to Leviticus and the Targum Onqelos to Numbers 8* (1988). **P. W. Harkins,** *St. John Chrysostom: On the Incomprehensible Nature of God* (1982). J. Havea, *Elusions of Control: Biblical Law on the Words of Women* (SemeiaSt 41, 2003). **R. E. Heine,** *Origen: Commentary on the Gospel According to John, Books 1–10* (1989). **R. C. Hill,** *Saint John Chrysostom: Homilies on Genesis 18-45* (1990). **M.A. Inch,** *Two Mosaic Motifs: Freedom Trek and Gentiles are Us* (2003). **C. F. Keil and F. Delitzsch,** *The Pentateuch* (repr., 1981). **M. L. Klein,** *The Fragment-Targums of the Pentateuch According to Their Extant Sources* (1980). **D. Krochmalnik,** *Schriftauslegung: Die Bücher Levitikus, Numeri, Deuteronomium im Judentum* (Neuer Stuttgarter Kommentar, AT 33, 2003). **G. W. H. Lamp and K. J. Woollombe,** *Essays on Typology* (1957). **W. W. Lee,** *Punishment and Forgiveness in Israel's Migratory Campaign* (2003). **N. Leibowitz,** *Studies in Bamidbar* (1980). **B. Levine,** *Numbers 1-20* (AB 4, 1993). **J. T. K. Lim,** *The Sin of Moses and the Staff of God: A Narrative Approach* (SSN, 1997). **J. Milgrom,** *The JPS Torah Commentary: Numbers* (1990). **J. Neusner,** *Sifr, to Numbers* (1986); *The Mishnah* (1988); *The Talmud of Babylonia* (1994-96). **D. Olson,** *Numbers* (1996). **W. G. Plaut,** *Numbers* (1979). **K. D. Sakenfeld,** *Numbers* (1995). **P. Schaff,** *Nicene and Post-Nicene Fathers: Saint Chrysostom*

(1978). **S. K. Sherwood,** *Leviticus, Numbers Deuteronomy* (Berit Olam, 2002). **A. Sperber,** *The Bible in Aramaic* (1959). **J. D. Thompson,** *A Critical Concordance to the Septuagint: Numbers* (The Computer Bible 55, 1998). **G. J. Wenham,** *Numbers* (1981); *Numbers* (OTG 5, 1997). **J. W. Wevers,** *Text History of the Greek Numbers* (1982).

T. B. DOZEMAN

THE PENTATEUCH

DEUTERONOMY

The fifth book of the Christian OT, in Jewish and Samaritan scriptures it is the last of the traditional books of Moses, which together comprise pentateuchal *Torah* (*hammissâ hômse tôrâ* [the five fifths of Torah], e.g., *b. Ḥag.* 14a). In addition to its many individual texts of liturgical, homiletical, and creedal import, two broad features of content account for the book's unusual significance in the history of biblical interpretation. First, the central portion of the book (4:14–28:68) consists of an ordered exposition of divinely authorized law, addressed by Moses to an Israelite plenary that is about to occupy a national homeland in Canaan. Second, this core legislation is promulgated in a framework of poignant theological and prophetic reflection, also in the first-person voice of Moses, on his own vocation and on Israel's as the perennial people of God. In short, the deuteronomic conjugation of covenantal theory and practice substantiates a normative sense of Torah as the constitutional legacy of Moses (Deut 29:10-15 [Heb. 9-14]; Deut 31:9-13; 33:4-5).

1. *Textual and Hermeneutical Foundations.* Some of the key issues pursued in modern historical-critical study of Deuteronomy—pertaining especially to the character and coherence of the book's contents and their relationships to other scriptural traditions—were intimated early on by the several communities of its ancient guardians and interpreters. The crux of the matter is how these communities variously identified and appropriated the Authority of "this Torah" (e.g., Deut 1:5; 4:8) or, with specific reference to its written form, "this book of the Torah" (e.g., Deut 30:10; 31:26; cf. 17:18-20; Josh 1:7-8).

a. *The Essene community of Qumran.* Apart from inner-scriptural testimony (2 Kings 22-23; Nehemiah 8-10), the scrolls of Hasmonean and Herodian periods, recovered from caves in the vicinity of Khirbet Qumran, provide the earliest data to confirm the role of Deuteronomy in shaping Judaic piety and theological politics. More than thirty manuscripts of the book, or excerpted portions thereof, have been identified among the fragmentary finds (cf. F. García Martínez [1994]). This number is well above extant witnesses to any other book of the Pentateuch or Prophets and is possibly exceeded only by Qumran exemplars of the Psalms. The textual horizon of these manuscripts is considerably wider than the tradition stabilized in the MT of Deuteronomy, displaying features that had previously been identified as Samaritan and septuagintal in type (e.g., 4QDeut^q and 5QDeut; see E. Ulrich [1992]). Some of these manuscripts, such as 4QDeut^j and 4Q Deut^n, can be classified as deutero-scriptural because they exhibit extracts from and rearrangements or paraphrases of the biblical text. Like the Nash Papyrus (comparable in date and textual character but of Egyptian provenance), they were apparently written for liturgical or scholarly use (J. Duncan [1992]; S. White [1990]; also DJD 14:7-142). Similarly, the manuscript known as 4Q *Testamonia* links together Deut 5:28-29; 18:18-19; Num 24:15-17; Deut 33:8-11; Josh 6:26—apparently as scriptural proof texts for prophetical—priestly leadership, whether individual or collective, in the succession of Moses. Other Qumran documents attest early forms of *Tefillin* (phylacteries) and *Mezuzot* (doorpost scroll) whose catena of passages include Deut 5:1–6:3 and 10:12-20 as well as the classical (rabbinic) pericopes of 6:4-9 and 11:13-21 (see Y. Yadin [1969]; J. Milik in *DJD* 6:34-85).

The difficulty in establishing sharp divides between biblical, deutero-scriptural, and derivative sectarian works among the Qumran finds is posed especially by documents that rewrite or imitate Pentateuchal literature. Some of these compositions have been called pseudo-deuteronomies: They take the form of testamentary addresses of Moses and are comparable to the already known *Testament [Assumption] of Moses*, which expansively recasts Deuteronomy 31–34 (J. Strugnell in *DJD* 19:131-36; D. Harrington [1973]). Even more dramatic is the comprehensive reworking of

Pentateuchal legislation in the Temple Scroll. This work includes deuteronomic laws drafted in the form of divine rather than Mosaic first-person speech, as though the text were a primal record of Sinaitic revelation—the pristine "Torah of YHWH" (Ezra 7:10; Jer 8:8)—on which Moses based his exposition of Torah (Exod 34:11-27; Deut 5:22-31; Y. Yadin [1983] 1:390-97).

Nevertheless, in works that expressly describe communal piety and polity, the Essenes claim to be strict constructionists of the Torah of Moses. They identify themselves as a remnant of faithful disciples who have covenanted to engage in diligent study and observance of this law's prescriptions (e.g., CD 15.2–16.6; 1QS 5.8-10; 8.15-26). To judge by the literary remains, however, this commitment was not expressed in the production of commentaries on either Deuteronomy or other juridical-cultic corpora in the Pentateuch. Nor is literalistic exegesis of Pentateuchal laws a significant feature even in the sectarian "Rules"—though certainly these works make liberal use of deuteronomic idioms, and they often cite and allude to specific texts (e.g., Deut 9:5 in CD 8.1-15; Deut 17:17 in CD 5.2; Deut 10:16 and 30:6 in 1QS 5.4-5). It seems that the Qumran community appropriated the Mosaic Torah less as a fixed text to be interpreted through exposition than as a revealed vision of divine providence. One way of honoring the fullness of that vision was to expand its literary manifestations; another was to implement it as a discipline for daily life, under the guidance of leaders who were supposed to exercise the inspired authority of Moses (e.g., CD 1.11-12; 3.12-17; 6.2-11; 1QpHab 8.1-3; cf. Deut 34:9). As the principal witness in Scripture to Moses' inheritable vocation and to his own recomposition of the revealed Torah, Deuteronomy supplied both the hermeneutical warrant and the literary template for these complementary ways in which the Essene community was faithful to Torah as a living tradition.

b. *Samaritan Pentateuch (Sam. Pent.)*. The *Pentateuch* alone comprises Samaritan scripture, which is called "holy *Torah*." Each of its five parts may be referred to as "this Holy Book"; individual parts are designated by number, Deuteronomy being the fifth book. Such circumspect terminology respects the Torah's coherent, even unitary character while safeguarding the authority of the whole as peerless revelation received through Moses.

Consistent with this viewpoint is the textual profile of the *Sam. Pent.*, now well illuminated by the Qumran scrolls (E. Tov [1989]; B. Waltke [1992]). The profile is also a principal reason for dating the *Sam. Pent.*'s discrete transmission only from the later Hasmonean or early Herodian period (F. M. Cross [1966]; J. Purvis [1968]). The text-base exhibits inner-Pentateuchal harmonizations, often identical to those attested in Qumran manuscripts (e.g., 4QpaleoExod[m] and 4QNum[b]). Typical are instances in which the first version of an event is filled out with variants from the Mosaic review of the same event in Deuteronomy: e.g., Exod 18:21-27 is reshaped in accord with Deut 1:9-18, and Deut 1:27-33 is interpolated following Num 13:33. In such fashion Scripture is made to interpret Scripture not only exegetically but also textually.

Some readings in the *Sam. Pent.* extend this general harmonizing proclivity in a peculiarly Samaritan direction. At the end of Deut 11:30, for example, the *Sam. Pent.* specifies the location of the oak of Moreh as "in front of Shechem," an identification based on Gen 12:6 (cf. *Sipre* Deut. 56, with the charge that this gloss in the *Sam. Pent.* is needless sectarian falsification of Torah). Much more elaborate—and comparable to reworked texts in 11QTemple—is the construction of a novel tenth commandment in *Sam. Pent.* versions of the Decalogue by interpolating after Exod 20:17 and Deut 5:21 a pastiche of readings adapted from Deut 11:29 + 27:2-7 + 11:30. The effect, no doubt intended, is to conjoin stipulations for a sanctuary on Mt. Gerizim, as Israel's mandatory and sole legitimate cult-place, to the zenith of Sinaitic revelation. Similarly, the Mosaic prescriptions in Deut 12:5, 14, 21 (etc.) were grammatically adjusted to read "the place that YHWH your God has chosen" [MT: "will choose"], since sacrificial worship at the "place" of Shechem had already been authorized and initiated at the time of God's appearance there to Abraham (Gen 12:6-7).

What was at stake in such contextual modifications of the *Sam. Pent.*, and may have contributed to their introduction, is illustrated in Josephus's account of a dispute between the Samaritan and the Jewish communities in Alexandria during the reign of Ptolemy Philometor (c. 150 B.C.E.). The matter in deadly contention was whether Scripture provided Mt. Gerizim or Zion/Jerusalem to be the site divinely chosen for an Israelite temple; according to Josephus, Ptolemy passed judgment in favor of the Jewish argument and executed the Samaritan opponents (*A. J.* 13.74-79; cf. 13.275-83). Whatever the truth of this account, the Samaritan case does not lack Pentateuchal support (Gen 33:18-20; Deut 11:29-30; 27:1-13) and is considerably stronger without the additional witnesses of Jewish scriptures to the inspired work of David and Solomon (e.g., 2 Samuel 6-7; 1 Kings 6-8). There is reason enough here for the restricted, or attenuated, Mosaic Canon of the Samaritans.

Early Samaritan hermeneutical traditions, to the extent that they can be recovered (R. Bóid [1988]; A. Tal [1989]), seem to bear closer resemblance to those of the Qumran community than to either the formal development of pharisaic-rabbinic halakah (authoritative guidance) or to the fundamentalism of the later Karaites. That is, the Mosaic Torah was appropriated by the Samaritan community as reliable testimony to the revelation that became full and preeminent at Sinai (Exod 34:1-27; Deut 10:1-5; 31:24-26). Some internal reshaping of the text of the Torah made it more perspicuous, at least in an early stage of its transmission. Samaritan religious practices, however, did not have to be legitimated through rigorous exegesis of this text (as in Karaism), nor did the Samaritans acknowledge a supplemental oral Torah per se. Rather, their traditional praxis was sufficiently warranted by pedagogical lore whose transmission they traced back to Moses. This hermeneutical perspective is, once again, shaped by interpretation of Deuteronomy (31:22, 28-29; 32:1-3, 44-47).

c. *Pharisaic-rabbinic scriptures.* Designations of Deuteronomy used in classical Jewish sources suggest a somewhat ambiguous understanding of its character. The book is most often identified by its incipit, i.e., the initial phrase of the editorial preface in 1:1-5: *ʾēlleh haddĕbārîm* (These [are] the words), which is commonly shortened to *dĕbārîm*, "Words." According to the traditional view, the whole Pentateuch consists of Moses' words; hence the more discrete sense of the appellation in 1:1 must be Moses' "words of reprimand" (*dibrê tôkāḥôt*) recognized to be a prophetical genre—which are recorded in the following chapters (Deuteronomy 1–3; also 29–32) as a prologue to his testamentary review of covenantal law (see *Sipre Deut* 1; Rashi). However, other authorities took "words" in 1:1 to refer to legal stipulations of the Torah proper, a topic reintroduced in Deut 4:44–5:1 and followed first by Moses' recall of the foundational divine words of the Decalogue and then by his amplification of them (so, e.g., Nachmanides [Ramban]). These alternatives intimate the pivotal position that Deuteronomy occupies between the earlier books of the Pentateuch and the Prophets.

The issue of the book's relationship to earlier Pentateuchal traditions is posed more sharply by the Hebrew appellation *Mishneh Torah* (e.g., *b. Meg.* 31b; cf. *Sipre Deut* 160). The sense can be construed either as "repetition of Torah," thus identifying the book as a general reprise of Pentateuchal legislation in its narrative setting; or as "supplemental Torah," identifying the deuteronomic polity as Moses' secondary elaboration of the Decalogue (Deut 4:1-2, 13-14; 5:28–6:2). These distinctive nuances are not insignificant: The first was emphasized in Jewish tradition and the latter by many Christian interpreters, who sometimes used it to relativize the authority of Mosaic legislation (see sec. 2 below). The Greek equivalent of *Mishneh Torah* is [*to*] *deuteronomion* (e.g., *T. Mos.* 1.8; Philo *Leg.* 3.174; see Eusebius *Hist. eccl.* 6.25.1-2), which yields, via Latin, the name "Deuteronomy." This Greek designation, apparently favoring the second nuance, was introduced into the Septuagint of Deut 17:18 as an interpretative title for the book of Mosaic Torah, most likely reflecting the Greek rendition of a similar expression in Josh 8:32 [LXX 9:5]: *to deuteronomion nomon Mouse*, "Deuteronomy, Moses' law."

Even apart from the Greek translation, however, the ambiguity of *Mishneh Torah* points to the hermeneutical significance of Deuteronomy in the extended, three-part scriptures of rabbinic Judaism. In a conventional sense, the book completes the principal codification of law authorized at Sinai/Horeb (cf. Deut 1:3, 5; 5:1–6:3). In a less conventional sense, it creates collective scriptural Torah by drawing earlier parts of the Pentateuch into its own unique self-identification as "[the book of] the Torah [of Moses]" (Deut 31:9-11, 24-26; see Neh 8:1-3). Moreover, this self-identification forms the referential link between the Pentateuch and the following collections of the *Nebiʾim* (both former and latter prophets), whose initial and concluding exhortations (Josh 1:1-9; Mal 4:4-6 [Heb 3:22-24]) reaffirm in deuteronomic idiom the efficacy of Mosaic Torah (see also, e.g., Josh 23:6; 1 Kgs 2:3; 2 Kgs 14:6; 23:25). The third scriptural division, the *Ketubim* (various writings), was also understood to give manifold witness to the continuing relevance of Torah in Israel's communal life (e.g., Neh 13:1-3; Psalm 1; 19; Dan 6:5; 9:11-14; cf. Eccl 12:13-14). Beyond these canonical corpora, the putative distillations of oral Torah into Mishnah (Instruction) and Talmud (Teaching) were deemed to be rabbinical permutations of the fuller Sinaitic revelation as transmitted and interpreted by Moses and his successors (Deut 17:8-11; 33:10; 34:9; *m. ʾAbot* 1; *Sipre* Deut. 351; *Pesiq. R.* 5).

The preeminent holiness, textual immutability, and insuperable authority of Pentateuchal Torah are fundamentals of rabbinic Judaism (e.g., *m. Meg.* 3.1; *b. ʿErub.* 13a; see Josephus *c. Ap.* 2.184-89). No less basic, however, is the hermeneutical strategy that opens this scriptural inner sanctum outward, extending its sanctifying power into the history of God's faithful people (W. Green [1987]; D. Kraemer [1991]). Accordingly, not Deuteronomy alone, but the rest of Scripture—Prophets and Writings, together with the complementary *Halakot* of oral Torah and even the rabbinical traditions that continue to interpret them—become in effect *Mishneh Torah*—repetition or, better, amplification of the divine words spoken to Israel's generations through the voice of Moses (see *b. Qidd.* 49a).

d. *Christian Scriptures.* The ordering of books in the Christian Bible, emergent in the late second century C.E., effectively prescribed a sequential, salvation-historical reading of the conjoined Jewish and apostolic Scriptures of the early church (e.g., Eusebius *Hist. eccl.* 4.26.12-14). This arrangement, which finally yielded Genesis to Malachi (with the Law and the Prophets absorbing the more fluid collection of the Writings) and Matthew to Revelation, reflects the narrative design that developed from early apostolic preaching (e.g., Acts 3:11-26; 13:13-41) into the more comprehensive periodization of history attested in the patristic rule of faith (e.g., Irenaeus *Proof*; see P. Blowers [1997]; R. Greer [1986] 126-54; R. Soulen [1996] 25-56). In this scheme the primal epoch of creation and fall has its endtime counterpart in the events of redemption and consummation. What stretches between primal and endtime epochs is preparation for the gospel—i.e., the scriptural history of Abraham's lineage through Isaac, Jacob, and the people Israel, separated from other nations but living among them as chosen witnesses to God's interim covenants and sublime promises that would come to universal fulfillment through the redemptive work of Christ (Luke 1:68-79).

In such canonical hermeneutics, Deuteronomy marks the transition or, better, forms a bond between the Pentateuchal and the prophetical segments of the extended protoevangelical narrative. The linkage is conceptual as well as serial. Although the nomistic character and contents of the deuteronomic Torah could scarcely be ignored, the work in its early Christian appropriation figures less as a corpus of perdurable divine legislation than as a farsighted testament, composed of oracular "words" (Deut 1:1 [Gr. *hoi logoi*]; 31:1, 28; 32:44-47; see J. Blenkinsopp [1977] 80-95; J. Barton [1986]). Here Moses, the principal instrument of divine guidance in Israel's constitutive experiences of exodus and covenant-making (e.g., Exod 3:7-12; 14:31; 34:10; Num 12:6-8; Deut 34:10-12), models the spiritual acuity of those who, in his succession (Deut 18:15-22), will also be empowered to impart knowledge of God's providential sovereignty, to warn of impending judgment, and to preach repentance that can lead to renewal of life (Deut 4:25-40; 31:16–32:47; cf. 2 Kgs 17:13; Neh 1:5-11; 9:26-31; Dan 9:3-19; Mal 4:4-6; Matt 3:1-3; 11:11-15; Acts 3:17-26; 7:35-53). The words of Deuteronomy thus inaugurate the testimony of Moses and the prophets; they shape a legacy that prefigures the efficacy of the gospel and articulates a desperate human need for it (Luke 16:29-31; 24:27, 44; John 1:45; 5:39-47; Acts 26:22; 28:23; 1 Pet 1:10-12; see also, e.g., *Barn.* 6.8-10; *1 Clem.* 43.1-6; Irenaeus *Proof* 28-30, 95-96; *Haer.* 3.12.11-5; and Tertullian *Apol.* 18.5; 19.1-4).

Characteristic, but still flexible, features of this hermeneutical profile are widely exhibited in NT sources. Portraits of Jesus' life and teaching in the Gospels identify, with varying degrees of clarity, prototypes in the intertwined careers of Moses and of early Israel (R. France [1989]; D. Hay [1990]; W. Meeks [1967]; D. Moessner [1983]). Among striking instances of this is the episode of Jesus' trial in the desert following his baptism, in which he employs Mosaic admonitions, summarizing the lessons of Israel's sojourn in the wilderness, to thwart Satan's wiles (cf. Matt 4:1-10 and Luke 4:1-12 with Deut 8:3; 6:13, 16). Both continuity of roles and supplantation are apparent in the Synoptic transfiguration accounts (Matt 17:1-13; Mark 9:2-13; Luke 9:28-36) and so too in reports of Jesus' authoritative teaching about what the law and the prophets demand (e.g., cf. Matt 5:17-20; 19:1-22; 22:34-40 with Deut 5:1-21; 6:4-5; 24:1-4; see Luke 16:16-17). Vocational supersession as well as metaphysical precession is explicit in the Johannine prologue, which juxtaposes promulgation of the law through Moses with manifestation of God's "grace and truth" in the work of Christ (John 1:17; Heb 3:1-6; 8). Similarly, displacement of the Mosaic law by the gift of God's righteousness, received through faith in Christ, is integral to the salvation-history sketched in the Pauline epistles (e.g., Rom 3:21-26; 10:1-4; 2 Cor 3:7-4:6; Phil 3:7-11; cf. Eph 2:11-22). This is stated most vituperatively in Paul's address to the Galatian Christians: He declares diligent observance of Torah (Gr. *nomos*)— which is the practical discipline of faith extolled as life-sustaining in deuteronomic discourse— to be a "yoke of slavery" (Gal 5:1), implicating any Gentiles who are persuaded to accept it in the covenantal curses from which Christ has already freed the spiritual heirs of Abraham (cf. Gal 3:6–4:7 with Deut 4:1-4; 11:26-28; 21:23; 27:26; 28:58-59). The argument is more extensive and artful in Paul's epistle to the Romans, a difference suited to the particular audience and issues treated. Here deuteronomic texts are prominent among those Paul cites and creatively reworks to construct a grand economy of salvation whose just denouement requires parity between faithful, Torah-observant Jews and believing Gentiles (cf. Rom 1:18-25; 3:29-30; 10:5-10, 19; 12:19; 15:8-12 with Deut 4:15-20; 6:4; 30:11-14; 32:4-6, 21, 35, 43; see R. Hays [1989] 34-83, 163-64).

2. *Interpretation of Deuteronomy in Traditional Jewish and Christian Sources (1st–15th cents.).* Commentary linked consecutively to the biblical text did not become a primary medium for interpretive study of Deuteronomy until the Middle Ages. By then the mainstreams of classical Judaic and Christian interpretations of the book's resources were well established— shaped during the centuries of Hellenistic antiquity through liturgical performance, preaching, and communal praxis as well as through scholarly apologetics and polemics, both extramural and internecine. The devastating blows to Jerusalem's Temple cultus and Jewish national aspirations struck by Rome in response to the revolts of 66–70 and 132–135 C.E. were critical factors in the divergence of these interpretive mainstreams.

a. *Formation of rabbinic and patristic orthodoxies (1st–5th cents.).* The appropriate role of Mosaic Torah in sustaining the communal faith and the discrete political identity of Israel in the midst of other nations was not Paul's preoccupation alone, of course, nor was it a new one in his era. Deuteronomy directly addressed some of the chief theological and cultural issues, especially in 4:1-40. The agenda for Israel's survival as the unique people of God, which is eloquently sketched in this preamble to the legislative corpus, was developed in both visionary and institutional forms from the exile through the extended Judean restoration of the later sixth and fifth centuries B.C.E. (e.g., Ezra 3:2; 7:11-26; Neh 10:28-31 [Heb 29-32]; Neh 13:1-3; Isa 51:4-8; 61:1-11; Jer 31:31-37). Moreover, the semi-autonomous polity of the Judean commonwealth, based on scriptural Torah and consolidated by Ezra and Nehemiah under Persian auspices, was apparently privileged as ancestral law in the wake of Alexander's conquest of the Near East (late 4th cent. B.C.E.; see Josephus A. J. 11.329-39). The polity seems to have retained this benign status through the first century and a half of Ptolemaic and Seleucid hegemony in Syro-Palestine, until it was undermined and forcefully abrogated during the reign of Antiochus IV Epiphanes (175–164 B.C.E.; see 1 Maccabees 1; 2 Maccabees 1–7; 4 Macc 3:20–4:26).

The latter crisis, with the successful Maccabean-led response to it and the often fractious politics of Hasmonean rule that ensued, is the starting point for Josephus's review of the centuries of Judean civil strife and international conflict that culminated during his own lifetime in Rome's destruction of the commonwealth (B. J. 1.17-30). Already in this account of the Jewish War (or First Revolt of 66–70 C.E.), but more expressly in his later works that define and defend the centrality of Torah in Jewish life, Josephus's theopolitical perspective is deuteronomic, again as epitomized by the paradigm of Deut 4:1-40 (see also Josh 1:1-9; 2 Kgs 17:7-20). Since its constitution in the time of Moses, Josephus maintained, the Jewish state prospered, or decreased and failed, according to the strict measure of its fidelity to God's will, articulated in the laws promulgated through Moses (e.g., A. J. 1.14; 4.176-93; C. Ap. 1.42-43; 2.45-47, 145-89). Judea's recent defeat by Rome is no exception, attributable to the latter's superior might and culture; rather, the Roman legions prevailed because they were implementing God's judgment on the divisive policies and deviant practices of Judea's tyrannical leadership (B. J. 1.9-12; 5.375-419; 6.38-41, 99-110; 7.358-60; cf. A. J. 20.215-18; see ʾAbot R. Nat. A 4).

Josephus's overview of Israel's Mosaic "constitution" (Gr. politeia) takes the form of a broad paraphrase of Deuteronomy 12–26, into which he interpolated some supplementary ordinances from earlier Pentateuchal corpora (A. J. 4.196-301). He emphasized the fairness and practicability of this ancestral legislation, occasionally adding juridical details that are not found in the biblical text but that are most often congruent with Pharisaic and later rabbinic interpretation (e.g., A. J. 4.219, 248, 254; see 13.297-98).

The influence of Deut 4:1-40 may also be discerned in the erudite reworking of the Greek Pentateuch authored by Philo, a leader of the Jewish community resident in Alexandria, Egypt, who flourished in the earlier first century C.E. (i.e., before the war between the Jewish state and Rome). Using terminology and philosophical concepts familiar to his Hellenized audience, Philo extolled at length the virtues of Moses and of Mosaic legislation. He argued that not only is Israel's polity both more ancient than and superior to the ancestral laws of other nations but also that it manifested from the outset the sublime ideals of reason, piety, equity, and amity celebrated in Platonic thought and pursued toward the ultimate goal of the intellect's freedom in the spiritual regimen of Stoicism (e.g., Mos. 1.156, 162; 2.12, 25-44, 50-51; Virt.; Prob. 41-47; cf. Deut 4:5-8). According to Philo's influential analysis, the Decalogue is a legislative précis consisting of divinely articulated general laws (Her. 167-68; Spec. 4.132); these ten stipulations serve as the main heads under which all other Pentateuchal ordinances may be arranged and interpreted as either oracular pronouncements of Moses or his own authoritative specifications of divine will (Mos. 2.187-91; cf. Deut 4:12-14; 5:22-6:3). This scheme for relating the specifics of Mosaic legislation to the moral precepts of the Decalogue facilitated Philo's claim that there is no real disparity between the universal natural order of divine law, idealized by Hellenistic culture, and such sacral rites as Passover that are peculiar features of Israel's experience, shaping its unique vocation as God's priesthood among the world's nations (e.g., Spec. 2.150-67; see Opif. 1.1-3). Conversely, although Philo made extensive use of allegory to exposit the universal significance of particular laws (e.g., Deut 23:1-2 [Heb 2–3] in Spec. 1.326-32), he insisted that the literal, practicable sense of Mosaic legislation should not be denigrated or exegetically abrogated (*Migr.* 89-93).

Philo's work, which brilliantly illuminates an intersection between first-century Judaism and Hellenistic culture, had formative influence on the development of the Alexandrian School of early Christian biblical scholarship. The principal architects of rabbinic Judaism, on the other hand, were the generations of Jewish scholars active at Jabneh and at other sites in Roman Palestine, who are known collectively as Tannaim (teachers, transmitters [of tradition]). Their labors extended from the beginning of the first century C.E. through the early third, when the Mishnah and the chief collections of Tannaitic Pentateuchal Midrash, including *Sipre* to the book of Deuteronomy, were stabilized in written forms. The achievement these works attest is the reconstitution of a coherent Jewish identity, one still resolute as to the insuperable authority, efficacy, and integrity of revealed traditions of Torah ("Torah from Heaven," *m. Sanh.* 10.1) and able to withstand at least interim loss of the Temple service as a means of divine grace and blessing (*ʾAbot R. Nat.* A 4, 14, 38).

The Mishnah documents the jurisprudential consolidation of rabbinic Judaism as an integrated system of faith and praxis. The key integrating factor is a rigorous discipline of piety that, in continuity with the themes of Pentateuchal legislation, interrelates sacral obligations—including those of the defunct Temple cultus—with civil duties and ethical responsibilities. One who resists the entrapments of worldly culture and follows this discipline (accepting "the yoke of Torah," *m. ʾAbot* 3.5; see *ʾAbot R. Nat.* A 20) serves God with the whole self in all aspects of personal and communal life; hence the Mishnah aptly begins with instruction about twice-daily recitation of the Shema, whose keynote in Deut 6:4-9 epitomizes this covenantal commitment of those who comprise Israel (*m. ʾAbot Ber.* 1-2).

The relationship between the Pentateuchal traditions of law and the Mishnah's tractates is complex. The Mishnah frequently cites scriptural sources, often as proof texts for particular arguments; and it sometimes links expository remarks to segments of text (e.g., the serial comments on Deut 26:13-15 in *m. Maʿaś.* 5.10-14, replicated in *Sipre* Deut. 303; see also *m. Soṭah.* 8 on Deut 20:2-9). On the whole, however, the work presents a complex reconfiguration of traditional Judaic polity, for the most part loosely arranged around scriptural loci, rather than an exegetical extension of Pentateuchal laws. For example, the tractate *Makkot* (Stripes), which derives its name from the practice of flogging regulated in Deut 25:1-3, treats various aspects of judicial due process and punishment, matters that are associated with the implementation of a number of Pentateuchal provisions (including Deut 19:1-13, 15-21). The archaic institution known as levirate marriage, sketched in Deut 25:5-10, is presupposed in tractate *Yebamot* (Brothers' Widows), which is largely concerned with contingencies and exemptions in application of the scriptural precedent (see, similarly, *m. Peʾah* on Deut 24:19-21 and *m. Šeb.* 10.3-7 on Deut 15:2). Note is sometimes taken of scholarly differences in interpretation of biblical regulations; a classic example is the dispute between the schools of Shammai and Hillel over the grounds for divorce allowed by Deut 24:1 (*m. Giṭ.* 9.10; see also 8.9).

Midrash *Sipre* to Deuteronomy provides a lucid expositional complement to the associative concatenations of the Mishnah's legal reasoning. *Sipre* is also an anthology of Tannaitic scholarship, composed in this case of selected interpretations and rulings of various rabbinical authorities and schools, attached segmentally to rubrics of the scriptural text (see R. Hammer [1986]; J. Neusner [1987]; S. Fraade [1991]). The legislative corpus of Deuteronomy 12:2–26:15 receives fullest treatment (secs. *pisqa* 60-303). Although some comments of antiquarian and homiletical character are included here (e.g., in secs. 148, 152, 275) most are concerned to give succinct definition to such matters as the logical sense, strict applicability, and continuing relevance of the scriptural ordinances as received and interpreted by the scribes and by their Tannaitic successors (e.g., secs. 153-54, 248, 285; see *m. Yad.* 4.3). Interconnections with the regulations and expository remarks of the Mishnah are both common and illustrative of the exegetical foundations of rabbinic orthopraxis (e.g., cf. *m. Ḥag.* 1.1-5 with sec. 143 on Deut 16:16-17, and *m. Sanh.* 2.4 with sec. 159 on Deut 17:17; cf. secs. 127-43 on Deut 16:1-17, providing a virtual textbook on method). Moreover, the value of *Sipre* as a complement to Mishnaic jurisprudence is greatly enhanced by sections of exposition devoted to portions of Deuteronomy that frame the central polity (specifically secs. 1-59 treating Deut 1:1-29; 3:23-29; 6:4-9; 7:12; 11:10-12:1; and secs. 304-57 on Deut 31:14; 32:1-52; 33:1-29; and 34:1-12). Sensitivity to theological and hermeneutical issues is sharply attested here, articulated often in view of Israel's threatened status among the world's nations and sometimes in apparent defense against the competing claims on scriptural traditions made by Samaritans and Christians (e.g., secs. 31, 56, 311-12, 336). Prevalent themes are that God has neither abandoned the sole legitimate lineage of Abraham, which extends through Jacob and his physical offspring, nor negated the efficacy of the Torah. In sum, the whole Torah, promulgated through Moses, remains Israel's unique and unifying inheritance, witnessing still to its favor with God (eloquently expounded in secs. 342-46 on Deut 33:2-5).

Tannaitic insistence that faithful observance of Torah continued to define the existence of Abraham's true heirs is one of the two major poles with reference to which patristic Christianity sought to establish an identity for the church as "the Israel of God" (Gal 6:16). The second pole is represented by otherwise diverse parties, eventually marginalized as heretical, who shared a view that the cultural idiosyncrasies of scriptural Torah made it largely irrelevant or even antithetical to the universal spiritual redemption effected through Christ. Negotiating a middle course that respected the revelatory import of Pentateuchal legislation while transcending many of its ostensible demands required both vigorous and flexible argumentation. Philo's agile hermeneutics had shown the way.

Themes that developed into characteristic patristic views on the significance of the Mosaic law are adumbrated in the *Epistle of Barnabas,* probably composed in the late first or early second century C.E. By then, destruction of the Temple in Jerusalem and further loss of Judean civil autonomy after the failed First Revolt had decisively altered the terms of the early apostolic debate regarding the extent to which observance of Torah was incumbent on either Jewish or gentile Christians (e.g., Acts 10:1–11:26; 15:1-29; cf. Jas 1:19–4:12). Most substantively, the traditional sacrificial cultus—revealed at Sinai and implemented under Moses' direction (e.g., Exod 40; Num 7–8)—had been physically abrogated, thus rendering key portions of the Torah no longer institutionally practicable. According to Barnabas, however, this did not negate Mosaic law; it confirmed that what the old cultus had imperfectly materialized was now spiritually realized through Christ's expiation of sins, a remission that transformed the church's membership into a new temple of God's indwelling presence (*Barn.* 4:11; 5:1-7; 8:1-3; 16:1-10; cf. 1 Cor 6:19; 2 Cor 6:14-18; Eph 2:19-22; Heb 7–11; 1 Pet 2:4-5). Accordingly, Christ repristinated Moses' work as mediator: He restored the covenant to conform with God's original intention, removing from it the heavy "yoke of necessity" imposed because of Israel's apostasy in the golden calf affair (*Barn.* 2:4-10; 4:6-8; 6:19; 14:1-6); and he unveiled the law's spiritual significance, which had become obfuscated by Jewish literalism (e.g., *Barn.* 10 on the dietary laws of Lev 11 and Deut 14:3-21). Freed from the incrustations of traditional Jewish praxis, the Decalogue especially undergirds the moral "law of Christ" (Gal 6:2), which guides the consecrated community along the "way of light" (*Barn.* 15; 19; see also *Did.* 1-2).

The costly second Judean revolt of 132–135 C.E., whose messianic nativism had significant Tannaitic support, sharpened the divide already evident in Barnabas between a Christian "we" and a Jewish "they" (e.g., *Barn.* 3:6; 8:7; 10:12; 13:1; see Justin *First Apology* 32; Eusebius *Hist. eccl.* 4.5-6; 4.8.4). From the later second through the fifth centuries, this polarization is exhibited in patristic apologetic and adversative writings that defend, often stridently, the church's claim to be the chosen legatee of ancient Israel's Scriptures and covenantal identity (Eusebius *Praep. ev.* 14.52; Augustine *Adv. Jud.* 3; 12; *Trin.* 1.13; *Maxim.* 2.10.1; 2.23.1-3). Two approaches to the significance of Pentateuchal law, distinguished in part by the interpretive uses they make of Deuteronomy, are represented in these sources. One of these approaches is identified with prominent Alexandrian scholars.

Alexandrian Christianity, which may have been the provenance of Barnabas, developed a catechetical curriculum indebted to Philo that integrated scriptural testimony to divine sovereignty with popular currents of Hellenistic learning. An eclectic Stoicism is the intellectual medium used by Clement of Alexandria to commend the ethical sublimity of biblical law in his *Paidagogos* and *Stromateis*, written at the close of the second century. The Word brought near to Israel in Mosaic legislation and in the new law manifest in Christ, the incarnate Word, are understood in these treatises to be complementary, successive stages in a divine pedagogy of saving knowledge (e.g., *Paid.* 1.9, 53-61; cf. Deut 30:11-14; John 1:14-18). As Philo had argued, Moses was a preeminent paradigm of wisdom and virtue; Moses' instructions to Israel, therefore, continue to provide a foundational education for Christian initiates in humanitarian values, preparing them for the advanced course in the soul's spiritual ascent taught by Christ (*Strom.* 1.23-26; 2.78-96; 2.105). Origen, who studied under Clement, made extensive use of allegory and typology to discern the figurative import of Pentateuchal traditions, while disparaging Jewish literalism as parochial (e.g., *Cels.* 1.47; 2.78; 4.49-53; 5.42-50; De Prin. 4.3.2.). In Origen's view, Deuteronomy—the "second law" that succeeds the cultic provisions of the Sinaitic covenant—is the type of Christ's moral law, just as Joshua, who succeeded Moses in the leadership of God's people, prefigures his namesake Jesus (*Princ.* 4.3.12-13; cf. Num 13:16; Deut 31:7-23; 34:9). In the earlier fifth century this position was elaborated by Cyril of Alexandria in his *Glaphyra*, extant portions of which include typological exposition of selected texts in Deuteronomy 21–31. For example, the strange expiatory ritual featuring an unworked heifer in 21:1-9 became intelligible to Cyril as a type of Christ's sacrificial atonement (*Glaph. in Deut.* 643-50).

A second strategy, shaped more by Pauline than by Philonic considerations, emphasized, not the metaphysical harmony of law and gospel, as did Alexandrian hermeneutics, but ostensible discord between them as well as perceived tensions within the Pentateuch. Justin's *Dialogue with Trypho,* set soon after the Second Revolt, exhibits the ambivalence toward Mosaic revelation that characterizes this approach. Although the polity revealed at Horeb specifically for the Jews is declared obsolete, some of the former legislation is acknowledged to remain "good, holy, and just" because it correlates with the new covenant universalized through Christ (e.g., *Dial.* 11, 45, 67). A number of works composed in the later second and third centuries attempt to differentiate between two or more categories of Pentateuchal legislation: Laws instituted by Moses or elaborated by his successors are deemed to be of questionable authority (see Deut 17:8-13; Matt 15:2; *m. Yad.* 4.2; *y. Sanh.* 11.3-4); only the Decalogue receives full approbation as efficacious instruction for the moral life of Christians (Ptolemaeus, *Letter to Flora*; Pseudo-Clementine *Homilies* 2.38-40; 3.41-51; *Didascalia Apostolorum* 1.6; 6.15-17; and, somewhat later in date, the *Apostolic Constitutions*). Irenaus, in his *Adversus Haereses*, develops an influential and relatively moderate form of this position. Especially on the basis of Deuteronomy 4–6, he distinguishes between the sufficient revelation to Israel of God's "natural precepts," encoded as the Decalogue, and two categories of supplemental legislation (Heb. *haḥuqqîm wehammišpāṭîm* [NRSV: the statutes and ordinances, e.g., Deut 4:1, 14, 45; 6:1] rendered in Latin by *caerimonias et iudicia* [the ceremonial and judicial laws]). The latter types were imposed through Moses as interim restraints on Israelite sinfulness; after Christ, they retain only figurative import (*Haer.* 4.15-17). This broad distinction, used to affirm Christian fidelity to the universal moral law as revealed to ancient Israel and to relativize Pentateuchal support for Jewish particularism, became a mainstay of patristic apologetics (see Tertullian *Adv. Jud.* 2-3; *Apol.* 21.1-3; Chrysostom Adv. Jud. 1.5; 6.6; *Stat.* 12; Augustine *Spir. et litt.* 36; *Adversus Faust. Manichaeum* 4.1-2; 6.2; 10:2-3; 16.10; 32.8-15).

b. *Medieval developments (6th–15th cents.).* By and large, interpretation of Deuteronomy during the Middle Ages conformed to the respective mainstreams of rabbinic and patristic orthodoxy. Important developments may be observed even so, especially in ways that traditional views of Moses' legacy were defended and, as became necessary after the turn of the millennium, adjusted to new intellectual circumstances.

Augustine's four-part *De doctrina christiana*, completed in 427, defined the curriculum for Christian biblical scholarship and teaching that prevailed through the Middle Ages and beyond. (The later medieval handbooks of Cassiodorus Senator, Isidore of Seville, and Hugh of St. Victor are in large measure revised editions of Augustine's work.) According to Augustine, Scripture must be understood and effectively exposited in order to fulfill its innate purpose, which is instruction in how to love God and neighbor. By giving careful attention to matters of historical context and to the diction of texts in their original languages, interpreters seek to understand what the inspired authors of Scripture intended to convey. If the "letter" of the text does not yield a sense in accord with the rule of charity, then the interpretation is either false or incomplete; recognition of semantic figurations and use of allegorical method may facilitate discernment of the text's true spiritual sense, which is the only one that can teach Christian morality and nurture faith worth propagating. In short, sound exposition of Scripture is the essential handmaid of practical theology.

This influential agenda helps to account for the unsystematic, disjunctive character of most medieval Christian commentaries on Deuteronomy (and some other biblical books as well): Such works are typically composed of sparse explanatory notes, mostly gleaned from earlier sources, recorded to assist expository study, teaching, and preaching by identifying spiritual tropes that a literal reading of the text might miss (see the commentaries ascribed to Bede [c. 700] and Rabanus Maurus [c. 850]). The earliest extant commentary on Deuteronomy of this type (known as catena) is attributed to Procopius of Gaza (c. 520); it consists in the main of paraphrased extracts from Alexandrian and other Greek patristic sources. Introductory notes, apparently influenced by Philo and Origen, sketch an overview of the book's significance: Read literally, Deuteronomy is a record of the covenantal legislation promulgated by Moses in Moab, supplementing the covenant already enacted at Horeb (citing Deut 29:1); read figuratively, the Mosaic polity points to the natural law of the cosmic "city of God" (citing Ps 87:3). Although most of the expository notes pertain to types and tropes (e.g., the two wives in Deut 21:15-16 connote the Jewish synagogue and the gentile church; Joshua is a figure of Jesus, who is the prophet like Moses announced in 18:15-19), "this Deuteronomy" in 17:18 (LXX) is identified—as Jerome, among others, had done (PL 25, 17B; commenting on the date in Ezek 1:1)—with the book found in the Jerusalem Temple during Josiah's reign and read aloud to the assembled people (2 Kgs 22:8; 23:21). Deuteronomy 32:1-43 receives the fullest treatment, testifying to the importance of this prophetic canticle in Christian as well as in Jewish liturgy and preaching (see Josephus *A. J.* 4.303-4; *Sipre Deut.* 306-33; *Roš. Haš* 31a).

Talmudic amplification of the Torah, in the form of commentary on the tractates of the Mishnah, was substantially complete by the end of the sixth century. The definitive Babylonian version (denoted by b. before the title of the tractate) includes at least oblique response to hermeneutical moves characteristic of patristic theology. Above all, the rabbinical sages insist that the whole Torah of Moses suffices to sustain Israel's sacral vocation, countering presumptions of Christians and others that new revelation has superseded it or that any of its components are "not from Heaven" or lack full, permanent, divine authorization (see *b. Sanh.* 99a; *b. Šabb.* 104a). Several deuteronomic texts provide the scriptural foundations for prosecution of this case. First,

Deut 33:1-5 establishes that Torah was neither revealed to the Gentiles nor meant for secondary appropriation by them; its 613 prescriptions and prohibitions (the numerical value of Torah plus two, which are the initial stipulations of the Decalogue addressed to the Israelite assembly at Sinai in divine first-person voice [Exod 20:2-6; Deut 5:6-10]) remain the legitimate possession of Jacob/Israel alone (*b. Sanh.* 59a-b; cf. *b. Mak.* 23b-24a; b. *ʿAbod. Zar.* 2b-3b; and compare *Sipre Deut.* 322, 343). Second, Deut 4:1-40 and Lev 18:2-5 frame reconsideration (see Sirach 24; Philo; Josephus) of how this covenantal legacy of law comports with general wisdom or rationalistic knowledge ostensibly shared among the world's cultured nations. On the basis of these texts the sages identify a significant difference between the Mosaic statutes [*ḥuqqîm*] and ordinances [*mišpātîm*], one that resembles the distinction represented by the Latin renderings "ceremonials" [*caerimonias*] and "judicials" [*iudicia*]. The ordinances are precepts that Jews, certainly, but also enlightened Gentiles should recognize to be prudent and just (Deut 4:5-8): They include rules for judicial due process and proscriptions of idolatry, blasphemy, murder, theft, and sexual immorality—all matters covered, according to rabbinical exegesis of Gen 2:16-17, by the so-called Noahic or Adamic laws (see *b. Sanh.* 56a-b; *Deut. Rab.* 2.25). The statutes, on the other hand, are sacral rites and regulations, such as the injunction against wearing garments woven of both wool and linen (Deut 22:11), that may be opaque to conventional reason and whose faithful observance honors God's rule but offends the minions of Satan (*b. Yoma* 67b). Torah's discrete, coherent purpose of sustaining Israel's relationship with God is thus violated by any attempt to extract from its corpora universal, natural precepts of morality or to set aside laws supposed to have only temporary or parochial import. Third, the Great Court instituted in accord with Deut 17:8-13 (see 1:9-18; Exod 18:13-26; Num 11:16-25) assumes the mantle of Moses in jurisprudential affairs (b. Sanh. 86b-89a). Because this court's decisions, based on Mosaic precedents, are deemed at once to be rulings intended by God (Deut 1:17; 15:1-2), it is unnecessary as well as illegitimate to revise the Torah by adding to or subtracting from its provisions (Deut 4:2). In sum, constitutional Torah encompasses its own authoritative interpretation (see *b. Sanh.* 87a; *b. Qidd.* 49b).

Other currents of Jewish interpretation of Deuteronomy, flowing from late antiquity through the Middle Ages, are represented in the major Aramaic Targumim, *Onqelos* (*Tg. Onq.*) and the freer, more expansive Palestinian versions, especially Neofiti (*Tg. Neof.*) and Pseudo-Jonathan (*Tg. Ps. J.*). The contemporizing style of these Targumim features paraphrase and adaptation (e.g., *Shekinah* replaces the indwelling divine name in Deut 12:5, etc.) but not allegory; figurative readings are few and usually intertextual in character (e.g., the toponyms "*Laban*" and "*Dizahab*" in Deut 1:1 are understood etymologically, in the senses "white" and "of gold" respectively, to connote the manna and golden-calf episodes [so already *Sipre* Deut. 1]; "Lebanon" in Deut 11:24 is read as an epithet of the Jerusalem Temple [*Tg. Neof.*; *Tg. Ps.-J.*]).

Although apparently redacted in the eighth or ninth century, *Midrash Debarim Rabbah* (*Deut. Rab.*, tr. J. Rabbinowitz) is another repository of older Palestinian-Jewish traditions, some taken over from *Sipre* and other Tannaitic sources. The work is composed of twenty-seven homilies linked to consecutive lectionary pericopes of Deuteronomy in the triennial cycle of sabbath readings. Exposition is diffuse, associative, and anecdotal, often incorporating elements of Folklore (e.g., Moses' encounter with Og [*Deut. Rab.* 1.24-25, on Deut 3:1-2; cf. *Tg. Neof.*; *Tg. Ps.*-J.]; the origin and import of the declaration in Deut 6:4 [*Deut. Rab.* 2.35; cf. *Sipre Deut.* 31]; and the extended account of Moses' death [*Deut. Rab.* 11.10; cf. *Sipre Deut.* 357; *Midrash Petirat Mošeh*]).

The broad turn that occurred in biblical scholarship during the eleventh and twelfth centuries toward closer, philologically informed engagement with the literal text affected exegetical style more than substance in the interpretation of Deuteronomy. The scholar known as Rashi made exemplary use of the method commonly called *peshat* to produce a spare, fluent, lucid exposition of the Pentateuch; but while the work eschews homiletic embellishments (of the kinds attested, e.g., in *Deut. Rab.*), it is vigilant in its defense of classical rabbinic interpretive traditions (giving frequent approbation to readings of *Sipre Deut.* and *Tg. Onq.*). A. Ibn Ezra, another early master of philological method, stated explicitly in the introduction to his Pentateuch commentary that he intended to uphold rabbinical orthodoxy, especially in matters of Mosaic law (*halakah*), against the extremes represented by the reductive, anti-traditionalist scripturalism of Karaite "distorters," on the one hand, and the illogical fantasies of Christian allegorists and of some Jewish homileticians on the other. He claimed scrupulous reason as his ally, and he did not refrain from identifying key Pentateuchal anachronisms—a number of them in Deuteronomy (esp. 1:2; 3:11; 34:6)—that would eventually be used to argue the case against Mosaic authorship (see 3a below). A century later the new style of exegetical study and discourse, still used in resolute advocacy of traditional Judaism, was brilliantly displayed in the work of Nachmanides. He often expressly called into question the interpretive views of Rashi and Ibn Ezra, sometimes even when they had ostensible support in classical sources, and argued for his own positions on grounds of their greater fidelity to contextual plain sense (see, e.g., his remarks on Deut 1:12, 25; 5:15; 6:2-3; 8:4; 29:29[28]). Yet Nachmanides was not a philosophical rationalist. More than occasionally he alluded to a spiritual sense—the mystical "way of truth" (Kabbalah)—which transcends but does not negate the rational contours of *peshat* (e.g., on Deut 4:21; 5:26; 32:20).

Duality of textual "letter" and "spirit" remained fundamental to Christian interpretation of the Pentateuch during this period and the rest of the Middle Ages, but renewed attention was given to Augustine's emphases on literary context and philology (which had anticipated key aspects of peshat) as necessary guides in the pursuit of right spiritual understanding (B. Smalley [1952]; K. Froehlich [1977]). The earlier twelfth-century works of Rupert of Deutz and of Hugh of St. Victor, different though they are, exhibit a shift away from disjointed tropology in favor of broad salvation-historical designs that highlight thematic continuities of Scripture. Still, the older eclectic style of the catena continued in the Glossa Ordinaria, which prevailed as a Christian expository resource from the eleventh through the thirteenth centuries (finally to be superseded in the 14th cent. by Nicholas of Lyra's *Postilla litteralis*). Annotations to Deuteronomy in the *Glossa* are quite mixed in character. Jerome, Augustine, Isidore of Seville, and Rabanus Maurus are often cited, but most comments are unattributed. A few display rudimentary knowledge of Hebrew (e.g., the note on Deut 16:1, naming Nisan as the month in which the exodus occurred). Many more identify figurative readings: for example, the eleven-day journey from Horeb to Kadesh-barnea symbolizes the move from the Mosaic law to the proclamation of the gospel in the preaching of the original apostles, minus Judas, of course (1:2); manna is a trope for Christ's body (8:3); the three cities of refuge to be appointed in the promised homeland signify faith, hope, and charity (19:2).

The line between classical Jewish and Christian approaches to Mosaic law was redrawn in the monumental syntheses constructed by Maimonides and by Thomas Aquinas. There is a close intellectual bond between these scholars. Influenced by the resurgence of Aristotelian philosophy as cultivated initially in Islam, each wanted to discern and describe comprehensively, to codify, how normative faith and religious praxis are grounded in the ultimate rationality of scriptural revelation.

The centerpiece of Maimonides' vast project is entitled, not coincidentally, Mishneh Torah—borrowing the descriptive Hebrew name for the book of Deuteronomy (see 1c above). In an earlier work, *The Book of the Commandments*, Maimonides first explained his criteria and then offered a schematic enumeration of the 613 perennial precepts of Pentateuchal Torah (i.e., 248 prescriptions and 365 prohibitions that Israel is covenantally obliged to observe in perpetuity). *Mishneh Torah* completes this codification (I. Twersky [1980]). Following the precedent of Deuteronomy (e.g., 1:5; 4:1; 29:1 [28:69]) Maimonides redrafted and exposited the authoritative extensions of the Mosaic Torah crystallized in classical rabbinic sources. His work not only reconfigured the provisions of the Talmud in order to make them more intelligible and accessible to Jewish practitioners but also bound them closely to their Pentateuchal loci, thereby countering the charges of the Karaites and others that rabbinical traditions had violated divine law by presumptuously adding to it. In both *Mishneh Torah* (esp. *Me'ilah* 8.8; *Melakim* 11-12) and his later, far more controversial *Guide of the Perplexed* (esp. 2.25, 39; 3.26-35, 51), Maimonides argued that the whole Torah was given to Israel to provide this people alone with a sufficient, practicable, and purposeful revelation of God's will, as complete and perdurable as the divine orders of creation. Each of the Torah's provisions has utility, though the reasons for some of them are not meant to be readily discerned lest human arrogance deem them too easy or idle: the ordinances [*mišpātîm*] establish rules of justice and guard against unhealthy and immoral acts; the statutes [*huqqîm*] shield Israel from idolatrous practices and opinions and prescribe the spiritual discipline that leads to communion with God.

Thomas Aquinas entered the Dominican order in 1243, a decade after the Dominicans had staged a public burning of Maimonides' *Guide*. Yet Thomas not only read this synthesis of biblical and philosophical theology, which many Jews as well as Christians considered dangerous (H. Ben-Sasson [1971]), but also acknowledged the value of its scholarship in his own masterwork (e.g., *Summa Theologiae* [*ST*] Ia2ae 101.1, 102.6.8). Nevertheless, the difference of emphasis separating these approaches to Mosaic law is intractable. According to Maimonides' analysis, the divinely legislated particularity of Israel's sacral identity, revealed through the Torah, remains cogent when articulated within an Aristotelian framework of universal wisdom. Conversely, Thomas's scholasticism understood the rational coherence of the "old law" to be an axiomatic witness, together with the rest of Scripture, to the all-encompassing scope of God's providence (see esp. *ST* Ia. I.6, citing Deut 4:6 as proof text).

Thomas's overview of the old law, although anticipated in important respects by Philo and Irenaeus, adverts directly to the hermeneutical agenda of Augustine (*ST* 1a2ae 98-105; cf. *On Charity*, art. 7). The central claim is that Scripture's moral legislation, epitomized in the Decalogue, reveals what sin had obscured: the natural, universal duties of humankind to love God and the neighbor as oneself (*ST* 1a2ae 100.3-5, 11). The Jewish people were chosen to receive this mandate in order to predispose them to reject idolatry and to encourage "a certain preeminence in sanctity" because Christ was to be descended from them (*ST* 1a2ae 98.2-6). Moreover, scholarly reason is able to discern how the principal categories of Mosaic law—the ceremonial statutes and the judicial ordinances—apply precepts of the moral law to the circumstances of ancient Israel's historical existence. Ceremonials were given to teach right worship of God in preparation for the advent of Christ, who is prefigured by them: For example, the literal sense of Deut 12:2-28 prescribes the unification of Israel's worship by restricting sacrifical service to one divinely chosen sanctuary; the spiritual sense signifies the unity of the church in Christ (*ST* 1a2ae 102.4). The literal sense alone suffices to show how the ordinances are designed to promote justice in human society. Although these rules have also been superseded by Christ's "new law" of grace, civil government may choose to reinstitute them on the grounds of their rational merit (*ST* 1a2ae 103-4; see, e.g., the use of Deut 17:6 and 19:15 as judicial exempla in *ST* 2a2ae 70.2). Thomas's form of the distinction between statutes and ordinances is momentous: It portends renewed conflict between ecclesial and civil claims to exercise the authority of Scripture.

3. *From the Reformation to the Present Day*. The taxonomy and the theological significance of biblical law received considerable attention during the Middle Ages; the particular character and purpose of the book of Deuteronomy did not. That began to change in the sixteenth century. Some German Reformers and, more successfully, Calvin and his heirs, who developed the Protestant Reformed tradition, appropriated Deuteronomy as a model for reconstruction of civil

society. Their experiments with theocractic government touched off a much wider debate that extended through the seventeenth and eighteenth centuries and whose results include works foundational to modern political theory. The debate also encouraged the development of a critical historiography of scriptural literature, setting the agenda of nineteenth- and twentieth-century biblical scholarship.

a. *Deuteronomic law in early Protestant exegesis, Reformed politics, and rationalist critiques (16th–18th cents.).* W. Tyndale's English Translation of the Hebrew Pentateuch (1530) is an exuberant witness to the confluence of Renaissance scholarship and evangelical zeal that reshaped Western Christendom during the sixteenth century. Tyndale stated in prefatory remarks that he intended his work to nurture renewal of personal faith among English laity but also to provide a mandate for both social reform and ecclesial revolution. He spurned allegorical interpretation because it veils the literal, practical import of Mosaic laws for the maintenance of the "common weal." Moses himself should be honored, not as "a figure of Christ," but as "an example unto all princes and to all that are in authority, how to rule unto God's pleasure and unto their neighbors' profit" (Mombert ed., 161 [archaic spelling modified here and below]). Deuteronomy receives particular approbation: "This is a book worthy to be read in day and night and never to be out of hands. For it is the most excellent of all the books of Moses. It is easy also and light . . . a preaching of faith and love: deducing the love to God out of faith, and the love of a man's neighbor out of the love of God" (Mombert, 517). Tyndale's sparse marginal notes to Deuteronomy usually offer benign explanations of words (e.g., the sense of "unclean" in 12:15), but rhetorical jabs at papal authority and clericalism of the kind that Henry VIII considered so treacherous as to earn Tyndale a sentence of death (carried out in 1536) are also liberally represented. At Deut 5:15, for example, he remarks that "God shows a cause why we ought to keep his commandments—the pope does not" (Mombert, 543; see also comments at 1:43; 6:18-19; 19:15; 23:18).

While working abroad on his translation of the Pentateuch, Tyndale observed social turmoil in Europe, instigated by Reformers like A. von Karlstadt M. Bucer and H. Zwingli, who invoked biblical legislation, especially the Decalogue and Deuteronomy, to authorize anti-Roman Catholic iconoclasm and broad political change. In sermons delivered in July of 1524, T. Münzer exhorted Saxon princes to use the sword to implement Deut 7:5-6, just as Judah's reforming kings Hezekiah and Josiah had effectively done (2 Kgs 18:4; 23:4-8). In one arena of the so-called Peasants' Revolt of 1524-25, Swabian serfs demanded that overlords grant them a measure of autonomy and economic relief, citing the "godly law" of Scripture (esp. Deut 12:8-12; 15:1-18; 26:12-15) to overturn the complicity of Roman imperial and canon law with oppressive feudalism (P. Blickle [1981]).

Luther remained substantially Thomistic in his approach to Mosaic law, although this is sometimes concealed by his strident rhetoric in countering the arguments of Karlstadt and others. His 1523 treatise, *On Secular Authority*, argues that "true Christians," those who are ruled by love of God and neighbor inscribed in their hearts, should need neither human government nor external codes to restrain them (citing Matt 5; 1 Tim 1:9). But liberated Christians also acknowledge—in accord with scriptural witnesses (esp. Rom 13; 1 Pet 2:13-17)—that civil rulers are divinely authorized to govern and to use the sword when necessary "to punish the wicked and protect the just" (H. Höpfl [1991] 7; *LW* 45, 87). Luther's response to the "enthusiasts" who "desire to govern people according to the letter of the law of Moses" was sharply stated in a sermon delivered in 1526 (*How Christians Should Regard Moses*; see also his treatise written in the same year, *Against the Heavenly Prophets*): "Moses is dead. His rule ended when Christ came." Even the Decalogue, Luther added, is not pristine "moral law"; its precepts pertain only to those specifically addressed, the ancestors of the Jews whom God delivered from Egypt (Exod 20:1; Deut 5:6). "We will regard Moses as a teacher, but we will not regard him as our lawgiver—unless he agrees with both the NT and the natural law" (*LW* 35, 165). For Luther, to be sure, Moses as teacher looms large: "If I were emperor, I would take from Moses a model for [my] statutes; not that Moses should be binding on me, but that I should be free to follow him in ruling as he rules" (*LW* 35, 166). More important than Moses' juridical acumen, however, is his testimony to what humanity could not learn through natural revelation alone: "the promises and pledges of God about Christ" (such as the prognosis of Moses' messianic counterpart in Deut 18:15-16 [*LW* 35, 168-69, 173; cf. *LW* 9, 176-90]).

In his Lectures on Deuteronomy (1525), Luther offered a quite positive assessment of Moses' work not only as harbinger of the gospel but also as practical lawgiver and effective teacher. He understood the book to consist of testamentary discourses, summarizing "the total Law and wisdom of the people of Israel," which Moses delivered over the course of perhaps as many as ten days (*LW* 9, 14, 60). The central portion of the book publishes Moses' authoritative exposition of the Decalogue: The three precepts of the "first table" (Deut 5:6-15 according to Luther's count and partition), concerned with right worship and godliness in civil affairs, are elaborated in Deuteronomy 6–18; the seven commandments of the "second table" (Deut 5:16-21) are more loosely treated in chapters 19–26 (*LW* 9, 63, 67, 193). Luther's exegetical style here is episodic and homiletical; though generally engaging the "literal" sense of the text, his exposition also includes considerable allegorizing (e.g., the single sanctuary is a trope for the unity of apostolic faith [*LW* 9, 126]; the proscription of women bearing arms or wearing male clothing in Deut 22:5 teaches that faith should not be perverted by works [*LW* 9, 224]).

Calvin's approach to Pentateuchal legislation resembles Luther's in some respects but is more consistently Thomistic (e.g., in using the traditional categories: moral, ceremonial, judicial) and also much bolder in advocating the law's import for contemporary Christian life. Editions of his Institutes, published between 1536 and 1559, are consonant in treating law and gospel as integral dispensations of divine grace. While these dispensations are historically conditioned, differing in their covenantal or administrative emphases, they are equally devoted to reconciliation between God and humankind; precepts of the Mosaic law, even those that are no longer obligatory, thus continue to provide the faithful with useful, practicable knowledge of God's sovereign will (*Institutes* 1.6.2; 2.7.3-15; 4.20.15-16). Similarly, while Calvin declared it foolish for any Christian commonwealth to constitute itself formally on the restrictive basis of the Pentateuchal revelation of divine or natural law, which had been promulgated specifically for ancient Israel, he nonetheless insisted that Moses' legislation authorizes civil government that is competent to defend "a public form of religion" as well as to secure social justice and judicial equity (*Institutes* 4.20.2-30; see Höpfl, 49-82).

It is not surprising, then, that Calvin—unlike Luther, but in line with Maimonides and Thomas Aquinas—wanted to systematize the scattered and ostensibly repetitious corpora of Mosaic law. The hermeneutical model he adapted in attempting to do so is the familiar one, which understands Mosaic legislation to amplify individual precepts of the Decalogue (see Philo; also Rashi on Exod 24:12, citing Saadia Gaon). This results in the contrived expository arrangement in Calvin's Harmony, which catalogs in decalogic order the nomistic traditions serialized in the books of Exodus through Deuteronomy. For example, under the rubric of the commandment prohibiting homicide, Calvin treated Deut 21:1-9 and 12:15-16, 20-25 as ceremonial supplements; many other deuteronomic rulings are included among those identified as judicial applications of the same prohibition (treated in this order: Deut 17:6; 19:15; 22:8; 24:7; 21:22-23; 25:1-3; 24:16; 20:10-18; 23:15-16; 22:6-7, 4; 19:1-13; cf. Philo *Spec.* 3.83-203).

Calvin's investment in this scheme is much more energetically displayed in his 200 *Sermons sur le Deutéronome*, preached on consecutive weekdays (from Mar. 20, 1555, through July 15, 1556) at the former cathedral of St. Peter in Geneva. The published transcriptions are introduced in a preface contributed by some of Calvin's fellow Genevan clergy, which hails

Deuteronomy as the grand summation of Pentateuchal law and a bastion for defense of true piety against the idolatries of Roman Catholicism. Polemic is also well represented in the sermons. While it is most often directed against the "papists," whose errors include turning the Lord's Supper into the Mass, also targeted are Jews and "Turks," who rightly abhor the veneration of images but who do not acknowledge Jesus to be "the law's soul" and "the living image of God, his Father" (*Sermon* 45 on Deut 6:1-4 [delivered July 19, 1555]; J. Calvin's *Sermons on the Ten Commandments*, 289-307; cf. *Institutes* 2.6.4; 4.18-19). Calvin's sermons on Deuteronomy 5 in this series exposit the Decalogue as the epitome of moral law. Because these moral provisions remain in full force for Christians, Moses' ceremonial and judicial applications of them should be received as authoritative guidance in such matters as relief from burdensome debts (Deut 15:1-11), a democratically constituted and accountable magistracy (16:18-20), neighborly assistance (22:1-4), restraints on usury and collateral (23:19-20; 24:10-13), fair wages (24:14-15), and honest business practices (25:13-16). Calvin made forceful sermonic use of these texts to indict egregious economic exploitation, especially of Protestant refugees from France, by Geneva's entrenched mercantile elite. Moreover, the timing of these sermons was politically cogent: In the election of February 1555 Calvin's allies regained majority on the Small Council of the Genevan Republic, leading to close collaboration in civil reforms with the consistory, an ecclesial court modeled by Calvin in large part on Deut 17:8-13 (on these issues and the era, see J. Calvin's *Sermons*, 13-29, and now esp. M. Valeri [1997]).

The shift during the middle decades of the sixteenth century toward deuteronomic theocracy in Calvin's Geneva was not unproblematic, of course, as the trial and execution of M. Servetus for heresy in 1553 may attest (Deut 13:6-11). Yet the Reform party claimed as principal motive, not imposition of theological orthodoxy on a diverse populace, but devotion to the political enfranchisement and economic ideals enacted into law for ancient Israel by God's preeminent prophet, Moses. Moreover, this commitment to a civil polity designed to implement what were supposed to be the timeless moral precepts of the Decalogue became a hallmark of Calvinist Reformed and Federal traditions generally (D. Steinmetz [1989]; D. Weir [1990], esp. 3-33). If Luther's Reformation reclaimed the gospel of God's egalitarian grace in Christ, Calvin's renewed the revolutionary social mandate of the Mosaic law. The mandate was exported when many who had found refuge in Geneva returned to their homelands—some to the Netherlands; some who came to be known as Huguenots to France; and others, the Marian exiles soon to be called Puritans and Presbyterians, to Elizabethan England and Scotland. Interpretation of Deuteronomy played an important role in the series of intellectual and often violent political struggles that ensued from the 1560s through the end of the eighteenth century.

The first century of conflict pitted the authority of Scripture—as warrant for a society constituted in accord with biblical notions of covenantal law, equity, and morality—against absolutist monarchical rule by divine right and its elitist corollaries, ecclesial prelacy and magisterial discretionary justice. Major impetus for this engagement in the English-speaking world came from the Marian exiles, among them M. Coverdale and his colleagues, whose Geneva Bible (1560) brought to completion Tyndale's annotated translation of the Hebrew and Greek Scriptures. The dedicatory epistle to Queen Elizabeth, dated Feb. 10, 1559, commends as examples of effective governance Josiah and other Judean rulers who reestablished "true religion" based upon God's Word (see also the 1556 "Confession of Faith" of Geneva's English congregation in A. Cochrane [1966] 127-30; and the 1558 tract of C. Goodman, one of the congregation's pastors, invoking Deuteronomy 13 and 17:14-20 against Queen Mary as a pagan Jezebel [E. Morgan [1965] 1-14]). Introductory notes to Deuteronomy identify the book as a discrete "second law," composed of "a commentarie or exposition of the ten commandments" in which Moses prescribes all that is necessary for faithful service of God and for the preservation of God's people (i.e., Moses' ceremonial and judicial laws). This understanding of Israelite polity provided a platform for the largely unsuccessful efforts of T. Cartwright and other Puritans during Elizabeth's reign (1558–1603) to rid the established church of practices not specifically sanctioned by their literal reading of Scripture (such as prelacy and its accoutrements of vestment, fixed liturgy, and social privilege) but also to institute deuteronomic laws as normative guidance for civil courts, particularly in capital cases (G. Haskins [1960] 145; D. McGinn [1949] 110-47). English Puritans and Presbyterians labored in concert to attain and expand these goals through the agency of Parliament, assisted by the Westminster Assembly, during the reign of Charles I (1625–46) and the eleven-year Interregnum, or Commonwealth, that followed his execution in January 1649.

In the same era English Puritans who established the Massachusetts Bay Colony made much less conflicted progress toward implementation of a civil polity inspired by Deuteronomy. With a view toward safeguarding the colony's freemen against arbitrary treatment by professional magistrates, pastor J. Cotton, at the request of the General Court, presented for consideration in 1636 a draft of "fundamental laws" based on Moses' "judicials," which he deemed to be still authoritative not only for Jews but also for the "new Israel" of Puritan Christians bound together in covenant with God (W. Ford [1902]; Morgan, 160-77; Haskins, 119-27). At least some of Cotton's proposals were adapted into the Massachusetts "Body of Liberties," enacted in 1641, which identifies foundational rights of citizenship (Morgan, 177-203). In article 94, for example, scriptural precedents are noted in the margins for crimes punishable by death (e.g., Deut 19:16, 18-19 in a case of false witness). In some other instances, articles paraphrase biblical laws without citing them (e.g., art. 43 limits punitive flogging to forty stripes [Deut 25:1-3]; art. 47 requires "two or three witness or that which is equivalent thereunto" to sustain a capital charge [Deut 19:15]; art. 90 prescribes that finders return lost property to rightful owners [Deut 22:1-3]). This populist document, expanded into the code of 1648 entitled "The Lawes and Liberties of Massachusetts," marks a substantial departure from English common law as well as from European traditions of Roman jurisprudence (Haskins, 136-47).

Anglican royalists were not alone in resisting what they perceived to be the inflexible biblical particularism of the Calvinist political agenda. In colonial Rhode Island, R. Williams (c. 1603–83) questioned the theological cogency of the Massachusetts model of governance. He maintained that Christian congregations are neither continuous with nor counterparts of ancient Israel, constrained by its sacral obligations; nor should a God whose beneficent sovereignty is universal be claimed as party to an exclusive civil covenant that compromises the integrity of individual consciences in matters of faith (*The Bloudy Tenent of Persecution* [1644]; see Morgan, 203-33). In response to the aggressive biblicism of Dutch Calvinists, who did much to encourage popular support of the House of Orange in the struggle against Spanish imperialism, jurist H. Grotius argued that Roman law continued to provide a sound, irenic, and internationally acceptable foundation for civil polity and public morality, whereas both the Decalogue and deuteronomic legislation had been addressed only to historical Israel (e.g., *De jure* [1645] 1.1.16, citing Deut 6:4 as proof text). Similarly, T. Hobbes mounted an elaborate defense of monarchy as "the most commodius government" in his *Philosophical Rudiments* (= *De Cive* [1642]), a position sharply restated during the Interregnum in Leviathan (1651). Human rights and the civil orders legitimately instituted to protect them are, he argued, grounded in natural law, of which Pentateuchal law is a historically conditioned manifestation. Although Hobbes denied that either the entire Pentateuch or Deuteronomy as a whole could be the authoritative work of Moses (citing Deut 34:6 and other anachronisms), he identified Deuteronomy 11–27 as an archaic Mosaic code establishing God's kingship over Israel, which was entrusted for interpretation to an aristocracy of clergy and elders (Deut 31:9-10, 26). He considered this document to be the book of the Law found again by the priest Hilkiah in Josiah's reign that gave rise to the reforms and renewal of covenant described in 2 Kings 22–23 (Rudiments 16.11-17; Leviathan chap. 33).

The historicizing approach to biblical traditions, adumbrated in the writings of Hobbes, is more programmatically exhibited in B. Spinoza's *Tractatus theologico-politicus* (pub. anonymously in 1670). Like Grotius's *De jure* earlier in the century, Spinoza's treatise is a plea for reason and tolerance in matters of both politics and religion—crafted here as a Cartesian response to the theocratic pretensions of Dutch Reformed clergy in their continuing efforts to suppress especially what the Synod of Dort (1618–19) had defined as the heterodoxy of the Remonstrant party (representing a more liberal Calvinist as well as Anabaptist theopolitical position). In his provocative analysis of the Pentateuch's nomistic traditions, Spinoza drew on the heritage of late medieval Jewish scholarship. He declared "useless and absurd" the attempt of Maimonides to salvage the revelatory authority of Mosaic-rabbinic jurisprudence for Jewish orthopraxis by accommodating primitive ceremonial precepts, as well as the Torah's ethical norms that Spinoza considered accessible to Gentiles and Jews alike through reason, to Aristotelian philosophy (*Treatise* [tr. Elwes] 79-80, 116-18, 190). On the other hand, Spinoza developed the evidence cryptically noted by Ibn Ezra in order to refute the "irrational" claim that Moses was the sole author of the Pentateuch (*Treatise* 120-27). It is important to observe, however, that Spinoza did not engage in wholesale deconstruction of Pentateuchal legislation. In his view the original Sinai/Horeb covenant instituted a democratic theocracy that almost immediately became a limited monarchy: Elected by the Israelite assembly to serve as its king and to exercise divine authority, Moses promulgated the civil polity preserved in Deuteronomy 6-28 (cf. Deut 5:22-33; *Treatise* 219-21). Spinoza directed particular attention to what he considered the eminently wise system of checks and balances in this Mosaic constitution: It enfranchises common citizens to be military leaders and judges, and it separates the function of levitical interpretation of the law from royal administration of it (*Treatise* 226-28, 235). Yet this rational polity of Moses was subverted through priestly control of Jewish government during the Second Commonwealth—a usurpation which, in effect, prefigured the hegemony sought by orthodox Calvinist clergy in Spinoza's own day (*Treatise* 236-56).

The influential writings of J. Locke in the final decades of the seventeenth century championing democracy and expansive religious tolerance should be counted in significant part as the secular harvest not only of his own Puritan heritage but also of Spinoza's reassessment of Mosaic traditions (L. Feuer [1958] 254-58). While Locke vigorously opposed royal absolutism, he also eschewed as frivolous traditional efforts to distinguish between Moses' moral, ceremonial, and judicial prescriptions for the purpose of identifying some still binding on Christians or any contemporary civil order. Locke argued that a society's positive laws should be humane, protecting natural rights, and grounded in reason rather than in privileged and privileging revelation; just laws obligate only those who consent to the government that enacts and enforces them (see esp. *Letter Concerning Toleration* [1689]).

Much political and religious thought of the eighteenth century participated in the renewed conflict between the ostensible demands of revelation and of reason (see Philo). One noteworthy attempt at compromise was M. Mendelssohn's Jerusalem (1783), which addressed the issues posed by Spinoza's critique of Maimonides. Mendelssohn insisted that Judaism, at least since the destruction of the Temple, is a superbly rational, non-dogmatic faith rather than a theopolitical commonwealth. This means that Jews are free to embrace enlightened modernity by participating with Gentiles in the quest for scientific knowledge, humanistic culture, and social well-being. Yet their separate religious identity as Jews remains contingent on adherence to the orthopractical traditions of Torah revealed to their ancestors through Moses; Jewish piety is viable in an age of reason.

Political themes of deuteronomism resounded strongly in Congregationalist and Presbyterian preaching during the era of the American Revolution and constitutional formation (C. Cherry [1971] 67-92; E. Sandoz [1991] 835-62). For example, S. Langdon's (1723–97) 1788 sermon on Deut 4:5-8 compared the emergent American states to the confederated tribes of Israel, and Moses' legislative wisdom to the work of the Constitutional Convention. Deuteronomy, he averred in the tradition of Tyndale, is a "pattern to the world in all ages" (Cherry, 93-105; Sandoz, 941-67). To be sure, such theo-political sentiments were not shared by all American patriots. In The Age of Reason (1794–95) T. Paine delivered what even many of his fellow Deists thought to be an intemperate attack on biblical authority and values. According to Paine, the Pentateuch is "an attempted history of the life of Moses... written by some very ignorant and stupid pretenders... several hundred years after the death of Moses..."; the literary character of Deuteronomy, with its interchange between the voices of a narrator and Moses, shows that the latter is not the book's author. This saves Deists, Paine declared, from the embarrassment of supposing that the moral justice of God is represented in Deuteronomy's brutal, xenophobic traditions.

b. *Development of the critical-historical agenda (19th–20th cents.).* The religio-historical interests of Reformed biblical Theology and of Enlightenment scholarship converge in the work of W. De Wette during the early decades of the nineteenth century (J. Rogerson [1992]). Three issues pertinent to an informed critical interpretation of Deuteronomy are identified in de Wette's dissertation (pub. 1805) and subsequently elaborated in editions of his Beiträge and Lehrbuch. First, Deuteronomy exhibits a literary and thematic profile that distinguishes it from the preceding books of the Pentateuch, which in de Wette's view were composed earlier. Second, this profile links Deuteronomy closely with Joshua and, to a lesser extent, with subsequent books of the former prophets. Third, deuteronomic legislation is characterized by a concern to unify ancient Israel's cultus and national life. This supports the position (reported, e.g., by Procopius of Gaza and revived by Hobbes, among others) that Deuteronomy preserves within its narrative framework the book of the law implemented in the seventh-century Judaean reforms of King Josiah.

During the second half of the nineteenth century, studies of such European scholars as E. Riehm (1854) and A. Kuenen (1861–65) made considerable progress in developing de Wette's three-part agenda. Riehm argued that the book of the Law (Deuteronomy 5–26; 28) rediscovered in Josiah's time represented reform policies initiated by Hezekiah in the late eighth century B.C.E. but the document itself he supposed to have been written during and in reaction to the reign of Manasseh, which followed. A more complex compositional history of Deuteronomy, interconnected with other components of the Pentateuch and with the former prophets, emerged from Kuenen's astute, thoroughgoing analysis of stylistic features and themes. Although on formal grounds Kuenen differentiated between the legislative corpus of Deuteronomy 12–26 and the hortatory introduction to it in chapters 5–11, he considered both to be the work of an early deuteronomist (designated D^1). This author, who was possibly the priest Hilkiah (2 Kgs 22:3-10), used identifiable sources—a prophetic narrative of Israel's early history (a composite of the tetrateuchal documents J and E), as well as sundry archaic laws preserved in Exodus 20–23—to design the reform program sponsored by Josiah (Hexateuch 24-32, 107-17, 214-20). According to Kuenen, another deuteronomist (D^2) later prefixed chapters 1–4 in order to sketch a historical setting and a rationale for the promulgation of the Torah ascribed to Moses. He discerned the work of this same author in Deuteronomy 27–34 and continuing through the book of Joshua, although he also identified even later elements of hexateuchal redaction, which include priestly strata associated with Ezra's postexilic reforms (*Hexateuch* 117-38, 165-73, 221-25).

Rhetorical features of Deuteronomy were also highlighted by other notable studies in this period. E. Reuss (1879) supported a Josianic dating of Deuteronomy, citing affinities of idiom and theological theme with the book of Jeremiah (e.g., Jer 11:1-13; 15:1). In his view the central corpus of Deuteronomy 5–26 is composed largely of religious instruction rather than of positive law per se; it originated as an expository reworking of Exodus 21–23 designed to promote priestly interests in theocratic centralization. In a similar vein A. Klostermann (1893) associated the book's contents with what he considered to be a long tradition of covenantal preaching (cf. Exod 24:7; Deut 33:9), here specifically formulated to win popular support for Josiah's policies. Outside the critical mainstream as regards the book's date of composition is the provocative study (1872) of P. Kleinert (1837–1920), who called attention to the coordinated series of editorial headings in Deut 1:1-5; 4:44-49; 29:1 [28:69]; and 33:1. This device suggested to him a classified collection of Mosaic traditions, perhaps compiled by the prophet Samuel as a testamentary archive to remind tribal Israel of its distinctive covenantal identity and to warn of the dangers posed by Canaanite practices, including monarchical excesses (cf. 1 Sam 8 with Deut 17:14-20).

The challenge at least implicit in earlier critical scholarship to traditional views of the authority and primacy of revealed Torah in the history of ancient Israelite religion was expressed forcefully in J. Wellhausen's *Prolegomena* (1885); *Geschichte Israels* [1878]). Hobbes and Spinoza, but also de Wette and most of Wellhausen's critical predecessors, had left some room for the Mosaic origins of Israel's civil polity and official cultus. Wellhausen's analysis left little such room, if any. In his view, a free-form spirituality or family piety was the earliest stage of Israelite religion; its features are residual in the narratives of Genesis and Judges. On the other hand, much of the later stages of religious development, which presuppose not only the politics of statehood but also the social ideals shaped by eighth-century Prophecy, is exhibited in the traditions of codified law and institutionalized worship that predominate in the books of Exodus through Joshua. The latest of these stages, as Kuenen, among others, had already recognized, is Judah's postexilic theocracy; it is expansively displayed in the priestly corpora that make Sinai the locus for the inauguration of the tabernacle cultus, with its elaborate system of sacrificial rites, a fixed liturgical calendar, and an exclusive Aaronid priesthood. This blatant retroversion takes for granted what Josiah accomplished, based on the book of the law—a document that had been drafted, in the guise of Mosaic authorship, to inspire him. Wellhausen did not doubt that the document in question is substantially attested in the self-conscious revisionism of Deuteronomy 12–26 (see esp. 12:8-12; 17:8–18:8).

Wellhausen's reconstruction, with Deuteronomy as its centerpiece, established the principal salient in a historical-critical and hermeneutical war that continued into the 1930s and has occasionally flared up since (W. Baumgartner [1929]; S. Loersch [1967]; H. Preuss [1982]; T. Römer [1994]). One of the early participants was W. R. Smith, who defended a Josianic date for Deuteronomy at the cost of his own professorial and ecclesiastical status in the Free Church of Scotland (R. Smend [1995]). Even so, Smith sought to bring Wellhausen's religio-historical views into closer accord with Reformed theology, arguing that a doctrine of inspiration need not be restricted to autographs but should rather embrace the coherent growth of scriptural traditions (*OT in the Jewish Church*; see already R. Simon's response to Spinoza, two cents. earlier.) S. Driver's erudite, long-lived commentary to Deuteronomy, first published in 1895, places greater emphasis on origination as the locus of authority. After reviewing the critical case for why Moses could not have been the book's author, Driver gave considerable attention to how the deuteronomic legislation and other collections of Pentateuchal Torah may still be interpreted as "moral, ceremonial, and civil" developments of "a Mosaic nucleus" (1901, lv-lvii). The nucleus was not otherwise identified.

The quest to recover the compositional history of Deuteronomy became a conspicuous feature in German scholarship of this period. C. Steuernagel (1894, 1896, 1900), W. Staerk (1894, 1924), A. Puuko (1910), and others tried to disentangle literary strata within Deuteronomy or to distinguish editions of the legislative corpus, especially on the basis of stylistic criteria like the use of second-person singular and plural forms of address to Israel (C. Begg [1979, 1994]).

J. Hempel (1914) and later F. Horst (1930) argued that the book's oldest stratum was a Temple document of Solomonic date that grew through multiple stages of redaction and accretion, culminating in the edition of the exilic deuteronomist (Kuenen's D^2). D. Hoffmann's commentary (1913, 1922) merits note in this context as an informed Jewish response to critical historiography. T. Oestreicher (1923) made an effort to sever the connection between Deuteronomy and Josiah's reforms, arguing that the book is much older than the seventh century and promotes religious purity, not a centralized cultus. Conversely, R. Kennett (1920) maintained that the centralizing legislation is a literary crystallization of Josiah's policies, with Deuteronomy being created in the late exilic or early restoration era (similarly G. Hölscher [1922], although he questioned some of the key reform measures attributed to Josiah).

An insightful line of argument recalling the position of Klostermann was developed during this period by A. Welch (1924, 1932). He linked proto-Deuteronomy to northern levitical traditions of religious instruction, which he thought could also be identified in the so-called Elohist document as well as in the later anti-Baalistic preaching of Hosea and Jeremiah; this older tradition was reworked in the Josianic era. G. von Rad took a similar approach in his form-critical studies on the origins and development of deuteronomic traditions (1929, 1938; see also 1948 and 1966; cf. H. Breit [1933]). The ceremony at Shechem, described in Deuteronomy 27, suggested to von Rad a recurrent event, a fall festival convened every seventh year to renew the covenant (see also 11:29; 31:9-13; Josh 8:30-35; 24:1-27). Such rites were supposed to include a historical retrospect and reproof, an exposition of covenantal law, an oath of allegiance, and an invocation of sanctions—features corresponding to the broad literary arrangement of Deuteronomy 7–28 ("The Form-critical Problem of the Hexateuch," 26-33). In his later work, von Rad identified levitical preaching as the primary medium through which these ancient liturgical traditions were shaped and transmitted and eventually recast in the Josianic era to promote cultic centralization (*Studies,* 60-73; cf. Deuteronomy, 23–27). Studies by F. Dumermuth (1950) and A. Alt (1953) offered additional support for the thesis that the core traditions of Deuteronomy antedate Josiah's reign and are of north Israelite provenance (see also Wright [1953] 323-26; F. McCurley [1974]; H. Ginsberg [1982]; M. Weinfeld [1985]).

M. Noth's historical-critical views complemented the form-critical work of von Rad in significant respects, lending weight to the notion, widely held at the middle of the twentieth century (C. North [1951]), that Wellhausen's reconstruction of the history of Israelite religion had been undermined. According to Noth, Pentateuchal traditions of law are not the idealistic creations of a civil state or of a royal establishment; rather, they presuppose a sacral community "Israel," the people of God, whose identity was primarily shaped through the centralized cultus of a tribal confederation in the pre-monarchical period (depicted in Joshua and Judges). The ceremony described in 2 Kgs 23:1-3 chronicles an attempt by Josiah, in the interests of Judah's political consolidation, to revive the erstwhile covenantal identity of Israel as set forth in the scroll recovered from the Temple. In effect, the liturgical instruction of Deuteronomy 5–30 was co-opted, "quite against the actual sense of its contents," to become a civil code enforced by the state ("Laws," 41-49; cf. von Rad, *Theology,* 1:195-231). Developing Kuenen's view of D^2, Noth also argued that Josiah's co-opting of the Torah was subsequently canonized in the work of an exilic historiographer who set the Temple Scroll in the narrative frame of Deuteronomy 1–4 and 31; this textual conjunction produced the initial Mosaic segment of a political history of Israel that extended through the destruction of both the northern kingdom in the later eighth century and the Judean successor state in the early sixth (*Deuteronomistic History;* cf. *Pentateuchal Traditions,* 156-75; von Rad, *Studies,* 74-91).

Before the middle of the twentieth century surprisingly little use was made of recovered traditions of cuneiform law and international diplomacy in critical interpretation of either Deuteronomy or of other corpora of Pentateuchal legislation. (On the important work of Alt and his students, which had emphasized the discrete sacral character and Israelite origins of apod-ictic prescriptions as opposed to the common ancient Near Eastern currency of casuistic jurisprudence, (see the review in W. Clark [1974] 103-16). In 1954 G. Mendenhall charted a new course of comparative study by demonstrating the close resemblance in structure and con-tents between Hittite suzerainty treaties of the Late Bronze Age and both the Decalogue of Exod 20:1-17 (cf. Exod 19:3-6; 24:1-8) and the Shechem pact described in Josh 24:1-27. He sug-gested that the genuinely archaic protocol of international treaties had been adapted to define a covenant relationship between the nascent league of Israelite tribes and their divine overlord; he also identified the protocol as vestigial in Deuteronomy, accounting for some of the striking themes and structural features that von Rad had considered indicative of a liturgical provenance ("Covenant Forms," 57-75; see also K. Baltzer [1964[2]; ET 1971] 1-38).

The line of inquiry initiated by Mendenhall and Baltzer—which was soon broadened to take into consideration Iron Age Assyrian and Aramean documents as well as Late Bronze Age sources—proved to be enormously productive, even in the short term (e.g., F. Fensham [1962]; G. E. Wright [1962]; D. McCarthy [1963]; W. Moran [1963]; D. Hillers [1964, 1969]; R. Frankena [1965]; Weinfeld [1972] 59-157; Cross [1973] 265-73; cf. P. Riemann [1976]). To be sure, some scholars have continued to defend Wellhausen's view that the concept of a covenant between Israel and its God is an ideological construction of the later monarchical period (L. Perlitt [1969]; E. Nicholson [1986]); some others have used the comparative data to claim sup-port for the Mosaic antiquity of the received deuteronomic textual corpus (M. Kline [1963]; P. Craigie [1976] 20-32, 79-83; J. McConville [1984]; cf. the responses of S. McBride [1973] 287-89; [1987] 236-38; A. Mayes [1979] 32-34; R. Clements [1989] 20-22). No doubt critical inter-pretation of deuteronomic traditions will continue to profit from comparative studies that make cogent use of Near Eastern contextual evidence (H. Tadmor [1982]; R. Westbrook [1985]; Weinfeld [1991] 6-9; Mendenhall and G. Herion [1992] 1180-88; E. Otto [1994]).

In the last decades of the twentieth century, the three major critical premises that de Wette's work on Deuteronomy identified in the earlier nineteenth century have been subjected to thor-ough scholarly reconsideration. A concise review of several broad trends in these multifaceted labors must suffice (McBride [1981] 536-39; Preuss; E. Cortese [1990]; Römer [1994]).

European scholarship has devoted considerable attention to analysis of the rhetorical con-tours of Deuteronomy, focusing especially on the textual segments framing the core legislation in chapters 12–26 (e.g., N. Lohfink [1963]; J. Plöger [1967]; P. Buis [1969]; R. Merendino [1969]; S. Mittmann [1975]; G. Seitz [1971]; F. García López [1978]; G. Braulik [1978]; D. Knapp [1987]; R. Achenbach [1991]). Much of this work, like the efforts of Steuernagel and others at the beginning of the twentieth century, has sought to discern not only the book's detailed literary design but also its history of composition. Component strata are identified on the basis of reasonable stylistic criteria—again, such as the conspicuous variation in second—person singular and plural forms of address (C. Minette de Tillesse [1962]; H. Cazelles [1967])—and clusters of paraenetic themes. Although the ostensible results are diverse and often too diachronically speculative and complex to be persuasive, they are supposed to favor exilic and even later Deuteronomistic stages of redaction as decisive for the book's formation (e.g., Lohfink [1985] 55-75; Mayes [1981]; U. Rütersworden [1987]; Braulik [1994] 151-64, 183-98). The general effects are an emphasis on theological and ideological dimensions of the developing traditions (rather than, e.g., their practical social and jurisprudential significance) and a weakening of the book's connections to the Josianic era (F. Crüsemann [1992; ET 1996] 204-12; Clements [1996]).

Other critical approaches have highlighted intertextual features that profile Deuteronomy in relationship to the coherent growth and crystallization of Pentateuchal traditions. While M. Noth and others had acknowledged the presence of scattered proto-deuteronomic materials or of an inchoate deuteronomic revision in parts of Exodus (esp. in 13:1-16; 19:3-9; and 32:7-14; see M. Caloz [1968]; C. Brekelmans [1966]), scholarship has entertained hypotheses regarding a more extensive deuteronomic or later deuteronomistic redaction of the Pentateuch (e.g., Perlitt [1969]; W. Fuss [1972]; W. Johnstone [1987]; E. Blum [1990]; cf. M. Rose [1981]; J. Van Seters [1991]; J. Blenkinsopp [1992] 186-94). A tighter focus on intertextual drafting and revision in juridical corpora has yielded provocative insights in the work of a number of other scholars (J. Milgrom [1976]; M. Fishbane [1985] 91-277, esp. 163-64, 195; Otto [1993, 1995]). To this category belongs the influential analysis of S. Kaufman (1978–79), which revived the traditional thesis (e.g., Philo, Luther, Calvin) that Deuteronomy 12–25 is a coherent, unified expansion of the Decalogue (Braulik [1985, 1991]; A. Rof, [1988]). Also of particular note is B. Levinson's 1997 study examining the hermeneutics involved in deuteronomic reworking of older laws, a recasting designed to promote centralizing reforms under the auspices of Mosaic authority.

Renewed attention to the sociopolitical implications of deuteronomic jurisprudence is another noteworthy trend—one that has generally favored preexilic circumstances as generative of the book's characteristic features (e.g., R. Wilson [1983]; L. Stulman [1990]; B. Halpern [1991]; N. Steinberg [1991]; C. Pressler [1993]; J. Tigay [1996] xx-xxvi; cf. the earlier studies of A. Causse [1933a, 1933b]). This trend, together with the others sketched above, may suggest that at the end of the twentieth century the right interpretive balance between diachronic analysis of deuteronomic traditions and recognition of the book's conceptual as well as structural coherence exists primarily in the eye of the critical beholder (cf. Mayes [1993]). If so, the interpretive situation invites further research and rigorous debate.

Bibliography: R. Achenbach, "Israel zwischen Verheissung und Gebot: Literarkritische Untersuchung zu Deuteronomium 5–11" (Europäische Hochschulschriften 23, 422, 1991). A. Alt, "Die Heimat des Deuteronomiums," *Kleine Schriften zur Geschichte des Volkes Israel* (1953) 2:250-75. **T. Aquinas,** *On Charity* [*De Caritate*] (1960); *Summa Theologiae*, vol. 29, *The Old Law* (Ia2ae, 98-105, 1969). **Augustine,** "Reply to Faustus the Manichaean [Adversus Faustum Manichaeum]," *St. Augustine: The Writings Against the Manichaeans and Against the Donatists* (NPNF, 1st ser. 4, 1887) 155-345; "In Answer to the Jews [Adversus Judaeos]," *Treatises on Marriage and Other Subjects* (FC 27, 1955) 387-414; "Answer to Maximinus the Arian" and "Answer to an Enemy of the Law and the Prophets," *Arianism and Other Heresies* (Works of St. Augustine 1, 18, 1990) 299-36, 339-56; *The Trinity* (Works of Saint Augustine 1, 5, 1991); "The Spirit and the Letter," *Answer to the Pelagians* (Works of St. Augustine 1, 23, 1996) 139-202; *Teaching Christianity* [*De Doctrina Christiana*] (Works of St. Augustine 1, 11, 1996). **O. Bächli,** *Israel und die Völker: Eine Studie zum Deuteronomium* (ATANT 41, 1962). **K. Baltzer,** *Das Bundesformular* (1964); ET, The Covenant Formulary in OT, Jewish, and Early Christian Writings [1971]). **J. Barton,** *Oracles of God: Perceptions of Ancient Prophecy in Israel After the Exile* (1986). **W. Baumgartner,** "Der Kampf um das Deuteronomium," *TRu NF* 1 (1929) 7-25. Bede, Explanatio in V. Librum Moisis (PL 91) 379-94. **C. Begg,** "The Significance of the *Numeruswechsel* in Deuteronomy: The 'Pre-history' of the Question," *ETL* 55 (1979) 116-24; "The Literary Criticism of Deut 4:1-40: Contributions to a Continuing Discussion," *ETL* 56 (1980) 10-55; "1994: A Significant Anniversary in the History of Deuteronomy Research," *Studies in Deuteronomy in Honour of C. J. Labuschagne* (VTSup 53, ed. F. García Martínez et al., 1994) 1-11. **H. H. Ben-Sasson,** "Maimonidean Controversy," *EncJud* (1971) 11:745-54. **H.V. Bennett,** *Injustice Made Legal: Deuteronomic Law and the Plight of the Widows, Strangers, and Orphans in Ancient Israel* (Bible in its World, 2002). **A. Bertholet,** *Deuteronomium* (KHC 5, 1899). **J. Blenkinsopp,** Prophecy and Canon: A Contribution to the Study of Jewish Origins (SJCA 3, 1977); The Pentateuch: An Introduction to the First Five Books of the Bible (ABRL, 1992). **P. Blickle,** *The Revolution of 1525: The German Peasants' War from a New Perspective* (1981). **P. M. Blowers,** "The Regula Fidei and the Narrative Character of Early Christian Faith," *Pro Eccl* 6 (1997) 199-228. **E. Blum,** *Studien zur Komposition des Pentateuch* (BZAW 189, 1990). **R. Bóid (M. N. Saraf),** "Use, Authority and Exegesis of Mikra in the Samaritan Tradition," *Mikra: Text, Translation, Reading, and Interpretation of the HB in Ancient Judaism and Early Christianity* (ed. M. J. Mulder and H. Sysling, CRINT 2, 1, 1988) 595-633. **G. Braulik,** *Die Mittel deuteronomischer Rhetorick: Erhoben aus Deuteronomium 4,1-40* (AnBib 68, 1978); "Die Abfolge der Gesetze in Deuteronomium 12–26 und der Dekalog," *Das Deuteronomium: Entstehung, Gestalt, und Botschaft* (BETL 68, ed. N. Lohfink, 1985) 252-72 (ET, "The Sequence of the Laws in Deuteronomy 12–26 and in the Decalogue," *Song of Power and the Power of Song: Essays on the Book of Deuteronomy* [ed. D. L. Christensen, 1993] 313-35); *Die deuteronomischen Gesetze und der Dekalog: Studien zum Aufbau von Deuteronomium 12-26* (SBS 145, 1991); *The Theology of Deuteronomy: Collected Essays* (Bibal Collected Essays 2, 1994). **H. Breit,** *Die Predigt des Deuteronomisten* (1933). **C. Brekelmans,** "Die sogenannten deuteronomischen Elemente in Genesis bis Numeri: Ein Beitrag zur Vorgeschichte des Deuteronomiums," (VTSup 15, 1966) 90-96. **W. Brueggemann,** *Deuteronomy* (Abingdon Old Testament Commentaries, 2001). **M. Bucer,** *De Regno Christi* (1550) (Martini Buceri Opera Latina 15, 1955). **J. Buchholz,** *Die Ältesten Israels im Deuteronomium* (GTA 36, 1988). **P. Buis,** *Le Deutéronome* (VSAT 4, 1969). **P. Buis and J. Leclercq,** *Le Deutéronome* (SB, 1963). **M. Caloz,** "Exode 13:3-16 et son rapport au Deutéronome," *RB* 75 (1968) 5-62. **J. Calvin,** *Mosis reliqui libri quatuor in formam harmoniae* (CR LII-LIII, 416, 1564; ET, *Commentaries on the Four Last Books of Moses, Arranged in the Form of a Harmony* [1852–55]); *Sermons sur le Deutéronome,* 1555-56 (CR LIII, 571-LVII, 232; ET, *The Sermons of M. Iohn Calvin Upon the Fifth Booke of Moses Called Deuteronomie* [1583]); *Institutes of the Christian Religion* (LCC 20-21, 1960); *J. Calvin's Sermons on the Ten Commandments* (ed. and tr. B. W. Farley, 1980); *The Covenant Enforced: Sermons on Deuteronomy 27 and 28* (ed. J. B. Jordan, 1990). **C. M. Carmichael,** *The Laws of Deuteronomy* (1974); *Law and Narrative in the Bible: The Evidence of the Deuteronomic Laws and the Decalogue* (1985). **A. Causse,** "L'ideal politique et social du Deutéronome: La fraternité, d'Israël," *RHPR* 13 (1933a) 289-323; "La transformation de la notion d'alliance et la rationalisation de l'ancienne coutume dans la rforme deutéronomique," *RHPR* 13 (1933b) 1-29. **H. Cazelles,** "Passages in the Singular Within Discourse in the Plural of Dt 1-4," *CBQ* 29 (1967) 207-19. **C. Cherry (ed.),** *God's New Israel: Religious Inerpretations of American Destiny* (1971). **A. Cholewinski,** *Heiligkeitsgesetz und Deuteronomium: Eine vergleichende Studie* (AnBib 66, 1976). **D. L. Christensen,** *Deuteronomy 1–11* (WBC 6A, 1991); *Deuteronomy 1:1–21:9* revised (WBC 6A, 2001); *Deuteronomy 21:10–34:12* (WBC 6B, 2002); (ed.), *A Song of Power and the Power of Song: Essays on the Book of Deuteronomy* (Sources for Biblical and Theological Study 3, 1993). **J. Chrysostom,** "The Homilies on the Statues," *St. Chrysostom* (NPNF 9, 1908) 315-514; *Discourses Against Judaizing Christians* [Adv. Iud.] (FC 68, 1979). **W. M. Clark,** "Law," *OT Form Criticism* (TUMSR 2, ed. J. H. Hayes, 1974) 99-139. **Clement of Alexandria,** *Christ the Educator* [*Paigogogos*] (FC 23, 1954); *Stromateis* (FC 85, 1991). **R. E. Clements,** "Deuteronomy and the Jerusalem Cult Tradition," *VT* 15 (1965) 300-312; *God's Chosen People: A Theological Interpretation of the Book of Deuteronomy* (1968); *Deuteronomy* (OTGu, 1989); "The Deuteronomic Law of Centralisation and the Catastrophe of 587 BC," *After the Exile: Essays in Honour of R. Mason* (ed. J. Barton and D. J. Reimer, 1996) 5-25; *The Book of Deuteronomy: A Preacher's Commentary* (Epworth Commentaries, 2001). **A. C. Cochrane (ed.),** *Reformed Confessions of the Sixteenth Century* (1966). **R. H. Connolly,** "Introduction," and "Notes," *Didascalia Apostolorum: The Syriac Version Translated and Accompanied by the*

Verona Latin Fragments (1929). **E. Cortese,** "Theories Concerning Dtr: A Possible Rapprochement," *Pentateuchal and Deuteronomistic Studies: Papers Read at the XIIIth IOSOT Congress, Leuven, 1989* (BETL 94, ed. C. Brekelmans and J. Lust, 1990) 179-90. **P. C. Craigie,** *The Book of Deuteronomy* (NICOT, 1976). **F. M. Cross,** "Aspects of Samaritan and Jewish History in Late Persian and Hellenistic Times," *HTR* 59 (1966) 201-11; *Canaanite Myth and Hebrew Epic: Essays in the History of the Religion of Israel* (1973). **F. Crüsemann,** *Die Tora: Theologie und Sozialgeschichte des alttestamentlichen Gesetzes* (1992; ET, *The Torah: Theology and Social History of OT Law* [1996]). **Cyril of Alexandria,** *Glaphyrorum in Deuteronomium liber* (PG 69, 1864) 645-78. U. Dahmen, *Leviten und Priester im Deuteronomium: Literarkritische und redaktionsgeschichtliche Studien* (BBB 110, 1996). **D. Daniell,** "Introduction," *Tyndale's OT: Being the Pentateuch of 1530, Joshua to 2 Chronicles of 1537, and Jonah* (1992). **W. M. L. de Wette,** *Dissertatio critico-exegetica qua Deuteronomiumn a prioribus Pentateuchi libris diversum, alius cuiusdam recentioris auctoris opus esse monstratur* (1805); *Beiträge zur Einleitung in das Alte Testament* (2 vols., 1806–7); *Lehrbuch die historisch-kritischen Einleitung in der kanonischen und apocryphischen Bücher des AT* (1840); ET, *A Critical and Historical Introduction to the Canonical Scriptures of the OT* [2 vols., 1843]). **P. Diepold,** *Israels Land* (BWANT 95, 1972). **A. Disse,** *Informationsstruktur im Biblischen Hebräisch: Sprachwissenschaftliche Grundlagen und exegetische Konsequenzen einer Korpusuntersuchung zu den Büchern Deuteronomium, Richter und 2 Könige* (Arbeiten zu Text und Sprache im alten Testament 56, 1998). **C. Dogniez and M. Harl,** *Le Deutéronome* (La Bible d'Alexandrie 5, 1986). S. R. Driver, *A Critical and Exegetical Commentary on Deuteronomy* (ICC 5, 1895, 1896, 1901). **F. Dumermuth,** "Zur deuteronomischen Kulttheologie und ihren Voraussetzungen," *ZAW* 70 (1950) 59-98. **J. A. Duncan,** "Considerations of 4QD in Light of the 'All Souls Deuteronomy' and Cave 4 Phylactery Texts," *The Madrid Qumran Congress* (STDJ 11, 1, ed. J. Trebolle Barrera and L. Vegas Montaner, 1992) 1:199-215. **Eusebius of Caesarea,** *Preparation for the Gospel* [*Praeparatio evangelica*] (2 vols., 1903; repr. 1981); *The Ecclesiastical History* (LCL, 2 vols., 1926). **L. H. Feldman,** *"Remember Amalek" : Vengeance, Zealotry, and Group Destruction in the Bible according to Philo, Pseudo-Philo, and Josephus* (HUCM 31, 2004). **F. C. Fensham,** "Malediction and Benediction in Ancient Near Eastern Vassal-treaties and the OT," *ZAW* 74 (1962) 1-9 (repr. in *A Song of Power and the Power of Song* [ed. D. L. Christensen, 1993] 247-55). **L. Feuer,** *Spinoza and the Rise of Liberalism* (1958). **S. Fisch (ed.),** *Midrash haggadol on the Pentateuch, Deuteronomy* (ET 1972). **M. A. Fishbane,** *Biblical Interpretation in Ancient Israel* (1985). **W. Ford,** "Cotton's 'Moses his Judicials,' " *Massachusetts Historical Society, Proceedings* (October 1902) 274-84. **S. D. Fraade,** *From Tradition to Commentary: Torah and Its Interpretation in the Midrash Sifre to Deuteronomy* (SUNY Studies in Judaica, 1991). **R. T. France,** *Matthew: Evangelist and Teacher* (1989). **R. Frankena,** "The Vassal-treaties of Esarhaddon and the Dating of Deuteronomy," *OTS* 14 (ed. P. A. H. de Boer, 1965) 122-54. **C. Frevel,** *Mit Blick auf das Land die Schöpfung erinnern: zum Ende der Priestergrundschrift* (Herders biblische Studien 23, 2000). **K. Froehlich,** " 'Always to Keep the Literal Sense of Holy Scripture Means to Kill One's Soul': The State of Biblical Hermeneutics at the Beginning of the Fifteenth Century," *Literary Uses of Typology from the Late Middle Ages to the Present* (ed. E. Miner, 1977) 20-48. **W. Fuss,** *Die deuteronomistische Pentateuchredaktion in Exodus 3-17* (BZAW 126, 1972). **F. García López,** *Analyse litteraire de Deuteronome, V-XI* (1978). **F. García Martínez,** "Les manuscrits du désert de Juda et le Deutéronome," *Studies in Deuteronomy in Honour of C. J. Labuschagne* (VTSup 53, ed. F. García Martínez et al., 1994) 63-82. **H. L. Ginsberg,** *The Israelian Heritage of Judaism* (TSJTSA 24, 1982). "Liber Deuteronomii," *Glossa Ordinaria* (PL 113) 446-506. **W. S. Green,** "Scripture in Rabbinic Judaism," *HBT* 9 (1987) 27-40. **R. A. Greer,** "The Christian Bible and Its Interpretation," *Early*

Biblical Interpretation (J. L. Kugel and R. A. Greer, LEC, 1986) 107-203. **H. Grotius,** *De jure belli et pacis* (1645; ET, *The Rights of War and Peace* [Universal Classics Library, 1901]). **R. Hammer (tr.),** *Sifre: A Tannaitic Commentary on the Book of Deuteronomy* (YJS 24, 1986); *Siphre ad Deuteronomium* (ed. L. Finkelstein, Corpus Tannaiticum 3, 3, 1939). **B. Halpern,** "Jerusalem and the Lineages in the Seventh Century B.C.E.: Kinship and the Rise of Individual Moral Liability," *Law and Ideology in Monarchic Israel* (JSOTSup 124, ed. B. Halpern and D. Hobson, 1991) 11-107. **J. Hamilton,** *Social Justice and Deuteronomy: The Case of Deuteronomy 15* (SBLDS 136, 1992). **D. J. Harrington,** "Interpreting Israel's History: The Testament of Moses as a Rewriting of Deuteronomy 31–34," *Studies on "The Testament of Moses": Seminar Papers* (ed. G. W. E. Nickelsburg, SCS 4, 1973) 59-70. **G. L. Haskins,** *Law and Authority in Early Massachusetts: A Study in Tradition and Design* (1960). **D. M. Hay,** "Moses Through NT Spectacles," *Int* 44 (1990) 240-52. **R. B. Hays,** *Echoes of Scripture in the Letters of Paul* (1989). **J. Hempel,** *Die Schichten des Deuteronomiums: Ein Beitrag zur israelitischen Literatur- und Rechtsgeschichte* (Beiträge zur Kultur- und Universalgeschichte 33, 1914). **M. D. Herr,** "Midrash," *EncJud* (1971) 11:1507-14. **S. Herrmann,** "Die Konstruktive Restauration: Das Deuteronomium als Mitte biblischer Theologie," *Probleme biblischer Theologie: G. von Rad zum 70. Geburtstag* (ed. H. W. Wolff, 1971) 155-70. **D. Hillers,** *Treaty-curses and the OT Prophets* (BibOr 16, 1964); *Covenant: The History of a Biblical Idea* (Seminars in the History of Ideas, 1969). **T. Hobbes,** *Leviathan* (1651); *Leviathan: Or, The Matter, Form, and Power of a Commonwealth, Ecclesiastical and Civil* (*English Works of T. Hobbes of Malmesbury 3*, ed. W. Molesworth, 1839); De Cive (1642)*Philosophical Rudiments Concerning Government and Society* (*English Works of T. Hobbes of Malmesbury 2*, ed. W. Molesworth, 1841). **D. Hoffman,** *Das Buch Deuteronomium* (2 vols., 1913, 1922). **G. Hölscher,** "Komposition und Ursprung des Deuteronomiums," *ZAW* 40 (1922) 161-225. **H. Höpfl,** *Luther and Calvin on Secular Authority* (Cambridge Texts in the History of Political Thought, 1991). **W. Horbury,** "OT Interpretation in the Writings of the Church Fathers," *Mikra: Text, Translation, Reading, and Interpretation of the HB in Ancient Judaism and Early Christianity* (CRINT 2, 1, ed. M. J. Mulder, 1988) 727-87. **F. Horst,** *Das Privilegrecht Jahwes* (FRLANT 28, 1930). **C. Houtman,** *Der Pentateuch: Die Geschichte seiner Erforschung neben einer Auswertung* (CBET 9, 1994) 279-342. **Hugh of St. Victor,** *De Scripturis et Scriptoribus Sacris* (PL 175) 9-28; *The Didascalicon of Hugh of St. Victor: A Medieval Guide to the Arts* (Records of Western Civilization, 1961, 1991). **A. Ibn Ezra,** *Pêrûše hattôra lerabbînû ᵓibn ʿezraᵓ* 3 (ed. A. Wieser, 1977). **Irenaeus of Lyon,** *Against Heresies* [*Adversus haereses*], (The Writings of Irenaeus 1, ANCL 5, 1, 1874); *Proof of the Apostolic Preaching* (tr. J. P. Smith, ACW 16, 1952). **J. Janzen,** "The Yoke That Gives Rest," *Int* 41 (1987) 256-68. **W. Johnstone,** "Reactivating the Chronicles Analogy in Pentateuchal Studies, with Special Reference to the Sinai Pericope in Exodus," *ZAW* 99 (1987) 16-37. **Josephus,** *Against Apion* [*Contra Apionem*] (Josephus 1, LCL, 1926) 161-411; *Jewish Antiquities* [*Antiquitates Judaicae*] (Josephus 4-9, LCL, 1926). **Justin Martyr,** *The Dialogue with Trypho* (Translations of Christian Literature, 1930). **A. von Karlstadt,** "On the Removal of Images and That There Should Be No Beggars Among Christians," *The Essential Carlstadt* (1522; ET, Classics of the Radical Reformation 8, 1995). **S. Kaufman,** "The Structure of the Deuteronomic Law," *Maarav* 1 (1978-79) 105-58. **M. Keller,** *Untersuchungen zur deuteronomisch-deuteronomistischen Namenstheologie* (BBB 105, 1996). **R. Kennett,** *Deuteronomy and the Decalogue* (1920). **P. Kleinert,** *Das Deuteronomium und der Deuteronomiker* (Untersuchungen zur alttestamentlichen Rechts- und Literaturgeschichte 1, 1872). **M. G. Kline,** *Treaty of the Great King: The Covenant Structure of Deuteronomy* (1963). **A. Klostermann,** "Das deuteronomische Gesetzbuch," *Der Pentateuch: Beiträge zu seinem Verständnis und seiner Entstehungsgeschichte* (1893, 1907) 154-428. **D. Knapp,** *Deuteronomium 4: Literarische Analyse und theologische Interpretation*

(GTA 35, 1987). **D. A. Knight,** "Deuteronomy and the Deuteronomists," *OT Interpretation: Past, Present, and Future* (ed. J. L. Mays et al., 1995) 61-79. **E. König,** *Das Deuteronomium* (KAT 3, 1917). **C. Kraemer,** "The Formation of Rabbinic Canon: Authority and Boundaries," *JBL* 110 (1991) 613-30. **D. Krochmalnik,** *Schriftauslegung: Die Bücher Levitikus, Numeri, Deuteronomium im Judentum* (Neuer Stuttgarter Kommentar, AT 33, 2003). **R. G. Kratz and H. Spieckermann (eds.),** *Liebe und Gebot: Studien zum Deuteronomium* (FRLANT 190, 2000). **A. Kuenen,** *Historische-kritisch Onderzoek naar het ontstaan en de verzameling van de Boeken den Ouden Verbonds 1.1* (1861, 1885; ET, *An Historico-critical Inquiry into the Origin and Composition of the Hexateuch: Pentateuch and Book of Joshua* [1886]). **G. Langer,** *Von Gott Erwählt-Jerusalem: Die Rezeption von Dtn 12 im frühen Judentum* (ÖBS 8, 1989). **N. Leibowitz,** *Studies in Devarim (Deuteronomy)* (1982). **J. D. Levenson,** "Who Inserted the Book of the Torah?" *HTR* 68 (1975) 203-33. **B. M. Levinson,** *Deuteronomy and the Hermeneutics of Legal Innovation* (1997). **B. Lindars,** "Torah in Deuteronomy," *Words and Meanings: Essays Presented to D. W. Thomas* (ed. P. R. Ackroyd and B. Lindars, 1968) 117-36. **J. Locke,** "A Letter Concerning Toleration [1689]," *The Works of J. Locke* (1823) 6:1-58. **S. Loersch,** *Das Deuteronomium und seine Deutungen: Ein forschungsgeschichtlicher überblick* (SBS 22, 1967). **N. Lohfink,** *Das Hauptgebot: Eine Untersuchung literarischer Einleitungsfragen zu Dtn 5-11* (AnBib 20, 1963); "Deuteronomy," *IDBSup* (1976) 229-32; (ed.), *Das Deuteronomium: Entstehung, Gestalt, und Botschaft* (BETL 68, 1985); *Die Väter Israels im Deuteronomium: Mit einer Stellungnahme von T. Römer* (OBO 111, 1991); *Theology of the Pentateuch: Themes of the Priestly Narrative and Deuteronomy* (1994). **M. Luther,** "Preface to the OT [1523]," *Word and Sacrament 1* (LW, 1960) 35:235-51-WA, DB 8, 11-31; "Against the Heavenly Prophets in the Matter of Images and Sacraments [1525]," *Church and Ministry 2* (LW, 1958) 40:73-223; *Wider die himmlischen Propheten, von den Bildern und Sacrament* (WA 18) 62-125, 134-214; "How Christians Should Regard Moses [1525]," *Word and Sacrament 1* (LW, 1960) 35:155-74; *Eyn Unterrichtung wie sich die Christen ynn Mosen sollen schicken* (WA 16) 363-93; *Lectures on Deuteronomy* (tr. R. R. Caemmerer, LW 9, 1960); *Deuteronomium Mosi cum annotationibus* (WA 14) 497-744. **S. D. McBride,** "The Yoke of the Kingdom: An Exposition of Deuteronomy 6:4-5," *Int* 27 (1973) 273-306; "Deuteronomium," *TRE* 8 (1981) 530-43; "Polity of the Covenant People: The Book of Deuteronomy," *Int* 41 (1987) 229-44 (repr. in *A Song of Power and the Power of Song* [ed. D. L. Christensen, 1993] 62-77). **D. J. McCarthy,** *Treaty and Covenant* (AnBib 21A, 1963, 1978[2]). **J. G. McConville,** *Law and Theology in Deuteronomy* (JSOTSup 33, 1984). **J. G. McConville and J. G. Millar,** *Time and Place in Deuteronomy* (JSOTSup 179, 1994). **F. R. McCurley,** "The Home of Deuteronomy Revisited: A Methodological Analysis of the Northern Theory," *A Light unto My Path: OT Studies in Honor of J. M. Myers* (GTS 4, ed. H. Bream et al., 1974) 295-317. **D. McGinn,** *The Admonition Controversy* (Rutgers Studies in English 5, 1949). **Maimonides,** *The Book of the Divine Commandments* (2 vols., tr. C. Chavel, 1940); *The Guide of the Perplexed* (tr. S. Pines, 1963). **J. Malfroy,** "Sagesse et loi dans le Deutéronome," *VT* 15 (1965) 49-65. **T. Mann,** *Deuteronomy* (Westminster Bible Companion, 1995). **A. D. H. Mayes,** *Deuteronomy* (NCB, 1979); "Deuteronomy 4 and the Literary Criticism of Deuteronomy," *JBL* 100 (1981) 23-51 (repr. in *A Song of Power and the Power of Song* [ed. D. L. Christensen, 1993] 195-224); "On Describing the Purpose of Deuteronomy," *JSOT* 58 (1993) 13-33. **W. A. Meeks,** *The Prophet-king: Moses Traditions and the Johannine Christology* (NovTSup 14, 1967). **M. Mendelssohn,** *Jerusalem oder über religiöse Macht und Judentum* (1783; ET, *Jerusalem, or On Religious Power and Judaism* [1983]). **G. E. Mendenhall,** "Ancient Oriental and Biblical Law," *BA* 17 (1954) 26-46; "Covenant Forms in Israelite Tradition," *BA* 17 (1954) 50-76. **G. E. Mendenhall and G. A. Herion,** "Covenant," *ABD* (1992) 1:1179-202. **R. P. Merendino,** *Das Deuteronomische Gesetz: Eine literarkritische, gattungs- und Überlieferungsgeschichtliche*

Untersuchung (BBB 31, 1969). **J. Milgrom**, "Profane Slaughter and a Formulaic Key to the Composition of **Deuteronomy**," *HUCA* 47 (1976) 1-17. **J.G. Millar**, *Now Choose Life: Theology and Ethics in Deuteronomy* (1999). **P. D. Miller**, "The Gift of God: The Deuteronomic Theology of the Land," *Int* 23 (1969) 451-65; "'Moses My Servant': The Deuteronomic Portrait of Moses," *Int* 41 (1987) 245-55; *Deuteronomy* (IBC, 1990); *Israelite Religion and Biblical Theology: Collected Essays* (JSOTSup 267, 2000). **C. Minette de Tillesse**, "Sections 'tu' et sections 'vous' dans le Deutéronome," *VT* 12 (1962) 29-87. **S. Mittmann**, *Deuteronomium 1,1-6, 3 literarkritisch und traditionsgeschichtlich Untersucht* (BZAW 139, 1975). **D. P. Moessner**, "Luke 9:1-50: Luke's Preview of the Journey of the Prophet Like Moses of Deuteronomy," *JBL* 102 (1983) 575-605. **J. I. Mombert (ed.)**, *W. Tyndale's Five Books of Moses Called the Pentateuch* (1967). **W. L. Moran**, "The Ancient Near Eastern Background of the Love of God in Deuteronomy," *CBQ* 25 (1963) 77-87. **E. Morgan (ed.)**, *Puritan Political Ideas, 1558–1794* (American Heritage Series, 1965). **T. Müntzer**, "Sermon Before the Princes [1524]," *Spiritual and Anabaptist Writers* (LCC 25, 1957) 47-70. **Nachmanides (Ramban)**, *Pêrûšê hattôra lerabbîmû moše ben nahaman, 3* (ed. C. Chavel, 1965; ET, *Commentary on the Torah: Deuteronomy* [1976]). **J. Neusner**, *Sifre to Deuteronomy: An Introduction to the Rhetorical, Logical, and Topical Program* (BJS 124, 1987). **R. D. Nelson**, *Deuteronomy: A Commentary* (Old Testament Library, 2002). **E. W. Nicholson**, *Deuteronomy and Tradition* (1967); *God and His People: Covenant and Theology in the OT* (1986). **C. R. North**, "Pentateuchal Criticism," *The OT and Modern Study* (ed. H. H. Rowley, 1951) 48-83. **M. Noth**, *Die Gesetze im Pentateuch: Ihre Voraussetzungen und ihr Sinn* (SKG.G 17, 2, 1940; ET, "The Laws in the Pentateuch: Their Assumptions and Meaning," *The Laws in the Pentateuch and Other Studies* [1966] 1-107); *Überlieferungsgeschichte des Pentateuch* (1948; ET, *A History of Pentateuchal Traditions* [1972]); *Überlieferungsgeschichtliche Studien* (1957) 1:1-110 (ET, *The Deuteronomistic History* [JSOTSup 15, 1981, 1991]). **T. Oestreicher**, *Das deuteronomische Grundgesetz* (BFCT 27, 4, 1923). **D. T. Olson**, *Deuteronomy and the Death of Moses: A Theological Reading* (OBT, 1994). **Origen**, *On First Principles* [*De Principiis*] (tr. G. W. Butterworth, 1936); *Contra Celsum* (tr. and ed. H. Chadwick, 1953). **E. Otto**, "Von Budesbuch zum Deuteronomium: Die deuteronomische Redaktion in Dtn 12-26," *Biblische Theologie und Gesellschaftlicher Wandel: FS für N. Lohfink* (ed. G. Braulik, W. Gross, and S. McEvenue, 1993) 260-78; "Aspects of Legal Reform and Reformulation in Ancient Cuneiform and Israelite Law," *Theory and Method in Biblical and Cuneiform Law: Revision, Interpolation, and Development* (ed. B. Levinson, JSOTSup 181, 1994) 160-96; "Gesetzesfortschreibung und Pentateuchredaktion," *ZAW* 107 (1995) 373-92; *Das Deuteronomium: politische Theologie und Rechtsreform in Juda und Assyrien* (BZAW 284, 1999); *Das Deuteronomium im Pentateuch und Hexateuch: Studien zur Literaturgeschichte von Pentateuch und Hexateuch im Lichte des Deuteronomiumrahmens* (Forschungen zum Alten Testament, 2000). **T. Paine**, *The Age of Reason* (1794–95; Carol ed., 1995). **J. Pakkala**, *Interolerant Monolatry in the Deuteronomistic History* (Publications of the Finnish Exegetical Society 76, 1999). **M. J. Paul**, "Hilkiah and the Law (2 Kings 22) in the 17th and 18th Centuries," *Das Deuteronomium* (BETL 68, ed. N. Lohfink, 1985) 9-12; *Het archimedisch punt van de Pentateuchkritiek: Een historisch en exegetisch onderzoek naar de verhouding van Deuteronomium en de reformatie van konig Josia (2 Kon. 22-23)* (1988). **L. Perlitt**, *Bundestheologie im Alten Testament* (WMANT 36, 1969); *Deuteronomium* (BKAT 5, 1990–); *Deuteronomium-Studien* (FAT 8, 1994). **R. F. Person, Jr.**, *The Deuteronomic School: Histroy, Social Setting, and Literature* (SBLSBS 2, 2002). **Philo of Alexandria**, "On the Creation [De Opificio Mundi]," "Allegorical Interpretation of Genesis II., III. [Legum Allegoria]," *Philo 1* (LCL, 1929); "On the Migration of Abraham [De Migratione Abrahami]," "Who Is the Heir of Divine Things [Quis Rerum divinarum Heres]," *Philo 4* (LCL, 1932); "Moses [De Vita

Mosis]," "On the Decalogue [De Decalogo]," "On the Special Laws [De Specialibus Legibus]," "On the Virtues [De Virtutibus]," "On Rewards and Punishments [De Praemiis et Poenis]," *Philo 6-8* (LCL, 1935–39); "Every Good Man is Free [Quod Omnis Probus Liber Sit]," *Philo 9* (LCL, 1941). **J. G. Plöger,** *Literarkritische, formgeschichtliche, und stilkritische Untersuchungen zum Deuteronomium* (BBB 26, 1967). **R. Polzin,** *Moses and the Deuteronomist: Deuteronomy, Joshua, Judges* (A Literary Study of the Deuteronomic History 1, 1980). **C. J. Pressler,** *The View of Women Found in the Deuteronomic Family Laws* (BZAW 216, 1993). **H. D. Preuss,** *Deuteronomium* (ErFor 164, 1982). **Procopius of Gaza,** *Commentarii in Deuteronomium* (PG 1865) 87:893-992. **Ptolemy,** "Letter to Flora," *Biblical Interpretation in the Early Church* (tr. and ed. K. Froehlich, Sources of Early Christian Thought, 1984) 37-43. **J. D. Purvis,** *The Samaritan Pentateuch and the Origin of the Samaritan Sect* (HSM 2, 1968). **A. F. Puukko,** *Das Deutronomium: Eine literarkritische Untersuchung* (BWAT 5, 1910). **Rabanus Maurus,** *Enarrationis super Deuteronomium* (PL 108) 837-998. **J. Rabbinowitz (tr.),** *Midrash Rabbah: Deuteronomy* (1939; Heb. ed. S. Liebermann, Midrash debarîm rabba [1974]). **G. von Rad,** *Das Gottsvolk im Deuteronomium* (BWANT 47, 1929); *Das formgeschichtliche Problem des Hexateuch* (BWANT 74, 1938; ET, "The Form-critical Problem of the Hexateuch," *The Problem of the Hexateuch and Other Essays* [1966]) 1-78; *Deuteronomium-Studien* (FRLANT 58, 1948; ET, *Studies in Deuteronomy* [SBT 1, 9, 1961]); *Theologie des Alten Testaments 1* (1957, 1960; ET, *OT Theology, vol. 1, The Theology of Israel's Historical Traditions* [1965]); "Deuteronomy," *IDB* (1962) 1:831-38; *Das fünfte Buch Mose: Deuteronomium* (ATD, 1964; ET, *Deuteronomy: A Commentary* [OTL, 1966]). **Rashi,** *Raš'y 'al hattôra* (ed. A. Berliner, 1905; ET, *Pentateuch with Tg. Onkelos, Haphtaroth, and Prayers for Sabbath and Rashi's Commentary: Deuteronomy* [n.d.]). **J. Reider,** *The Holy Scriptures: Deuteronomy, with Commentary* (1937). **E. Reuss,** *L'histoire sainte et la loi* (1879). **E. Reuter,** *Kultzentralisation: Entstehung und Theologie von Dtn 12* (Athenaums Monografiens 87, 1993). **S. L. Richter,** *The Deuteronomistic History and the Name Theology* (BZAW 318, 2002). **E. K. A. Riehm,** *Die Gesetzgebung Moisis im Lande Moab* (1854). **P. Riemann,** "Covenant, Mosaic," *IDBSup* (1976) 192-97. **A. Rof,** "The Strata of the Law About the Centralization of Worship in Deuteronomy and the History of the Deuteronomic Movement," *Congress Volume, Uppsala, 1971* (VTSup 22, 1972) 221-26; "The Monotheistic Argumentation in Deuteronomy 4:32-40: Contents, Composition, and Text," *VT* 35 (1985) 434-45; "The Arrangement of the Laws in Deuteronomy," *ETL* 64 (1988) 265-87. **A. Rofé,** *Deuteronomy: Issues and Interpretations* (OT Studies, 2002). **J. W. Rogerson,** *W. M. L. de Wette: Founder of Modern Biblical Criticism: An Intellectual Biography.* (JSOTSup 126, 1992). **T. Römer,** *Israels Väter: Untersuchungen zur Väterthematik im Deuteronomium und in der deuteronomistischen Tradition* (OBO 99, 1990); "The Book of Deuteronomy," *The History of Israel's Traditions: The Heritage of M. Noth* (ed. S. L. McKenzie and M. P. Graham, JSOTSup 182, 1994) 178-212. **M. Rose,** *Der Ausschliesslichkeitsanspruch Jahwes: Deuteronomische Schultheologie und die Volksfrömmigkeit in der späten Königszeit* BWANT 106, 1975); *Deuteronomist und Jahwist: Untersuchungen zu den Berührungspunkten beider Literaturwerke* (ATANT 67, 1981). **Rupert of Deutz,** "In Deuteronomium," *De Trinitate et Operibus Eius* (PL 167) 917-1000. **U. Rüterswörden,** *Von der politischen Gemeinschaft zur Gemeinde: Studien zu Dt 16,18-18,22* (BBB 65, 1987). **J. A. Sanders,** "Deuteronomy," *The Books of the Bible* (ed. B. W. Anderson, 1989) 1:89-102. **E. Sandoz (ed.),** *Political Sermons of the American Founding Era: 1730–1805* (1991). **L. S. Schearing and S. L. McKenzie,** *Those Elusive Deuteronomists: The Phenomenon of Pan-Deuteronomism* (JSOTSup 268, 1999). **F. W. Schultz,** *Das Deuteronomium* (1859). **G. Seitz,** *Redaktionsgeschichtliche Studien zum Deuteronomium* (BWANT 93, 1971). **S. K. Sherwood,** *Leviticus, Numbers, Deuteronomy* (Berit olam, 2002). **A. R. Siebens,** *L'origine du code deutéronomique* (1929). **R. Simon,**

Histoire critique du Vieux Testament (1678; ET, *A Critical History of the OT* [1682]). **D. E. Skweres,** *Die Rückverweise im Buch Deuteronomium* (AnBib 79, 1979). **B. Smalley,** *The Study of the Bible in the Middle Ages* (1952). **R. Smend,** "W. R. Smith and J. Wellhausen," *W. R. Smith: Essays in Reassessment* (ed. W. Johnstone, JSOTSup 189, 1995) 226-42. **G. A. Smith,** *The Book of Deuteronomy* (1918). **W. R. Smith,** *The OT in the Jewish Church* (1881, 1892). **J. P. Sonnet,** *The Book within the Book: Writing in Deuteronomy* (BibInt Series 14, 1997). **R. K. Soulen,** *The God of Israel and Christian Theology* (1996). **B. de Spinoza,** *Tractatus theologico-politicus* (1670; ET R. H. M. Elwes, *A Theologico-political Treatise* [1951]). **W. Staerk,** *Das Deuteronomium: Sein Inhalt und seine literarische Form. Eine kritische Studie* (1894); *Das Problem des Deuteronomiums: Ein Beitrag zur neuesten Pentateuchkritik* (BFCT 29, 2, 1924). **N. Steinberg,** "The Deuteronomic Law Code and the Politics of State Centralization," *The Bible and the Politics of Exegesis: Essays in Honor of N. K. Gottwald on His Sixty-fifth Birthday* (ed. D. Jobling et al., 1991) 161-70. **D. Steinmetz,** "The Reformation and the Ten Commandments," *Int* 43 (1989) 256-66. **C. Steuernagel,** *Der Rahmen des Deuteronomiums: Literarcritische Untersuchungen ∞ber seine Zusammensetzung und Entstehung* (1894, 1923); *Die Entstehung des deuteronomischen Gesetzes* (1896, 1901); *Deuteronomium und Josau* (HKAT 1, 3, 1, 1900, 1923). **L. Stulman,** "Encroachment in Deuteronomy: An Analysis of the Social World of the D Code" *JBL* 109 (1990) 613-32. **H. Tadmor,** "Treaty and Oath in the Ancient Near East: A Historian's Approach," *Humanizing America's Iconic Book* (SBLBSNA 6, ed. G. M. Tucker and D. A. Knight, 1982) 127-52. **A. Tal,** "Samaritan Literature," *The Samaritans* (ed. A. Crown, 1989) 413-67. **Tertullian,** *An Answer to the Jews* [*Adversus Iudaeos*] (The Writings of Tertullian, ANCL 18, ed. A. Roberts and J. Donaldson, 1870) 3:202-49; *Apology* [De Spectaculis] (LCL, 1931); *Apology* (LCL, 1953). **A. Thiel,** *In der Schule Gottes: die Ethik Calvins im Spiegel seiner Predigten über das Deuteronomium* (1999). **J. D. Thompson,** *A Critical Concordance to the Septuagint: Deuteronomy* (The Computer Bible 57, 1998). **J. H. Tigay,** *Deuteronomy: The Traditional Hebrew Text with the New JPS Commentary* (JPS Torah Commentary, 1996); "The Significance of the End of Deuteronomy (Deut 34:10-12)," *Texts, Temples, and Traditions: A Tribute to M. Haran* (ed. M. Fox et al., 1996) 137-43. **E. Tov,** "Proto-Samaritan Texts and the Samaritan Pentateuch," *The Samaritans* (ed. A. Crown, 1989) 397-407. **I. Twersky,** *Introduction to the Code of Maimonides* (*Mishneh Torah*) (*YJS* 22, 1980). **E. Ulrich,** "Pluriformity in the Biblical Text, Text Groups, and Questions of Canon," *The Madrid Qumran Congress* (ed. J. Trebolle Barrera and L. Vegas Montaner, STDJ 11, 1, 1992) 1:23-41. **M. Valeri,** "Religion, Discipline, and the Economy in Calvin's Geneva," *SCJ* 28 (1997) 123-42. **J. Van Seters,** "Confessional Reformulation in the Exilic Period," *VT* 22 (1972) 448-59; "The Conquest of Sihon's Kingdom: A Literary Examination," *JBL* 91 (1972) 182-97; "The So-called Deuteronomistic Redaction of the Pentateuch," *Congress Volume, Leuven, 1989* (ed. J. Emerton, VTSup 43, 1991) 58-77. **T. Veijola,** *Moses Erben: Studien zum Dekalog, zum Deuteronomisums und zum Schriftgelehrtentum* (BWANT 8, 2000). **J. Vermeylen,** *Le Dieu de la Promesse et le Dieu de l'Alliance: Le dialogue des grandes institutions théologiques de l'Ancien Testament* (LD 126, 1986). **M. Vervenne and J. Lust (eds.),** *Deuteronomy and Deuteronomic Literature: FS C. H. W. Brekelmans* (BETL 133, 1997). **B. K. Waltke,** "Samaritan Pentateuch," *ABD* (1992) 5:932-40. **M. Weinfeld,** *Deuteronomy and the Deuteronomic School* (1972); "The Emergence of the Deuteronomic Movement: The Historical Antecedents," *Das Deuteronomium: Entstehung, Gestalt, und Botschaft* (ed. N. Lohfink, BETL 68, 1985) 76-98; *Deuteronomy 1–11* (AB 5, 1991); "Deuteronomy, Book of," *ABD* (1992) 2:168-83. **D. Weir,** *The Origins of the Federal Theology in Sixteenth-century Reformation Thought* (1990). **A. C. Welch,** *The Code of Deuteronomy: A New Theory of Its Origin* (1924); *Deuteronomy: The Framework of the Code* (1932). **J. Wellhausen,** (*Prolegomena zur*) *Geschichte Israels* (1878, 1883; ET, *Prolegomena to the History of Israel* [1885]); *Die*

Composition des Hexateuchs und der historischen Bücher des Alten Testaments (1889, 1899).
R. Westbrook, "Biblical and Cuneiform Law Codes," *RB* 92 (1985) 247-64. **J. W. Wevers,**
Notes on the Greek Text of Deuteronomy (SBLSCS 39, 1995); (ed.), *Studies in the Text
Histories of Deuteronomy and Ezekiel* (Mitteilungen des Septuaginta-Unternehmens 26, 2003).
S. A. White, "The All Souls Deuteronomy and the Decalogue," *JBL* 109 (1990) 193-206.
J. N. M. Wijngaards, *The Dramatization of Salvific History in the Deuteronomic Schools*
(OTS 16, 1969). **T. M. Willis,** *The Elders of the City: A Study in the Elder-laws in Deuteronomy*
(SBLMS 55, 2001). **R. Wilson,** "Israel's Judicial System in the Preexilic Period," *JQR* 74
(1983) 229-48. **G. E. Wright,** "The Book of Deuteronomy: Introduction and Exegesis," *IB*
(1953) 2:309-537; "The Lawsuit of God: A Form-critical Study of Deuteronomy 32," *Israel's
Prophetic Heritage* (ed. B. W. Anderson and W. Harrelson, 1962) 26-67. **Y. Yadin,** *Tefillin from
Qumran* (XQPhyl 1-4) (1969); *The Temple Scroll* (3 vols., 1983). **K. Zobel,** *Prophetie und
Deuteronomium: Die Rezeption prophetischer Theologie durch das Deuteronomium* (BZAW
199, 1992).

S. D. McBRIDE

THE FORMER PROPHETS

Joshua

The text of Joshua raises acute questions as to what context is appropriate for its interpretation. Is Joshua essentially a complete and integrated book that can properly stand on its own and be viewed in and for itself? Or is it only sensible to see its contents as part of something else: whether the Pentateuch, from which it may be a lost conclusion or a detached appendix; or the narratives of the former prophets, which may offer a single deliberately planned story? Of course, the second alternative simply pushes back the equally vital question of to what extent the larger text of which Joshua might be a part might itself be an integrated work, rather than a haphazard deposit of tradition. How much or how little structure or planning can be detected in Joshua or in its supposed wider context?

Answers to questions like these determine whether we give priority to aesthetic or historical attempts to understand the book. Is this text more like persons with whom we may readily deal and interact on the terms in which they present themselves? Or is it more like those people about whom we have to learn something of their family and their past before we can cope with the puzzle they represent? It may be impatience with such preliminaries that has led many readers to advocate simply taking the text as it is, as tradition or the canon have handed it down.

1. *Interpretation Within the Text, or What Is the Text?* Such an apparently straightforward approach founders on the facts as disclosed by text-critical studies. The Hebrew (MT) and Greek (LXX) texts of Joshua, preserved separately by synagogue and church after their ancient division, exhibit significant differences; and only some of these are the result of random mistakes. The importance of the Septuagint (LXX) of Joshua as evidence for the history of the Hebrew text before it was standardized in Masoretic (MT) tradition has been appreciated at least since J. Hollenberg (1876). The important work of S. Holmes (1914), in part a defense of Hollenberg, broke ground in glimpsing the implications for the book's literary history of some of the divergences between the ancient texts. Yet M. Margolis's magisterial treatment of the textual history of the Greek Joshua (1931–38) and M. Noth's influential commentary on the Hebrew text (1938) combined to marginalize the significance of the LXX for the understanding of the Hebrew Joshua.

A series of studies returning to and advancing Holmes's insights was inaugurated by H. Orlinsky (1969); and contributions have accelerated through the efforts of A. G. Auld, A. Rofé, E. Tov, L. Greenspoon, and J. Floss. (These have received thorough methodological grounding in the detailed and vital work by J. Trebolle-Barrera [1986], illustrating in portions of Judges, Samuel, and Kings the close relationship between textual criticism and literary history.) The implications of these studies have not yet reached a wide readership. R. Boling's textual notes (AB 6, 1982) diligently note variation between Hebrew and Greek texts and the divergent evidence of the available Qumran material. And several of the results of the above-mentioned scholars have been incorporated piecemeal in T. Butler's more important commentary (1983). However, a full-scale treatment of the whole book of Joshua from this perspective has still to be published; and K. Bieberstein (1995) and C. den Hertog have urged caution.

2. Ea*rlier Interpretation of the Texts.* Ben Sira epitomizes Joshua in a few verses (beginning of Sirach 46): the successor to Moses, the one who as a deliverer deserved his name, the one who brought Israel into its inheritance, the one splendid in fighting the Lord's battles. The passage from which most detail is drawn is Josh 10:10-15, in which Joshua defends the Israelites from the Amorites by commanding the sun to stand still, whereby hailstones fall from the sky and annihilate this enemy.

The NT takes no explicit opportunity to exploit the fact that Joshua and Jesus share the same name—a feature prominent in patristic interpretation. The letter to the Hebrews (Heb 4:8) contrasts the "rest" offered by Jesus with what could not have been provided in full by Joshua because Psalm 95 sees it as incomplete. The great review of examples of faith passes over Joshua in two verses (Heb 11:30-31). James's letter (Jas 2:25) also mentions Rahab's "justification by works," while the Gospel of Matthew (Matt 1:5) counts her among the ancestors of the Messiah.

Josephus's account of Joshua in his *Jewish Antiquities* is mostly a rather wordy paraphrase of the whole text of the biblical book. Some of its additions and, even more, its omissions are interesting. The twelve stones at Gilgal form an altar; but there is absolute silence on the circumcision episode, and the Passover is barely mentioned. More understandably the account of land division is both shorter and more orderly than in Joshua 13–21, with the survey by geometricians (cf. 18:1-10) at its head. As if to compensate, the dispute over the eastern altar is even more leisurely than Joshua 22.

Origen's *Homilies on Joshua,* perhaps his latest work (around 250 C.E.), stressed the first Joshua/Jesus as greater than the dead Moses of the law. The theme is already found in Justin Martyr and Irenaeus, but it appears to have been Origen's detailed exposition that had the most influence during this period. The changing of the leader's name from Hoshea was prophetic. The crossing of the Jordan was a procession with priestly ritual, not the undisciplined mob at the Red Sea. Moses settled only two-and-a-half tribes, and outside the land, while Joshua settled the majority, including the Levites, in the land.

Origen's other key theme has already been suggested: the spiritualizing of the land and the struggles within it. It is the soul that is the real area of conflict; heaven is symbolized by the promised land and its "rest." This interpretation permitted Origen to oppose both the heretical disjunction between the cruel God of the HB and the loving one of the NT as well as the fleshly literalism of the Jews. A fine example is the more "dignified" interpretation he is able to give of the second circumcision of the people before the first Passover in the promised land. In fact, his commentary on John had already mentioned the obvious literal sense of the passage. Here, however, Origen remarked that Jews must be asked how a second circumcision is possible. For Christians, for whom the law is spiritual, the difficulties of the passage are resolved: The first circumcision marked the passage from idolatry to the Mosaic law; the second, accomplished by the stone that is Christ, marked the passage from the law and the prophets to the gospel faith. Theodore of Mopuestia indulged in a similar polemic when he suggested that Jews are regrettably unable to see that the circumcised perished and the uncircumcised were saved: the fathers died, and it was their sons who received the object of the promise.

F. Langlamet (1979) has provided a masterly survey of Rahab as she has been discussed in ancient and modern times—by the rabbis, among the fathers of the church, and in more recent scholarship. Rabbis and early fathers almost outdid each other in the significance they found in this woman and her story. For some of the rabbis she was one of the four most beautiful women in the world (with Sarah, Abigail, and Esther); for others, one of the four most seductive (with Ruth, Jael, and Saul's daughter Michal). Her profession of faith was linked with those of Moses, Jethro, and Naaman; Joshua married her; and eight prophets were descended from her (including Jeremiah and Ezekiel in different lists). In short, as ideal proselyte, she was an example to all the nations of the world: Any waverer could be challenged, "Are you worse than Rahab?" Christian fathers made some similar points (beginning with Matt 1:5) and noted also that she was saved by her faith and her hospitality; the scarlet cord given her by the messengers of Joshua/Jesus was a sign of salvation by the Lord's blood; and her example is endorsed by Jesus' statement to religious leaders of his time that publicans and courtesans proceed them into the kingdom.

The divinely instigated treatment of the Canaanites has long been a problem for commentators, whether as a straightforward moral issue or as a precedent from within their own Scriptures felt by politically vulnerable Jews to be all too dangerous in Christian hands. Medieval rabbis suggested that Joshua, before his invasion, had offered the inhabitants of Canaan by letter a three-fold invitation to submit.

Calvin's commentary on the book, from the closing months of his life in 1563/64, happens to be his last literary work. His long experience as a leader and his failing health both illumine his exposition. The removal of Moses, "as if God, after cooping up his people in a corner, had left his work in a shapeless and mutilated form," and his replacement by Joshua "suggests the very useful reflection, that while men are cut off by death, and fail in the middle of their career, the faithfulness of God never fails."

Again, on the dispute in chapter 22 over the altar of the Transjordanian tribes, he comments ironically, but firmly: "Nothing was farther from their intention than to innovate in any respect in the worship of God. But they sinned not lightly in attempting a novelty, without paying any regard to the high priest, or consulting their brethren, and in a form which was very liable to be misconstrued." Leadership and literary sensitivity combine to influence his discussion of how the two closing speeches by Joshua are related: In chapter 24 Joshua "explains more fully what he before related more briefly. For it would not have been suitable to bring out the people twice to a strange place for the same cause."

3. *Earlier Modern Discussion: Joshua and Pentateuch.* The synthesis of J. Wellhausen on the composition of the Hexateuch, which was to remain authoritative for sixty years, was heavily indebted to two immediate predecessors. In 1874 Hollenberg declared that Pentateuchal Criticism gave new life to the study of Joshua. In a detailed article he argued first that Joshua 1; 8:30-35; 23; and parts of 24 had been composed by the deuteronomist, who had added Deuteronomy 1–4 and portions of the final chapters to the basic speech of Moses in Deuteronomy 5–28; and then that this major author had also made numerous smaller contributions to the "Jehovistic" Joshua traditions. A. Kuenen (1886) was to concur in almost all details, although he argued against ascribing this deuteronomic recension to a single author. Wellhausen's movement (toward the end of his influential study) from Pentateuch to Joshua was introduced in carefully chosen words: Unlike Judges–Kings, Joshua was an appendix to the Pentateuch that assumed it at all points—without the same material being edited in it the same way. In fact, he was to argue that the sources had been more substantially altered in the editing of Joshua than in the Pentateuch. In his discussion of the deuteronomist's role, Wellhausen made only minor alterations to the proposals of Hollenberg and Kuenen, agreeing with Hollenberg that deuteronomic style could be found even in late additions unrepresented in the LXX (e.g., 20:4-6).

The commentary of C. Keil and Franz Delitzsch (1869), while admitting that Joshua is more closely connected to the Pentateuch in form and content than to those books that follow, insists that it is not a literary appendix: Their relationship is like that of Joshua to Moses. Even if it was not composed until some time after Joshua's death, this does not affect its historico-prophetic character; both the content and form of the book show it to be an independent and simple work composed with historical fidelity as well as a work that is as thoroughly pervaded with the spirit of HB revelation as is the Pentateuch.

The third volume of A. Dillman's Hexateuch commentary on Numbers–Joshua (1886) is more sympathetic to Wellhausen and Kuenen. Once separated from the more authoritative Pentateuch, Joshua had not been so carefully corrected, hence its many preferable LXX readings. However, historically it cannot be separated from the Pentateuch. He offers some arguments against preferring the LXX just because it is shorter.

C. Steuernagel's third volume on the historical books (1900) covers Deuteronomy–Joshua and offers a concluding introduction to the Hexateuch. Five sections of the latter concern composition, and only one treats the book of Joshua as historical source: The miraculous and popular form in which religious conviction clothes itself in the book is worthless for the political history of Israel; it has meaning for the history of religion only as a sign that Israel was a people with lively religious thought.

The earlier Cambridge Bible volume by G. Maclear on the AV (1880) stands very much in the Greek patristic tradition, with Joshua presented as a "type" prefiguring Jesus the Christ. He notes that the undoubtedly terrible severity of the work of Joshua was often used as an objection against HB morality, but quotes H. Ewald: "It is an eternal necessity that a nation such as the majority of the Canaanites then were, sinking deeper and deeper into a slough of discord and moral perversity, must fall before a people roused to a higher life by the newly awakened energy of unanimous trust in Divine Power." Maclear continues: "When ... God entrusted the sword of vengeance to Joshua, was ever campaign waged in such an unearthly manner as that now inaugurated by the leader of the armies of Israel?" And he ends by quoting a sermon of T. Arnold: "The Israelites' sword in its bloodiest executions, wrought a work of mercy for all the countries of the earth ... they preserved unhurt the seed of eternal life."

G. Cooke's later volume (1878, 1917), based on the RV, is a whole thought-world away. After an account of the book's literary origins very like that of Wellhausen, he explains that the deuteronomic redactor "tells about Joshua, not as he really was, but as the writers of the seventh century pictured him; the portrait, if it can be called one, is not a study from the life, but the creation of a fervid believer and patriot. We may be sure that nothing like the wholesale slaughter of the natives and irresistible victories of the Israelites ever took place ... Far more ancient and vivid than anything we find in the OT is the picture of early Canaan given by the Amarna tablets." Like Hollenberg, Kuenen, and Wellhausen, he is good in his treatment of the LXX.

The divorce between the message of Joshua and the facts of history was already clear in Steuernagel and Cooke. It was not successfully overcome by J. Garstang, despite that archaeologist's attempts in the Foundations of Biblical History (1931). However, a more enduring historical response was to come from his German colleagues.

4. *The Legacy of Alt and Noth*. A. Alt's three volumes of Kleine Schriften (1953–59) contain a dozen major papers relevant to the historical evaluation of Israel's settlement, the role of Joshua, and most distinctively the topographical information in the book, behind which he detected archival administrative source material (from the end of the Judaean monarchy in the case of the town lists in 15:21-62). Noth adopted Alt's methods and argued (1935) that a list of Judaean localities in twelve districts had been combined with a system of tribal boundaries to produce most of the material in Joshua 13–19. Their studies provided the methods and set the standards for the major works that followed by J. Simons (1959), Y. Aharoni (1967), and Z. Kallai (1967).

In his commentary on Joshua (1938) Noth reaffirmed that the topographical material had had its own prehistory and argued that even the narratives had a literary background distinct from Genesis, in which deuteronomistic affiliations were most easily detectable. He then addressed (1943) all the biblical narratives where consensus recognized the deuteronomist's editing, arguing first that Joshua–Kings represented a self-contained whole: The retrospective and anticipatory passages (Joshua 1; 23; Judges 2; 1 Samuel 12; 2 Kings 17) had no exact parallels in the HB and had much in common with each other in subject. "If we take the perfectly sound approach of interpreting the relatively simple and clear conditions in Joshua–Kings, without regard to the findings of literary criticism elsewhere, and postpone discussing the very controversial 'Hexateuch' questions in their application to Joshua, we can reach only one conclusion."

However, Joshua 1 is certainly not the beginning. The links of this chapter with the Moses story and in particular the account of the settlement of some tribes in Transjordan show that these matters have already been treated in the deuteronomist's work. Noth found that with little difficulty the chronological details in the other books can be seen to square with the information in 1 Kgs 8:1 that the Temple was dedicated 480 years after the exodus. (In the case of Joshua this depends on his claim that Josh 14:10 is part of a passage once linked to the deuteronomist's 11:23!) His review of the deuteronomist's contribution to the account of the occupation of Cisjordan differs little in essence from Hollenberg's (1874). A series of separate etiological stories relevant to the Israelites' successful incursion had been combined into a well-rounded whole with a few heroic legends. The deuteronomist obviously took over the whole of this and altered it only by adding an introduction and epilogue and some supplementary material.

In a significant comment on the nature of the composition, Noth writes that these deuteronomistic passages, "brought in at every suitable opportunity... come to make good literary sense if they are not just the monotonously repeated statement of the pet idea of an 'editor,' intended to accompany and interpret a piece of tradition already existing in finished form, but rather meant to play a part in transforming elements totally diverse in form, scope and content, into a single literary unit." The fact that despite these elements the separate parts of the work seem disunited and heterogeneous is explained because the deuteronomist consciously committed himself to using the material available to him. Novelty and faithfulness hand in hand!

In 1953 Noth published a fresh edition of his commentary on Joshua, stating more decisively what he had anticipated in 1938: that the book should be read independently of the Pentateuch (i.e., Genesis–Numbers). G. von Rad, S. Mowinckel, and G. Fohrer (1968) continued to assert close links between Joshua and the Pentateuch. Auld (1980) and M. Rose (1981) responded, suggesting that even more of the Pentateuch depended on material in Joshua than Noth had claimed.

Noth's thesis of a Deuteronomistic History was to capture the imagination of almost all nonconservative scholars, although important details of his argument were challenged by many followers. Commentaries on Joshua for over thirty years (e.g., by H. Hertzberg [1953]; J. Gray [1967, 1986]; J. Miller and G. Tucker [1974]; and J. Soggin [1972]) operated within his structure. R. Smend (1971) challenged Noth's view that the addition of the topographical traditions was achieved editorially by anticipating in Josh 13:1 the deuteronomist's words in 23:1 about Joshua's age. His reversal of the relationship of these two verses allowed him to propose (a) that the deuteronomistic history (DtrH) did contain a report of land division and (b) that Joshua 23 was simply the most detailed of several additions to the original history by a second deuteronomistic editor (DtrN). W. Dietrich was to follow with a study on Kings (1972), interposing a third prophetic redaction (DtrP).

Their lead was followed by T. Veijola (1977) and summarized by Smend (1978). F. M. Cross's discussion (1973) focused on the later chapters of Kings and led him to propose that the original deuteronomistic history was composed in honor of Josiah before the fall of Judah. This history was brought up to date during the exile and supplemented with elements more critical of kingship. Cross's more summary views have been adjusted and advanced by R. Nelson (1981a, 1981b). H.-D. Hoffmann (1980), in a study of the religious reforms related by the deuteronomist, argued against both these trends: (a) that the deuteronomistic history was a unity (but for quite insignificant exceptions), and (b) that very much more of Joshua–Kings had been drafted by the deuteronomist than Noth had allowed. A. Mayes (1983) proposed that with a little adjustment on each side the similarities between the Smend and Cross "schools" would be clear.

Unhappily for our purposes, with the exception of Smend's article (1971) and, of course, Noth's original epoch-making commentary, very little of the above discussion has actually been based on close study of Joshua. There is a real danger that the study of this book is now quite as much at the mercy of broader theories about a deuteronomistic history as it was once misread as the conclusion of a Hexateuch.

Soggin's introduction and his commentary on Judges have endorsed the modifications argued by Smend and his followers. The volume by Boling and G. E. Wright, by contrast, stands more in the American tradition of Cross and Nelson. Unhappily, it is also a very uneven volume: The introduction was prepared by Wright before his death in 1974 and was out of date on its publication in 1982; then, since Boling did not write the introduction, the methods underlying his puzzling approach to matters of textual and literary history remain rather obscure despite further exposition (1983, 1985).

Different stages of the discussion were well reviewed by individual scholars: E. Jenni (1961), A. Radjawane (1974), Smend (1978), Auld (1980), T. Butler (1983), Mayes, and H. Weippert (1985), whose survey of what she in nice understatement calls a polyphonic situation, includes studies up to 1981. When considering studies that mention the deuteronomist in Joshua subsequent to those reviewed by Weippert, "chaotic" might be a more adequate term than "polyphonic." J. Van Seters (1983) attributes most of Joshua–Kings to an exilic deuteronomist, supplemented by a late anti-monarchic author; while B. Peckham (1984) attributes most of Joshua–Samuel to the second deuteronomist, seeing his work as a monumental commentary built into and onto a once brief narrative of Deuteronomy 1. And C. Begg (1986) confidently talks of the "deuteronomisticity" of Joshua 7–8 on the basis of its structural contribution to the whole, whether words and ideas from Deuteronomy are found in it or not.

Each of these scholars believed in a deuteronomistic history—but not in Noth's—and each in a different one. Was it time to revalue this currency or to move on to a different standard? Two collaborative projects, one on the legacy of Noth and the other on Israel's constructing its own history, led to valuable publications edited by S. L. McKenzie and M. P. Graham (1994) and A. De Pury, T. Römer, and J.-D. Macchi (1996). C. Schäfer-Lichtenberger (1995) provided a wealth of documentation in her careful comparison of Joshua and Solomon; Auld (1995) also reviewed some Joshua issues in the light of his work on Kings.

5. *A Literary Reading?* R. Polzin's (1980) attempt to read the first half of the deuteronomistic history (Deuteronomy–Judges) after the example of the Russian "formalist" literary critics may have been underrated. He offers sensitive and attractive readings of many parts of Joshua. The text is studied "as it is," unreconstructed, mostly by attention to the shifting perspectives or points of view in different "planes" of the text: phraseo-logical, temporal, spatial, psychological and ideological. The reader is invited into ever-richer readings of the text; and the deepest, the ideological level, is reached through the more superficial. Polzin makes particular use of the interplay between the narrator, God, and Moses or Joshua, especially when one is quoting, and sometimes slightly misquoting another.

The detail of the Rahab story (chap. 2) is allowed to interrupt the action of conquest so long because, once it is seen that the story of Rahab is really the story of Israel told from the point of view of a non-Israelite, then the larger themes of the justice and mercy of God vis-á-vis Israel can be recognized as central to the story and to its position as the initial episode in the deuteronomist's account of the occupation of the land. The valuable distortions brought about by constant shifts in perspective offer the reader a much more adequate image of the occupation of the land as the fulfillment of God's word than the flat, universalized, and pat evaluations of the voice of authoritarian dogmatism, the reflexes of whose simplistic ideology can still be heard in the categorical assertions of, say, 4:10b. Chapter 22 helps us see why the two-and-a-half tribes are so prominent in the book: They are like the other "aliens"—Rahab, the Gibeonites, Caleb, the Levites—and dependants in the book of Joshua. All of them are representative versions of the same typology: The Transjordanian tribes are a permanent representation of the obedience to God's law that never quite makes it. As Phinehas testifies to these "outcasts": "We know this day...that you have saved the people of Israel from the hand of the Lord."

M. Greenberg (in Y. Kaufmann [1985]) has noted how Kaufmann's reading of Joshua, while less critical historically, was holistic before that became fashionable. There is sensitive, but less coordinated, literary comment in Boling, Butler, and Auld (1984), who draw attention to humor and irony and warn against too straight a reading of the text. Butler, a master of fair-minded review, encourages the search for historical development in the interpretation of the Joshua traditions and claims that their "final, canonical message . . . is made clear by the Deuteronomistic structural markers." It is vital that the import of the book of Joshua be sought in its text and not in a reconstruction of whatever history may underlie it. The commentaries of Boling and E. Hamlin (1983) commend a liberationist Joshua who owes more to the historical endeavors of G. Mendenhall (1962) and N. Gottwald (1979) than to close reading of the biblical book.

Polzin's reading of Deuteronomy–Judges (complemented by subsequent volumes on the books of Samuel) has received valuable support from the articles by D. Gunn (1987) and L. Rowlett (1992) and the volumes by L. Eslinger (1989), L. Hawk (1991), G. Mitchell (1993), and E. Mullen (1993). Rowlett particularly neatly sketches contrasts such as the fate of outsider Rahab and insider Achan with respect to the Jericho "ban" or of insider Transjordanians on the wrong side of the Jordan and outsider Gibeonites on the right side. R. Carroll (1992) analyzes the myth of the empty land. N. Winther-Nielsen (1995) has made a thorough appeal to discourse analysis as a more objective umpire among the competing witnesses cited by synchronic and diachronic readers alike.

None of the commentaries of the 1990s has embraced these newer literary approaches, although each is novel in its own way. M. Ottosson (1991) reads Joshua as a plea for a new David in the period of Josiah. His interest in the topographical chapters is reflected also in J. Svensson's dissertation (1994). V. Fritz (1994), whose work replaces that of Noth in the HAT series, remains remarkably faithful to the broad lines of his predecessor's approach, although the deuteronomist, whether Josianic or exilic, now displaces Noth's early monarchic Sammler as the first collector of the materials. He too offers a fresh account of the topographical materials.

S. Ahituv's modern Hebrew volume (1995) is intended as a "scientific" commentary but also for a wide readership in Israel. It unpacks idioms from the older tongue, offers a transcription of all the Joshua Qumran fragments, and explores several issues with contemporary resonance: the conquest and the question of the land left over; the Canaanite "ban": halakha and fact; the righteous generation of the conquerors; the dating of the geographical lists. The bibliography is quite detailed on such points of interest but makes little concession to more literary approaches. A commentary by R. Hess (1996) emphasizes evidence for early dating but is well informed and judicious throughout. These commentaries make little use of the more radical historical assessments by G. Ahlström (1993), R. Coote (1987), P. Davies (1992), N. Lemche (1988), T. Thompson (1992), and K. Whitelam (1996); and Ahituv in particular is more at home with compatriot historians like W. Weinfeld (1993) and N. Na'aman (1994).

6. *The Challenge of the Textual Facts.* Tov (1981 and repeatedly) has drawn attention to the relevance of the LXX for the literary history of the Bible. His discussion (1986) of the strange story of the altar on Ebal, which appears in a different position in the Hebrew and Greek Bibles—suggests that this is a late addition to the narrative, filed differently by different editors. The apparent link in 4Qjosh[a] of the end of this story with the beginning of Josh 5:2-3 has allowed A. Kempinsky (1993), Rofé (1994), and Auld (1995) to give this discussion a new twist. Then Tov developed a series of arguments (1987) to support the claim that the shorter LXX Vorlage has (by and large) been expanded into the longer familiar Hebrew rather than shortened from it. He assumes, apparently without argument, that the short Hebrew text translated into Greek around 200 B.C.E. had existed for centuries. However, might the familiar expanded Hebrew instead be much more recent than often thought?

Auld's studies on the tribal lists (1980, 1987) and those of M. Wüst (1975), whose major project remains only half published, have suggested that much of the historico-geographical information in Joshua 13–21 on the division of the land between the various tribes of Israel is more heavily reedited and harmonized than Alt and Noth allowed—or Aharoni and Kallai, who have largely followed their methods. Kallai did not take the opportunity of the translation of his major study (Hebrew, 1967) to answer some of these criticisms. However, E. Cortese (1990) has been very critical of Auld's work. G. Garbini (1988) has argued that details suggesting the Persian period are not so much supplements to an older tradition as indicators of the age of much of the biblical narrative tradition.

The discussion between Rofé and M. Rösel over the traditions that interlock at the end of Joshua and the beginning of Judges, but rather differently in the MT and the LXX, is quite vital for answering the first question posed in this article: In what context should we view the book of Joshua—in and for itself, or as part of a longer story, whether we call that a deuteronomistic history or not? Tov has been soberly providing the text-critical tools. Others must try to stand on his shoulders and attempt a riskier view. Two samples are the detailed study of Joshua 2 by Floss and Trebolle's correlation of textual and literary work at the beginning of Judges. That is where the most exciting action may be in Joshua studies in the next years.

Bibliography: **Y. Aharoni,** *The Land of the Bible* (1967). **S. Ahituv,** *Joshua: Introduction and Commentary* (Mikra LeYisra'el, 1995). **G. W. Ahlström,** *The History of Ancient Palestine* (1993). **G. A. Alt,** *Kleine Schriften zur Geschichte des Volkes Israel* (3 vols., 1953–59). **A. G. Auld,** "Joshua: The Hebrew and Greek Texts" (VTSup 30, 1979) 1-14; *Joshua, Moses, and the Land* (1980); *Joshua, Judges, and Ruth* (Daily Study Bible, 1984); "Tribal Terminology in Joshua and Judges," *Le Origini di Israele* (1987) 87-98; "Reading Joshua after Kings," *Words Remembered, Texts Renewed: Essays in Honour of J. F. A. Sawyer* (JSOTSup 195, ed. J. Davis, 1995); *Joshua Retold: Synoptic Perspectives* (1998). **C. T. Begg,** "The Function of Josh 7:1-8, 29 in the Deuteronomistic History," *Bib 67* (1986) 320-34. **K. Bieberstein,** *Lukian und Theodotion im Josuabuch, mit einem Beitrag zu den Josuarollen von Hirbet Qumran* (BNB 7, 1994); *Josua—Jordan—Jericho: Archäologie, Geschichte, und Theologie der Landnahmeerzählungen Josua 1-6* (OBO 143, 1995). **R. G. Boling,** "Levitical History and the Role of Joshua," *The Word of the Lord Shall Go Forth* (ed. C. L. Meyers and M. O'Connor, 1983) 241-61; "Levitical Cities: Archaeology and Texts," *Biblical and Related Studies Presented to S. Iwry* (ed. A. Kort and S. Merschauser, 1985) 23–32. **R. G. Boling and G. E. Wright,** *Joshua* (AB 6, 1982). **J. Briend,** "Les sources de l'histoire deut,ronomique: Recherches sur Jos 1-12," *Israël construit son histoire: L'historiographie deutéronomiste à la lumière des recherches récentes* (Le Monde de la Bible 34, ed. A. de Pury, T. Römer and J. D. Macchi, 1996) 343-74. B.J. Bruce (trans.), *Origen: Homilies on Joshua* (ed. C. White; FC 105, 2002). **T. C. Butler,** *Joshua* (WBC 7, 1983). **J. Calvin,** *Commentaries on the Book of Joshua* (Calvin Translation Society, 1984). **R. P. Carroll,** "The Myth of the Empty Land," *Ideological Criticism of Biblical Texts* (Semeia 59, ed. D. Jobling and T. Pippin, 1992) 79-93. **J. Cazeaux,** *Le refus de la guerre sainte: Josué, Juges et Ruth* (1998). **G. A. Cooke,** *The Book of Joshua in the RV* (CBC, 1878, 1918). **R. B. Coote,** "The Book of Joshua," *NIB* (1998) 2:553-719. **R. B. Coote and K. W. Whitelam,** *The Emergence of Early Israel in Historical Perspective* (1987). **E. Cortese,** "Gios 21 e Giud 1 (TM o LXX?) e l'abbottonaura del Tetrateuco con l'Opera deuteronomistica," *RivB 33* (1985); *Josua 13-21: Ein priesterschriftlicher Abschnitt im deuteronomistichen Geschichtswerk* (OBO 94, 1990). **F. M. Cross,** *Canaanite Myth and Hebrew Epic* (1973). **P. R. Davies,** *In Search of "Ancient Israel"* (JSOTSup 148, 1992). **K. De Troyer,** *Rewriting the Sacred Text* (Text-critical Studies 4, 2003). **W. Dietrich,** *Prophetie und Geschichte* (FRLANT 108, 1972). **A. Dillmann,** *Numeri, Deuteronomium, Josua* (KHC, 1886). **J. E. Erbes,** *The Peshitta and the Versions : A Study of the Phesitta Variants in Joshua 1–5* (Studia Semitica Upsaliensia 16, 1999). **L. Eslinger,** *Into the Hands of the Living God*

(JSOTSup 84, 1989). **J. P. Floss,** *Kunden oder Kundschafter: Literaturwissenschaftliche Untersuchung zu Jos 2, vol. 1, Text, Schichtung, ?berlieferung* (ATSAT 16, 1982); *vol. 2, Komposition, Redaktion, Intention* (ATSAT 26, 1986). **G. Fohrer,** *Introduction to the OT* (1968). **R. E. Friedman,** *The Exile and Biblical Narrative: The Formation of the Deuteronomistic Band Priestly Works* (HSM 22, 1981). **V. Fritz,** *Das Buch Josua* (HAT 1, 7, 1994). **G. Garbini,** *History and Ideology in Ancient Israel* (1988). **J. Garstang,** *Joshua–Judges* (1931). **N. K. Gottwald,** *The Tribes of Yahweh: A Sociology of the Religion of Liberated Israel, 1250–1050 B.C.E.* (1979). **J. Gray,** *Joshua, Judges, and Ruth* (NCBC, 1967; 1986). **L. J. Greenspoon,** *Textual Studies in the Book of Joshua* (HSM 28, 1983); "The Qumran Fragments of Joshua: Which Puzzle Are They Part of and Where Do They Fit?" *Septuagint, Scrolls, and Cognate Writings* (SBLSCS 33, ed. G. J. Brooke and B. Lindars, 1992). **H. Gressmann,** *Die Anfänge Israels* (von 2. Mose bis Richter und Ruth) (1922). **D. M. Gunn,** "Joshua and Judges," *The Literary Guide to the Bible* (ed. R. Alter and F. Kermode, 1987). **E. J. Hamlin,** *Inheriting the Land: A Commentary on the Book of Joshua* (ITC, 1983). **J. G. Harris,** *Joshua, Judges, Ruth* (NIB Commentary, OT 5, 2000). **L. D. Hawk,** *Every Promise Fulfilled: Contesting Plots in Joshua* (Literary Currents in Biblical Interpretation, 1991); (ed.) *Joshua* (Berit Olam, 2000). C. J. den Hertog, "Studien zur griechischen übersetzung des Buches Josua" (diss., Giessen, 1995). **H. W. Hertzberg,** *Die Bücher Josua, Richter, Ruth* (ATD 9, 1953). R. Hess, *Joshua* (TOTC, 1996). **H. D. Hoffman,** *Reform und Reformen unters zu e. Grundthema d. deuteronomist* (ATANT 66, 1980). **J. Hollenberg,** "Die deuteronomischen Bestandtheile des Buches Josua," *TSK 47* (1874) 462-506; *Der Charakter der alexandrinischen übersetzung des Buches Josua* (1876). S. Holmes, *Joshua, the Hebrew and Greek Texts* (1914). **E. Jenni,** "Zwei Jahrzehnte Forschung an den Büchern Josua bis Könige," *TRu 27* (1961) 1-32, 87–146. **Z. Kallai,** *Historical Geography of the Bible: The Tribal Territories of Israel* (1967; ET 1986). Y. Kaufmann, *The Biblical Account of the Conquest of Canaan* (preface by M. Greenberg, 1985). **C. F. Keil and F. Delitzsch,** *Joshua, Judges, and Ruth* (1869). **A. Kempinsky,** " 'When History Sleeps, Theology Arises': A Note on Joshua 8:30-35 and the Archaeology of the 'Settlement Period' " (Malamat Volume, ErIsr 24, 1993) 175–83. **A. Kuenen,** *The Origin and Composition of the Hexateuch* (1886). F. Langlamet, "Rahab," *DBSup 6* (1979) 1065–92. **K. Latvus,** *God Anger, and Ideology: The Anger of God in Joshua and Judges in Relation to Deuteronomy and the Priestly Writings* (JSOTSup 279, 1998). **N. P. Lemche,** *Ancient Israel: A New History of Israelite Society* (The Biblical Seminar, 1988); "The OT-A Hellenistic Book?" *SJOT 7* (1993) 163–93. **S. L. McKenzie and M. P. Graham** (eds.), *The History of Israel's Traditions: The Heritage of Martin Noth* (JSOTSup 182, 1994). **G. F. MacLear,** *The Book of Joshua* (CBC, 1890). **M. A. Margolis,** *The Book of Joshua in Greek* (1931-38). **A. D. H. Mayes,** *The Story of Israel Between Settlement and Exile: A Redactional Study of the Deuteronomistic History* (1983). **G. E. Mendenhall,** "The Hebrew Conquest in Palestine," *BA 25* (1962) 66–87. **J. M. Miller and G. M. Tucker,** *The Book of Joshua* (CBC, 1974). **G. Mitchell,** *Together in the Land: A Reading of the Book of Joshua* (JSOTSup 134, 1993). S. Mowinckel, *Erwägungen zur Pentateuch Quellenfrage* (1964); *Tetrateuch-Pentateuch-Hexateuch: Die Berichte über die Landnahme in den drei altisraelitischen Geschichtswerken* (BZAW 90, 1964). **E. T. Mullen, Jr.,** *Narrative History and Ethnic Boundaries: The Deuteronomistic Historian and the Creation of Israelite National Identity* (SemeiaSt, 1993). **N. Na'aman,** *Borders and Districts in Biblical Historiography: Seven Studies in Biblical Geographic Lists* (JBS 4, 1986); "The Conquest of Canaan in the Book of Joshua and in History," *From Nomadism to Monarchy: Archaeological and Historical Aspects of Early Israel* (ed. I. Finkelstein and N. Na'aman, 1994) 218-81. **R. D. Nelson,** *The Double Redaction of the Deuteronomistic History (*JSOTSup 18, 1981); "Josiah in the Book of Joshua," *JBL 100* (1981) 531-40; Joshua (OTL, 1997). **E. Noort,** *Das Buch Josua: Forschungsgeschichte und*

Problemfelder (Erträge der Forschung 292, 1998). **M. Noth,** "Studien zu den historisch-geographischen Dokumenten des Josuabuches," *ZDPV 58* (1935) 185–255; *Das Buch Josua* (HAT 1.7, 1938, 1953); *Überlieferungsgeschichtliche Studien 1* (1943; ET of pt. 1, *The Deuteronomistic History* [JSOTSup 15, 1981]). Origen, *Homélies sur Josu, (*SC 71, ed. A. Jaubert, 1960). **H. M. Orlinsky,** "The Hebrew Vorlage of the Septuagint of the Book of Joshua" (VTSup 17, 1969) 187–95. **M. Ottosson,** *Josuaboken: En programskrift for davidisk restauration* (Studia Biblica Upsaliensia I, 1991). **B. Peckham,** "The Composition of Joshua 3–4," *CBQ 46* (1984) 413-31. **R. Polzin,** *Moses and the Deuteronomist: A Literary Study of the Deuteronomic History, vol. 1, Deuteronomy, Joshua, Judges* (1980). **C. Pressler,** *Joshua, Judges, Ruth* (WBC, 2002). **A. de Pury, T. Römer and J.-D. Macchi (eds.),** *Israël construit son histoire: L'historiographie deut,ronomiste à la lumière des recherches récentes* (Le Monde de la Bible 34, 1996). **G. von Rad,** "The Promised Land and Yahweh's Land in the Hexateuch" (1943), his *The Problem of the Hexateuch and Other Essays* (1966) 79-93; "Hexateuch oder Pentateuch," *VF* (1947/50) 52–56. **A. N. Radjawane,** "Das deuteronomistische Geschichtswerk: Ein Forschungsbericht," *TRu 38* (1974) 177–216. **A. Rof,** "The End of the Book of Joshua According to the Septuagint," *Henoch 4* (1982) 17-36; "The Editing of the Book of Joshua in the Light of 4QJosh^a," *New Qumran Texts and Studies Relating to the Bible* (ed. J. G. Brooke, 1994). **M. Rose,** *Deuteronomist und Jahwist: Untersuchungen zu den Berührungspunkten beider Literaturwerken* (ATANT 67, 1981). **L. Rowlett,** "Inclusion, Exclusion, and Marginality in the Book of Joshua," *JSOT 55* (1992) 15–23. **C. Schäfer-Lichtenberger,** *Josua und Salomo: Eine Studie zu Autorität und Legitimität des Nachfolgers im Alten Testament* (VTSup 58, 1995). **H. Seebass,** "Zur Exegese der Grenzbeschreibungen von Jos. 16,1-17, 13," *ZDPV 100* (1984) 70-83; "Josua," *BN 28* (1985) 53–65. **J. Simons,** *The Geographical and Topographical Texts of the OT* (1959). **R. Smend,** "Das Gesetz und die Völker," *Probleme Biblischer Theologie* (ed. H. W. Wolff, 1971) 494-509; *Die Entstehung des Alten Testaments* (1978). **J. A. Soggin,** *Joshua* (OTL, 1972); *Introduction to the OT* (OTL, 1976). **C. Steuernagel,** *Deuteronomium und Josua und allgemeine Einleitung den Hexateuch* (HAT, 1900). **J. Svensson,** *Towns and Toponyms in the OT, with Special Emphasis on Joshua 14–21* (ConBOT 38, 1994). **J. D. Thompson,** *A Critical Concordance to the Septuagint: Joshua* (The Computer Bible 58, 1998). **T. L. Thompson,** *The Early History of the Israelite People* (SHANE 4, 1992). **E. Tov,** *The Text-critical Use of the Septuagint in Biblical Research* (JBS 3, 1981); "The Growth of the Book of Joshua in the Light of the Evidence of the LXX Translation," *Studies in Bible* (ScrHier 31, ed. S. Japhet, 1986) 321-39; "Some Sequence Differences Between the MT and LXX and Their Ramification for the Literary Criticism of the Bible," *JNSL 13* (1987) 151-60; *Textual Criticism of the HB* (1992a); "4QJosh^b," *Intertestamental Essays in Honour of J. T. Milik* (ed. Z. J. Kapera, 1992b). **J. Trebolle Barrera,** "Historia del Texto de los Libros Historicos e Historia de la Redaccion Deuteronomistica (Jueces 2,10-3,6)," *Salvacion en la Palabra: Targum-Derash-Berith* (ed. D. Muñoz Leon, 1986) 245–55. **E. Ulrich,** "4QJosh^a and Joshua's First Altar in the Promised Land," *New Qumran Texts and Studies Relating to the Bible* (ed. J. G. Brooke, 1994). **M. N. Van der Meer,** *Formation and Reformulation: The Redaction of the Book of Joshua in the Light of the Oldest Textual Witnesses* (VTSup 102, 2004). **J. Van Seters,** *In Search of History* (1983). **T. Veijola,** *Die ewige Dynastie: David und die Entstehung seiner Dynastie nach der deuteronomistichen Darstellung* (AASF B/193, 1975); *Das Königtum in der Beurteilung der deuteronomistischen Historiographie* (AASF B/198, 1977). **J.C. de Vos,** *Das Los Judas : über Entstehung und Ziele der Landbeschreibung in Josua 15* (VTSup 95, 2003). **B. G. Webb,** *The Book of Judges: An Integrated Reading* (JSOTSup 46, 1987). **M. Weinfeld,** *The Promise of the Land: The Inheritance of the Land of Canaan by the Israelites* (1993). **H. Weippert,** "Das deuteronomistiche Geschichtswerk: Sein Ziel und Ende in der neueren Forschung," *TRu 50* (1985) 213-49. **J.**

Wellhausen, "Pentateuch and Joshua," *EncBrit 18* (1885) 9:505-14; *Die Composition des Hexateuchs* (1899). **K. W. Whitelam,** *The Invention of Ancient Israel: The Silencing of Palestinian History* (1996). **N. Winther-Nielsen,** *A Functional Discourse Grammar of Joshua* (ConBOT 40, 1995). **M. H. Woudstra,** *The Book of Joshua* (NICOT, 1981). **M. Wüst,** *Untersuchungen zu den siedlungsgeographischen Texten des Alten Testaments, vol. 1, Ostjordanland* (BTAVO 9, 1975). **K. L. Younger, Jr.,** *Ancient Conquest Accounts: Study in Ancient Near Eastern and Biblical History Writing* (JSOTSup 98, 1990).

A. G. Auld

THE FORMER PROPHETS

Judges

1. *Introduction.* "And what more shall I say?" we read in Hebrews 11. "For time would fail me to tell of Gideon, Barak, Samson, Jephthah...who through faith conquered kingdoms, enforced justice, received promises." Time, however, has not noticeably failed others intent on idealizing these "famous men," "whose hearts did not fall into idolatry and who did not turn away from the Lord" (Sir 44:1; 46:11). In the process, as a history of Judges interpretation shows, many disturbing realities have been precluded—mass murder, fratricide, and gender-based violence, to name but a few. Of course, idealization has not been the only means to preclude. Many other interpretive paradigms have sufficed.

Interpretation always proceeds from particular investments of belief and horizons of meaning. For example, Judges has been read to underpin ideologies of anti-semitism, nationalism, and patriarchy, among others. Some indication of these ideological dimensions will be a concern of this survey.

2. *The Early Christian Church.* Few references to Judges are found in the ante-Nicene period of the Christian church. Those who referred to Judges during this time did so primarily in regard to its recurring plot pattern of transgression-punishment-deliverance. Tertullian, for example, recounted this cycle to demonstrate that God disciplines according to established rules of devotion, particularly against idolatry (*Scorpiace* chap. 3). Exceptionally, Clement of Alexandria's *Stromata* used a chronology that included Judges in order to establish the greater antiquity of "Jewish institutions and laws over the philosophy of the Greeks" (chap. 21).

Such Christian attempts to uphold Judaism tended to decline abruptly, however, during the Nicene and post-Nicene periods. The most popular text seems to be the story of Gideon and the fleece (Judges 6), read as an allegorical history of God's grace, first with Israel and then with Christians. Of the ten substantial references to Judges (seven involving Gideon) in Augustine's works, for example, five are cases in point. In line with both Ambrose (*Of the Holy Spirit*, bk. 1) and Jerome (*Letter* 58), he claimed that the fleece on the first morning describes Judaism before Christ, in which "grace was hidden in a cloud, as the rain in the fleece" (*Sermon* 81.9). Concerning the second morning he wrote, "Like the rain in the fleece it [grace] was latently present, but is now patently visible amongst all nations as its 'floor,' the fleece being dry—in other words, the Jewish people having become reprobate" (*On Original Sin* chap. 29). In his sermon on Psalm 72 he added, "But that the above nation under the name of a fleece is signified, I think is either because they were to be stripped of the authority of teaching, just as a sheep is stripped of its skin, or because in a secret place He was hiding that same rain."

Other interpretations invoke stories in Judges as a means to encourage Christians in times of suffering. Athanasius, for example, referred in his Circular Letter to the sending of pieces of the Levite's raped concubine to the twelve tribes (Judg 19:29-30) as a precedent for sharing the suffering experienced in his own community with the wider church body.

With Jerome began a focus on the women of Judges, which, together with the anti-Jewish allegory of the fleece, would persevere into modern times. In *Against Jovinianus*, for example, he commended women not to marry by appeal to Samson, who was "once shaven bald by a woman," and to the preference for "the fidelity of the father Jephthah to the tears of the virgin daughter" (bk. 1).

Later, as Christian monasticism gained greater popularity, we find J. Cassian interpreting the ambidextrous Ehud as an allegory for the devotional life: "The inner man consists of two parts, and if I may be allowed the expression, two hands...The saint has for his right hand his spiritual achievements...He has also a left hand, when he is entangled in the toils of temptation" (*The Conferences*, pt. 1, chap. 10).

For the Christian church moving into the Middle Ages, allegory became an important reading strategy offering (highly creative) support of many and various interests and arguments. Yet in comparison to commentary on other historical books of the HB, Judges received little attention. Moreover, the readings it did host were limited primarily to a few of its many stories, those of Gideon being most popular.

3. *Rabbinic Judaism.* While a chronological account of Jewish interpretation of Judges is a highly problematic undertaking, a general survey shows its history to involve a tradition-dependent accumulation of dialogue across time between biblical texts, precursive readings, and imaginative rereadings. Rabbinic literature on Judges lives in a tension between, on the one hand, celebration of the sacred indeterminacy of biblical language and, on the other hand, submission to the authority of precursive interpretation. It is always both subordinate and subversive in relation to tradition as it spreads out from its biblical foundation with layer after layer of new insight (*hiddush*).

The story of Jael and Sisera (Judges 4–5) provides a good example of this interpretive dialogue. Where the Tannaitic *Midrash ha-Gadol* speaks only of Sisera's fateful intoxication by Jael's beauty and voice, Pseudo-Philo takes the language of intoxication a step further, adding that "Jael took wine and mingled it with the milk" (*L.A.B.* 31:6-7). In another direction, the Babylonian Talmud posits that Jael surrendered herself to Sisera's passion in order to make him more vulnerable to her assault (*b. Yebam.* 103a-103b; *b. Nazir*, 23b). In reference to the maternal allusions in the Hebrew of this story, the medieval *Rimze Haftarot* further advises that the milk Sisera drank was actually from Jael's breast (L. Ginzberg [1913] 198).

Compared to Christian theological tradition, rabbinic Judaism appears to place a high value on the activity of reading, over and above the specific conclusions derived. On the other hand, the study of Judges has also sometimes been related to particular Jewish confessional crises. Sisera, for example, is identified with Alexander the Great in some early rabbinic literature (Ginzberg [1913] 195). A related concern pervading the literature on Judges is the threat of a religious syncretism, e.g., Jephthah and his contemporaries are severely criticized for their ignorance of the Torah and the resulting tragedy (human sacrifice). The Ephraimites are no better, according to the same tradition, for their human sacrifices to Baal set the precedent for Jephthah's horrifying act. In fact, according to Tosefta Targum, the Ephraimites deserved to be slaughtered, "for they were addicted to idolatry, particularly to the worship of an idol called Sibboleth, which name was so much on their lips that they involuntarily said Sibboleth when they intended to say Shibboleth" (Judg 12:6; cf. *Seder Eliahu Rabbah*, 11, 456).

Likewise, Gideon is severely criticized for his idolatrous act of setting up an ephod after defeating the enemy. According to Pseudo-Philo, this act put God in a predicament: "God said, 'When he destroyed the sanctuary of Baal, then all men said: Let Baal avenge himself. Now, therefore, if I chastize him for the evil he did against me, ye will say: It was not God who chastized him but Baal because he sinned aforetime against him'" (*L.A.B.* 36.3-4). The story of Gideon and the fleece, which supports an anti-Semitic polemic in Christian interpretation, received comparatively little attention—and no allegorical interpretation—in Jewish study. By the same token, the judges most frequently criticized as least worthy within the rabbinical tradition—Gideon, Samson, Jephthah (Ginzberg [1913] 201)—are three of the four adulated in Hebrews.

Josephus, on the other hand, writing from a different confessional horizon (apologetics) than many rabbinic writers, was very reluctant to criticize any of the judges, including Jephthah (*A.J.* 5.257-66) and Gideon (*A.J.* 5.213-32; cf. his positive rendering of Samson and Manoah, *A.J.* 5.275-317, which is again contrary to other rabbinical criticism).

Although Christian and Jewish interpretations of Judges are in many ways quite distinct from one another, both traditions join in regarding with patriarchal suspicion the women Jael and Deborah. Especially is this true of Deborah in Jewish writings of many periods, from Talmud to Zohar. Inordinately self-possessed, according to several authorities she summoned Barak to her instead of going to him. Moreover, according to these sources, she spoke so much of herself in her song that the spirit of prophecy (apparently an oppressively deferential spirit when it comes to women) departed from her for a while during its composition (*b. Pesaḥ* 66b; *Zohar* 3, 21b-22a). In the Talmud it is further written, "Pride is unbecoming in women; the prophetesses Deborah and Huldah were proud women, and both bore ugly names" (*b. Meg.* 14b).

4. *The Christian Middle Ages.* While some medieval Christian scholars of the HB began looking to rabbinic modes of interpretation (especially the Victorines), most Christian use of Judges was typological. Such reading of the *"Vetus" Testamentum* centered meaning ostensibly in the *"Novum" Testamentum* and effectively in Christology (and its practical applications) as formulated by the church, and this monopoly on the Christ who monopolized Scripture served the church in its increasing struggle to maintain its social and political centrality. Moreover, the church's subserving of the meaning of the "old" to the "new" lent itself surreptitiously to the larger cultural and political purpose of distinguishing a homogeneous Christian Europe from the threats, real or imagined, of Islam and Judaism, both of which advocated authority in the "old." Thus, in the pictorial *Speculum humanae salvationis* of the fourteenth and fifteenth centuries, we find the sacrifice of Jephthah's virgin daughter prefiguring the dedication of Mary's virginity (chap. v), Samson's mass slaughter with the jawbone prefiguring Jesus prostrating his enemies with a single word (John 18:6; chap. xvii), and Samson carrying off the gates of Gaza prefiguring Jesus breaking out of the guarded tomb (chap. xxviii). Especially noteworthy here are the parallel interpretations of Mary and Jesus as conquerors of the devil, prefigured by Jael's piercing of Sisera and Samson's rending of the lion, respectively (chaps. xxix and xxx; see A. Wilson and J. Wilson [1984]; for the similar *Biblia Pauperum*, see R. Milburn [1969] and H. Musper [1961]). This literature reflects the popularity of Mary in the devotional spirituality of the times, which has in turn brought positive attention to the women of Judges.

5. *From the Protestant Reformation to Modernity.* Judges received comparatively little attention during the Protestant Reformation. In fact, even such prolific commentators as Luther and Calvin wrote no commentaries on the book. Rather, Judges was used by these and other Christian theologians primarily in support of points made from other texts.

Both Luther and Calvin, like their classic Christian precursors, used the story of Gideon more than any other text in Judges. And while Luther principally opposed allegorical interpretations, his reading of the story of Gideon's fleece reflects a normative tradition indebted to the readings of Augustine, Ambrose, and Jerome over a thousand years earlier. Like them, Luther was concerned to show the Jews of the law to be skinned dry and reprobate, with the grace of God now flowing freely over the rest of the world's floor. He wrote, "If you hear and see any figure of the Law, it will appear altogether flesh and thick, but when you will have separated it from the spirit, you will behold the skin in which the flesh was, but the flesh has been emptied... Yet the flesh was in that skin. And Gideon's fleece received the dew, that is, with the letter stripped off, the law is spiritual... Therefore the former is judgment, the latter righteousness... the former hardness, the latter sweetness" (*First Lectures on the Psalms*, Ps 104:2 [319]).

Calvin, on the other hand, cited the Gideon stories in his commentaries (especially on Isaiah and Jeremiah), not as allegory, but rather as a means to prepare the faithful for impending judgment and destruction. In his commentary on Jer 44:29-30, for example, he wrote, "Gideon was torpid, but when he saw by this miracle that victory would be given him, he boldly took the work assigned to him" (1950, 561). Hardly a bold reading until one contrasts it with those of Augustine and Luther.

Nevertheless, while shying away from such allegories, Calvin continued the tradition of hermeneutical suspicion regarding the women of Judges. In his commentary on 1 Tim 2:12 ("I permit no woman to teach or to have authority over men") he wrote, "If any one bring forward, by way of objection, Deborah and others of the same class ... the answer is easy: Extraordinary acts done by God do not overturn the ordinary rules of government, by which he intended that we should be bound" (cf. his commentary on Mic 6:5). We would note, however, that Calvin did not follow Jerome in preferring Jephthah's fidelity over the daughter's lament. "Jephthah was punished for his own folly when in hasty fervor he conceived a rash vow" (*Institutes* 4.13.3).

Following the early Reformers within the Christian tradition, interpretation moved generally in two divergent directions. In one direction scholars found themselves increasingly immersed in Enlightenment modes of rationality, moving rapidly toward the dawn of so-called higher criticism where questions concerning historical context became paramount. Among these scholars B. de Spinoza (1634–77) is perhaps the most well known. As with other texts treated in his *Tractatus theologico-politicus* (1670), Spinoza read Judges in terms of its references to ostensive history. Thus he focused on references in Judges to chronology in order to argue that the building of the Temple by Solomon took place 162 years later than claimed in 1 Kings 6 and that all of the historical books of the HB were written by Ezra rather than by Moses (128-37).

With the rise of rationalism over the next century or so, the Hebrew Scriptures came under increasing attack from outside the confessional Jewish and Christian communities. In addition to Spinoza's program for ascertaining a "trustworthy history of Scriptures," these readings involve an indignantly enlightened moral-evaluative dimension. Thus the prolific champion of deism, Voltaire, deployed the book of Judges as an instance of the primitive anthropomorphism, polytheism, and moral depravity that he saw enshrined in the Bible of the establishment church and religion that he was attacking. But his critical attempts to skewer Christian orthodoxy on the failings (as he argued them) of its HB foundations slide often into an uncritical deprecation of Judaism, ancient and contemporary, which has justifiably raised against him the charge of anti-Semitism. In fact, of all the biblical characters open to his scathing assault, Jephthah received the most critical attention (*Ages,* 211). In his *Dictionnaire philosophique* (1764), for example, Voltaire submited Jephthah as the primary example of the brutality of primitive religion with its *dieu sanguinaire* (religion) and purported to show that the story of Jephthah and his daughter proves human sacrifice to be an established part of Jewish faith (*Jephté*)—a rhetorical flourish the danger of which this defender of the persecuted seemed to ignore.

In the other direction, many Christian scholars interpreted the stories of Judges as lessons for daily Christian life. Given the apparent lack of substantial interpretations of Judges throughout the history of the Christian church, R. Roger's highly popular *Commentary on Judges* (1615) is remarkable. It avoids theological allegory, walking instead through the details of every story in search of lessons for living in true Christian piety. Thus from Jael we learn that "no bonds of familiarity and equity are so neerely joined together, and so just, but that if God for causes best knowne to him, commands otherwise, they are to be broken" (225). In Gideon's quest for a "double signe" we learn that God returns our weakness and distrust with lovingkindness (343). And concerning the loss of Jephthah's daughter as a result of his "rash" and "unbeseeming" vow, we must remember that all we have has been given to us by God for our stewardship, lest we become too attached to our possessions (578).

6. *The Modern Period.* Under the impact of historical criticism Judges became a mine of source-critical hypotheses, primarily in German-speaking Christian scholarship, but increasingly, as the nineteenth century elapsed, elsewhere in Europe and the United States. The pentateuchal sources, J, E, and D were discovered in the book, along with independent sources, mostly the work of "later hands." In this vein of criticism, in Judges as in Exodus "doublets" abound, including the elaborate intertwining of whole parallel stories (e.g., a "Gideon" story and a "Jerubbaal" story; cf. G. Moore [1898] 173-77); T. Cheyne treated the two separately in his article on Gideon [1899–1903]). Redactional stages are multiple and complex.

Commentaries, monographs, and scholarly surveys in dictionaries became dense thickets of disentangled verses, largely impenetrable to the non-specialist reader.

By the mid-twentieth century little had changed. The prevailing view was still akin to K. Budde's—namely, that an early collection of disparate stories was edited and framed in a deuteronomistic redaction. Few scholars believed anymore that the early book was the product of J and E (see König in *HDB*, 811), although these sources were minutely described later by C. Simpson (1957), and J was traced again with ingenuity through Judges and Samuel with more sensitivity to the difficulties by H. Schulte (1972). There was argument over the existence of a kernel pre-deuteronomistic "savior book" (see esp. Richter [1963, 1964]), and the provenance of the so-called appendix (chaps. 17–21) was frequently disputed. The presence of the Deuteronomist (D), on the other hand, continued to be recognized (to this day), particularly in the so-called framework passages that recount a "cycle" of apostasy-oppression-repentence-deliverance. Interest in D strengthened with the widespread acceptance of M. Noth's hypothesis of a Deuteronomistic History (1943), a carefully fashioned work reaching from the beginning of Deuteronomy to the end of Kings. As a result, much mid- and late-twentieth-century scholarly argument on Judges has concerned the precise extent of deuteronomistic material, the stages of deuteronomistic editing, and the nature of the "pre-deuteronomistic" book (see A. G. Auld [1984]; U. Becker [1990]; G. Boling [1985]; A. Mayes [1983, 1985]; M. O'Brian [1989, 1994]).

Throughout the historical-critical period no critical work on Judges was complete without an extensive exploration of its chronology, both internally and in relation to the larger history of Israel. As a thirteenth-century B.C.E. date for the exodus gained popularity toward the end of the nineteenth century, strategems were devised and details enumerated to condense the four centuries or so of the book's expressed chronology into the two centuries demanded by the new theory.

Text-critical and philological questions in Judges as in other books of the period were accorded significant attention in monographs and commentaries. The beginnings of scholarly archaeology opened up new possibilities for addressing questions of realia, although archaeological discussion of Judges is much more noticeable in twentieth-century discussion. Of much greater importance to nineteenth-century commentators, scholarly and popular alike, was the increasing accessibility of the Middle East, and of Palestine in particular, to European and American travelers. Commentary became an occasion to invoke wine presses, millstones, buildings, wild and domestic animals—in short, the paraphernalia of nineteenth-century Palestinian, especially bedouin, life—to illustrate the text of Judges as of other biblical books. (The popular engravings of Dor, are characteristic of this interest.) Particular features of the narrative found explanation in general "oriental" and especially bedouin custom (see, e.g., W. R. Smith on kinship and marriage [1893]). "Sheykhs" and "emirs" rode at the head of "nomad Arab clan(s)" (Smith, 1184a, 1504b).

A marked tone of cultural and moral superiority pervaded much (though by no means all) of this comment in scholarly and popular works alike. Not surprisingly this often took a Eurocentric form, as when one scholar, explaining the panic that struck the Midianite army confronting Gideon, observed that the hero's plans "were admirably adapted to strike a panic terror into the huge and undisciplined nomad host... We know from history that large and irregular Oriental armies are especially liable to sudden outbursts of uncontrollable terror" (Smith, 1183b).

Early Israelite civilization, religion, and morality were considered "untaught" and "barbarous" (C. Geikie [1884]), from an "uncultured" time of "dubious light" (R. Horton [1899]). We are reminded of Voltaire. The Canaanites of the cities, rich in civilization (though, alas, hotbeds of voluptuousness and wickedness), were contrasted with the sons of the desert, rough, rude, and continuing unpolished in manners despite "a slowly advancing refinement of life and custom" (R. Kittel [1909] 94-95; cf. 62).

Sometimes class attitudes shaped the discussion. Writing of Samson, Budde could not help observing that the man's characteristic behavior – including cultivating brute strength, chasing and being unfaithful to women, brawling, eating and drinking to excess, and lying—was still extant as a standard of a certain people, being the behavior of the ideal country hero, as many readers, "especially those who have been brought up in the country, will be able to substantiate" (K. Budde, *HDB*, 380).

Sexism was commonplace. Throughout the nineteenth century and well into the twentieth, the mass of readings on the women of Judges, whether popular or scholarly, continued to reflect a deep ambivalence concerning their praiseworthiness. Of Jael, for example, Geikie wrote, "The end was noble enough; the means brave to a marvel; but the heart that could have planned and carried them out was anything rather than that of a woman" (140). On the other hand, Horton was of the view that to say Jael's action was not praiseworthy is to "lower our whole estimate of Deborah herself," since Deborah called her "blessed" (126). And while G. Matheson (1907) would not join in Deborah's approbation of Jael's dastardly deed, he wrote, "I should like to apply some ammonia to the stain in the robe of Deborah," whose wrath could be felt only by such an "intensely soft nature" (163-64).

Where some readers condemned Jephthah's vow as rash (see also rabbinic interpretation above), others persisted in affirming the tragic consequence, commending the father's "faithful fulfillment" of his vow (C. Kraft [1962] 1018; cf. 821) and praising the daughter's willingness to die for her father's integrity. No man could have put it better than A. Whyte (1905), who wrote that the young women who journeyed to commemorate her at that mountain altar each year "came back to be far better daughters than they went out. They came back softened, and purified, and sobered at heart. They came back ready to die for their fathers, and for their brothers, and for their husbands, and for their God" (31).

In general terms, the perception of early Israel's religious and moral life as being "primitive" reflects a longstanding conviction about evolution through the history of civilization. The theological expression of this view in Christian thought is the doctrine of progressive revelation, much invoked throughout the modern period of Judges interpretation to explain events in the stories that are perceived as morally and religiously troubling, if not positively offensive. Recurrent cases in point are the violent dispossession of the Canaanites, the "treachery" of Ehud and Jael, Gideon's acquisition of the golden ephod, Jephthah's sacrifice of his daughter, the Levite's treatment of his concubine, the tribes' slaughter of the inhabitants of Jabesh Gilead, the rape of the young women of Shiloh, and Samson's behavior generally. Struck by "the low level of the morals of the period, even according to ancient standards" (Kraft, 1022), it is reassuring for one to be able to think of these times as merly times of imperfect glimmerings, "pointing to the perfect religion and morality" (König, *HDB*, 820). Of course, it is not altogether difficult either, along this line of reasoning, to make the jump from moral condescension toward "early Judaism" to an "enlightened" (i.e., Christian) disdain for the Judaism of the interpreter's own time. We are reminded again of Voltaire.

Drawing on the theme of tribal disunity ("In those days there was no king in Israel; a man would do what was right in his own eyes" [21:25]) many scholars of the modern period, especially in Germany, have read the book of Judges as a commentary on the formation of the nation state, mandating political and religious unity as the precondition of success. For Kittel, writing in Breslau in 1892, it was "a time of struggle with great tasks, which were recognised by only a few individuals, and to which even they were not equal. But... after going astray more than once in the sphere of politics and religion, a people of such original strength and so lofty a destiny must eventually find its way to its high goal" (68). The last battle against the Canaanites "brought about the glorious union of the tribes of Israel under Barak and Deborah" and Deborah's song was "a fire kindled at the holy flame of ardent enthusiasm for Israel, and purest, most fervent love for Yahv, and his people" (72). Or as H. Schultz (1892, 144-51) puts it, citing the song of Deborah, "The enemies of Israel are the enemies of Jehovah, and they who fight for the national cause fight for God" (148).

For many historians, therefore, the failures of polity in the period of the judges were eventually rectified by the centralized state and military machine of David. Ironically, but not surprising in light of notions of manifest destiny and the sovereignty issues of the "war between the states," such interpretations have also been popular among American scholars, persisting into the latter part of the twentieth century. They have found favor too among Israeli scholars, for whom David's "unification" of the land and capture of Jerusalem is a defining point in a "national" history (the "Jerusalem 3000" celebrations owe much to this conceit). On the other hand, immensely popular during the middle part of the twentieth century was Noth's theory that a twelve-tribe league, or "amphictyony," organized around a central shrine was the model of political organization during the Judges period. This idealization of polity, articulated in Depression era Germany on the eve of the Third Reich, was built as much from scant sources outside Judges as from meager evidence in the book itself. It met with fatal criticism on that score in the 1970s (e.g., Mayes [1974]).

With few exceptions work on Judges since the mid nineteenth century, influenced by historical criticism, is noteworthy for failure to sustain any extended interpretation of the stories comprising the book. Rarely have the narratives been interpreted as coherent "stories" through close and sustained attention to the elements constituting the story world itself. Sensitivity to rhetorical features of the text, except perhaps in the case of the Song of Deborah, has been sporadic at best. Largely, the text has been examined for clues to possible political (i.e., national and tribal leadership, wars, property) and institutional reconstruction of the purported history of the "period." Like much interpretation of Genesis during this period, any story disclosed is usually the story of "tribal movements." Where attention has been paid to other social and personal dimensions—e.g., to characterizaton (motivation or interpersonal relationships)—the interpeter rarely draws on a reading of the story beyond the immediate context. Frequently such issues are settled by appeal to some general (often tenuous) notion of customs and conditions in the "period." The extensive scholarly invocations of culpable "fertility religion," for example, scarcely match the subject's virtual absence from the surface text.

There have been several major reasons for the failure to interpret at the level of the narrative as story. One is the assumption that what is being constructed in the interpretive act is history (usually of the positivist, patriarchal kind indicated above). Another is the fragmenting effect (observed by many conservatives) of source criticism: Often there has been no agreed-upon surface narrative to interpret. A third reason is that the guild of biblical scholars, through control of hiring; promotion; and, above all, public presentation and publication of research, long denied legitimacy to methods other than those developed in the historical-critical vein. The disruption of this interpretive monopoly coincided in the 1970s with the reformation of the Society of Biblical Literature and the American Academy of Religion in North America and the foundation of new publishing outlets in the United States and Great Britain that were open to nontraditional research.

7. *New Directions*. In historical studies the 1970s and 1980s saw growing support, particularly in North America, for the hypothesis that internal peasant rebellion, as opposed to conquest from outside the land, should be central to any explanation of the "emergence" of Israel and hence to any understanding of the people's experience of oppression in the Judges period (G. Mendenhall [1973] and then, developing the social dimensions of the hypothesis, N. Gottwald [1979]). Feudal domination by a city-state ruling class was successfully overthrown

by an underclass of peasants and displaced persons. This situation was classically illustrated (according to the theory) by the account of the war against Jabin and Sisera in the Song of Deborah, for many years widely thought to be the oldest text in the HB (though well-founded skepticism has been expressed by N. Lemche [1991], among others).

Often including in their reconstructions some element of the internal rebellion model, historians have moved away from the W. F. Albright school's attempts to correlate the destruction levels of Late Bronze Age cities with the stories of conquest in Joshua and Judges 1–2 and toward viewing the emergence of Israel in Early Iron Age Palestine as a gradual settlement in non-populated areas (as earlier, A. Alt [1925]). Some scholars have invoked the model of a "segmentary society" to describe the resulting autonomous communities (J. Flanagan [1981]; N. Lohfink [1983]; A. Malamat [1973]).

More radically, others argue that the biblical accounts of conquest, of the "Judges period," of Saul, David, Solomon, and indeed much of the "monarchic period" are historically unreliable constructions deriving from the exilic or postexilic period and are useful chiefly as sources for understanding that later period (e.g., P. Davies [1992]; Lemche [1985]; T. Thompson [1994]; see V. Fritz and Davies [1996]; L. Grabbe [1997]). Certainly archaeological evidence from the Early Iron Age seems to have borne out a pattern of basically peaceful expansion and has failed to distinguish ethnic difference between the inhabitants of the new settlements in the central highlands and others in the region who, according to the biblical account, ought to be ethnically distinct "Canaanites" (cf. I. Finkelstein [1991]; M. Skjeggestad [1992]). Nor is there undisputed corroborating evidence for virtually any part of the biblical account of Judges, Samuel, or the early chapters of Kings. At the very least, serious obstacles confront those who wish to draw on the text of Judges for any historical reconstruction of "Israel" in the Early Iron Age.

In his 1975 commentary Boling observed that at the root of earlier difficulties with the "low morality" of Judges 19–21 was the unwillingness of critics to allow the writers "anything resembling a Mosaic conscience" (278). His reading, brief as it is, nevertheless marks a significant break with his own (historical-archaeological) interpretive tradition by recognizing that the narrator's treatment of characters, institutions, and events might be consistently sardonic or ironic ("tragicomedy" and "grim humor" are his terms; 1975, 277; 1985, 216). He also sees a significant thematic relationship between the story of the Levite in Gibeah and that of Lot in Sodom (Genesis 19), whereas the usual procedure has been to dismiss the one story as merely a tendentious imitation of the other (cf. J. Wellhausen [1878] 235-37, where Judges imitates Genesis). Both these strategies, reading through irony and reading intertextually, have become characteristic features of a whole new phase of interpretation of Judges that has dominated late twentieth-century criticism.

A shift began in the 1970s and was marked from about 1980. New readings emerged that attended to the final form of the text, to its literary (including rhetorical and aesthetic) dimensions, and increasingly to its moral and ideological implications for contemporary as well as for ancient readers. Such readings have been cultivated by Jewish and Christian scholars as well as by others standing outside any confessional position. Scholars working in schools of English or comparative literature have provided major impetus for change (e.g., R. Alter [1981]; M. Bal [1988a, 1988b]; K. Gros Louis [1982]; M. Sternberg [1985]). J. Crenshaw's lively monograph on Samson (1978), attentive to its aesthetic qualities, heralded a spate of presentations and publications on literary dimensions of Judges 13–16 from J. C. Exum (1980, 1981, 1983) most prolifically, and others (e.g., E. Greenstein [1981]; J. Vickery [1981]). Other parts of the book began to receive similar attention, especially Judges 4–5, 10–12, and 19–21 (e.g., Alter; Y. Amit [1990]; Bal; Exum; D. Fewell and D. Gunn [1993]; S. Niditch [1993]; P. Trible [1984]; Sternberg). Readings of the book as a whole began to appear (e.g., Bal; M. Brettler [1989]; Exum; D. Gooding [1982]; Gunn [1987]; J. Hamlin [1990]; D. Jobling [1986]; L. Klein [1988];

90

R. Polzin [1980]; B. Webb [1987]; cf., more than a decade earlier, J. Lilley [1967]). Critics adopted a variety of approaches but increasingly explored reader-oriented interpretations.

Interest in tensive voices and ironic perspectives is characteristic of early literary criticism of Judges in this period. Among readings of the book as a whole, one of the first and most influential was a study by Polzin using (Russian) formalist literary-critical methodology to analyze Deuteronomy–Judges. He viewed Judges in terms of an ideological struggle between "authoritarian dogmatism" (adhering strictly to an original authoritative law) and "critical traditionalism" (sustaining a tradition by critically reinterpreting it).

Jobling's extended structuralist analysis of Judges and deuteronomic political theory has also proved to be a prescient study. Instead of dissipating the often-observed pro- and anti-monarchical strains in the book into redactional layers, he holds them in tension in Levi-Straussian fashion. The book thus construes its account of polity in a way that is neither "pro" nor "anti," nor, for that matter, "balanced." It is a construction that opens for its exilic audience possibilities for creating a new "political theology" for its own situation.

Webb's monograph, which saw the book as addressing the issue of Yahweh's failure to give Israel the whole land as promised, attends to complexities of structure as a clue to meaning. He showed themes of Israel's apostasy and Yahweh's refusal to be "used" by Israel reaching a climax in the Samson episode and treated the final chapters as a coda resonating with many ironic references to the main story.

Gunn traces unifying threads in the book and explores its sardonic play with themes of language, security, patriarchy, and violence. Klein configures the book as an ironic spiral ("the widening gyre") of anti-Yahwism and the displacement of integrity by territory until "mere anarchy is loosed upon the world" (quoting W. B. Yeats).

The new veins of criticism also began to show in commentary writing, especially in series addressing an audience beyond the academic guild. Hamlin's book is notable: He interprets in terms of liberation and cross-cultural reading (with a Southeast Asian focus), drawing freely on Gottwald (Israel's formation through revolution), on literary-critical method, and on feminist criticism.

It would, of course, have been difficult for biblical studies to remain totally isolated from the major challenge of post-modernist thought with which other disciplines had been confronted. It was doubly difficult to maintain the status quo given the entry of growing numbers of women into the academic field of biblical studies and (complementarily) the growing number of women seeking advanced theological education.

By 1990 the impact of women's writing (usually feminist) about Judges was marked. Amit, Bal, A. Brenner (1990), F. van Dijk-Hemmes (1989), Exum, Fewell, E. Fuchs, J. Hackett (1985), Klein, Niditch, and Trible, among others, often utilize non-traditional, predominantly literary-critical modes of interpretation. Most press their readers to reevaluate the place of women in Judges and to confront the ideological dimensions of the book's recurrent conjunction of women and violence. Among the first was Trible, whose "literary-feminist" readings of Jephthah's daughter and the Levite concubine direct attention sharply away from the male protagonists to the plight of the women in these "texts of terror" in a vein of formalist rhetorical criticism influenced by J. Muilenburg's teaching and writing in the 1960s. Trible's essays have had wide influence not only within the academy but also, both directly and indirectly, with a large audience of other, particularly church-connected, readers.

Bal's analysis of traditional studies of the death of Sisera (*Murder and Difference* [1988]) relentlessly exposes the ideological, especially patriarchal, biases of "neutral" and "objective" scholarship. Her study of the book as a whole (*Death and Dissymmetry* [1988]) deconstructs the customary coherence, seen in a pattern of holy war, and reads for a countercoherence, seen in a pattern of murder. With others she sees gender-based violence shaping the book. Radically, she affirms the women who kill men. In a world where men have disproportionate power over body, life, and language, these women introduce a countervailing anger. They kill "for" the women victims. Bal's writing in these works and elsewhere has strong underpinnings in contemporary critical theory and is marked by a keen sensitivity to ideological complexities in the reading of texts as also by illuminating shifts in disciplinary perspective. Thus, in "A Body of Writing: Judges 19" she considers relationships among death, women, and representation through an analysis of narrative argumentation that includes a Rousseau short story and a sketch by Rembrandt. Her work is probably the single most creative force at play in present studies of Judges.

Feminist criticism continued into the 1990s its concentration on the female figures of Judges, as Brenner's collection (*A Feminist Companion to Judges* [1993, 1999]) well illustrates: The stories of Deborah, Jephthah's daughter, Samson's mother, and the Levite's woman in Judges 19 receive particular attention. The volume also exemplifies the growing recourse to rabbinic materials as sources for critical reflection. A growing diversity of approaches to biblical criticism is a mark of the decade, and Judges is no exception. Yee's *Judges and Method* (1995), for example, chooses to discuss narrative, social-scientific, feminist, structuralist, deconstructive, and ideological criticism. At the same time, in the definition and application of these approaches, there is often significant overlap: Fewell's deconstructive (but also narrative, feminist, and ideological) reading of Achsah and the "(e)razed city of writing" in Yee's volume is a case in point. Elsewhere K. Stone (1996) shows the advantage of bringing an anthropological frame to bear on questions of gender, as he discusses honor and shame in Judges 19. Several scholars have used folklore studies to illuminate the story of Samson, among other texts in Judges, with particular interest in the trickster figure (Niditch, C. Camp and C. Fontaine [1990]; G. Mobley [1997]). F. Deist (1996) in South Africa struggles with issues of cultural translation and transformation: How can such a narrative of violence and ethnic ridicule as the Ehud story be "Scripture" ("Murder in the Toilet")?

At the same time, formalist literary analysis of the book has continued to be elaborated, sometimes in conjunction with redactional ("diachronic") criticism as most notably in R. O'Connell's (1996) extensive account of the "rhetorical purpose" of the Judges "compiler/redactor." This purpose to enjoin readers to endorse a divinely appointed Judahite king who upholds such deuteronomistic ideals as the need to expel foreigners and to maintain Yahweh's cult and covenant O'Connell infers from formal structures and "motivic patterns" recurring throughout the book's narrative framework and from patterns of plot structure and characterization in the plot-based deliverer stories and ending.

Critics are increasingly interested in Judges' connections with other biblical texts. Thus, Fewell (1997) reads Judges as a rewriting of Genesis for the purpose of constructing postexilic identity and accordingly constructs her own essay dialogically as a play of past and present voices. Earlier, Fewell and Gunn (1993) attempted to write Judges into a deconstructive reading of the "subject" of Genesis–Kings as a whole, recasting the story into one of women and children. Camp (1998) traces the literary and ideological connections of Judges even further by locating the Samson story in a widespread textual web that includes narrative, law, and wisdom. Drawing on anthropology, literary criticism, and social history, she seeks through the figure of "strangeness" to nuance traditional scholarly constructions of Israelite identity as well as to complicate the analysis of power offered by feminist criticism.

Exum's further analyses of the stories of Jephthah and Samson (1993) have helped bring issues of subjectivity and "the gaze" into focus. The step to study of the Bible as a "viewed" artifact is a short one. Exum (1996) returns to Samson and Delilah ("Why, Why, Why, Delilah?"), as do J. Koosed and T. Linafelt ("How the West Was Not One" [1996]), in a methodological turn toward contemporary culture, Bible, Western art, and film, for example. Such writing marks another significant shift in current biblical studies (see also Bal, above, and A. Bach, Biblical Glamour and Hollywood Glitz [1996]).

As post-modern critical theory continues to pervade the study of Judges, hermeneutical questions have become profoundly important. Clearly, new horizons of meaning are in view. Clearly too, the politics of reading are changing.

Bibliography: S. **Ackerman**, *Warrior, Dancer, Seductress, Queen: Women in Judges and Biblical Israel* (AB, 1998). A. **Ages**, "Voltaire's Biblical Criticism: A Study in Thematic Representations," *Studies on Voltaire and the Eighteenth Century 30* (1964) 205-21. A. **Alt**, "The Settlement of the Israelite Tribes in Palestine," *Essays in OT History and Religion* (1925; ET 1966) 133-69. R. **Alter**, *The Art of Biblical Narrative* (1981). Y. **Amit**, "Judges 4: Its Contents and Form," *JSOT 39* (1987) 89-111; "The Story of Ehud (Judg 3:12-30): The Form and the Message," *Signs and Wonders* (ed. J. C. Exum, 1989) 97-123; "Hidden Polemic in the Conquest of Dan: Judges xvii-xviii," *VT 40* (1990) 4-20; *The Book of Judges: The Art of Editing* (1992; ET 1998); *The Book of Judges: The Art of Editing* (Biblical Interpretation 38, 1999). G. **Auld**, *Joshua, Judges, and Ruth* (1984); "Gideon: Hacking at the Heart of the OT," *VT 39* (1989) 257-67. A. **Bach**, *Biblical Glamour and Hollywood Glitz* (= Semeia 74, 1996). M. **Bal**, *Lethal Love: Feminist Literary Readings of Biblical Love Stories* (ISBL, 1987); *Death and Dissymmetry: The Politics of Coherence in the Book of Judges* (Chicago Studies in the History of Judaism, 1988a); *Murder and Difference: Gender, Genre, and Scholarship on Sisera's Death* (ISBL, 1988b); (ed.), *Anti-Covenant: Counter-Reading Women's Lives in the HB* (JSOTSup 81, 1989); "Dealing/With/Women: Daughters in the Book of Judges," *The Book and the Text: The Bible and Literary Theory* (ed. R. Schwartz, 1990) 16-39; "A Body of Writing: Judges 19," *A Feminist Companion to Judges* (ed. A. Brenner, 1993) 208-30. R. **Bartelmus**, "Forschung am Richterbuch seit M. Noth," *TRu 56* (1991) 221-59. R. **Bayley**, "Which Is the Best Commentary? 14. The Book of Judges," *ExpTim 103* (1991–92) 136-38. U. **Becker**, *Richterzeit und Königtum: Redaktionsgeschichtliche Studien zum Richterbuch* (BZAW 192, 1990). W. **Bluedom**, *Yahweh versus Baalism: A Theological Reading of the Gideon Abimelech Narrative* (JSOTSup 329, 2001). R. G. **Boling**, *Judges* (AB 6A, 1975); "Judges, the Book of," *Harper's Bible Dictionary* (ed. P. J. Achtemeier, 1985). T. A. **Boogaart**, "Stone for Stone: Retribution in the Story of Abimelech and Shechem," *JSOT 32* (1985) 45-56. A. **Brenner**, *The Israelite Woman: Social Role and Literary Type in Biblical Narrative* (The Biblical Seminar 2, 1985); "A Triangle and a Rhombus in Narrative Structure: A Proposed Integrative Reading of Judges iv and v," *VT 40* (1990) 129-38; (ed.), *A Feminist Companion to Judges* (1993, new series 1999). M. **Brettler**, "The Book of Judges: Literature as Politics," *JBL 108* (1989) 395-418; *The Book of Judges* (Old Testament Readings, 2002). K. **Budde**, in *Dictionary of the Bible* (ed. J. Hastings, 5 vols., 1898–1904), 380. J. **Calvin**, *Commentaries on the Epistles to Timothy, Titus, and Philemon* (1948); *Commentaries on the Book of the Prophet Jeremiah and the Lamentations* (1950); *Institutes of the Christian Religion* (1960). C. V. **Camp**, *Wise and Strange: Reading the Bible with the Strange Woman* (1998); and C. R. **Fontaine**, "The Words of the Wise and Their Riddles," *Text and Tradition: The HB and Folklore* (ed. S. Niditch, 1990) 127-52; *Women, War, and Metaphor: Language and Society in the Study of the HB* (Semeia 61, 1993). T. K. **Cheyne** and J. S. **Black** (eds.), *Encyclopaedia Biblica: A Critical Dictionary of the Literary, Political, and Religious History, the Archaeology, Geography, and Natural History of the Bible* (4 vols., 1899–1903). J. L. **Crenshaw**, *Samson: A Secret Betrayed, a Vow Ignored* (1978). P. R. **Davies**, *In Search of "Ancient Israel"* (JSOTSup 148, 1992). P. L. **Day**, "From the Child is Born the Woman: The Story of Jephthah's Daughter," *Gender and Difference in Ancient Israel* (1989) 58-74. F. **Deist**, "Murder in the Toilet (Judg 3:12-30): Translation and Transformation," *Scriptura 58* (1996) 263-72. W. G. **Dever**, "How to Tell a Canaanite from an

Israelite," *The Rise of Ancient Israel* (ed. H. Shanks, 1993) 26-60. **B. J. Diebner**, "Wann sang Deborah ihr Lied? Überlegungen zu zwei der Ältesten Texte des TNK (Ri 4 und 6)," *ACEBT* (1995) 106-30. **F. Van Dijk-Hemmes**, "Interpretaties van de relatie tussen Richeteren 4 en 5," *Proeven van Vrouwenstudies Theologie I* (1989) 149-213. **J. C. Exum**, "Promise and Fulfillment: Narrative Art in Judges 13," *JBL 99* (1980) 43-59; "Aspects of Symmetry and Balance in the Samson Saga," *JSOT 19* (1981) 2-29; "The Theological Dimension of the Samson Saga," *VT 33* (1983) 30-45; "'Mother in Israel': A Familiar Figure Reconsidered," *Feminist Interpretation of the Bible* (ed. L. Russell, 1985) 73-85; "Judges," *HBC*, 245-61; "The Tragic Vision and Biblical Narrative: The Case of Jephthah," *Signs and Wonders: Biblical Texts in Literary Focus* (ed. J. C. Exum, 1989) 59-83; "The Center Cannot Hold: Thematic and Textual Instabilities in Judges," *CBQ 52* (1990) 410-29; *Fragmented Women: Feminist (Sub)versions of Biblical Narratives* (1993); *Plotted, Shot, and Painted: Cultural Representations of Biblical Women* (JSOTSup 215, 1996); *Was sagt das Richterbuch den Frauen?* (SB 169, 1997). **D. N. Fewell**, "Judges," *The Women's Bible Commentary* (ed. C. A. Newsom and S. H. Ringe, 1992) 67-77; "Deconstructive Criticism: Achsah and the (E)razed City of Writing," *Judges and Method: New Approaches in Biblical Studies* (ed. G. A. Yee, 1995) 119-45; "Imagination, Method, and Murder: Un/Framing the Face of Post-Exilic Israel," *Reading Bibles, Writing Bodies: Identity and the Book* (ed. T. K. Beal and D. M. Gunn, 1997) 132-52; and **D. M. Gunn**, "Controlling Perspectives: Women, Men, and the Authority of Violence in Judges 4 and 5," *JAAR* (1990) 389-411; *Gender, Power, and Promise: The Subject of the Bible's First Story* (1993). **I. Finkelstein**, "The Emergence of Israel in Canaan: Consensus, Mainstream, and Dispute," *SJOT 5* (1991) 47-59. **J. W. Flanagan**, "Chiefs in Israel," *JSOT* (1981) 47-73; *David's Social Drama: A Hologram of Israel's Early Iron Age* (SWBA, 1988). **V. Fritz** and **P. R. Davies** (eds.), *The Origins of the Ancient Israelite States* (JSOTSup 228, 1996). **E. Fuchs**, "The Literary Characterization of Mothers and Sexual Politics in the HB," *Feminist Perspectives on Biblical Scholarship* (BSNA 10, ed. A. Y. Collins, 1985) 117-36; "Marginalization, Ambiguity, Silencing: The Story of Jephthah's Daughter," *JFSR 5* (1989) 35-45. **C. Geikie**, *OT Characters* (1884). **L. Ginzberg**, *The Legends of the Jews* (7 vols., 1913). **D. W. Gooding**, "The Composition of the Book of Judges," *ErIsr 16* (1982) 70-79. **N. Gottwald**, *The Tribes of Yahweh: A Sociology of the Religion of Liberated Israel, 1250–1050 B.C.E.* (1979). **L. L. Grabbe** (ed.), *Can a "History of Israel" Be Written?* (JSOTSup 245, 1997). **E. L. Greenstein**, "The Riddle of Samson," *Prooftexts 1* (1981) 237-60. **K. R. R. Gros Louis** with **J. S. Ackerman** (eds.), *Literary Interpretations of Biblical Narratives* (2 vols., 1982). **P. Guillaume**, *Waiting for Josiah: The Judges* (JSPSup 385, 2004). **D. M. Gunn**, "Joshua and Judges," *The Literary Guide to the Bible* (ed. R. Alter and F. Kermode, 1987) 102-21; "Samson of Sorrows: An Isaianic Gloss on Judges 13–16," *Reading Between Texts: Intertextuality and the HB* (Literary Currents in Biblical Interpretation, ed. D. N. Fewell, 1992) 225-53. **J. A. Hackett**, "In the Days of Jael: Reclaiming the History of Women in Ancient Israel," *Immaculate and Powerful: The Female in Sacred Image and Social Reality* (The Harvard Women's Studies in Religion, ed. C. W. Atkinson et al., 1985) 15-38. **J. Hamlin**, *At Risk in the Promised Land: A Commentary on the Book of Judges* (ITC, 1990). **J. G. Harris, C. A. Brown, M. S. Moore**, *Joshua, Judges, Ruth* (NIB Commentary 5, 2000). **J. Hastings** (ed.), *A Dictionary of the Bible* (4 vols., 1898–1902). **R. F. Horton**, *Women of the OT: Studies in Womanhood* (1899). **J. G. Janzen**, "A Certain Woman in the Rhetoric of Judges 9," *JSOT 38* (1987) 33-37. **D. Jobling**, "Deuteronomic Political Theory in Judges and 1 Samuel 1–12," *The Sense of Biblical Narrative: Structural Analyses in the HB II* (JSOTSup 39, 1986) 44-87. **G. Josipovici**, "The Rhythm Falters: The Book of Judges," *The Book of God: A Response to the Bible* (1988) 108-31. **M. R. Kelley** and **J. Wittreich** (eds.), *Altering Eyes: New Perspectives on Samson Agonistes* (2002). **R. Kittel**, *A History of the Hebrews 2* (1909). **L. R. Klein**, *The*

Triumph of Irony in the Book of Judges (JSOTSup 68, 1988). **J. R. Koosed** and **T. Linafelt**, "How the West Was Not One: Delilah Deconstructs the Western," *Biblical Glamour and Hollywood Glitz* (SemeiaSt, ed. A. Bach, 1996) 167-81. **C. F. Kraft,** "Jephthah" and "Judges, Book of," *IDB* (1962) 2:820-21, 1013-23. **S. Lasine**, "Guest and Host in Judges 19: Lot's Hospitality in an Inverted World," *JSOT 29* (1984) 37-59. **K. Latvus**, *God, Anger, and Ideology: The Anger of God in Joshua and Judges in Relation to Deuteronomy and the Priestly Writings* (JSOTSup 279, 1998). **N .P. Lemche**, *Early Israel: Anthropological and Historical Studies on the Israelite Society Before the Monarchy* (VTSup 37, 1985); *The Canaanites and Their Land: The Tradition of the Canaanites* (JSOTSup 110, 1991). **J. P. U. Lilley**, "A Literary Appreciation of the Book of Judges," *TynBul 18* (1967) 94-102. **N. Lohfink**, "Die segmentären Gesellschaften Afrikas als neue Analogie für das vorstaatliche Israel," *Bibel und Kirche* 2, 2 (1983) 55-8. **M. Luther**, *Luther's Works, vol. 11, First Lectures on the Psalms* (ed. H. L. Oswald, 1976). **S. L. McKenzie** and **M. P. Graham** (eds.), *The History of Israel's Traditions: The Heritage of M. Noth* (JSOTSup 182, 1994). **A. Malamat**, "Tribal Societies: Biblical Genealogies and African Lineage Systems," *AES 14* (1973) 126-36. **D. Marcus**, *Jephthah and His Vow* (1986). **G. Matheson**, *Representative Women of the Bible* (1907). **V. H. Matthews**, *Judges and Ruth* (New Cambridge Bible Commentary, 2004). **A. D. H. Mayes**, *Israel in the Period of the Judges* (SBT 29, 1974); *The Story of Israel Between Settlement and Exile: A Redactional Study of the Deuteronomistic History* (1983); *Judges* (OTGu, 1985). **G. E. Mendenhall**, *The Tenth Generation: The Origins of the Biblical Tradition* (1973). **R. L. P. Milburn**, "The 'People's Bible': Artists and Commentators," *CHB 2* (ed. G. W. H. Lampe, 1969) 280-308. **G. Mobley**, "The Wild Man in the Bible and the Ancient Near East," *JBL 116* (1997) 217-33. **G. F. Moore**, *A Critical and Exegetical Commentary on Judges* (ICC, 1898). **J. Muilenburg**, "Form Criticism and Beyond," *JBL 88* (1969) 1-18. **D. F. Murray**, "Narrative Structure and Techniques in the Deborah-Barak Story (Judges iv 4-22)," *Studies in Historic Books of OT* (VTSup 30, ed. J. A. Emerton, 1979) 155-89. **H. T. Musper**, *Die Urausgaben der holländischen Apokalypse und Biblia pauperum* (1961). **H. -D. Neef,** *Deboraerzählung und Deobralied: Studien zu Jdc 4,1–5,31* (Biblish-theologische Studien 49, 2002). **S. Niditch**, "The 'Sodomite' Theme in Judges 19–20: Family, Community, and Social Disintegration," *CBQ 44* (1982) 365-78; "Eroticism and Death in the Tale of Jael," *Gender and Difference in Ancient Israel* (ed. P. L. Day, 1989) 43-57; "Samson as Culture Hero, Trickster, and Bandit: The Empowerment of the Weak," *CBQ 52* (1990) 608-24; *Text and Tradition: The HB and Folklore* (1990); *Underdogs and Tricksters: A Prelude to Biblical Folklore* (New Voices in Biblical Studies, 1990). **M. Noth**, *The Deuteronomistic History* (1943; ET JSOTSup 15, 1981); *The History of Israel* (1954; ET 1960). **M. A. O'Brian**, *The Deuteronomistic History Hypothesis: A Reassessment* (OBO 92, 1989); "Judges and the Deuteronomistic History," *The History of Israel's Traditions: The Heritage of M. Noth* (JSOTSup 182, ed. S. L. McKenzie and M. P. Graham, 1994) 235-59. **R. H. O'Connell**, *The Rhetoric of the Book of Judges* (VTSup 63, 1996). M. O'Connor, "The Women in the Book of Judges," *HAR 10* (1986) 277-93. **D. Olsen**, "The Book of Judges," *NIB* (1998) 2:553-719. **D. Penchansky**, "Staying the Night: Intertextuality in Genesis and Judges," *Reading Between Texts: Intertextuality and the HB* (Literary Currents in Biblical Interpretation, ed. D.N. Fewell, 1992) 77-88; "Up for Grabs: A Tentative Proposal for Doing Ideological Criticism," *Semeia 59* (1992) 35-42. **R. Polzin**, *Moses and the Deuteronomist: Deuteronomy, Joshua, Judges* (A Literary Study of the Deuteronomic History, pt. 1, 1980). **C. Pressler**, *Joshua, Judges, Ruth* (WBC, 2002). **A. Reinhartz**, "Samson's Mother: An Unnamed Protagonist," *JSOT 55* (1992) 25-37. **W. Richter**, *Traditionsgeschichtliche Untersuchungen zum Richterbuch* (BBB 18, 1963); *Die Bearbeitung des "Retterbuches" in der deuteronomistischen Epoche* (BBB 21, 1964). **R. Rogers**, *A Commentary on Judges* (1615). **P. Schaff** (ed.), *The Nicene and Post-Nicene Fathers, 1st ser.*

(14 vols., 1956); and **H. Wace** (eds.), *The Ante-Nicene Fathers* (10 vols., 1952, 1961); *The Nicene and Post-Nicene Fathers, 2nd ser.* (14 vols., 1952, 1961). **T. J. Schneider**, *Judges* (Berit Olam, 2000). **H. Schulte**, "Das Richterbuch," Die Entstehung der Geschichtschreibung im Alten Israel (BZAW 128, 1972) 77-105). **H. Schultz**, *OT Theology: The Religion of Revelation in Its Pre-Christian Stage of Development* (1892). **C. A. Simpson**, *Composition of the Book of Judges* (1957). **M. Skjeggestad**, "Ethnic Groups in Early Iron Age Palestine: Some Remarks on the Use of the Term 'Israelite' in Recent Research," *SJOT* 6 (1992) 159-86. **W. F. Smelik**, *The Targum of Judges* (OTS 36, 1995). **W. R. Smith**, *Kinship and Marriage in Early Arabia* (1903); and **J. M. Fuller** (eds.), *A Dictionary of the Bible* (3 vols., 1893). **B. Spinoza**, *A Theologico-Political Treatise* (2 vols., 1951). **M. Sternberg**, *The Poetics of Biblical Narrative: Ideological Literature and the Drama of Reading* (ISBL, 1985). **K. Stone**, *Sex, Honor, and Power in the Deuteronomistic History* (JSOTSup 234, 1996). **J. D. Thompson**, *A Critical Concordance to the Septuagint: Judges* (The Computer Bible 60, 1998). **T. L. Thompson**, *The Early History of the Israelite People: From the Written and Archaeological Sources* (SHANE 4, 1994); "Historiography of Ancient Palestine and Early Jewish Historiography: W.G. Dever and the Not So New Biblical Archaeology," *The Origins of the Ancient Israelite States* (JSOTSup 228, ed. V. Fritz and P.R. Davies, 1996) 26-43. **P. Trible**, *Texts of Terror: Literary-feminist Readings of Biblical Narratives* (OBT 13, 1984). **J. Vickery**, "In Strange Ways: The Story of Samson," *Images of Man and God: OT Short Stories in Literary Focus* (Bible and Literature Series 1, ed. B.O. Long, 1981) 58-73. **Voltaire**, *Dictionnaire philosophique portatif* (1764). **B. G. Webb**, *The Book of the Judges: An Integrated Reading* (1987). **J. Wellhausen**, *Prolegomena to the History of Israel* (1878; ET 1885). **A. Whyte,** *Bible Characters: Gideon to Absalom* (1905). **A. Wilson** and **J. L. Wilson**, *A Medieval Mirror: Speculum humanae salvationis, 1324–1500* (1984). **G. Yee** (ed.), *Judges and Method: New Approaches in Biblical Studies* (1995).

T. K. BEAL AND D. M. GUNN

THE FORMER PROPHETS

Ruth

The book of Ruth tells the story of a Moabite woman who marries into an Israelite family fleeing from a famine in Judah. Subsequently becoming a widow, she returns with her widowed mother-in-law to Bethlehem and while gleaning in the fields at harvest time meets and eventually marries a wealthy relative, later giving birth to King David's grandfather.

From the earliest period down to the time of the medieval Jewish commentators, the primary interest of exegesis was in telling the biblical story and, to this end, in explaining any difficulties in the biblical text. Thus, in the ancient versions the text was expanded at various points by the introduction of comments that provided reasons for occurrences or actions or otherwise filled in perceived gaps in the story. This process reached its apogee in the Targum, which as a result of these expansions is more than twice as long as the Hebrew text of the HB.

In rabbinic literature there was also an interest in locating the events of the biblical story in history. Some early rabbis took the use of the plural "judges" in Ruth 1:1 to indicate the period of Deborah and Barak (*Ruth Rab.* 1.1), whereas in the Targum and in the Talmud (*b. B. Bat.* 91a) Boaz was identified with the judge Ibzan. Ruth was given a royal genealogy and said to be a daughter or granddaughter of Eglon (Judges 3), king of Moab (*Ruth Rab.* 2.9.).

Various passages in the story were used for didactic and homiletic purposes, a major interest in this area being the derivation of rules for proselytes. Especially in the Targum, where Ruth's declaration of fidelity to Naomi (Ruth 1:16-17) is expanded into a catechism, in each phrase of which Ruth indicates her acknowledgement and acceptance of some consequence of her conversion, Ruth was seen as a model proselyte. Perhaps this accounts for the custom of reading the book at the festival of Shavuot, first recorded in the post-Talmudic tractate *Soferim*. Or perhaps the development of Ruth as a model proselyte may have occurred in parallel with the development of Shavuot from a harvest festival to a commemoration of the giving of the law. The traditional explanation, that Ruth is read at Shavuot because that is when King David died (*Ruth Rab.* 3.2), is hardly realistic, while the fact that the main action in the story takes place at the time of harvest is hardly in itself a sufficient basis for the custom's origin.

Aside from the statement in the baraita of *b. B. Bat.* 14b-15a that Samuel wrote Ruth, no interest was displayed during this period in the question of authorship. One opinion on the purpose of the book is recorded (*Ruth Rab.* 2.14): "R. Ze'ira said, 'This scroll tells us nothing of cleanliness or of uncleanliness, either of prohibition or permission. For what purpose then was it written? To teach how great is the reward of those who do deeds of kindness.'"

For the major part of the modern period, the main focus of interest has been on the book's date and purpose. To date it on the basis of its language has proved difficult. On the whole, the language is good classical Hebrew, which has often been taken to indicate a preexilic date; however, it includes some Aramaisms and other features generally considered to be late. Several specimens of archaic forms are found only in the speech of Boaz and Naomi, and the suggestion has been made that they represent a literary device that has these older people speak in an old-fashioned way, rather than being an indication of when the book was composed.

The question of date has usually been considered in conjunction with that of purpose, and a wide range of conclusions have been reached. The theory that gained the widest currency—that the book was written as a protest against the policy of Ezra and Nehemiah on intermarriage between the people of Judah and those of surrounding territories—suffers from the problem that not only is there no hint of polemic in the book but that it may equally well be read as propaganda in support of that policy, saying in effect that marriage with foreigners is permissible if they first become proselytes. This problem of the book's ambivalence was recognized already when the idea that the book opposes Ezra and Nehemiah's policy was first broached (see L. Bertholdt [1812–19] 2:2356); notwithstanding its widespread currency, it is doubtful whether the theory will hold.

Many of the proposals made in the present century have proved (or will undoubtedly prove) to be ephemeral and must be seen as monuments to passing fashions in biblical studies. Attempts to explain the story as a fertility cult drama (W. Staples [1936–37]; H. May [1939]) found no lasting acceptance. The proposal that the origin of the book should be located in the Solomonic enlightenment (R. Hals [1969]), which was based on a comparison of the book's theological ideas with those found in other writings attributed to that period, was deprived of its foundation when the concept of the Solomonic enlightenment passed out of fashion. Some other suggestions are that Ruth was written possibly by Jehoiada the priest in order to compare its heroine with another foreign widow, Athaliah, to the disadvantage of the latter (M. Crook [1948]) or that the book's origin should be associated with Jehoshaphat's reformation (E. Campbell [1975]).

The theory that the book had the historical purpose of providing King David with a genealogy has proved a little more durable than most, but the often-stated opinion that the connection with David is secondary (most recently, A. Phillips [1986]) would mean that the original composition must have had another purpose. This opinion, which relies on the supposition that because the birth of Ruth's child is greeted with the saying "A son has been born to Naomi" (Ruth 4:17), the child's name should have some connection with the name Naomi, is not necessarily sound, for the statement is not precisely identical in form with any of the other texts in which a child's name is explained by a saying of the person who bestows the name. It remains plausible that the connection with David made in 4:17 is original, although many scholars believe the genealogy of 4:18-22 to be secondary. However, it does not follow from this that the name and nationality of Ruth, at the very least, must be accurate historical data (see A. Anderson [1978] 172). That conclusion, resting on the assumption that Moabite ancestry would have carried a stigma, is questionable in view of the fact that the law of Deut 23:3-4, which is the basis of this thinking, was clearly never applied to the Davidic dynasty, as it ought to have been, on account of Rehoboam's mother, who was an Ammonite (1 Kgs 14:21).

The suggestion that the purpose of the book was to register a legal precedent goes back to the beginning of the modern period. Bertholdt, who has been credited with the invention of the "anti-Ezra" theory, actually thought that the book's purpose was to extend the obligation to marry a childless widow to kinsmen other than the nearest and the rights to such marriage to foreign women who had embraced the Israelite religion. Even if it is not considered to constitute the purpose of the book, the juridical background to the story has attracted a great deal of interest. The chief exegetical problem is the relation between the situation reflected in chap. 4 and the HB laws on marriage, inheritance, and the redemption of property. There was for a time a widespread tendency to understand Ruth's remarriage as a form of levirate marriage that applied to a more distant relative than the brother-in-law specified in the law of Deut 25:5-10; and the concept of a redeemer-marriage, in which the obligation to marry a widowed kinswoman was combined with the right to redeem the property of her first husband, gained some currency.

More recently, however, the trend has been to move away from the search for juridical precision and to see that the connection between marriage and redemption was created by the storyteller and did not necessarily have any existence as a legal institution. Questions have also been raised as to whether there is any levirate element in Ruth's second marriage. This has been increasingly denied in recent years, especially by those who have examined the textual problem posed by the existence of the kĕtîb and qĕrê form, representing respectively a first person and a second person singular verb, in Ruth 4:5 (see D. Beattie [1971]; J. Sasson [1979]; B. Green [1982]). Scholars who have recognized in this phenomenon two alternative readings have decided that the ketîb must represent the original reading and that no obligation to marry Ruth was imposed on the nameless redeemer. Although others continue to follow the tradition of reading the *qěrê*, which had hitherto been all but unanimous, no one has yet offered any considered argument in its support. The presence of a levirate element has also been denied on other grounds (see R. Gordis [1974] 246; Anderson, 183).

These developments should be seen as part of the trend toward a greater concern with literary values, which may be said to have begun with H. Gunkel. One of the earliest exercises in detecting symmetrical structures in biblical literature dealt with Ruth (see S. Bertman [1965]), and it soon attracted the attention of feminist literary critics (see P. Trible [1978]). A notable development was the application to Ruth of V. Propp's morphological analysis of Russian fairy tales (see Sasson; P. Milne [1986]), while a number of other significant contributions to understanding the literary art of Ruth have been made in recent years (e.g., M. Bernstein [1991]; D. Fewell and D. Gunn [1988, 1989]; Fewell [1990]).

Bibliography: **A. A. Anderson**, "The Marriage of Ruth," *JSS 23* (1978) 171-83. **D. R. G. Beattie**, "Kethibh and Qere in Ruth 4:5," *VT 21* (1971) 490-94; *Jewish Exegesis of the Book of Ruth* (JSOTSup 2, 1977). **M. J. Bernstein**, "Two Multivalent Readings in the Ruth Narrative," *JSOT 50* (1991) 15-26. **L. Bertholdt**, *Historisch-kritische Einleitung in die sammtlichen kanonischen und apokryphischen Schriften des Alten und Neuen Testaments* (6 vols., 1812–19). **S. Bertman**, "Symmetrical Design in the Book of Ruth," *JBL 84* (1965) 165-68. **J. Bos**, *Ruth, Esther, Jonah* (1986). **A. Brenner** (ed.), *Ruth and Esther: A Feminist Companion to the Bible* (FCB second series 3, 1999). **E. F. Campbell, Jr.**, *Ruth: A New Translation with Introduction, Notes, and Commentary* (AB 7, 1975). **M. B. Crook**, "The Book of Ruth: A New Solution," *JBR 16* (1948) 155-60. **K. Farmer**, "The Book of Ruth," *NIB* (1998) 2:889-946. **D. N. Fewell**, *Compromising Redemption: Relating Characters in the Book of Ruth* (1990); and **D. M. Gunn**, "'A Son Is Born to Naomi!': Literary Allusions and Interpretation in the Book of Ruth," *JSOT 40* (1988) 99-108; "Boaz, Pillar of Society: Measures of Worth in the Book of Ruth," *JSOT 45* (1989) 45-59. **I. Fischer**, *Rut: übersetzt und ausgelegt* (Herders theologischer Kommentar zum Alten Testament, 2001). **R. Gordis**, "Love, Marriage, and Business in the Book of Ruth," *A Light Unto My Path: OT Studies in Honor of J. M. Myers* (ed. H. N. Bream et al., 1974) 241-64. **B. Green**, "The Plot of the Biblical Story of Ruth," *JSOT 23* (1982) 55-68. **H. Gunkel**, *Reden und Aufsätze* (1913). **R. M. Hals**, *The Theology of the Book of Ruth* (1969). **J. G. Harris**, *Joshua, Judges, Ruth* (NIB, OT 5, 2000). **A. Ibn Ezra**, *Abraham Ibn Esras Kommentare zu den Büchern Kohelet, Ester und Rut*, ed. D.U. Rottzoll (Studia Judaica 12, 1999). **M. C. A. Korpel**, *The Structure of the Book of Ruth* (Pericope: Scriptures as Written and Read in Antiquity 2, 2001). **A. LaCoque**, "Ruth," *The Feminine Unconventional: Four Subversive Figures in Israel's Tradition* (1990). **A.-J. Levine**, "Ruth," *Women's Bible Commentary* (ed. C. A. Newsom and S. H. Ringe, 1992). **T. A. Linafelt**, *Ruth* (Berit Olam, 1999). **H. Matthews**, *Judges and Ruth* (New Cambridge Bible Commentary, 2004). **H. G. May**, "Ruth's Visit to the High Place at Bethlehem," *JRAS* (1939) 75-78. **P. J. Milne**, "Folktales and Fairy Tales: An Evaluation of Two Proppian Analyses of Biblical Narrative," *JSOT 34* (1986) 35-60. **J. M. Myers**, *The Linguistic and Literary Form of the Book of Ruth* (1955). **K. Nielsen**, *Ruth* (OTL, 1997). **A. Phillips**, "The Book of Ruth: Deception and Shame," *JJS 37* (1986) 1-17. **C. Pressler**, *Joshua, Judges, and Ruth* (WBC, 2002). **K. D. Sakenfeld**, *Ruth* (Interpretation, 1999). **J. M. Sasson**, *Ruth: A New Translation with a Philological Commentary and a Formalist-Folklorist Interpretation* (1979). **W. E. Staples**, "The Book of Ruth," *AJSL 53* (1936–37) 145-47. **T. and D. Thompson**, "Some Legal Problems in the Book of Ruth," *VT 18* (1968) 79-99. P. Trible, "A Human Comedy," *God and the Rhetoric of Sexuality* (OBT 2, 1978) chap. 6. **Y. Zakovitch**, *Das Buch Rut: ein jüdischer Kommentar* (SBS 177, 1999).

D.R.G. BEATTIE

THE FORMER PROPHETS

1 and 2 Samuel

1. *Pre-modern Interpretations.* Originally, there was one book called Samuel. The Septuagint divided it, along with the book of Kings, into two, creating four books of "Kingdoms." The Vulgate followed this designation, but the division did not enter into manuscripts of the HB until 1488 and not into printed editions until D. Bomberg's *Rabbinic Bible* of 1516/17. The Babylonian Talmud (*b. B. Bat.* 14b) ascribed the authorship of this one book to Samuel; 1 Chr 29:29 attributes authorship to Samuel, Gad, and Nathan. This view of authorship was widely called into question in the eighteenth century.

The NT cites a number of passages from the books of Samuel (1 Sam 12:22; 2 Sam 5:2; 7:8, 14; 22:3, 50), in addition to many other allusions to the text. Among the Greek fathers, commentaries and/or sermons were written by Origen, Chrysostom, Theodoret, and Pseudo-Gregory the Great. Ambrose wrote an apology dealing with David's relationship to Bathsheba and Uriah, while Charlemagne's identification of himself with King David gave new popularity to the books of Samuel and Kings. An anonymous and widely used commentary on the Vulgate, *Quaestiones Hebraicae in Libros Regum* (9th cent.), was falsely attributed to Jerome in the eleventh century. The author of this commentary was probably brought up as a Jew but had converted to Christianity. Pseudo-Jerome rejects the standard Christian interpretation of 1 Sam 13:1 (Ishbosheth was one year old when Saul began his reign, and he reigned over Israel for two years after Saul's death) and then cites the standard Jewish interpretation: Saul began his reign when he was as innocent as a year-old infant and continued in that state for two years. This commentary was used by Rabanus Maurus in the ninth century and by Andrew of St. Victor and S. Langton in the twelfth century.

During the Renaissance and the Reformation Nicholas of Lyra and T. Cajetan wrote commentaries, and Calvin authored a series of sermons on 1 Samuel. J. Bugenhagen (1485–1558), Luther, a pastor and a theologian in his own right, published a commentary on Samuel in 1524. In the seventeenth century there were commentaries by Sanctius, I. Menochius (1575–1655), Malvenda, and C. à Lapide, all Roman Catholic, as well as by E. Schmid, a Protestant. H. Grotius also commented on Samuel in his *Annotate ad Vetus Testamentum* (1644).

2. *Modern Interpretations.* The nineteenth and twentieth centuries have seen vigorous critical study of the book that can be summarized under six major categories.

a. The text of Samuel. The MT of Samuel seems to have been severely damaged by *homoioteleuton* and other similar mistakes in antiquity. In the nineteenth and early twentieth centuries, O. Thenius (1842; ET 1898), J. Wellhausen (1871), and S. Driver (1913) attempted to improve the text, relying primarily on evidence from the Septuagint. When it was discovered that the Dead Sea Scrolls often preserved Hebrew readings that previously had only been conjectured on the basis of the Greek (F. M. Cross [1973]), textual critics collated the Qumran texts with the MT and studied the Septuagint with renewed seriousness. Several commentaries and monographs have advanced the discussion significantly on the basis of the Qumran scrolls and the Septuagint (P. McCarter [1980–84]; R. Klein [1983]; E. Ulrich [1978]).

Within the Greek manuscript tradition, textual critics now distinguish between the OG, a second-century B.C.E. translation made in Egypt on the basis of a Hebrew text; the proto-Lucianic recension, a revision of the OG toward the Hebrew text as preserved in Palestine in the first-century B.C.E.; and the *kaige* recension, a first-century CE revision of the Greek on the basis of a Hebrew text very close to the MT. The *kaige* has now replaced the OG in standard copies of the LXX for 2 Sam 10:1–24:25.

b. Source criticism. During the nineteenth century the influence of pentateuchal studies and the search for continuous sources extended to the books of Samuel. C. Gramberg detected two sources, Ra and Rb; Thenius increased these to five. Wellhausen described the two sources in the story of Saul's rise to power as pro-monarchical and anti-monarchical. The pro-monarchical source (1 Sam 9:1–10:16, early joined to 11:1-11, 15 and chaps. 13–14) portrayed kingship as the high point of Israel's history and the greatest blessing of Yahweh, while for the writer of the postexilic anti-monarchical source (1 Sam 7:1–8:22; 10:17-27; 12:1-25, with 11:13-14 serving as a bridge between the two sources), the request for a king was sinful, and Israel was conceived as a theocracy. In his 1902 commentary *Die Bucher Samuel erklärt*, K. Budde placed these sources in an earlier period and attributed them to the sanctuaries of Gilgal and Mizpah. The pro-monarchical source he considered J (Yahwist); the anti-monarchical, E (Elohist). R. Smend and O. Eissfeldt (1966) traced the L (*Laienquelle*, or lay source), J, and E sources throughout Samuel. In last decades of the twentieth century, this search for sources continuing (or similar to) the Pentateuchal sources has been eclipsed by other concerns, although a source-critical interpretation was revived by B. Halpern (1981, 171).

   c. Pre-deuteronomistic documents. H. Gressmann raised doubts about the existence of extended sources running throughout the books of Samuel (see the ET of his article in D. Gunn [1991]). Subsequently, other scholars have identified coherent pre-canonical documents dealing with specific issues, written for one situation but given a new interpretation by inclusion in the structure of the books we call 1 and 2 Samuel. Contemporary scholarship has sought to determine the original limits of these documents, their date, and their original intention, although some scholars would deny that such sources can be easily isolated from the final Dtr forms of one material (see R. Carlson [1964]).

   i. Samuel at Shiloh. These materials, while not as unified as some of the other pre-canonical documents discussed below, antedate the composition of the Deuteronomistic History. They consist of an account of Samuel's marvelous birth (chap. 1), the sins of the sons of Eli (chap. 2), and the vocation of Samuel (chap. 3). The Song of Hannah (2:1-10) was originally a poem sung after a national military victory before it was ascribed to Hannah and is later echoed in Mary's song in Luke 2:46-55. Deuteronomistic notices have been added in 2:27-36 and 3:11-14. It is difficult to determine the function of most of this material outside of its present context, although McCarter considers chapter 1 an original part of the Saul cycle because of the pun in v. 20 and attributes large portions of chap. 2 to the ark narrative.

   ii. The ark narrative. L. Rost (1926; ET 1982) identified an ark narrative in 1 Sam 4:1b–7:1 and in 2 Samuel 6 that described the loss of the ark to the Philistines, the havoc it caused when deposited in Dagon's temple, its restoration to Israel, and its eventual procession to and deposit in Jerusalem. He thought this narrative was a cultic myth for the Jerusalem Temple written by a priest active in the reign of David or Solomon. A. Campbell (1975) accepted the identification of the limits for this document proposed by Rost, although he believed that its central theological idea was a reflection on the end of the pre-monarchical epoch. P. Miller and J. Roberts (1977), followed in large part by McCarter, believe that the ark narrative did not originally include 2 Samuel 6 (note the tension between Kiriath-jearim in 1 Sam 7:1 and Baale-Judah in 2 Sam 6:2) but that it did include portions of 1 Samuel 2 (vv. 12-17, 22-25; possibly vv. 27-36). In this understanding the narrative shows that God's displeasure with the priests of Shiloh led to the defeat at Ebenezer but also reaffirms Yahweh's power in a time of apparent defeat. The God of Israel does not go into eclipse with God's people but uses their calamities as a foil for God's mightiest acts. These scholars date the ark narrative to an early period in David's reign before his defeat of the Philistines. During the exilic period this narrative showed what God could do with the broken community of Israel (R. Gordon [1984]).

   iii. The rise of Saul. The story of Saul's search for the lost asses of his father, Kish, which leads to his anointing as "prince" (*nāgîd*) by Samuel (1 Sam 9:1–10:16), comes, at least in large part, from early tradition, while the reports of his judge-like victory over the Ammonites and his deliverance of Jabesh-gilead in 1 Sam 10:27b–11:15 describe an alternative route by which he became king. The other parts of chaps. 7–12 may have undergone Deuteronomistic editing (see below), but the underlying stories of prophetic denunciation of royal self-aggrandizement (1 Sam 8:11-18) or of Saul's being chosen by lot or because of his stature (1 Sam 10:17-27) also have the ring of primary traditions. I. Mendelsohn (1956) dated the prophetic denunciation to Samuel's own time, whereas F. Crüsemann (1978) located it in the early monarchical period. While chap. 12 is clearly a Deuteronomistic editorial speech (see below), D. McCarthy (1978) and others have detected older traditions lying within and behind the present text. Anecdotes from Saul's Philistine wars are preserved in 13:2-7a, 15b-23; 14:1-46.

iv. History of David's rise. The history of David's rise has also been considered an independent document and extends, in one common understanding, from 1 Sam 16:14 to 2 Sam 5:10. McCarter dates this document to the time of David and proposes that it testifies to the legitimacy of David as Saul's successor and attempts to allay the fears of the tribe of Benjamin, which was suspicious of this new king (cf. the Shimei incident and Sheba's revolt). The dynastic idea, which developed under Solomon, is not yet present. McCarter cites the Hittite *Apology of Hattushilish*, which sought to legitimize the rule of a king who had usurped the power of his predecessor. T. Mettinger (1976) dates this document to the period after Solomon's death when the king in Jerusalem tried to assert control over all Israel after the breakup of the national unity that had existed during the time of David and Solomon. J. Grønbaek (1971) locates it in the era of Baasha of the northern kingdom. Both Mettinger and Grønbaek believe that it begins with 1 Sam 15:1, while Mettinger and A. Weiser (1966) include parts of 2 Samuel 6–7.

v. The succession narrative. This document, commonly identified as 2 Samuel 9–20 and 1 Kings 1–2, recounts the court history of David and of Solomon's ascension to the throne despite the fact that Adonijah was older than he. Rost also included in this account 2 Sam 6:16, 20-23; 7:11b, and 16 and dated it to the time of Solomon. McCarter considers only 1 Kings 1–2 as a succession narrative, attributing parts of 2 Samuel 9–20 to other documents from the time of David (the story of Absalom's revolt in 2 Samuel 13–20, the revenge of the Gibeonites in 2 Sam 21:1-14, and David's patronage of Meribbaal in 2 Sam 9:1-13). E. Würthwein (1974), T. Veijola (1975, 1977), and F. Langamet (1981) believe that the materials favorable to Solomon are secondary and that the document was originally critical of Solomon. J. Van Seters (1983) places this material very late and sees it as an anti-messianic insertion.

vi. The appendix in 2 Samuel 21–24. The diverse materials in these chapters have often received inadequate attention or have been dismissed as miscellaneous accretions to the end of the books of Samuel. Recent studies have called attention to the significant and orderly arrangement of these chapters:

21:1-14 famine story
  21:15-22 warrior exploits
    22:1-51 psalm dealing with mighty acts of God for and through David
    23:1-7 oracle about enduring dynasty
  23:8-39 warrior exploits and warrior list
24:1-25 plague story

The psalm in 2 Samuel 22 (cf. Psalm 18) celebrates divine deliverance, contrasting with accounts of human weakness in the lists of warrior exploits that precede and follow it. According to this psalm David was blameless, while 2 Sam 23:1-7 reports the everlasting covenant God made with him and his dynasty.

d. A prophetic redaction. A number of scholars (Weiser; B. Birch [1976]; McCarter) detect a redactional layer within the books of Samuel that gave the stories a prophetic interpretation before their inclusion in the Deuteronomistic History. According to McCarter this eighth-century prophetic history viewed the advent of kingship as a concession to the wanton demands of the people. This northern writer, prepared to acknowledge the legitimacy of David, also felt that kings should be subject to the instruction of a prophet. Birch ascribes the following passages dealing with Saul to prophetic circles writing after the fall of the northern kingdom: 1 Sam 9:15-17, 20-21, 27–10:1, 5–8, 16b; 10:17-19, 25; 11:12-14; 12:1-5; 13:7b-15; 15:1-35. He also argues that the contribution of this redactor was more important than that of the deuteronomistic historian.

   e. The Deuteronomistic History. In 1943 M. Noth portrayed Joshua, Judges, Samuel, and Kings as part of a deuteronomistic history written in Judah after 562 B.C.E. (the last date mentioned in 2 Kgs 25:27) and before the return from the Babylonian exile in 538 B.C.E. According to him this document attempted to justify to the exilic generation the destruction of the northern and the southern kingdoms. Israel had sought after other gods and had not held to the ideal of one central sanctuary, despite frequent warnings by the prophets.

   Noth and most subsequent commentators have found fewer deuteronomistic comments in Samuel than elsewhere in the Deuteronomistic History (Veijola is an exception). The date and unity of this redaction as well as its purpose are now understood quite differently from Noth's original proposal.

   Cross identified a preexilic deuteronomistic redaction (Dtr^1), completed before the death of Josiah. The writer of this document called the remnants of the northern kingdom to return to Judah and to Yahweh's sole legitimate shrine in Jerusalem and extended the claims of the Davidic monarchy to all Israel. The final form of the deuteronomistic history was completed in mid-exile (Dtr^2; for details see R. Nelson [1981]). The Göttingen school (Smend; W. Dietrich [1972]; and Veijola) has detected three layers of redaction in this history, ascribing all of them to the time of the exile: A prophetic redaction (DtrP) added certain prophetic emphases to the original history (DtrG or DtrH). A final, nomistic redaction (DtrN) stressed compliance with the requirements of the Mosaic law.

   In the last decades of the twentieth century, almost all studies have differed from Noth in finding positive elements in Dtr. H. W. Wolff (1975) thought that Dtr meant to challenge its audience to repent and so experience Yahweh's favor anew. The repentance initiated by Samuel in 1 Sam 7:3 led to defeat of the Philistines, whereas the confession of sins in 1 Sam 12:19 persuaded Samuel to promise that God would not abandon the people and that he, Samuel, would continue to pray for them. Cross believed Dtr^1 celebrated the promises to David in addition to its judgment on the sin of Jeroboam. For him Dtr^1 was a propaganda document for the Josianic reform. Although G. von Rad probably erred in attributing almost a messianic significance to the release of Jehoiachin, many other scholars see this release as a signal that the promise to David was still alive as far as the deuteronomistic historian was concerned.

   Samuel's farewell speech in 1 Samuel 12 and the oracle of Nathan and David's response in 2 Samuel 7 serve as indicators of the historian's own point of view, even if one or both of these chapters may have existed prior to their incorporation in Dtr. In 1 Samuel 12 Samuel shows that he and Yahweh are innocent, while the request for a king is categorized as a failure to look to Yahweh for help in time of need. Still, life under a king could have been blessed if Israel's conduct had been obedient. The righteousness of Yahweh could thus adjust itself to the new condition of monarchy. Yahweh would also show the divine righteousness by sending prophets like Samuel to pray and teach. The threat in the final verse of this chapter had no doubt become reality by the time the Deuteronomistic Historian wrote, "If, however, you persist in acting wickedly, both you and your king will be swept away."

   The final forms of the oracle of Nathan (2 Sam 7:1-17) and of David's prayer (2 Sam 7:18-

29) provide another great Deuteronomistic interpretation, whatever role earlier versions of this chapter may have played (see McCarter, 224-31, who finds a primitive document from the court of Solomon in vv. 1a, 2-3, 11b-12, and 13-15a; a prophetic editing in vv. 4-9a and v. 15b; and a Deuteronomistic redaction in vv. 1b, 9b-11a, 13a, and 16). The dynastic promise to David is frequently referred to throughout the rest of Samuel and the books of Kings (e.g., 1 Kgs 11:34-36); it is also anticipated in passages contained in the history of David's rise (e.g., 1 Sam 24:20; 25:28). Yahweh established a permanent sacred site for the Israelites in order to give them rest. With the establishment of the monarchy also came the erection of the Temple. The themes of kingship and Temple persist until the end of the Deuteronomistic History.

f. A literary reading of the books of Samuel. The methods summarized in sections a-e are primarily diachronic attempts to interpret the text of 1-2 Samuel either through its prehistory (sources or identifiable pre-Deuteronomistic documents), through one or more redactions (prophetic and/or Deuteronomistic), or through recovering a superior text from one damaged by haplography and other vicissitudes of textual transmission. Many later studies of Samuel, however, have focused more on the present shape of the MT and on narrative critical method. Some of these provide a synchronic reading of the text; other readings have attempted to blend modern literary analysis with diachronic observations. D. Damrosch (1987), for example, argues for the mutually beneficial interplay of historical and literary study and even hopes to integrate comparative, text-historical, and literary study. McCarter, by way of contrast, divided his discussion of the Goliath story into two sections: (a) 17:1-11, 32-40, 42-48a, 49, 51-54 and (b) 17:12-31, 41, 48b, 50, 55-58; 18:1-5, 10-11, 17-19, 29b-30. The second section (b) is lacking in Codex Vaticanus and is interpreted by McCarter as an alternative account of David's arrival and early days in court, which has been interpolated into the primitive narrative. He considers it excursus material. Damrosch argues that the second section (b) is in fact older and once served as a structuring device for the pre-deuteronomistic version of the history of David's rise. When the deuteronomistic historian constructed a new story (a), he had two choices, both of which he tried: He threw out the old story, putting only (a) in the text (cf. the text presumed by LXX), and he inserted his new story (a) into the old (b), resulting in the MT. Damrosch bases these conjectures on sensitive literary analysis of the narrative.

The great variety of modern literary-critical or structuralist readings of Samuel cannot be described in the space here provided (see the review article by R. Polzin [1989] dealing with biblical studies and the humanities). The studies on Samuel by C. Conroy (1978), J. Fokkelman (1986), Gunn (1991), J. Jackson (1965), B. Long (1981), Polzin (1989), and J. Rosenberg (1987) illustrate these approaches. In addition feminist literary biblical scholars have sought to reveal how issues of gender affect the interpretation of the text (see A. Brenner [1994]).

Synchronic and diachronic approaches have made great advances in the understanding of the books of Samuel. While some scholars have stressed one or more methods to the virtual exclusion of the others, there is an increasing awareness that both approaches, with all their sub-disciplines, need to be used in creative tension as the history of the interpretation of the books of Samuel moves on into the twenty-first century.

Bibliography: R. Alter, *The David Story: A Translation with Commentary* (1999). **A. A. Anderson,** *2 Samuel* (WBC 11, 1989). **P. S. Ash,** *David, Solomon and Egypt: A Reassessment* (JSOTSup 297, 1999). **S. K. Beitenhard,** *Des Königs General: die Heerfürertraditionen in der vorstaatlichen und frühen staatlichen Zeit und die Joabgestalt in 2 Sam 2–20; 1 Kön 1–2* (OBO 163, 1998). **B. C. Birch,** *The Rise of the Israelite Monarchy: The Growth and Development of 1 Samuel 7–15* (SBLDS 27, 1976); "The First and Second Books of Samuel," *NIB* (1998) 2:947-1383. **A. Brenner** (ed.), *A Feminist Companion to Samuel and Kings* (1994, new series 2000). **T. L. Brodie,** *The Crucial Bridge: The Elijah-Elisha Narrative as an Interpretive*

Synthesis of Genesis–Kings and a Literary Model for the Gospels (2000). **K. Budde**, *Die Bücher Samuel* (KHC 8, 1902). **A. F. Campbell**, *The Ark Narrative (1 Samuel 4–6; 2 Samuel 6): A Form-critical and Traditio-historical Study* (SBLDS 16, 1975); *1 Samuel* (FOTL 7, 2003). **R. A. Carlson**, *David, the Chosen King: A Traditio-historical Approach to the Second Book of Samuel* (1964). **J. Cazeaux**, *Saül, David, Salomon: Le Royauté et le destin d'Israël* (2003). **C. C. Conroy**, *Absalom! Absalom! Narrative and Language in 2 Samuel 13–20* (AnBib 81, 1978). **J. E. Cook**, *Hannah's Desire, God's Design: Early Interpretations of the Story of Hannah* (JSOTSup 282, 1999). **F. M. Cross**, *Canaanite Myth and Hebrew Epic: Essays in the History of the Religion of Israel* (1973); and **S. Talmon** (eds.), *Qumran and the History of the Biblical Text* (1975). **F. Crüsemann**, *Der Widerstand gegen das Königtum* (WMANT 49, 1978). **H. J. Dallmeyer**, *David, ein Königsweg: psychoanalytisch-theologischer Dialog über einen biblischen Entwicklungsroman* (2002). **D. Damrosch**, *The Narrative Covenant: Transformations of Genre in the Growth of Biblical Literature* (1987). **W. Dietrich**, *Prophetie und Geschichte: Eine Redaktionsgeshichtliche Untersuchung zum deuteronomistischen Geschichtswwerk* (FRLANT 108, 1972). **S. R. Driver**, *Notes on the Hebrew Text and the Topography of the Books of Samuel* (1913). **O. Eissfeldt**, *The OT: An Introduction* (1966). **M. Elat**, *Samuel and the Foundation of Kingship in Ancient Israel* (1998). **M. J. Evans**, *1 and 2 Samuel* (NIB Commentary, OT 6, 2000). **A. A. Fischer**, *Von Hebron nach Jerusalem: Eine redaktionsgeschichtliche Studie zur Erzählung von König David in II Sam 1–5* (BZAW 335, 2004). **J. P. Fokkelman**, *Narrative Art and Poetry in the Books of Samuel: A Full Interpretation Based on Stylistic and Structural Analyses, vol. 2, The Crossing Fates* (1986). **R. P. Gordon**, *1 and 2 Samuel* (1984). **B. Gosse**, *Structuration des grands ensembles bibliques et intertextualité à l'époque perse: de la redaction sacerdotale due livre d'Isaïe à la contestation de la Sagesse* (BZAW 246, 1997). **B. Green**, *How Are the Mighty Fallen? A Dialogical Study of King Saul in 1 Samuel* (JSOTSup 365, 2003). **J. H. Grønbaek**, *Die Geschichte von Aufstieg Davids (1. Sam 15–2 Sam 5): Tradition und Composition* (1971). **D. M. Gunn**, *The Story of King David: Genre and Interpretation* (JSOTSup 6, 1978); (ed.), *Narrative and Novelle in Samuel: Studies by H. Gressmann and Other Scholars, 1906–23* (1991). **B. Halpern**, *The Constitution of the Monarchy in Israel* (HSM 25, 1981); *David's Secret Demons: Messiah, Murderer, Traitor, King* (2001). **G. Hens-Piazza**, *Of Methods, Monarchs, and Meanings: A Socio-rhetorical Approach to Exegesis* (1996). **J. J. Jackson**, "David's Throne: Patterns in the Succession Story," *CJT* 11 (1965) 183-95. **D. Jobling**, *1 Samuel* (Berit olam, 1998). **J. Klein**, *David versus Saul: ein Beitrag zum Erzählsystem der Samuelbücher* (BWANT, 2002). **R. W. Klein**, *1 Samuel* (WBC 10, 1983); *Textual Criticism of the OT: The Septuagint After Qumran* (1974). **H. H. Klement**, *II Samuel 21–24: Context, Structure, and Meaning in the Samuel Conclusion* (2000). **F. Langamet**, "Affinités Sacerdotales, Deutéronomiques, Élohistes dans l'histoire de la Succession (2 S 9-20; 1 R 1-2)," *Mélanges Bibliques et Orientaux en l'honneur de M. H. Cazelles* (ed. A. Caquot and M. Delcor, 1981) 223-46. **B. Lehnart**, *Prophet und König im Nordreich Israel: Studien zur sogenannten vorklassischen Prophetie im Nordreich Israel anhand der Samuel-, Elija- und Elischa-Überlieferungen* (VTSup 96, 2003). **B. O. Long**, "Wounded Beginnings: David and Two Sons," *Images of Man and God: OT Short Stories in Literary Focus* (ed. B. O. Long, 1981) 26-34. **L. L. Lyke**, *King David with the Wise Woman of Tekoa: the Resonance of Tradition in Parabolic Narrative* (JSOTSup 255, 1997). **P. K. McCarter, Jr.**, *1 and 2 Samuel* (AB 8-9, 1980–84). **D. J. McCarthy**, *Treaty and Covenant* (1978). **I. Mendelsohn**, "Samuel's Denunciation of Kingship in the Light of Accadian Documents from Ugarit," *BASOR* 143 (1956) 17-22. **T. N. D. Mettinger**, *King and Messiah: The Civil and Sacral Legitimation of the Israelite Kings* (ConBOT 8, 1976). **P. D. Miller, Jr.**, and **J J. M. Roberts**, *The Hand of the Lord: A Reassessment of the "Ark Narrative" of 1 Samuel* (1977). **P. D. Miscall**, *1 Samuel: A Literary Reading* (1986). **C. E. Morrison**, *The*

Character of the Syriac Version of the First Book of Samuel (Monographs of the Peshita Institute 11, 2001). **I. Müllner**, *Gewalt im Hause Davids: die Erzählung von Tamar und Amnon* (Herders Biblische Studien 13, 1997). **D. F. Murray**, *Divine Prerogative and Royal Pretension: Pragmatics, Poetics and Polemics in a Narrative Sequence about David* (2 Samuel 5.17–7.29 (JSOTSup 264, 1998). **R. D. Nelson**, *The Double Redaction of the Deuteronomistic History* (JSOTSup 18, 1981). **S. Nicholson**, *Three Faces of Saul: An Intertextual Approach to Biblical Tragedy* (JSOTSup 339, 2002). **K. L. Noll,** *The Faces of David* (JSOTSup 242, 1997). **M. Noth**, *The Deuteronomistic History* (1943; ET, JSOTSup 15, 1981). **E. H. Peterson**, *First and Second Samuel* (Westminster Bible Companion, 1999). **M. Pietsch**, *"Dieser ist der Spross Davids" : Studien zur Rezeptionsgeschichte der Nathanverheissung im alttestamentlichen, zwischentestamentlichen und neutestamentlichen Schriftum* (WMANT 100, 2003). **R. Polzin**, "1 Samuel: Biblical Studies and the Humanities," *RStR* 15 (1989) 297-313; Samuel and the Deuteronomist: 2 Samuel (1989). **A. de Pury** and **T. Römer** (eds.), *Die Sogenannte Thronfolgegeschichte Davids: neue Einsichten und Anfangen* (OBO 176, 2000). **J. Rosenberg**, *"1 and 2 Samuel," The Literary Guide to the Bible* (ed. R. Alter and F. Kermode, 1987). **L. Rost**, *The Succession to the Throne of David* (1926; ET 1982). **A. Saltman**, *Pseudo-Jerome: Quaestiones on the Book of Samuel* (SPB 26, 1975). **A. Salveson**, *The Books of Samuel in the Syriac Version of Jacob of Edessa* (Monographs of the Peshita Institute, 10, 1999). **W. M. Schiedewind**, *Society and the Promise to David: The Reception History of 2 Samuel 7.1-17* (1999). **S. Seiler,** *Die Geschichte von der Thronfolge Davids (2 Sam 9–20; 1 Kön 1–2): Untersuchungen zur Literarkritik und Tendenz* (BZAW 267, 1998). **H. J. Stoebe**, *Das Erste Buch Samuelis* (KAT 8, 1, 1973). **O. Thenius**, *Die Bücher Samuels* (KEH 4, 1842; ET 1898). **J. D. Thompson**, *A Critical Commentary to the Septuagint: Kings I* (The Computer Bible 61, 1999); *A Critical Commentary to the Septuagint: Kings II* (The Computer Bible 62, 1999). **I. Tomoo**, *History and Historical Writing in Ancient Israel: Studies in Biblical Historiography* (1999). **E. C. Ulrich, Jr.**, *The Qumram Text of Samuel and Josephus* (HSM 19, 1978). **J. Van Seters**, *In Search of History* (1983). **T. Veijola**, *Die Ewige Dynastie: David und die Enstehung seiner Dynastie nach der Deuteronomistischen Darstellung* (1975); *Das Königtum in der Beurteilung der Deuteronomistischen Historigraphie: Eine Redaktionsgeschichtliche Untersuchung* (1977). **A. Weiser**, "Die Legitimation des Königs David: Zur Eigenart und Enstehung der Sogenannten Geschichte vom David's Aufstieg," *VT* 16 (1966) 325-54. **J. Wellhausen**, *Der Text der Bücher Samuelis Untersucht* (1871). **H. W. Wolff**, "The Kergyma of the Deuteronomic Historical Work," *The Vitality of OT Traditions* (1975) 83-100. **E. Würthwein,** *Die Erzählung von der Thronfolge Davids-theologische oder Politische Geschichtsschreibung?* (ThSt 115, 1974).

R. W. Klein

THE FORMER PROPHETS

1 and 2 Kings

The history of interpretation of the book(s) of Kings extends over two and a half millennia. At the beginning of that history stand what might be called "interpretative rewritings." Of these, the earliest is the book of Chronicles, more specifically 2 Chronicles, which covers the same period, from the accession of Solomon to the exile, as does 1–2 Kings. Writing sometime in the postexilic era, the chronicler retold the narrative he found in Kings so as to heighten, for example, the cultic factor and the doctrine of "immediate retribution." Subsequently, at the end of the first century C.E., Josephus, in his *Antiquities of the Jews*, compiled the material of both Kings and Chronicles into a composite historical account designed to elicit the interest and sympathy of a Hellenistic audience for the Jewish story. Such rewritings are notable for the freedom with which they handle the content and wording of the book they are "interpreting" for their contemporaries.

1. *Patristic Period.* The first five centuries of Christian history, both in the East and in the West, are not particularly rich in large-scale, systematic interpretations of Kings. From this period there are, however, two works worthy of special mention. The oldest of these, a more or less verse-by-verse commentary on Kings, is attributed to the preeminent Syrian church father Ephraem (d. 373), although the genuineness of the work is questioned. While it does not disregard the historical, literal dimension of the text, the commentary gives primary interest to an allegorical reading of Kings wherein the book's persons and events become symbolic foreshadowings of happenings in the life of Christ and of the church.

The procedure of a second patristic author, Theodoret, bishop of Cyrene (d. 457) was quite different. His Greek work on Kings consisted of a series of some 125 mostly brief questions and answers. The questions, virtually always evoked by a literal reading of the text, concern such issues as the localization of sites mentioned, the meaning of particular expressions, and theological/moral difficulties implicit in a given passage. Allegorizing is virtually absent.

2. *Medieval Period.* Within the exegetical millennium extending from c. 500 to c. 1500 separate Jewish and Christian currents may be distinguished. Included in the former are the outstanding figures of Rashi (d. 1105) and D. Kimhi (d. 1235), whose concise comments evidence a profound knowledge of Hebrew and a command of the entire biblical corpus that enabled them to resolve problems in one text by adducing a parallel passage.

A representative figure among the fairly numerous Christian medieval authors on Kings is Rabinus Maurus (d. 856), whose commentary exemplifies features common to many other writers. First, his exegesis was oriented to the Vulgate; his rudimentary Hebrew is displayed in his (sometimes fanciful) explanations of the meanings of proper names. More noteworthy is his predominantly allegorical approach to the text. Finally, Rabanus's interpretation shows itself to be very much part of a school tradition; he copied out extended sections from such earlier writers as Bede and Isidore of Seville, just as his own discussions would be taken over in later presentations. However, the picture of medieval Christian exegesis furnished by Rabanus needs to be complemented by reference to other tendencies at work in the period. Richard of St. Victor (d. 1173), for example, offered an explicitly "literal" reading of the account of Solomon's Temple in 1 Kings 6–7; he likewise authored an attempt to resolve the many chronological problems involved in correlating the reigns of the Israelite and Judean kings. Similarly, at the end of the period Nicholas of Lyra (d. 1349) introduced the Hebrew erudition of Rashi and Kimhi into Christian scholarship.

3. *Early Modern Period.* Christian exegesis in the period c. 1500–c. 1800 was marked by a variety of developments: confessional antagonisms, greater knowledge of biblical and Semitic

languages (e.g., Arabic), the ever-clearer domination of the historical-literal over the allegorical approach, and an emerging consciousness that the Hebrew *textus receptus* needed to be treated critically. All these features, to some degree, manifested themselves in the three Kings commentaries that may be cited as representative of this period. The earliest of these, dating from 1624, by the Spanish Jesuit G. Sanchez, runs to over 700 folio pages. Sanchez's (Latin) verse-by-verse commentary displays his broad familiarity with the biblical material, classical literature, and the exegetical tradition, both Christian and Jewish. Allegorizing is minimal, although moral/theological problems suggested by the text are discussed in detail.

Protestant interpretation for this period includes the treatment of Kings in the 1708 commentary on the historical books by the Dutch scholar J. Le Clerc (Clericus), who gave his own Latin translation of the original text, with accompanying notes that regularly cite the Hebrew in addition to the LXX and Vulgate renditions. Philological rather than theological questions were the primary focus of Le Clerc's attention; occasionally, however, he proposed an emendation of the received Hebrew text. A final early modern author, the French Benedictine A. Calmet, produced a multi-volume commentary on the entire Bible. Calmet's work has the character of a summarizing compendium of all previous scholarship and gives a French translation of the Vulgate, with regular reference to the Hebrew where the Vulgate fails to reproduce it accurately. The fact that Calmet's commentary is written in the vernacular rather than in Latin presages later scholarly practice. Of interest, too, is his citation of ethnographic parallels and reports by contemporary Holy Land travelers in elucidating the biblical material.

4. *Contemporary Period.* The overall exegetical epoch from c. 1800 until the present is designated as the critical period of biblical scholarship. During this period the tendencies of the preceding era have come still more strongly to the fore (e.g., the MT is being subjected to ever more venturesome criticism). At the same time, various more or less novel factors have made themselves felt in contemporary scholarship. Negatively, there has been a marked decline of interest in a theological reading of the text. Positively, archaeological discoveries and the decipherment of hitherto unknown languages are providing exegetes with new resources. Scholars have become intensely conscious of the problems surrounding the historical reliability of the biblical reports. Above all, however, the period is characterized by the attempt to reconstruct the history of the formation of the biblical books.

Accordingly, the following survey will concentrate on various views concerning the literary process whereby the books of Kings attained their present form. More particularly, it will focus on divergent conceptions regarding the number and nature of the overarching redactions that produced a "book of Kings" comparable in content and extent to ours. By way of background to this discussion, it may be noted that there are three points about the composition history of Kings that seem beyond dispute: (1) The book is a composite in which one must distinguish between the level of the sources (see the explicit references to these in 1 Kgs 11:41; 14:19, 29, etc.) and that of the compiler-editor. (2) Kings underwent Deuteronomistic editing, as the recurring linguistic and thematic affinities with Deuteronomy indicate. (3) Given the reference to Jehoiachin's 561 B.C.E. release in 2 Kgs 25:27-30, the book in its present form cannot be older than the middle of the Babylonian exile. These parameters, however, still allow for much scholarly variation regarding the redaction history of Kings, as the following attempt at classification will make clear.

a. *A single exilic Deuteronomistic edition.* The simplest of the views to be examined holds that the book of Kings, in basically its current shape, originated during the exile as the work of a Deuteronomist who compiled pre-existing materials, both annalistic compendia and prophetic narratives, and added to these various reflective comments. Naturally, this view allows for later, minor, occasional additions to the Deuteronomist's work, just as it recognizes that the materials used had already undergone a process of expansion, combination, etc. The exilic

Deuteronomistic redactor remains all-important, however, in that previously there existed no "book of Kings" comparable to ours and subsequently the book received only minimal retouching. Today, this view is identified especially with M. Noth (1943), for whom the exilic Deuteronomistic redactor in Kings was the editor of the whole complex of Deuteronomy–Kings, the Deuteronomistic History (Dtr).

But in fact the Nothian view of the formation of Kings is essentially that of various earlier commentators—e.g., C. Keil (1846), O. Thenius (1849), K. Bähr (1868), H. Klostermann (1887), W. Barnes (1908), and S. Landersdorfer (1927)—even though they did not stress the "Deuteronomistic" character of the exilic redactor to the degree Noth did. Since 1943 this view has had its advocates both among writers on Kings—Noth (1968), J. Montgomery and H. Gehman (1951), A. van den Born (1958), M. Rehm (1979, 1982), T. Hobbs (1985), and J. McConville (1989)—and among authors on the Deuteronomistic history in general—H.-D. Hoffmann (1980) and J. Van Seters (1983). Of these, Hoffmann in particular has provided a detailed restatement of Noth's conception in response to alternative views that have emerged primarily since 1970. In doing so, however, Hoffmann "transfers" to the Deuteronomist large amounts of material that for Noth pertained to the Deuteronomist's sources.

b. *Multiple exilic/postexilic Deuteronomistic editions.* The next distinct group of authors stands the closest to Noth's view. In particular, they agree with him that it was a deuteronomist, working during the exile, who first assembled a book of Kings like ours. At the same time, these scholars believe that the present book evidences such diverse focal points and perspectives that it cannot derive from a single Deuteronomistic editor. Rather, it originated via a process of supplementation in which one or more later Deuteronomists inserted material—whether pre-existing or composed by themselves—into the work of the first Deuteronomistic editor.

Already A. Šanda (1911—12) distinguished between a first Deuteronomistic editor who worked shortly after 587 B.C.E. and a later supplementer from the period 500–400 who interpolated, e.g., 1 Kgs 8:44-51; 2 Kgs 21:7-14; 23:26-27; 25:22-30. In more recent scholarship this conception is associated above all with what might be called the "Göttingen school" of R. Smend, Jr. (1971). Smend and his students distinguish three exilic Deuteronomistic redactors (in Kings and in Dtr in general), each having a distinctive interest, i.e., DtrH (the Deuteronomistic Historian), DtrP (the Prophetic Deuteronomist who inserted various pre-existing prophetic stories into Kings), and DtrN (the Nomistic Deuteronomist).

Three major commentators opt for this model in elucidating the redaction history of Kings: E. Würthwein (1977, 1984), G. Jones (1984), and G. Hentschel (1984, 1985). Würthwein and Hentschel further reckon with a large body of "late Deuteronomistic" material, while the former likewise emphasizes that both DtrP and DtrN have to be seen as ciphers covering the activities of several related but distinct hands. With Würthwein, Noth's single exilic Deuteronomistic editor becomes a whole series of exilic/postexilic Deuteronomists.

c. *A preexilic Deuteronomistic redactor.* The next group of scholars agree with Noth that the first, major, encompassing redactional activity that gave us a book of Kings was Deuteronomistic. They diverge from him (as well as from the authors cited in sec. b above) on the question of whether that activity started only during the exile (with Noth they admit a Deuteronomistic exilic redaction). Against such a supposition, they point to various Deuteronomistically formulated passages (see e.g., 1 Kgs 8:8, 14-44; 11:39; 15:4-5; 2 Kgs 8:18-19) that seem to presuppose the continued existence of the Temple and the Davidic dynasty. The resultant theory of an initial, preexilic Deuteronomistic edition has a long history and comes in several variants. Among its earlier advocates there is some discrepancy as to how early or late in the preexilic era it is to be dated. I. Benzinger (1899) ascribed it in general terms to the period 621-597. Other commentators placed it more specifically in the reign of Josiah: R. Kittel (1900), O. Eissfeldt (1922), N. Snaith (1954), J. Robinson (1972, 1976). Still others assigned the preexilic Deuteronomist to late in Jehoiakim's reign: C. Burney (1903), A. Kamphausen (1909), and J. Gray (1964).

However, the notion of a preexilic Deuteronomistic redaction of Kings has become closely associated with the wider thesis advocated by the American scholars F. M. Cross (1973) and R. Nelson (1981) that a first edition of Dtr as a whole was produced under Josiah to support his political and religious initiatives. Contemporary Kings commentaries reflecting the influence of the Cross-Nelson thesis include those of S. De Vries (1985) and M. Cogan and H. Tadmor (1988). The thesis is likewise adopted in the monographs of A. Mayes (1983), I. Provan (1988), M. O'Brien (1989), and S. McKenzie (1991). It must be noted, however, that Provan, unlike the other authors mentioned, holds that, while written in Josiah's time, the initial Deuteronomistic redaction did not go beyond 2 Kings 18–20 and that the whole of 2 Kings 21–25 derived from the exilic Deuteronomist. O'Brien, who finds the conclusion of the Josianic Deuteronomist in 2 Kgs 23:25, approximates the view of the Göttingen school in his identification of a whole series of exilic/postexilic Deuteronomistic redactions, the most significant of which is the third, "nomistic" one. For McKenzie, the Josianic book of Kings underwent a variety of disparate amplifications at different times.

d. *Pre-Deuteronomistic editions.* There remains a group of scholars who diverge still more markedly from Noth in that they posit a pre-Deuteronomistic "book of Kings" that was subsequently expanded by one or more Deuteronomistic editors. This communality aside, however, these scholars go their own ways in their more specific conceptions of the pre-Deuteronomistic editorial process. A first, older group held that there existed a "Yahwistic" book of Kings (and of Genesis–Kings as a whole) in which were combined the concluding segments of the earlier sources that begin in Genesis. This theory came to the fore in the early 1920s in Germany. Its advocates disagreed, however, regarding how many sources the Yahwistic book of Kings combined as well as where in Kings the termination points of these sources occur (and hence also the *terminus a quo* for their datings).

Benzinger (1921) and G. Hölscher (1923, 1952) affirmed that the pre-Deuteronomistic book of Kings represented a combination of two sources: J and E. For Benzinger, J's strand continues down to Hezekiah, while E's extends to Josiah's reform. But according to Hölscher, J reaches no further than the breakup of the united monarchy, whereas E has its conclusion in 2 Kgs 25:30 and so is to be dated to the exile. R. Smend, Sr. (1921) and Eissfeldt (1934) both thought in terms, rather, of three sources they designated respectively as J, J^2, and E; and L (the "lay source"), J, and E as the component strands in the pre-Deuteronomistic historical book that encompassed Genesis–Kings. In Smend's analysis J^1's final extant occurrence is in 2 Kgs 4:8-37, J^2's in 2 Kings 9–10, and E's in 2 Kgs 6:8-23. Eissfeldt, by contrast, contented himself with arguing that the pre-Deuteronomistic sources likely extended into Kings, without making any detailed attempt to partition the book's material among them. Despite its earlier popularity, the theory of Eissfeldt et al. apparently lacks any contemporary advocate.

In its more recent formulations, the theory of a pre-Deuteronomistic edition of Kings conceives a redactional stage that might be called "proto-Deuteronomistic." According to A. Jepsen (1953, 1956) the Deuteronomistic ("Nebiistic") redaction of Kings (c. 560) was preceded by a priestly one (c. 580). This priestly redaction, in turn, incorporated and combined two preexisting works, a "synchronistic chronicle" (from Hezekiah's time) and the "Annals of the Kings of Judah and Israel" (from the reign of Manasseh). The priestly redactor anticipated later Deuteronomistic concerns in, for example, his preoccupation with the problem of worship on the high places. In his edition of the commentary of J. Fichtner, K. Fricke (1964, 1972) adopts Jepsen's conception.

Other authors locate the initial Deuteronomistic redaction, with its stress on the problem of the high places, in the reign of Hezekiah (H. Weippert [1985], A. Lemaire [1986], and E. Exnikel

[1996]). Of these authors, Lemaire identifies a series of further textual blocks put together by still earlier editors in the material of 1 Kings, e.g., a history of the early divided monarchy assembled around 850 with a view to generating support for the political and religious endeavors of Jehoshaphat.

From the above it is apparent that contemporary scholarship is far from having reached unanimity regarding the redaction history of the book of Kings. It is understandable, then, that in a major commentary on the book covering 1 Kings 1–7 (M. Mulder [1987]), the question of how many Deuteronomistic redactions can be distinguished is left provisionally open. It is equally comprehensible that such recent works on Kings as those of Nelson (1987, 1988), Provan (1995), and J. Walsh (1996) opt for a synchronic approach in which the focus of attention is the book in its extant form.

Bibliography: P. S. Ash, *David, Solomon, and Egypt: A Reassessment* (JSOTSup 297, 1999). **K. C. Bähr,** *The Books of the Kings* (1868; ET, Commentary on the Holy Scriptures OT 6, 1986). **W. E. Barnes,** *The First Book of Kings* (CBSC, 1908). **I. Benzinger,** *Die Bücher der Könige* (KHC 9, 1899), *Jahvist und Elohist in den Königsbücher* (BWANT NF 2, 1921). **A. van den Born,** *Köningen* (BOT, 1958). **T. L. Brodie.** *The Crucial Bridge: The Elijah–Elisha Narrative as an Interpretive Synthesis of Genesis–Kings and a Literary Model for the Gospels* (2000). **P. Buis,** "Rois (Livre des)," *DBSup 10* (1985) 695-740. **C. F. Burney,** *Notes on the Hebrew Text of the Books of Kings* (1903). **C. Camp,** *The Women's Bible Commentary* (1992) 96-109. **J. Cazeaux,** *Saül, David, Salomon: Le Royauté et le destin d'Israël* (2003). **M. Cogan** and **H. Tadmor,** *II Kings: A New Translation* (AB 11, 1988). **R. Coote,** *Elijah and Elisha in Socio-literary Perspective* (SemeiaSt, 1992). **F. M. Cross,** *Canaanite Myth and Hebrew Epic: Essays in the History of the Religion of Israel* (1973). **S. De Vries,** *1 Kings* (WBC 12, 1985). **O. Eissfeldt,** *Die Bücher der Könige* (HSAT 1, 1922); *The OT: An Introduction Including the Apocrypha and Pseudepigrapha and also the Works of Similar Type from Qumran. The History of the Formation of the OT* (1934; ET 1965). **E. Exnikel,** *The Reform of King Josiah and the Composition of the Deuteronomistic History* (OTS 33, 1996). **J. Fichtner** and **K. D. Fricke,** *Das erste Buch von den Königen* (BAT 12:1, 1964); *Das zweite Buch von den Königen* (BAT 12:2, 1972). **J. Gray,** *I and II Kings: A Commentary* (OTL, 1964). **G. Hentschel,** *1 Könige* (NEB 10, 1984); *2 Könige* (NEB 11, 1985). **T. R. Hobbs,** *2 Kings* (WBC 13, 1985). **G. Hölscher,** "Das Buch der Könige, seine Quellen und seine Redaktion," *Eucharisterion: Studien zur Religion und Literatur des Alten und Neuen Testaments* (FS H. Gunkel, ed. H. Schmidt, FRLANT NF 19, 1923) 1:159-213; *Geschichtsschreibung in Israel: Untersuchungen zum Jahvisten und Elohisten* (1952). **H. D. Hoffmann,** *Reform und Reformen* (ATANT 66, 1980). **A. Jepsen,** *Die Quellen des Königbuches* (1953, 1956). **G. H. Jones,** *1 and 2 Kings: Based on the RSV* (2 vols., NCBC, 1984). **A. Kamphausen,** *Die Bücher der Könige* (HSAT 1, 1909). **C. F. Keil,** *Commentar über die Bücher der Könige* (1846). **J. Keinänen,** *Traditions in Collision: A Literary and Redaction-Critical Study on the Elijah Narratives 1 Kings 17–19* (2001). **R. Kittel,** *Die Bücher der Könige* (HKAT 1:5, 1900). **H. A. Klostermann,** *Die Bücher Samuelis und der Könige* (KK A:3, 1887). **S. Landersdorfer,** *Die Bücher der Könige* (HS 3:2, 1927). **A. Lemaire,** "Vers l'histoire de la rédaction des livres des rois," *ZAW 98* (1986) 221-36. **B. O. Long,** *2 Kings* (FOTL 10, 1991). **J. G. McConville,** "Narrative and Meaning in the Book of Kings," *Bib 70* (1989) 31-49. **S. L. McKenzie,** *The Trouble with Kings: The Composition of the Book of Kings in the Deuteronomistic History* (VTSup. 42, 1991). **A. D. H. Mayes,** *The Story of Israel Between Settlement and Exile: A Redactional Study of the Deuteronomistic History* (1983). **J. A. Montgomery** and **H. S. Gehman,** *A Critical and Exegetical Commentary on the Book of Kings* (ICC, 1951). **M. J. Mulder,** *Koningen 1* (COT, 1987). **R. D. Nelson,** *The Double Redaction of the Deuteronomistic History* (JSOTSup 18, 1981); *First and Second Kings*

(Interpretation, 1987); "The Anatomy of the Book of Kings," JSOT 40 (1988) 39-48. **M. Noth**, *Überlieferungsgeschichtliche Studien (1943; ET, The Deuteronomistic History* [JSOTSup 15, 1981]); *Könige* (BKAT 9:1, 1968). **M. A. O'Brien**, *The Deuteronomistic History Hypothesis: A Reassessment* (OBO 92, 1989). **R. F. Person**, *The Kings–Isaiah and Kings–Jeremiah Recensions* (BZAW 252, 1997). **I. W. Provan**, *Hezekiah and the Books of Kings: A Contribution to the Debate About the Composition of the Deuteronomistic History* (BZAW 172, 1988); *1 and 2 Kings* (NICOT, 1995). **M. Rehm**, *Das erste Buch der Könige: Ein Kommentar* (1979); *Das zweite Buch der Könige: Ein Kommentar* (1982). **G. Rice**, *Nations Under God: A Commentary on the Book of 1 Kings* (ITC, 1990). **J. Robinson**, *The First Book of Kings* (CBC, 1972); *The Second Book of Kings* (CBC, 1976). **A. Sanda**, *Die Bücher der Könige* (EHAT 9:1-2, 1911-12). **R. Smend, Sr.**, "JE in den geschichtlichen Büchern des Alten Testaments," *ZAW* 39 (1921) 181-217. **R. Smend, Jr.**, "Das Gesetz und die Völker: Ein Beitrag zur deuterono-mistischen Redaktionsgeschichte," *Probleme biblischer Theologie* (FS G. von Rad, ed. H. W. Wolff, 1971) 494-509. **N. H. Snaith**, "The First and Second Books of Kings: Introduction and Exegesis," *IB* (1954) 3:1-18. **O. Thenius**, *Die Bücher der Könige* (KEH 9, 1849). **J. D. Thompson**, *A Critical Concordance to the Septuagint: Kings III* (The Computer Bible 63, 1999); *A Critical Concordance to the Septuagint: Kings IV* (The Computer Bible 64, 1999). **J. Van Seters**, *In Search of History: Historiography in the Ancient World and the Origins of Biblical History* (1983). **D. Volgger**, *Verbindliche Tora am einzigen Tempel: zu Motiv und Ort der Komposition von 1.2 Kön (Arbeiten zu Text und Sprache im Alten Testament 61, 1998).* **J. T. Walsh**, *1 Kings* (Berit Olam, 1996). **H. Weippert**, "Das deuteronomistische Geschichtswerk," *TRu* 50 (1985) 213-49. **M. C. White**, *The Elijah Legends and Jehu's Coup* (BJS 311, 1997). **D. J. Wiseman**, *1 and 2 Kings* (TOTC 9, 1993). **E. Würthwein**, *1 Könige 1–16* (ATD 11:1, 1977); *1 Könige 17–2 Könige 25* (ATD 11:2, 1984).

C. T. BEGG

THE WRITINGS

1 and 2 Chronicles

The feature of Chronicles that has most determined the course of its study is that in certain ways it is a "doublet"—a description of the history of Israel that has already been told, mainly in the books of Samuel–Kings. Although repetition does occur elsewhere in the Bible, it is never as extensive as here; and it is with this idiosyncrasy that the interpretation of the book has had to struggle from its very beginning.

The earliest attempt to address the problem is to be found in the book's title in the Septuagint: *Paraleipomenon*—"[the book of the things] that remained." The assumption is that the information contained in Chronicles relates to matters omitted from the other historical books for unspecified reasons; presumably this information was to be considered as valid as that provided in the parallels and based on the same or similar sources. This view of Chronicles, while affirming its authority, presents it essentially as a supplement to the other historical books and thereby plays down its significance. Whether consciously or not, this attitude greatly influenced the understanding of the literary nature of Chronicles and established its secondary position in the annals of scholarly activity. The echoes of this approach are heard in the nineteenth century, from J. G. Eichhorn (1780–83) onward (see D. Mathias [1977]), in various learned attempts to define the books' goals and indicate the sources.

1. *Early Jewish Interpretation.* In early Jewish exegesis Chronicles occupied a marginal position (E. Ben Zvi [1988]). Although its Aramaic Targum is attributed to "Rav Yoseph," a sage of the third century, it did not receive its final form before the eighth century (R. Le Déaut and J. Robert [1971] 24-25). No midrashic composition was ever written for Chronicles; the compilation of homiletic interpretations, mostly of the genealogical material, found in *Yalqut Shimoni* (secs. 1072-85), illustrate how little interest the book evoked. The attitude of the sages was that "the book of Chronicles was given for study only" (*Lev. Rab.* 1:3)—that is, not to be "read" (T. Willi [1972] 16). From the outset the book, and especially its genealogies, was reserved for the setting of the learned (*b. Pesaḥ* 62b) and not for liturgical or popular use.

Only a few medieval Jewish commentaries are known. A short commentary by an anonymous pupil of Saadia Gaon dates from the tenth century, and a more comprehensive commentary, from the literal school of northern French exegesis, probably written in Narbonne around the middle of the twelfth century, was published in the rabbinic Bible under the name of Rashi. The latter, while showing some midrashic inclination, contains many insightful remarks regarding the chronicler's goals and literary methods. The commentary by D. Kimhi (Redak, 1160-1235) was probably his first exegetical work, which he claims to have written because "a scholar from Gerona, a pupil of my lord father, asked me to interpret the book." In his prologue, Kimhi explains the need for such a commentary: "I have not seen that any of the exegetes has endeavored to interpret it, but here in Narbonne I have found a number of commentaries on this book; the names of their authors are unknown to me."

Also noteworthy of mention are a midrashic commentary by R. Samuel ben Nissim Masnut (thirteenth cent.) and the commentary of Gersonides (R. Levi ben Gershon, 1288-1344), published in some of the editions of the rabbinic Bible. An unpublished commentary by R. Benjamin of Rome (1295-1335) exists in several manuscripts. There are a few late medieval and Renaissance commentaries, among them the "Mezudoth": "Mezudath David" and "Mezudath Zion." This commentary, written in the seventeenth century by D. and Y. Altschuler, although in fact but an epigone of Kimhi, is published in all editions of the rabbinic Bible. From more modern times one should mention the commentary of "HaGRA"—an acronym for Hagaon Eliahu from Vilna (1720-97)—found in the appendix of several editions of the rabbinic Bible.

2. *Early Christian Interpretation*. Chronicles hardly fared better in the Christian scholarly milieu. Although highly recommended by Jerome, who stated that anyone claiming to know Scripture without having a knowledge of Chronicles ridicules himself (*Epist.* 53.8; PL 22:548; A. Saltman [1978] 11), the book in fact received little attention. Of the church fathers only Theodoret of Cyrrhus (5th cent.) devoted to it a worthwhile commentary (see the critical edition by N. Marcos and J. Busto Saiz [1984]), although later Western medieval circles took more note. The "general Christian consensus" (Saltman, 17) is represented by three influential works: Pseudo-Jerome's *Questiones Hebraicae in Paralipomenon* (the authenticity of which was already denied by Nicholas of Lyra, but which was brought to the attention of a wider public by J. Martianay in the late seventeenth cent.) and the more original work of Rabanus Maurus were both written in the ninth century (Maurus around 830; Pseudo-Jerome, who is sometimes identified as a converted Jew, somewhat earlier), and both works were incorporated into the twelfth century *Glossa Ordinaria*.

Also noteworthy is the somewhat later commentary of S. Langton, archbishop of Canterbury, written around 1200 and recently published by Saltman (1978). Two works of his older contemporaries, R. Niger and Peter the Chanter, are still unpublished (Saltman, 15, 22). From the thirteenth and fourteenth centuries are the *Postillae* of Hugh of St. Cher (d. 1264), whose commentary on Chronicles is, according to Saltman, "an abridgement of Langton's" but nevertheless "shows some technical advance" (45-46). A more original and influential commentary was that of Nicholas of Lyra (1270-1349), best known for its heavy reliance on Jewish sources, especially Rashi; Nicholas's work was published in 1471-72. For subsequent developments until the dawn of modern criticism see the references in E. Curtis (1910, 49-50) and J. Goettsberger (1974, 22-23).

3. *Nineteenth-century Interpretation*. The first comprehensive treatment of Chronicles in modern biblical scholarship was W. De Wette's "Historical-critical study of the book of Chronicles" published in 1806 as the first part of his *Beiträge zur Einleitung in das Alte Testament*. De Wette's study and the questions he posed determined the course of research for a long time, and their influence is felt forcefully even today. The central question he raised concerned the historical reliability of Chronicles. Although the issue of historical reliability is of relevance to any historical source and in time has indeed been applied to the entire biblical evidence, it was first and most vigorously broached regarding Chronicles, the "doublet" of earlier historiography. In principle, although not explicitly, de Wette followed B. Spinoza in assigning to Chronicles little or no value (Spinoza [1670] 146, in the Elwes translation). Behind de Wette's treatise lay, not an interest in Chronicles, but rather the opposite: a wish to deny as forcibly as possible the book's reliability.

The subject with which de Wette was concerned was the composition of the Pentateuch: Was it composed by Moses, as claimed by tradition, or by a later, anonymous author? De Wette's standard method was the juxtaposition of literary and historical facts according to the following logic: If indeed composed by Moses, the Pentateuch would have made some impression on historical reality, and its impact would be discerned in the descriptions of the period following the conquest of Canaan. Such traces, however, are almost completely absent from Joshua–Kings; on the other hand, they are abundantly manifest in Chronicles. Accepting the historicity of Chronicles would mean, then, that the Pentateuch was indeed composed by Moses. De Wette directed his efforts toward disproving the chronicler's evidence by systematically comparing it with Samuel–Kings. His results can be subsumed under two categories: the chronicler's lack of literary qualification, his work being characterized by "imprecision," "negligence," and "compilatory manner," and his ideological motives ("tendencies"), which made history ancillary to certain political and religious goals. Among these de Wette mentioned "Levitism," the significance of the cult, love for Judah and hatred of Israel, and a fondness for miracles. De Wette's conclusions are stated categorically: Chronicles is worthless as historiography.

De Wette's forceful and unequivocal statement gave rise to an energetic discussion regarding the value and reliability of Chronicles. The scholarly world of the day divided into two camps over the issue: the critical school, which followed de Wette and went at times to even further extremes (C. Gramberg [1823]); and the conservative school, which endeavored to defend the book as a reliable witness for the early history of Israel (represented most strongly by C. Keil [1833]). This debate reached its climax in the work of J. Wellhausen (1878); in the meantime its effects were clearly seen in the vascillating use of Chronicles as a supplementary source in "histories of Israel" and works on related subjects throughout the nineteenth century (see M. P. Graham [1990]).

The discussion of historical reliability was closely accompanied by the problem of sources. Although essentially an independent aspect of the historical-critical inquiry, this subject had been consistently discussed in the context of reliability (see, at great length, D. Mathias [1977]). In its most neutral form the question was, How much of Chronicles was composed by its author, and to what degree did he employ earlier sources? What kind of sources did he use, and in what way? And more specifically, what is the relationship between the chronicler's actual source material and the allusions to sources that one finds abundantly in his presentation?

This subject, however, when applied to the question of reliability, took an apologetic turn; for even if one grants that the chronicler himself was a late, careless, and tendentious author, one may, by regarding the bulk of his material as derived from ancient, authoritative sources, still preserve in the final analysis the book's value and authority. The eager discussion of sources thus became one more facet of the more burning issue of reliability. From the outset the general evaluation of the chronicler's use of sources was positive: He followed substantially the course of events as outlined in Samuel–Kings, of which his presentation is quite often an almost literal repetition. Regarding this common material, it has often been asked if the chronicler used Samuel–Kings in their present canonical form or whether he had at his disposal an earlier or later recension.

While J. Eichhorn and his followers assumed a common source for both Samuel–Kings and Chronicles (*Einleitung*, [1787] 2:450-550; this view was restated by Hänel-Rothstein in 1927 and recently reintroduced by B. Halpern [1981]), de Wette and his school insisted on the canonical form of Samuel–Kings as the chronicler's source for the common material. This latter attitude, more than the former, raised a further question regarding the non-parallel material: Did the chronicler rely on earlier sources, or is this additional material his own free composition?

While the most extreme views in this respect were expressed (e.g., C. Gramberg; C. C. Torrey [1896]), the reliance on some kind of source for the non-parallel material—in particular for the genealogical preface—was generally accepted; the conclusions drawn were, however, by no means unequivocal. Attention was then focused on further aspects of the problem: How many sources were used? Of what nature and origin? How reliable were they? The phenomenon of the chronicler's allusions to sources was brought heavily into play: Were his authorities indeed prophetical writings as he claims? Do the general titles he cites refer to the canonical books of Samuel–Kings or to any other book or books of similar nature and origin?

In the course of the nineteenth-century debate on this issue, every conceivable answer was brought forward, from the claim that the citation of sources was fully and completely reliable, the chronicler having indeed made use of the books—prophetic or historical—that he mentioned, to the equally extreme conclusion that he used at most one rather dubious source, "the Midrash of the book of Kings" (2 Chr 24:27), as unreliable as Chronicles itself, and that allusions to sources were merely a literary device devised to promote the chronicler's authority.

The critical study of Chronicles was occupied to a lesser degree with the question of authorship. The traditional view expressed by the statement that "Ezra wrote his book and the genealogy of Chronicles up to him," and the Talmudic note that the book was completed by Nehemiah the son of Hachaliah (*b. B. Bat.* 15a), is itself ambiguous. Pseudo-Rashi presents this view in his prologue as "Ezra wrote this genealogical book with the sanction of Haggai, Zechariah and Malachi" (Saltman, 51), ignoring the identification of Ezra with Malachi (*b. Meg.* 15a; *Tg. Jonathan* Malachi 1:1). Kimhi, by contrast, identified the book as "the Chronicles of the kings of Judah" mentioned in the book of Kings and attributed to Ezra only its later inclusion in the canon (Kimhi, prologue).

Among Christian exegetes Ezra figures as either the author of Chronicles (John of Salisbury [c. 1115–80]; R. Niger) or its editor, the author himself being anonymous (Langton and others; see Saltman, 23). Spinoza relegated the book to the period of the Maccabees (146). The more conservative views of the eighteenth and nineteenth centuries preserve the attribution of Chronicles to Ezra without making too strong a connection between the two books and, in particular, without allowing the discussion of Chronicles to have any great influence on the study of Ezra–Nehemiah.

A significant turning point came with the 1832 work of L. Zunz, who came to the study of Chronicles from an altogether different angle. His interest lay with post-biblical Jewish literature, and his book *Die Gottesdienstlichen Vorträge der Juden* portrays the history of Jewish midrashic literature down to the fourteenth century. Following his basic assumption of continuity in Jewish spiritual creativity, Zunz sought the beginnings of Midrash in the Bible itself and found them in Chronicles. Here again his study was facilitated by the nature of the book as "repetition," which enabled him to uncover the midrashic elements of chronistic exegesis.

According to Zunz, Ezra is referred to in the third person in the book that bears his name and so, contrary to the traditional view, could not have been its author. However, Zunz had no objection to the opinion, likewise traditional, that one and the same author wrote both Ezra–Nehemiah and Chronicles. He further emphasized the similarity between these books by pointing to their linguistic affinities, common stylistic features, methods of composition, and certain characteristic views, all of which proved, according to him, the thesis of common authorship. On the basis of these assumptions Zunz's conclusion was almost self-evident: It was not Ezra who wrote both books but "the chronicler," a later writer whose literary idiosyncrasies were most evident in the book of Chronicles. This view (reached independently also by F. Movers [1834]) was eventually adopted almost unanimously and had far-reaching consequences, not so much for Chronicles as for the books of Ezra–Nehemiah (S. Japhet [1985] 88-92).

The way taken by nineteenth-century research arrives via K. Graf (1866) at Wellhausen. Graf's point of departure for the study of Chronicles and his conclusions regarding the general reliability of the book resemble those of de Wette, but since he dealt with the details his approach was more cautious and less dogmatic. Wellhausen was therefore correct in presenting himself as a follower of de Wette, although his actual work is influenced in equal measure by that of Graf.

For Wellhausen, as for de Wette, the discussion's point of departure lay, not in an interest in Chronicles itself, but in the problem of historical reliability in relationship to the composition of the Pentateuch. The central question for Wellhausen was, not this composition as a whole, but the formation of the priestly document; employing de Wette's method, he sought the traces of priestly material in the historical narrative and concluded that these are absent from the former prophets, while they are abundantly manifest in Chronicles. Consequently, he went on to disprove the authenticity of the chronicler's history, pronouncing it a tendentious "Judaizing of the past," a result of priestly theology and interests, including the idealization of David and Solomon in the spirit of the time; the centrality of the cult and its personnel; the concept of "the twelve tribes" as "all Israel"; and the "historical pragmatism" expressed by a developed doctrine of retribution. Although Wellhausen did not categorically deny the chronicler's use of additional materials, he considered the discussion of this matter greatly overworked and limited these sources to one major work, "the Midrash of the book of Kings," of the same historical and spiritual provenance as Chronicles. In all, Wellhausen showed scant interest in questions pertaining to the book and mentions its relationship to Ezra–Nehemiah only in passing.

4. *Twentieth-century Interpretation*. The development of research in the twentieth century follows two major lines. One is the continuation of former research, as befits a living scholarly tradition. This is evident not so much in the answers reached as in the handling of the same questions: historical reliability, sources, and authorship; and in the use of the same terminology: priestly history, historical pragmatism, Levitism, Tendenz, and so on. The other approach is innovative, i.e., the study of Chronicles in the light of interests that are entirely or relatively new. These in turn have their impact on the way in which the already established questions are addressed.

The question of historical reliability was inherited by scholars whose main interest was neither in literary problems nor in the history of religious institutions but in the reconstruction of the early history of Israel; to this end these scholars endeavored to enlist as many sources as possible. Although in principle there seemed to be a consensus regarding the tendentious nature of Chronicles, increasingly an attempt was made to salvage from this category as much information as possible and to ascribe an ever greater measure of historical reliability to the book. Here several factors come into play: On the one hand is the unwavering recognition that the intentions and motives of the chronicler make every additional detail the object of suspicion from the outset. On the other hand, the broadening of historical horizons; the accumulation of archaeological evidence – material as well as epigraphic – from throughout the ancient Near East; the reluctance to ascribe historical material to the "creative imagination" of an author or to his supposed sources; and the better understanding of the chronicler's literary method all imply that there must be some nucleus of fact within the guise of even the most tendentious descriptions.

The beginning of a conscious change of attitudes within the critical school is to be seen in Winckler (1892), followed by W. F. Albright (1921, 1955) and his pupils, especially J. Bright. The rehabilitation of Chronicles and the almost unhesitating reference to it as a historical source reach a zenith in the work of some Israeli scholars, initiated by B. Mazar and followed by Y. Aharoni, H. Reviv (1989), and others. A more moderate approach to the same issue is shown also by such European scholars as K. Galling and W. Rudolph. Between the two extremes— complete denial and full acceptance—all possible variations have found expression. In more recent times, however, an increasing reaction questioning the reliability of Chronicles is gradually setting in. The works of P. Welten (1979), C. North (1974), and R. Klein (see Japhet [1985] 98-99) remind us that the issue has not reached its final resolution.

Regarding the questions of authorship and date, several new contributions have been made. The most prevalent views for the date of the chronicler have ranged between the late Persian period (early 4th cent. B.C.E.) and the early Hellenistic (3rd cent. B.C.E.), depending on the scholar's convictions concerning the supposed historical and theological background of the chronicler's work, the evidence of the genealogical and cultic material, the book's relationship to Ezra–Nehemiah, specific details of chronological consequence, and the scholar's general view of the development of biblical literature. In this category the "earliest" position is that of Albright (1921), who regarded Ezra as the author of Chronicles.

An altogether different approach, resembling in a way (probably unconsciously) the early Jewish views, has been the dating of Chronicles as far back as the restoration period in the second half of the sixth century B.C.E. For example, according to A. Welch (1939), who regards Chronicles as having undergone a thorough priestly editing, "the annotator belonged to the generation which followed the Return from Exile" (155), while the original author "belonged to the community which had never been in Exile" (157). The original composition of the book thus is actually contemporary with Ezekiel's vision of the future and the Deuteronimistic historiography.

A different reasoning is followed by those who seek the actual historical circumstances that served as the political background in the chronicler's assumed eschatological aspirations. These are found in the hopes attached to the figure of Zerubbabel during the early period of the restoration (D. N. Freedman [1961]; F. M. Cross [1975]; J. Newsome [1975]). As the book contains sections that are certainly later (the genealogy of Jehoiachin, 1 Chr 3:17-24; the list of priestly divisions, 1 Chronicles 24, and so on), the inevitable literary corollary would be a conception of the book's composition either as abounding in editorial or secondary material (Welch) or as resulting from complex literary evolution (Cross, see below).

One aspect of the problem of authorship is the chronicler's relationship to Ezra–Nehemiah. This problem, which seemed to have been completely settled at the beginning of the twentieth century, has been reopened for discussion (Japhet [1968]). This reevaluation has been motivated mainly by two factors: a greater awareness of the linguistic-stylistic developments of late biblical Hebrew, in particular as a result of the discovery of the Qumran scrolls and the study of the Samaritan Pentateuch and rabbinic Hebrew; and second, a growing appreciation of the theological views and literary method of Chronicles and Ezra–Nehemiah, factors that highlight the respective peculiarities and unique character of each composition. Although the traditional view of common authorship has not been abandoned (see among others R. Polzin [1976] and the commentaries of D. Clines [1984] and A. Gunneweg [1985; 1987] on Ezra–Nehemiah), it seems that more and more scholars distinguish between Chronicles and Ezra–Nehemiah, either as separate works by one author (Willi, 180; Welten, 4) or, more often, as compositions completely independent of each other in authorship and provenance. While the similarities between the two have been explained as owing to the general background of the Persian period, their peculiar features—linguistic, historical, and theological—have been emphasized anew (M. Segal [1942/43]; Japhet [1968]; H. Williamson [1977]; R. Braun [1979, 1986]; T. Eskenazi [1986, 1988]; etc.).

The most important aspect of the study of Chronicles in the twentieth century, however, is a change in the general approach to the book. No longer merely a "supplement" to earlier historiography, an "ancillary source" for the reconstruction of the history of Israel, or a corollary of the critical study of the Pentateuch, Chronicles has been studied for its own sake as an integral part of biblical literature in which it claims a position in its own right. The catalyst for this change was probably an increasing interest in biblical theology, in the framework of which the theology of Chronicles was studied, not as an instrument to prove the book's *Tendenz*, but on its own theological merits and for its special position within the religion of Israel. While it is difficult to assess the influence of J. Swart (1911), this new direction is indicated in Hänel's introduction to his commentary (1927) and receives decisive expression in G. von Rad's 1930 monograph.

Von Rad's attitude toward Chronicles should be understood in the framework of his general approach to biblical theology. Regarding as his task the demonstration of the HB's relevance for present-day Christianity, he undertook to explain the relationship between the HB and the NT in terms of internal development and put great emphasis on demonstrating the continuity of the theological process. The novelty of his position may be understood by comparing it to that of Wellhausen, for whom, from the vantage point of Christianity, the book of Chronicles might as well not have been included in Scripture and was a product of "Judaizing of the past" rather than of authentic Israelite spirit. For von Rad, by contrast, no book of the HB is without value for Christianity. Moreover, the "chronistic work" (Chronicles + Ezra–Nehemiah) occupies a very special position within biblical literature, reaching to the end of the HB period. To exclude its theological testimony would be paramount to severing the line of continuity at a crucial point.

Von Rad made an impressive attempt to portray the theology of the Chronicler as an integral part of biblical theology, emphasizing the influence of Deuteronomic rather than priestly predecessors, focusing his theology in the figure of David, and summing up the book as "the Law of David," an intermediate stage between the "Law of Moses" and "the Law of Jesus" (1930,

136). Von Rad's monograph pointed the way to an intensive preoccupation with the chronicler's theology—with special attention given to the problem of eschatology—and formed a point of departure for all subsequent theological studies of the book.

Individual theological facets as well as comprehensive themes have been intensively studied (A. Noordtzij [1940]; J. Botterweck [1956]; A. Brunet [1959]; Freedman; W. Stinespring [1961]; North [1963]; P. Ackroyd [1967, 1973]; R. Braun [1971, 1973]; R. Mosis [1973]; J. Newsome [1975]; Japhet [1977, 1978]; Williamson [1977]; and so on). Even studies oriented in the direction of other interests found the need to take into consideration the unfolding of the book's religious thought.

Another line of development was introduced with the inception and flourishing of form criticism, the fruits of which for the study of Chronicles may be seen in three major directions: (a) The least energetically pursued has been the search for new genres within the literature of Chronicles. The most influential attempt was made by von Rad, who classified the specific addresses of Chronicles as "Levitical sermons" ("Levitische Predigt," 1934). Although this concept and its assumed *Sitz im Leben* have prompted justifiable criticism (Mathias [1984]; R. Mason [1984]), von Rad's statements nevertheless drew attention to the formal peculiarity of the chronistic speeches—in addition to their significance as expressions of the chronicler's theology (O. Plöger [1957]). Another genre, not restricted to Chronicles, but abundantly evidenced there, was identified as the "installation genre" (D. McCarthy [1971]).

(b) A more significant contribution has been made by the study of Chronicles in the framework of tradition history, forcefully presented by M. Noth (1943; ET 1987). Noth attempted to unfold the historical development of biblical traditions in their entirety and dealt respectively with the Pentateuch (1948) and the Deuteronomistic and the Chronistic compositions, thus putting Chronicles on an equal footing with earlier historiography. Noth's methodological presupposition led him to regard even the literary format of biblical compositions as evidence of a "tradition-history" process; he analyzed in the historical works three literary stages: sources, the authentic work of the author (Deuteronomistic or Chronistic), and later accretions. Conceiving of the historical compositions as strongly bound to actual political situations, Noth connected them to particular political impulses—in the case of Chronicles, to the polemic against the Samaritans. The concept of a "chronistic work" encompassing also Ezra–Nehemiah is of primary importance as the anti-Samaritan attitude attested in Ezra–Nehemiah is at most only implied in Chronicles (see Willi, 190-94; Japhet [1977] 278-85; Braun [1977]), although often read into the text.

For the understanding of the literary composition of Chronicles, Noth's influence cannot be overestimated. His literary analysis, which resulted in the labeling of many sections in Chronicles (and Ezra–Nehemiah) as "post-chronistic," seemed to present a useful solution to one of the most problematic features of Chronicles—its heterogeneity. Noth's scheme was immediately adopted by several influential scholars, and its effects are seen not only in the studies that explicitly follow his lead (the commentaries of W. Rudolph [1955] and J. Myers [1965]; the monographs of Willi and Mosis and others) but also elsewhere. Galling's hypothesis of two chroniclers and the reconstruction of the chronicler's work in three stages by F. M. Cross probably owe their motivating force to Noth's work.

(c) Another effect of form criticism may be observed in the increased awareness of the overall nature of the book. The Hebrew name for Chronicles—*Dibrê-hayyāmîmas*—as well as the Latin title, clearly reflect an understanding of the book as "history" and its author as a "historiographer" (see Langton on 2 Chr 10:2; Kimhi, prologue). For a long time this view was hardly questioned. Of the nineteenth-century scholars only Zunz deviated from this general consensus and related the book to the midrashic activity of the people of the Great Assembly. Without clear literary definitions it was linked to Midrash by W. Barnes (1896). The question of the book's literary form was consciously resumed in the research of the twentieth century and is evident in a wide range of studies. Willi conceives of Chronicles as an *Auslegung*, an exegesis of written Scriptures characterized by midrashic features (53-66). In his general approach he follows Zunz's presuppositions, but his study—greatly influenced by Movers—is much more detailed, accounting for all the minute differences between Chronicles and earlier material. Taking another tack, Goulder proffers the idea that the Chronistic work as a whole was composed for liturgical purposes as a series of sermons, to be read aloud as lections along with the weekly Torah portions (202-24). Brunet described the chronicler's method as *"procédé rabbinique"* (1953, 491), while Welten defines the book of Chronicles as a "free, parabolic writing of history" similar to the book of Judith (206), which might be understood as a "historical Midrash."

Again, differently, Chronicles features prominently in M. Fishbane's (1985) general survey of inner-biblical exegesis. Without analyzing the book's literary genre, but rather appreciating the chronicler's activity as evidenced from his work, the chronicler has been presented as a theologian—his work being almost a theological essay for the benefit of his contemporaries (Ackroyd [1977] 24: "The first OT theologian"; Mosis, 14-16)—or a preacher (Mason). At the same time, the definition of Chronicles as historiography has been reexamined and reasserted not only by those who adhere to its reliability (see J. Liver, 1956), but also by scholars who are fully aware of the theological message of the work (see R. Duke [1990]). They regard the chronicler as basically a historian and the literary nature of his work first and foremost as historiography (Noth, 166, 172; E. Bickerman [1962] 22-29; Japhet [1977] 426-31).

Interest in Chronicles has not been limited to these "mainstream" topics; other aspects and specific subjects, some directly relevant to the parallel nature of the book, have engaged scholarly attention. A first fruit of this interest is the handbooks, which present the parallel texts with or without the evidence of the ancient versions, and further helpful material (see among others P. Vannutelli [1931–34]; A. Bendavid [1967]; J. Kegler and M. Augustin [1984]). More germane to the actual content are studies in the realms of text and language. The parallel character of Chronicles made it a natural point of departure for all studies of textual transmission.

The existence of two and sometimes more versions of the same text within the MT serves as the best illustration of the problem of textual transmission and stabilization. Kimhi, in his commentary on 1 Chr 1:6-7, already indicates the chronistic evidence for the interchangeability of letters that are orthographically or phonetically similar. Chronicles features prominently in all studies of this nature, e.g., those of Friedrich Delitzsch, G. Gerleman (1948), and M. Rehm (1937), with the work of the latter devoted more specifically to the textual transmission of Chronicles and Samuel–Kings. In the same general category may be included studies devoted more specifically to the ancient versions, the particular attraction of which, in the case of Chronicles, lies in the multiplicity of textual witnesses and the more general conclusions regarding translation and transmission that may be drawn. Thus note should be taken of some of the works on the Targum (K. Kohler and M. Rosenberg [1870]; Le Déaut and Robert), the Peshitta (S. Fraenkel [1879]; Barnes), the comprehensive work on the Septuagint (L. Allen [1974]), and the study of the Vulgate (B. Neteler [1899]; R. Weber [1945]).

The discovery of the Dead Sea Scrolls has evoked new interest in this field. The categorical classification of orthographic, linguistic, stylistic, or theological variants has always been a matter of controversy (see W. Lemke [1965]). This question has been further complicated by the evidence of the scrolls, and in particular of 4QSam[a]. The concept of "variant" and the complicated process of textual transmission should be reexamined in view of the accumulating material. Early interest in the language of Chronicles focused mainly on its vocabulary, which served as an indication of the linguistic similiarity between Chronicles, Ezra–Nehemiah, and the priestly source. Lists to that effect were promulgated by S. Driver (Introduction to the

Literature of the OT [1891] 535-40) and Curtis (28-36; see their reexamination by Williamson [1977] 37-59). A pioneering study, more linguistically oriented, is that of A. Kropat (1909).

The growing interest in post-biblical Hebrew, encouraged by the discovery of the Qumran material, inspired as well a greater attention to late biblical Hebrew, of which Chronicles is the largest biblical corpus. The book's language, although no doubt reflecting the stylistic idiosyncrasies of its author, could no longer be regarded as merely an individual stylistic expression; it has been gradually recognized as the important representative of a general linguistic stratum. However, although great progress has been achieved in this field (e.g., E. Kutscher [1959]; Japhet [1966/67]; Bendavid [1971]; A. Hurvitz [1972]; W. Watson [1972]; Polzin; M. Throntviet [1982]), it seems that a more systematic description of late biblical Hebrew is now indicated. Many pertinent questions must be addressed, e.g., the extent of Aramaic influence on Hebrew and the survival of the latter as a living language in the postexilic period, the simultaneous influence of other Semitic and non-Semitic languages, the actual transition from biblical to rabbinic Hebrew, and so on. The responses to these questions, taking into full consideration the Chronistic material, will contribute to a clearer picture of this stage in the development of the Hebrew language.

Among the more specific subjects of interest in Chronicles two may be mentioned:

(a) The genealogies of Chronicles were the focus of interest for the ancients, as is seen in both Jewish and Christian evidence (Willi, 14-26). In modern scholarship two conflicting approaches to this material can be detected. One is a very explicit lack of interest, to the extent of denying this material authenticity and historical value (Noth, Welch, Rudolph, Willi, et al.). The other is a certain fascination, prompting repeated attempts to decipher this material's genealogical code, to learn its geographical-historical-ethnological background, and to clarify its sociological significance. The genealogy of Judah in particular (see Wellhausen's 1870 dissertation; Noth's discussion [1934]; and recently Williamson [1979]; and G. Galil [1983]) and the socio-historical and literary aspects of the lists are repeatedly the subject of new studies (e.g., G. Richter [1914]; M. Johnson [1969]; R. Wilson [1975]; Liver [1968]; M. Razin [1977])—which have by no means exhausted the material's potential.

(b)The topic of prophecy has attracted growing attention in recent decades, as is in fact illustrated by the recent study of Mathias describing the attitudes of nineteenth-century scholars to this subject (112-302). Although often described as a "priestly history," in contrast to the Deuteronomistic "prophetic history," Chronicles in fact assigns to prophets an important role. Many prophets who are not mentioned in earlier biblical material are here introduced; they appear before and address the king and people; they are alluded to as having recorded the history of their period; their fate is sometimes described; they are presented as communicating God's commandments to the people; and the title "prophets" is also given to the singers.

What, then, was the chronicler's familiarity with the phenomenon of prophecy? Was it a living institution of his day, or was he working with traditional and literary material? How authentic is his evidence concerning the names, deeds, words, and lives of the prophets? What social and religious functions does the chronicler attribute to them? Are figures like David and Solomon regarded as prophets? How is the chronicler's attitude here related to other biblical and post-biblical views? Some of these questions have been dealt with to some degree in studies dedicated to this subject (see, e.g., Newsome; Petersen, 55-96; Japhet [1977]; Willi, 215-44; R. Micheel [1983]; I. Seeligmann [1978]; J. Weinberg [1978]; Y. Amit [1982/83]), but it seems that here, too, a fuller portrayal of the subject is still a desideratum.

Concluding this review, which is by no means exhaustive, it seems fitting to draw the reader's attention to the tide of commentaries on Chronicles that have appeared in recent years in different languages, standards, and scopes, and from so many points of view, seeming to meet any existing or expected need.

Bibliography: P. R. Ackroyd, *The Chronicler in His Age* (1990). **W. F. Albright**, "The Date and Personality of the Chronicler," *JBL* 40 (1921) 104-24; "The Judicial Reform of Jehoshaphat," A. Marx Jubilee Volume (ed. S. Lieberman, 1950) 61-82. **L. C. Allen**, *The Greek Chronicles* (VTSup 25, 27, 1974). **Y. Amit**, "The Role of Prophecy and the Prophets in the Teachings of Chronicles," *Beth Mikra* 28 (1982/83) 113-33 (Hebrew). **P. S. Ash**, *David, Solomon and Egypt: A Reassessment* (JSOTSup 297, 1999). **W. E. Barnes**, "The Midrashic Element in Chronicles," *Expositor* 5th ser., 4 (1896) 426-39; *An Apparatus Criticus to Chronicles in the Peshitta Version* (1897). **A. Bea**, "Neuere Arbeiten zum Problem der biblischen Chronikbüchern," *Bib* 22 (1941) 46-58. **C. Begg**, *Josephus' Story of the Later Monarchy* (BETL 145, 2000). **A. Bendavid**, *Biblical Hebrew and Mishnaic Hebrew* (1967); *Parallels in the Bible* (1972). **E. Ben Zvi**, "The Authority of 1–2 Chronicles in the Late Second Temple Period," *JSP* 3 (1988) 59-88. **E. J. Bickermann**, *From Ezra to the Last of the Maccabees* (1962). **J. Botterweck**, "Zur Eigenart der chronistischen David-geschichte," *TQ 136* (1956) 402-35. **R. L. Braun**, "Solomonic Apologetic in Chronicles," *JBL* 92 (1973) 503-16; "Solomon, the Chosen Temple Builder: The Significance of 1 Chronicles 22, 28, and 29 for the Theology of Chronicles," *JBL* 95 (1976) 581-90; "A Reconsideration of the Chronicler's Attitude Toward the North," *JBL* 96 (1977) 59-62; "Chronicles, Ezra and Nehemiah: Theology and Literary History," VTSup 30 (1979) 52-64; *1 Chronicles* (WBC, 1986). **A. M. Brunet**, "Le Chroniste et ses Sources," *RB* 60 (1953) 483-508; 61 (1954) 349-86; "La Théologie du Chroniste Théocratie et Messianism," *BETL* 12 (1959) 384-97. **A. Caquot**, "Peut-on parler de messianisme dans l'oeuvre du Chroniste?" *RTP* 16 (1966) 110-20. **D. J. A. Clines**, *Ezra, Nehemiah, Esther: Based on the RSV* (NCB, 1984). **F. M. Cross**, "A Reconstruction of the Judean Restoration," *JBL* 94 (1975) 4-18. **E. L. Curtis** and **A. A. Madsen**, *A Critical and Exegetical Commentary on the Books of Chronicles* (ICC, 1910). **F. Delitzsch**, *Die Lese- und Schreibfehler im Alten Testament* (1920). **N. Dennerlein**, *Die Bedeutung Jerusalems in den Chronikbüchern* (BEATAJ 46, 1999). **W. M. L. De Wette**, *Kritischer Versuch über die Glaubwördigkeit der Bücher der Chronik, mit Hinsicht auf die Geschichte der Mosaischen und Gesetzgebung: Ein Nachtrag zu den Vaterschen Untersuchunger über den Pentateuch* (1806). **R. K. Duke**, *The Persuasive Appeal of the Chronicler* (JSOTSup 88, 1990). **J. E. Dyck**, *The Theocratic Ideology of the Chronicler* (BibInt 33, 1998). **J. G. Eichhorn**, *Einleitung in das Alte Testament* (3 vols., 1780–83). **J. C. Endres**, *Chronicles and Its Synoptic Parallels in Samuel, Kings, and Related Biblical Texts* (1998). **T. C. Eskenazi**, "The Chronicler and the Composition of 1 Esdras," *CBQ* 48 (1986) 39-61; *In an Age of Prose: A Literary Approach to Ezra–Nehemiah* (SBLMS 36, 1988). **M. Fishbane**, *Biblical Interpretation in Ancient Israel* (1985). **S. Fraenkel**, "Die syrische Übersetzung zu den Büchern der Chronik," *JPT* 5 (1879) 508-36, 720-59. **D. N. Freedman**, "The Chronicler's Purpose," *CBQ* 23 (1961) 436-42. **J. Fries**, *"Im Dienst am Hause des Herrn": Literaturwissenschaftliche Untersuchungen zu 2 Chr 29–31; zur Hiskijatradition in Chronik* (ATSAT 60, 1998). **G. Galil**, "The Genealogy of the Tribe of Judah" (diss., Jerusalem, 1983), Hebrew. **K. Galling**, *Die Bücher der Chronik, Esra, Nehemia* (ATD, 1954). **G. Gerleman**, *Synoptic Studies in the OT* (1948). **J. Goettsberger**, *Die Bücher der Chronik oder Paralipomenon* (1939). **M. D. Goulder**, *Midrash and Lection in Matthew* (1974) 202-24. **K. H. Graf**, "Das Buch der Chronik als Geschichtsquelle, *"Die Gesichtlichen Bücher des Alten Testments* (1866) 114-247. **M. P. Graham**, *The Utilization of 1 and 2 Chronicles in the Reconstruction of Israelite History in the Nineteenth Century* (SBLDS 116, 1990); (ed.), *The Chronicler as Historian* (JSOTSup 238, 1997); (ed.), *The Chronicler as Theologian: Essays in Honor of Ralph W. Klein* (JSOTSup 371, 2003). **C. P. W. Gramberg**, *Die Chronik nach ihrem geschichtlichen Charakter und ihrer Glaubwördigkeit neu geprüft* (1823). **A. H. J. Gunneweg**, *Esra* (KAT 19, 1, 1985); *Nehemia* (KAT 19, 2, 1987). **B. Halpern**, "Sacred History and Ideology: Chronicles' Thematic Structure—Indications of an Earlier

Source," *The Creation of Sacred Literature: Composition and Redaction of the Biblical Text* (ed. R. E. Friedman, 1981). **A. Hanspach**, *Inspirierte Interpreten: das Prophetenverständnis der Chronikbücher und sein Ort in der Religion und Literatur zur Zeit des Zweiten Tempels* (ATSAT 64, 2000). **K. Hognesius**, *The Text of 2 Chronicles 1–16: A Critical Edition with Textual Commentary* (ConB 51, 2003). **P. K. Hooker**, *First and Second Chronicles* (Westminster Bible Companion, 2001). **A. Hurvitz**, *The Transition Period in Biblical Hebrew* (1972), Hebrew. **S. Japhet**, "Interchanges of Verbal Roots in Parallel Texts in Chronicles," *Lesonenu* 31 (1966/67) 165-79, 261-79 (Hebrew); "The Supposed Common Authorship of Chronicles and Ezra–Nehemiah, Investigated Anew," *VT* 18 (1968) 330-71; *The Ideology of the Book of Chronicles and Its Place in Biblical Thought* (1977; ET BEATAJ 9, 1989); "Conquest and Settlement in Chronicles," *JBL* 98 (1979) 205-18; "The Historical Reliability of Chronicles: The History of the Problem and Its Place in Biblical Research," *JSOT* 33 (1985) 83-107; *1 Chronik* (Herders theologischer Kommentar zum Alten Testament, 2003). **J. Jarick**, *1 Chronicles* (Readings, 2002). **E. Jenni**, "Aus der Literatur zur chronistischen Geschichtsschreibung," *TRu* 45 (1980) 97-108. **M. D. Johnson**, *The Purpose of the Biblical Genealogies* (SNTSMS, 1969) 37-76. **W. Johnstone**, *1 and 2 Chronicles* (JSOTSup 253-54, 1997); *Chronicles and Exodus: An Analogy and Its Application* (JSOTSup 275, 1998). **I. Kalimi**, *Zur Geschichtsscheibung des Chronisten* (BZAW 226, 1995). **J. Kegler** and **M. Augustin**, *Synopse zum chronistischen Geschichtswerk* (BEATAJ 1, 1984). **C. F. Keil**, *Apologetische Versuch über Bücher der Chronik und über die Integrität des Buches Esra* (1833). **R.W. Klein**, "Abijah's Campaign Against the North (2 Chronicles 13): What Were the Chronicler's Sources?" *ZAW* 95 (1983) 210-17. **G. Knoppers**, *1 Chronicles* (AB, 2004). **K. Koch**, "Das Verhältnis von Exegese und Verkünigung anhand eines Chroniktextes," *TLZ* 90 (1965) 659-70. **K. Kohler** and **M. Rosenberg**, "Das Targum zur Chronik," *JZWL* 8 (1870) 72-80, 135-63, 263-78. **A. Kropat**, *Die syntax des Autors der Chronik* (BZAW 16, 1909). **E. Y. Kutscher**, *The Language and Linguistic Background of the Isaian Scroll* (1959; ET 1974). **A. L. Laffey**, "1 and 2 Chronicles," *Women's Bible Commentary* (eds. S. Ringe and C. Newsom, 1992) 110-15. **R. Le Déaut** and **J. Robert**, *Targum des Chroniques* (AnBib 51, 1971). **W. E. Lemke**, "The Synoptic Problem in the Chronicler's History," *HTR* 58 (1965) 349-63. **J. Liver**, "History and Historiography in the Book of Chronicles," *FS A. Biram* (1946), Hebrew; *Chapters in the History of the Priests and the Levites* (1968). Hebrew **D. J. McCarthy**, "An Installation Genre?" *JBL* 90 (1971) 31-42. **S. L. McKenzie**, *The Chronicler's Use of the Deuteronomistic History* (HSM 33, 1985). **N. F. Marcos**, *Scribes and Translators: Septuagint and OL in the Book of Kings* (1994). **R. Mason**, "Some Echoes of the Preaching in the Second Temple?" *ZAW* 96 (1984) 221-35. **F. J. Matera**, *II Chronicles: A Commentary* (NTL, 2004). **D. Mathias**, "Die Geschichte der Chronikforschung im 19. Jahrhundert" (diss., Leipzig, 1977); " 'Levitische Predigt' und Deuteronomismus," *ZAW* 96 (1984) 23-49. **R. Micheel**, *Die Seher- und Prophetenüberlieferungen in der Chronik* (BBET 18, 1983). **R. Mosis**, *Untersuchungen zur Theologie des chronistischen Geschichtswerkes* (1973). **F. K. Movers**, *Kritische Untersuchungen über die biblische Chronik* (1834). **J. M. Myers**, *Chronicles* (AB, 1965). **B. Neteler**, *Die Bücher der Chronik der Vulgata und des Hebräischen Textes* (1899). **J. D. Newsome**, "Toward a New Understanding of the Chronicler and His Purposes," *JBL* 94 (1975) 201-17. **A. Noordtzij**, "Les intentions du Chroniste," *RB* 49 (1940) 161-68. **R. North**, "Theology of the Chronicler," *JBL* 82 (1963) 369-81; "Does Archaeology Prove Chronicles Sources?" *A Light Unto My Path* (ed. H. Bream, 1974) 375-401. **M. Noth**, "Die Ansiedlung des Stammes Juda auf den Boden Palästinas," *PJ* 40 (1921) 104-24; *Überlieferungsgeschichtliche Studien* (1943; ET 1981, 1987). **K. Peltonen**, *History Debated: The Historical Reliability of Chronicles in Pre-Critical and Critical Research* (2 vols., Publications of the Finnish Exegetical Society 64, 1996). **D. Petersen**, Late Israelite Prophecy: Studies in Deutero-prophetic Literature and Chronicles (*SBLMS 23*, 1976). O. Plöger, "Reden und Gebete im deuteronomistischen und chronistischen Geschichtswerk," *FS für G. Dehn* (ed. W. Schneemelcher, 1957) 35-49. **R. Polzin**, *Late Biblical Hebrew: Toward an Historical Typology of Biblical Hebrew Prose* (1976). **G. von Rad,** *Das Geschichtsbild des chronistischen Werkes* (*BWANT* 4, 3, 1930); "The Levitical Sermon in I and II Chronicles," *FS für O. Procksch* (1934) 113-24; *ET The Problem of the Hexateuch and Other Essays* (1966) 267-80. **L. Randellini**, "Il Libro delle Cronache del decennio 1950–60," *RivB* 10 (1962) 136-56. **M. Razin**, *Census Lists and Genealogies and Their Historical Implications for the Times of Saul and David* (1977). **M. Rehm**, *Textkritische Untersuchungen zu den Parallelstellen der Samuel–Königsbücher und der Chronik* (ATA 13, 3, 1937). **H. Reviv**, *The Elders in Ancient Israel: A Study of a Biblical Institution* (1989). **G. Richter**, "Untersuchungen zu den Geschlechtsregistern der Chronik," *ZAW* 34 (1914) 107-41; 49 (1931) 260-70; 50 (1932) 130-41. **J. W. Rothstein** and **J. Hänel,** *Das erste der Chronik* (KAT, 1927). **W. Rudolph**, *Chronikbücher* (HAT, 1955). **A. Saltman** and **S. Langton,** *Commentary on the Book of Chronicles* (1978). **A. Schoors,** *Die Königreiche Israel und Juda im 8. und 7. Jahrhundert v. Chr.: die assyrische Krise* (Biblische Enzyklopädie 5, 1998). **I. L. Seeligmann,** "Der Auffassung von der Prophetie in der deuteronomistischen und chronistischen Geschichtsschreibung," VTSup 29 (1978) 254-84; "The Beginnings of Midrash in the Books of Chronicles," *Tarbiz 49* (1979/80) 14-32 (Hebrew). **M. H. Segal**, "The Books of Ezra and Nehemiah," *Tarbiz 14* (1942/43) 81-88 (Hebrew). **B. Spinoza**, *Theologico-Political Treatise* (1670). **W. F. Stinespring**, "Eschatology in Chronicles," *JBL* 80 (1961) 209-19. **J. Swart**, "De Theologie van Kronieken" (diss., Groningen, 1911). **J. D. Thompson**, *A Critical Concordance to the Septuagint: Chronicles I* (The Computer Bible 65, 1999); *A Critical Concordance to the Septuagint: Chronicles II* (The Computer Bible 66, 1999). **M. A. Throntviet**, "Linguistic Analysis and the Question of Authorship in Chronicles, Ezra, and Nehemiah," *VT* 32 (1982) 201-16; *When Kings Speak: Royal Speech and Royal Prayer in Chronicles* (SBLDS 93, 1987). **C. C. Torrey**, The Composition and Historical Value of Ezra–Nehemiah (*BZAW* 2, 1896). **A. G. Vaughn**, *Theology, History, and Archaeology in the Chronicler's Account of Hezekiah* (Archaeology and Biblical Studies 4, 1999). **P. Vannutelli**, *Libri Synoptici Veteris Testamenti* (1931–34). **W. G. E. Watson**, "Archaic Elements in the Language of Chronicles," *Bib* 53 (1972) 191-207. **R. Weber**, *Les ancienne versions latines du deuxième livre des Paralipomènes* (1945). **J. P. Weinberg**, "Die 'ausserkanonischen Prophezieungen' in den Chronikbüchern," *Acta Antiqua* 26 (1978) 387-404. **A. C. Welch**, *The Work of the Chronicler* (1939). **J. Wellhausen**, *De gentibus et familiis Judaeis quae 1. Chr 2.4. enumerantur* (1870); *Prolegomena to the History of Israel* (1878; ET 1885). **P. Welten**, "Lade-Tempel-Jerusalem: Zur Theologie der Chronikbücher," *Textgemäss: Aufsätze und Beiträge zur Hermeneutik des Alten Testaments* (ed. A.H.J. Gunneweg and O. Kaiser, 1979) 169-83. **G. Wilda**, "Das Königsbild des chronistischen Geschichtswerk" (diss., Bonn, 1959). **T. Willi,** Die Chronik als Auslegung (FRLANT 106, 1972). **H. G. M. Williamson**, "The Accension of Solomon in the Books of Chronicles," *VT* 26 (1976) 351-61; "Eschatology in Chronicles," *TynBul* 28 (1977) 115-54; *Israel in the Books of Chronicles* (1977); "The Origins of the Twenty-four Priestly Courses: A Study of 1 Chronicles xxiii-xxvii," *VTSup* 30 (1979) 251-68; "Sources and Redaction in the Chronicler's Genealogy of Judah," *JBL* 98 (1979) 351-59; *1 and 2 Chronicles* (NCBC, 1982). **R. R. Wilson**, "The OT Genealogies in Recent Research," *JBL* 94 (1975) 169-89. **H. Winckler**, "Bemerkungen zur Chronik als Geschichtsquelle," *Alttestamentliche Untersuchungen* (1892) 157-67. **S. Zalewski**, *Solomon's Ascension to the Throne: Studies in the Books of Kings and Chronicles* (1981), Hebrew. **L. Zunz**, *Die Gottesdienstlichen Vorträge der Juden* (1832).

S. JAPHET

THE WRITINGS

Ezra and Nehemiah

1. *Relationship to Other Texts.* There is considerable controversy concerning the distinction between composition and interpretation with regard to the books of Ezra and Nehemiah because of the apocryphal work known as 1 Esdras (Ger., 3 Esra). First Esdras includes a Greek translation of 2 Chronicles 35–36; Esdra; and Neh 8:1-12. Included in Esdras, however, is an account not found in the canonical books of a contest of wisdom between three guardsmen at the court of Darius that resulted in Zerubbabel's mission to Jerusalem. Other minor additions and differences in order and chronology exist in 1 Esdras.

On the one hand, some scholars have argued that this work represents a translation of the original ending of the chronicler's history and that the present books developed only subsequently (opinions about this process differ; see, e.g., C. C. Torrey [1910]; S. Mowinckel [1964–65] 1-28; K. Pohlmann [1970]; F. M. Cross [1975]). If this were the case, of course, 1 Esdras could tell us nothing about the early interpretation of Ezra and Nehemiah. Many scholars, however, reject this view and regard 1 Esdras as possibly a fragment of a work compiled from various sources for purposes of its own (R. Hanhart [1973]; W. In der Smitten [1973]; H. Williamson [1977], 12-36, and [1983]; A. van der Kooij [1991]). The centrality of the Temple and its restoration in 1 Esdras have long been noted, and A. Gardner (1986) has linked this theme with the purpose of giving comfort and succor to the faithful during the Maccabean crisis. If this is true, it indicates that from an early date a major theme in Ezra and Nehemiah was interpreted paradigmatically—if not indeed typologically—in terms of the restoration of the people of God and their sanctuary in times of trouble.

It is worth noting that in later centuries 1 Esdras was frequently preferred as a source for the restoration period to the Septuagint version of the canonical books of Ezra and Nehemiah. It was used by Josephus as the basis for his account (*A.J.* 11.1-158), perhaps because of its superior Greek style, while in the early centuries of the Christian church there are undoubtedly more surviving references to it than to Ezra and Nehemiah (see J. Myers [1974] 17-18; M. Goodman in G. Vermes et al. [1987] 714).

Apart from the disputed evidence of 1 Esdras, early Jewish interpretation of Ezra and Nehemiah focused largely on the use of their central characters in subsequent apocryphal tradition. The use of Ezra's name in the pseudonymous *Apocalypse of Ezra* (2 Esdras 3–14 = 4 Ezra) shows a comparable development to that noted in connection with 1 Esdras. The work represents an attempt to come to terms with the fall of Jerusalem and the destruction of the Temple in 70 C.E. Although a number of visions provide assurance that Israel's distress will soon be brought to an end, the climax appears with the miraculous restoration of the Scriptures to Ezra. This illustrates that Ezra's outstanding qualities as a scribe (as recorded, e.g., in Ezra 7:10) had already made a deep impression and had become a source for fruitful reflection; hopes for a restoration of the Temple could take second place to the study of Scripture as a focus for Jewish life (for this and other later, mainly Christian, pseudepigraphical literature related to Ezra (see J. Charlesworth, 516-604).

Not surprisingly, in the case of Nehemiah it was his restoration of the walls of Jerusalem that made the greatest impression, initially as part of the restoration started by Zerubbabel and Jeshua (Sir 49:11-13). The lack of chronological distinction in this passage is not new with Ben Sira, however (U. Kellermann [1967] 114) but continues a line of historical interpretation whose origins are to be found already in the biblical text (Williamson [1985] xlviii-xlix). There is thus no good reason to suppose that Ben Sira knew the Nehemiah source in isolation or that his surprising omission of a reference to Ezra is due to anything other than reasons of selection in view of his overall purpose. It is of further interest to note that in a letter cited in 2 Macc 1:10–2:18, which doubtless rests on earlier material, Nehemiah is credited with both the restoration of the Temple and the collection of books "about the kings and prophets, and the writings of David, and the letters of kings about votive offerings" (2 Macc 2:13). However, this apparent "takeover" by Nehemiah of other major elements in the restoration, attributed in the biblical text to Zerubbabel and Jeshua (Temple restoration) and to Ezra (scribal activity), is due more to claims for legitimacy among the rival priestly groupings under the Hasmoneans than to biblical interpretation proper.

2. *Early Jewish and Christian Interpretation.* In Jewish writings of the subsequent centuries, any appreciation based on an approach to these books as a whole, such as we have noticed above to a limited extent, becomes lost from sight among occasional references to the exploits of the various leading characters. It is true that in the Talmud a number of legal rulings are said to derive from the time of the return from Babylon, as are the founding of the Great Assembly and the age of the Soferim, and that this attests an appreciation of the age of Ezra and Nehemiah as one of major restoration; but there is little in this that can be explicitly associated with the literature. Similarly, the several references to Ezra's restoring the forgotten law (*b. Sukkah* 20a) or to his changing the style of writing (*b. Sanh.* 21-22) may owe as much to later tradition as to biblical interpretation.

More noteworthy are discussions over chronology (e.g., of Neh 1:1 and 2:1 and the identification of the Persian kings in *b. Roš Haš.* vv. 3-4), the identification of Nehemiah with Shealtiel, which shows continuing flexibility in the role and date of Nehemiah (*b. Sanh.* 38a), the identification of Ezra with Malachi based on comparable conditions prevailing in their days (*b. Meg.* 15a), and especially discussions of authorship. In the well-known passage *b. B. Bat.* 15a we are told, "Ezra wrote the book that bears his name and the genealogies of the Book of Chronicles up to his own time"; this was believed to include Nehemiah and is supported by the opinion expressed by R. Jeremiah b. Abba in *b. Sanh.* 93b that although the book of Nehemiah was narrated by Nehemiah it was called by Ezra's name because of the way in which Nehemiah claimed credit for himself.

Not until the medieval period do we find a return to more extended consideration of Ezra and Nehemiah with the commentaries of Rashi and A. Ibn Ezra, followed by those mentioned in G. Bartolocci's *Bibliotheca Magna Rabbinica* 4, by R. Simeon ben Joiakim, by Joseph ben David Ibn Yahya (1538), and by Isaac ben Solomon Jabez (end of 16th cent.).

Apart from a few occasional references there is little evidence regarding the interpretation of Ezra and Nehemiah in the Christian tradition of the earliest centuries. Working on the basis of 1 Esdras, Pseudo-Cyril of Alexandria (5th cent.) spoke of the "new Zerubbabel, who is Jesus Christ," and from the few lines of Isidore of Seville (7th cent.) that survive it seems likely that he pursued a similar approach. Unless this silence is severely misleading, the work of the Venerable Bede (8th cent.) stands out as a remarkable and unique achievement for its time, for his commentary on these books stretches to some 150 printed pages and is generally described as an *Expositio Allegorica*. In his preface Bede referred to Jerome's opinion that the deeds of Ezra and Nehemiah prefigured those of Christ and foreshadowed things that should be done to the church. It is not uncommon to find such characterizations of the work as that of M. Laistner: "The work is figurative in the spiritual mode, that is, it sees in the restoration of Jerusalem a figure of the return to grace of the repentant sinner" (1957, 120). It should be emphasized, however, that this is true only of Bede's hermeneutic. The commentary itself gives full (if inevitably sometimes misguided) attention to the tasks of biblical scholarship. Josephus, for instance, is cited not only for extra-biblical background material but also in an attempt to solve the problems of Ezra 4. The chronological difficulties at Ezra 6:14 are appreciated, the identification of the months at Neh 1:1 and 2:1 are discussed (though without finding the problems that have troubled more recent commentators), the topography of Jerusalem is given due attention at Nehemiah 3, and so on. It would thus be a distortion to imply that Bede was concerned only with allegorical interpretation.

3. *From the Sixteenth Century to the Modern Era.* After Bede we have no information until the sixteenth century. No exposition of these works from the leaders of the Reformation is known, but it seems probable from occasional references in other works that they would have regarded the accounts primarily as examples for Christian living. Of their place in the history of salvation, however, Calvin was evidently not particularly impressed: "Then Ezra and Nehemiah followed them, the authority of whom was great among the people; but we do not read that they were endued with the Prophetic gift" (Preface to Haggai).

Despite this, the sixteenth and seventeenth centuries saw the publication of many commentaries, both Roman Catholic and Protestant, and among them for the first time some explicitly intended for a lay readership. For instance, J. Pilkington left a "Godlie Exposition" on the first five chapters of Nehemiah at his death in 1575 (his commentary on Ezra, to which he referred at Neh 2:20, was lost). He regarded the two books as separate compositions by the authors whose names they bear (an opinion that has only recently been revived independently by J. VanderKam [1992] and D. Kraemer [1993]). His exposition is highly discursive and generally edifying in nature, Nehemiah being "a worthie paterne for all courtiers to follow" (6). Since he claimed to write especially for "the unlearned" (12), we learn little about his attitude to more erudite matters, although a clue is furnished in his introduction to Nehemiah 3. After explaining that it would not be profitable for his readers were he to go through all the names mentioned, he added in parentheses, "though the learned may with pleasure picke out good lessons of them by Allegorical interpretation of the places, etc." (45).

Quite different in tone is the learned commentary of C. Làpide (= van den Steen [1645]), in which for the first time a thorough knowledge of classical sources with their many references to the wider history of the Persian Empire and its kings is brought to bear on the interpretation of these books. Làpide was also well read in earlier Christian interpreters and was confident enough to take issue with them when he saw fit; e.g., he disagreed with Bede over the identification of "the Province" at Ezra 2:1, arguing that it refers to Babylon (just as "the city" could refer to Rome in his own day) and not to Judah, as the allegorical method had led Bede to suppose. Furthermore, Lapide was not afraid to compare the ancient versions with the MT in an elementary form of textual criticism. It is not surprising, therefore, to find that Làpide's commentary is largely a scholarly attempt to do justice to the plain meaning of a historical text, dealing at some length, for instance, with the questions of the identity of the various Persian kings. Only occasionally does his hermeneutic come through. In contrast with Calvin, he insisted that Ezra was a prophet (because he wrote Scripture), and elsewhere he referred to both Ezra and Nehemiah as types of Christ. On the few occasions where he adopted this approach in the text, he used the formula allegorice (allegorically) and tropologice (metaphorically) to apply the passage to Christ and the behavior of Christian believers respectively. Only at Neh 8:11 ("the joy of the LORD is your strength"), however, do his remarks become properly homiletical.

It is often suggested that the modern era of critical biblical scholarship is best represented first by J. G. Eichhorn's introduction (1803[3]). With regard to Ezra and Nehemiah, however, there is no fundamental advance here over the much earlier introduction of J. Carpzov (1741), both writers being concerned largely with such basic issues as authorship (about which they add little to the discussions already noted except for a somewhat fuller use of internal evidence) and authenticity. And when a significant step forward was achieved a few decades later, it had the ironic effect of diverting attention away from Ezra and Nehemiah and onto the books of Chronicles, books that from the time of W. De Wette, at the start of the nineteenth century, to J. Wellhausen, near its close, were the real focus of attention in the great debates about the composition of the Pentateuch as representing postexilic historical writing.

L. Zunz (1832) for the first time set out a full case for the common authorship of Chronicles, Ezra, and Nehemiah based on four principal arguments—namely, the overlap between the end of 2 Chronicles and the beginning of Ezra, the testimony of 1 Esdras, the similarity of Hebrew style, and the common religious outlook of the books in question. Although this argument was not accepted by everyone (see, e.g., the introduction to C. Keil's commentary on Chronicles [1870]); nevertheless, at the end of the century C.C. Torrey could reasonably begin his important monograph of 1896 with the words, "It is at present generally agreed that Chronicles-Ezra-Nehemiah originally formed one book, which was put in its final form by the author of the book of Chronicles, commonly called 'the Chronicler.'" Indeed, this assumption remained virtually unchallenged until the late twentieth century. It is thus not surprising that throughout most of the nineteenth century, and with the partial exception of commentaries like those of E. Bertheau (1862) and Keil (1870), interest in Ezra and Nehemiah focused on their historical testimony regarding the restoration rather than on more specifically literary or theological concerns; for an outstanding example, see E. Meyer (1896), whereas by contrast K. Graf (1866), writing explicitly on the historical books of the HB, gave no sustained attention to Ezra and Nehemiah. It should be noted that in 1890 A. Van Hoonacker first advanced the theory that he continued to elaborate during the next thirty years and that is still a major unresolved issue in the history of the period: that Ezra's mission should be dated to the reign of Artaxerxes II, later, therefore, than the mission of Nehemiah. For summaries that reach opposite conclusions, see H. Rowley (1965) and Williamson (1987, 55-69).

4. *Modern Research*. The next major turning point in the interpretation of these books came with Torrey's monograph of 1896, which he followed with a series of essays collected in 1910. Since this marks the start of the modern period of research, the discussion will be clearer if a purely chronological survey is abandoned in order to treat the major sections of the books: Ezra 1–6, the Ezra memoir, and the Nehemiah memoir.

a. *Ezra 1–6*. Since the overwhelming majority of scholars since Zunz have accepted the argument that the editor of Ezra 1–6 was the chronicler, attention has been focused mainly on the question of the authenticity of the documents incorporated into this narrative. In the same year that Torrey expressed considerable skepticism in this regard, Meyer set out a more conservative line of approach, at least with regard to the Aramaic documents in chaps. 4–6, that has been further refined in the intervening decades and now commands a considerable degree of consensus (cf. L. Grabbe [1991] and [1992] 32-36). This is to compare the texts with indubitably authentic documents of the Achaemenid period with regard to their language, their political and historical verisimilitude, and their literary shape or genre. The latter half of the twentieth century has seen not only the publication of still additional texts but also a considerable advance in the form-critical analysis of the whole corpus of letters written in Imperial Aramaic (see P. Alexander [1978]; P. Dion [1979]; J. Fitzmyer [1979]; and J. White [1982]). Similarly, the authenticity of the inventory of Temple vessels in 1:9-11 is generally accepted.

Much greater doubt remains, however, over the Hebrew version of Cyrus's edict in 1:2-4 (though see E. Bickerman [1946]), while no agreement has been reached concerning the precise historical setting of the long list in Ezra 2 of those who returned from Babylon. An attractive theory that has gained a good deal of support is that of K. Galling (1951), who suggested that it was drawn up as part of the Jewish response to Tattenai's inquiry (5:3-4, 10) about who was engaged in the rebuilding of the Temple.

The chronicler, then, is believed to have drawn on an Aramaic source (4:6-6:12) and some other material to construct his account of the early return and restoration. Doubts persist over whether chap. 3 is a parallel account to that in chaps. 5–6 or whether the two passages should be taken sequentially. The author's purpose is to be seen as part of a larger concern to present the postexilic Jewish theocracy as the legitimate heir of the preexilic monarchy (e.g., W. Rudolph [1949]; O. Plöger [1959]).

The last half of the twentieth century, however, has seen a strong challenge to the view that Ezra and Nehemiah are to be regarded as part of the chronicler's work (see S. Japhet [1968]; Williamson [1977] 5-70; for a more nuanced position, Cross [1975]), and many of those currently writing in this field have embraced this new (rather, revitalized older) approach. Not many have yet worked through its implications for Ezra 1–6 (though see R. Braun [1979]; B. Halpern [1990]), but Williamson (1983) has proposed that these chapters were written after the combining of the accounts concerning Ezra and Nehemiah as the last major stage in the composition of the books as a whole. Taking a high view of the authenticity of all the alleged documents in Ezra 1–6, he argues that a much later editor worked directly from the firsthand sources, which were preserved in the Temple archives. The only information he had at his disposal was in these sources, together with what he could glean from such other biblical books as Haggai and Zechariah. This accounts for the large gaps in his information (e.g., regarding the return journey) as well as for some of the apparent historical confusion. Writing in the early Hellenistic period, his purpose would have been to defend the legitimacy of the Jerusalem Temple against its newly established Samaritan rival on Mt. Gerizim.

b. *The Ezra memoir.* With regard to the material about Ezra, attention has chiefly been focused on the relationship between the literature and the historical Ezra. Four main views may be distinguished, with the first and most radical that of Torrey. Until the end of the nineteenth century, the Ezra material was generally taken at face value; but in his monograph and subsequent publications Torrey subjected it to the most searching criticism. Because of its Hebrew style he concluded that it could not be distinguished from the editorial hand of the remainder of Chronicles, Ezra, and Nehemiah. He concluded, therefore, that there was no Ezra source; Ezra was no more than a figure of the chronicler's imagination. In the modern period, Grabbe (1994), in particular, remains skeptical about the history of Ezra.

Although much discussed, Torrey's views were not followed by many scholars in their entirety (but see G. Hölscher, HSAT(K)). However, one aspect of his analysis has continued to attract widespread support. He argued that the Ezra material was originally written in the order Ezra 7–8; Nehemiah 8; Ezra 9–10; Nehemiah 9–10, and that its present order was the result of mistakes by later copyists. (This view, of course, is unacceptable to those who hold that 1 Esdras, which places Nehemiah 8 after Ezra 10, represents the original ending of the chronicler's work.) Torrey was obliged to speak of later copyists' errors because in his opinion the chapters had been written from scratch by the editor of the books as a whole. Those who, by contrast, accept that the editor was here reworking an independent source have been able to transfer Torrey's reconstruction to that source and to investigate the potentially more fruitful suggestion that the editor rearranged them into their present order for purposes of his own.

A second approach was developed independently by M. Noth (1943) and A. Kapelrud (1944). Literary and historical considerations led Noth to believe that the edict of Artaxerxes in Ezra 7:12-26 and the list in 8:1-14 of those who accompanied Ezra on his journey to Jerusalem were both sources that were available to the chronicler, as, of course, was the Nehemiah memoir. On the basis of this material the chronicler himself wrote the whole of the Ezra account. This suggestion explained why the style so closely resembles the chronicler's, why Nehemiah 8 appears where it does (the chronicler wrote it for that setting for theological reasons), and why part of the account is in the first person (inconsistent imitation of Nehemiah).

Kapelrud, meanwhile, undertook a study of the Hebrew style of the Ezra narrative. Like Torrey he concluded that it must be attributed to the hand of the chronicler, but at the same time he allowed the probability that some earlier tradition underlay the account. Kapelrud was not as specific as Noth about this, however, and his stylistic analysis is also open to criticisms of method. It is not surprising, therefore, that Noth's form of this theory has had the most influence, especially on the more recent major studies of Kellermann (1967) and W. In der Smitten

(1973). The attraction of this approach is that it enables scholars to discount the possibility of an Ezra source while nevertheless holding on to the historicity of Ezra himself.

The third approach to the Ezra material is that of S. Mowinckel. As with the Nehemiah memoir, Mowinckel had published a monograph on Ezra as early as 1916, but since it was in Norwegian it was inaccessible to most scholars (though see F. Ahlemann [1942–43]). He returned to these books at the end of his life, however, publishing three monographs in German (1964–65) that are of great importance for all aspects of the interpretation of Ezra and Nehemiah. Regarding Ezra, his opinion was more conservative than that of Noth; but paradoxically it was far from traditional. Finding some editorial comments in the Ezra material, Mowinckel argued that this editor is the chronicler; therefore, he must have been working on an already existing text—an Ezra source. Mowinckel could find no reason, however, to attribute this to Ezra. It was, he thought, the work of an admirer who had been a young man during Ezra's activity and who years later wrote an idealized version of the events for purposes of edification. Since history was not its main aim, allowances should be made for all manner of legendary embellishment. Needless to say, Mowinckel had no difficulty in citing other examples of narratives that use the first-person singular but that are not autobiographical.

Fourth, there have always been scholars who have held to a more traditional approach (e.g., H. Schaeder [1930]; Rudolph [1949]; K. Koch [1974]; Williamson [1985]; J. Blenkinsopp [1988]; K. Hoglund [1992]). That is to say, they accept that the material about Ezra was originally written by Ezra in the first person throughout in order to give an account of his work to the Persian king. It was later reworked by an editor (whether the chronicler or another), who among other things cast some of it in the third person. However, since Torrey's time all but the most conservative (e.g., F. Kidner [1979]; F. Fensham [1982]) have agreed that Nehemiah 8 (and perhaps 9–10) was once an integral part of the Ezra material in Ezra 7–10. Furthermore, if the view that Ezra and Nehemiah were not part of the chronicler's work is correct, then a major plank in the arguments of those who deny the existence of an Ezra source is removed.

Alongside these literary concerns, historical and theological disagreements have continued with regard to Ezra's mission. Some scholars held that Ezra's mission should be dated to the seventh year of Artaxerxes I or II while others argued that he came in either the twenty-seventh or the thirty-seventh year of Artaxerxes I, thus viewing his reforms as building more closely on the work of Nehemiah (see Rudolph [1949]; V. Pavlovsky [1957]; J. Bright [1959] 375-86; for a searching criticism of this view, see J. Emerton [1966]). Also noteworthy is the suggestion of Schaeder (1930) that Ezra was the "secretary of state for Jewish affairs" at the Achaemenid court prior to his mission and Koch's more speculative view (1974) that he came with high hopes of reestablishing the community of the full twelve tribes of Israel around the holy center of the Jerusalem Temple—a view that implies that he failed in his mission rather more disastrously than later interpretation might have led us to expect. (For a fuller exposition and discussion of these views, see Williamson [1987] 69-76.) Finally, one should not overlook the continuing discussions of the identity of the book of the law that Ezra brought with him, whether it was the Pentateuch in its finished form or one of its major constitutive sources, such as P or D, or some other quite separate document since lost to us. (For full surveys of research, see Kellermann [1968] and C. Houtman [1981].) Alongside this, attention has turned to a consideration of the interpretation of the law evident in this material and its formative influence in the development of later Jewish hermeneutics (D. Clines [1981]; M. Fishbane [1985]; Williamson [1988] 25-38).

c. *The Nehemiah memoir.* In contrast to the Ezra material, the authenticity of the Nehemiah memoir has been widely accepted. Discussion has centered, rather, on the question of its genre and purpose. It was Mowinckel (1916, Norwegian; GT 1923), who first pointed out that the term "Nehemiah memoir" is inappropriate as a technical literary classification; he suggested instead that the work might be more appropriately compared with a number of ancient Near Eastern royal inscriptions in which various kings commemorate their achievements. G. von Rad (1964) later endeavored to refine this thesis by comparing the memoir instead to various tomb and temple inscriptions from Egypt that date from roughly the same period as Nehemiah and that recall in first-person narrative the duties of senior officials faithfully performed, often in spheres of public life closely resembling those of Nehemiah (see Blenkinsopp [1987]).

An alternative approach takes the distinctive "remember" formula as its starting point and finds the closest parallels to the Nehemiah memoir in the common votive or dedicatory inscriptions known in several Aramaic dialects from later times. Problems for this view that have never been faced, however, are the disparity in length between these brief inscriptions and the Nehemiah memoir and the fact that Nehemiah never asked God to remember his greatest achievement, the building of the wall.

Another suggestion is that Nehemiah needed to write in order to justify himself to the Persian king. Based more on the contents of the text than on formal analogies with other sources, this view suggests that accusations had been leveled against Nehemiah by some of his opponents. The main problem here, however, is that the document appears to be addressed directly to God rather than to the king. In a major study of the whole topic, Kellermann (1967) has sought to avoid this objection by comparing the Nehemiah memoir with the type of psalm known as "the prayer of the accused." The differences between the two bodies of material he explains on the basis of the particular circumstances in which Nehemiah was placed.

As an alternative to this whole approach, Williamson (1985, xxiv-xxviii) has suggested that the Nehemiah memoir developed in two distinct stages, the first a report to the king on Nehemiah's first year in office and the second a later reworking of this report in votive style in order to claim credit for his achievements as a whole. (It is observed that most of the accounts of Nehemiah's accomplishments are paralleled by third-person narratives elsewhere in the book that ascribe the same reforms to the community at large under priestly leadership.) On this view it will not be surprising that attempts to compare the Nehemiah memoir as a whole with other unified texts have never proved fully convincing.

5. *New Approaches.* It will be apparent from this survey of work on Ezra and Nehemiah during the twentieth century that most attention was directed to specific literary and historical issues rather than to the interpretation of the books as a whole and that such consideration as there has been of this latter topic has been subsumed under the umbrella of the books of Chronicles. There are several indications, however, that this is likely to change (see the useful survey of T. Eskenazi [1993]): first, the challenge already mentioned to the common authorship of Chronicles, Ezra, and Nehemiah; second, the rise of the canonical approach (B. Childs [1979]; J. Shaver [1992]), which believes that interpretation should start from the study of the books as we now have them and the mutual influence of the text and the believing community on their formation and understanding; third, more sophisticated application of insights from the social services as well as archaeology (see, e.g., Tolletson and Williamson [1992]; J. Weinberg [1992]; Hoglund [1992]; and the many essays in P. Davies [1991] and T. Eskenazi and K. Richards [1994]); and finally, the general rise in HB scholarship of a more genuinely literary approach that seeks to understand the books in their present shape regardless of the processes that led to their formation (A. Gunneweg [1981]; see also his important commentary [1985]; Eskenazi). Work in all these fields as it affects Ezra and Nehemiah is only beginning, but there is every prospect that the coming years will see in consequence a genuine advance in the literary and theological interpretations of these books.

Bibliography: **P. R. Ackroyd**, *I and II Chronicles, Ezra, Nehemiah* (TBC, 1973); *The Chronicler in His Age* (1991). **F. Ahlemann**, "Zur Esra-Quelle," *ZAW 59* (1942–43) 77-98.

P. S. Alexander, "Remarks on Aramaic Epistolography in the Persian Period," *JSS 23* (1978) 155-70. **L. C. Allen**, *Ezra, Nehemiah, Esther* (NIB Commentary, 2003). **L. W. Batten**, *A Critical and Exegetical Commentary on the Books of Ezra and Nehemiah* (ICC, 1913). **Bede**, *Bedae Venerabilis Opera*, Pars II/2A (ed. D. Hurst, CCSL, 1969) 235-392. **P. R. Bedford**, *Temple Restoration in Early Achaemenid Judah* (JSJSup 65, 2001). **E. Bertheau**, *Die Bücher Esra, Nehemia, und Ester* (KEH, 1862). **A. Bertholet**, *Die Bücher Esra und Nehemia* (KEH, 1902). **J. A. Bewer**, *Der Text des Buches Ezra* (1922). **E. J. Bickermann**, "The Edict of Cyrus in Ezra 1," *JBL* 65 (1946) 249-75. **J. Blenkinsopp**, "The Mission of Udjahorresnet and Those of Ezra and Nehemiah," *JBL* 106 (1987) 409-21; *Ezra–Nehemiah* (OTL, 1988). **M. J. Boda**, *Praying the Tradition: the Origin and Use of Tradition in Nehemiah 9* (BZAW 277, 1999). **D. Böhler**, *Die heilige Stadt in Esdras und Esra–Nehemia: zwei Konzeptionender Wiederherstellung Israels* (OBO 158, 1997). **R. A. Bowman**, "Introduction and Exegesis to the Book of Ezra and Nehemiah," *IB* (1954) 3:551-819. **R. L. Braun**, "Chronicles, Ezra, and Nehemiah," VTSup 30 (1979) 52-64. **J. Bright**, *A History of Israel* (1959). **L. H. Brockington**, *Ezra, Nehemiah, and Esther* (NCBC, 1969). **J. G. Carpzov**, *Introductio ad Libros Historicos Veteris Testamenti* (1741). **J. H. Charlesworth** (ed.), *OTP 1*. **B. S. Childs,** *Introduction to the OT as Scripture* (1979). **D. J. A. Clines**, "Nehemiah 10 as an Example of Early Jewish Biblical Exegesis," JSOT 21 (1981) 111-17; *Ezra, Nehemiah, and Esther* (NCBC, 1984). **R. J. Coggins**, *The Books of Ezra and Nehemiah* (CBC, 1976). **F. M. Cross**, "A Reconstruction of the Judean Restoration," *JBL* 94 (1975) 4-18. **P. R. Davies** (ed.), *Second Temple Studies, vol. 1, Persian Period (*1991). **P. E. Dion**, "Les types épistolaires hébréo-araméens jusqu'au temps de Bar-Kokhbah," *RB* 86 (1979) 544-79. **M. Duggan**, *The Covenant Renewal in Ezra–Nehemiah* (SBLDS 164, 2001). **J. G. Eichorn**, *Einleitung in das Alte Testament II* (1803). **J. A. Emerton**, "Did Ezra Go to Jerusalem in 428 BC?" *JTS NS* 17 (1966) 1-19. **T. C. Eskenazi**, "The Structure of Ezra–Nehemiah and the Integrity of the Book," *JBL* 107 (1988) 641-56; *In an Age of Prose: A Literary Approach to Ezra–Nehemiah* (SBLMS 36, 1988); "Current Perspectives on Ezra–Nehemiah and the Persian Period," *CurBs* 1 (1993) 59-86. **T. C. Eskenazi** and **K. H. Richards** (eds.), *Second Temple Studies, vol. 2, Temple and Community in the Persian Period* (1994). **F. C. Fensham**, *The Books of Ezra and Nehemiah* (NICOT, 1982). **M. Fishbane**, *Biblical Interpretation in Ancient Israel* (1985). **J. A. Fitzmyer**, "Aramaic Epistolography," *A Wandering Aramean: Collected Aramaic Essays* (1979) 183-204. **K. Galling**, "The Eroman list' According to Ezra 2–Nehemiah 7," *JBL* 70 (1951) 149-58; *Die B∞cher der Chronik, Esra, Nehemia* (ATD, 1954); *Studien zur Geschichte Israels im persischen Zeitalter* (1964). **A.E. Gardner**, "The Purpose and Date of 1 Esdras," *JJS* 37 (1986) 18-27. **G. F. Gordon** (ed.), *Ezra and Nehemiah* (1999). **L. L. Grabbe**, "Reconstructing History from the Book of Ezra," *Second Temple Studies, vol. 1, Persian Period* (ed. P. R. Davies, 1991) 98-106; *Judaism from Cyrus to Hadrian* (1992); "What Was Ezra's Mission?" *Second Temple Studies, vol. 2, Temple and Community in the Persian Period* (ed. T. C. Eskenazi and K. H. Richards, 1994) 286-99. **K. H. Graf**, *Die geschichtlichen Bücher des Alten Testaments: Zwei historisch-kritische Untersuchungen* (1866). **A. H. J. Gunneweg**, "Zur interpretation der Bücher Esra–Nehemia," VTSup 32 (1981) 146-61; *Esra* (KAT, 1985); *Nehemia* (KAT, 1987). **B. Halpern**, "A Historiographic Commentary on Ezra 1–6," *The HB and Its Interpreters* (W. H. Propp et al., BJuS 1, 1990) 81-142. **R. Hanhart**, "Zu Text und Textgeschichte des ersten Esrabuches," *Proceedings of the Sixth World Congress of Jewish Studies* (ed. A. Shinan, 1973) 1:201-12. **K. G. Hoglund**, *Achaemenid Administration in Syria-Palestine and the Missions of Ezra and Nehemiah* (SBLDS 125, 1992). **G. Hölscher**, "Die Bücher Esra und Nehemia," HSAT(K) 2:491-562. **C. Houtman**, "Ezra and the Law," OTS *21* (1981) 91-115. **W. T. In der Smitten**, *Esra: Quellen, Überlieferung, und Geschichte* (SSN 15, 1973). **D. Janzen**, *Witch-hunts, Purity, and Social Boundaries: the Expulsion of the Foreign Women in Ezra 9–10* (JSOTSup 350). **S.**

Japhet, "The Supposed Common Authorship of Chronicles and Ezra–Nehemiah Investigated Anew," *VT 18* (1968) 330-71; "Sheshbazzar and Zerubbabel," *ZAW* 94 (1982) 66-98; 95 (1983) 218-29; "'History' and 'Literature' in the Persian Period," *Ah, Assyria: Studies in Assyrian History and Ancient Near Eastern Historiography Presented to H. Tadmor* (ed. M. Cogan and I. Eph'al, 1991) 174-88; "The Temple in the Restoration Period: Reality and Ideology," *USQR* 44 (1991) 195-251. **A.S. Kapelrud,** *The Question of Authorship in the Ezra-Narrative: A Lexical Investigation* (1944). **C. Karrer,** *Ringen um die Verfassung Judas: eine Studie zu den theologisch-politischen Vorstellungen im Esra-Nehemia-Buch* (BZAW 308, 2001). **U. Kellermann,** *Nehemia: Quellen, Überlieferung, und Geschichte* (BZAW 102, 1967); "Erwägungen zum Problem der Esradatierung," *ZAW 80* (1968) 55-87; "Erwägungen zum Esragesetz," *ZAW 80* (1968) 373-85. **C. F. Keil,** *Biblischer Commentar ∞ber die nachexilischen Geschichtsücher: Chronik, Esra, Nehemiah, und Esther* (1870). **F. D. Kidner,** *Ezra and Nehemiah* (TOTC, 1979). **R. W. Klein,** "Ezra and Nehemiah in Recent Studies," *Magnalia Dei: The Mighty Acts of God* (ed. F. M. Cross et al., 1976) 361-76. **K. Koch,** "Ezra and the Origins of Judaism," *JSS* 19 (1974) 173-97. **A. van der Kooij,** "On the Ending of the Book of 1 Esdras," *VII Congress of the IOSCS* (ed. C. E. Cox) 37-49; "Zur Frage des Anfangs des 1. Esrabuches," *ZAW* 103 (1991) 239-52. **D. Kraemer,** "On the Relationship of the Books of Ezra and Nehemiah," *JSOT* 59 (1993) 73-92. **M. L. W. Laistner,** *Thought and Letters in Western Europe* (AD 500-900) (1957). **C. à Lapide,** *Commentaria in Scripturam Sacram 4* (1645, 1877) 200-261. **F. Michaeli,** *Les livres des Chroniques, d'Esdras et de Néhémie* (CAT, 1967). **E. Meyer,** *Die Entstehung des Judenthums* (1986). **S. Mowinckel,** *Ezra den Skriftlaerde* (1916); *Statholderen Nehemia* (1916); "Die vorderasiatischen Königs- und Fürsteninschriften," *Eucharisterion: H. Gunkel zum 60. Geburtstage* (FRLANT 36, 1923) 278-322; *Studien zu dem Buche Ezra–Nehemia I–III* (1964–65). **J. M. Myers,** *I and II Esdras* (AB, 1974). **A. Noordtzij,** *Ezra–Nehemia* (1951). **M. Noth,** *Überlieferungsgeschichtliche Studien* (1943; ET, *The Chronicler's History* [1987]). **V. Pavlovsky,** "Die Chronologie der Tätigkeit Esdras: Versuch einer neuen Lösung," *Bib* 38 (1957) 275-305, 428-56. **J. Pilkington,** *A Godlie Exposition upon Certaine Chapters of Nehemiah* (1585). **O. Plöger,** *Theokratie und Eschatologie* (WMANT 2, 1959; ET, *Theocracy and Eschatology* [1968]). **K. F. Pohlmann,** *Studien zum dritten Esra* (FRLANT 104, 1970). G. von Rad, "Die Nehemia-Denkschrift," *ZAW* 76 (1964) 176-87. **H. H. Rowley,** "The Chronological Order of Ezra and Nehemiah," *The Servant of the Lord and Other Essays on the OT* (1965) 137-68. **H. E. Ryle,** *The Books of Ezra and Nehemiah* (CBSC, 1893). **W. Rudolph,** *Esra und Nehemia* (HAT, 1949). **H. H. Schaeder,** *Esra der Schreiber* (1930). **R. J. Saley,** "The Date of Nehemiah Reconsidered," *Biblical and Near Eastern Studies: Essays in Honor of W. S. Lasor* (ed. G. A. Tuttle, 1978) 151-65. **H. Schneider,** *Die Bücher Esra und Nehemia* (HSAT, 1959). **D. Schwiderski,** *Handbuch des nordwestsemitischen Briefformulars: ein Beitrag zur Echtheitsfrage der aramäischen Briefe des Ezrabuches* (BZAW 295, 2000). **B. E. Scolnic,** *Chronology and Papponymy: A List of the Judean High Priests of the Persian Period* (SFSHJ 206, 1999). **J. R. Shaver,** "Ezra and Nehemiah: On the Theological Significance of Making Them Contemporaries," *Priests, Prophets and Scribes: Essays on the Formation and Heritage of Second Temple Judaism in Honour of J. Blenkinsopp* (ed. E. Ulrich et al., 1992) 76-86. **D. C. Siegfried,** *Esra, Nehemia, und Esther* (HKAT, 1901). **J. D. Thomson,** *A Critical Concordance to the Septuagint: Nehemiah* (The Computer Bible 67, 1999). **K. D. Tolletson** and **H. G. M. Williamson,** "Nehemiah as Cultural Revitalization: An Anthropological Perspective," *JSOT* 56 (1992) 41-68. **C. C. Torrey,** *The Composition and Historical Value of Ezra–Nehemiah* (BZAW 2, 1896); *Ezra Studies* (1910). **A. Van Hoonacker,** "Néhémie et Esdras, une nouvelle hypothèse sure la chronologie de l'époque do la restauration," *Le Muséon* 9 (1890) 151-84, 317-51, 389-401. **J. W. H. Van Wijk-Bos,** *Ezra, Nehemiah, and Esther* (Westminster Bible Companion, 1998). **J. C. VanderKam,** "Ezra–Nehemiah or Ezra and Nehemiah?" *Priests,*

Prophets, and Scribes: Essays on the Formation and Heritage of Second Temple Judaism in Honour of J. Blenkinsopp (ed. E. Ulrich et al., 1992) 55-75. **R. de Vaux**, "The Decrees of Cyrus and Darius on the Rebuilding of the Temple," *The Bible and the Ancient Near East* (1971) 63-96. **G. Vermes, F. Millar,** and **M. Goodman,** *HJPAJC* (E. Schürer 3, 2, 1987). **J. W. Watts**, *Persia and Torah: The Theory of Imperial Authorization* (SBLSymS 17, 2001). **J. P. Weinberg**, *The Citizen-Temple Community* (1992). **J. L. White** (ed.), *Studies in Ancient Letter Writing* (Semeia 22, 1982). **H. G. M. Williamson**, *Israel in the Books of Chronicles* (1977); "The Composition of Ezra i-vi," *JTS* NS 34 (1983) 1-30; *Ezra, Nehemiah* (WBC, 1985); *Ezra and Nehemiah* (OTGu, 1987); "History," *It Is Written: Scripture Citing Scripture. Essays in Honour of B. Lindars, SSF (ed. D. A. Carson and H. G. M. Williamson,* 1988) 25-38. **L. Zunz**, *Die gottesdienstlichen Vorträge der Juden* (1832).

H. G. M. WILLIAMSON

THE WRITINGS

Esther (and Additions)

1. *Introduction.* No other biblical book has occasioned as much strong feeling and scholarly debate over its historicity, canonical status, textual integrity, and theological and moral stature as has the book of Esther. Excluded by some Jews from their canon of the first century CE (and possibly from that of the second or even the third), Esther was gradually accepted as canonical by both Jews and Christians, only to be virtually ignored by the latter even as Jews increasingly venerated the *Megillah*, as they called it. Judaism developed a rich talmudic and midrashic tradition about the book, while Christians were divided, first into Eastern and Western camps, and then later into sharply contrasting Protestant and Roman Catholic perspectives. All this becomes more understandable when one realizes that in the MT of Esther, God is not mentioned (yet the Persian king is referred to 190 times in 167 verses!); nor are such key Jewish concepts as prayer, temple, Jerusalem, or covenant (fasting is the only religious practice mentioned!). Moreover, the Greek version has two radically different texts (the Septuagint, or B-text; and the A-text), neither of which closely corresponds to the MT, plus six additions (Add Esth), which appreciably affect the book's purpose, dramatic appeal, appearance of authenticity, and religious and moral character. Jews and Protestants have regarded the Add Esth "apocryphal," while Roman Catholics, since the decrees of the Council of Trent in 1546, have called them "deuterocanonical."

Esther's Add Esth (107 verses) differ from one another—and from the canonical sections—in purpose, content, and style. They consist of Add Esth A: Mordecai's dream (vv. 1-11) and a conspiracy uncovered by him (vv. 12-17); B: the royal edict composed by Haman for the destruction of the Jews (vv. 1-7); C: the prayers of Mordecai (vv. 1-11) and Esther (vv. 12-30); D: Esther's dramatic unannounced audience with the king (vv. 1-16); E: the royal edict dictated by Mordecai (vv. 1-24); and F: an explanation of Mordecai's dream (vv. 1-10) and the book's colophon (v. 11).

2. *Early Jewish Interpretations.* Although the earliest form of the Esther story may go back to the fourth century B.C.E., its Hebrew text probably took its final form in the early or middle Hellenistic period (331–168 B.C.E.). Nonetheless, Esther was one of the last books of the Hebrew Bible to be canonized. The Essene community at Qumran (c. 150 B.C.E.–68 C.E.) did not regard it as canonical, for not even a fragment of it has been found there (J. Milik 1992) nor was Purim part of their liturgical calendar. At least two rabbis in the third century (*b. Meg.* 7a) and two in the third/fourth (*b. Sanh.* 2) also regarded the book as noncanonical, and it is not found in the second-century Jewish Greek translations of Aquila, Symmachus, or Theodotion. The Jewish historian Josephus evidently accepted Esther's canonicity, however, for he paraphrased it and Add Esth B-E in his *Jewish Antiquities* (c. 94 C.E.) and added additional material to it.

3. *The Early Christian Era.* Esther was not quoted by Jesus or alluded to by any New Testament writer. Even though included in the canonical lists of a few Eastern church fathers (notably, Origen, Epiphanius, Cyril of Jerusalem, the Laodicene Canons [343-381], the Apostolic Canons [380], the Synod of Trullo [692], John of Damascus and of most Western fathers, ranging from Hilary to Isidore of Seville as well as the councils of Hippo (393) and Carthage (397), it was rarely alluded to, let alone quoted.

The fathers virtually ignored the book. Some exceptions include Clement of Rome (1 *Clem.* 55), Clement of Alexandria (*Strom.* 4:19), Athanasius of Alexandria (*Fourth Festal Letter*), the author of the *Apostolic Constitutions* (5.3.20), Origen (*Peri proseuchēs* 13.2), Jerome (A*pologeticum ad Pammachius*), and Paulinus Nolanus (*Carmina* 26.95; 28.27). Augustine commented on the book (*De divinis scripturis* 130), including Add Esth D 8 (*De civitate Dei* 18.36, *De gratia Christi et de peccato originali* 1.24)

4. *The Medieval Period. a. Jewish*. Traditional rabbinic exegesis continued during this period. A radically different type of scholarship that rejected this style of rabbinic exegesis and emphasized a literalistic interpretation of Scripture was that of Rashi, who emphasized lexical and grammatical analysis. Using much the same approach, the greatest of all Arabic-Jewish exegetes, A. ibn Ezra also wrote a commentary on Esther. This literalistic approach to Scripture was productive, but short-lived, with the thirteenth century rise of the esoteric, mystical Kabbalah that emphasized allegorical and midrashic interpretations.

b. *Christian*. Rabanus Maurus's *Expositio in librum Esther* (836) marked the appearance of the first full-length commentary on Esther (the canonical sections only) offering largely allegorical interpretations, e.g., the "linen and purple cords" in Esth 1:6 represent "mortification of the flesh" and "the blood of the martyrs," respectively.

Devotional and homilectical concerns prevailed over exegetical ones, e.g., the commentaries of Walafrid Strabo and Hugh of St. Victor. R. Tuitiensis (1135) regarded the book as essentially historical, but continued allegorical interpretations. Relying on the work of Rashi and Ibn Ezra, Nicholas of Lyra§ made the major medieval contribution to the critical study of Esther with his *Postillae perpetuae*.

5. *The Renaissance-Reformation Period*. a. *Jewish*. Virtually unaffected by the intellectual revolution then going on among Christian scholars, Jewish commentators continued their midrashic approach to Scripture.

b. *Christian*. With the West's discovery of classical languages and literature, plus the Protestants' insistence on Scripture as the sole Authority for doctrines, the second half of the sixteenth century witnessed a strong emphasis on the study of the Bible in its original Hebrew and Greek, although most Roman Catholic scholars still used the Vulgate. Thus Roman Catholics continued to study the Add Esth while Protestants increasingly ignored them.

Following the earlier interpretations of the fathers, many Roman Catholics continued the allegorical approach (especially the idea that Queen Esther was a type of the Virgin Mary); but others showed a strong interest in textual and historical matters, notably, J. Menochius (1630), who also utilized Jewish and Protestant scholarship. J. de la Haye's *Biblia Maxima* (1660) was a compendium of Roman Catholic study for the previous 150 years.

Protestants, too, regarded Esther as essentially historical but employed allegory less, preferring to emphasize the book's literal, historical, and grammatical aspects. Neither Calvin nor Luther wrote a commentary on the book. The latter's attitude toward it is still sometimes quoted with approval: "I am so hostile to this book [2 Macc] and to Esther that I could wish that they did not exist at all; for they judaize too greatly and have much pagan impropriety" (*Table Talks*, 24).

S. Münster's Latin translation of Esther (1546) was based on the Hebrew text. Critical studies were also made by scholars like H. Grotius (1644), who cited such classical sources as Herodotus's *History of the Persian Wars* and Josephus, while S. Pagninus (1556), the Westminster Assembly's *Annotations* (1657), and others continued along more devotional or homiletical lines. M. Poole's§ *Synopsis criticorum aliorumque Sacrae Scripturae interpretum* (1669) included the critical insights of both Protestant and Roman Catholic scholarship for the past century and a half.

6. *The Post-Reformation Period*. The next 150 years was a period of retrenchment and theological narrowness for both churches during which little scholarly progress was made on Esther by either Roman Catholics or Protestants. Although B. Spinoza's *Tractatus theologico-politicus* (1670) demonstrated a genuinely critical spirit, it exerted little influence on his own compatriots, let alone on Christians.

7. *The Modern Period*. a. *Die Aufklärung, or the Enlightenment*. Under the influence of German rationalists and English Deists (Deism), biblical books were scrutinized with a most

critical eye. "Lower criticism" was advanced by J. H. Michaelis[§] (1720), B. Kennicott (1776–80), and G. de Rossi (1784–88), all of whom collated variants of the Hebrew text, although most of the manuscripts were unfortunately of a late medieval date.

Considerable progress was also made in the area of higher criticism: the who, what, where, when, and why of a biblical book. When J. D. Michaelis (Esther [1783]) conceded that one could be "a perfect [*vollkommener*] Lutheran" and yet have doubts about the historicity of the book, J. Semler had already made an all-out attack on its historicity, characterizing the book as "a Jewish romance" or novel, a view to which a majority of scholars still subscribe.

The sustained attack on the book's historicity and its "unacceptable moral tone" by scholars like J. G. Eichhorn (1780) and A. Niemeyer (1782), who first made the often repeated observation that Queen Vashti was the only decent person in Esther, elicited conservative responses on the part of J. Vos (1775) and others. Increasingly, Christian scholars were divided into two camps: those contesting Esther's historicity and those defending it, the latter position more often taken by Roman Catholics.

b. *The nineteenth century. i. Jewish.* Jewish scholars began addressing some of the same problems as Christians, sometimes in the same journals, e.g., J. Bloch (1877, 1866), B. Hause (1879), and J. J. de Villiers (1893).

ii. Christian. Conservative treatments of Esther appeared in Jahn (1803), J. Scholz (1845), C. Keil (1873, very scholarly and ultra-conservative), A. Scholz (1892, scholarly but allegory-laden), and E. Kaulen (1890).

Liberal treatments included W. de Wette (1817), H. Ewald (1843), T. Nöldeke (1868), E. Reuss (1890); T. Cheyne (1893), E. Kautzsch (1896), and E. Schürer (1898–1901), and V. Ryssel (1887, the best of the liberal treatments).

As part of his efforts to reconstruct the Urtext of the LXX, P. Lagarde (1883) "proved" that Esther's A-text was part of the Lucianic recension of the LXX, a view that universally prevailed among scholars until the discovery of the Dead Sea Scrolls, when various apocryphal and pseudepigraphical works (Pseudepigrapha) now appeared in Semitic form. Protestants, too, exhaustively treated the Add Esth and regarded them as composed in Greek (so O. Fritzsche 1851, J. Fuller 1888, and Ryssel [1900] 193-212).

The nineteenth century's (and the twentieth's) decipherment of various cuneiform scripts and languages, as well as the excavation of various archaeological sites and their artifacts, contributed much toward illuminating the book's Achaemenid setting but little toward confirming its historicity. During this same period scholars began looking for Purim's origins in pagan sources, in some Greek, Babylonian, or, especially, Persian festival—but without conspicuous success.

The critical work of the nineteenth century was actually best summarized in three works appearing in 1908: P. Haupt and L. Paton, (1908a, 1908b), the latter being the most comprehensive and detailed discussion in English thus far of the book's history of interpretation and its problems of higher and lower criticism

c. *The twentieth century.* Especially after the works of Paton, Haupt, and H. Gunkel (1916), the literary aspects of Esther became the primary concern of scholars, with some even arguing that the Joseph narrative in Genesis (A. Meinhold 1976, 72-93) or the Moses story in Exodus 1-12 (G. Gerleman 1970–73) provided the paradigm for Esther's plot and all its details of "fact."

While the dominant theory among liberal scholars at the turn of the century was that Esther was "pure" fiction, in the twentieth century (especially the second half), the "combination theory" gained ascendancy—that is, the book is a combination of fiction and "fact," the combining of a harem tale about Vashti, a Mordecai story, and an Esther/Hadassah story, the latter two stories being independent tales with a possible core of historicity to each. Thus Esther is a historical novel in which literary considerations determine the plot and details of fact (so H. Bardtke 1963, C. Moore 1971, 1992, S. Berg 1979, and D. Clines 1984). The book provides a lifestyle for Jews of the Diaspora (W. L. Humphreys 1973).

i. Jewish. In some respects, Jewish scholarship on Esther is more impressive than either Roman Catholic or Protestant studies, if only because of its marked increase in both quantity and scope. Some Jewish scholars were still concerned with the centuries-long Judaic approaches to Esther; e.g., L. Ginzberg (1939); H. Freedman and M. Simon (1939); J. Brown (1976); and B. Grossfeld (1983). But apart from J. Hoschander (1923), who was concerned with establishing the full historicity of the book, Jewish scholars became primarily interested in problems of higher criticism, especially those concerning the historical origins and theological meaning of Purim: N. Doniach (1933), S. Ben-Chorin (1938), J. Lewy§ (1939), T. Gaster (1950), S. Besser (1969), J. Lebram (1972), R. Herst (1973), and A. Cohen (1974). Their consensus is that although God is not mentioned in Esther and Purim may well be of pagan origin, the book has a genuinely religious meaning, veiled though it may be.

But Jewish scholars had other concerns as well; e. g., A. Yahuda, "The Meaning of the Name Esther" (JRAS [1946] 174-78); S. Talmon, " 'Wisdom' in the Book of Esther" (VT 13 [1963] 419-55), which viewed Esther as a historicized wisdom tale; E. Bickerman, Four Strange Books of the Bible (1967); S. Zeitlin, "The Books of Esther and Judith: A Parallel" in M. Enslin's The Book of Judith (1972); and R. Gordis (1974, 1976, 1981), who hypothesized that the book was written by a gentile chronicler. S. Berg's study (1979) is, to date, the best rhetorical analysis of Esther and clearly shows that the MT in its present form is an integrated and literary whole whose themes are those of power, loyalty to God and Israel, the inviolability of the Jewish people, and reversal.

In contrast to previous centuries, Jewish articles featured the Greek text, including the Add Esth; e.g., Bickerman, (1944, 1950) and E. Tov(1982),which argued that Esther's A-Text is a recension of the LXX corrected toward a Hebrew (or Aramaic) text quite different from the MT.

ii. Christian. Commentaries continuing the liberal tradition included those of A. Streane (1907); B. Anderson (1954); G. Knight (1955); H. Ringgren (1958), and H. Bardtke (1963), the most scientific and complete German commentary on Esther in the last two hundred years; Moore (1971); G. Gerleman (1970–73); W. Fuerst (1975); and J. Cragham (OTM, 1982). Roman Catholic commentaries, often more conservative and frequently containing Add Esth, included those of J. Schildenberger, Das Buch Esther (HSAT 4.3 [1941]); L. Soubigou, Esther traduit et comment, (1952); A. Barucq, Judith-Esther (1959); and B. Girbau, La Biblia (1960).

Separate and detailed studies of the Add Esth were made by J. Gregg (1913, 665-84), and F. Roiron (1916), the latter arguing that Add Esth B and E are the actual Greek edicts of Haman and Mordecai respectively; and R. Pfeiffer§ (1949). But thanks to the catalytic study of the problem by C. C. Torrey (1944), scholars, while granting a Greek origin for Add Esth B and E, have increasingly argued for a Hebrew or Aramaic *Vorlage* for such interpolations as Add Esth A, C, D, and F (so E. Ehrlich 1955 69-74, Moore 1973, R. Martin 1975).

In contrast to the previous one hundred years, scholars increasingly maintained that the A-text is a separate and independent translation of another Semitic text, not a recension of the LXX (Torrey 1944, Moore 1967 351-58; and Clines 1984). In a foreshadowing of Vatican II, L. Soubigou (Esther 1952, 581-82, 597) noted that Roman Catholic scholars must accept as doctrinally true the inspirational character of Add Esth, but not that they were part of the original book.

Now, however, the legitimate, centuries-old distinctions between Jewish scholarship on Esther and that of Christians (including Catholic versus Protestant) are no longer useful. It is now much more the academic or methodological perspective rather than the theological or religious orientation that determines the nature and character of any particular study of Esther. Redaction and literary criticism (e.g., C. Dorothy [1989]; M. Fox [1991]; L. Day [1995]; K. Craig [1995]), feminist scholarship (such as A. LaCoque 1990; K. Darr 1991; W. Phipps 1992; S. White 1992; A. Bellis 1994), and computer-generated studies (J. Miles 1985 and K. Jobes 1996) dominate the field of Esther studies—for now.

Recent commentaries on Esther (and the additions) include Berlin (2000) and Crawford (2003a, 2003b). Thompson has developed concordances for Esther (1999, 2002). Fountain (2002) studies the MT, LXX, and A versions of Esther from a reader-response perspective. Brenner (1999) is a collection of feminist analyses of Esther. Glickman (1999) studies the figure of Haman in Midrashic interpretation. Rottzoll (1999) translates and provides commentary on the medieval Jewish exegete Ibn Ezra's Esther commentary. Harvey (2003) discusses morality within Esther's different textual recensions. Kossmann (2000) studies Esther from the perspectives of history of traditions and redactional history. Layzer (2001) compares the figure of Esther with figures in Irish folk tales to study the relationship of Celtic myth, Irish folktales, and biblical hero stories. Beal (Linafelt and Beal 1999) uses rhetorical criticism to investigate anti-Judaism in Esther and the contemporary questions raised by the text concerning sexism, ethnocentrism, and national identity.

Bibliography: B. W. Anderson, "The Book of Esther," *IB* (1954) 3:823-74. **H. Bardtke,** *Das Buch Esther* (KAT 17, 5, 1963); *Luther und das Buch Esther* (1964). **T. K. Beal**, *The Book of Hiding: Gender, Ethnicity, Annihilation, and Esther* (1997). **A. O. Bellis**, *Helpmates, Harlots, and Heroes: Women's Stories in the HB* (1994). **S. Ben-Chorin**, *Kritik des Estherbuches* (1938). **S. B. Berg**, *The Book of Esther: Motifs, Themes and Structure* (SBLDS 44, 1979). **A. Berlin**, *Esther: The Traditional Hebrew Text with the New JPS Translation* (JPS Bible Commentary, 2001), "The Book of Esther and Ancient Storytelling," *JBL* 120 (2001) 3-14. **S. Besser**, "Esther and Purim—Chance and Play" *CCARJ 16* (1969) 36-42. **E. Bickerman**, *Four Strange Books of the Bible* (1967); "The Colophon of the Greek Book of Esther," *JBL* 63 (1944) 339-62; "Notes on the Greek Book of Esther," *PAAJR* 20 (1950) 101-33). **J. Bloch**, *Hellenistische Bestandtheile im biblischen Schriftthum, eine kritische Untersuchung über Abfassung, Charakter, und Tendenzen des Buches Esther* (1877); "Der historische Hintergund und die Abfassungszeit des Buch Esther," *MGWJ* (1886). **D. Börner-Klein** and **E. Hollender**, trans., *Rabbinische Kommentare zum Buch Ester* (2000). **A. Brenner** (ed.), *Ruth and Esther* (Feminist Companion to the Bible, Second Series 3, 1999). **J. M. Brown**, *Rabbinic Interpretations of the Characters and Plot of the Book of Esther: As Reflected in Midrash Esther Rabbah* (1976). **D. J. A. Clines**, *The Esther Scroll: The Story of the Story* (1984). **A. Cohen**, " 'Hu Ha-goral': The Religious Significance of Esther," *Judaism 23* (1974) 87-94. **J. M. Cohen**, "Purim and Adloyada," *JBQ* 29 (2001) 259-62. **K. M. Craig, Jr.**, *Reading Esther: A Case for the Literary Carnivalesque* (Literary Currents in Biblical Interpretation, 1995). **S. W. Crawford**, "Esther," *NISB* (2003a) 689-701; "Esther (The Greek Version Containing the Additional Chapters)," *NISB* (2003b) 1401-1417. **K. P. Darr**, *Far More Precious Than Jewels: Perspectives on Biblical Women* (1991). **L. Day**, *Three Faces of a Queen: Characterization in the Books of Esther* (JSOTSup 186, 1995). **K. DeTroyer**, *The End of the Alpha Text of Esther: Translation and Narrative Technique* (SBLSCS 48, 2000); *Rewriting the Sacred Text* (Text-critical Studies 4, 2003). **W. Dommershausen**, *Die Estherrolle* (SBM 6, 1968). **N. Doniach**, *Purim or the Feast of Esther: An Historical Study* (1933). **C. V. Dorothy**, *The Books of Esther: Structure, Genre, and Textual Integrity* (JSOTSup 187, 1989, 1997). **J. G. Eichhorn**, *Einleitung ins Alte Testament* (3 vols., 1780–83). **H. Ewald**, *Geschichte des Volkes Israel bis Christus* (1843). **A. K. Fountain**, *Literary and Empirical Readings of the Books of Esther* (Studies in Biblical Literature 43, 2002). **M. V. Fox**, *The Redaction of the Books of Esther* (SBLMS 40, 1991). **H. Freedman** and **M. Simon**, *Midrash Rabbah 9* (1939)

1-124. **S. Frolov**, "Two Eunuchs, Two Conspiracies, and One Loyal Jew: the Narrative of Botched Regicide in Esther as Text- and Redaction-critical Test Case," *VT* 52 (2002) 304-325. **W. J. Fuerst**, *The Books of Ruth, Esther, Ecclesiastes, the Song of Songs, Lamentations* (CBC, 1975). **J. Fuller**, "Esther," *Apocrypha of the Speaker's Commentary*, vol. 1 (ed. H. Wace, 1888). **T. Gaster**, *Purim and Hanukkah in Custom and Tradition* (1950). **G. Gerleman**, *Esther* (BKAT 21, 1970–73). **L. Ginzberg**, *The Legends of the Jews 4* (1913) 365-448; *6* (1928) 451-81; *7* (1939). **E. R. Glickman**, *Haman and the Jews: A Portrait from Rabbinic Literature* (1999). **R. Gordis**, *Megillat Esther: The Masoretic Hebrew Text with Introduction, New Translation and Commentary* (1974); "Studies in the Esther Narrative," *JBL 95* (1976) 43-58; "Religion, Wisdom and History in the Book of Esther—A New Solution to an Ancient Crux," *JBL 100* (1981) 359-88. **L. Greenspoon** and **S. W. Crawford**, eds., *The Book of Esther in Modern Research* (JSOTSup 380, 2003). **J. A. F. Gregg**, "The Additions to Esther," *APOT 1* (1913) 665-71. **H. Grossfeld**, *The First Targum to Esther* (1983). **H. Gunkel**, *Esther* (1916). **H. M. Hager**, *Or ha-ḥamah: 'al Megilat Ester ve-Shelah ha-kadosh, Masekhet Megilah* (1997). **C. D. Harvey**, *Finding Morality in the Diaspora?: Moral Ambiguity and Transformed Morality in the Books of Esther* (BZAW 328, 2003). **P. Haupt**, *Critical Notes on Esther* (1908). **B. Hause**, "Noch einmal das Buch Esther," *JBL* 8 (1879). **R. Herst**, "The Purim Connection," *USQR 28* (1973) 139-45). **J. Hoschander**, *The Book of Esther in the Light of History* (1923). **W. L. Humphreys**, 'Apodictic Prohibition: Some Observations,' *JBL 92* (1973) 211-23; "The Story of Esther and Mordecai: an Early Jewish Novella," in *Saga, Legend, Tale, Novella Fable*, ed. G. W. Coats (1985) 97-113; "The Story of Esther in its Several Forms: Recent Studies," *RSR* 24 (1998) 335-342. **K. H. Jobes**, *The Alpha-Text of Esther: Its Character and Relationship to the Masoretic Text* (SBLDS 153, 1995). **S. B. J. A. Kluger**, *Sefer Ma'amar Ester: 'al Megilat Ester* (2003). **G. F. Knight**, *Esther, Song of Songs, Lamentations: Introduction and Commentary* (TBC, 1955). **R. Kossmann**, *Die Esthernovelle: Vom Erzählten zur Erzählung: Studien zur Traditions- und Redaktionsgeschichte des Estherbuches* (VTSup 79, 2000). **M. Kuyama**, "Origen and Esthe: a Reflection on the 'Anti-Jewish' Argument in Early Christian Literature," *Studia Patristica XXXIV: Historica, biblica, theologica et philosophica* (2001) 424-35. **A. LaCoque**, *The Feminine Unconventional: Four Subversive Figures in Israel* (1990). **P. Lagarde**, *Librorum Veteris Testamenti Canonicorum* (1883). **J. Lebram**, "Purimfest und Estherbuch," *VT 22* (1972) 208-22. **B. D. Lerner**, "No Happy Ending for Esther," *JBQ* 29 (2001) 4-12. **J. D. Levenson**, *Esther: A Commentary* (OTL, 1997). **J. Lewy**, "Old Assyrian puru'um and purum," *RHA 5* (1939) 117-24; "The Feast of the 14th Day of Adar," *HUCA 14* (1939) 127-51. **T. Linafelt** and **T. K. Beal**, *Ruth and Esther* (Berit Olam, 1999). **R. Martin**, "Syntax criticism of the LXX additions to the book of Esther," *JBL* 94 (1975) 65-72. **A. Meinhold**, "Die Gattung der Josephsgeschichte und des Estherbuches : Diasporanovelle I und II," *ZAW* 88 (1976) 72-93. **J. D. Michaelis**, *Esther* (1783). **J. R. Miles**, *Retroversion and Text Criticism: The Predicability of Syntax in an Ancient Translation from Greek to Ethiopic* (SBLSCS 17, 1985). **J. T. Milik**, "Les Modeles Aram,ens du Livre d'Esther dans La Grotte 4 de Qumran," *RdQ 15* (1992) 321-99. **C. A. Moore**, *ZAW* 79 (1967) 351-58; *Esther* (AB 7B, 1971); *JBL 92* (1973) 382-93; *Daniel, Esther, and Jeremiah: The Additions* (AB 44, 1977); 'Esther,' *ABD* (1992) 2:626-43. **A. Niemayer**, *Charakteristick der Bibel* (1782). **T. Nöldeke**, *Die Alttestamentliche Literatur* (1868). **L. B. Paton**, "A Text-critical Apparatus to the Book of Esther" (*Old Testament and Semitic studies in memory of William Rainey Harper*, vol. 2 (R. F. Harper, F. Brown, G. F. Moore, eds., 1908[a]); *A Critical and Exegetical Commentary on the Book of Esther* (ICC, 1908[b]). **W. E. Phipps**, *Assertive Biblical Women* (Contributions in Women's Studies 128, 1992). **H. Ringgren**, *Das Buch Esther* (ATD 16, 1958). **D. U. Rottzoll**, *Abraham Ibn Esras Kommentare zu den Büchern Kohelet, Ester und Rut* (SJ 12, 1999). **J. Schildenberger**, *Das Buch Esther*, HSAT 4.3 (1941). **A. Scholz**, *Commentar über das Buch Esther mit seinen*

Zusätzen (1892). **D. ben Se'adyah**, *Midrash ha-be'ur: 'al ḥamishah ḥumshe Torah, ha-hatorot u-Megilat Ester*, 2 vols. (1998, 1999). **Y. B. S. Shelomoh**, *Sefer be'erot ha-mayim* (1998). **M. Simon**, "Megillah: Translated into English with Notes, Glossary, and Indices," *Babylonian Talmud* (1938). **L. Soubigou**, *Esther traduit et comment* (1952). **A. W. Streane**, *The Book of Esther, With Intro and Notes* (CBSC, 1907). **S. Talmon**, "'Wisdom' in the Book of Esther," *VT* 13 (1963) 419-55). **J. D. Thompson,** *A Critical Concordance to the Septuagint: Esther* (The Computer Bible 68, 1999); *A Critical Concordance to the Apocrypha: Esther* (The Computer Bible 104, 2002). **C. C. Torrey**, "The Older Book of Esther," *HTR 37* (1944) 1-40. **E. Tov**, "The Lucianic Text of the Canonical and the Apocryphal Sections of Esther," *Textus* 10 (1982) 1-25. **W. Vischer**, *Esther* (TEH 48, 1937). **H. M. Wahl,** "Das Buch Esther als methodisches Problem und hermeneutische Herausforderung: eine Skizze," *BibInt* 9 (2001), 25-40. **F. S. Weiland**, "Historicity, Genre, and Narrative Design in the book of Esther," *BSac* 159 (2002) 151-65; "Literary Conventions in the Book of Esther," *BSac* 159 (2002) 425-35. **S. A. White**, "Esther: A Feminine Model for Jewish Diaspora," *Gender and Difference in Ancient Israel* (ed. P. Day, 1989) 161-77; *Women's Bible Commentary* (eds. C. A. Newsom and S. H. Ringe, 1992) 124-29. **E. Yadid**, *Sheva 'ha nevi'ot: Sarah, Ḥanah, Devorah, Miryam, Avigayil, Huldah, Ester* (2002). **A. Yahuda,** "The Meaning of the Name Esther," *JRAS* (1946) 174-78. **S. Zeitlin**, "The Books of Esther and Judith: A Parallel," *The Book of Judith* (ed. M. Enslin, 1972).

C. A. MOORE

THE WRITINGS

Job

Wherever we turn in the history of Western thought, we find Job: The Talmud, ath-Tha'labi's (d. 1035) "A Discourse of the Prophet Ayyub and His Trials," and W. Blake's (1757-1827) *Illustrations of the Book of Job* (1826) all demonstrate an enduring fascination with this tragic figure. From Gregory the Great to Calvin and from C. Jung to E. Wiesel (b. 1928), the image of Job haunts every attempt to explain suffering and to justify God's actions. Job's story has captivated the human imagination and has forced its readers to wrestle with the most painful realities of human existence.

1. *Patristic Interpretations of Job.* Like many books of the HB, the book of Job finds its earliest Christian reading in the NT. The Synoptic Gospels (Matt 19:26; Mark 10:27; and Luke 1:52), Paul (1 Cor 3:19; Phil 1:19; 1 Thess 5:22; 2 Thess 2:8), James (5:11), and the Apocalypse (Rev 9:6) refer explicitly or implicitly to the Joban text. These citations describe God's power, the "foolishness" of divine wisdom, the desire for death, and the famous "steadfastness" or "patience" of Job.

In the early church major commentaries on Job did not appear until the third century. One of the most important exegetes to initiate the reading of the book was Origen. Unfortunately no commentary of his on Job survives; however, scholars have culled more than 300 citations from his writings, often accompanied by detailed exegesis. In the fourth and fifth centuries several major commentaries or sermons on Job appeared, including those by Ambrose, Chrysostom, Augustine, and Julian of Eclanum (d. c. 454). Although these texts do not appear to have exercised major influence on the medieval Joban tradition, nonetheless, several themes emerge that characterize the patristic image of Job, some of which recur in medieval interpretations.

Job's virtue was a common theme. Both Origen and Chrysostom stressed that Job was a just man who feared God before the law was given to Moses. Chrysostom argued that before the law Job practiced evangelical doctrine and manifested an interior detachment (1 Tim 6:7), proving that for the just man there is no law (1 Tim 1:9) and that Christ did not come to teach anything new or unprecedented.

Perhaps it is this emphasis on Job's virtue that elicited teachings about free will from the Job text. Origen insisted on Job's free will and explained the mystery of evil in terms of the initial fall of preexistent souls; his Job became a prototype of the Christian martyr. In Chrysostom's various statements on Job, he too argued for Job's freedom as opposed to any fatalistic solution to the problem of evil. These discussions about free will found further expression in the Pelagian debates of the fifth century. Augustine's *Adnotationum in Job* was written between 399 and 404, before the outbreak of the Pelagian controversy. According to Augustine the story of Job portrays suffering as a test of the just person, which becomes exemplary for all subsequent Christian readers. In the later context of the anti-Pelagian controversy, Augustine's Job knew the universality of sin and recognized that the righteous person could expect no reward for right conduct. Moreover, by a special revelation Job learned the universal economy of salvation in a world where divine justice surpasses all earthly justice. Not surprisingly, Job played a different and more central role for Augustine's Pelagian opponents. As P. Brown notes, "Job was the hero of the Pelagians: he was a man suddenly stripped of the heavy artifice of society and capable of showing to the world the raw bones of a heroic individuality" (1967, 349). Julian of Eclanum is an example of an anti-Augustinian reading of Job. His *Expositio Libri Job* was influenced by Chrysostom, just as other Pelagians were influenced by the Latin translation of Chrysostom's homilies. Thus, by the mid-fifth century Job became a figure around whom theologians debated sin, justice, and human freedom (C. Kannengiesser [1974] 1218-22).

Many of these commentators considered suffering a providential benefit. For Augustine, Job's scourges were evils all the elect must endure as a test. Origen also portrayed the suffering of the righteous as a divine gift meant to heal and strengthen the sufferer, and Chrysostom placed Job's afflictions within the context of providence. All historical and natural events lie under the justice and goodness of God's providence; angels and demons render account to God, and creation also testifies to God's care.

But why would a providential God permit the devil to afflict the righteous? For Chrysostom this dilemma was exemplified in Job, while for Ambrose it was personified by Job and David (*De interpellatione Job et David*). Both authors gave the fullest expression to the view of suffering as beneficial, medicinal, and pedagogical. Chrysostom explained that the devil acts by God's permission in order to inflict "a terrible and hard pedagogy." Both he and Ambrose depicted this pedagogy in terms of athleticism: Suffering effects spiritual fortitude. To describe the muscular benefit of suffering, Ambrose drew on 2 Cor 12:9 and described Job "as an athlete of Christ" who attained greater glory through temptation. Job "was stronger when sick than he had been when healthy," and both Job and David found "strength in their afflictions." Chrysostom also saw Job as an "athlete of God" and his story as a battle fought in a stadium; God was Job's "trainer," and the devil was his adversary. Job, therefore, was the great victor.

Finally, these authors also associated Job's suffering with wisdom. Visual metaphors denoting insight and knowledge describe the experiences of Ambrose's Job and David. Job's friends are said to have suffered from "feeble insight," while the afflicted Job "spoke in mysteries," made "distinctions in the spirit," and uttered truths according to a knowledge of God's judgments. The insight and discernment gained by Job and David led to a wisdom that gave them a deeper perception into reality, a perception that allowed them to see the vanity and illusory nature of earthly prosperity and power. Unlike the wicked, Job and David were not "drunk" with the abundance of worldly possessions, but were wise in the knowledge that "abiding things cannot follow unless earthly things have failed."

Both Chrysostom and Ambrose related Job's suffering to a wisdom equated with detachment. Chrysostom's Job was the model of philosophy, the sage who was glorious in adversity because he had always been detached in prosperity. (Chrysostom continued this theme of wisdom in his interpretation of the whirlwind speech. At this point Job discovered true wisdom-namely, his own human weakness and the fear of God.) Ambrose also equated the wisdom of suffering with detachment. The adversaries of Job and David enabled them to transcend the "waves" or "sea" of this temporal, ever-fluctuating world. Thus, in the lives of Job and David, Ambrose found an expression of that ancient identification between suffering and freedom: A real and muscular suffering leads to a truer perception of reality that, in turn, frees the sufferer from earthly entanglements.

2. *Medieval Commentaries on Job.* In the Middle Ages Job appeared in poetry, mystery plays, liturgy, and biblical exegesis. The medieval era inherited the portrayal of Job as a warrior or *athleticus Dei* from sources like Prudentius's (d. c. 410) *Psychomachia*. In the various medieval reworkings of the Joban legend, we find Job as a wise man, a prophet, and a philosopher. He was even portrayed as the patron saint of persons suffering from worms, skin diseases, and melancholy; and he was the patron saint of Music. The cult of Job flourished from the fourteenth to the sixteenth centuries due to the ravages of the plague and the spread of syphilis; indeed, syphilis became known as "le mal monsieur saint Job." Finally, in the liturgy Job played a major role in the Office of the Dead, particularly in the Matins of the Dead or the Dirge proper. In this liturgical setting many medieval clergy and laity experienced the book of Job on a daily basis (L. Besserman [1979] 56-65, 71).

The precritical exegetical tradition divides into two trajectories in the Christian West: the allegorical tradition established by Gregory the Great and the literal tradition formulated most decisively by Thomas Aquinas. Between their works stands the interpretation of the great Jewish philosopher Maimonides.

These readings of Job vary greatly from one another. Different exegetical methods as well as different philosophical and theological presuppositions make the world of precritical Joban exegesis seem labyrinthine. Despite these differences, however, medieval (and Reformation) commentaries examine topics that gravitate around issues of suffering, justice, history, and providence. More important, a unifying feature runs throughout all of these commentaries-namely, the concern with perception or understanding. Fundamentally, all Joban exegetes had to answer a basic question: What did Job understand that made him perceptually superior to his friends? The term perception does not mean that epistemology drives exegesis. For medieval and Reformation commentators the issue of perception expressed a deeper concern regarding the more explicit subjects of suffering, justice, and providence. What can the sufferer, who stands within history, perceive about the self, God, and reality? Can suffering, especially inexplicable suffering, elevate human understandings about God and the self? Are evil and injustice really matters of perspective? Is there a darker side of God and of reality that we must confront before wisdom can be found? The question that permeates the precritical Joban tradition is not how one knows, but what one knows.

Repeatedly these commentaries are suffused with terminology referring to what the human mind can know via the imagery of sight, given a certain perspective aided by revelation and illumined by faith. In all the commentaries the perceptual opposition inherent in the Joban story is central: Some speakers are perceptive, while others are not. Empirical evidence is not ultimate; for these exegetes there is a depth dimension to reality that transcends purely sensory, historical, and experiential ways of knowing. They all expressed a theme native to the book of Job: Things are not what they seem.

Gregory's *Moralia in Iob* was composed for a monastic audience and dates from the late sixth century. He interpreted Job as a multi-layered text with innumerable literal, allegorical, and moral meanings. As the model for how one should endure suffering, Gregory's Job often collapses the literal and moral senses of the text: He is the literal embodiment of moral truth. For Gregory and his successors, however, Job was not the only moral exemplar in the story; his friends also dispensed lofty truths. But how does one account for the fact that Job's friends were reproved by God in 42:7-8? Gregory answered by arguing that Job's friends said many true things but misapplied them to Job because they did not understand that his suffering was not punishment for past sins. Moreover, Elihu was corrected in chapter 38 but was not included in the divine rebuke of "Eliphaz and his two friends." Elihu's words were arrogant, then, but often true. These exegetical solutions were to recur in various fashions in late medieval and Reformation (Christian) commentaries on Job.

Job's speeches also created hermeneutical problems. The justice of Job's suffering was guaranteed, according to Gregory, by increased merit in the afterlife. The problem was Job's behavior during his scourges. Two verses govern Gregory's exegesis of Job's laments: the Satanic challenge in 2:5 and the divine affirmation in 42:7. For Gregory these verses ensured that Job did not blaspheme under trial; to accuse him of cursing God was to say that Satan won the celestial contest recounted in the prologue. Such an accusation was also to deny God's final words.

These exegetical moves allowed Gregory to portray Job as the model for virtuous suffering and interior ascent. By combining the Neoplatonic hierarchy of being with his presuppositions about the enlightening and liberating power of suffering, Gregory read the book as a description of that arduous inner ascent toward God undertaken by the elect. He assumed that Job's ascent created an inward perception of reality made possible only by the double movement of turning inward and rising to a higher level of being, which is effected through suffering. Thus Job's "complaints" become words about the vanity of earthly prosperity. By embracing suffering he manifested the virtue of detachment, insight, and inner freedom. Rejoicing over the brevity and harshness of life, Gregory's Job escaped the dreaded danger of "tranquility." According to Gregory, Job knew that providence is most indiscernible when the good prosper and the wicked suffer because suffering frees the elect from the world and leads to wisdom. Hence Job discovered an anthropological wisdom that allowed him deeper insight into the self and the proper home of the soul on the eternal realm.

Gregory read the book of Job as a description of both the human condition and human history. For the sufferer standing within time the historical realm must be renounced in order to ascend to a higher perceptual reality. Gregory's identification of Job's virtue with detachment shows that the realm of time, change, and exteriority is the "exile" or "Egypt" of the present life. Gregory's view of history, however, was more complex than is first apparent, as is revealed on the allegorical level of the text. His portrayal of Job as a prophet and his many typological interpretations turn the mind, not toward the eternal, but "downward" toward a providential history. It is true that as the "literal" and "moral" Job ascended he expressed contempt for and freedom from the temporal world. But as the "allegorical" and "prophetic" Job ascended, he looked down on a typological history and recounted or foretold God's redemptive acts. As one who suffered unjustly, for example, Job inevitably became a type of Christ. This redemptive history, centered in the crucifixion, consisted of events that took place in time.

The whirlwind speech provides the most striking example of this temporal downward perspective gained from the eternal viewpoint. In Gregory's reading of chaps. 38-41, Job either remained on the historical level or typified the church. In both cases God addressed him through history. From the whirlwind God recounted God's salvific acts throughout history, foretold Christ's victory over Satan (demonstrated by God's power over Behemoth and Leviathan), and promised the final defeat of the antichrist. From this higher perceptual level granted in the whirlwind speech, Job sought the protection of God against the "Ancient Enemy" and thereby also saw that history is not utterly rejected; the devil is defeated by Christ in history. Sacred history creates a philosophy that both affirms the historical realm and relegates it to the lowest level of reality. By seeing the book of Job as allegorically relating sacred history, Gregory's allegorical-typological interpretation reclaims a part of historical existence as redemptive. Furthermore, this theory of history becomes a hermeneutical device that casts the Joban story in terms of perception, perspective, and the limitations posed by time. Thus, as Gregory's readers penetrate the meaning of the text, they rise with Job toward the eternal and contemplate the truths buried deeply within the realm they left behind.

Maimonides provided a very different reading of Job, as found in book 3 of the *Guide of the Perplexed* (c. 1185-90). According to Maimonides, the story of Job is not historically true but is a parable about the true meaning of providence. Since providence is one of the "secrets of the law," he explained this parable in a closely guarded and cryptic way.

At the beginning of his ordeal Maimonides' Job was morally righteous but not wise: He knew the deity only by "the acceptance of authority." Struck by inexplicable suffering, he fell into the error of "Aristotelianism," which Maimonides identified as the belief that God had abandoned the human race. Job's speeches, then, were not expressions of detachment but, rather, cries of despair. In his rendering of the Joban story, Maimonides traced Job's progress from traditional authoritative religion to despair and finally to wisdom.

By saying that Satan was the cause of Job's despair, Maimonides argued that Job's suffering was due to "imagination" or error. The deluding power of imagination is broken by Elihu's angel (33:23, 29), identified as the Active Intellect or the Tenth Intelligence. Human intellects who attain perfection are capable of intermittent union with the Active Intellect, during which the Active Intellect exercises "providence" over them. In the book of Job, Maimonides found proof that "providence is consequent upon the intellect."

Maimonides' Job attained this union with the Active Intellect in the whirlwind speech. Here Job gained a wisdom that made him reject his former errors and accept the limitations of human knowledge. As he moves from imagination to wisdom, his confession becomes the hermeneutical key to the story. Previously he imagined that happiness consisted of health, wealth, and children. In chap. 42, however, he expresses his new "correct apprehension," whereby he realizes that those things he had imagined to be happiness were not the goal of life. For Maimonides, then, Job did not gain this perception through suffering. Rather, he suffered because he was ignorant, since suffering belongs to the realm of Satan, matter, and imagination; he had overestimated the good belonging to the sphere of time and change. His wisdom freed him from the illusions that cause suffering.

Job's "correct apprehension" was identical to Maimonides' "revised Aristotelianism"; i.e., the knowledge that providence does extend to some individuals who are capable of union with the Active Intellect. This wisdom detached Job from his adversaries and made him reject his earlier beliefs (shared by his friends) and his earlier despair. Most important, he learned the equivocal nature of language about God. A naturalistic reading of the "prophetic" revelation of the whirlwind speech allowed Maimonides to argue that human knowledge cannot move beyond the sphere of nature. Terms like providence, purpose, and knowledge cannot be applied to God in the way they can be applied to humans. Maimonides, then, portrayed Job's deepening insight, not in terms of "ascent," but in terms of restriction and incomprehensibility; Job's highest point of understanding was to confess what he could not know. In his newly gained perception of reality, he learned the limits of human knowledge. But, as Maimonides concluded, "If a man knows this [the equivocal nature of terms about God] every misfortune will be borne lightly by him."

Whereas Gregory interpreted Job allegorically and Maimonides read the book parabolically, Thomas's *Expositio super Iob ad litteram* (c. 1260-64) expounded the text according to the literal sense. Like Maimonides, Thomas saw the Joban story as a book about providence. However, while Maimonides denied personal immortality, Thomas made this belief the message of the book, i.e., that Job believed in personal immortality, while his friends (except Elihu) denied the afterlife. Thus 19:25 becomes the hermeneutical key to the book. Nonetheless, Thomas maintained that the issue at the center of the controversy between Job and his friends was the perception of order. For Thomas the presence of a just and good order in nature and in history is inseparable from a faith in providence. Doubts about providence arose regarding human events because "no certain order" appeared in them.

Thomas argued that because Job's friends (to varying degrees) denied immortality they restricted providence to the earthly life. To defend the justice of this earthly providence, they were forced to conclude that Job's adversities were due to sin. In the friends Thomas saw what we now call the deuteronomic view of history; i.e., that history is justly ordered, intelligible, and predictable as God punishes sin and rewards virtue. Thomas did not want to discard this theory altogether. He too admired the wisdom of Job's opponents, and to reclaim it he argued that on many crucial points Job agreed with his accusers.

Nonetheless, Thomas thought Job's friends were wrong and that their error was a perceptual one: They claimed to see within history an order that is not always discernible. The justice they professed to see is often reserved to the afterlife. Thomas's Job spoke rightly about God because his faith in immortality provided him with a perceptual superiority over that of his friends, a superiority based on the link between the doctrine of personal immortality and a justly ordered history. The afterlife functions as an extension of history so that God can exercise justice after death. Without immortality the proof for divine justice remains within history, as the friends argued.

Exegetically Thomas presented Job's belief by giving his laments the same literal reading as did Maimonides. Job's complaints were honest and experiential observations about human events if those events are judged without a doctrine of personal immortality. Thomas's Job showed that if providence is restricted to history, then disorder is the true character of that providential rule. Thus to restrict providence to history is to accuse God of injustice. This problem of God's injustice disappears, however, if there is an afterlife where God remedies historical injustices; hence Job's complaints became, for Thomas, a defense of divine justice. Moreover, he illustrated Job's ultimate faith in providence through the interpretation of Behemoth and Leviathan. Like Gregory, Thomas identified the great beasts as Satan; the story of Job thereby became a part of that providential drama involving God and Satan that has raged throughout history. By taking Leviathan "with a hook" God defeated Satan through the "hook" of Christ's incarnation. History, then, is the arena of God's redemptive action.

Thomas, therefore, both agreed and disagreed with his predecessors. As did Maimonides, he interpreted the book of Job in terms of providence. Unlike Maimonides, he affirmed God's individual providence and identified personal immortality as the belief that gave Job perceptual superiority. Like Gregory, he interpreted Behemoth and Leviathan as Satan, thereby connecting the end of Job's story with the prologue. However, Thomas's spirituality of suffering differed from that of Gregory. Thomas repeated Gregory's explanation for Job's afflictions, i.e., that God permitted Satan to punish Job in order to manifest his virtue. He also stated that trials contribute to salvation, but he gave no sense that Job rejoiced in his suffering. Thomas saw Job as "impeded" by pain. His Job did not ascend through suffering and affliction or turn his soul inward, thereby curing his perception and directing him to the eternal, for the process of suffering did not alter Job's perception. It was Job's faith in immortality that allowed him a deeper perception of reality. And, finally, by extending "history" to the afterlife Thomas affirmed, not the equivocal, but the analogous nature of justice. His use of immortality as a heuristic device functioned to delay divine justice, not to make it utterly unknowable.

3.Sixteenth-century Commentaries on Job. The late Middle Ages and the sixteenth century inherited both the Gregorian and the Thomistic Joban interpretations, as is evident in varying degrees in the works of Nicholas of Lyra and Denis the Carthusian (1402-71). In the sixteenth century we can see the growing importance of the Thomistic literal tradition. T. Cajetan's *In librum Iob commentarii* and Oecolampadius's *In librum Iob exegeme* both provide literal interpretations demonstrating knowledge of Maimonides and Thomas. Both exegetes stated that the book of Job is a debate about the nature of divine providence.

Calvin's *Sermons sur le livre de Job* (1554-55) represents the Reformation interest in the book and also shows the influence of the Thomistic literal tradition (probably known indirectly). Calvin too read the Joban story in terms of providence, portraying Job as the lone defender of immortality against Eliphaz, Bildad, and Zophar. Calvin's Job vindicated God's providence by extending divine justice to the afterlife. Most important, Calvin used the doctrine of immortality to set up the same perceptual opposition between Job and his friends as did Thomas. Accordingly, the friends (except Elihu) were wrong because they restricted providence to history and concluded that all suffering is punishment for past sins. This restriction made them misperceive the nature of history; to defend God's justice they claimed that history appears ordered. Job, however, knew that history often seems confused; providence is not always discernible, and sometimes God "hides" while the wicked prosper. Calvin stretched to the breaking point the perceptual tension inherent in the book. Job's suffering drove him toward a deeper awareness of the darker side of God and confronted him with two aspects of divine hiddenness: the inscrutability of God's justice and the incomprehensibility of divine providence.

Calvin argued that Job encountered two levels of God's justice-namely, that revealed in the law and a higher secret justice, which, according to Eliphaz in 4:18, can condemn even the purity of the angels. Since Job knew he was not being punished according to the lower justice of the law, his search for the cause of his afflictions led him to confront the "secret" justice of God. Calvin developed this theory of a twofold justice to defend God's acts; since God's will is the rule of justice, even those acts that transcend the justice of the law are righteous. Job's experience showed that there is no continuity between the infinite and the finite. While God's lower justice was revealed in the law, the higher justice was imperceptible to Job's mind, which left Job's God nearly eclipsed by his own inscrutability.

The idea of a twofold justice may have guaranteed God's justice, but it left Calvin's Job with a feeling of unrelenting dread expressed by his suspicion that God was exercising an "absolute power," a term Calvin interpreted to mean a cruel power unregulated by mercy and justice. To alleviate Job's dread Calvin mitigated his own exegetical device of God's twofold justice by asserting that at no time, including in the case of Job, does God ever act according to secret justice. God commits to judge only according to the lower justice of the law. But by blunting this theory, Calvin left Job at the whirlwind speech with no answer to his suffering because he knew nothing of the celestial contest recounted in the prologue. Calvin emphasized this dilemma by refusing to interpret Behemoth and Leviathan as Satan, hence Job never understood his situation allegorically through reference to God's battle with the devil. Calvin's Job seemed truly within the realm of incomprehensibility.

Nonetheless, Calvin refused to renounce completely the visibility and knowability of God. The imagery of nature that pervades the book of Job allowed Calvin to end his sermons by appealing to the revealed world of creation and thereby to find grounds for trust in a God who seemed to be receding into total darkness. To relieve this darkness Calvin juxtaposed nature and history as an opposition between revelation and hiddenness. For Calvin the order visible even in fallen creation served to demonstrate the providence of God over the cosmos. Therefore, in contrast to the incomprehensibility of God's actions in history stands the beauty and order in nature. But while one can appeal rightly to nature as proof of God's providence, it is wrong to claim to perceive this same order in history. Calvin cited this perceptual error, exemplified by Bildad's words in chapter 18, to show that Job's friends were wrong in failing to acknowledge the present disorder in history. In contrast, Job had faith in what he could not see-that is, in God's ultimate restoration of order.

In Calvin's literal exegesis of the whirlwind speech, however, God argues on the basis of nature. Here Calvin combined visibility and invisibility by placing within nature a dialectic between hiddenness and clarity. Nature reflects the wisdom of divine providence; however, it also transcends human understanding and leaves us with only a glimpse of God's providence. In short, the very majesty of nature infuses it with a kind of hiddenness.

According to Calvin, the use of nature in the whirlwind speech shows that the governing of history requires a wisdom and justice beyond that revealed in the cosmos. Still, despite the ultimate incomprehensibility of both nature and history, he left the faithful Job with a promise-namely, that the same God who governs the order of creation is powerful and wise enough to govern history and to bring order out of confusion. On the basis of the revelation of nature, Calvin's Job trusted that God is ordering human events with justice. Therefore, Calvin concluded by holding out the promise of continuity between God's revelation in creation and his governance of history.

4. *The Modern Period.* The seventeenth and eighteenth centuries produced an abundance of translations of Job into Latin, Greek, and several modern European languages (English, French, German, Italian, Spanish), as well as paraphrases, many of which were in verse (see D. Clines [1989] lxix-lxxv). Perhaps the most noteworthy is the translation by E. Smith (1776-1806; completed 1803; pub. 1810). Not only was it one of the first translations of a biblical book into English published by a woman but also one of the best translations of Job between the KJV and the late nineteenth century.

Although the question of the historicity of the story of Job had already been raised in rabbinic and medieval Jewish interpretation (*b. B. Bat.* 15a; *Genesis Rab.* 57; Maimonides), the issue became a topic of contention in the eighteenth century, with J. Le Clerc (1731) arguing for the fictive character of the Job story and A. Schultens (1737) defending its historicity. In England W. Warburton published an eccentric but widely circulated study (2 vols., 1737-41) in which he argued for the book of Job as an allegory of the political situation of the Jews after the Babylonian captivity. The eminent Hebraist R. Lowth refuted Warburton (1765), defending the antiquity and non-allegorical nature of Job.

Lowth's influential lectures on Hebrew poetry (1753) mark an important stage in the literary analysis and appreciation of Job. Arguing against a tradition that understood the book as analogous to Greek tragedy (maintained both by Theodore of Mopsuestia in the 4th cent. and by Theodore de Beza in the 16th), Lowth held that Job did not fit the formal criteria of Greek tragedies. The artistic quality of the book should be judged, rather, according to criteria appropriate to Hebrew poetry. In particular, Lowth praised Job for the poet's descriptive power in expressing character and manners, sentiments, and descriptions of natural phenomena.

European Romanticism of the eighteenth and nineteenth centuries was intrigued with the book in varied ways. Strongly influenced by Lowth, J. G. Herder (1782-83) championed its nature poetry as an example of the sublime. The French Romantic poet A. de Lamartine (1790-1869) interpreted Job as a type of the Promethean poet, passionate and eloquent, the embodiment of a humanity capable and worthy of dialogue with the divine. The most influential interpreter from the Romantic period, however, is W. Blake, whose famous *Illustrations* actually constitute more of a rewriting than an interpretation.

The meaning of Blake's illustrations has been variously interpreted, though all interpreters seek the key in his poetry and other writings. Blake used the account of Job to depict what he elsewhere calls the cleansing of "the doors of perception." Blake understood Job in his initial state as fundamentally failing to apprehend the nature of God, the world, and human existence. His outward piety is merely life according to "the letter" rather than "the spirit," represented in the first engraving by Job's holding the book of the Law on his lap (ill. 1). Thus, Blake's Job is not perfect and upright, as is the biblical Job, but misguided and a sinner. His sufferings serve to give him gradual awareness of his pride and his misperception of reality (ill. 6-11). God's appearance to Job from the whirlwind (ill. 13) serves as the critical moment of recognition for Job, who now sees the true God, the Divine Imagination. Although the book of Job makes no further reference to Satan the Accuser after chapter 2, Blake depicts a scene in which Satan is cast down from heaven into flames, along with figures who represent the errors that had characterized Job and his wife at the beginning of the book (ill. 16). In another departure from the biblical narrative, the penultimate illustration depicts Job telling his three daughters the story of his experience (ill. 20). The crucial role of art in disclosing truth is emphasized by the wall panels to which Job points, paintings that depict scenes from his story. The final illustration, portraying Job's restoration, echoes the first. Job's children are gathered around him, but he no longer sits with the book of the Law on his lap. Rather, they all stand and play the musical instruments that in the first illustration had been hung on the branches of a tree.

Job also figured in philosophical discourse of the modern period. Already in 1584 the commentary on Job by the Spanish Augustinian theologian D. de Zúñiga (*Didacus à Stunica* [1536-98]) had interpreted Job 9:6 as scriptural grounds for Copernicus's view that the earth revolves around a stationary sun. Zúñiga went on to argue for Copernicanism on scientific grounds as well; as a consequence, his commentary was condemned by the Roman Catholic Church in 1616 until the objectionable passage was removed (R. Blackwell [1991] 26-27, 122-23, 185-86). T. Hobbes (1651) drew on the divine speeches in Job not only for the image of Leviathan as symbol of the state but also as an illustration of sovereign power that does not justify itself by reference to law or reason. For the most part, however, Job played a role in debates over theodicy. G. Leibniz (1710) briefly referred to Job as an example of one who improperly complains of unjustified evil because he fails to see the divine purposes, whereas Voltaire's article on Job in the *Dictionnaire Philosophique* (1764) satirizes the inanities of Job's comforters and their philosophical defenders. Although Voltaire considered the book of Job to be one of the most precious of all antiquity, he argued that it was written by an Arab, a claim that provided him with the occasion to make several anti-Jewish remarks. I. Kant's critique of Liebniz (1791) differentiated between "doctrinal theodicy," the attempt to discern the moral intentions of God from the world of experience by speculative reason, and "authentic theodicy," which is grounded in the practical knowledge of God as revealed. For Kant Job served as an example of authentic theodicy: His integrity elicits the divine revelation from the whirlwind, which manifests the resistance of the purposes of God to the operations of speculative reason. Job's faith, grounded on moral conduct and acknowledging the limits of reason, however, forms the basis of an authentic theodicy.

G. W. F. Hegel (1770-1831) referred to Job only briefly (ET 1895), citing him as an example of one who recognizes the contradiction between his righteousness and his condition of suffering and yet brings his discontent "under the control of pure and absolute confidence" in the harmony of God's power. Although the restoration of Job's happiness, which follows upon his submission, cannot be demanded as a right, nevertheless it reflects "this unity [of God] which brings about a state of well-being proportionate to the well-doing" (2:193). S. Kierkegaard (1813-55) treated Job in two writings, both published in 1843. In *Repetition* Job figures as the example of one who undergoes an "ordeal." In Kierkegaard's writings this term describes an experience that does not belong to the aesthetic, ethical, or dogmatic realm of existence but is, rather, transcendent, as it "places a person in a purely personal relationship of opposition to God" (210). Job's ordeal ends, however, as he receives in an unexpected manner the possibility of repetition-that is, of taking up his life again. In *Edifying Discourses* Kierkegaard explicitly treated only the Job of the prose tale, although in effect he read the entire book through the lens of Job's action in uttering the words in 1:21 ("The LORD gave; the Lord took; blessed be the name of the Lord"). Provocatively, Kierkegaard attempted to recover these words from their status as pious clich, and to read them within the narrative context as a radical form of the fear of God.

As critical biblical scholarship became a more self-conscious discipline during the late eighteenth century and in the nineteenth, it wrestled not only with the book's meaning but also increasingly with the investigation of the textual, historical, and comparative issues that became the hallmark of scientific biblical criticism at this time. These issues have largely set the agenda for the study of Job until the present. The apparent success of source-critical analysis of the Pentateuch in the nineteenth century led to an interest among biblical scholars in uncovering the compositional history of other biblical books. Job lent itself readily to such analysis. The stylistic and theological incongruity of the prose narrative (1:1-2:13; 42:7-17) with the poetic dialogue led scholars to posit separate compositions. Earlier critics who had anticipated the discussion of the compositional history of Job (R. Simon [1685]; A. Schultens [1737]) suggested that the dialogue was the oldest part of the book, the prose framework a later addition, a position that continued to have supporters (W. de Wette [1807]; S. Lee [1837]; K. Kautzsch [1900]; N. Tur-Sinai [1957]). More commonly, the prose tale was assumed to be an old written or oral tale that was taken over by the author of the dialogue as a narrative setting. (This view was established and given its classic shape by the work of J. Wellhausen [1871]; T. Cheyne [1887]; K. Budde [1896]; B. Duhm [1897]; P. Volz [1902].) Others, readily admitting the stylistic differences, saw no reason to posit different compositional stages or different authorship, arguing that "one and the same man can tell a story when necessary and sing when necessary" (E.

Dhorme [1926; ET 1967] lxv; cf. S. Driver and G. Gray [1921]; G. Hölscher [1937]). Virtually all agreed, however, that the character Job and certain aspects of his story were drawn from an ancient legendary tradition.

Even more consensus existed that the Elihu speeches constituted a later addition to the book, added either by the author at a later date (A. Merx [1871]; E. Sellin [1919]; R. Gordis [1965]) or, more commonly, by another author (J. G. Eichhorn [1803]; de Wette [1843]; Cheyne [1887]; Driver [1913]; E. Dhorme [1926]; E. König [1929]), which continues to be the broad consensus. A few scholars have, however, attempted to argue for the Elihu speeches as part of the book's original design (Budde [1876]; C. Cornill [1892]; G. Wildeboer [1895]; cf. N. Habel [1985]).

Enthusiasm for recovering the book's compositional history led scholars into increasingly subtle arguments for considering the wisdom poem in chap. 28, as well as one or both of the divine speeches, as later additions. The third cycle of speeches in the dialogue, which lacks the regularity of the first two and assigns material to Job that seems inconsistent with his earlier views, was reconstructed in various ways. None of these positions, however, garnered the same degree of consensus as the proposals concerning the prose frame tale or the Elihu speeches.

Whereas earlier discussions of Job had looked for literary parallels and perhaps influence in Greek literature, the recovery of ancient Near Eastern texts in the late nineteenth century shifted the focus to alleged parallels from ancient Egypt and particularly Mesopotamia. The most important of these were texts portraying a righteous or emblematic sufferer like Job, especially the so-called Babylonian Job, properly known by its first line as *Ludlul bel nemeqi*; the *Babylonian Theodicy* (first published in 1875 and 1895, respectively; see W. Lambert [1960]); other fragmentary Akkadian texts (Lambert [1960]), including one from Ugarit (J. Nougayrol [1968]); and a Sumerian composition (S. Kramer [1953]). Of these the one with the strongest similarities to Job is the *Babylonian Theodicy*. Composed c. 1000 B.C.E., it consists of a poetic dialogue between a sufferer and his friend. In a series of eleven alternating speeches the sufferer laments his condition while the friend attempts to provide explanations and give advice. Unlike Job, the *Babylonian Theodicy* has neither a frame narrative nor a theophany; nevertheless, stylistic and thematic similarities to the dialogue portion of Job are significant.

Opinion has remained divided as to whether *Ludlul bel nemeqi*, the *Babylonian Theodicy*, and other such texts can be considered sources for or influences on the composition of Job (C. Kuhl [1953]; J. van Dijk [1953]; H. Gese [1958]; J. Gray [1970]; H. Müller [1978]). These texts, however, have encouraged a comparative investigation of why the issue of acute and apparently inexplicable suffering became such a problem in the Semitic cultures of the ancient Near East: possibly as a crisis in the wisdom tradition's ideology of the act-consequence relationship (Gese); as an intrinsic problem of a religious system that posited the gods as the guarantors of an order of justice (K. van der Toorn [1985]); as a consequence of changing conceptions of the gods (W. von Soden [1965]; T. Jacobsen [1976]); or as a response to sudden political or socioeconomic upheaval (R. Albertz [1981]).

The recovery of ancient Near Eastern literary and religious materials, including graphic art, has also permitted the recognition and clarification of a variety of mythological motifs (M. Pope [1965, 1973]; G. Fuchs [1993]), in particular the role of the animals in the divine speeches as evocative of the realm of the chaotic (O. Keel [1978]). Although the prominence of legal terminology in Job's speeches had long been recognized, ancient Near Eastern texts that clarify the structure of legal process and technical terminology have been important in recent efforts to argue for the centrality of the forensic metaphor in Job's understanding of his situation (H. Richter [1959]; S. Scholnick [1975]; M. Dick [1979]; Habel; E. Greenstein [1996]).

Whereas the Akkadian texts have had the greatest impact on issues pertaining to Job's religious and intellectual context, the discovery of the Ugaritic texts provided new resources for investigating linguistic problems. The poetic sections of the book were shown to preserve many archaic linguistic features (D. Robertson [1972]), and a number of obscure words and expressions have been clarified by reference to Ugaritic cognates and parallels (Pope; L. Grabbe [1977]). What was perceived as excessive and ill-disciplined application of comparative linguistics to Job on the part of some scholars (M. Dahood [1962]; A. Blommerde [1969]; A. Ceresko [1980]; W. Michel [1987]), however, has provoked a backlash, leading the most recent commentators to be cautious about either emending the text of Job or replacing the traditional definitions of Hebrew words with new definitions based on comparative Northwest Semitic linguistics.

Among the Dead Sea Scrolls are four fragmentary manuscripts of Job (2Q15, 4Q99, 4Q100, 4Q101). Although these manuscripts contain relatively little of the text, they do establish that the Elihu speeches were a part of the book by the turn of the era. One of the manuscripts (4Q101) is written in paleo-Hebrew (P. Skehan et al. [1992]). Since this script is usually reserved for books of the Torah, its use in 4Q101 may reflect the tradition of Mosaic authorship (see b. B. Bat. 14b-15a). In addition, two manuscripts preserve portions of an Aramaic Targum of Job (4Q157 and 11QtgJob), which appears to have been translated from a text closely similar to the MT, although the end of 11QtgJob differs significantly from the MT, both in detail and in extent, ending with lines corresponding to Job 42:9-11 (M. Sokoloff [1974]; G. Fohrer [1963b]).

Categorizing the interpretations of the book's meaning that have characterized late nineteenth- and twentieth-century biblical and theological scholarship is difficult, given the immense amount of critical literature and the subtle variations of interpretation. Nevertheless, some general observations can be made. One distinction might be made between those who see the meaning of Job as involving the fate of certain ideas and those who see the book less about theology than about religious experience. These positions need not be mutually exclusive, however. Although very few scholars argue that the book attempts to provide a positive rational theodicy (Cornill), a number have argued that its purpose is to contradict the doctrine of retribution (de Wette; Driver [1913]) or, more forcefully stated, to claim that retributive justice is not a part of God's plan for the world (M. Tsevat [1980]). Closely related are those analyses that interpret the content and imagery of the divine speeches more broadly as a refutation of Job's assumptions and expectations concerning the nature of the world and God's interaction with it (Habel; C. Newsom [1996]) or a repudiation of the image of God preserved in the dominant traditions of Israelite piety and salvation history (T. Jacobson [1976]; F. M. Cross [1973]). In these readings the problem presented by Job is considered to be rooted in a false or inadequate perception of reality; and the solution, communicated through the divine speeches, involves a shift to a more adequate paradigm of understanding.

More common is the view that the book's purpose is to examine the religious dilemma of the one who suffers inexplicably (M. Buber [1942; ET 1949]; M. Susman [1946]; C. Westermann [1956; ET 1981]; Fohrer [1963a]; H. Rowley [1958-59]; S. Terrien [1958]; R. Gordis [1965]; Clines). The quest for an intellectual solution is not just futile but ultimately beside the point. The problem presented by Job is the sense of acute isolation from God, an isolation that is overcome through the encounter with God at the book's climax. Interpreters who take this approach tend to see the significance of the divine speeches less in terms of their cognitive content than in their function as the Divine's self-disclosure. As Buber put it, "God offers Himself to the sufferer who, in the depth of his despair, keeps to God with his refractory complaint; He offers Himself to him as an answer" (195).

R. Otto (1917; ET 1923, 1958) gave a quite different estimation of the nature of the encounter with God as an experience of the holy, "the mysterium, presented in its pure, non-rational form" (79). Like Otto, P. Berger (1967) speaks of Job's being overwhelmed by his encounter with

God, although Berger characterizes the encounter as the purest example of a masochistic theodicy. In K. Barth's reading, Job begins with a knowledge of God as "Elohim" – that is, God as known through the various qualities that may be predicated through experience and tradition. Job's sufferings at God's hand confound his understanding, as his angry but bewildered protests indicate. In the theophany, however, Job encounters "Yahweh"—that is, God as unique Personality, the radical Subject, who cannot be comprehended in terms of the moral and metaphysical categories Job and his friends presumed. Barth suggests that in the revelatory moment Job knows the "two gods," Elohim and Yahweh, as one; however, it is Job's submission before the divine Subject that is the expression of true faith. In this submission Job finds reconciliation and freedom.

C. Jung's *Answer to Job* (1952; ET 1954) does not so much attempt to interpret the biblical text as to read it as an expression of the human unconscious in its effort to grapple with the phenomena of good and evil and their relationship (x). What the drama of Job explores, according to Jung, is the disclosure of the nature of Yahweh as "an antinomy—a totality of inner opposites" (7). Yahweh lacks self-consciousness and thus is not a moral being; yet Yahweh is dimly aware that "a somewhat keener consciousness based on self-reflection" (13) does exist in humanity. This awareness explains the hidden jealousy that underlies Yahweh's willingness to yield to the doubting thought represented by Satan. Although Job submits before Yahweh's might, the accomplishment of the book has been not only to reveal Yahweh's dual nature but also to initiate a process of dialectic within God. There is not much movement in God's resolution of the inner antinomy within the book of Job; however, Jung sees the process continuing in God's union with primordial wisdom (Job 28), incarnated in the virgin Mary. Through this union "Job and Yahweh were combined in a single personality. Yahweh's intention to become man, which resulted from his collision with Job, is fulfilled in Christ's life and suffering" (46).

During the twentieth century a wide range of literature, both serious and popular, has drawn on the story of Job. Perhaps the most significant of these literary responses is F. Kafka's (1883-1924) *The Trial* (1925; ET 1937). Although not explicitly linked by intertextual references, connections between *The Trial* and the book of Job have been noted by both theological and literary critics (M. Buber [1964]; M. Susman [1929]; N. Frye [1957]). The relationship may be more complex than often assumed, however (S. Lasine [1992]). The Joban figure is Joseph K., who is arrested one morning for an unspecified crime. He passes through an endless bureaucratic hierarchy, trying to gain access to the court that has accused him; but he never gets beyond the lowest layers of this massive judiciary system. Finally, he is executed without ever having confessed to guilt or knowing the reasons for his arrest. This complex novel, open to many interpretations, shows one trait clearly: a story similar to Job's is told in terms of the inability to understand, delusion, the loss of self-knowledge, blindness, and the inaccessibility of the transcendent. Joseph K. never finds the insight, understanding, or perspective needed to allow him an escape from his nightmare. Not accidentally does *The Trial* bear the quality of a dream from which one cannot wake up. The judge for whom K. searches never becomes visible, hence K.'s situation remains inscrutable: He "dies like a dog," his end signifying a complete lack of redemptive insight. There is no depth dimension to reality that becomes accessible to the human mind. The confidence in noetic perception that in various ways permeates precritical commentaries has vanished.

Other twentieth-century interpreters have also stressed the elusiveness of God, even in the encounter with Job in the whirlwind and in the fact that the book ends without Job's ever knowing what precipitated the disasters that inexplicably befell him. Job's situation thus appears to have affinities with the existentialist tradition, especially in its absurdist mode (D. Cox [1978]). In R. Frost's (1874-1963) *A Masque of Reason*, when God finally reveals to Job in heaven the reason for his torment ("I was just showing off to the Devil"), Job comments that "I expected more than I could understand and what I get is almost less than I can understand" (1945, 11:327, 331-33).

A somewhat different post-WWII reading of Job is present in A. MacLeish's (1892-1982) play J. B. (1956), which was culturally influential during the 1950s and 1960s. For MacLeish the Joban figure, J. B., confronts, not God, but the meaninglessness of the universe. The problem is not God's injustice but God's absence. The play's post-religious, humanistic perspective is articulated by J. B.'s wife, Sarah, who tells him, "You wanted justice and there is none-only love." When J. B. observes, "He does not love. He Is," Sarah replies, "But we do. That's the wonder" (151-52). The answer to the meaninglessness of the universe is not to be sought in God but in the human act of blowing on "the coal of the heart" (153).

MacLeish's distinctly humanistic engagement with Job contrasts with the post-Holocaust reading of Job in Wiesel's play *The Trial of God* (1979). The Joban figure is an innkeeper named Berish, the survivor of a seventeenth-century Russian pogrom. Wandering Jewish actors agree to put on a Purim farce, but the innkeeper insists that it be a legal proceeding in which God is put on trial. In order to stage the play a defender of God must be found. The character who agrees to take this role, "Sam," is eventually revealed to be Satan. Before his identity is disclosed, however, Sam has seductively articulated not only arguments in favor of God's righteousness reminiscent of Job's three friends but also rationalizations characteristic of modern theological interpreters of the book. Against these discredited theodicies Wiesel places the defiant faithfulness of Berish, who paradoxically insists that he will not renounce his Judaism but with his dying breath will protest the injustice of a God who stands by while his children are murdered.

God's failure to answer directly Job's cry for justice in the world has also provoked a line of philosophical and theological interpretation that rejects the book's apparent resolution, which is merely "a cover for the heresy Job so fearlessly wanted to proclaim," i.e., "the exodus of man from Yahweh" (E. Bloch [1968; ET 1972] 113, 118), a rejection of all theodicy (D. Soelle [1973; ET 1975]; T. Tilley [1991]; cf. J. Crenshaw [1984]). Biblical scholars who argue for such an interpretation as intrinsic to the book base their arguments in part on the linguistic ambiguity of Job's reply to God in 42:6 (D. Robertson [1977]; J. Curtis [1979]).

A similar dissatisfaction with the divine speeches is evident in analyses that read Job in light of R. Girard's (b. 1923) understanding of mimetic rivalry and the scapegoat mechanism (1985). The violence directed against Job by neighbors and exemplified in the friends' increasing hostility toward him can be seen as a means of shifting the potentially disruptive desire to imitate and ultimately displace a model who is also a rival. The hostility directed toward such a person can be effective as a means of social stabilization only if the object of hostility recognizes himself or herself as guilty and thus takes on the role of scapegoat. Girard believes that Job disrupts this process by insisting on his innocence and demanding vindication. Yet the God who would defend victims, whom Job invokes, is not the God who replies to Job. Girard thus argues that the divine speeches are not original to the book but a later attempt to neutralize Job's subversive words. J. Williams (1992), however, more ingenuously acknowledges the unity of the book but argues that the divine speeches are simply bad theology.

The difference of approach between Girard and Williams also illustrates a significant recent shift in biblical scholarship's understanding of the book. Earlier historical-critical analysis raised the problem of the book's unity by drawing attention to the sharply different styles and perspectives it contains. If it could no longer be naively read as a unity, the book nevertheless could be read as a sort of diachronic dialogue, as various hands interpolated characters and speeches or otherwise altered its shape and sequence. This approach continues to have its defenders, especially among European scholars (A. de Wilde [1981]; V. Maag [1982]; J. Vermeylan [1986]; J. van Oorschot [1987]), and provides the basis for such ingenious readings as that of B. Zuckerman (1991). Zuckerman posits that the poetic dialogue was originally written as a parody of an old oral folktale about a silently enduring hero. The disturbing poem with its excessively vocal Job attracted a series of interpretive supplements (the wisdom poem of chap. 28, the Elihu speeches, and finally, a written version of the old folktale). The authors of these supplements, however, failed to understand the parody of the poem. Thus the book of Job consists of a dialogue of misreading.

In general, however, accounts of the book of Job based on a redaction-critical model have come to be increasingly out of favor, at least in English-language scholarship, since the mid-1970s. This reaction emerges in part out of dissatisfaction with traditional historical criticism's tendency to fragment the text and its failure to provide an integrated interpretation of the book as a whole (F. Andersen [1976]; J. Janzen [1985]; J. Hartley [1988]). Increasingly, the final-form readings have been self-consciously informed by one or another model of literary criticism. Habel's 1985 commentary, indebted to Anglo-American New Criticism, provides a reading of the entire book, including the Elihu speeches, as a literary unity. This reading stresses the unifying function of the plot, the pervasive forensic metaphor, foreshadowing, and verbal and dramatic irony that work to produce "a literary whole integrating prose and poetic materials into a rich paradoxical totality" (9). Clines's 1989 commentary, by contrast, is more conscious of the role of the reader in producing different but legitimate readings. In an article published just a year later (1990), Clines outstripped his own modestly reader-oriented approach with a deconstructionist reading, demonstrating how the book as a whole undermines the positions it affirms about suffering and the moral order in a way that prevents any determinate meaning. Published in the same year, E. Good's commentary draws on reader-oriented and post-structuralist approaches, especially the work of R. Barthes (1915-80), to champion a model of reading that is a form of play with a resolutely open text. For Good the book of Job is an indeterminate text that continually subverts the attempt to find in it a unitary truth. Ironically, literary readings, which were introduced in order to provide an alternative to the fragmentary and contradictory readings produced by historical-critical approaches, have themselves come to stress the fragmentary and contradictory nature of Job, as of all texts.

Contemporary scholarship's growing awareness of the role of the reader and of specific interpretive communities has had two other consequences for Job scholarship. The first is an increased interest in interpretations that are self-consciously based in concrete social or ideological communities. Thus readings of Job have been produced from the perspective of Latin American liberation theology (G. Gutiérrez [1986; ET 1987]; J. Pixley [1982]), African American hermeneutics (S. Reid [1990]), feminism (I. Pardes [1992]; Newsom), and political dissidence (W. Safire [1992]). Although these readings differ from one another in many particulars, they tend to be strongly favorable not only to the character of Job but also to the divine speeches and to the response Job makes to them. This affirmation contrasts sharply with the ambivalence or rejection of the book that one encounters in certain Marxist and post-Holocaust readings (Bloch; R. Rubenstein [1969-70]; Wiesel).

The second consequence of the interest in interpretive communities has been an increased attention to the history of the reception of Job. In the last quarter of the twentieth century, numerous critical editions and translations of works by important figures in the history of interpretation have appeared (e.g., Didymus the Blind, Julian the Arian, Gregory the Great, Thomas Aquinas, and Saadia) as well as monographs and articles on particular periods and interpreters (J. Baskin [1981]; J. Lamb [1995]; S. Schreiner [1986, 1988, 1989, 1994]; M. Yaffe [1979-80]). Clines's commentary contains an extensive bibliography of works on Job from the patristic period to the present. Complementing the textual record is the collection and analysis of graphic depictions of Job from antiquity to the present published by Terrien (1996). Although the history of the book's reception has not yet been extensively integrated into biblical scholarship, it is likely to have a much greater impact on Job studies than in the previous period when historical-critical scholarship privileged the attempt to recover the meaning of the book for its original audience.

Bibliography: M. Adriaen (ed.), *S. Gregorii Magni Moralia in Iob* (CCSL 143, 143A, 143B, 1979-85). **R. G. Albertson**, "Job and Ancient Near Eastern Wisdom Literature," *Scripture in Context 2* (ed. W. W. Hallo et al., 1983) 213-30. **R. Albertz**, "Der sozialgeschichtliche Hintergrund des Hiobbuches und der Babylonischen Theodizee [Ludlul bel nemeqi]," *Die Botschaft und die Boten* (ed. J. Jeremias and L. Perlitt, 1981) 349-72. **L. Alonso Schökel and J. D. Sicre Díaz**, *Job, comentario theológico y literario* (Nueva Biblia Española, 1983). **F. Andersen**, *Job: An Introduction and Commentary* (TOTC, 1976). **J. Barr**, "The Book of Job and Its Modern Interpreters," *BJRL* 54 (1971-72) 28-46. **K. Barth**, *Hiob* (BibS[N] 1966 = *Kirchliche Dogmatik* 4, 3, 1). **J. R. Baskin**, "Job as Moral Exemplar in Ambrose," *VC* 35 (1981) 222-31; "Rabbinic Interpretations of Job," *The Voice from the Whirlwind* (ed. L. G. Perdue and W. C. Gilpin, 1992) 101-10. **P. Berger**, *The Sacred Canopy: Elements of a Sociological Theory of Religion* (1967). **L. Besserman**, *The Legend of Job in the Middle Ages* (1979). **T. de Beza**, *Jobus commentario et paraphrasi illustratus* (1583). **P. Bishop**, *Jung's Answer to Job : A Commentary* (2002). **R. J. Blackwell**, *Galileo, Bellarmine, and the Bible* (1991). **E. Bloch**, *Atheism in Christianity: The Religion of the Exodus and the Kingdom* (1968; ET 1972). **A. C. M. Blommerde**, *Northwest Semitic Grammar and Job* (BibOr 22, 1968). **P. R. L. Brown**, *Augustine of Hippo: A Biography* (1967). **M. Buber**, *The Prophetic Faith* (1942; ET 1949); *Darko shel mikra* (1964), Hebrew. **K. Budde**, *Beiträge zur Kritik des Buches Hiob* (1876); *Das Buch Hiob* (1896, 1913). **A. Ceresko**, *Job 29-31 in the Light of Northwest Semitic: A Translation and Philological Commentary* (BibOr 26, 1980). **T. K. Cheyne**, *Job and Solomon* (1887). **D. J. A. Clines**, *Job 1-20* (WBC 17, 1989), with extensive bibliography, lxiii-cxv; "Deconstructing the Book of Job," *What Does Eve Do to Help?* (JSOTSup 94, 1990). **S. L. Cook**, ed., *The Whirlwind: Essays on Job, Hermeneutics and Theology in Memory of Jane Morse* (JSOTSup 336, 2001).**C. H. Cornill**, *Introduction to the Canonical Books of the OT* (Theological Translation Library 23, 1907). **D. Cox**, *The Triumph of Impotence: Job and the Tradition of the Absurd* (AnGr 212, 1978). **J. Crenshaw**, *A Whirlpool of Torment: Israelite Traditions of God as an Oppressive Presence* (OBT 12, 1984). **F. M. Cross**, *Canaanite Myth and Hebrew Epic* (1973). **J. B. Curtis**, "On Job's Response to Yahweh," *JBL* 98 (1979) 497-511. **C. Dagens**, *Saint Grégoire le Grand* (1977). **M. Dahood**, "Northwest Semitic Philology and Job," *The Bible in Current Catholic Thought* (ed. J. L. MacKenzie, 1962) 55-74. **A. Damico and M. D. Yaffe** (tr. and ed.), *Thomas Aquinas: The Literal Exposition on Job* (CRSS 7, 1989). **S. F. Damon**, *Blake's Job* (1966). **E. Dassmann**, *RAC 15* (1991) 366-442. **W. de Wette**, *A Critical and Historical Introduction to the Canonical Scripture of the OT* (2 vols., 1843). **E. Dhorme**, *A Commentary on the Book of Job* (1926; ET 1967). **M. B. Dick**, "The Legal Metaphor in Job 31," *CBQ* 41 (1979) 37-50; "Job 31, the Oath of Innocence, and the Sage," *ZAW* 95 (1983) 31-53. **J. J. A. van Dijk**, *La sagesse Suméro-Accadienne* (1953). **S. R. Driver**, *Introduction to the Literature of the OT* (1913). **S. R. Driver and G. B. Gray**, *The Book of Job* (ICC, 1921). **B. Duhm**, *Das Buch Hiob* (KHC, 1897). **J. Ebach**, "Hiob/Hiobbuch," *TRE 15* (1986) 360-80. **J. G. Eichhorn**, *Einleitung in das Alte Testament (*1803). **G. Fohrer**, *Das Buch Hiob* (KAT 16, 1963a); "4QOrNab, 11QTgJob und die Hioblegende," *ZAW* 75 (1963b) 93-97. **R. Frost**, *A Masque of Reason* (1945). **N. Frye**, *Anatomy of Criticism: Four Essays* (1957); *The Great Code: The Bible and Literature* (1982). **G. Fuchs**, *Mythos und Hiobdichtung: Aufnahme und Umdeutung altorientalischer Vorstellungen* (1993). **H. Gese**, *Lehre und Wirklichkeit in der alten Weisheit: Studien zu den Sprüchen Salomos und zu dem Buche Hiob* (1958). **R. Girard**, *Job: The Victim of His People* (1985; ET 1987). **N. Glatzer**

(ed.), *The Dimensions of Job: A Study and Selected Readings* (1969). **E. M. Good**, *In Turns of Tempest: A Reading of Job with a Translation* (1990). **L. E. Goodman** (ed. and tr.), *The Book of Theodicy: Translation and Commentary on the Book of Job by Saadiah ben Joseph al-Fayyumi* (YJS 25, 1988). **R. Gordis**, *The Book of God and Man: A Study of Job* (1965); *The Book of Job: Commentary, New Translation, and Special Studies* (Moreshet Series 2, 1978). **L. Grabbe**, *Comparative Philology and the Text of Job: A Study in Methodology* (SBLDS 34, 1977). **F. Gradl**, *Das Buch Iob* (Neuer Stuttgarter Kommentar, AT 12, 2001). **J. Gray**, "The Book of Job in the Context of Near Eastern Literature," *ZAW* 82 (1970) 251-69. **E. Greenstein**, "A Forensic Understanding of the Speech from the Whirlwind," *Texts, Temples, and Traditions: A Tribute to M. Haran* (ed. M. V. Fox et al., 1996) 241-58. **G. Gutiérrez**, *On Job: God-Talk and the Suffering of the Innocent* (1986; ET 1987). **N. Habel**, *The Book of Job* (OTL, 1985). **D. Hagedorn** (ed.), *Der Hiobkommentar des arianers Julian* (PTS 14, 1973). **U. Hagedorn** and **D. Hagedorn** (eds. and tr.), *Johannes Chrysostomos Kommentar zu Hiob* (PTS 35, 1990). **U. Hagedorn, D. Hagedorn** and **L. Koenen**, (eds. and tr.), *Didymus der Blinde: Kommentar zu Hiob* (Tura-Papyrus) (1985). **J. Hartley**, *The Book of Job* (NICOT, 1988). **G. W. F. Hegel**, *Lectures on the Philosophy of Religion* (ET, 3 vols., 1895). **J. G. Herder**, *Vom Geiste der Ebr"ischen Poesi* (1782-83). **T. Hobbes**, *Leviathan* (1651). **G. Hölscher**, *Das Buch Hiob* (HAT 1, 17, 1937). **R. A. Hubble**, *Conversation on the Dung Heap: Reflections on Job* (1998). **T. Jacobsen**, "Second Millennium Metaphors: The Gods as Parents. Rise of Personal Religion," *Treasures of Darkness: A History of Mesopotamian Religion* (ed. T. Jacobsen, 1976) 145-64. **J. Janzen**, *Job* (IBC, 1985). **C. Jung**, *Answer to Job* (1952; ET 1958). **A. Künzli**, *Gotteskrise: Fragen zu Hiob, Lob des Agnostizismus* (Rowohlts Enzyklopädie, 1998). **F. Kafka**, *The Trial* (1925; ET 1937). **C. Kannengiesser**, "Job chez les Peres," *DS* 8 (1974) 1218-24. **I. Kant**, *The Failure of All Philosophical Attempts Towards a Theodicy* (1791). **H. E. Kaufmann**, *Die Anwendung des Buches Hiob in der rabbinischen Agadah* (1893). **K. Kautzsch**, *Das sogennante Volksbuch von Hiob und der Ursprung von Hiob cap. I. II. XLII, 7-17* (1900). **O. Keel**, *Jahwes Entgegnun an Hiob* (FRLANT 121, 1978). **J. Kegler**, "Hauptlinien der Hiobforschung seit 1956," *Der Aufbau des Buches Hiob* (ed. C. Westermann, 1977) 9-25. **S. Kierkegaard**, *Edifying Discourses* (1843; ET 1943); *Repetition* (1843; ET 1983). **E. König**, *Das Buch Hiob* (1929). **S. N. Kramer**, "Man and His God: A Sumerian Variation on the 'Job' Motif," *VT* 3 (1953) 170-82. **C. Kuhl**, "Neuere Literarkritik des Buches Hiob," *TRu* 21 (1953) 163-205, 267-317. **H. J. Laks**, "The Enigma of Job: Maimonides and the Moderns," *JBL* 83 (1964) 345-64. **A. de Lamartine**, *Cours familier de litt,rature 2* (1956). **J. Lamb**, *The Rhetoric of Suffering: Reading the Book of Job in the Eighteenth Century* (1995). **W. G. Lambert**, *Babylonian Wisdom Literature* (1960). **S. Lasine**, "Job and His Friends in the Modern World," *The Voice from the Whirlwind* (ed. **L. G. Perdue and W. C. Gilpin**, 1992), 144-55, 247-51. **J. Le Clerc**, *Veteris Testamenti Libri Hagiographi: Jobus, Davidis Psalmi, Salomonis Proverbia, Concionatrix et Canticum Canticorum* (1731). **L. Leclercq**, "Job," *DACL* 7, 2 (1927) 2554-70. **S. Lee**, *The Book of the Patriarch Job* (1837). **G. Leibniz**, *Theodicy* (1710). **J. Levenson**, *The Book of Job in Its Time and in the Twentieth Century* (1972). **A. Lo**, *Job 28 as Rhetoric: An Analysis of Job 28 in the Context of Job 22-31* (2003). **R. Lowth**, *De sacra poesi Hebraeorum Praelectiones Academicae* (1753); *Letter to the Right Reverend Author of the Divine Legation of Moses* (1765). **V. Maag**, *Hiob: Wandlung und Verarbeitung des Problems in Novelle, Dialogdichtung, und Spätfassungen* (FRLANT, 1982). **A. MacLeish**, *J. B.* (1956). **J. Manley** (ed.), *Wisdom, Let Us Attend: Job, the Fathers, and the OT* (1997). **A. Merx**, *Das Gedicht von Hiob: Hebräischer Text* (1871). **J. H. Michaelis**, *Notae in Jobum* (1720). **W. L. Michel**, *Job in the Light of Northwest Semitic 1* (BibOr 42, 1987). **H. P. Müller**, "Keilschriftliche Parallelen zum biblischen Hiobbuch," *Orientalia* 47 (1978) 360-75; *Das Hiobproblem: Seine Stellung u. Entstehung im alten Orient und im AT* (Erträge der Forschung 84, 1995). **D.-W. Nam**, *Talking* *about God: Job 42:7-9 and the Nature of God in the Book of Job* (Studies in Biblical Literature 49, 2003). **C. A. Newsom**, "Job," *The Women's Bible Commentary* (ed. C. A. Newsom and S. H. Ringe, 1992) 130-36; "Considering Job," *CurBs* 1 (1993) 87-118; "The Book of Job" *NIB* (1996) 4:319-637; *The Book of Job: A Contest of Moral Imagination* (2003). **J. Nougayrol**, "(Juste) souffrant (R.S. 25.460)," *Ugaritica* 5 (1968) 265-83. **J. van Oorschot**, *Gott als Grenze: Eine literar- und redaktionsgeschichtliche Studie zu den gottesreden des Hiobbuches* (BZAW 170, 1987). **R. Otto**, *The Idea of the Holy* (1923). **I. Pardes**, *Countertraditions in the Bible: A Feminist Approach* (1992). **J. Pixley**, *El libro de Job: Comentario biblico latino-americano* (1982). **M. Pope**, *Job: Introduction, Translation, and Notes* (AB 15, 1965, 1973). **Y. Pyeon**, *You Have Not Spoken What is Right about Me: Intertextuality and the Book of Job* (Studies in Biblical Literature 45, 2003). **S. Reid**, "Suffering and Critical Awareness: The Foundation of a Quest for Witnesses," *Experience and Tradition: A Primer in Black Biblical Hermeneutics* (1990) 85-138. **H. Richter**, *Studien zu Hiob: Der Aufbau des Hiobbuches dargestellt an den Gattungen des Rechtslebens* (ThA 11, 1959). **D. Robertson**, *Linguistic Evidence in Dating Early Hebrew Poetry* (SBLDS 3; 1972); *The OT and the Literary Critic* (1977). **H. H. Rowley**, "The Book of Job and Its Meaning," *BJRL* 41 (1958-59) 167-206, his *From Moses to Qumran* (1963) 141-83. **R. Rubenstein**, "Job and Auschwitz," *USQR* 25 (1969-70) 421-37. **C. Rudolph**, *Violence and Daily Life: Reading, Art, and Polemics in the* Cîteaux Moralia *in Job* (1997). **W. Safire**, *The First Dissident: The Book of Job in Today's Politics* (1992). **S. H. Scholnik**, "Lawsuit Drama in the Book of Job" (diss., Brandeis University, 1975). **S. E. Schreiner**, "'Through a Mirror Dimly': Calvin's Sermons on Job," *CTS* 21 (1986) 175-93; "'Where Shall Wisdom Be Found?' Gregory's Interpretation of Job," *ABenR* 39 (1988) 321-42; "Exegesis and Double Justice in Calvin's Sermons on Job," *CH* 58 (1989) 322-38; *Where Shall Wisdom be Found? Calvin's Exegesis of Job from Medieval and Modern Perspectives* (1994). **A. Schultens**, *Liber Iobi* (1737). **E. Sellin**, *Das Problem des Hiobbuches* (1919). **D. Shepherd**, *Targum and Translation : A Reconsideration of the Qumran Aramaic Version of Job* (SSN 45, 2004). **R. Simon**, *Histoire critique du Vieux Testament* (1685). **P. Skehan et al.**, *Qumran Cave 4.IV: Paleo-Hebrew and Greek Biblical Manuscripts* (DJD 9, 1992). **E. Smith**, *The Book of Job: A Facsimile Reproduction* (1996). **W. von Soden**, "Das Fragen nach der Gerechtigkeit Gottes im Alten Orient," *Mitteilungen der Deutschen Orient-Gesellschaft zu Berlin* 96 (1965) 41-59. **D. Soelle**, *Suffering* (1973; ET 1975). **M. Sokoloff**, *The Targum to Job from Qumran Cave XI* (Bar Ilan Studies of Near Eastern Languages and Culture, 1974). **J. D. Soloveitchik**, *Out of the Whirlwind: Essays on Mourning, Suffering and the Human Condition* (D. Shatz, ed., Meotzar Horav 3, 2002). **M. Susman**, "Das Hiob-Problem bei F. Kafka," *Der Morgen* 5 (1929) 31-49; *Das Buch Hiob und das Schicksal des jüdischen Volkes* (1946). **S. Terrien**, *Job: Poet of Existence* (1958); *The Iconography of Job Through the Centuries: Artists as Biblical Interpreters* (1996). **Theodore of Mopsuestia**, *In Jobum,* PG 66:697-98. **J. D. Thompson**, *A Critical Concordance to the Septuagint: Job* (The Computer Bible 69, 1999). **T. Tilley**, *The Evils of Theodicy* (1991). **K. van der Toorn**, *Sin and Sanction in Israel and Mesopotamia: A Comparative Study* (SSN 22, 1985). **H. Tremblay**, *Job 19:25-27 dans la Septante et chez le pères grecs : unanimité d'une tradition* (Etudes bibliques, New Series, 47 ; 2002). **M. Tsevat**, *The Meaning of the Book of Job and Other Biblical Studies* (1980). **N. H. Tur-Sinai**, *The Book of Job: A New Commentary* (1957, 1967). **J. Vermeylen**, *Job, ses amis et son Dieu: La légende de Job et ses relectures postexiliques* (StB 2, 1986). **J. Voltaire**, *Dictionnaire Philosophique* (1764). **P. Volz**, *Hiob und Weisheit* (1902, 1921). **R. Wasselynck**, "Les compilations des 'Moralia in Job' du VIIᵉ au XIIᵉ siècle," *RTAM* 29 (1962) 5-32; "Les `Moralia in Job' dans les ouvrages de morale du haut moyen âge latin," *RTAM* 31 (1964) 5-31. **W. Warburton**, *The Divine Legation of Moses* (2 vols., 1737-41). **J. Wellhausen**, review of A. Dillmann, *Hiob, JDTh* (1871) 555. **C. Westermann**, *The Structure of the Book of Job: A Form-*

Critical Analysis (1956; ET 1981). **J. A. Wharton**, *Job* (Westminster Bible Companion, 1999). **E. Wiesel**, "Job: Our Contemporary," *Messengers of God: Biblical Portraits and Legends* (1976); *The Trial of Job* (1979); *Job ou Dieu dans le tempete* (1986). **A. de Wilde**, *Das Buch Hiob* (OTS 22, 1981). **G. Wildeboer**, *Die Literatur des Altes Testament nach der Zeitfolge ihrer Entstehung* (1895). **J. Williams**, *The Bible, Violence, and the Sacred: Liberation from the Myth of Sanctioned Violence* (1992). **A. Wright**, *Blake's Job: A Commentary* (1972). **M. D. Yaffe**, "Providence in Medieval Aristotelianism: Moses Maimonides and Thomas Aquinas on the Book of Job," *Hebrew Studies* 20-21 (1979-80) 62-74. **B. Zuckerman**, *Job the Silent: A Study in Historical Counterpoint* (1991). **D. de Zúñiga**, *Commentaria in librum Job* (1584).

C. A. Newsom and S. E. Schreiner

THE WRITINGS

Psalms

1. *Early Jewish Interpretation*. Some of the headings of the psalms reflect a work of exegesis already in HB times. In thirteen of the headings connections are made with episodes in David's life; other examples include the application of an individual's thanksgiving to a communal celebration (Psalm 30). The Greek and Syriac versions attest the fluidity of such headings as interpretation developed, with the Greek showing a marked tendency to tone down the Hebrew's bold depiction of God. The Dead Sea Scrolls from both before and during NT times include numerous portions of psalm texts as well as compositions where phrases from the psalms are echoed or applied. David is strongly presented as the author of the psalms in general. Correspondence is assumed between the experiences of the psalmists and those of the Qumran community, and the leader who prays in the *Hodayot* (hymns) uses phrases from Psalms 22, 41, and 69, as does the NT.

Lines of exegesis can also be followed in the Targum, which gives the sense in Aramaic with many turns of interpretation. "You are my son" in Ps 2:7b, for example, is rendered as "Beloved as a son to a father are you to me, pure as if this day I had created you." The Targum also subdues the Hebrew's bold portrayals of God and God's activity. Interpretation can further be traced in references to the psalms in the Mishnah and in the Talmud, where the prophetic aspect is maintained. The old Jewish exegesis, however, is most richly represented by the *Midrash Tehillim*, which has preserved much ancient Palestinian teaching.

Sometimes the Midrash comments on every phrase of a psalm; in other cases, only on the opening and on the end. While there are comments on plain matters like the meanings of rare words, most interest is shown in spiritual truths, parables, and hidden meanings. For "I will rejoice in thee" (Ps 9:2), it is noted that the Hebrew spelling of "in thee" has the numerical value of twenty-two, the number of letters of the alphabet in which the Torah is written. Thus a hidden meaning refers to the joy of knowing God through Scripture. By a combination of 1:3 and 119:99 we are led to the case of a rabbi who was forever "transplanting" himself to different circles of Torah sages. Thus he found numerous "channels of water" to nourish his inner life and so "gained understanding from [so *min* is taken!] the abundance of teachers."

2. *Early Christian Interpretation*. The NT provided a massive foundation for subsequent exegesis, citing the psalms some seventy times (mostly from the Greek version) as prophetic of the messianic events. As in Jewish tradition, David is taken to be the chief author, by inspiration referring beyond his own life to Christ and his people. In the same tradition the NT writers were usually content to seize on meanings suggested by isolated phrases or verses, though there may be some cases where a larger context was taken into account. The vivid imagery of the psalms provided a potent expression of the vocation, suffering, and exaltation of Jesus as divine Son and Messiah.

Teachers of the second century continued this understanding, citing the psalms in letters and homilies for doctrinal and ethical purposes. Origen, the dominant commentator in the third century, explained the psalms with glosses, homilies, and commentaries. Although most of these have not survived, important examples of his expositions were used by other writers and appear in the popular "chains" compiled from the works of various writers. In such a chain on Psalm 119 (Greek 118), Origen was given pride of place, though no doubt his copious style of commenting on every essential word has been abbreviated. He took this psalm's alphabetic scheme as pointing to the elementary practice of the way of God and (because of the eightfold strophic patterns) to the attainment of contemplative fulfillment; beginning and end go together. Here David speaks for the one who follows the way of union with Christ the eternal Word, who is also named in the psalm's references to God's law, mouth, salvation, mercy, justice, face, hand, and name. Very seldom did Origen refer to the circumstances of David, who became, rather, the prototype of the monk, the spiritual warrior who endures humiliation in his ascetic struggle with Satan. Many commentators were to follow Origen in the exegesis developed by the Alexandrian School from Philo's approach: Like the body and the soul, Scripture had both a plain and a mystical sense; and the latter was given the most attention.

The opposing tendency of stressing the plain meaning, which characterized the tradition of the Antiochene School, produced an exegesis more congenial to modern critics, with emphasis on the text, grammatical sense, and historical setting. The best example is the commentary of Theodore of Mopsuestia; an early work, it boldly takes David to be anticipating future Jewish history down to Maccabean times. Also in the Antiochene tradition was Chrysostom, who wrote enthusiastically of the psalms as coming "first, last and midst" in the life and worship of his day and left fifty-eight eloquent homilies on them. Although Basil of Caesarea later adhered to literal interpretation, his homilies on the psalms are closer to Origen. In Psalm 45 he took the prophet to be addressing Christ, with the myrrh (45:8) alluding to Christ's burial. The queen (45:9) is the church, also the soul joined to the Word. "Hearken O daughter and see" (45:10) enjoins the church to contemplation.

Jerome was a great translator of the psalms, but his contribution to their exegesis is disputed. His collection of brief learned notes (*commentarioli*) is drawn from Origen's works, as he says himself. The many commentaries on the psalms confidently attributed to him until the last half of the twentieth century were thought to be extempore addresses to his monks in Bethlehem, which a hearer wrote down. It now seems more likely that Jerome translated Origen's homilies, occasionally interposing his own comments (see M.-J.Rondeau [1982-85] 155-61). If so, these commentaries provide samples of the wealth of exposition, vibrant with the love of Christ, that Origen addressed to a daily gathering in the Basilica of Caesarea.

Augustine was decidedly inclined to go beneath and beyond the mundane sense. His ample and varied discourses on the psalms hardly rank as scientific exegesis, but as spiritual dialogue with the texts they are of towering importance. His conversion had been greatly aided by listening to the singing of the psalms. Just as the antiphons and doxologies constantly oriented them in the Christian service, so also Augustine read them in constant recollection of Christ, while David receded from view. He took "Blessed is the man" of Ps 1:1 to refer to Christ "the Lord Man" (*Homine Dominico*); "in the LORD's Law" (1:2) means that Christ is not subject to the law and does not need its outer letter; "in his season" (1:3) means after he has been glorified; "the LORD knows his way"-such knowing is true being.

3. *The Middle Ages.* For much of this period, in East and West, the church was content with compilations from earlier commentators, Augustine being especially influential. "Practice hurried far ahead of theory," commented Franz Delitzsch, for church and community lived deeply in the constantly recited psalms. J. Neale and R. Littledale, who made a remarkable chain (1860-74) from the works of this period, wrote more warmly, "There is . . . a perfect treasure of mythology locked up in medieval commentaries and breviaries . . . the beauty of which grows upon the student."

Following the achievements of the Masoretes in textual and grammatical work and stimulated by controversy with the "heretical" Karaites and by Arab civilization, a new era of Jewish exegesis began. Saadia included the psalms in the commentary with his translation of the HB into Arabic. His was a sober, reasoned approach, respecting context. This line of exegesis continued with Rashi, A. Ibn Ezra, and D. Kimhi; later ages would profit from their philological knowledge, their recording of older Jewish lore, and their engagement with the plain sense of the text. Kimhi often took issue with christological interpretations and on Psalm 2 advised his students on how to answer Christians regarding the "Son" in this psalm.

4. *The Reformation*. Luther's first lectures at Wittemberg were expositions of the psalms. His style shows some continuity with tradition, although the standard four levels of sense (literal, symbolic, moral, and mystical) tend to flow into the principal sense of Christ the Word. Luther provided specially printed Latin texts for the students and from his own prepared copy dictated explanatory glosses to be written around and between the lines. According to custom, he supplemented these brief notes with "scholia," more extensive remarks on selected points that connected with issues of theology and garnered scriptural support. Both the glossed texts and the separate manuscript of scholia have been preserved in Luther's hand.

Luther often expounded psalms in later years; and various expositions, given in lectures, sermons, or in the family circle, were published from notes made by his followers. These reveal a great exegete who truly lived both in the psalm and in the struggles of his time. On Psalm 2, the raging of the nations, the apparent weakness of God's cause, and its ultimate triumph all illuminate the suffering and the hopes of the Lutheran movement. On Psalm 51, Luther followed the title, taking good account of David's situation with Bathsheba; yet he was more concerned with the psalm's lessons about "the whole of sin," "the root and tree of sin," and the gospel of forgiveness.

Calvin's commentary (tr. 1845-49) is of outstanding competence. Marked by orderly and sober argument, it is more akin to modern historical-critical works in its sense of history than with the interpretations of his contemporaries. Calvin was determined to find, not just any truth, but the truth of the passage at hand. To that end the plain sense, indispensable where Scripture is treated as sole authority, is applied effectively in ethical and religious teaching, as when he expounded from Psalm 1 the subtle process of moral degeneration. Yet he did not neglect the correspondence of the old and new kingdoms of God. Beyond an immediate circumstance of battle, David through Psalm 20 was understood to be calling for continual prayer for the kingdom of Christ.

Both Luther and Calvin tended to depict the psalms as doctrine and admonition, and their successors were increasingly inclined to make sound doctrine the overriding concern. The flood of Protestant exegesis had its counterpart in Roman Catholic circles; knowledge of Semitic languages flourished, but the detailed expositions of the time tended to be pedantic.

5. *Critical Foundations in the Eighteenth Century*. With a revival in humanist learning some scholars approached the HB in a more detached spirit, discarding the "papistical" grip of the Protestant churches. The foundations of modern criticism were laid in the advancement of comparative philology, textual and literary criticism, and the study of antiquity. R. Lowth's (1753) analysis of Hebrew poetry was directly important for psalm study, and B. Kennicott's (1776-80) collations of Hebrew manuscripts and his notes on the psalms all fed into the work of subsequent commentators.

If the passionate voice of the psalms was somewhat muted during this period of classical elegance, a corrective arose in the work of J. G. Herder, whose *Vom Geist der ebräischen Poesie* (1782-83) treats many psalms with understanding and sympathy. With "simplicity of heart" (*Einfalt des Herzens*) one enters the world of the ancient poet, breathing the good air of primitive origins. Herder greatly influenced the following centuries and not least the key commentators W. De Wette and H. Gunkel.

6.*The Nineteenth Century*. During this period great strides were made in textual and philological study and in the knowledge of the ancient world and of the development of HB literature. An era of influential German commentaries opened with that of de Wette (1811), and its second edition (1823) was improved philologically by use of H. Gesenius's new Hebrew dictionary. Unlike most scholars of the century, de Wette thought that few psalms revealed historical circumstances and that it was better to propose nothing of the kind than to overrun the evidence. Instead, he offered an aesthetic criticism, appraising each psalm as a lyrical expression of feeling and intuition, which led him to develop the classification of the poems by placing them in six categories similar to those Gunkel would more thoroughly work out a century later.

Nevertheless, the trend toward supposed historical precision continued. Suggested datings became ever later, and any connection with David seemed increasingly unlikely. Most of the psalms were associated with postexilic, frequently Maccabean, times. The themes of ungodly oppressors, kingship, and love of God's law were taken as sure signs of postexilic conflicts and were placed near the end of the era. Resemblances to the prophets and to other Scriptures indicated the dependence of late writers on hallowed texts. Such views were given incisive expression in the commentary of B. Duhm (1899, 1922); admirable in its scientific clarity, it is marred by its low estimate of the psalms and by scathing remarks about Jewish piety.

E. Hengstenberg, "father of the reactionaries" (according to C. Briggs), produced a dogmatic commentary in four volumes (1842-47). Franz Delitzsch only gradually came to terms with modern ideas of the HB's development; his reasoned conservatism and rabbinical learning have given his commentary on Psalms (1859-60; ET 1894) enduring value. F. Baethgen's commentary (1892) represents the typical moderate work of the century: Emending the text through comparison of the versions, he took account of the metrical structure, related the texts to history down to Maccabean times, and gave little room to spiritual appreciation.

7. *Form Criticism.* Characteristic twentieth-century study of the psalms has been based on a method of systematic sorting. The approach is variously referred to as the history or study of forms, classes, or types (*Gattungen*, genres), and its champion was Gunkel (1862-1932). He explained that the primary law for all science is that an object cannot be understood in isolation but must be seen in its context. In relation to the psalms, this is accomplished by gathering comparable material from the ancient world and by identifying and analyzing the main types of psalms through thorough inner-biblical comparisons. Gunkel conceived of each type as having arisen from a recurring situation in worship that determined the type's elements of thought ("motifs") and forms of speech. He believed it possible to trace the history of the types, their development, and in some cases their rebirth in mixed forms, which would give broad guidance for dating a psalm. In cases where the types had grown away from the original ceremonies, they still preserved this fixed wording and patterns of thought.

Gunkel's outline of the types in his commentary (1929, 1X) begins with the hymns used to glorify God during the ceremonies in the sanctuary before the assembly and sung by the choir or expert soloist. A variation of the hymns praising the sanctuary itself he called elsewhere "songs of Zion." Additional types include "songs rendered on the feast-day when they celebrated Yahweh's throne-ascension"; the people's songs of lament (or complaint, *Klage*), sung with rites at the sanctuary in times of national need to express grief and implore mercy; the king's songs, of various kinds that have in common rendition by a court singer in the festivities for the king and his house; the individual's songs of lament/complaint, sung by an individual (not the corporate figure Israel) in personal need and originally including rites performed in the sanctuary. Corresponding to these are the individual's song of thanks, in which a saved person pours out thanks and praise in the sanctuary while presenting offerings. Smaller types include blessings, curses, songs of pilgrimage, Israel's songs of victory, Israel's songs of thanks, and holy legends (parts of Psalms 78, 105, and 106).

To these Gunkel added some that were not originally from the tradition of psalmody but came to be combined with it: prophetic poems and wisdom poetry. Finally he listed "mixtures," in which later writers freely drew on various types, and "liturgies," in which different types were set side by side because of the alternation of voices in worship.

Gunkel's heartfelt wish that the "dam" holding his fellow scholars from recognizing the forms and their importance would burst was amply granted. In time form criticism became fundamental for most commentators, and many works were devoted to revision or refinement of the classes he set out. The very conception of "thanksgiving" was deprecated by C. Westermann (1953; ET 1965), who preferred to see Gunkel's hymns as "descriptive praise" and his song of thanks as "narrative/declarative praise." F. Crüsemann's (1969) thorough study of hymnic forms concluded that although Gunkel's communal thanksgivings should be considered as hymns, the class of individual thanksgivings should be retained. Distinctions among the individual's songs of lament have been proposed: pleas (which praise God), complaints (where God is blamed), protective psalms (anticipating danger), etc. Gunkel's songs from Yahweh's throne-ascension have been differentiated and distributed through a wide range of periods.

The greatness of Gunkel's exposition did not arise solely from this approach. He was above all a passionate and sensitive interpreter. His ambition was to be the mouth of ancients, expressing for our age what the Hebrew poets had felt in the depths of their hearts.

8. *The Study of Function.* Form criticism took account not only of patterns of expression but also of the functions in society that had molded them. It was especially in regard to these functions that S. Mowinckel contributed much to interpretation.

a. *Enthronement Psalms.* Especially fruitful was Mowinckel's view of the songs for Yahweh's throne-ascension, in which he saw, not songs based on prophecies of Second Isaiah, but the expression of an ancient ingredient in worship, the climax of the festal days. Action in worship was first and foremost that of God. As Yahweh had asserted power in the beginning, so now on the festal day these psalms proclaimed that Yahweh was manifested as sovereign over all-Yahweh and no other has "become king." The beginning and the festal day were one, and divine light shone forward on days to come. Renewal touched all aspects of life founded in the classic past: creation, covenant, liberation, settlement. From many other psalms, HB texts, and rabbinic sources, Mowinckel filled out his picture of the annual observances that covered the transition to the agricultural new year in September-October, antecedents of the Jewish festivals of New Year, Atonement, and Booths.

All this offered vivid insights into the HB world. The public religion focused in the festivals was viewed sympathetically at last in its age-long work of nurturing, inspiring, and creating; and the psalmody that expressed it appeared with new importance, no longer as a mere late echo of the prophets. Mowinckel's work, however, met with some hostility. He was said to be reading the HB too mythologically, after the pattern of the Babylonian new year festival through which the creator, Marduk, subjugated chaos and was honored as king of the gods. But Mowinckel's reconstruction has a wide basis in the HB. Striking analogies from surrounding peoples serve to give us a proper perspective of the ancient world.

b. *The King's Psalms.* The function of another type of psalm-the king's songs-now seemed due for reconsideration. Gunkel had strongly argued that nine complete psalms and parts of others were included in this category and had been used in ceremonies of the preexilic kings; they were not later compositions concerning the people (as a royal figure), the Messiah, or Maccabean high priests and kings. Within the framework of the reconstructed autumn festival it seemed that the function of these psalms could be further pursued. In 1927 H. Schmidt envisaged how, along with Yahweh, the Davidic ruler also symbolically defeated his enemies and entered his kingdom anew. Mowinckel was notably restrained in the use of these psalms for reconstructing the autumn festival; however, he granted the likelihood that the ruler's installation was celebrated and then annually commemorated in the festival through the use of these psalms.

The matter was followed up by A. Johnson (1955, 1967). A true interpreter, his method was to present his view through a chain of psalms that he translated and expounded. In this way he traced the lines of sacred drama within the festival, maintaining that it represented Yahweh's defeat of the forces of darkness and death that through the kings of the nations had attacked his city and throne-center, Zion. The Davidic king served Yahweh by leading the defenders but tri-

umphed only after coming near defeat. At first Johnson found the purpose of the drama especially in the annual revitalizing of society. Subsequently he emphasized that it signaled an ultimate reality, the great day to come, which already challenged the contemporary ruler and people.

c. *Psalms of Lament.* Discussion has continued on the function of the individual's songs of
lament (see J. Croft [1987]). Whereas Gunkel had thought that the extant examples represented a development away from the original cultic setting, Mowinckel in his early work saw them
as still set in rites of cleansing and healing at the Temple, in which their imprecations were a
defense against the injurious wishes or spells of the enemies. Schmidt (1928), and later W.
Beyerlin (1977), found the cultic situation of some of these psalms in the trials held at the
Temple: They were prayers for vindication. L. Delekat (1967) saw the supplicants rather as
seekers of asylum at the Temple. E. Gerstenberger (1980) thinks of rites in the sufferer's own
locality, amid his primary group but led by a local seer.

Another line of interpretation for these psalms was advocated by H. Birkeland in 1933 and
soon came to have the weighty support of Mowinckel. The worshiper is generally taken to be
Israel's leader, usually a king; prayer is being offered in the Temple or at a field sanctuary in
time of crisis-invasion, plotting, and so forth. J. Eaton (1976, 1986) has worked over the materials with more emphasis on the ideas and language of royal traditions and found much that
favors the royal interpretation, explaining the interplay of individual and community, of regular cult and sudden crisis, of harsh warfare and tender piety. Others who have favored passing
beyond the limits of Gunkel's royal class include A. Bentzen, M. Dahood, J. Gray, Johnson, J.
Day, P. Craigie (1983), and M. Goulder (1990).

d. *Wisdom Psalms.* The situations behind the later stages of psalmody have also received
attention. The currents of both wisdom schooling and Torah piety seem to run stronger in the
psalms during the postexilic era. Mowinckel saw the bulk of psalmody as passing into the care
of collectors who were learned sages and scribes, forerunners of Ben Sirah; a few of their own
compositions then entered the collection, pieces they had composed in their schools to edify
their disciples or to bring to the Temple in thanksgiving. They employed the old proverb forms
but also exalted Yahweh's Torah. One school of thought, especially in France and in Catholic
Germany, has given the greatest weight to the activity of the scribes in the Persian and Greek
periods, seeing most of the psalms as their reuse of older elements.

9. *Current Concerns.* Progress continues in the publication of such comparable materials as
hymns and prayers from Babylonia and Egypt, poetry from Ugarit, and evidence of temples and
musicians. Dahood's commentary (1966-70) is remarkable for its exploitation of comparisons
with Ugaritic, though many of its novel proposals on text and translation must be regarded as
only experimental. From Ugaritic studies also, O. Loretz has developed the method of colom-
etry: He divides a psalm into its cola, examines the total number of letters in each colon, and
so hopes to identify secondary expansions. The structuralist approach has produced some
minute analyses of psalms; repetitions and parallelisms are taken to mark alternating or con-
centric patterns. Structure is found also in the interplay of persons; analysis of images and figures contributes to the disclosure of the psalm's shape and movement as well. Interest thus
shifts from a psalm's origin to its rhetoric and symbolic world.

The structure of the psalter as a whole has also received close attention. With a fresh respect
for the final shape of Scripture, scholars have pondered anew the links of wording and ideas
between adjacent psalms, moods characterizing groups of psalms, and the strategic positions of
psalms with decisive themes.

H. J. Kraus (1960, 1979) demonstrated how, after all, a theological appreciation of the psalms
could be achieved in harmony with modern study; after an interval of centuries it seemed that
the exegetical fullness of the great Reformers was reviving. Several studies have further eval-

uated the psalms' theology of Temple and royal house, and there are signs of renewed appreciation of the ancient interpreters. Not just the anticipations of modern research are to be valued but also those imaginative encounters where the Origens, Augustines, and Midrashists were prompted by the psalms to see deep into the divine world.

Bibliography: A. **Aejmelaeus** and U. **Quast,** tr., *Der Septuaginta-Psalter und seine Tochterübersetzungen: Symposium in Göttingen 1997* (MSU 24, 2000). L. C. **Allen**, *Psalms 101-150* (WBC 21, 1983). **Augustine** (Bishop of Hippo), *Enarrations in Psalmos* (F. Gori, ed., CSEL 93, 95, 2001). B. J. L. **Baethgen**, *Die moderne Bibelkritik und die Autorität des Gotteswortes* (1892). **Basil**, *St. Basil: Exegetic Homilies* (FC 46, tr. A. C. Way, 1963). J. **Becker**, *Wege der Psalmenexegese* (SBS 78, 1975). W. **Beyerlin**, *Die Rettung der Bedrängten in den Feindpsalmen der Einzelnen auf institionelle Zusammenhänge untersucht* (FRLANT 99, 1977). H. **Birkeland**, *Die Feinde des Individuums in der israelitischen Psalmenliteratur: Ein Beitrag zur Kenntnis der semitischen Literatur- und Religionsgeschichte (1933); The Evildoers in the Book of Psalms* (1955). W. C. **Bouzard**, *We Have Heard with Our ears, O God: Sources of the Communal Laments in the Psalms* (SBLDS 159, 1997). W. G. **Braude**, *The Midrash on Psalms* (2 vols. YJS 13, 1959). A. **Brenner** and C. R. **Fontaine**, eds., *Wisdom and Psalms* (FCB, Second Series 2, 1998). G.M. **Browne**, *Collectio psalterii Bedae Venerabili Adscripta* (Bibliotheca scriptorum Graecorum et Romanorum, 2001). C. H. **Bullock**, *Encountering the Book of Psalms: A Literary and Theological Introduction* (2001). J. **Calvin**, *J. Calvin's Commentary on the Book of Psalms* (2 vols., tr. J. Anderson, 1845-49); *La Chaîne Palestinienne sur le Psaume 118* (SC 189, tr. M. Harl, 1972). R. J. **Clifford**, *Psalms 1-72* (Abingdon Old Testament Commentaries, 2002); *Psalms 73-150* (Abingdon Old Testament Commentaries, 2003). R. L. **Cole**, *The Shape and Message of Book III (Psalms 73-89)* (JSOTSup 307, 2000). A. C. **Coxe** (ed.), *Saint Augustin: Expositions on the Book of Psalms* (1888, repr. 1979). P. C. **Craigie**, *Psalms 1-50* (WBC 19, 1983). S. J. L. **Croft**, *The Identity of the Individual in the Psalms* (JSOTSup 44, 1987). F. M. **Cross**, *Studies in Ancient Yahwistic Poetry* (new edn., 1997). F. **Crüsemann**, *Studien zur Formgeschichte von Hymnus und Danklied in Israel* (WMANT 32, 1969). U. **Dahmen**, *Psalmen- und Psalter-Rezeption im Frühjudentum: Rekonstruktion, Textbestand, Struktur und Pragmatik der Psalmenrolle 11Qpsa aus Qumran* (STDJ 49, 2003). L. **Delekat**, *Asylie und Schutzorakel am Zionheiligtum: Eine Untersuchung zu den privaten Fiendpsalmen* (1967). R. **Devreesse** (ed.), *Le commentaire de Théodore de Mopsueste sur Psaumes* (I-LXXX) (1939); *Les anciens commentateurs grecs des Psaumes* (1970). W. M. L. **de Wette**, *Kommentar über die Psalmen* (1811). B. **Duhm**, *Psalms* (KEH 14, 1899, 1922). J. H. **Eaton**, *Kingship and the Psalms* (1976, 1986); *Psalms of the Way and the Kingdom* (JSOTSup 199, 1995). D. **Erasmus**, *Expositions of the Psalms* (D. Baker-Smith, ed., M.J. Heath, tr., Collected Works of Erasmus 63, 1997). A. C. **Feuer**, *Tehillim: A New Translation with Commentary Anthologized from Talmudic, Midrashic, and Rabbinic Sources* (2 vols., 1985). P. W. **Flint**, *The Dead Sea Psalms Scrolls and the Book of Psalms* (STDJ 17, 1997). E. **Gerstenberger**, "Psalms," *OT Form Criticism* (ed. J. H. Hayes, TUMSR 2, 1974); *Der bittende Mensch: Bittritual und Klagelied der Einzelnen im Alten Testament* (WMANT 51, 1980). M. **Goulder**, *The Prayers of David: Psalms 51-72* (JSOTSup 102, 1990). **Gregory of Nyssa**, *Sur les titres des psaumes* (Sources chrétiennes 466, 2002). A. **Grund**, *"Die Himmel erzählen die Herrlichkeit Gottes" : Psalm 19 im Kontext der nachexilischen Toraweishiet* (WMANT 103, 2004). H. **Gunkel**, *Die Psalmen* (1929); *Introduction to Psalms* (1933; ET 1998). R. G. **Haney**, *Text and Concept Analysis in Royal Psalms* (Studies in Biblical Literature 30, 2002). S. **Hendrix**, *Ecclesia in Via: Ecclesiological Developments in the Medieval Psalms Exegesis and the "Dictata Super Psalterium" of M. Luther* (SMRT 8, 1974). E. W. **Hengstenberg**, *Commentary on the Psalms* (1842-47; ET 1850). J. G. **Herder**, *The Spirit of*

Hebrew Poetry (2 vols. 1782-83; ET 1833). **W. L. Holladay**, *The Psalms Through Three Thousand Years: Prayerbook of a Cloud of Witnesses* (1993). **F.-L. Hossfeld**, *Psalmen* (Herders Theologischer Kommentar zum Alten Testament , 2000). **D. M. Howard, Jr.,** *The Structure of the Psalms 93-100* (Biblical and Judaic Studies 5, 1997). **A. G. Hunter**, *Psalms* (Old Testament Readings, 1999). **Jerome,** *The Homilies of St. Jerome* (FC 48, 57, tr. M. E. Ewald, 1964, 1965). **A. R. Johnson**, "The Psalms," *The OT and Modern Study: A Generation of Discovery and Research* (ed. H. H. Rowley, 1951) 162-209; *Sacral Kingship in Ancient Israel* (1955, 1967). **B. Kennicott**, *Vetus Testamentum Hebraicum cum variis lectionibus* (2 vols., 1776-80). **D. Kimhi,** *The Longer Commentary of Rabbi D. Kimhi on the First Book of Psalms* (tr. R. G. Finch, 1919); *The Commentary of Rabbi D. Kimchi on Psalms CXX-CL* (tr. J. Baker and E. W. Nicholson, 1973). **H. J. Kraus**, *Psalmen* (2 vols., BKAT 15, 1960, 1979; ET 1987-89); *Theology of the Psalms* (1979; ET 1986). **R. de Langhe** (ed.), *Le Psautier: Ses origines, ses probl?mes litt,raires, son influence* (OBL 4, 1962). **M. Luther**, *Luther's Works: First Lectures on the Psalms* (2 vols., tr. H. C. Oswald, 1974). **C. Mandolfo**, *God in the Dock: Dialogic Tension in the Psalms of Lament* (JSOTSup 357, 2002). **J. C. McCann**, *A Theological Introduction to The Book of Psalms: The Psalms as Torah* (1995); "The Book of Psalms," *NIB* (1996) 4:639-1280. **J. L. Mays**, *The Lord Reigns: A Theological Handbook to the Psalms* (1994). **S. Mowinckel**, *Psalmenstudien I-VI* (1921-24); *The Psalms in Israel's Worship* (2 vols., 1962). **E. Mühlenberg**, *Psalmenkommentare aus der Katenenüberlieferung* (3 vols., 1975-78). **R.E. Murphy**, *The Gift of the Psalms* (2000). **J. M. Neale** and **R. F. Littledale**, *A Commentary on the Psalms from Primitive and Medieval Writers* (4 vols., 1860-74). **R. Lowth**, *De sacra poesi Hebraeorum Praelectiones Academicae* (1753). **P. H. A. Neumann** (ed.), *Zur neueren Psalmenforschung* (WdF 192, 1976). **J. S. Preus**, *From Shadow to Promise; OT Interpretation from Augustine to the Young Luther* (1969), esp. 151-271. **Rashi**, *Rashi's Commentary on Psalms* (M.I. Gruber, tr., South Florida Studies in the History of Judaism 161, 1998). **S. B. Reid**, *Listening In: a Multicultural Reading of the Psalms* (1997). **M. J. Rondeau**, *Les commentaires patristiques du Psautier* (IIIe siècles) (2 vols., 1982-85). **A. D. Savage**, *D'Aubigné's Meditations sur les Pseaumes* (Studies in Reformed Theology and History, New Series, 8, 2002). **K. Schaefer**, *Psalms* (Berit Olam, 2001). **H. Schmidt**, *Die Thronfahrt Jahves am Fest der Jahreswende im alten Israel* (1927); *Das Gebet der Angeklagten im AT* (BZAW 49, 1928). **K. Seybold**, *Studien zur Psalmenauslegung* (1998). **H. Spieckermann**, *Heilsgegenwart: Eine Theologie der Psalmen* (FRLANT 148, 1989). **S. R. A. Starbuck**, *Court Oracles in the Psalms: the So-called Royal Psalms in their Ancient Near Easter Context* (SBLDS 172, 1999). **D. C. Steinmetz**, "Luther as an Interpreter of the Psalms," *Luther and Staupitz: An Essay in the Intellectual Origins of the Protestant Reformation* (1980) 50-67. **B. L. Tanner**, *The Book of Psalms through the Lens of Intertextuality* (Studies in Biblical Literature 26, 2001). **M. E. Tate**, *Psalms 51-100* (WBC 20, 1990). **Theodoret (Bishop of Cyrrhus),** *Theodoret of Cyrus: Commentary on the Psalms* (R.C. Hill, tr., Fathers of the Church 101, 2000). **J. D. Thompson**, *A Critical Concordance to the Septuagint: Psalms* (The Computer Bible 90, 2001). **N. Van Deusen**, ed., *The Place of the Psalms in the Intellectual Culture of the Middle Ages* (SUNY Series in Medieval Studies, 1999). **C. Westermann**, *The Praise of God in the Psalms* (1953; ET 1965).

J. H. EAYTON

THE WRITINGS

Proverbs

The Masoretic title Proverbs of Solomon (*mis̆lê s̆elōmōth*, subsequently abbreviated to as *mis̆lê*, as in modern printed editions of the HB), which is already found in Greek translation in the Septuagint (Codex Alexandrinus), probably indicates that the heading in 1:1 ("The proverbs of Solomon, son of David, king of Israel") was understood quite early to be an attribution of the entire book to Solomon, despite the contrary indications of the sectional headings in 10:1 and 25:1, which might seem to indicate that he wrote only some parts of it, and the statements in 30:1 and 31:1, which appear to deny Solomonic authorship altogether for the final sections. However, this view was not universally accepted by early Jewish scholars, who took seriously the statement in 25:1 that "these also are proverbs of Solomon which the men of Hezekiah copied" (or "edited"). Indeed, in the famous statement about the authorship of the biblical books in the Talmud (*b. B. Bat.* 14b-15a) the Solomonic claim to authorship is ignored: It is there unequivocally stated that it was Hezekiah and his "college" who wrote Proverbs (*mis̆lê*) as well as certain other books. Evidently, then, the phrase "proverbs of Solomon" was not always taken at face value—an anticipation of the modern view that, like the phrase "a psalm of David" attached to some of the psalms, it is intended merely to indicate that the book belongs to a particular class of literature, in this case one to which Solomon was traditionally supposed to have contributed (1 Kgs 4:32; Heb 5:12). In later Judaism too the Solomonic attribution was not taken as necessarily foreclosing discussion about authorship: D. Kimhi, for example, in the eleventh century CE suggested that Isaiah might be the author of the book.

According to the Talmud (*b. Šabb.* 30b) and *ʾAbot R. Nat.* (chap. 1) some objections were initially raised about the worthiness of Proverbs to be included in the canon—not , however, on doctrinal grounds, but rather because it contained contradictions (e.g., between 26:4 and 26:5) and also included unduly vivid descriptions (e.g., the seduction scene in 7:7-20) that might be morally harmful to its readers. After the first century C.E. its canonical status within the *Kethubim* was not questioned; it was translated, like the other canonical books, into a number of languages. Of these translations the Greek text is noteworthy for a number of additions to the Hebrew, some of which appear to represent deliberate attempts to modify the character of the original by moralistic and pietistic comment and by toning down some of its supposed sensuality.

In the classical and medieval periods Proverbs was frequently cited in both Jewish and Christian literature, especially in the Talmud, the NT, and the early Christian fathers. Passages like Prov 22:20-21 (LXX) provided Origen legitimation for reading multiple meanings into biblical texts. In general, however, the book was prized by both Jews and Christians as a source of simple moral and religious truths and practical advice rather than being used to establish or confirm particular religious doctrines.

In the late Middle Ages, the Reformation period, and the seventeenth and eighteenth centuries, various critical theories were proposed by scholars that in many ways anticipated later critical work. Among others, Nicholas of Lyra, whose *Postillae* (1326) long remained influential, interpreted 25:1 as meaning that Hezekiah's men made a second collection of Solomon's unpublished proverbs and added it to those previously made in Solomon's own time; P. Melanchthon (1497–1560) understood the proverb form as specifically designed to function as a teaching device and also compared the book with the works of the Greek authors Theognis and Phocylides; and T. Hobbes (1651) sketched a history of the composition of the book in several stages, of which the latest was to be dated in the postexilic period or in the reign of Josiah at the earliest. But the modern critical interpretation of Proverbs really began with J. G.

Eichhorn's *Einleitung in das Alte Testament* (1783, 1824), in which he employed stylistic criteria to assign the various sections of the book to different pre-exilic periods. He also put forward a theory of the development of the proverb form from its origins as domestic regulations laid down by heads of families to its formation into collections of pious admonitions for general use.

Throughout the nineteenth century opinion remained divided on the question of whether Proverbs was substantially pre-exilic or postexilic in date. A. Hartmann's (1774–1838) argument—based partly on the presence of Aramaisms in the book and partly on its supposed identification of wisdom with the law—that the book is an example of late Jewish piety was particularly influential. The pendulum began to swing in the opposite direction with the discovery of texts from Egypt and Mesopotamia that were remarkably similar both in form and theme to the biblical book of Proverbs and of great antiquity. The Egyptian *Instruction of Ptahhotep*, first published in 1847, was described by the French Egyptologist F. Chabas in 1858 as "the oldest book in the world." But it was not until A. Erman and H. Gressmann argued (in 1924) that the recently discovered *Instruction of Amenemope* had actually been used as a model by the author of an entire section of Proverbs (22:17–24:22) that it began to be recognized that Israel's wisdom literature, and in particular the book of Proverbs, was not the product of the unaided Israelite genius but rather a late flowering of a much older literary tradition common to the peoples of the ancient Near East. Further studies (e.g., that of P. Humbert [1929]) made this abundantly clear.

The implications of these discoveries for the study of Proverbs soon became apparent. There was no doubt that the Egyptian "instructions" were textbooks composed for use in schools connected with the royal court to educate young men of the upper class destined for high civil service. In view of the now-proven dependence of at least part of Proverbs on this type of literature, together with the references in the book to kings and to the royal entourage and the didactic tone of much of the book, it was concluded that its origins were to be looked for in similar circles in preexilic Israel. This remained the prevailing opinion for more than a generation. It was further strengthened by G. von Rad's hypothesis that in the reign of Solomon Israel had passed through a period of rapid cultural change (the so-called Solomonic enlightenment) brought about by contacts with Egypt as a result of Solomon's organization of the new national state of Israel on Egyptian models. Some parts of the book, however, especially chaps. 1–9, were universally believed to be postexilic additions (see sec. 5).

The following topics have been particularly prominent in discussion of the book in the last half of the twentieth century:

1. *Provenance.* The view that the milieu from which the book emerged was the royal court with its "wisdom school" was challenged, especially by E. Gerstenberger (1965). He argued that the instructional material in the book originated, not in schools, but in rules of conduct that had governed tribal life in pre-monarchical Israel (*Sippenweisheit*). However, this view was rejected by H. J. Hermisson (1968) and others on the grounds that the short proverbs in the book are of a highly artistic character quite unlike the "popular" wisdom sayings embedded in the historical and prophetical books of the HB and also that the organization and customs of early Israelite tribal society are extremely obscure. A third view is that the collections of proverbs may have been intended for the edification of a class of educated farmers whose interests were wider than those of the professional scribe or teacher (U. Skladny [1962]; R. Whybray [1974]). It has been pointed out that the "royal" and "court" sayings in the book are far less numerous than those concerned with more general topics. No consensus has been reached on the question of the provenance of the book, but it may be said that these three views are not necessarily mutually exclusive. In this connection there has been a lengthy but also inconclusive discussion

about the evidence for the existence of schools in preexilic Israel (Whybray [1974]; B. Lang [1979]; A. Lemaire [1981]; J. Crenshaw [1985]).

2. *The Nature and Function of the Proverb.* Much of the earlier discussion was impeded by a failure to achieve agreement about the nature and function of the short proverbs that make up most of the book. In retrospect it is arguable that this failure was due to an excessive reliance on form-critical analysis as an interpretative tool. Amid the many different forms capable of classification it was stressed that there is a fundamental distinction between the "sentence" (*Aussagewort*), which makes a statement about some aspect of life based on observation or experience without drawing an explicit moral (e.g., 14:4; 16:8), and the "admonition" (*Mahnwort*), which is couched in the form of advice, either positive or negative (warning), often accompanied by a statement of the reason for that advice (e.g., 19:20; 27:1). This differ-ence of form was taken to be an indication of a fundamental difference of origin and function, the admonition being strictly educational in purpose while the sentence was simply a general observation whose purpose was difficult to determine precisely and whose origin was much more problematical (the discussion about its "popular" provenance, already stimulated by O. Eissfeldt in 1913, still continues and seems unlikely to lead to a general consensus of opinion).

In the last decades of the twentieth century, the significance of the formal difference between these two types of proverbs has been questioned. It was observed long ago but not always taken into account by the form critics that the great majority of the sentences are not simply neutral observations about a particular aspect of reality but imply, no less than the direct admonitions, the desirability of adopting specific modes of behavior. It is only their form (indicative rather than imperative) that is different. This is true of popular sayings in every age, including our own: No distinction is perceived between the functions of sentences like "A stitch in time saves nine" and admonitions like "Don't count your chickens before they are hatched."

This observation has led a number of writers (e.g., J. Williams [1981]; C. Fontaine [1985]) to suggest that progress toward understanding the nature and function of the short proverbs in the book can best be made by asking more general questions, in light of the world-wide use of proverbs, about the proverb form as a whole. In other words, why has this brief, encapsulated form of speech been chosen as a vehicle for comment about the world and society? These writ-ers imply that the distinctions usually made between "folk sayings," "rules of conduct," "teach-ing Proverbs," and the like are too rigid and conceal the fact that the proverb is a natural and universal form of speech not confined to any particular class or situation. It is not a primitive form later superseded by more elaborate philosophical discourse but one that continues to exist side by side with other forms of speech.

Williams, citing a comment made by Paschal about the reason for the brevity and fragmen-tary character of his *Pensées,* suggested that the unsystematic form of proverb literature, with its fragmentary commentary on particular, very limited aspects of the world and society, is espe-cially appropriate to a fragmented world—a reply to those scholars who have understood Proverbs as expressing the notion of an all-embracing, divinely established order, of which either Yahweh or Wisdom is the guardian (see sec. 4 below). Fontaine went further, seeing the proverb as not only springing from a perception of a lack of order but also as having a positive function: It is used to create pockets of order in the world or to restore order where it has bro-ken down. In such a view the admonitions and sentences in Proverbs, although they may have originated in different circumstances, have a common function and are not to be fundamental-ly distinguished from one another. The real distinction is to be made between proverb literature as a whole and longer poems like those in chaps. 1–9 that do indeed attempt to subsume expe-rience of the world in a systematic theology in which divine wisdom guards and controls a coherent world order.

3. *Developments in the Concepts of Wisdom in Proverbs*. A somewhat different attempt to distinguish between types of material that make up the mass of proverb literature in the book was made by a number of scholars, including von Rad (1957; ET 1962) and W. McKane (1970), who claimed that in these chapters are to be found two different concepts of wisdom, the one superimposed on the other. In their earliest form these chapters taught a purely pragmatic, amoral kind of wisdom based wholly on human reason and similar to the kind underlying the policies of the politicians in the early Israelite monarchy portrayed in 1 Samuel (McKane called this "old wisdom"). In the course of time this was transformed under the influence of the pre-exilic prophets into an exposition of a highly moral Yahwism by the addition of new, more religious sayings to the original collections. This estimate of Israel's "old wisdom," however, runs counter to what has long been known about the character of ancient Near Eastern wisdom literature in general, in which all human conduct was regarded as subject to the scrutiny of the gods, who judged it by distinctly moral standards. In the last decades of the twentieth century, most scholars reject the idea of a non-religious and amoral wisdom in early Israel since this would have been a unique phenomenon. It is true that there are contradictory or incompatible statements in these chapters on the moral level, but artibitrarily to classify these as though each were a complete expression of a religious or moral standpoint is to ignore the complexity of the currents of thought present in any given society.

4. *The Theology of Proverbs*. The theology of the book and its place in the theological world of the OT have been variously assessed. Some scholars (H. Gese [1958]; H. Schmid [1966]) see it as expressing a view of the world as a divinely ordered system within which all things work for the best but which it is folly to transgress. This was believed by C. Kayatz (1966) to be akin to the concept of *Maat* in Egypt. It must be recognized, however, that chaps. 1–9 (see sec. 5) are on a quite different plane from the rest of the book. As has already been pointed out (sec. 2), it is questionable whether any systematic theological point of view is to be found in chaps. 10–31.

On the whole these chapters take the optimistic position that righteous conduct, which is frequently equated with wisdom and is generally attainable by those who pursue it, reaps its own reward, while the wicked and foolish will perish miserably. This belief is not peculiar to Proverbs but is found elsewhere in the OT and appears to have been generally accepted in Israel, at least during the pre-exilic period. In these chapters Yahweh is seen as the guarantor of this principle. Whether in this role Yahweh is also regarded as a judge who dispenses retribution personally in the form of rewards and punishments is disputed. K. Koch (1955) maintained that this is not so: These proverbs reflect a belief that human actions contain within themselves the seeds of their own consequences, which ensue by a kind of automatic process. No agreement has been reached on this question, which lies beyond the study of Proverbs per se.

5. Chapters 1–9. The distinctive character of these chapters was recognized from very early times. Instead of the short proverbs predominant in the rest of the book, they consist almost entirely of longer poems. Three of these—1:20-33; 8; 9:1-6 + 13-18—are entirely unique in that they personify wisdom as a woman who claims to have been associated with Yahweh from before the creation of the world, builds a house, and offers life and happiness to men. Biblical feminists (C. Newsom [1989]; C. Camp [1985, 1988]; Fontaine [1992]) have noticed that folly is also personified as a woman. Both Wisdom and Folly cry out in the streets, hoping to lead young men on opposite journeys, one wise, another foolish. Since it is difficult to distinguish between the two women, women in general are suspect.

For a long time modern scholarship was virtually unanimous in regarding these chapters as postexilic and as the latest addition to the book based on considerations of both form and content. In the last half of the twentieth century, it has been recognized that they do not constitute a single block of material. Although the poems in which wisdom is personified represent a relatively late wisdom theology anticipating still later developments in which "the entire theological thinking of later Judaism came more or less under the sway of wisdom" (von Rad), it has not been demonstrated that the remainder of the material consists of a series of instructions from a teacher to a pupil on the pattern of the earlier Egyptian instructions (Whybray [1965]; Kayatz).

In 1986 Lang offered a new explanation of the figure of personified Wisdom that speaks for a preexilic origin of chaps. 1, 8, and 9. These chapters, he argues, have been adapted from poems composed in praise of an Israelite goddess who was worshiped independently of Yahweh as the patroness of scribal education. This thesis, only one of a succession of attempts to derive the figure of personified Wisdom from Near Eastern female divinities, was to some extent anticipated in 1955 by W. F. Albright, who proposed a Canaanite goddess of wisdom as the prototype of this figure.

Bibliography: W. F. Albright, "Some Canaanite-Phoenician Sources of Hebrew Wisdom," (VTSup 3, 1955) 1-15. **C. V. Camp,** *Wisdom and the Feminine in the Book of Proverbs* (Bible and Literature 11, 1985); "Wise and Strange: An Interpretation of the Female Imagery in Proverbs in the Light of Trickster Mythology," *Semeia* 42 (1988) 14-36; *Wise, Strange, and Holy: The Strange Woman and the Making of the Bible* (JSOTSup 320, 2000). **R. J. Clifford,** *Proverbs: A Commentary* (Old Testament Library, 1999). **V. Cottini,** *La vita futura nel libro dei Proverbi: Contributo alla storia dell'esegesi* (1984). **J. L. Crenshaw,** "Education in Ancient Israel," *JBL* 104 (1985) 601-15; *Education in Ancient Israel* (ABRL, 1998). **O. Eissfeldt,** *Der Maschal im Alten Testament* (BZAW 24, 1913). **A. Erman,** "Eine ägyptische Quelle der 'Sprüche Salomos,'" *SPAW* (1924) 86-93. **C. Fontaine,** *Traditional Sayings in the OT* (1982); "Proverb Performance in the HB," *JSOT* 32 (1985) 87-103; "Proverbs," *The Women's Bible Commentary* (ed. C. A. Newsom and S. H. Ringe, 1992) 145-52. **M. V. Fox,** *Proverbs 1-9: A New Translation with Introduction and Commentary* (AB 18A, 2000). **E. Gerstenberger,** *Wesen und Herkunft des "apodiktischen Rechts"* (WMANT 20, 1965). **H. Gese,** *Lehre und Wirklichkeit in der alten Weisheit* (1958). **E. Ginsburg,** *Proverbs: a New Translation with a Commentary Anthologized from Talmudic, Midrashic, and Rabbinic Sources* (1998). **H. Gressmann,** "Die neugefundene Lehre des Amen-em-ope und die vorexilische Spruchdichtung Israels," *ZAW* 42 (1924) 272-96. **H. J. Hermisson,** *Studien zur israelitischen Spruchweisheit* (WMANT 28, 1968). **T. Hobbes,** *Leviathan* (1651). **P. Humbert,** *Recherches sur les sources égyptiennes de la littérature sapientiale d'Israël* (1929). **C. Kayatz,** *Studien zu Proverbian 1-9* (WMANT 22, 1966). **K. Koch,** "Gibt es ein Vergeltungsdogma im alten Testament?" *ZTK* 52 (1955) 1-42; *Um das Prinzip der Vergeltung in Religion und Recht des Alten Testaments* (Wege der Forschung 125, 1972). **B. Lang,** "Schule und Unterricht im alten Israel," *ETL* 51 (1979) 186-201; *Wisdom and the Book of Proverbs* (1986). **A. Lemaire,** *Les écoles et la formation de la Bible dans l'ancien Israël* (OBO 39, 1981). **W. McKane,** *Prophets and Wise Men* (SBT 44, 1965); *Proverbs: A New Approach* (1970). **A. Müller,** *Proverbs 1-9: der Weisheit neue Kleider* (BZAW 291, 2000). **C. A. Newsom,** "A Woman and the Discourse of Patriarchal Wisdom: A Study of Proverbs 1-9," *Gender and Difference in Ancient Israel* (ed. P. L. Day, 1989) 142-60. **J. B. Pritchard** (ed.), *Ancient Near Eastern Texts Relating to the OT* (1969). **G. von Rad,** *OT Theology 1* (1957; ET 1962); *Wisdom in Israel* (1970; ET 1972). **R. Schäfer,** *Die Poesie der Weisen: Dichtomie als Grundstruktur der Lehr-und Weisheitsgedichte in Proverbien 1-9* (WMAN 77, 1999). **A. Scherer,** *Das weise Wort und seine Wirkung: eine Untersuchung zur Komposition und Redaktion von Proverbia 10:1-22* (WMAN 83, 1999). **H. H. Schmid,** *Wesen und Geschichte der Weisheit* (BZAW 101, 1966). **U. Skladny,** *Die ältesten Spruchsammlungen in Israel* (1962). **J. D. Thompson,** *A Critical Concordance to the Septuagint Proverbs* (The Computer Bible 70, 1999). **R. C. Van Leeuwen,** "The Book of Proverbs," *NIB* (1997) 5:17-

264. **R. N. Whybray**, *The Intellectual Tradition in the OT* (BZAW 135, 1974); *The Composition of the Book of Proverbs* (JSOTSup 168, 1994); *Proverbs* (NCB, 1994); *The Book of Proverbs: A Survey of Modern Study* (1995). **J. G. Williams**, *Those Who Ponder Proverbs* (1981).

R. N. WHYBRAY

THE WRITINGS

Qohelet (Ecclesiastes)

Qohelet is named in the title verse of the book (1.1; cf. also 1:12): "The words of Qohelet, the son of David . . . " The English spelling "Ecclesiastes" comes from the Greek version: "The words of Ecclesiastes, the son of David . . . " (1.1), and is related to *ekklēsia* ("congregation," or "assembly").

1. *Authorship and Date*. Virtually all commentators until modern times ascribed the book to Solomon. A. Ibn Ezra (12th cent.), however, mentioned (and rejected) an opinion that the author was an "assembly" (understanding the name *qôhelet* as *qehillâ*) of Solomon's disciples who included their own, often contradictory, opinions.

Maimonides (middle 12th cent.) ascribed the epilogue to "those who edited the book," indicating that he considered Qohelet to be a later collection of Solomon's teachings (see Japhet and Salters). Luther judged the book to be non-Solomonic on grounds of literary unevenness. H. Grotius (1644, 1:258) determined, on the basis of the book's haphazard composition and late language, that Qohelet is not Solomonic but rather a postexilic collection of various opinions. By the middle of the nineteenth century scholars commonly accepted the book's postexilic (and thus non-Solomonic) dating.

With few exceptions commentators since the late nineteenth century place Qohelet in the Hellenistic period (4th-3rd cent.). The arguments are linguistic (the book shows late usages and numerous Aramaisms; see sec. 2) and conceptual (Qohelet shows a late stage in the development of wisdom thought; see, e.g., S. Blank [1970] xv-xxv). Some scholars also base this dating on presumed Greek influence in language and thought (see sec. 5) as well as on various putative historical references. C. Whitley (1979, 122-46) places Qohelet after Ben Sira in the middle of the second century (but see Reif [1981]). H. Graetz proposed a Herodian dating, but such dating has been excluded by the discovery of second-century fragments of Qohelet among the Dead Sea Scrolls (J. Muilenburg [1954]).

2. *Language*. Grotius was apparently the first to remark on the late character of Qohelet's language, observing that it contains many Aramaisms and postexilic locutions. Franz Delitzsch catalogued these features and characterized Qohelet's language as bearing a mishnaic stamp and being no earlier than Ezra-Nehemiah. Most recent commentators have affirmed this assessment (for a survey of late locutions see Delitzsch [1875] 190-206; and Gordis [1968] 59-68). R. Gordis describes Qohelet's language as a transition between classical biblical and mishnaic Hebrew (see also Whitley, 119-48). D. Fredericks (1987) argues that the evidence usually adduced for a postexilic dating can be explained in other ways and favors an exilic or preexilic date. B. Isaksson suggests that Qohelet's language may be a popular dialect of the First Temple period. C. L. Seow (1997, 11-20) places it specifically in the Persian period.

Two theories try to explain the strangeness of Qohelet's language as literally foreign. M. Dahood (1952, 1958, 1962, 1966) claimed that Qohelet's language and orthography are northern (Phoenician) in character and point to a northern locale for its authorship. F. Zimmermann (1945–46; 1949–50; 1973, 98-122) and H. Ginsberg (1961), developing a suggestion of F. Burkitt (1922), argued that Qohelet is a mechanical, often erroneous and awkward, translation from Aramaic. They contend that numerous awkward locutions make better sense if retroverted to Aramaic then translated correctly back to Hebrew (sometimes after emendation as well). Gordis (1952; 1968, 399-403), Whitley (42-49, 106-10), and F. Piotti argued against both theories in detail, claiming that better explanations for the difficult words and phrases are available. A. Schoors's detailed examination of Qohelet's morphology and syntax (1992) argues that the language is late biblical Hebrew and that the other theories either treat the data atomistically (Fredericks), assume too many mistranslations (Ginsberg), or misinterpret the epigraphic and linguistic evidence (Dahood). (See further the survey by F. Bianchi [1993].)

Special mention should be made of F. Ellermeier's studies of Qohelet's syntax (1967, 161-306) and Ginsberg's insights into Qohelet's idiosyncratic vocabulary (1961, 13-18). D. Michel (1989) examines the literary functions of Qohelet's linguistic usages, and W. Delsman (1982) brings together data on Qohelet's language. Isaksson (1989) applies structural and discourse analysis to aspects of Qohelet's syntax, particularly the verbal system, and explains the distinctive series of qatal verbs as characteristic of the "autobiographical" genre. Schoors surveys Qohelet's orthography, morphology, and syntax in detail.

3. *Unity of Composition.* The inconsistencies in Qohelet (e.g., he both affirms divine justice [8:12b-13] and points to its violation [9:11-12a, 14]), which have been at the center of Qohelet exegesis since at least the first century CE, have given rise to theories that posit additional voices besides Qohelet's in the book.

An older approach—followed, e.g., by Jerome, J.G. Herder, J.G. Eichhorn, and J. K. C. Nachtigal (1753–1819), saw the book as a dialogue between Qohelet and one or more people of lesser wisdom such as a pupil or a fool. (See also the paragraph on Perry [1993] below.) Alternatively, the unorthodox opinions were considered as statements of erroneous ideas that Qohelet quotes in order to refute them. (This approach is common in traditional Jewish commentary; A. Ibn Ezra, for example, says that 9:4b and 9:10 are claims of others that Qohelet rejects.) L. Levy and, most extensively, Gordis have maintained the book's unity by regarding the orthodox opinions as unmarked quotations of various sorts that Qohelet opposes or refutes; this suggestion has been widely accepted.

Another line of interpretation finds various secondary additions (always of orthodox glossators) imbedded in Qohelet's words. K. Siegfried's analysis is often mentioned because it represents the extreme of fragmentation: two "Qohelets," two glossators, a group of glossators of indefinite number, two editors, and two epiologists. More moderate and widely accepted are the analyses of A. McNeile, L. Podechard, and G. A. Barton, who distributed various orthodox passages between a *Ḥāsîd* (a pietist, whose additions speak of God's justice and the need for human piety [e.g., Eccl. 2:26ab; 3:17; 7:26b; 8:11-13; and the "second epilogue," 12:13-14]) and a *Ḥākām* (a wise man, whose additions defend the value of wisdom [e.g., Eccl 1:2; 7:27-28; 12:8; and the "first epilogue," 12:9-11]). In this way Qohelet is made to appear as consistently skeptical as he is consistently pious in most traditional commentaries. Most of the recent commentators hypothesize a few additions, usually without identifying the group affiliation of their authors. For example, K. Galling, W. Zimmerli, and Ellermeier identify a few phrases and sentences as secondary (e.g., Eccl 1:16a; 2:7b; 4:17b; 11:9b; plus two epilogues). Gordis marks no interpolations in the body of the book (1:2-12:8).

Virtually all modern scholars assign the epilogue, 12:8-14 (or 9-14), to a later glossator, whom they commonly identify as the book's editor (Maimonides was the first to do this). Many discern two (12:9-11 + 12-14) or three epilogues (12:9-11 + 12 + 13-14). Delitzsch and M. Fox (1977; 1987, 311-27) see in the epilogue a shift to the voice of the author, who has previously quoted Qohelet, a persona.

4. *Literary Structure and Form.* The structure of Qohelet has been placed everywhere on a continuum from a more or less random collection of sayings and meditations to a well-organized discourse whose parts are subordinated to a single design. On the latter end of the continuum, various interpreters, e.g., M. Thilo (1923), A. Miller (1934), Ginsberg, G. Castellino (1968), and most notably, A. Wright (1968) have proposed different well-conceived designs to describe the book's structure. Wright emphasized formal characteristics, in particular repetitions, as an approach to discovering the book's structure, which he saw as an intricate, well-articulated, hierarchical design. In subsequent studies (1980, 1983) he found intricate numeri-

cal patterns coordinated with the design (e.g., *hbl*, "vanity," has the numerical value of thirty-seven and occurs this number of times). N. Lohfink (1980) finds a palindromic structure in the book as a whole. Most commentators since the end of the last century regard the book as a collection of aphorisms and longer units without much overall organization; e.g., Delitzsch, Zimmerli, H. Hertzberg, Gordis, O. Loretz, A. Lauha, and most emphatically, K. Galling (1932, 1969). Ellermeier (1967, 131-41) provides a useful tabulation of the unit demarcation according to the major modern commentaries and attempts to isolate the editorial means (22-124)-namely, thematic concepts and key words-used to order the originally independent units (fifty-six, according to his analysis). Michel (1989) argues that 1:3-3:15 is a coherent unit expressing the basics of Qohelet's thought. Statements later in the book that do not agree with the message of that unit are citations of other opinions, which Qohelet rejects or relativizes.

Commentators who deny the presence of an overall structure see the book's unity as residing in the cohesiveness of the author's thought, attitudes, tone, and style (Delitzsch, Galling, Hertzberg, Gordis, and many others; on style see in particular Loretz [1980] 135-217). Loretz also identifies a group of recurrent *topoi* as a source of cohesiveness (1980, 196-212). Zimmerli (1974) argued that the book of Qohelet, while not a well-structured tractate on a single theme, is not a mere collection of sayings; for there are relations in content among contiguous units.

The genre of the book as a whole has been variously identified. The view implicit in much of traditional exegesis is that the book is or consists of preachment since it is words Solomon preached in his wanderings ("Qohelet" is understood as *maghîl*, "assembler" of the congregation). Others, understanding the name *qôhelet* to allude to an assembly of sayings, regarded the book as a collection of teachings. Some interpreters of the eighteenth and nineteenth centuries (e.g., M. Mendelssohn and J. Döderlein), spoke of the book as a philosophical discourse or treatise. Others of that period, most notably Herder, described the book as a philosophical dialogue or symposium. The latest representative of that view is Miller (1934), who argued that the book is a condensed literary rendering of a school disputation or discussion and that this form is the principle of its structure. Miller (1934), A. Allgeier (1925), and Lohfink (1980) have classified Qohelet as a diatribe. It has also been compared to a journal or "confession," like Pascal's *Pensées* (Murphy [1955]) or Marcus Aurelius's *Meditations* (Rudolph [1959]).

Various literary forms within the book have been described in greatest detail by Ellermeier (1967, 48-93). He labels the basic form the *mashal*, a broad grouping he subdivides into "sentences" (including proverbs and artistic sayings) and "reflections" of various sorts, the latter composed of various form elements (statements, questions, self-presentation). R. Murphy (1981, 127-30) identifies the following forms: wisdom saying, instruction, reflection, example story, woe oracle, blessing. Loader (1979) says that the book is composed of thirty-eight chiastic structures and sixty polar structures, the latter being patterns of tension between an idea of "general *hokmâ* and another view (i.e., Qohelet's) or a contrary fact."

5. *Foreign Influence*. The peculiarity of Qohelet's thought and style has led some scholars to look to foreign influences as the sources of his special character.

a. *Greek*. G. Zirkel (1792) was the first to propose that Qohelet was influenced by Greek thought, language, and literature. He was followed by numerous commentators, especially in the late nineteenth to early twentieth centuries, including Graetz, Allgeier, G. Wildeboer, and Levy. Certain phrases were thought to be Grecisms (e.g., "under the sun, "*hypo ton hēlion*" = "do good," *la ʿasôt tob* or *eu prattein*). Ranston (1923, 1925) emphasized the indirect influence of Theognis and Hesiod (noting especially the latter's doctrine of the "right time"). More recently, Braun (1973) has argued for extensive stylistic, structural, and philosophical parallels between Qohelet and a broad range of Greek writers, in particular Homer, Theognis, Euripides, and Menander. Whitley (165-75) emphasizes Epicurean influence (e.g., God's remoteness, reluctance to communicate with man; life ends with the body; hedonistic advice). M. Hengel sees Qohelet as responding to the impact of the spiritual crisis of early Hellenism and as fusing the popular views of the Greek "bourgeoisie" with traditional wisdom and with Qohelet's own observations (1974, 125). Lohfink finds Greek influence in Qohelet's motifs, ideas, language, and style. He maintains that the inspiration for the book was Greek education, but that the background and values were Hebrew wisdom (1980, 10). Other writers, e.g., Podechard, Hertzberg, Gordis, and M. Fox, grant only a vague and general contact of Qohelet with his Hellenistic environment (against the theory of Greek influence, see Loretz [1964] 45-57). In contrast, Schwienhorst-Schönberger (1996) examines Qohelet's thought in its Hellenistic and Jewish contexts to determine the ways in which it draws upon and is in tension with both. The pivotal question of both Hellenistic philosophy and Qohelet is the nature of human happiness and the limitations of its possibilities, especially with respect to the individual life. In contrast to Greek wisdom, Qohelet does not believe in the absolute autonomy of the inner realm. Man cannot create happiness but can only receive it from God.

b. *Mesopotamian.* H. Grimme (1905) was the first to observe the similarity of 9:7-10 to Gilgamesh X, iii (*ANET* 90a; Old Babylonian), the alewife's advice to Gilgamesh to enjoy life in the face of inevitable mortality. Loretz (1964, 90-134) made the case for a Mesopotamian background (to the exclusion of other influences) most thoroughly. He emphasized certain parallels with Babylonian literature, in particular Ludlul (*ANET* 435-37), the "Pessimistic Dialogue" (*ANET* 437-38), the Babylonian Theodicy (*ANET* 438-40), and above all Gilgamesh (*ANET* 72-99). Among the parallels he noted are the concern with the problem of divine justice; the motif of "wind/breath" (*hebel*; Babylonian *saru*), in the sense of nothingness, transience; and the problem of "name" and memory. A. Shaffer (1967, 1969) found Qohelet's "threefold cord" saying (4:12) in "Gilgamesh and Hubaba."

c. *Egyptian.* P. Humbert (1929) almost alone strongly advocated an Egyptian background for Qohelet, even suggesting that the author had traveled to Egypt. The parallels he noted include the theme of royal authorship (as in Amenemhet [*ANET* 418-19] and the instruction for Merikare [*ANET* 414-18]); pessimistic and skeptical texts, e.g., the "Dispute Over Suicide" (*ANET* 405-10) and the "Song of the Harper" (*ANET* 467; this includes a *carpe diem* comparable to Eccl 9:7-9); complaints about old age (cf. *Ptahhotep* [*ANET* 412a, Eccl 12:1-6]). B. Gemser (1960) pointed to parallels with the Demotic *Instructions of Onchsheshonqy*, including the near-identity of *Onchsheshonqy* 19.10 (advice to cast one's bread upon the water) with Eccl 11:1. Loretz (1964, 57-89) disputes Egyptian influence altogether.

6. *Teaching.* The major divide in Qohelet interpretation lies between the traditional exegesis of this book (from the 1st cent. to the 18th or 19th, together with that of many modern religious conservatives) and its modern exegesis (18th–20th cents.). Most of the main ideas that modern interpretation ascribes to Qohelet can be found, with different emphases, in the interpretations of the earliest exegetes—a fact that seems to show that the essential themes of the book are clear. Traditional interpreters, believing that the book was Solomon's, found in it an affirmation of such orthodox beliefs as Solomon could be assumed to teach. Modern interpreters emphasize the book's skepticism and pessimism and commonly view it both as an attack on earlier orthodoxies (of the wisdom school) and as evidence for the failure of the regnant intellectual and religious systems. The following survey looks at a sampling of significant commentators, with emphasis on the modern period. C. Ginsburg's commentary includes an extensive survey of all exegesis until 1860. For early and medieval Jewish commentary see Schiffer (1884). For patristic commentaries see E. Plumptre (1881, 83-97), S. Holm-Nielsen (1974), and Murphy (1982). For later works see Galling (1934), Blank (1970), S. Breton (1973), and J. Crenshaw (1983).

a. *Traditional interpretations.* Three presuppositions common to all early Qohelet exegesis are: (1) Solomon is the author; (2) "vanity of vanities" is to be understood against the perspective of a belief in immortality; and (3) tensions in the book show that Solomon was in dialogue with others (Murphy [1982] 331-32).

The earliest statement of Qohelet interpretation is found in the epilogue (12:9-12), which appraises Qohelet's teachings, along with the other words of the wise, cautiously but appreciatively. The epilogue speaks of Qohelet as one sage among many, not as intolerably skeptical or heterodox. (Sheppard [1977] discusses the epilogist's concept of canon, arguing that he thematizes the book in order to include it within a canon-conscious definition of sacred wisdom.)

It seems that Ben Sira knows of Qohelet and uses his teachings, as he does other inspired writings, often giving a characteristic twist to Qohelet's words but showing no awareness of heterodoxy in them (e.g., Eccl 3:11 and Sir 39:16, 33; Eccl 3:15 and Sir 5:3; Eccl 8:1 and Sir 13:24; Eccl 9:10 and Sir 14:11-12). According to many scholars, the Wisdom of Solomon refers to Qohelet when it castigates the "ungodly" for advocating hedonism (as well as oppression of the righteous) as a response to mortality (Wis 1:16–2:24). However, if the description of the ungodly in that passage were meant to represent Qohelet's teaching, it would be such a distortion that it would be ineffective even as polemic.

The translation of Qohelet in the Septuagint is extremely literalistic and may even be Aquilan (Graetz, McNeile, Barthélemy [1963]; but see Hyvärinen [1977] 88-99, 112). The translation (and later glossators within the Greek tradition) shows some attempts at moralistic improvement, as in adding a "do not" in the advice of 11:9a. According to G. Bertram (1952), the Greek translation tends to make Qohelet's teaching more abstract, theological, and psychological than does the MT. Humans are regarded as burdened by a sense of sin and spiritual unrest. The theme of the book becomes the complaint against the vanity and willfulness of the human spirit, and Qohelet acquires a unified theological meaning it lacked before. (Many of the qualities Bertram sees in the Greek translation may, in fact, be in the original. For a study of the text of the Greek and its relation to the Hebrew, see McNeile [1904] 115-69.)

The Syriac too (see Kamenetzky [1904]; Schoors [1985]) is highly literalistic. It reveals little of an underlying interpretation except in its understanding of the sense of individual sentences.

According to a later account, at the end of the first century CE the Tannaim, troubled by contradictions in the book, debated Qohelet's status as inspired Scripture. They accepted its legitimacy because it begins and ends in words of Torah (b. Šabb. 30b). The rabbis also considered withdrawing Qohelet because some of its words – they mention 11:9a and 1:3 – might "cause an inclination to heresy" (Qoh. Rab. i. 4). In both cases the danger envisioned lay in the susceptibility of these verses to misinterpretations that might have practical consequences rather than in actual ideological skepticism.

There is virtual unanimity among the pre-modern Jewish interpretations (in the Talmud, the Midrash, the Targum, and the medieval commentaries) on the basic teachings of the book: All works of this world are trivial; humans and their works are ephemeral. One must be resigned to God's will, for all God's works are good. All that is worthwhile is quiet enjoyment of one's lot, good deeds, and study of Torah. People will receive appropriate recompense for their deeds, if not in this life, then in the next.

The highly paraphrastic Aramaic translation, the Targum (c. 6th cent.), weaves Qohelet's words into a coherent moralistic homily and interprets his teachings as lessons drawn from Israel's history (viewed prophetically). It opens by relating that when Solomon grew arrogant because of his wealth, God sent Ashmodai, king of demons, to depose him. Solomon went wandering through the land preaching repentance and obedience to the commandments. In his preaching he prophesied the division of the kingdom, the destruction of the Temple, and Israel's exile and said, "Vanity of vanities . . . " In other words, Solomon's pessimistic statements are thought to address specific historical crises rather than the nature of the world itself. The paraphrase consistently imposes an orthodox assertion of divine justice on the text; for example: "And indeed I have seen sinners who are buried and blotted out of this world, from the holy place where the righteous dwell" (8:10a). Similarly 8:15 is made to praise the joy of obedience to Torah. Misfortunes in this life are explained by astrological influences and by God's decrees.

Qohelet is one of the books most frequently quoted in midrashic literature. Individual verses are quoted for homiletical purposes with little reference to the message of the book as a whole. The way the book is quoted shows that it is understood as a repudiation of the value of earthly matters in favor of a life of Torah study.

The *Midrash Qohelet Rabbah* (c. 7th cent.) is more exegetical than most Midrashim. As exegesis it is atomistic, but in general it understands Qohelet as teaching that humanity is ephemeral and without substance, that one should devote one's life to good deeds and to the study of Torah, and that reward and punishment await in the next life.

The early Christian commentators took essentially the same approach. However, they placed greater emphasis on the devaluation of this life and its pleasures and believed that salvation through Christ is Qohelet's implied solution to the failure of temporal values.

Ibn Ezra (12th cent.) may be taken as representative of medieval Jewish Qohelet exegesis. Like most traditional commentators, Ibn Ezra was disturbed less by the apparently unorthodox character of Qohelet's teachings than by the apparent contradictions in the book, which he systematically undertook to resolve (see his comment on 7:3). He understood Solomon as teaching that all human works are transient and insignificant. Only the fear of God, reached through the acquisition of wisdom (= Torah) can bring happiness. God's work is perfect, but there are imperfections in the world due to imperfections in the recipients of God's goodness. Ibn Ezra's commentary is infused with philosophical and astronomical ideas as well as with careful grammatical observations.

Bonaventure (13th cent.) may be taken as a representative medieval Christian commentator. He wrote that Qohelet maintains the vanity of earthly creatures—who are vain insofar as they are changeable—in order to teach contempt for this world. Still, earthly creatures have some reality and goodness. Since God alone possesses intransmutable repose, true life and happiness can be found in God only (summary in Ginsburg [1970] 109).

b. *Modern interpretations.* One may summarize the core of Qohelet's teaching as perceived by most commentators since the end of the nineteenth century—excluding religious and homiletical expositors—as follows: Qohelet is pessimistic and skeptical. He declares the futility of human labor, the triviality of wealth, the transience of human life, and the impossibility of true wisdom. He attacks the doctrine of reward and punishment. All this constitutes a polemic against the wisdom school, which had become overconfident, rigid, and dogmatic and which had made unjustified claims to possess knowledge. Qohelet commends wisdom for its relative practical value and urges fear of God and moderate enjoyment of life's pleasures.

Modern interpreters commonly regard Qohelet as representing (or initiating) a general crisis in the wisdom school and in Judaism as a whole. (There is some vacillation as to whether he is responding to a crisis in wisdom literature—unattested elsewhere, except perhaps in Job—or initiating a crisis, which shows no signs of persistence beyond him.) Qohelet's negativism is then often taken as demonstrating the inadequacy of HB religion and clearing the way for the new message of Christianity. A few commentators, however, find a message more affirmative of God's goodness and of the value of human life.

The following epitomes of a sampling of modern interpreters highlight the themes the commentators consider most significant:

Delitzsch (1875, 179-90): All things on earth are vanity; humanity's labor achieves nothing enduring. The striving after secular knowledge, pleasure, riches, and wisdom is unsatisfactory.

God is just, but things happen contrary to his justice. The most desirable thing for humanity is to enjoy life, but only within the limits of the fear of God, which is the highest duty. Qohelet testifies both to the power of revealed religion, grounded in an unshakable faith, and to the inadequacy of HB religion.

Pedersen (1930, 344-70): Qohelet is symptomatic of a crisis in Israel's late period, when earlier harmonies between nature and humanity and between God and humanity had broken down. The interior and the exterior no longer correspond: One may have all the external blessings but lack happiness. God becomes more and more sublime, while humans become more and more lowly and lacking influence on events, which are under God's arbitrary control. The principal virtue is now fear of God and resignation to the divine will. Qohelet nevertheless recommends enjoyment of life as well as perseverance in trying all possibilities. In this way his skepticism is inseparable from his piety.

Ginsberg (1955; 1961; 1963, 21-27): All is futility, zero. Death renders nugatory the advantages of wisdom and other talents. The same emotions, experiences, and activities recur endlessly. God determines the time when every event will occur. Humans may try to discover this time, but they cannot succeed. The only real value in life is the use of material goods for enjoyment.

Gordis (1955, 112-14): Qohelet believes in God but cannot accept the platitudes of the conventional wisdom teachers. He thinks that justice in human affairs is elusive and that truth is unattainable. All that is certain is that human beings desire happiness; since God created them, the furthering of their pleasure must be the divine purpose.

H. Gese (1963): Wisdom undergoes a crisis in Qohelet. Earlier wisdom assumed that the good or evil a person experiences is just another aspect of the good or evil he or she does. Qohelet recognizes no such connection. The result is a structural change of outlook, consisting of the distancing of the person—the "I"—from the event, i.e., the estrangement of individuals from all that happens to them and about them. Time—the passage of "right moments"—is hidden from humans, to whom life is now opaque. But through fear of God the estrangement may be replaced by an openness to time, meaning an acceptance of whatever comes upon one. This openness includes accepting enjoyment of life, not as an automatic consequence of virtue, but as the direct gift of God.

Hertzberg (1963, 222-38): Qohelet presents three recurrent and decisive ideas: (1) God's exclusivity. God, who is a sort of *fatum* devoid of personal characteristics, determines everything. (2) Earthly vanity. All strivings for wisdom, wealth, happiness—all human activity—is nothing. (This idea is shaped in direct dependency on Genesis 2-4.) (3) Pleasure. The only human possibility is to accept the present as it is and to take passively whatever happiness is given. The main point of the book is (2)—humanity's utter nothingness. This complete negation makes Qohelet the most disturbing messianic prophecy of the HB.

Lohfink (1980): Man is an ephemeral being in an unchanging world, with whose oppressive fullness he cannot cope (cosmology, Eccl 1:4-11). Happiness is powerful, but in the face of death all human abilities and achievements are a "vapor." Happiness is allotted by God, not securely produced by man, who must enjoy what he is given in the fear of God (anthropology, 1:12-3:15). Observations of social injustice and fragmentation reinforce the anthropology of "vapor" and "fear of God" (social criticism, 3:16–4:16; 5:7–6:10). In the middle of the book, Qohelet also offers a critical evaluation of piety (religious criticism, 4:17–5:6). The basic dogmas of wisdom, in particular that of just recompense, are undermined (ideological criticism, 6:11–9:6). The fear of God alone can guide humankind. Humans cannot comprehend God's work, hence they may think it arbitrary and amoral. Humans must manage the best they can, accept what the moment brings, and enjoy God's gifts (ethics, 9:7–12:7). The book ends with two orthodox appendices (12:8-11, 12-14).

Crenshaw (1987): Qohelet directs a radical, unrelentingly negative attack on the traditional beliefs of the sages. He repudiates wisdom's claim to secure one's existence and denies that there is any moral order. Chance determines everything, including the time of death; and the future—indeed, all of reality—remains utterly hidden. Divine justice is not in evidence. Qohelet can merely recommend enjoying life's little pleasures in order to soothe the troubled spirit; this, at least, has God's approval.

Murphy (1992): A variety of attitudes are heard in Qohelet. These are sometimes contradictory, sometimes in dialogue. Qohelet affirms the values of life, wealth, toil, and wisdom; but these values prove inadequate when seen under the shadow of death. Qohelet is often in conflict with traditional wisdom teaching, especially its claim to provide security; yet he affirms wisdom and remains within its traditions, employing its methods and literary genres. It is because Qohelet loved life and wisdom that he was grieved by death and by life's vanity.

Fredericks (1993): Qohelet speaks of the transient human realm of reality, not the eternal. He is not skeptical or pessimistic, though he recognizes the evanescence (*hebel*) of human labor and its products. He offers ways of coping with transience, finding value in wisdom, in the joy of work, and above all, in simple pleasures, which are humanity's major consolation. The duty of humans is to resign themselves to God's will and to accept circumstances beyond their control.

T. Perry (1993): The book is a dialogue between a pious sage-narrator, the "Presenter" (P), who transmits and debates the wisdom of the skeptical persona, Kohelet (K). K is the man of experience. He is deterministic and skeptical and rejects wisdom and faith, except insofar as they emerge from his own experience. He teaches that we should embrace pleasure because it is within our power to do so and should fear God because of human ignorance. P, the man of faith, uses K's words to provoke thought and as the basis for argument. P affirms the value of labor, pleasure, and wisdom. God is to be feared because God is unpredictable; divine justice and freedom are not bound by human conceptions of justice. At the end, P modifies his own position by recognizing that life is vanity; but we are to fear God as the ground of our transience.

C. L. Seow (1997): Humans cannot control events or their destiny, for everything is *hebel*, meaning that everything is beyond human apprehension and comprehension. (The full meaning of *hebel* is anything that is superficial, ephemeral, insubstantial, incomprehensible, enigmatic, inconsistent, or contradictory.) In spite of God's distance, he is related to humanity and has given it the possibilities of each moment. Hence people must accept what happens to them and respond spontaneously to life, even in the midst of uncertainties, and accept both the possibilities and limitations of being human.

T. Longman (1998): Qohelet (a fictional persona) is distinguished from the book of Ecclesiastes. Qohelet's message is skeptical and pessimistic; but the message of the book is determined by the authorial voice in 12:9-14, which is an affirmation of faith: Life is meaningless without God. Verses 13-14, moreover, introduce an eschatological perspective. Longman places Qohelet's words in the genre of fictional autobiographies found elsewhere in ancient Near Eastern literature.

Fox (1999): The central concern of the book of Ecclesiastes is meaning. What unites all of Qohelet's specific complaints is the collapse of meaning, which is revealed in the contradictions that pervade life. Qohelet fully intends the contradictions he describes (which exegesis has usually tried to eliminate); they demonstrate to him life's absurdity. Qohelet is frustrated that life cannot be "read," that the multiplicity of disjointed deeds and events cannot be drawn together into a coherent narrative with its own significance. Qohelet also tries to reconstruct and recover meanings, albeit local and restricted ones. Even if the world as a whole lacks meaning and purpose, humans have the potential to possess passing moments of goodness and clarity. These are brief, limited, and uncertain; but they are enough to make life worth living.

Bibliography: A. **Allgeier,** *Das Buch des Predigers oder Koheleth* (HSAT 6, 2, 1925). D. **Barthélemy,** *Les Devanciers d'Aquila* (VTSup 10, 1963). C. G. **Bartholomew,** *Reading Ecclesiastes: Old Testament Exegesis and Hermeneutical Theory* (AnBib 139, 1998). G. A. **Barton,** *The Book of Ecclesiastes* (ICC, 1908). A. **Barucq,** *Ecclésiaste* (1968). G. **Bertram,** "Hebräischer und griechischer Qohelet," *ZAW* 64 (1952) 26-49. F. **Bianchi,** "The Language of Qohelet: A Bibliographical Survey," *ZAW* 105 (1993) 210-23. G. **Bickell,** *Der Prediger über den Wert des Daseins* (1884). E. **Bickerman,** *Four Strange Books of the Bible* (1967). S. H. **Blank,** "Prolegomenon," *The Song of Songs and Coheleth* (Library of Biblical Studies, ed. C. D. Ginsburg, 1970). R. **Brandscheidt,** *Weltbegeisterung und Offenbarungsglaube: literar-, form- und traditionasgeschichtliche Untersuchung zum Buch Kohelet* (Trierer theologisches Studien 64, 1999). R. **Braun,** *Kohelet und die frühhellenistische Popularphilosophie* (BZAW 130, 1973). S. **Breton,** "Qoheleth Studies," *BTB* 3 (1973) 22-50. K. **Budde,** *Der Prediger* (KEH 18, 1922). S. **Burkes,** *Death in Qoheleth and Egyptian Biographies of the Late Period* (SBLDS 170, 1999). F. C. **Burkitt,** "Is Ecclesiastes a Translation?" *JTS* 23 (1922) 22-28.   D. **Buzy,** "La Notion du bonheur dans l'Ecclésiaste," *RB* 43 (1934) 494-511; *L'Ecclésiaste* (1946). G. **Castellino,** "Qohelet and His Wisdom," *CBQ* 30 (1968) 15-28. E. S. **Christianson,** *A Time to Tell: Narrative Strategies in Ecclesiastes* (JSOTSup 280, 1998). J. L. **Crenshaw** (ed.), *Studies in Ancient Israelite Wisdom* (1976), with prolegomenon by Crenshaw; "The Shadow of Death in Qoheleth," *Israelite Wisdom: Samuel Terrien Festschrift* (ed. J. G. Gammie et al., 1978) 205-16; (ed.), *Theodicy in the OT* (1983), with intro. by Crenshaw; *Ecclesiastes* (OTL, 1987). M. J. **Dahood,** "Canaanite-Phoenician Influence in Qoheleth," *Bib* 33 (1952) 30-52, 191-221; "Qoheleth and Recent Discoveries (Qumran)," *Bib* 39 (1958) 302-18; "Qoheleth and Northwest Semitic Philology," *Bib* 43 (1962) 349-65; "The Phoenician Background of Qoheleth," *Bib* 47 (1966) 264-82; "The Phoenician Contribution to Biblical Wisdom Literature," *The Role of the Phoenicians in the Interaction of Mediterranean Civilizations* (ed. W. A. Ward, 1968) 123-48. E. F. **Davis,** *Proverbs, Ecclesiastes, and the Song of Songs* (Westminster Bible Companion, 2002). F. S. **Delitzsch,** *Koheleth* (1875; ET 1877). K. J. **Dell,** "Ecclesiastes as Wisdom: Consulting Early Interpreters," *VT* 44 (1994) 301-29. W. C. **Delsman,** "Zur Sprach des Buches Koheleth," *Von Kanaan bis Kerala* (ed. W. C. Delsman et al., 1982) 341-65. J. C. **Döderlein,** *Salomons Prediger und Hohes Lied* (1784). A. B. **Ehrlich,** *Randglossen zur hebräischen Bibel* 7 (1914, repr. 1968) 55-108. F. **Ellermeier,** "Die Entmachtung der Weisheit im Denken Qohelets," *ZTK 60* (1963b) 1-20; *Qohelet, Teil 1, Abschnitt 1* (1967). S. **Eppenstein,** *Aus dem Kohelet-Kommentar des Tanchum Jerushalmi (1888).* S. **Euringer,** *Der Masorahtext des Koheleth kritisch untersucht* (1890). J. **Fichner,** *Die altorientalische Weisheit in ihrer israelitisch-jüdischen Ausprägung* (BZAW 62, 1933); *Gottes Weisheit* (1965). M. V. **Fox,** "Frame-narrative and Composition in the Book of Qohelet," *HUCA* 48 (1977) 83-106; "Aging and Death in Qohelet 12:1-7: A Three-fold Interpretation," *JSOT* 41 (1988) 55-77; *Qohelet and His Contradictions* (JSOTSup 71, 1989); "Wisdom in Qoheleth," *In Search of Wisdom* (ed. L. G Perdue et al., 1993) 115-32; *Tearing Down and Building Up: A Rereading of Qohelet* (1998); *A Time to Tear Down and a Time to Build Up: A Rereading of Ecclesiastes* (1999). D. C. **Fredericks,** *Qohelet's Language* (1987); *Coping with Transience: Ecclesiastes on Brevity in Life* (1993). T. **Frydrych,** *Living under the Sun: Examination of Proverbs and Qoheleth* (VTSup 90, 2002). K. **Galling,** "Kohelet-Studien," *ZAW* 50 (1932) 276-99; "Stand und Aufgabe der Kohelet-Forschung," *TRu* 6 (1934) 355-73; *Prediger Salomo* (HAT I, 18, 1940, 1969); *Die Krise der Aufklärung in Israel* (1952). B. **Gemser,** "The Instructions of Onchsheshonqy and Biblical Wisdom Literature," *Congress Volume, Oxford, 1959* (VTSup 7, 1960) 102-28 (= Crenshaw [1976] 134-60). H. **Gese,** "Die Krisis der Weisheit bei Kohelet,"

Les Sagesses du Proche-Orient ancient (1963) 139-51 (ET in Crenshaw [1983] 141-53). **H. L. Ginsberg**, "The Structure and Contents of the Book of Koheleth," *Wisdom in Israel and in the Ancient Near East* (VTSup 3, 1955) 138-49; *Kohelet* (1961), Hebrew; "The Quintessence of Koheleth," *Biblical and Other Studies* (ed. A. Altmann, 1963) 47-59. **C. D. Ginsburg**, *The Song of Songs and Coheleth* (1861, repr. 1970). **E. Glasser**, *Le Procès du bonheur par Qohelet* (1970). **R. Gordis**, "Quotations as a Literary Usage in Biblical, Oriental, and Rabbinic Literature," *HUCA* 22 (1949) 157-219; "Koheleth: Hebrew or Aramaic?" *JBL* 71 (1952) 93-109; *Koheleth: The Man and His Word* (1955, 1968); "Was Koheleth a Phoenician?" *JBL* 74 (1955) 103-14. **H. Graetz**, *Kohélet* (1871). **H. Grimme**, "Babel und Qoheleth-Jojakhin," *OLZ* 8 (1905) 432-38. **H. Grotius**, *Opera* (1644, 1679). **A. P. Hayman**, "Qohelet, the Rabbis, and the Wisdom Text from the Cairo Genizah," *Understanding Poets and Prophets* (ed. A. G. Auld, JSOTSup 152, 1993). **M. Hengel**, *Judaism and Hellenism*, (tr. J. Bowden, 1974). **J. G. Herder**, *Briefe das Studium der Theologie betreffend* 11 (1780-90). **H. W. Hertzberg**, *Der Prediger* (KAT NF 17, 4, 1963). **S. Holm-Nielsen**, "On the Interpretation of Qoheleth in Early Christianity," *VT* 24 (1974) 168-77. **P. Humbert**, *Recherches sur les sources Égyptiennes de la littérature sapientiale d'Israël* (1929). **K. Hyvärinen**, *Die Übersetzung von Aquila* (ConBOT, 1977). A. Ibn Ezra, *Abraham Ibn Esras Kommentar zu den Büchern Kohelet, Ester, und Rut* (ed. D.U. Rottzoll, Studia Judaica 12, 1999). **B. Isaksson**, *Studies in the Language of Qoheleth* (1987). **S. Japhet** and **R. Salters**, *The Commentary of R. Samuel ben Meir, Rashbam, on Qoheleth* (1985). **J. Jarick**, *Gregory Thaumaturgos' Paraphrase of Ecclesiastes* (1990); *A Comprehensive Bilingual Concordance of the Hebrew and Greek Texts of Ecclesiastes* (1993). **O. Kaiser**, "Beiträge zur Kohelet-Forschung," *TRu* 60 (1995) 1-31; "Die Botschaft des Buches Kohelet," *ETL* 71 (1995) 48-70; *Gottes und der Menschen Weisheit: gesammelte Aufsätze* (BZAW 261, 1998). **N. Kamano**, *Cosmology and Character: Qoheleth's Pedagogy from a Rhetorical-Critical Perspective* (BZAW 312, 2002). **A. S. Kamenetzky**, "Die P'sita zu Koheleth," *ZAW* 24 (1904) 181-239. **P. Kleinert**, "Sind im Buche Koheleth ausserhebräische Einflüsse anzuerkennen?" *TSK* 56 (1883) 761-82. **M. A. Klopfenstein**, "Die Skepsis des Qohelet," *TZ* 28 (1972) 97-109. **R. Kroeber**, *Der Prediger* (1963). **G. Kuhn**, *Erklärung des Buches Koheleth* (BZAW 43, 1926). **D. J. Lane**, "Peshitta Institute Communication XV: 'Lilies that fester . . . ': The Peshitta Text of Qoheleth," *VT* 29 (1979) 481-89. **A. Lauha**, *Kohelet* (BKAT 19, 1978); "Die Krise des religiösen Glaubens bei Kohelet," *Congress Volume, Oxford, 1959* (VTSup 7, 1960) 183-91. **M. Leahy**, "The Meaning of Ecclesiastes [12:2-5]," *ITQ* 19 (1952) 297-300. **L. Levy**, *Das Buch Qoheleth: Ein Beitrag zur Geschichte des Sadduzäismus, kritisch untersucht* (1912). **J. A. Loader**, *Polar Structures in the Book of Qohelet* (BZAW 152, 1979). **N. Lohfink**, *Kohelet* (Die Neue Echter Bibel, 1980); "*Melek, sallît* und *môsel* bei Kohelet und die Abfassungszeit des Buchs," *Bib* 62 (1981) 535-43; "Grenzen und Einbindung des Kohelet-Schlussgedichts," *AT Forschung und Wirkung* (FS H. G. Reventlow, 1994); "Freu dich, Jüngling—doch nicht, weil du jung bist . . . (Koh 11,9-12, 8)," *BibInt* 3 (1995) 158-89; "Les Épilogues du livre de Qohélet et les débuts du canon," *Ouvrir les Écritures* (FS P. Beauchamp, ed. P. Bovati and R. Meynet, 1995); *Qoheleth: a Continental Commentary* (tr. S. McEvenue, 2003). **T. Longman, III,** *The Book of Ecclesiastes* (NICOT, 1998). **O. Loretz**, "Zur Darbietungsform der 'Ich-Erzählung' im Buche Qohelet," *CBQ* 25 (1963) 46-59; *Qohelet und der alte Orient* (1964); "Altorientalische und kanaanäische Topoi im Buche Kohelet," *UF* 12 (1980) 267-86. **D. Lys**, *L'Ecclésiaste ou que vaut la vie?* (1977). **D. B. MacDonald**, "Eccl 3:11," *JBL* 18 (1899) 212-15; *The Hebrew Philosophical Genius* (1936). **A. H. McNeile**, *An Introduction to Ecclesiastes* (1904). **M. Mendelssohn**, *Koheleth* (1787; ET 1845). **D. Michel**, *Qohelet* (EdF 258, 1988); *Untersuchungen zur Eigenart des Buches Qohelet* (1989). **Midrash Rabba**, vol. 8, *Ecclesiastes* (ET ed. H. Freedman and M. Simon, tr. A. Cohen, 1983). **A. Miller**, "Aufbau und Grundproblem des Predigers," *Miscellanea Bib* 2 (1934) 104-22. H. G. Mitchell,

"'Work' in Ecclesiastes," *JBL* 32 (1913) 123-38. **J. A. Montgomery**, "Notes on Ecclesiastes," *JBL* 43 (1924) 241-44. **J. Muilenburg**, "A Qohelet Scroll from Qumran," *BASOR* 135 (1954) 20-28. **H. P. Müller**, "Wie sprach Qohälät von Gott?" *VT* 18 (1968) 507-21. **R. E. Murphy**, "The *Pensées* of Coheleth," *CBQ* 17 (1955) 304-12; "Form Criticism and Wisdom Literature," *CBQ* 31 (1969) 475-83; "Qohelet's 'Quarrel' with the Fathers," *From Faith to Faith* (FS D. G. Miller, ed. D. Y. Hadidian, 1979) 235-45; *Wisdom Literature: Job, Proverbs, Ruth, Canticles, Ecclesiastes, and Esther* (FOTL 13, 1981); "Qohelet Interpreted: The Bearing of the Past on the Present," *VT* 32 (1982) 331-37; *Ecclesiastes* (WBC, 1992). **A. Neher**, *Notes sur Qohélét* (1951). **F. Nötscher**, *Kohelet* (1954); "Schicksal und Freiheit," *Bib* 40 (1959) 446-62. **G. S. Ogden**, *Qohelet* (1987). **T. A. Perry**, *Dialogues with Kohelet* (1993). **J. Pedersen**, "Scepticisme israélite," *RHPR* 10 (1930) 317-70. **B. Pennacchini**, "Qohelet ovvero il libro degli assurdi," *Euntes Docete* 30 (1977) 491-510. **E. Pfeiffer**, "Die Gottesfurcht im Buche Kohelet," (FS H. W. Hertzberg, 1965) 133-58. **F. Piotti**, "Osservazioni su alcuni usi linguistici dell'Ecclesiaste," *BeO* 19 (1977a) 49-57. **O. Plöger**, "Wahre die richtige Mitte; solch Mass ist in allem das Beste!" (FS H. W. Hertzberg, 1965) 159-73. **E. H. Plumptre**, *Ecclesiastes* (1881). **L. Podechard**, *L'Ecclésiaste* (1912). **G. von Rad**, *Wisdom in Israel* (1972). **O. S. Rankin**, "The Book of Ecclesiastes," *IB* (1956) 5:3-88. **H. Ranston**, "Koheleth and the Early Greeks," *JTS* 24 (1923) 160-69; *Ecclesiastes and the Early Greek Wisdom Literature* (1925). **S. Reif**, review of C. F. Whitley, *Koheleth: His Language and Thought*, *VT* 31 (1981) 120-26. **M. Rose**, *Rien de nouveau : nouvelles approches du livre de Qoheleth* (OBO 168, 1999). **F. Rousseau**, "Structure de Qohelet I 4-11 et Plan du Livre," *VT* 31 (1981) 200-217. **D. Rudman**, *Determinism in the Book of Ecclesiastes* (JSOTSup 316, 2001). **W. Rudolph**, *Vom Buch Kohelet* (1959). **J. C. Rylaarsdam**, *Revelation in Jewish Wisdom Literature* (1946). **G. D. Salyer**, *Vain Rhetoric: Private Insight and Public Debate in Ecclesiastes* (JSOTSup 327, 2001). **J. F. A. Sawyer**, "The Ruined House in Ecclesiastes 12: A Reconstruction of the Original Parable," *JBL* 94 (1975) 519-31. **S. Schiffer**, *Das Buch Kohelet, nach der Auffassung der Weisen des Talmud und Midrasch und der jüdischen Erklärer des Mittelalters I* (1884). **H. H. Schmid**, *Wesen und Geschichte der Weisheit* (BZAW 101, 1966) 186-96. **A. Schoors**, "Kethibh-Qere in Ecclesiastes," (OLA 13, 1982) 215-22; "The Peshitta of Kohelet and Its Relation to the Septuagint," (OLA 18, 1985) 347-57; *The Preacher Sought to Find Pleasing Words, pt. 1, Grammar* (OLA 41, 1992); *Qohelet in the Context of Wisdom* (BETL 136, 1998). **L. Schwienhorst-Schönberger**, "Kohelet: Stand und Perspektiven der Forschung," *Das Buch Kohelet: Studien zur Struktur, Geschichte, Rezeption, und Theologie* (ed. L. Schwienhorst-Schönberger, 1977) 5-38; *Nicht im Menschen gründet das Glück* (Koh 2:42): *Kohelet im Spannunbgsfeld jüdischer weisheit und hellenistischer Philosophie* (Herders biblische Studien 2, 1996). **R. B. Y. Scott**, *Proverbs, Ecclesiastes* (AB 18, 1965). **C. L. Seow**, *Ecclesiastes* (AB 18C, 1997). **J. J. Serrano**, "I Saw the Wicked Buried (Eccl 8, 10)," *CBQ* 16 (1954) 168-70. **A. Shaffer**, "The Mesopotamian Background of Qohelet 4:9-12," *EI* 8 (1967) 246-50; "New Light on the `Three Ply Cord,'" *EI* 9 (1969) 159-60. **G. T. Sheppard**, "The Epilogue to Qoheleth as Theological Commentary," *CBQ* 39 (1977) 182-89. **K. Siegfried**, *Prediger und Hoheslied* (HAT 2, 3, 2, 1898). **C. L. Seow**, *Ecclesiastes: A New Translation with Introduction and Commentary* (AB 18C, 1997). **J. Steinmann**, *Ainsi Parlait Qohèlèt* (1955). **A. Strobel**, *Das Buch Prediger (Kohelet)* (1967). **E. Tamez**, *Cuando los Horizontes se Cierren = When the Horizons Close: Re-reading Ecclesiastes* (tr. M. Wilde, 2000). **C. Taylor**, *The Dirge of Coheleth* (1874). **M. Thilo**, *Der Prediger Salomo* (1923). **C. C. Torrey**, "The Question of the Original Language of Qoheleth," *JQR* 39 (1948-49) 151-60. **W. Sibley Towner**, "The Book of Ecclesiastes," *NIB* (1997) 5:265-360. **N. H. Tur-Sinai**, *The Literal Meaning of Scripture 4b* (1962). **T. Tyler**, *Ecclesiastes* (1899). **P. Volz**, "Koheleth," *Hiob und Weisheit* (1921). **C. F. Whitley**, *Koheleth: His Language and Thought* (1979). **G. Wildeboer**, "Der Prediger," *Die*

Fünf Megillot (K. Budde et al., 1898) 109-68. **J. G. Williams**, *Those Who Ponder Proverbs* (1981); "What does It Profit a Man? The Wisdom of Koheleth," *Judaism* 20 (1971) 179-93 = Crenshaw (1976) 375-89. **H. Witzenrath**, *Süss ist das Licht* (1979). **E. Wölfel**, *Luther und die Skepsis* (1958). **A. G. Wright**, "The Riddle of the Sphinx: The Structure of the Book of Qoheleth," *CBQ* 30 (1968) 313-34; "The Riddle of the Sphinx Revisited: Numerical Patterns in the Book of Qoheleth," *CBQ* 42 (1980) 38-51; "Additional Numerical Patterns in Qohelet," *CBQ* 45 (1983) 32-43. **Yahya** (Yosef ben David ibn Yahya), *Perus Hames Hammegillot* (1539), Hebrew. **M. Zer-Kavod**, *Qohelet* (1973), Hebrew. **T. Zimmer**, *Zwischen Tod und Lebensglück: eine Untersuchung zur Anthropologie Kohelets* (BZAW 286, 1999). **W. Zimmerli**, "Zur Struktur der alttestamentlichen Weisheit," *ZAW* 51 (1933) 177-204 (= Crenshaw [1976] 175-207); *Das Buch des Predigers Salomo* (ATD 16, 1, 1962); "Ort und Grenze der Weisheit im Rahmen der alttestamentlich Theologie," *Les Sagesse du Proche-Orient Ancien* (1963) 121-38 (= Crenshaw [1976] 314-26); "Das Buch Kohelet-Traktat oder Sentenzensammlung?" *VT* 24 (1974) 221-30. **F. Zimmermann**, "The Aramaic Provenence of Qohelet," *JQR* 36 (1945-46) 17-45; "The Question of Hebrew in Qohelet,*" JQR* 40 (1949-50) 79-102; *The Inner World of Qohelet* (1973). **G. Zirkel**, *Untersuchungen über den Prediger mit philosophischen und kritischen Bemerkungen* (1792). **R. B. Zuck**, *Reflecting with Solomon* (1994), anthology of articles.

M. V. Fox

THE WRITINGS

Song of Songs (Canticles)

The Song of Songs is one of the oddest books of the Bible. Eight chapters of love lyrics, including many repeating phrases and images that seem to hint at an underlying structure, it nevertheless contains no readily apparent narrative. Instead, a series of amorous images speak of the love between a man (identified as "the king" or "Solomon") and his beloved (named only as "my sister," "my bride," or occasionally "the Shulamite"). Nor is the inclusion of this text in the canon of the Bible readily understandable, for it tells no sacred history, makes no theological points, and does not mention God. In spite of these peculiarities, Song of Songs is part of all known versions of the biblical text. The MT has many examples of *hapax legomena*; consequently, the Septuagint, based on an undiscovered Hebrew original, contains divergent readings. Subsequent translations into Latin and modern vernaculars are also variant at a number of points, depending on the text from which they were translated. In response to this textual confusion Greek and Latin manuscripts used by Christians show a number of strategies for making sense of the poetry, notably inserting rubrics identifying the speakers as "God," "the church," "the synagogue." This scribal custom is perhaps the first instance of interpretation.

It is equally clear that Song of Songs is included in the Bible because of an ancient tradition, common to Judaism and Christianity, of reading the text allegorically. Rabbi Akiba defended the book at the discussions of the canon held by Jewish scholars at Jamnia in the first century C.E. with the much-quoted words: "The whole world is not worth the day on which the Song of Songs was given to Israel, for all the Scriptures are holy, but the Song of Songs is the Holy of Holies" (*m. Yadayim* 3:5). Rabbinic interpretation, as found in the Midrashim and the Targumim, tends to follow one of two basic readings: The book is understood as the song of love between God and Israel given to Moses with the law at Mount Sinai or as the song of love revealed at the building of the ark of the covenant. These interpretations were the basis for an extremely rich tradition of Jewish commentary and provided important clues for the Christian understanding of the text.

1. *Early Interpretations.* The first important Christian commentator on Song of Songs was Origen of Alexandria, who was widely acclaimed as the author of two interpretations, although these survive only in part and in Latin translation. Extant are two homilies on Cant 1:1–2:14 translated by Jerome and parts of a commentary (to Cant 2:15) in the Latin version of Rufinus (fl. 399-401). Both works show the clear influence of Jewish interpretation and have been linked to Origen's study with rabbis in Alexandria) and especially in Caesarea of Palestine. The most striking evidence of this influence is Origen's assumption that Song of Songs tells a divine love story. Like Jewish interpreters he understood the book's deeper meaning with great flexibility as the love between God and the soul, or Christ and the church, or both. This ease with multiple, non-systematic understandings of a sacred text is congruent with his discussion of the fundamentals of biblical interpretation in bk. 4 of his *De Principiis*.

Origen's homilies and commentary differ at some points but in general provide a consistent interpretation. Both works stress that the title evokes the "Holy of Holies," as evidence of the book's importance. Both describe the text as an *epithalamium*, a wedding song written to celebrate the spiritual marriage of God and the Christian soul or the Christian people. The commentary is more detailed and explicit about the nature of this spiritual love than are the homilies and refers more evidently to Jewish teachers. Both texts, but especially the homilies, were widely circulated and quoted in the Middle Ages in spite of doubts about Origen's orthodoxy that reached a peak with his condemnation by the Second Council of Constantinople in 553, 300 years after his death.

The Origenistic approach to biblical exegesis in general was greatly boosted in the West by its incorporation in the works of the fourth-century bishop Ambrose of Milan. Ambrose wrote no commentary on Song of Songs but cited the text frequently in his writings, with spiritual understandings taken from Origen. These comments were gathered into one book by the twelfth-century Cistercian author William of St. Thierry. An otherwise unknown contemporary of Ambrose named Aponius, thought to be of Syrian origin, is the author of a Song of Songs commentary with many similarities to Origen's. In the Greek-speaking Christian world Origen's allegorical interpretation was widely spread through the work of the Cappadocian bishop Gregory of Nyssa, whose commentary presented an allegorical reading through Cant 6:9.

Origen's allegorical understanding of Song of Songs, however influential, did not receive universal acceptance in the early Christian exegetical tradition. The fifth-century Syrian exegete Theodore of Mopsuestia, a member of the independent theological tradition known as the Antiochene School, is credited with an interpretation that denied any spiritualizing of the text, reading it instead as Solomon's defense of his marriage to an Egyptian princess in the face of the criticism of his people. Theodore apparently understood the Song to be literally carnal and worthy of inclusion (at best) among the deuterocanonical books of the Bible. Unfortunately, this intriguing minority opinion has been lost. Only hints of Theodore's interpretation remain in the writings of his opponents, who were many and powerful: His views may have provoked the attack of Theodoret of Cyrrhus on those who do not believe in the spiritual meaning of the poems and certainly played a role in Theodore's condemnation at the first Council of Constantinople in 550 (over a century after his death and three years before Origen's condemnation). His literal or "carnal" interpretation seems to have influenced another lost Song of Songs commentary, that of Julius of Aeclanum (d. 454), the Pelagian foe of Augustine's waning years.

2. *The Early Middle Ages.* From the sixth through the twelfth centuries, Song of Songs enjoyed an unmatched flowering of interest. Nearly one hundred commentaries and a series of homilies on the text are extant, many still in unprinted manuscripts. The book's popularity during this period is a result of the relevance of Origen's allegorical interpretation to the dominant monastic culture. Why a spiritual understanding of these biblical love poems struck such a chord has yet to be fully explored, but the wealth and variety of interpretations of the love between God and the church or God and the soul suggests a multifaceted answer.

Three Song of Songs commentaries written before the Carolingian period set the tone for this tradition. That of Justus of Urguel, written in northern Spain before 546, gives an essentially ecclesiological interpretation but understands several verses, notably Cant 4:12, "a garden enclosed is my sister, my spouse," as references to the Virgin Mary. Gregory the Great, openly following Origen, wrote two homilies on the first eight verses that were widely admired by later medieval exegetes. Gregory took advantage of the difficulties of his text to theorize on the nature of allegorical representations of truth; his dictum that allegory is "a sort of machine which draws one up to God" is a favorite tag of later medieval interpreters. His interpretation was most widely circulated, not as an independent text, but as part of the compendium of his writings assembled by his disciple Paterius. The third early medieval expositor of Song of Songs is the eighth-century Northumbrian Bede. The middle five books of his seven-part commentary constitute a complete verse-by-verse explication. Book one is a refutation of the Pelagian position on free will, directed against the teachings of Julius of Aeclanum. Book seven presents a collection of comments on Song of Songs taken from the writings of Gregory the Great. The central five books are solidly ecclesiological; the whole taken together should be understood as an educational treatise on the sanctity of the church and on the lack of saving grace outside it. Bede's interpretation was known to later centuries mostly through the abridgement of Alcuin of York, another English scholar, whom Charlemagne put in charge of ninth-century school reforms.

Biblical exegesis was the major form of theological writing in the Carolingian age. Song of Songs did not figure prominently in this intellectual enterprise, but one treatise from that period proved to be very important for the subsequent tradition of the book's interpretation. The commentary of Haymo (also Haimo or Aimo) of Auxerre, *Commentarium in Cantica Canticorum* (PL 117, 295-358) stressed that the text represents a relationship between the church and God, although Haymo allowed for the possibility that it may represent God's relationship with the individual Christian soul, perhaps showing in this the influence of Origen. Haymo's commentary also shows at some points readings having to do with the end times, thus giving evidence of the application of the famous "four senses of scripture" of J. Cassian (historical, allegorical, tropological, anagogical) that were widely applied to biblical texts in the later Middle Ages. This treatise was held in high regard for many centuries and was avidly read and copied even after the great flowering of interest in Song of Songs in the twelfth century because it reflects so well the spirit of early medieval biblical commentary. The Middle High German paraphrase of William of Ebersberg in the eleventh century was the first interpretation of the book to enter the tradition of vernacular literature.

Haymo was also the basis for two very different Latin Song of Songs commentaries from the eleventh century, those of John of Mantua and Robert of Tombelinia. John's commentary, primarily concerned with the soul as the beloved of God, characterizes the book as a "doctrine of contemplation." Robert concentrated his interpretation almost exclusively on the spiritual marriage of God and the soul, a union besieged by the corruption found in both the world and the church. This shift from ecclesiological to spiritual interpretation anticipates the later medieval tradition.

3. *The Twelfth Century.* Twelfth-century commentaries on Song of Songs are extremely numerous and varied. This is seen very clearly in the *Glossa Ordinaria*, the popular running gloss on the Bible that became increasingly standardized in the later Middle Ages. The most important version of the gloss on Song of Songs names wide-ranging sources, including Jerome, Theodoret, Rupert of Deutz (a contemporary author), and Origen. This marks both the explicit reentry of Origen into the tradition and the common acceptance of the Mariological interpretation found in Rupert's treatise. Both Origen's and Rupert's versions of the gloss make clear the predominance of spiritual over ecclesiological interpretations in this century.

No interpretation of the book is more famous than the eighty-six homilies by the Cistercian abbot Bernard of Clairvaux. Probably intended for study by fellow monks rather than for preaching in a liturgical setting, this series of homilies treats the text only to Cant 3:1; but this eloquent description of the love between God and the human soul approaches the language of mystical union. Bernard understood the book on three levels equivalent to three stages of spiritual ascent, opening the possibility for a literal, or carnal, reading of the text. But this reading is in some ways the most metaphoric of all the possible interpretations, since it minimalizes human love, portraying it as a cheap imitation of the love of God, which passes all understanding (Phil 4:7). Bernard's influence on his age can be seen in a wave of Cistercian commentaries that followed and complemented his treatment. A commentary by the English Cistercian Gilbert of Hoyland begins at Cant 3:1, where Bernard's homilies end. Bernard's secretary, Geoffrey of Auxerre was also solicited by the order to finish Bernard's truncated work; he declined the task but did compose a commentary on the complete text that includes a short gloss for each verse for those who needed to quickly find an interpretation.

A more systematic attempt to relate levels of meaning in Scripture to Song of Songs is found in the commentaries of Honorious Augustoduniensis (*Expositio in Cantica canticorum*, PL 172, 347-495; *Sigillum Beatae Mariae ubi exponuntur Cantica Canticorum*, PL 172, 496-518). The two prefaces of his treatise deal at length with the question of levels of understanding. In the first, Cassian's fourfold sense is invoked: Historically, the book speaks of Solomon and Pharaoh's daughter; allegorically, it depicts the incarnation and the love between Christ and the church; tropologically, it shows either the mystical union of Christ and the soul or the marriage of human will to divine laws; anagogically, it speaks of the union of the heavenly and the earthly church at the resurrection of the dead. In the second preface the allegorical and moral senses are conflated into a drama of redemption, making Song of Songs the nuptial poem that celebrates the elevation of humanity (as individuals but also collectively as the church) to be the bride of God. All four of Cassian's senses function together in this understanding, and again human sexual passion is understood as a metaphor for the love of God. Honorius's lengthy exposition begins with four senses for each verse; but by the middle of the second chapter this cumbersome method is cast aside in favor of an ecclesiological reading with occasional references to the other senses.

Another important twelfth-century tradition, Mariological interpretation, is also ultimately linked to an ecclesiological understanding. Single verses had been adapted for use in liturgies of the Virgin Mary as early as the fourth century; by the twelfth, the propers for the Feast of the Assumption were taken directly from the text. Commentaries on the book's liturgical use for Marian feasts were written by Honorius and by the Parisian Augustinian canon Hugh of St. Victor. Several systematic explications that understood the bride as the Virgin Mary also date from this period, notably those of Rupert of Deutz, William of Newburgh, and Alan of Lille, all stressing the role of the Virgin in the incarnation of Christ and so as the mother of the church. An anonymous Middle High German commentary known as the St. Trudpert Song of Songs, addressed to a community of nuns, offered a Mariological interpretation as a model of a pious soul. As the last of the medieval traditions of Song of Songs interpretation, Mariological readings may seem more innovative than they really were, for the primary Christian understanding of the book continued to be that it depicts the love between God and the church and/or God and the soul.

4. *The Scholastic Period.* With the waning of monastic culture and the rise of the scholastic tradition in the thirteenth century, Song of Songs commentaries were adapted to the scholastic method. An early example is found in the Aurora, a versified Bible begun in Reims before 1200 by the canon Peter Riga and completed by the deacon Aegidius of Paris about a decade later, which drew on entirely traditional sources, including Origen. William of Auvergne (c. 1180–1249), a master of theology at the University of Paris, used the scholastic posing of antitheses to present a dark twist on the traditional ecclesiological reading, stressing the corruption of the church of his day. Even mystical and Mariological interpretations were subjected to the rigors of the scholastic method in the commentaries of the Franciscan P. Olivi and of the Oxford scholar A. Neckham. The Postilla of Nicholas of Lyra, a fourteenth-century Franciscan, acknowledged that Jewish scholars understood the bride to be the people of Israel, even as Christians understood her to be the Roman Catholic Church. This is one of the few references since Origen to the tradition of Jewish commentary on the text, although the celebrated commentary of Rashi, who wrote in the late eleventh century, and that of his grandson, Samuel ben Meir, were known by medieval Christians.

5. *The Early Modern Period.* The disavowal of both monastic and scholastic exegesis by the biblical scholars of the Protestant Reformation is the beginning of a split in Song of Songs interpretation. Luther tried to tread a thin line between unacceptable medieval allegorizing and the equally disturbing literal sense. His commentary reflects political concerns: The bridegroom is God, but the bride is the Christian state in harmonious union with secular and divine powers. Other Protestant exegetes were willing to go further. S. Castellio claimed that the poems only celebrated human sexual love and were not worthy of a place in the canon, a position that led

him into conflict with Calvin and to expulsion from Geneva. Calvin took Song of Songs to portray human love, if divinely inspired. Later Protestant authors often read it as showing the love between Christ and the church, as did T. Wilcocks (1624) and J. Durham (1723), or followed Nicholas of Lyra's historical/allegorical reading, as did T. Brightman, J. Cotton, and J. Cocceius. By the end of the seventeenth century, this Protestant reading had also influenced such Roman Catholic interpreters as J. Bossuet (1693), whose claim that the text should be read as a historical narrative of Solomon's wedding feast contrasts to the mystical explications of John of the Cross and Teresa of Avila in the sixteenth century, and of his contemporary Françis de Sales.

6. *Modern Interpretations.* Allegorical readings of Song of Songs, Protestant and Roman Catholic, are found in the eighteenth century in such authors as J. Wesley, who read the text as describing the love between God and the church, and J. M. Guyon, who read it as representing the love between God and the soul. But an emerging critical consensus, of which J. G. Herder is an important representative, focused attention on the poems as literature, emphasizing structural and linguistic analysis. By the middle of the nineteenth century the tools of "scientific" biblical study and the discovery of ancient Near Eastern literature enabled scholars to ask new questions about the book.

Several nineteenth-century scholars cited similarities between the Song and Syrian wedding poetry as the key to its meaning, but this has not been widely accepted. Also controversial but far more established is the position that Song of Songs is related to ancient cultic rituals, especially those connected with divinities of fertility that flourished in the ancient Near East. The similarities between the book and cultic literature of Mesopotamia, Egypt, and Ugarit has been elaborated by such twentieth-century scholars as E. Ebeling, T. Meek, S. Kramer, and M. Fox (1985). M. Pope (1977) has given a complex summary of these parallels and suggested others. Clues to the book's meaning found in Jewish mystical texts, especially the *Zohar,* have been presented by G. Scholem and elaborated by R. Patai (1967). Although not universally accepted, this work has been influential for more traditional Christian expositors.

Roman Catholic commentators have taken a number of different positions on questions of both the origin and the allegorical understandings of the text. A. Robert (1963) argued that the poems are a midrash on the history of Israel and are therefore essentially allegorical in nature, not just according to a tradition of interpretation. P. Parente (1944), citing many examples from the long tradition of Christian exegesis, characterized the Song of Songs as "an allegorical representation of various mystical states." A. Rivera (1951) revived the Mariological interpretation as the literal meaning, since the description of the bride fits the Virgin Mary singularly well, especially in her relation to the church. It is striking that none of these interpretations is particular to the modern era. Another contemporary Roman Catholic scholar, R. Murphy, has argued strongly against allegorizing on any level, citing the precedent of Theodore of Mopsuestia. For R. Murphy the Song celebrates the sanctity of human love and the virtues of devotion and fidelity.

Most Protestant commentary in the last half of the twentieth century also agrees that these are songs of human love. E. Young, H. Rowley, and R. Laurin (1962) all describe the book as an affirmation of the goodness and dignity of human love, while stressing that the same details of sexuality can be understood as profane or pure, depending on one's spiritual state. Reading the Song as human love poems is also common in modern Jewish commentaries, notably those of I. Bettan (1950), R. Gordis, and H. Ginsberg. W. Phipps (1974) has issued a scathing denunciation of traditional allegories, blaming them for "the plight of the Song of Songs." The interpretation of D. Lys (1968) portrays the book as sexual and sacred, its eroticism a deliberate reminder that sexuality is part of both creation and covenant. Lys thus follows K. Barth in reading the Song as a commentary on Genesis 2. P. Trible (1978) understands the book as expanding and completing the creation of sexuality described in Genesis 2–3 by describing human love without male dominance, female subordination, or sexual stereotyping; however, C. Exum (2000), R. Weems (1992, 1997), V. Burrus (2003) and S. D. Moore (2000, 2003) discuss violence and misogynist tendencies in the book.

What is clear from both this biblical book and many of its interpretations is that Song of Songs speaks of the power and mystery of love. Perhaps the true meaning of the text is destined to remain complex, controversial, and elusive.

Bibliography: P. S. Alexander, *The Targum of Canticles* (The Aramaic Bible 17A, 2003). Apponius, *Commentaire sur le Cantique des cantiques* (3 vols.; tr. B. de Vregille and L. Neyrand, Sources chrétiennes 420, 421, 430, 1997-1998). **R. Alter,** "The Song of Songs: an Ode to Intimacy," *BR* 18 (2002) 24-32, 52. **Association catholique française pour l'étude de la Bible**, *Les nouvelles voies de l'exégèse : en lisant le Cantique des cantiques* (Lectio Divina 190, 2002). **F. B. A. Asiedu**, "The Song of Songs and the Ascent of the Soul: Ambrose, Augustine, and the Language of Mysticism," *VC* 55 (2001) 299-317. **A. W. Astell**, *The Song of Songs in the Middle Ages* (1990). **N. Ayo**, *Sacred Marriage: The Wisdom of the Song of Songs* (1997). **J. D. Baildam**, *Paradisal Love: Johann Gottfried Herder and the Song of Songs* (JSOTSup 289, 1999). **I. Bettan**, *The Five Scrolls: A Commentary on the Song of Songs, Ruth, Lamentations, Ecclesiastes, and Esther* (1950). **F. Black**, "Beauty or the Beast? The Grotesque Body in the Song of Songs," *BibInt* 8 (2000) 302-23. **A. Bloch** and **C. Bloch**, *The Song of Songs: a New Translation with Introduction and Commentary* (1998). **J. B. Bossuet**, *Libri Salomonis, Canticum Canticorum* (1693). **A. Brenner**, *The Song of Songs* (OTG, 1989); ed., *A Feminist Companion to the Song of Songs* (FCB 1, 1993); and **C. R. Fontaine**, eds., *The Song of Songs: A Feminist Companion to the Bible* (FCB Second Series 6, 2000). **V. Burrus** and **S. D. Moore**, "Unsafe Sex: Feminism, Pornography, and the Song of Songs," *BibInt* 11 (2003) 24-52. **M. Caleo**, *Il controcantico di Origene* (2000). **R. J. DeSimone**, *The Bride and Bridegroom of the Fathers: an Anthology of Patristic Interpretations of the Song of Songs* (Sussidi patristici 10, 2000). **M. Dove**, " 'Merely a Love Poem?' Common Sense, Suspicion, and the Songs of Songs," in *Feminist Poetics of the Sacred* (ed. F. Devlin-Glass and L. McCredden, 2001) 151-64. **J. Durham**, *Clavis Cantici, or an Exposition of the Song of Solomon* (1624). M. Engammare, *Le Cantique de Cantiques . . . la Renaissance: Étude et Bibliographie* (1993). **J. C. Exum**, "Abuse, Desire and the Body: Ezekiel and the Song of Songs," *BibInt* 8 (2000) 205-323; "Seeing Solomon's Palanquin," *BibInt* 11 (2003) 301-316. **Ezra ben Solomon (of Gerona)**, *Perush Shir ha-shirim = Commentary on the Song of Songs* (tr. S. Brody, 1999). **A. Feuillet**, *Comment lire le Cantique des Cantiques: étude de théologie biblique et réflexions sur une méthode d'exégèse* (1999). **M. V. Fox**, *The Song of Songs and the Ancient Egyptian Love Songs* (1985). **L. ben Gershom**, *Commentary on Song of Songs* (tr. M. Kellner, Yale Judaica series, 28, 1998). **R. Gordis**, *The Song of Songs and Lamentations: A Study, Modern Translation, Commentary* (1974). **A. C. Hagedorn**, "Of Foxes and Vineyards: Greek Perspectives on the Song of Songs," *VT* 53 (2003) 337-352. **S. C. Horine**, *Interpretive Images in the Song of Songs: from Wedding Chariots to Bridal Chambers* (Studies in the Humanities 55, 2001). **A. Lacocque**, *Romance, She Wrote: a Hermeneutical Essay on the Song of Songs* (1998). **R. B. Laurin**, "The Life of True Love: The Song of Songs and Its Modern Message," *Christianity Today* 6 (1962) 10/1062-11/1063. **R. F. Littledale**, *A Commentary on the Song of Songs from Ancient and Mediaeval Sources* (1869). **T. Longman**, *Song of Songs* (NICOT, 2001). **D. Lys**, *Le plus beau chant de la creation: Commentaire du Cantique des Cantiques* (LD 41, 1968). **E. A. Matter**, *The Voice of My Beloved: The Song of Songs in Western Medieval Christianity* (1990). **E. Menn**, "Thwarted Metaphors: Complicating the Language of Desire in the Targum of the Song of Songs," *JSJ* 34 (2003) 237-73. **K. Modras,**

ed., *The Art of Love Lyrics: In Memory of Bernard Couroyer, OP and Hans Jacob Polotsky, First Egyptologists in Jerusalem* (Chaiers de la Revue biblique 49, 2000). **S. D. Moore**, "The Song of Songs in the History of Sexuality," *CH* 69 (2000) 328-49. **C. Mopsik**, tr., *Le Zohar: Cantique des Cantiques* (1999). **S. S. Ndoga** and **H. Viviers**, "Is the Woman in the Song of Songs Really That Free?" *HvTSt* 56 (2000) 1286-1307. **Nicholas of Lyra**, *The Postilla of Nicholas of Lyra on the Song of Songs* (ed. J.G. Kiecker, 1999). **R. A. Norris, Jr.**, *The Song of Songs: Interpreted by Early Christian and Medieval Commentators* (2003). **F. Ohly**, *Hohelied-Studien: Grundzüge einer Geschichte der Hoheliedauslegung des Abendlandes bis um 1200* (1958). **Origen**, *Omelie sul Cantico dei cantici* (ed. M. Simonetti, Scrittori greci e latini, 1998). **P. P. Parente**, "The Canticle of Canticles in Mystical Theology," *CBQ* 6 (1944) 142-58. **R. Patai**, *Man and Temple in Ancient Jewish Myth and Ritual* (1967); *The Hebrew Goddess* (1968). **W. E. Phipps**, "The Plight of the Song of Songs," *JAAR* 42 (1974) 82-100. **M. H. Pope**, *Song of Songs: A New Translation and Commentary* (AB, 1977). **A. Rickenmann**, *Sehnsucht nach Gott bei Origenes: ein Weg zur verborgenen Weisheit des Hohenliedes* (2002). **W. Riedl**, *Die Auslegung des Hohenliedes in der jüdischen Gemeinde und der griechischen Kirche* (1898). **H. Riedlinger**, *Die Makellosigkeit der Kirche in den lateinischen Hoheliedkommentaren des Mittelalters* (BGPTM 37, 1958). **P. A. Rivera**, "Sentido mariologi-co del Cantar de los Cantos," *EM* 1 (1951) 437-468. **A. Robert** and **R. Tournay**, *La Cantique des Cantiques: Traduction et commentaire* (1963). **G. Scholem**, *Jewish Gnosticism, Merkabah Mysticism, and Talmudic Tradition* (1960); *Major Trends in Jewish Mysticism* (1961); *On the Kabbalah and Its Symbolism* (1965). **J. D. Thompson**, *A Critical Concordance to the Septuagint: Song of Solomon* (The Computer Bible 72, 1999). **P. Trible**, *God and the Rhetoric of Sexuality* (1978). **D. Turner**, *Eros and Allegory: Medieval Exegesis of the Song of Songs* (1995). **C. E. Walsh**, *Exquisite Desire: Religion, the Erotic, and the Song of Songs* (2000). **R. J. Weems**, "Song of Songs," *Women's Bible Commentary* (ed. C. A. Newsom and S. H. Ringe, 1992); "Song of Songs," *NIB* (1997) 5:361-434. **T. Wilcocks**, *An Exposition Upon the Book of Canticles* (1624).

E. A. MATTER

THE LATTER PROPHETS: MAJOR

Isaiah

Isaiah is traditionally the first of the Major Prophets (Sir 48:23-25) and holds a unique position in both Judaism and Christianity. The book of Isaiah is prominent in the Jewish prophetic lectionaries, and its manuscripts, as well as Isaiah commentaries, are well represented among the Dead Sea Scrolls. It is the most often quoted book from Scripture in the NT and contains the text Jesus reads and reflects on near the beginning of his ministry at his synagogue in Nazareth (Luke 4:16-30). Its unique status in Christian tradition is reflected in the view expressed by Jerome in the introduction to his commentary that Isaiah should be called an evangelist rather than a prophet, because he writes about Christ and the church in such a way as to make one think he is "telling the story of what has already happened, rather than foretelling what is still to come."

1. *Ancient and Medieval Interpretations.* The earliest Greek version of Isaiah (c. 140 B.C.E.) contains significant references to the Jewish community in Egypt (e.g., 10:24; 19:18-25) and freely modifies descriptions of the kings of Assyria (8:11; 36:20) and Babylon (14:18-20) to fit the behavior and ultimate fate of the oppressor Antiochus IV Epiphanes (175-164 B.C.E.; cf. Dan 11:36, alluding to Isa 8:11; 10:23, 25). Greek words for "law" (8:20; 33:6), "metropolis" (1:26), "fortune" (65:11), "light" (26:9; 53:11), and "knowledge" and "wisdom" (11:2; 33:6) introduce Hellenistic theology and prepare the path from Hebrew Scripture to subsequent Christian and Gnostic developments. The choice of Greek *parthenos*, "virgin," for ʿ*almâ*, "young woman," in 7:14 is the best known and most influential example of this.

Frequent quotations from Isaiah throughout the sectarian literature of the Qumran community, including the remains of six Isaiah commentaries (*pesharim*) and an anthology of "Words of Consolation" based on Isaiah 40–55 illustrate the importance of the book and the way in which it was interpreted there. Isaiah 7:17 is applied to the departure of the "new Israel" from corrupt Judah, and 40:3 to the setting up of their community in the desert. References to the sect's opponents are found in many passages (e.g., 5:11-14; 10:12-14; 19:11-12; 24:17). Isaiah 52:7 and 61:1 are applied to the leader of the heavenly host, called Melchizedek, who will come to execute judgment on the "spirits of Baal" on the eschatological Day of Atonement (Leviticus 25).

The Targum of Isaiah, which reflects Jewish understanding of the book from several centuries before Christ to about 200 C.E., inserts explanatory references to the Torah (e.g., 2:5; 9:5; 30:15; 50:10; 63:17), *Gehenna* (e.g., 33:14; 53:9; 65:5-6; 66:24), and the resurrection of the dead (e.g., 26:19; 42:11; 45:8; 57:16). Also typical of targumic style are the avoidance of anthropomorphisms (e.g., 63:1-3) and the prosaic explanation of metaphors (e.g., 5:17; 9:18; 12:3; 55:1). Like Christian interpretations of Isaiah, it also contains a very high number of explicit messianic references (e.g., 9:5; 11:1; 16:1; 42:1; 52:13), but the sufferings in 52:13–53:12 are those of Israel, not the Messiah.

The apocryphal *Martyrdom of Isaiah* (1st cent. C.E.) contains the tradition that the prophet was sawn in half by Manasseh, known to Jewish and Christian authors from the second century (see Heb 11:37), and an account of his journey to the seventh heaven, where he sees God and the future life, death, and resurrection of Christ.

Although it was through his translation that Jerome made his greatest contribution to the history of interpretation, fine scholarship, greatly assisted by a knowledge of Hebrew and rabbinic sources, soon established his commentary on Isaiah as the most respected and influential in Western Christendom. An example will illustrate his exegetical skill. The "ox and the ass at their master's crib" (1:3) had already in Jerome's day found their way into the nativity story, but he developed the theme by linking 1:3 with a vision of the new age in 32:20. The fact that the two animals are working together proves that now the law is no longer binding (Deut 22:10), and if the ox stands for Israel with the yoke of the law on its neck and the ass for the Gentiles weighed down by the burden of their sins, then the point of that vision of a new age where "the ox and the ass range free" is all the more poignant. Most subsequent commentators on Isaiah down to modern times draw heavily on Jerome.

The commentary by Cyril of Alexandria should be evaluated more as a theological treatise than as a work of exegesis, as his powerful descriptions of God's beneficence (p. 25) and omnipotence (pp. 40-41) illustrate. But his critical use of Jewish legend (e.g., 6:2; 38:1; 40:1) and Jerome is interesting, as are his references to Roman victories over the Jews (6:11-13; 27:4, 10; 66:24) and to the *Pax Romana* (2:1-5).

The influential writings of Isidore of Seville (c. 560–636) are largely dependent on Jerome and illustrate how the book of Isaiah was interpreted in medieval Christian tradition. His polemical *Isaiae testimonia de Christo domino*, much used by medieval scholars and artists, is a prime example, finding in Isaiah almost every detail of the life of Christ. The annunciation in 7:14 is followed by the celebration of the birth of the Savior in the city of David (9:6). His Davidic ancestry is referred to in 11:1 and also in 16:1 (see AV; the rock of the Moabite desert refers to Ruth). Isaiah is the only HB prophet to make specific mention of the virginity of the mother of the messiah. In addition to the Immanuel prophecy in 7:14 (cf. Matt 1:23), the important proof text was 53:8, where "his generation" referred to the virgin birth as well as to the divine nature of Christ. The dry ground from which a young plant miraculously springs up provides another expression of this doctrine (53:2; cf. 45:8). The flight into Egypt is referred to in 19:1 and the arrival of the magi in 60:6. There are several references to Christ's baptism (11:1; 42:1; 61:1; cf. Mark 1:9-11) and the healing miracles (34:5-6; 53:4; cf. Matt 8:17). References to the passion are frequent, too: his purple robe (63:1), his silence before his executioners (53:7), the cross carried on his shoulders (9:6), and his words of forgiveness from the cross (53:12). Isaiah ends, like Matthew, with the sending forth of apostles to the nations (66:19). The pre-existence of the Son of God is referred to in 66:7-9 and his divinity in 9:6 (cf. 53:8). The three persons of the Trinity are mentioned individually in 42:1 and 48:16 and celebrated in the threefold repetition of "Holy" in the Sanctus (6:3). Up to the twelfth century most Christian exegesis remained within the tradition established by Jerome and Isidore.

Of the great medieval Jewish commentaries, that of Rashi (1040–1105) is the most influential in subsequent Jewish and Christian tradition, frequently quoted, for example, by Nicholas of Lyra. Like his two successors, the much traveled A. Ibn Ezra and D. Kimhi, he combined literal interpretation with a respect for rabbinic tradition and sought to refute christological interpretations (e.g., 7:14; chaps. 52–53), while at the same time understanding the text in the light of contemporary events and current Jewish messianic expectation (e.g., 11:1). Ibn Ezra is the most original of the three and even questions the Isaianic authorship of some of the Babylonian prophecies in 40–66 (40:1).

The commentary on Isaiah by Andrew of St. Victor is a significant example of medieval Christian scholarship. The prologue contains a unique "character study" of the prophet illustrating what a lively imagination can create out of scanty legends: "he suffered unto death . . . for justice's sake . . . he was willing rather to lose his life, with honour, by exquisite torture, a way of death unheard of . . . than suppress the truth for fear of fleeting death." He frequently cites Jewish interpretations as the "literal sense" of the text, even in the case of such "Christian" passages as 7:14; 11:1; and chap. 53. His exegesis was considered scandalous by contemporaries but appreciated by scholars of a later age, including Nicholas of Lyra.

Luther's lectures on Isaiah, delivered between 1527 and 1530, divide the book into two parts: chaps. 1–39, in which the prophet is "a historical prophet and leader of the army," and chaps. 40-66, where "the prophet is the most joyful of all, fairly dancing with promises." Despite frequent anti-Jewish interpretations (e.g., on 2:22; 4:3; 25:2; 29; 33), he makes considerable use of Hebrew, the Jewish sources, Jerome, Nicholas of Lyra, and other Hebraists, and brands some traditional Christian interpretations as "childish errors" (1:3) and "twisted" (45:8). But at 7:14 he argues that although the Hebrew word ʿalmâ does not mean "virgin," the verse nonetheless must refer to a virgin birth since otherwise it would be no miraculous sign. Chapter 53 (beginning in *Luther's Bible* at 52:13) he describes as the "foremost passage on the suffering and resurrection of Christ." The "our . . . us . . . for us" in vv. 4-6 "should be written in letters of gold."

Embarrassed by the publication not long before of John Knox's pamphlet against the government of women, in 1559 Calvin dedicated the second edition of his commentary on Isaiah to Queen Elizabeth of England, citing 49:23, along with the examples of Huldah and Deborah, as scriptural authority for the role of queens in government and as "nursing mothers of the Church."

2. *Isaiah in Art.* A few illustrations of how Isaiah was interpreted in medieval Christian art and architecture reveal which aspects of the Isaianic tradition were taken up as of particular theological, social, or political significance in the period. First, there is the influence of the cult of the virgin Mary upon the interpretation of Isaiah. The earliest representation of Isaiah, a second-century catacomb painting in Rome, shows the prophet seated opposite the Virgin and Child. An unusually spirited representation of Isaiah at what was once the main entrance to the Cathedral of Notre Dame at Souillac in southwest France, opposite a statue of the patriarch Joseph, represents virginity and chastity (Gen 39:10). Here and in many other contexts he bears a scroll on which the words of Isa 7:14 are inscribed. Among the Major Prophets of the HB depicted on a window in Chartres Cathedral, Isaiah is shown carrying Matthew on his shoulders (Matt 1:23). Representations of the vision of God among the *seraphim* (6:1-4) were also common in Byzantine and medieval art.

The ancestry of Jesus held a particular fascination for medieval artists, living as they did in a society in which kings and knights set great store by their lineage, and in this context Isa 11:1 acquired special significance. The entrance to many European cathedrals is flanked by the ancestors of the Messiah, each symbolically clutching a branch of the "Tree of Jesse," and elaborate representations based on 11:1 and Matt 1:1-17 are among the most popular motifs in medieval Christian art. A Chartres window provides possibly the most beautiful example: At the bottom Jesse, grandson of Ruth and father of David, is lying asleep. A tree rises from his body, and at its top the Virgin and Christ are surrounded by seven doves symbolizing the seven gifts of the spirit that "will rest upon him" (Isa 11:2). There are other examples in Amiens, Reims, Troyes, Le Mans, and elsewhere.

A seventeenth-century development of the "Jesse Tree" motif in Troyes Cathedral was inspired by Isa 63:3. Following Augustine's interpretation, the artist has depicted Christ in the winepress, his blood flowing out into a chalice. From his breast rises a new family tree, the true vine, carrying in its branches the twelve apostles, related by the sacramental blood of Christ this time, not by the ancestral blood of Jesse. Another interpretation of this verse from a church in Conches depicts Christ standing alone on a winepress, which is clearly designed to make one think of the cross. Suffering is also uppermost in a striking sculpture in Dijon by Claus Sluter, dating to c. 1400, in which Isaiah, old, bareheaded, and contemplative, bears a scroll with 53:7 inscribed on it. Perhaps there was a tradition that the author of chap. 53 was an older, more solemn Isaiah than the jubilant proclaimer of the nativity in the earlier chapters. The lively Souillac statue and Michelangelo's Isaiah on the ceiling of the Sistine Chapel are young, though this may be for aesthetic rather than exegetical or theological reasons.

3. *Isaiah in Music.* Isaiah's traditional association with the Advent and Christmas liturgies is also reflected in music. "O come, O come, Immanuel" (*Veni Immanuel*) is an arrangement of

Isa 7:14; 9:1; 11:1; 22:22; and 59:20, and the Latin of 45:8 provided the extremely popular antiphon *Rorate coeli.* The political associations of the *Rorate* are reflected in a version by W. Byrd (c. 1542–1623), composed at a time when his fellow Roman Catholics were being persecuted. He also composed *Ne irascaris,* another motet with political overtones on an Isaianic theme (Isa 64:9-10), soon after the martyrdom of E. Campion in 1581.

In addition to cantatas for Advent, Christmas, and Epiphany based on traditional passages like Isa 40:3-5; 9:6; and 60:6-7 (although in German now, rather than Latin), J. Bach also composed a political one on 58:7 on behalf of Protestant refugees from Salzburg who were seeking asylum in Leipzig. The first two parts of Handel's *Messiah* (1741) are largely made up of direct quotations from Isaiah in the KJV combined with other passages of Scripture in a brilliant text by the librettist C. Jennens. Handel's highly original overture, expressing "a mood without hope . . . and the violent, fruitless upward striving of the oppressed," provides a perfect context for the opening words of Isaiah 40. Common to Handel and Isaianic tradition was a compassion for the poor and needy, which makes his interpretation of 40:11 (with 35:5-6); 52:7; and chap. 53 especially effective.

Examples of nineteenth-century musical interpretations of Isaiah include the superb setting of parts of chap. 40, including "Alles Fleisch es ist wie Gras" in Brahms's *German Requiem* (1857–68), and the "Battle Hymn of the Republic" (1862), written by the women's rights campaigner J. Ward Howe on themes from Isa 63:1-3 and 30:28 combined with Rev 19:15.

A number of twentieth-century works composed or commissioned by Jews, including Martinu's *The Prophecy of Isaiah* (premiere, Jerusalem 1963), pick up the recurring Zion motif in Isaiah (e.g., 2:2-5; 26:1-6; 40:9-11; 52:1-2; 62; 65:17-25). Chapters 40–55 have provided the inspiration for some of the best-known and best-loved Christian hymns composed in the 1970s, mostly by Roman Catholics, and now regularly sung at folk masses and other Christian gatherings throughout the English-speaking world. These include settings of 43:1-7; 49:15; 52:7; 54:10; and 55:12.

4. *Modern Scholarship.* H. Grotius rejected the traditional christological interpretation of many passages (e.g., 7:14; 9:6; 11:1-2; 42:1; 53) in favor of philological exegesis. The theologian and orientalist J. Cocceius found some remarkable historical references in Isaiah (e.g., the death of Constantine in 19:2 and of Gustavus Adolphus in 33:7). The epoch-making two-volume commentary by C. Vitringa (c. 1659–1722) introduced notions of literary unity, structure, composition, purpose, and even reader response, while R. Lowth's influential *Isaiah: A New Translation* with a preliminary dissertation and notes (1778) also achieved a new sensitivity to the literary and aesthetic qualities of Isaiah.

But it was with the question of authorship that the age of modern critical scholarship can be said to have begun. Apart from a few remarks by Ibn Ezra (see above), it was not until the eighteenth century that scholars seriously suggested that the prophet Isaiah was not the sole author of the book that bears his name. A commentary by J. Döderlein's (1775, 1789) and the pioneering HB introduction of J. G. Eichhorn (1780–83; ET 1888) put forward the view that the author of Isaiah 40–66 lived in sixth-century B.C.E. Babylon. The destruction of Jerusalem and the Babylonian exile are presupposed, not foretold (44:26-28; 48:20-21; 49:19-21, etc.). The style and imagery of chaps. 40–66 have a distinctiveness and unity that separate them from 1–39: e.g., repeated imperatives (40:1; 51:9; 52:1, 9); "the servant of the Lord" (42:1; 44:1, 21; 49:3; 52:13, etc.); the personification of Zion (40:9-11; 49:14-18; 52:1-2; 54:1-8; 66:7-14). There are theological innovations such as explicit monotheism (44:6, 8; 45:5, 6, 14, 18, 21, 22), a new emphasis on cosmology (40:12-17; 45:18-19; 51:9-11), and a reinterpretation of the exodus traditions (43:1-2; 48:20-21; 52:11-12), which are not found in eighth-century prophecy.

The identification of a "Second Isaiah" or "Deutero-Isaiah" as the author of chaps. 40–66 caused much less of a furor than did challenges to the Mosaic authorship of the Pentateuch, published at about the same time, and was almost universally accepted by Protestant and Roman Catholic scholars alike by the end of the nineteenth century. In 1908, however, the Pontifical Biblical Commission issued a decree rejecting the evidence for the multiple authorship of Isaiah, but this ultra-conservative view was finally abandoned by Roman Catholic scholars in 1943 following the papal encyclical *Divino afflante spiritu*. There have been several attempts by conservative scholars to defend the unity of Isaiah, such as those of O. Allis (1950) and E. Young (1965-72), but most twentieth-century commentaries handle chaps. 1–39 and chaps. 40–66 separately, and a number of scholars have written separate commentaries on Deutero-Isaiah alone.

B. Duhm's brilliant commentary (1892, 1922) contained a number of conclusions on date and authorship, primarily directed at discovering the original Isaiah, but pointing to features of the book that are today almost universally accepted. The situation was much more complicated than had been assumed previously. The *ipsissima verba* of Isaiah were held to occur mostly within two "collections" (chaps. 1–12 and 28–33) and a "historical appendix" (chaps. 36–39). Deutero-Isaiah composed chaps. 13–14 and 34–35 (as well as 40–55) during the Babylonian exile, and a third Isaiah (Trito-Isaiah), living in the time of Malachi (c. 490), was the author of chaps. 56–66. Of chapters 24–27 Duhm says, "Isaiah could as well have written the Book of Daniel as this text," and dates its final form to 127 B.C.E. The general importance of these insights for the interpretation of Isaiah cannot be overestimated, even though the historical accuracy of some of them may be disputed. Duhm's analysis of an eighth-century prophetic core in the book combining relentless demands for social justice (e.g., 1:10-20; 5:8-23; 6:9-11; 10:1-4; 28:1-4; 29:13-14; 30:1-17) with messianic visions of a better age to come (e.g., 2:2-6; 9:1-6 [Eng. 2-7]; 11:1-8; 32:1-5, 15-20) is impressive. His use of Daniel, "Maccabean" psalms, Enoch, and other intertestamental literature to elucidate passages such as those about Jews in Egypt (19:16-25) and the resurrection of the dead (26:19; 53:11; 66:23-24) is also suggestive.

Duhm is best remembered for his identification of the four "Songs of the Servant of Yahweh" (42:1-4; 49:1-6; 50:4-11; 52:13-53:12). He argued that they were clearly distinct in thought and style, although not unrelated to the rest of Deutero-Isaiah, and could be removed from their present context without leaving any gaps. In the songs, especially in the last one, the "Servant" is an individual, while in the rest of Deutero-Isaiah he is named as the people Jacob/Israel (41:8-9; 44:1, 21, etc.). "Israel" in 49:3 has to be removed as a gloss. The "Servant Songs" were written in the first half of the fifth century, after Job and before Malachi, and in that context Duhm identified the Servant with a prophetic teacher of the law (cf. Mal 2:5-6; Isa 57:1). His use of Job, Malachi, Trito-Isaiah, Ezra-Nehemiah, and some of the "Torah-Psalms" (e.g., 119) greatly illuminates the exegesis of the "Servant Songs" whether or not one accepts his conclusions.

Since Duhm, no other part of Isaiah has been more discussed than these "Servant Songs." If we accept his assumption that they are to be taken together and tell the story of an individual chosen by God (42:1; 49:1, 4, 5) to bring justice and salvation to the ends of the earth (42:1, 4; 49:6), who suffers humiliation, persecution, and death (49:4; 50:6; 53:2-11), but is later exalted (49:3; 52:13; 53:12), then the main question is likely to be who he is. Early proposals included Cyrus, Zerubbabel, Jehoiachin, Moses, and Deutero-Isaiah himself. The author may have had some ideal figure in mind, reflecting such contemporary events as the release of Jehoiachin from prison in 560 B.C.E. (2 Kgs 25:27-30) and perhaps his own personal experiences, but transcending them. His highly original use of the exodus motif would lend support to the theory that the servant is a "New Moses" willing to suffer for his people (Exod 32:32; Deut 1:9-12). I. Engnell found traces of the myth and ritual of divine kingship in the "Songs," including a description of the suffering of the servant in language reminiscent of a Babylonian ritual (50:6), his death and rising again (53:7-12), and the fertility motif (53:2). Traditional messianic interpretations of the first and last of the "Servant Songs" (see above) have also been extended by some to the other two in such a way as to trace the life story of a suffering messiah (closely parallel to that of Christ) through the four poems.

In addition to all these individual interpretations, there have been attempts to keep the continuity between the "Songs" and the rest of Deutero-Isaiah and to argue for a corporate interpretation. The community "Israel/Jacob" is addressed as an individual in many passages outside the "Songs" (40:27; 41:14; 43:1; 44:1, etc.). There are close parallels between the Servant Songs and the rest of Isaiah 40–55 (e.g., 44:1 to 49:1), not to mention the specific identification of the Servant as "Israel" in 49:3, which, whether it is a gloss or not, proves that a corporate interpretation is possible. The *reductio ad absurdum* of this line of argument was reached with the "fluid" theory that the Servant is both an individual and the community and that a distinction between them is a modern European one.

The "Servant Song" problem hinged on Duhm's assumption that the four passages in question must be taken together as telling a single story, and its fascination for modern (almost exclusively Christian) scholars was greatly increased by correspondences between that story and the Gospels. In effect, much of the exegesis of these passages in the twentieth century has been, often unintentionally, the modern critical equivalent of early Christian interpretations. Once Duhm's assumption is questioned (Mettinger), the differences between one "Song" and another appear more striking than those between the "Servant Songs" and the rest of Isaiah. The first passage becomes just another messianic prophecy in the traditional Isaianic mold (cf. 9:1-6 [Eng. 9:2-7]; 11:1-5; 32:1-5), especially if 42:2 is interpreted impersonally as "there will be no more crying . . . in the street" (D. Jones). Isaiah 49:1-6 and 50:4-9 are autobiographical: Either the prophet himself or the community (as in 40:27; 49:1, 21) is speaking. The "Suffering Servant" poem in 52:13–53:12 is what it has always been, a unique theological statement on suffering. Isaiah 52:13 exploits the language of Isaiah's vision of God in 6:1 (cf. 57:15); and 53:4-6 uses the technical terminology of the atonement ritual in Leviticus 16, no matter who the "Servant of the Lord" is.

Much modern scholarship since Duhm has been devoted to literary form, and this has yielded some useful results for the interpretation of Isaiah. R. Scott's (1957) identification of "embryonic oracles" ("brief, striking, enigmatic and marked by a strong rhythm, verbal symmetry, paronomasia, assonance and a preponderance of sibilant and guttural sounds") sought to get back to the pre-literary stage of prophetic revelation (e.g., 5:7; 7:9; 8:3-4; 9:17; 30:15). It was proposed that the famous dynastic prophecy in 9:1-6 (Eng. 9:2-7) contains the remains of the five royal names of Egyptian enthronement protocol. J. Begrich's identification and analysis of the priestly "Salvation Oracle" (*Heilsorakel*), developed in C. Westermann's commentary (1969), greatly assists the literary appreciation of Isaiah. Thus 41:14-16 is in the form of a priest's response to an individual lament such as Psalm 22:7-9 (Eng. 22:6-8; cf. Isa 43:1-7; 44:1-5; 54:4-8). Study of hymns (e.g., Exod 15:1-18; Deut 32:1-43; Psalms 8, 19) and especially the "Enthronement Psalms" (e.g., 74; 89; 93; 94-100) has illuminated Deutero-Isaiah's use of creation motifs in language about the new exodus (e.g., Isa 42:5-9, 10-17; 43:14-21; 44:23-28; 45; 51:9-11; 52:7-12).

The Assyrian invasions of Samaria and Judah in the eighth century B.C.E. have been the subject of a number of historical and literary studies that take into account contemporary Assyrian documents. Isaiah 8:23 (Eng. 9:1) has been presumed to contain reference to Tiglath-pileser III's invasions of 734–732 and to the creation of three Assyrian provinces subsequently established in Gilead, Galilee, and the coastal region (2 Kgs 15:29). Sennacherib's destruction of all the cities of Judah except Jerusalem in 701 (2 Kgs 18:13; Isa 36:1) is referred to in many passages, reflecting the fear of an approaching army (5:26-30; 10:28-32; 37:1-4) and the scenes of destruction surrounding Jerusalem (1:7-9; 8:7-8). The almost wholly fictitious account of Jerusalem's miraculous victory in that year (2 Kgs 19:35-37; Isa 37:36-38) was probably composed at a time of national revival under Josiah (640–609). The Isaiah version entirely omits reference to Jerusalem's surrender (cf. 2 Kgs 18:14-18).

Recent work on the so-called Isaiah Apocalypse (24–27) suggests that, although it exhibits few of the literary characteristics of the later Jewish apocalypses (e.g., Daniel; Enoch; 2 Esdras; Revelation), it does contain apocalyptic eschatology, possibly traceable to the struggle between hierocratic and visionary parties in Judaism from the sixth century B.C.E. on (cf. 56:9-57:13; 60:19-20; 66:1-4, 17-24). But Ugaritic studies, which have thrown light on the language and mythology of passages like 25:6-8 (cf. 2:2-4) and 27:1, remind us of the antiquity of these traditions.

Interest in the structure and purpose of larger literary units (e.g., chaps. 1–12; 1–35; 2–4; 13–23) has led to renewed consideration of the literary and theological unity of the book of Isaiah as a whole. Emphasis on the Babylonian material in chaps. 13–14 and 34–35 as well as in 40–55 and the function of chaps. 36–39 as a transition passage linking the Assyrian to the Babylonian period suggests some deliberate editorial control of the Isaianic material. Recurring phrases and motifs, like "the Holy One of Israel," "high and lifted up" (6:1; 52:13; 57:15) Zion/Jerusalem, "faith," "justice," and "righteousness," give the book a thematic unity, as do such passages as 1:4-6 (cf. 53:1-9); 6:1-9 (cf. 40:1-8); 9:2 (cf. 60:1-2); and 11:6-9 (cf. 65:25), where early themes are developed later.

5. Some Recent Developments. Twentieth-century human rights activists and freedom fighters have found inspiration in Isaianic visions of, and calls for, justice and peace. The pronouncement of the Second Vatican Council (1962–65) on justice and peace begins with a quotation from Isa 32:17 (*Gaudium et Spes* 70), and in the whole revolution within the Roman Catholic Church that followed Vatican II, Isaiah has played a prominent role, increasingly being depicted as the prophet of justice and peace, rather than the prophet of the nativity and the passion.

In *Marx and the Bible* (1971) by J. Miranda, Isaiah is the most often quoted HB book next to Psalms, but a passage like 7:14, so popular in an earlier age, is not even mentioned, while 11:3-4 completely eclipses 11:1-2. His interpretations of "rulers of Sodom" (1:10) in terms of injustice (cf. Ezek 16:49), rather than in sexual terms, and "wickedness" in 58:9 as a pragmatic social term rather than a magical or mystical one are motivated by concern for the politically oppressed. Similar considerations lead to an interpretation of the word play in 5:7 (the Hebrew words for "justice" and "bloodshed" sound similar, as do the words for "righteousness" and "cry") as having a more concrete and at the same time more poignant meaning elucidated by the following verse. Passages like 43:1; 44:2; and 45:9-11, in which the liberation of Israel from oppression is described as an act of creation, are given new force by the bias of liberation theologies and are applied to issues of justice and freedom in this world.

Another example of how certain texts have taken on a new significance in light of post-Vatican II developments is to be found in the feminist interpretation of Isaiah. P. Trible (*Texts of Terror* [1984]) applies verses from Isaiah 53 to suffering women. R. Reuther (*Sexism and God-talk* [1983]) identifies women among "the afflicted . . . the brokenhearted . . . the captives . . . those that are bound" of 61:1 (cf. Luke 4:27).

Of the few biblical passages in which the feminine nature of God is described, most are in Isaiah, and these, too, have now taken on a new significance. The image of a God who suffers for us as a woman suffers the pangs of childbirth appears twice in Isaiah (42:14; 45:10). Another feminine image in Isaiah is that of a mother's love for her child (49:15), which may be compared with the final vision of Zion as a mother dandling her baby on her knee, while God is the midwife (66:7-14). The Hebrew word translated "compassion" is etymologically related to a word for "womb" and is undoubtedly used to special effect here (49:13, 15). Feminine imagery is unusually prominent in Isaiah, not only in the way God is described, but also in the way the people of God are addressed as a woman (feminine singular) in passages like 40:9; 51:17; 52:1; 54:1; and 60:1. This uniquely effective feature of Isaianic style was not fully recognized until modern feminist interpreters appreciated its significance.

Bibliography: S. Ackerman, "Isaiah," *Women's Bible Commentary* (ed. C. A. Newsom and S. H. Ringe, 1992) 161-68. **P. R. Ackroyd**, "Isaiah 36-39: Structure and Function," *Von Kanaan bis Kerala: Festschrift für Prof. Mag. Dr. Dr. J. P. M. van der Ploeg* (1982) 3-21. **O. T. Allis**, *The Unity of Isaiah: A Study in Prophecy* (1950). **J. Alobaidi**, tr., *The Messiah in Isaiah 53: The Commentaries of Saadia Gaon, Salmon ben Yeruham, and Yefet ben Eli on Is 52:12 – 53:12* (Bible dans l'histoire 2, 1998). **D. A. Baer**, *When We All Go Home: Translation and Theology in LXX Isaiah 56-66* (2001). **K. Baltzer**, *Deutero-Isaiah: A Commentary on Isaiah 40-55* (Hermeneia, 2001). **H. M. Barstad**, *The Babylonian Captivity of the Book of Isaiah: "Exilic" Judah and the Provenance of Isaiah 40-55* (1997). **J. Barton**, *Isaiah 1-30* (OTG, 1995). **J. Begrich**, *Studien zu Deuterojesaja* (1938). **W. H. Bellinger** and **W. R. Farmer**, eds., *Jesus and the Suffering Servant: Isaiah 53 and Christian Origins* (1998). **W. A. M. Beuken**, "The Main Theme of Trito-Isaiah: 'The Servants of Yahweh,'" *JSOT* 47 (1990). **J. Blenkinsopp**, *Isaiah 1-39* (AB 19, 2000). **P. E. Bonnard**, *Le Second Isaïe* (1972). **H. J. Bosman** and **H. van Grol**, eds., *Studies in Isaiah 24-27: The Isaiah Workshop = de Jesaja Werkplaats* (Oudtestamentische studiën 43, 2000). **L. Bronner**, "Gynomorphic Imagery in Exilic Isaiah (40-66)," *Dor le Dor 12* (1983-84) 71-83. **C. C. Broyles** and **C. A. Evans** (eds.), *Writing and Reading the Scroll of Isaiah: Studies of an Interpretive Tradition* (2 vols., VTSup 70, 1997). **T. K. Cheyne**, *Introduction to the Book of Isaiah* (1895). **B. S. Childs**, *Isaiah and the Assyrian Crisis* (1967); *Isaiah* (OTL, 2001). **R. E. Clements**, *Isaiah and the Deliverance of Jerusalem* (JSOTSup 13, 1980); *Isaiah 1-39* (1980); "The Unity of the Book of Isaiah," *Int* 36 (1982); "Beyond Tradition-History: Deutero-Isaianic Development of First Isaiah's Themes," *JSOT* 31 (1985). **R. Clifford**, *Fair Spoken and Persuading: An Interpretation of Second Isaiah* (1984). **D. J. A. Clines**, *I, He, We and They: A Literary Approach to Isaiah 53* (1976). **E.W. Conrad**, *Reading Isaiah* (OBT 27, 1979). **J. C. Döderlein**, *Esaias ex recensione textus hebrae ad fidem codd. quorundam mss. et versionum antiquarum latine vertit notasque varii argumenti subiecit* (1775, 1789). **B. Doyle**, *The Apocalypse of Isaiah Metaphorically Speaking : A Study of the Use, Function, and Significance of Metaphors in Isaiah 24-27* (BETL 151, 2000). **S. R. Driver** and **A. Neubauer**, *The Fifty-third Chapter of Isaiah According to the Jewish Interpreters* (2 vols., 1876–77). **B. Duhm**, *Das Buch Jesai, Übersetzt und erklärt* (HKNT 3/1, 1892, 1922). **J. Eaton**, "The Isaiah Tradition," *Israel's Prophetic Tradition: Essays in Honour of Peter R. Ackroyd* (1982) 58-76. **J. G. Eichhorn**, *Introduction to the Study of the OT* (1780–83; ET 1888). **O. Eissfeldt**, *The OT: An Introduction* (1934; ET 1965) 303-46. **I. Engnell**, "The Ebed Yahweh Songs and the Suffering Messiah in Deutero-Isaiah," *BJRL* 31 (1948) 54-93. **G. Fohrer**, "The Origin, Composition, and Tradition of Isaiah I–XXXIV," *ALUOS* 3 (1962) 3-38 = BZAW 99 (1967) 113-47. **F. Giesebrecht**, *Beiträge zur Jesajakritik* (1890). **P. Grelot**, *Les Poèmes du Serviteur* (LD 103, 1981). **E. Hammershaimb**, "The Immanuel Sign," *StTh* 3 (1949) 124-42. **P. D. Hanson**, *Isaiah 40-66* (1995). **A. J. Heschel**, *The Prophets* (1962) 61-97, 145-55. **H. Irsigler**, *Vom Adamssohn zum Immaneuel : Gastvorträge Pretoria 1996* (Arbeiten zu Text und Sprache im Alten Testament 58, 1997). **B. Janowski** and **P. Stuhlmacher**, eds., *Der leidende Gottesknecht* (FAT 14, 1996). **J. Jensen**, *The Use of Torah by Isaiah* (CBQMS 3, 1973). **D. R. Jones**, "II-III Isaiah," *PCB* 516-36. **O. Kaiser**, *Isaiah 1–12* (OTL, 1983); *Isaiah 13–39* (OTL, 1974). **J. Kerman**, *The Masses and Motets of William Byrd* (1980) 40-44. **A. Kerrigan**, *St. Cyril of Alexandria, Interpreter of the OT* (AnBib 2, 1952). **R. Kilian**, *Jesaja 1–39* (EdF 200, 1983). **M. A. Knibb** (ed.), "Martyrdom and Ascension of Isaiah," *OTP* 2:143-76. **A. van der Kooij**, *The Oracle of Tyre: the Septuagint of Isaiah XXIII as Version and Vision* (VTSup 71,

1998). **M.C.A. Korpel** and **J.C. de Moor**, *The Structure of Classical Hebrew Poetry : Isaiah 40-55* (Oudtestamentische studiën 41, 1998). **A. Labahn**, *Wort Gottes und Schuld Israels: Untersuchungen zu Motiven deuteronomistischer Theologie im Deuterojesajabuch mit einem Ausblick auf das Verhältnis von Jes 40-55 zum Deuteronomismus* (BWANT 143, 1999). **J. P. Larsen**, *Handel's Messiah* (1957); *Luther's Works* (ed. **J. Pelikan** and **H.C. Oswald**, 16 [1969]; 17 [1972]). **T. L. Leclerc**, *Yahweh is Exalted in Justice: Solidarity and Conflict in Isaiah* (2001). **N. Lohfink** and **E. Zenger**, *The God of Israel and the Nations: Studies in Isaiah and the Psalms* (tr. E.R. Kalin, 2000). **W. Ma**, *Until the Spirit Comes: The Spirit of God in the Book of Isaiah* (JSOTSup 271, 1999). **E. Male**, *Religious Art in France: Thirteenth Century* (1913). **R. F. Melugin**, *The Formation of Isaiah 40-55* (BZAW 141, 1976); and **M. A. Sweeney**, eds., *New Visions of Isaiah* (JSOTSup 214, 1996). **T. Mettinger**, *A Farewell to the Servant Songs* (1983). **W. R. Millar**, *Isaiah 24-27 and the Origin of Apocalyptic* (HSM 11, 1976). **S. Mowinckel**, *He That Cometh* (1956) 96-124, 155-257. **G. R. North**, *The Suffering Servant in Deutero-Isaiah: An Historical and Critical Study* (1948); *The Second Isaiah* (1964). **H. Odeberg**, *Trito-Isaiah* (1931). **D. W. Parry** and **E. Qimron**,eds., *The Great Isaiah Scroll (IQIsa^a): a New Eidtion* (STDJ 32, 1999). **R. F. Person**, T*he Kings-Isaiah and Kings-Jeremiah Recensions* (BZAW 252, 1997). **P. Pulikottil**, *Transmission of Biblical Texts in Qumran: The Case of the Large Isaiah Scroll 1QIsa^a* (JSPSup 34, 2001). **G. von Rad**, *OT Theology* 2 (1965) 238-62. **E. I. J. Rosenthal**, "The Study of the Bible in Medieval Judaism," *CHB* 2 (1969) 252-79. **H. H. Rowley**, *The Servant of the Lord, and Other Essays on the OT* (1952). **J. Van Ruiten** and **M. Vervenne**, eds., *Studies in the Book of Isaiah* (BETL 132, 1997). **L. Ruszkowski**, *Volk und Gemeinde im Wandel: eine Untersuchung zu Jesaja 56-66* (FRLANT 191, 2000). **J. F. A. Sawyer**, "Blessed Be My People Egypt (Isa 19:24-25)," *A Word in Season: Essays in Honour of William McKane* (ed. J. D. Martin and P. R. Davies, 1986) 57-71; "The Daughter of Zion and the Servant of the Lord in Isaiah: A Comparison," *JSOT* 44 (1989) 89-107; *The Fifth Gospel: Isaiah in the History of Christianity* (1996). **R. L. Schultz**, *The Search for Quotation: Verbal Parallels in the Prophets* (JSOTSup 180, 1999). **R. B. Y. Scott**, "The Literary Structure of Isaiah's Oracles," *Studies in OT Prophecy: Presented to Professor Theodore H. Robinson* (ed. H. H. Rowley, repr. 1957) 175-86. **I. L. Seeligmann**, *The Septuagint Version of Isaiah (1948)*. B. Smalley, *The Study of the Bible in the Middle Ages* (1983) 112-95. **C. R. Seitz**, *Zion's Final Destiny : The Development of the Book of Isaiah* (1991) ; *Isaiah 1-39* (1993); "The Book of Isaiah 40-66," *NIB* 6 (2001). **P. A. Smith**, *Rhetoric and Redaction in Trito-Isaiah* (VTSup 62, 1995). **J. F. Stenning**, *The Targum of Isaiah* (1949). **J. Stiebert**, *The Construction of Shame in the Hebrew Bible: The Prophetic Contribution* (JSOTSup 246, 2002). **M. Sweeney**, *Isaiah 1-4 and the Post-Exilic Understanding of the Isaianic Tradition* (BZAW 171, 1988); *Isaiah 1-39* (FOTL 16, 1996). **M. E. Tate**, "The Book of Isaiah in Recent Study," in *Forming Prophetic Literature: Essays on Isaiah and the Twelve in honor of John D.W. Watts*, ed. J.W. Watts and P.R. House (JSOTSup 235, 1996). **C. C. Torrey**, *The Second Isaiah* (1928). **G. M. Tucker**, "The Book of Isaiah 1-39," *NIB* 6 (2001). **J. Van Ruiten** and **M. Vervenne** (eds.), *Studies in the Book of Isaiah* (FS W. A. M. Beuken, BETL 132, 1997). **G. Vermes**, *The Dead Sea Scrolls in English* (1987) 61-62, 88, 267-70, 300-301. **J. Vermeylen**, *Du Prophète Isaïe à l'Apocalyptique, Isaïe, I-XXXV, miroir d'un demi-mill,narīe d'experience religieuse en Israel* (Études Bibliques, 2 vols., 1977-78) ; (ed.), *The Book of Isaiah-Le Livre d'Isaïe: Les oracles et leurs relectures. Unité, et complexité, de l'ouvrage* (BETL 81, 1989). **A. Watson**, *The Early Iconography of the Tree of Jesse* (1934, repr. 1978). **C. Westermann**, *Isaiah 40-66* (1969). **J.W. Whedbee**, *Isaiah and Wisdom* (1971). **L. H. M. van Wieringen**, *The Implied Reader in Isaiah 6-12* (*BibInt* series 34, 1998). **B. Wiklander**, *Prophecy as Literature: A Text-linguistical and Rhetorical Approach* (ConBOT 22, 1984). **P. Wilcox** and **D. Paton-Williams**, "The Servant Songs in Deutero-Isaiah," *JSOT* 42 (1988). **H. Wildberger**, *Isaiah 1-12* (tr. T.H. Trapp, 1991);

Isaiah 13-27 (1997). **H. G. M. Williamson**, *The Book Called Isaiah : Deutero-Isaiah's Role in Composition and Redaction* (1994); *Variations on a Theme: King, Messiah, and the Servant in the Book of Isaiah* (1998). **E. J. Young**, *The Book of Isaiah* (NICOT, 1965-72).

J.F.A. SAWYER

THE LATTER PROPHETS: MAJOR

Jeremiah (Interpretation through the 19th Century)

The history of interpretation of the book of Jeremiah is highly complex, beginning within the biblical book itself since the canonical text is represented by at least two different traditions, the MT and the LXX. Because the latter is significantly shorter than the former and also has large parts of the text in a different order, it is now widely agreed that the MT probably reflects an expanded version of a shorter Hebrew *Vorlage*, now represented by the Greek text. While the MT does not contain more chapters or even more oracles than its Greek counterpart, it contains 3,097 words not represented in the LXX, while only 307 words in the LXX have no corresponding parallel in the MT. The MT tends to expand the divine epithets (e.g., "Yahweh of Hosts, the God of Israel," rather than simply "the Lord") as well as the name of Jeremiah (almost always "Jeremiah the prophet" in the MT). Another difference between the two editions is the order of the text; the oracles against the foreign nations in chaps. 46–51 follow 25:38 in the LXX and are presented in a different order. It has further been suggested that the book has undergone extensive Deuteronomistic editing and that such prose passages as 52:1-34 (paralleled by 2 Kgs 24:18–25:30) that did not originally belong to the oracles of Jeremiah have been added.

Outside the book the first specific mention of the prophet in the HB is found in 2 Chr 35:25, where Jeremiah is reported to lament the death of Josiah, and in 2 Chr 36:12, where King Zedekiah is said not to have shown humility before the prophet. The first of these two occurrences seems to associate Jeremiah with the origin of a custom of lamenting as well as with the book of Lamentations. This tradition is also reflected in the LXX translation of Lamentations, which identifies Jeremiah as its author (Lam 1:1), and many subsequent interpretations of the book of Jeremiah treat it in conjunction with the book of Lamentations. Another direct reference to Jeremiah found in 2 Chr 36:22 and Ezra 1:1 pertains to his prediction about the end of the Babylonian exile. This tradition is expressed more specifically in Dan 9:2, which refers to the seventy-year duration of the exile (Jer 25:11-12; 29:10). It is unclear whether a similar reference to seventy years of exile in Zech 1:12 and 7:5 was taken from the book of Jeremiah or whether the author of these passages relied on an independent tradition.

In the Apocrypha, Sir 49:6-7 mentions Jeremiah's prediction of the destruction of Jerusalem as well as his mistreatment by the people. This emphasis on Jeremiah's persecution was to become quite significant for later interpretations of the book, being used to illustrate the stubbornness of the people to whom he prophesied, and is also reflected in several later traditions of Jeremiah's martyrdom. Another, quite different, motif that emerges in the reception of the book in the Apocrypha is that of Jeremiah as an intercessor on behalf of the people. In 2 Macc 15:12-16, where he appears to the high priest Onias and Judas Maccabeus as they are preparing for battle, he is described as a man distinguished by gray hair and dignity who loves the family of Israel and prays for the people and the city of Jerusalem. A third tradition is indicated by 2 Macc 2:1-8, which speaks of Jeremiah making provisions for the rededication of the Temple after the exile. He is reported to have hidden the tent and the ark of the covenant, along with the Temple altar, as well as having instructed the people to preserve some of the Temple fire while in exile and not to forget the law. This exhortation is also reflected in the apocryphal *Letter of Jeremiah* (*Baruch* 6), in which Jeremiah admonishes the exiles against idol worship and which is influenced by the book of Jeremiah, especially chapters 10 and 29.

1. *Early Jewish Interpretation.* While the Qumran community was undoubtedly aware of the book of Jeremiah, as is attested by several fragments, it displayed remarkably small interest in either the figure of Jeremiah or the canonical book. Thus, although the *Damascus Document*

(CD) cites both Isaiah and Ezekiel, it makes no reference to Jeremiah. Attempts to establish a relationship between the "new covenant" of CD and Jeremiah 31 have proved inconclusive. The only quotations from Jeremiah in any Qumran writings are found in the *Hodayoth* (1HQ), and even here the evidence is sparse (1QH 5:7, 22; 25:17; Jer 12:3; 15:1; 16:16). It is noteworthy, however that textual fragments of the book from the second century B.C.E. have been found at Qumran, some of which reflect the MT tradition, while others seem to represent a Hebrew version of the shorter LXX text, lending strength to the theory that the Greek text of Jeremiah is not an abridgement of the MT but is indeed based on an older, shorter Hebrew text.

More significant is the interest in Jeremiah displayed by other early Jewish traditions like the *Paralipomena* of Jeremiah, a work from the second or third century C.E. that elaborates on a number of traditions from the canonical book, especially Jeremiah's conflict with Zedekiah, already noted in 2 Chr 36:12. Jeremiah's designation as "the chosen one of God" may be based on Jer 1:5. Likewise, the emphasis of the Paralipomena on his priestly status may be related to Jer 1:1, although it is likely based on a hagiographic legend about the prophet. Similarly, the *Vita of Jeremiah*, written after 70 C.E., derives much of its biographical information from the book of Jeremiah but also provides its own legends. The reference to Anathoth as Jeremiah's birthplace is inferred from Jer 1:1, while the report of his death in the Egyptian town of Tahpanhes is only loosely based on chapter 43. While the canonical book only mentions that he stayed in Tahpanhes, the *Vita of Jeremiah* observes that he was stoned by the people of Israel in Egypt and was buried near the house of the pharaoh. The text further mentions that Alexander the Great moved Jeremiah's bones to Alexandria, where their presence made all snakes and crocodiles disappear. Other legends found in the *Vita*, e.g., Jeremiah's hiding of the ark, parallel the same tradition as 2 Macc. 2:1-8, while the reference to the return of the glory of God, which had left Zion along with the ark, after all nations have come to venerate the cross is certainly based on a later Christian reworking of the text.

References to Jeremiah by the Jewish historian Eupolemos, transmitted by Eusebius (*Praeparatio evangelica* 9.39), largely follow the biblical text with a few minor exceptions—namely, that Nebuchadnezzar was encouraged to attack Judah by Jeremiah's prophecies of doom and that he brought all the Temple treasures to Babylon, while Jeremiah kept the ark of the covenant along with the tablets of the law. Similarly, Josephus (*A. J.* 10.78.11) based his description of Jeremiah on the HB but emphasized that he, like Ezekiel, was of priestly descent, a tradition also known from the Paralipomena of Jeremiah.

Philo spoke very highly of Jeremiah, devoting more attention to him than to any other biblical prophet. His reading of the book, based on the LXX text, was highly allegorical and platonic, centering on spiritual ideals and the edification of the soul. The interpretive key for Philo was the discernment of certain abstract principles signified by the more literal meaning of the text. Thus, e.g., Jer 15:10 is interpreted as a reference to the struggle of the wise against the dangers to the soul, using the weapons of reason alone (*On the Confusion of Tongues* 44.49-51). Similarly, he read Jer 3:4 as an allusion to God as the father of spiritual ideas and of wisdom (*On the Cherubim* 49, 51).

In rabbinic literature Jeremiah is the paradigmatic prophet of doom. Thus *b. Ber.* 57b associates Ezekiel with wisdom, Isaiah with consolation, and Jeremiah with condemnation. On the other hand, Jeremiah is also seen as an intercessor on behalf of the people, a tradition already found in 2 Maccabees, and is frequently associated with Moses, although he declined the opportunity to assume leadership over the people of Israel (*Mattot* 91d). In *b. Meg.* 14b and *b. ʿArak.* it is also reported that Jeremiah returned the ten northern tribes to the fold of a united kingdom and that Josiah was the last king to govern both Israel and Judah. In addition to such midrashic materials, the book of Jeremiah is frequently used in the development of rabbinic *halakhah*; thus certain legislative traditions are connected to it-e.g., *b. B. Bat.* 160b uses 32:44

as the biblical basis for several purchase documents. Similarly, *b. Sanh.* 11:5 and *t. Sanh.* 14:14 refer to the dispute between Jeremiah and Hananiah (Jeremiah 28) to explain the characteristics that distinguish true from false prophets.

The Talmud seems to place the book of Jeremiah at the beginning of the Major Prophets in the canon, preceding Ezekiel and Isaiah, rather than between the two. The reason for this arrangement is explained theologically in *b. Ber.* 57b, which notes that Jeremiah speaks exclusively of punishment and destruction, Ezekiel begins with destruction but ends with restoration and hope, and Isaiah is entirely concerned with restoration and hope. Of liturgical significance for the synagogue service are *Pesiq. Rab. Kah.* 13 and *Pesiq. Rab.* 2, both of which present readings from the book of Jeremiah to be read before the commemoration of the destruction of the Temple. Although these texts focus on Jeremiah's oracles of judgment against Judah and Jerusalem, each concludes with a more hopeful reference to the eventual restoration of Zion.

2. *Early Christian Interpretation.* In the past it was assumed that many of Paul's writings were heavily influenced by Jeremiah. Certain theological concepts and rhetorical devices were assumed to be derived directly from the book, e.g., the image of the law written into the heart of the people (Jer 31:33), the prophet's appointment while still in his mother's womb (1:5), and above all the concept of a new covenant (31:31). However, while there appears to be a certain intertextual relationship between the Pauline letters and the book of Jeremiah, a direct literal dependence of the former upon the latter is difficult to prove since such images and concepts were undoubtedly part of a larger religio-literary frame of reference that was not exclusive to Jeremiah. On the other hand, it cannot be disputed that the early Christian community was familiar with Jeremiah's concept of a "new covenant" since the LXX text of Jer 31:31-34 is cited almost verbatim by Heb 8:8-12.

In the Gospels Jeremiah is mentioned only in Matt 16:14, which states with regard to the identity of Jesus, "some say John the Baptist, but others Elijah, and still others Jeremiah or one of the prophets," indicating that Jeremiah was a highly revered figure in the first century C.E. Revelation 17–18, a vision of the destruction of Babylon, employs a number of images from Jeremiah 50–51 (judgment against Babylon) as well as from 25:10 (the silence of brides and bridegrooms). The use of Jeremiah in Revelation is based, however, on imagery rather than on direct textual quotation.

The apostolic fathers showed remarkably little interest in Jeremiah. Unlike their early Jewish counterparts they did not develop the themes of judgment and restoration central to the book, since the destruction of the Jerusalem Temple in 70 C.E. had less direct impact on the gentile Christian community. If a particular motif in Jeremiah was used, it was the critique of Israel's sacrificial cult in 7:21-23, cited along with other biblical passages in *Barnabas* 2:5-8 to demonstrate the superiority of the Christian faith over the Jewish religion. This polemical use of Jeremiah as well as of other passages of the HB also characterizes many subsequent Christian readings. Thus Cyprian (*Testimoniorum libri III ad Quirinum*, CSEL 3.1) used Jeremiah's call for the people to circumcise their hearts rather than their flesh (4:4) along with other citations (2:13, 6:10, 8:7-9) to illustrate the Jewish misinterpretation of the HB and of the Israelites' covenant with God. Interestingly, Tertullian employed the same motif of circumcised hearts (4:4) against Marcion's opposition to the HB as Christian Scripture. While Tertullian used this image to demonstrate the newness of the Christian covenant, he emphasized at the same time the impossibility of acknowledging the old covenant on which the new is built (*Marc.* 1.20.4; 4.1.6; 4.11.9; 5.4.10; 5.13.7; 5.19.11).

Prominent among the early church fathers is Jeremiah's use by Origen, especially in his Homilies (*Homiliae in J.*, GCS 3.1-194; GCS 8.290-317). Because these homilies were delivered in a liturgical setting, they systematically cite and explain passages from the LXX text of Jeremiah, mostly from chaps. 1–25, often with intertextual references to other HB or NT texts.

Like many early Christian writers Origen did not place much emphasis on the textual material after chap. 26 (largely prophetic oracles against foreign nations), with the exception of chap. 31, which announces the making of a new covenant, seen by Origen and others as referring to the Christian gospel. Origen's interpretation of Jeremiah, as of other biblical texts, is firmly based on his anthropological understanding of humanity as constituted by body, soul, and spirit, which corresponds to a historical, moral, and mystical sense of Scripture respectively. These three senses must be understood as consistently interdependent rather than as individual layers of meaning. A significant passage in this regard is Jer 18:14-16 (NRSV): "Does the snow of Lebanon leave the crags of Sirion? Do the mountain waters run dry, the cold flowing streams? But my people have forgotten me, they burn offerings to a delusion; they have stumbled in their ways, in the ancient roads, and have gone into bypaths, not the highway, making their land a horror, a thing to be hissed at forever. All who pass by it are horrified and shake their heads." Origen equated the fountain of mountain waters with Christ and stated that the believer must thirst for all three fountains of water (i.e. the historical, moral, and mystical senses of Scripture) in order to find any source of water at all (*Homiliae in J.* 18:9). Although he used the same passage to suggest the insufficiency of the Jewish religion, which rejects Christ and recognizes only one fountain of knowledge, he did not refrain from using Jewish traditions of textual transmission and interpretation. On a purely literary level, since he was well trained in philological matters, he often appealed to the Hebrew text of Jeremiah (*Homiliae in J.* 20:2, 13:2, 14:3). His hermeneutic principles of exegesis and his readings are very close to the allegorical interpretations of Philo of Alexandria, and it must be assumed that he was familiar with the principles of Alexandrian Jewish exegesis, although his own readings were always integrated into the larger tradition of the early church. Thus his allegorical interpretations tended to be christological—e.g., his reading of the gentle lamb led to the slaughter in Jer 11:19.

The most prolific ancient commentator on Jeremiah was Theodoret of Cyrrhus (10 books, PG 81, 495-806). In contrast to the Alexandrian Origen, Theodoret followed the Antiochene exegetical tradition, which largely rejected allegorizing and spiritual readings of the biblical text. As such he read the book of Jeremiah, not in terms of ideas of spiritual edification, but rather in terms of its references to the destruction of Jerusalem, the Babylonian exile, and the announcement of a new covenant, which is also addressed to the gentile world. While Theodoret did not completely avoid christological typologies in his readings of Jeremiah, he tended to subordinate such readings to the more historical sense of the passage in question; thus, following Ephraem the Syrian (*Ephraem Syri Opera* 2:141A), he read the messianic oracle of 23:5 as referring primarily to Zerubbabel and only secondarily to Christ.

In the Western church Jerome likewise rejected excessively allegorizing interpretations of the biblical text. Furthermore, writing in the Latin tradition, he was significantly more critical of the LXX than were his Eastern counterparts, as is reflected in his translation of the Vulgate on the basis of Hebrew texts rather than on the traditional Greek. With regard to Jeremiah he observed that the LXX had been corrupted by copyists to such an extent that its meaning is entirely lost (*Jer. comm. prol.* 2). His interpretation of the book is, like that of Theodoret, based on the historical points of reference that can be derived from the text. Only some passages that were accepted by the church as clearly pointing beyond their immediate historical context, e.g., Jer 11:19, were read as christological pronouncements (*Jer. comm.* 2.110).

Another interpretive principle was emphasized by the Cappadocian Basil the Great, who focused primarily on the book's moral or ethical aspects. Thus, the reference to the lusty stallions in Jer 5:8, seen by several previous writers as an allegorical image for the unfaithful Israelites (cf. e.g., Clement of Alexandria, *Paedagogus* 1.15.1.77.1; 2.89.2) was viewed as a condemnation of sexual excesses. Similarly, the mention of God's nearness in 23:23 was read as an exhortation to base one's behavior on the awareness that all actions are carried out in the presence of God (*De Jejunio Homilia* 1, 9, PG 31 [1885] 181).

Like most of the church fathers, Augustine's interest in Jeremiah was surprisingly small. He cited the book relatively infrequently and did not write a commentary on it. However, it is perhaps interesting to note that he summarized the prophet's life and works in reference to the history of Rome in the sixth century B.C.E., setting up a comparative history and chronology between Israel and Rome (*City of God* 18.33).

3. *The Medieval Period.* During the early Middle Ages only two significant commentaries were written on the book of Jeremiah, one by Odo of Cluny (PL 133, 517-638) and the other by the Carolingian scholar Rabanus Maurus (*PL* 111, 793-1182). While most medieval commentators interpreted the biblical text on the basis of the Quadriga, or four senses of Scripture, the historical or literal sense was generally emphasized in the reading of Jeremiah. This is especially true for Rabanus, whose commentary follows that of Jerome. This tradition is also represented in the *Glossa Ordinaria*, a production of the biblical text with extensive interlinear and marginal glosses that dominated most of medieval biblical interpretation. In the case of Jeremiah most of the glosses seem to derive from Rabanus and Jerome, although it is not entirely clear whether Jerome is in fact cited directly or, as is more likely, indirectly as quoted by Rabanus.

Illustrative of the pervasiveness of this approach to the book in the West during the Middle Ages is also Thomas Aquinas's commentary *Expositio Super Ieremiam et Threnos* (mid-13th cent.). This work, like his commentary on Isaiah, both based on lectures Aquinas delivered in Cologne while he was still studying with Albert, belongs to the genre of rapid or "cursory" readings of the biblical text, focusing on the literal sense with only some marginal notations or "collations" pertaining to spiritual or pastoral applications.

4. *Reformation and Later.* The Reformers seemed to take more interest in the book of Jeremiah and especially in the life of the prophet. Thus Luther, in his *Preface to the Prophet Jeremiah* (1532; *Works of M. Luther with Introductions and Notes* 6 [1982] 408-11), focused on the rejection of Jeremiah by his people and argued that this illustrates the "wickedness of the Jews." In addition to such anti-Jewish sentiments, however, Luther also observed that Jeremiah was not entirely a prophet of doom but also promised hope, in the immediate sense through the return of the people from exile but also through the announcement of Christ and his kingdom. Similarly, Calvin (*Commentaries on the Book of the Prophet Jeremiah and the Lamentations* [1563]; ET 1620) emphasized the idea of the new covenant of Jeremiah 31 and its fulfillment in Christ, already proposed by many of the church fathers. Furthermore, Calvin, like Luther, took interest in the personal life of the prophet and the struggles he faced. In his *Sermons on Jeremiah* (1549; ET 1990), which are fairly eclectic and exegetically rather free, he compared the Babylonian threat against Jeremiah's Jerusalem to the Roman Catholic threat against his own Geneva during the Reformation, noting that both he and Jeremiah were struggling for the glory of God against the enemies of the faith. Other commentaries on Jeremiah written during the sixteenth and seventeenth centuries include works by J. Oecolampadius (1533); J. Bugenhagen (1546); F. Castro Palao (1608); J. Maldonato (1609); C. Sanctius (1618); M. Ghislerius (1623); and J. Alting (1687).

The eighteenth century witnessed a renewed interest in the book. Most significant are the commentaries by W. Lowth (*A Commentary upon the Prophecy and Lamentations of Jeremiah* [1728]) and B. Blayney (1784). While Lowth was largely concerned with the book's historical sense, along with the explanation of theological key ideas, which he explored through intertextual references to other biblical books in the HB and the NT, his commentary also points to new developments in the history of biblical interpretation. First, he incorporated discussions on textual variants with regard to both the order of the chapters in the LXX and the MT and the specific lexical meaning of words and expressions, appealing to Greek, Aramaic, and Syriac translations in order to achieve a greater semantic depth in his reading. While such textual concerns are by no means new, since ancient interpreters like Origen and Jerome were already cognizant of other textual traditions, the pervasiveness of the Vulgate as the authoritative text in the West had put such concerns on hold until the Renaissance. It was not until the Reformation and the development of humanism that questions pertaining to the biblical text were addressed. This new element in biblical interpretation, then, came to its full fruition during the eighteenth century; and Lowth's commentary on Jeremiah is representative of this movement.

More significant, Lowth also began the subdivision of the text into smaller source units or collections. While he did not question that virtually all textual material in the book ultimately came from the prophet, he suggested that Jeremiah's oracles were written down in different collections and were only later combined into the canonical book sometime after the Babylonian exile. Most significant is the collection referred to in 36:2, where Jeremiah is commanded by God in the fourth year of King Jehoiakim to write down all of the prophecies he had to this date spoken against Israel, Judah, and the nations. Lowth argued that this collection was in fact written down by Jeremiah, whereas the oracles delivered after this point up to the fall of Jerusalem were subsequently written down by Jeremiah's disciple Baruch in a collection described in Jer 1:3. A third collection, noted in chaps. 42–44 and describing events after the fall of Jerusalem, was added after the exile, possibly by Ezra, along with some other textual material; e.g., the historical summary of Jeremiah 52, which is chiefly taken from 2 Kings 24–25. Although this division into different collections is still very tentative, it does point toward some of the major source-critical questions central to the interpretation of the book during the first half of the twentieth century, especially by B. Duhm and S. Mowinckel.

Also noteworthy about Lowth's commentary is his emphasis on the need to interpret the biblical text in the context of its historical setting. Thus, although even he did not avoid reading Jeremiah's reference to the new covenant in chap. 31 christologically with reference to the Pauline letters and to Heb 8:8 and 10:16, he did not view Jer 11:19 ("like a gentle lamb led to the slaughter") as a proleptic reference to the suffering of Christ. Instead, he noted that this expression connotes an image of false security or insensibility to danger and even cited a similar expression used in Homer's *Odyssey* in support of his reading.

Blayney's commentary, written toward the end of the eighteenth century, is based on the exegetical principles developed by W. Lowth's son Robert and was intended to do for the book of Jeremiah what R. Lowth had done with Isaiah (1778). The main innovation of this approach was a concern with such stylistic features as acrostics and parallelisms, which Blayney tried to preserve in his English translation. He noted that he had attempted to be faithful to the general sense of the Hebrew text "but also to express each word and phrase by a corresponding one as far as the genius of the two languages would admit," indicating in his notes a literal reading in cases where his translation required a free rendering for stylistic purposes (*Jeremiah and Lamentations*, iv). Most of Blayney's translation is presented in poetic style, in which he tried to preserve the Hebrew parallelism wherever possible, and in cases where no parallelism could be found, he showed sensitivity to the rhythmic and metrical proportions of the text.

This does not mean that Blayney exclusively followed the MT in his translation. In fact, his commentary reflects an even stronger concern with text-critical issues than does that of W. Lowth, and he frequently referred to textual work done by R. Lowth and B. Kennicott in his attempt to reconstruct the original text of Jeremiah's oracles. Thus, in his discussion of the new covenant in chap. 31, he referred to Heb 8:8, not for theological or christological reasons, but rather for text-critical purposes, since the NT passage reflects the LXX text of Jeremiah almost verbatim. Likewise, his notes are primarily concerned with grammatical and philological issues, which he addressed with reference to other Semitic languages like Syriac, Aramaic, and even Arabic. Furthermore, in order to explain the meaning of certain expressions, he referred not only to other books of the Bible but also to such non-biblical authors as Herodotus, Homer, and Horace.

Many of the questions addressed during the eighteenth century received fuller attention in the nineteenth. Especially Lowth's observations about the different collections contained in the book of Jeremiah were the subject of much debate, and different suggestions were made as to how many collections can be identified and how they are best subdivided (J. G. Eichhorn [1803] 116-86; H. Ewald [1840]; F. Hitzig [1841]; F. Movers [1837]). To this was added the question of authenticity. While Lowth and Blayney still viewed most oracles in the book as deriving from the prophet himself, several nineteenth-century scholars attributed some material to later periods. Movers suggested that 10:1-16 as well as chaps. 30–31 and 33 were not in fact genuine prophecies by Jeremiah but were more likely composed by the author of Isaiah 56–66. This view was also adopted by W. De Wette (1817) and by F. Hitzig, whose commentary on Jeremiah was one of the most significant of that century, although strongly opposed by E. Hengstenberg (1829–35; ET 1836–39). Movers's argument was largely based on the observation that Zech 8:7-8 quotes from Jer 31:7-8, 33 and speaks in Zech 8:9 of the author as one who lived in the days when the foundations of the Temple were laid, which led him to the conclusion that these chapters from Jeremiah must have been written by a contemporary of Zechariah. Similarly, Movers and De Wette suggested that the oracles against Babylon in Jeremiah 50–51 do not appear to be genuine, since they contain many interpolations. This was also the view taken by H. Ewald, who had accepted the other chapters rejected by Movers as genuine Jeremiah prophecies, but who proposed that chaps. 50–51 were composed by an author imitating the prophet's style.

Also debated was the authorship of Jeremiah 46–51, the second section of oracles against the nations. Eichhorn was the first to suggest that these chapters, which constitute the last section of the book in the MT before the historical summary of chap. 52, but which follow the first section of oracles against foreign nations (25:15-38) in the LXX, may not have been composed by Jeremiah. He initially proposed that Jeremiah had incorporated the words of earlier prophets into his own composition (*Repertorium für biblische und morgenländische Litteratur* 1 [1777]) but later revised his opinion and argued instead that these chapters are from a later editor (1803). Movers and Hitzig proposed, on the other hand, that only a small core of chaps. 46–51 goes back to the prophet and that this was subsequently expanded during the exile, especially chaps. 50–51.

Another point of debate that emerged during the nineteenth century was the lack of order among the oracles in Jeremiah. Already Blayney had argued that the present order of the book is a rather jumbled arrangement of prophecies from the reigns of Jehoiakim and Zedekiah and that the original order of Jeremiah's oracles must have been disturbed by an ancient editor. Similarly, Eichhorn proposed that Jeremiah might have written his oracles on single scrolls and, in an effort to provide the exiles in Babylon with a copy of his prophecies, dictated them to a follower without paying attention to their chronological order. Another approach was taken by Ewald, who was less concerned with the book's historical coherence than with its poetical structure or unity. He noted that many portions are introduced by the recurring formula "the word which came to Jeremiah from the LORD" (7:1; 11:1; 18:1; 21:1; 25:1; 30:1; 32:1; 34:1; 34:8; 35:1; 40:1; 44:1) or "the word of the LORD which came to Jeremiah" (14:1; 46:1; 47:1; 49:34) as well as by other introductory formulas that have a more historical value (36:1; 37:1; 37:2). Two further sections are thematically distinct and are thus lacking an introduction altogether (23:1; 45:1), while 1:1 serves as a superscription to the first chapter of the book. As a result, the book can be subdivided into twenty-two separate and independent units, which for the poetical section are further divisible into stanzas of seven to nine verses often separated by phrases like "the LORD said also to me."

The turn of the century witnessed an influential, seminal study by Duhm (*Das Buch Jeremia* [KHC 11, 1901]), who analyzed the book on the basis of prose and poetry portions and proposed that it consisted of three independent compositional sections. The first of these contains Jeremiah's prophecies (280 verses), which are entirely in poetic form, while the second part contains his biography (220 verses) in prose as composed by his disciple Baruch. The third and largest portion (850 verses), he suggested, was added by later editors. Even though the question of different collections of oracles as well as the distinction between poetry and prose material had already been addressed in the eighteenth century, Duhm's study was the first to apply to Jeremiah systematically the principles of historical-critical source analysis as outlined by J. Wellhausen with regard to the Pentateuch. Duhm's exegesis thus set the tone for much of twentieth-century scholarship on the book of Jeremiah.

Bibliography: G. L. Berlin, "The Major Prophets in Talmudic and Midrashic Literature" (diss., St. Mary's, 1976). **B. Bernheimer**, "Vitae prophetarum," *JAOS* 55 (1935) 200-203. **B. Blayney**, *Jeremiah and Lamentations: A New Translation with Notes Critical, Philological, and Explanatory* (1784). **W. Bousset** and **H. Gressmann**, *Die Religion des Judentums im späthellenistischen Zeitalter* (HNT 21, 1966). **J. Bowman**, "Prophets and Prophecy in Talmud and Midrash," *EQ* 22 (1950) 107-14, 205-20, 255-75. **F.H. Colson**, "Philo's Quotations from the OT," *JTS* 41 (1940) 237-51. **A. H.W. Curtis** and **T. Romer** (eds.), *The Book of Jeremiah and Its Reception* (BETL 128, 1997). **J. Darling**, *Cyclopaedia Bibliographica: A Library Manual of Theological and General Literature, and Guide to Books for Authors, Preachers, Students, and Literary Men* (1854) 645-66. **E. Dassmann**, *RAC* 17 (1996) 543-631. **G. Delling**, *Jüdische Lehre und Frömmigkeit in den Paralipomena Jeremiae* (BZAW 100, 1967). **W. de Wette**, *A Critical and Historical Introduction to the Canonical Scriptures of the OT* (1817; ET 1843). **J.G. Eichhorn**, *Einleitung in das Alte Testament 3* (1803(r³) 116-86; **E. E. Ellis**, *Paul's Use of the OT* (1957). **H. Ewald**, *Die Propheten des alten Bundes* (3 vols., 1840-41). **E. Fascher**, "Jerusalems Untergang in der urchristlichen und altkirchlichen Überlieferung," *TLZ* 89 (1964) 81-98. **M. Gibson**, "The Twelfth-century Glossed Bible," *StPatr* 23 (1989) 232-44; "The Glossed Bible," *Biblia Latina Cum Glossa Ordinaria: Facsimile Reprint of the Editio Princeps A. Rusch of Strassburg 1480*, 81 (1992) vii-xi. **F. D. Gotch**, *Cyclopedia of Biblical Literature 4* (1866) 495-99; *The Popular and Critical Bible Encyclopaedia and Scriptural Dictionary 2* (1913) 221-23. **S. Granild**, "Jeremia und das Deuteronomium," *StTh* 16 (1962) 135-54. **P. Häuser**, "Barnabas 9:6 und Jer 9:25-26 (LXX)," *TQ* 97 (1915) 499-508. **T. R. Hayward**, "Jewish Traditions in Jerome's Commentary on Jeremiah and the Targum of Jeremiah," *PIBA* 9 (1985) 100-120; *The Targum of Jeremiah: Introduction, Translation, and Commentary* (The Aramaic Bible 12, 1987). **J. Heinemann**, "A Homily on Jeremiah and the Fall of Jerusalem (Pesiqta Rabbini, Pisqa 26)," *The Biblical Mosaic: Changing Perspectives* (ed. R. Polzin and E. Rothmann, 1982) 27-41. **E. Hengstenberg**, *Christology of the OT, and a Commentary on the Predictions of the Messiah by the Prophets* (3 vols. 1829-35; ET 1836–39, 1864–72). **S. Herrmann**, *TRE* 16 (1986) 568-86. **F. Hitzig**, *Die Prophet Jeremia* (KEH 3, 1841). **C. Kannengiesser**, "Les citations bibliques du traité, athanasien sur l'incarnation du Verbe et les 'Testimonia,'" *La Bible at les Pères: Colloque de Strasbourg, 1969* (ed. M. Aubineau et al, 1971) 135-60; *Dictionnaire de Spiritualit, 8* (1974) 889-901; "L'interprétation de Jérémie dans la tradition alexandrine," *StPatr* 12 (TU 115, 1975) 317-20. **A. S. Kapelrud**, "Der Bund in den Qumran-Schriften,"*Bibel und Qumran* (ed. S. Wagner, 1968) 137-49. **G. Kisch**, *Pseudo-Philo's* "Liber antiquitatum biblicarum" (PMS 10, 1949). **J. R. Lundbom**, *ABD* (1992) 3:706-21. **F. Lurz**, "Jeremia in der Liturgie der Alten Kirche," *Ecclesia Orans 9* (1992)

141-71. **J. Lust**, "Messianism and the Greek Version of Jeremiah," *VII Congress of the International Organization for Septuagint and Cognate Studies* (ed. C. Cox, 1991) 87-122. **U. Luz**, "Der alte und neue Bund bei Paulus und im Hebräerbrief," *EvTh* 27 (1967) 318-36. **A. Marmorstein**, "Die Quellen des neuen Jeremia-Apocryphons," *ZNW* 27 (1928) 327-37. **E. A. Matter**, "The Church Fathers and the Glossa Ordinaria," *The Reception of the Church Fathers in the West: From the Carolingians to the Maurists* (ed. I. D. Backus, 1997) 83-111. **R. Meyer,** "Paralipomena Jeremiae," *RGG 3* (1959) 102-3. **F. Movers**, *De utriusque Vaticiniorum Jeremiae recensionis indole et origine* (1837). **Origen**, *Homilies on Jeremiah* (tr. J.C. Smith ; FC 97, 1998). **M. Pesty**, "La Septante et sa lecture patristique, un example: Jer‚mie 3,22–4,1," *Rashi, 1040-1990: Hommage . . . E. E. Urbach* (ed. G. Sed-Rajna, 1993) 173-82. **L. Prijs** (ed.), *Die Jeremia-Homilie Pesikta Rabbati Kap. 26: Eine synagogale Homilie aus nachtalmudischer Zeit über den Propheten Jeremia und die Zerstörung des Tempels* (StDel 10, 1966). **E. Schadel**, *Origenes: Die griechisch erhaltenen Jeremia Homilien* (Bibliothek der griechischen Literatur 10, 1980). **N. Schmid**, *Encyclopaedia Biblica 2* (1901) 2372-95. **S. Soderlund**, *The Greek Text of Jeremiah: A Revised Hypothesis* (JSOTSup. 47, 1985). **H. O. Thompson**, *The Book of Jeremiah: An Annotated Bibliography* (ATLA Bibliographies 25, 1996). **J. D. Thompson,** *A Critical Concordance to the Septuagint Jeremiah* (The Computer Bible 74, 2000). **K. J. Torjesen**, *Hermeneutical Procedure and Theological Method in Origen's Exegesis* (1985). **J. P. Torrell**, *Saint Thomas Aquinas 1* (1996) 27-28, 337. **C. C. Torrey**, *The Lives of the Prophets* (JBLMS 1, 1946). **E. Tov**, *The Septuagint Translation of Jeremiah and Baruch: A Discussion of an Early Revision of the LXX of Jeremiah 29–52 and Baruch 1:1–3:8* (HSM 8, 1976); "Exegetical Notes on the Hebrew Vorlage of the LXX of Jeremiah 27 (34)," *ZAW* 91 (1979) 73-93; "The Literary History of the Book of Jeremiah in Light of Its Textual History," *Empirical Models for Biblical Criticism* (ed. J. Tigay, 1985) 211-37; "The Jeremiah Scrolls from Qumran," *RevQ* 14 (1989) 187-204; "Three Fragments of Jeremiah from Qumran Cave 4," *RevQ* 15 (1992) 530-41. **C. Wolff**, *Jeremia im Frühjudentum und Urchristentum* (TU 118, 1976); "Irdisches und Himmlisches Jerusalem: Die Heilshoffnung in den Paralipomena Jeremiae," *ZNW* 82 (1991) 147-58. **J. Ziegler**, "Jeremia Zitate in Väter-Schriften: Zugleich grundsätzliche Betrachtungen über Schrift-Zitate in Väter-Ausgaben," *Theologie aus dem Geist der Geschichte* (FS B. Altaner, 1958) 347-57.

A. SIEDLECKI

THE LATTER PROPHETS: MAJOR

Jeremiah (20th and 21st Century Interpretation)

Jeremiah's call to be a prophet is located in the thirteenth year of Josiah (c. 626 B.C.E.), but controversy has raged around this date. Noted in both Jer 1:2 and 25:3, this double occurrence of the date creates difficulties for those who suppose that "thirteen" arises from a textual corruption of "twenty-three" and that the call of Jeremiah took place in 616 rather than 626 B.C.E. The hypothesis of accidental corruption falls if the two notices are independent of each other, but even if one is derived from the other, it has to be assumed that the prior one was corrupted before it became the source of the dependent one. Other dates have been produced by literary-critical analysis coupled with textual emendation, the most common being 609 B.C.E. (F. Horst [1923]; J.P. Hyatt [1951]; and W. Holladay [1986–89]), although 605 has also been proposed (C. Whitley 1964]). It has been argued that Jer 1:2 should be deleted and that "He was active in the reign of Jehoiakim" (1:3) marks the beginning of Jeremiah's prophetic activity. The general reason for dissatisfaction with 626 is that a long period of prophetic inactivity between 621 and 609 has to be supposed. The representation of a call in 626 is said to be a consequence of deuteronomic interference guided by a desire to associate Jeremiah with the reform of Josiah. The necessity of assuming the inactivity of the prophet over a long period has encouraged the view that there is a case for the application of Occam's razor and for the conclusion that Jeremiah began his work in 609, and that 626 was perhaps the year of his birth.

Bearing on Jeremiah's biography is the problem of the "enemy from the north," if it is supposed that the original reference was to the Scythians. Here we stand on controversial ground. There is a reference to an enemy from the north in Jer 1:14, and the passages B. Duhm (1901) entitled "Scythian Songs" (4:5-8, 11-17, 19-21, 23-26, 29-31; 6:1-5, 22-26; 8:14-17; 10:19-22). Some scholars still hold the view that the "enemy from the north" referred originally to the Scythians, who had overrun Palestine and were maintaining a hostile presence there at the time of Jeremiah's call in 626. Even if there was an earlier enemy from the north, the only one present in the book of Jeremiah is Babylon, and the exegesis of the above passages should be pointed in that direction. A. Welch (1928) solved the problem by arguing that the enemy was part of a scheme depicting eschatological judgment.

Although the beginnings of Jeremiah's ministry remain in some doubt, there is no compelling alternative to a 626 date for his call. The presentation of his subsequent career is more straightforward, however. He was active in the reigns of Jehoiakim and Zedekiah until the exile of 587 and after the fall of Jerusalem was coerced by Johanan son of Kareah into going to Egypt (43:1-7). The description of him as "a prophet to the nations" (1:5) has troubled commentators; special pleading is required to reconcile this with Jeremiah's concentration on the Judean community. While there is probably some connection between "prophet to the nations" and the oracles against foreign nations that are part of the book (chaps. 46–51), there are different views about the relation of these oracles to the historical Jeremiah (see B. Huwyler's survey [1997]). W. Rudolph (1947, 1968(r)¯3) took a positive view and included them in his source A and also in the contents of the scroll of 605 (36:1). The most probable conclusion is that the phrase "prophet to the nations" is primarily a description of a Jeremiah corpus containing the oracles against foreign nations and that it sets us at a distance from the historical Jeremiah. There is, however, an argument that these oracles represent the earliest phase of Jeremiah's prophetic activity and that he was a "nationalistic" prophet before he became a prophet of "doom."

1. *Contents.* Poetic oracles of doom directed against Judah feature prominently in Jeremiah 1–25. These threats are supported and justified by legal arguments and indictments, and the poetry is interspersed with small and large passages of prose. The longer prose passages are rep-

resented by chap. 7, which has only one verse of poetry (v. 29) and is generally anti-cultic in tone; also by chap. 11, which has a more transparent deuteronomic/deuteronomistic character ("deuteronomic" is used of prose that has affinities with the book of Deuteronomy, and "deuteronomistic" of prose whose particular associations are with the vocabulary, word strings, and style of the framework of Joshua–2 Kings).

The prose in Jeremiah 1–25 has generally been identified as having deuteronomic or deuteronomistic affinities (see the essays in W. Gross [1995]) and has commonly been distinguished from the prose of the so-called Baruch biography, sometimes described as a passion narrative because it describes Jeremiah's suffering in the fulfillment of his prophetic vocation. According to Rudolph, Baruch's work is represented in these chapters by 19:1-10, 14-15 and 20:1-6, but it appears principally in chapters 26–51 (26; 28; 29; 34:1–38:28a; 38:28b–40:6; 40:7-43:12; 44; 45; 51:59-64). This leaves as the principal remainder of the second half of the book prophecies of hope for the restoration of Jerusalem (chaps. 30-33); an account of an abortive rising against Babylon that involved Jeremiah in symbolic action (chap. 27—Rudolph's source A); a report of how Zedekiah reneged on the freeing of slaves (34:8-22—Rudolph's source C); a narrative of Jeremiah's encounter with the Rechabites (chap. 35—also source C); and the oracles against foreign nations already mentioned (chaps. 46–51). Chapter 52 is a historical note on the fall of Jerusalem derived from 2 Kgs 24:18–25:30.

A special category of material, mostly poetry, is constituted by the "laments" or "complaints," whether those exploring the anguish Jeremiah felt in the pursuit of his prophetic vocation (8:18-23; 12:1-5; 15:10-21; 17:9-18; 20:7-9) or those in which he appears in a communal context as an intercessor (e.g. 14:2-10; 14:17–15:4). The oracles against foreign nations have a poetic form and are differently located in the Hebrew and Greek texts: chaps. 46–51 in the Hebrew and 25:15-31 in the Greek (Septuagint). Jeremiah 25:1-13 has been widely regarded as the conclusion of the preceding part of the book and has been drawn into discussions about the contents of the two scrolls mentioned in chapter 36: the one destroyed by Jehoiakim (vv. 1-8) and the enlarged scroll written again by Baruch (vv. 27-32). "In this book" (25:13) is taken as a reference to either the first or the second scroll. But 25:1-13 will fit as a conclusion to the preceding part of the book only if "that land" (v. 13) is emended to "this land," and here the wish is father to the thought. "That land" refers to Babylon just as "that nation" does in v. 12. Jeremiah 25:1-13 is an introduction to the oracles against foreign nations, and it appears immediately before them in the order of the Septuagint.

The contents of the scrolls have been differently identified by Rudolph with (a) oracles of doom against Judah, including some prose, and (b) oracles against foreign nations (chaps. 45–49). O. Eissfeldt (1964; ET 1965) speculated that the scrolls were made up of the prose in chaps. 1–25 and amounted to a considered retrospect of the oracles Jeremiah had delivered over a period of twenty-three years (25:3). A similar view appears in B. Childs (1979).

2. *Criticism.* A source theory formulated by S. Mowinckel in 1914 was subsequently adopted by Rudolph and others and has gained wide acceptance. The three sources are specified as A, B, and C, with the extent of the B source indicated above. B is ascribed to Baruch, Jeremiah's "scribe"; it is biographical in character and is narrated in the third person. Source A, according to Rudolph, consists of sayings of Jeremiah largely made up of oracles of doom addressed to Judah in chaps. 1–25 but including threats directed against foreign nations (chaps. 46–49). It is comprised for the most part of poetry, but prose is not excluded (e.g. 3:6-13; 14:14-16; 23:25-32).

The C source is mostly identified with the prose interspersed with the poetry in Jeremiah 1-25 (7:1–8:3; 11:1-14[17]; 16:1-13; 17:19-27; 18:1-12; 21:1-10; 22:1-5; 25:1-14) and otherwise only at 34:8-22, 35. It is said to consist of sayings of Jeremiah that have undergone a deuteronomic or deuteronomistic editing and do not retain their original linguistic constituents. J.

Bright (1965) questioned the view that the prose of source C is deuteronomic or deuterono-mistic in the exact sense that has been supposed, describing it generally as sixth century. H. Weippert (1973) has examined individual items of vocabulary and word strings of source C in order to show by lexicographical and exegetical arguments that there are significant differences between this prose and that of the book of Deuteronomy or the deuteronomistic historical liter-ature. Her object is the highly particular one of reclaiming the prose of the postulated source C for the historical Jeremiah—nothing less than the prophet's prose style.

The C source is mainly located in the first half of the book and the B source in the second half. B has been represented as a contemporary historical source that enables us to make imme-diate contact with the historical prophet Jeremiah. It is an account and interpretation of his prophetic activity by Baruch that has the advantage of presence at and involvement in great issues as they emerged and developed. The true prophet is wrapped in an environment of dark-ness and misunderstanding in which the truth does not prevail over falsehood; consequently, he is marked out for alienation, suffering, and failure. In contrast, C is said to be a view of the prophet in retrospect, one that has historical value but is colored by the conditions and concerns of the Jewish community in Babylon. What scholars make of the historical Jeremiah is influ-enced by the theological problems with which they wrestle and the methods they adopt to solve these problems. They seek to do this in agreement with a deuteronomic view of the prophetic office that gives high priority to its intercessory function. The eventuation of exile has sealed the truth of Jeremiah's predictions of doom, but the failure of this true prophet to make an effec-tive impact on the late pre-exilic community he addressed is a theological problem that calls for clarification.

The validity of this kind of distinction between the B and C sources has been called into ques-tion, with doubts arising as to whether its linguistic basis is assured—whether the prose of source B can be sharply distinguished from the prose of source C—as well as to whether the historical background of B is different from that of C. In 1970 E. Nicholson urged that a setting in the exilic community should also be assumed for B and that it is the circumstances and con-cerns of this period that are being addressed. He argued for both sources that a more sensitive exegetical appreciation of the literature will identify processes of reflection by the exilic com-munity that will generate a reinterpretation of the activity of the historical Jeremiah.

The view that the book of Jeremiah has been largely expanded by deuteronomic or deuteron-omistic (Dtr) editors and that it has been shaped into a coherent theological whole by the work-ing out of leading principles was earlier considered by Hyatt but is associated particularly with W. Thiel (1973, 1981). Applying especially to the relation between the poetry and prose in Jeremiah 1–25, it has been argued by Thiel in great detail. An important assumption of his method is that prose compositions attributed to Dtr inhere within a kernel or core, which may be poetry or may be critically reconstructed into poetry by Thiel, but which may also be prose. The composition that arises from these processes of expansion and transformation may be small, medium, or large, for Thiel supposes that the work of Dtr has an all-embracing charac-ter and that there is a master plan in which the units of composition are like the bricks of an edi-fice.

Thiel's contribution to the elucidation of the relations between poetry and prose in Jeremiah 1–25 is a notable one, but the question that ought to be asked is whether the book has as high a degree of literary or theological organization as he represents. There is something to be said for more localized investigations that keep very close to the text and do not have such high expectations of disclosing cohesive compositions shaped by broad theological principles. Whether one envisions a piece of poetry that generates prose, there is a virtue in seeking nar-row exegetical explanations that are not disengaged from the details of the text. The argument will then be that prose expansions that are contiguous (or almost contiguous) with a piece of poetry or prose are precisely attempts at exegetical elucidation of verses to which they are adjacent in the extant text, and that this is the primary, local understanding that is needed.

This view, founded on exegetical considerations, is reinforced by what the book of Jeremiah discloses about the history of the Hebrew text. The argument is that there are secondary prose additions and that they have the character of exegetical expansions of poetry or prose already established in the Jeremiah corpus. The text-critical support for this is made possible, in the first place, because the text of the Septuagint in Jeremiah is shorter than that of the MT. This would have no text-critical significance if it were supposed that this state of affairs has been produced by abbreviations of the Hebrew text in the Septuagint. Although this should not be ruled out entirely as an explanation of individual cases, for the most part the shortness of the Greek text is accounted for by the fact that the Hebrew *Vorlage* used by the Alexandrian translators of the Septuagint was shorter than the MT. A comparison of the MT with the Septuagint in the book of Jeremiah will reveal that the history of the Hebrew text involves a process of addition and expansion. The hypothesis that a secondary exegetical expansion of the Jeremiah corpus occurred is not, therefore, merely speculative; its probability is indicated by hard textual evidence. Jeremiah 10:1-16 is a particularly interesting example because a Hebrew text fragment found in Cave 4 at Qumran (4QJer[b]) corresponds to the text of the Septuagint, where it differs from the MT. In this case it can be asserted categorically that the Septuagint derives from a Hebrew text shorter than that of the MT. There is good reason for holding that 10:1-16 was built up by successive additions, each generated by the preexisting text or part of it. The Septuagint does not represent vv. 6-8, and v. 9 is located within v. 5 of the MT; however, the general point is that a secondary exegetical expansion is supported by the textual tradition.

3. *Exegesis.* Weippert's view of the prose in the book of Jeremiah foreshortens the processes of composition. If the prose is largely to be attributed to Jeremiah, by implication the corpus had, more or less, achieved its extant shape during his lifetime, an extra-linguistic factor that makes Weippert's view on the authorship of the prose difficult to accept. It is hard to believe that the extant Jeremiah corpus had so brief a history of composition when indications are rather that the processes of composition that brought the corpus to its final shape proceeded by installments over a long period. The stages are difficult to recover because there are haphazard factors at work, and it should not be supposed that this long period of growth was everywhere guided by a literary master plan, by a systematic theology, or by a canonical intention.

Rudolph's interest, like that of Weippert, is focused on the historical prophet Jeremiah; but Rudolph does not suppose that the prose of his source C is Jeremiah prose. Nevertheless, although Rudolph analyzes the prose of source C as deuteronomic, his exegetical use of this source is focused on the prophet Jeremiah and the historical conditions of his ministry, not on the reinterpretation of the prophet by the Jewish exilic community. Hence his assumption is that the linguistic transformation that has taken place in source C has not obliterated Jeremiah's sayings and that what is deuteronomic in their presentation can be peeled off to disclose the content of his utterances in the historical circumstances of the late preexilic period.

The same is partly true of Nicholson's attitude toward source B. He has two strings on his bow, however; and although he is concerned to emphasize that the historical Jeremiah and the background of the late preexilic period have not been obliterated, his main exegetical point is to throw light on aspects of the reinterpretation of the historical Jeremiah against the background of exilic conditions. Whereas the historical Jeremiah is Rudolph's focus in his exegetical use of source C, Jeremiah as construed by the exilic community is Nicholson's exegetical focus in his handling of source B. The other side of Nicholson's concern is historical rather than exegetical. He urges that by transporting the exegesis of source B from late preexilic Jerusalem to the Babylonian exile he is not denying its value as a historical source. The extant exilic shape that discloses its exegetical significance can be peeled off to leave a reliable historical residue.

Thiel's assumptions remove us more decisively from the historical context of Jeremiah's ministry because his exegetical investigations are largely directed toward the elucidation of a comprehensive theology imposed on the Jeremiah corpus by his Dtr editor. His view that the processes involved in the composition of the book are long and complicated is realistic, and these processes carry us into exilic and even postexilic times.

4. *The Suffering Prophet.* It has been generally supposed that of all the prophetic books Jeremiah gives us the best access to the humanity of a prophet and that this window opens perceptions that contribute to an especially profound prophetic theology (see the older works of J. Skinner and G. A. Smith). The individual "laments" or "complaints" (discussed above) have been regarded as one such mode of access; but this view has been challenged by H. G. Reventlow (1963), who describes this expectation and the interpretation it encourages as a psychological fallacy. He argues that the so-called individual laments do not give us an insight into the tensions the prophetic vocation created in an individual prophet, and that they reveal only the cultic language appropriate in the mouth of a prophet discharging a representative intercessory function on behalf of the community. It has already been indicated that there are communal laments in the book of Jeremiah, but there are also individual laments describing the anguish of the prophet that cannot be metamorphosed into communal laments.

So far as communal laments are concerned, it is unlikely that the theology they project is attributable to the prophet Jeremiah. The theme "interdict on intercession," which appears in 14:2-9 and 14:17–15:4, is also present at 7:16 and 11:14. Instead of enlisting this feature as evidence of Jeremiah's originality in contrast to the cultic models he employs, this interdict should be seen as an attempt by the exilic community to throw light on troubling theological problems. The "interdict on intercession" formula enabled them to affirm their theology of prophecy, in which the prophet appeared as an effective intercessor, and at the same time to explain the disaster of exile and to embrace Jeremiah as a true prophet.

The individual laments are a different matter, however, demanding an interpretation that focuses on the human cost of prophetic responsibility as it was endured by the historical Jeremiah. But this protest against the contradictions of the prophetic vocation and the anguish these generate should not be interpreted negatively, not, e.g., at Jer 12:1-5 or at any other place where they rise to the surface. A view that puts the emphasis on Jeremiah's rebelliousness can cause distortion. Jeremiah is represented as having rebelled in 12:14 and in similar contexts where his words throb with the pain of a commitment that seems to be wrecked by circumstances he cannot defeat. We are told that this is the voice of a prophet who has lost his way, whose words are an expression of his willfulness, and who must repent and return to Yahweh, as he is required to do in 12:5 (cf. 14:19). Neither in these passages nor at 20:7, where Jeremiah accuses Yahweh of having deceived him, can the anguish of a prophet be reduced to mere human sinfulness without inflicting major theological damage. These passages teach us not to divorce the human from the divine in a theology of prophecy. The profundity of prophetic truth grasped by Jeremiah is not separable from his human anguish, and "word of God" must not be taken so literally that it is divorced from the discovery of prophetic truth at great human cost. The interpretation of "word of God" in these laments as no more than the activity of a speaking God who finally intervenes to chide the prophet for his waywardness results in great theological impoverishment. Jeremiah could not have appropriated the truth that the prophetic vocation is full of suffering, that there would be no remission, and that the burdens of sorrow would become heavier without enduring the strife and struggles expressed at 12:1-4; 15:10, 15-18; or 20:7.

The idea that Yahweh has deceived Jeremiah has to be linked with Jeremiah's conviction that Yahweh has also deceived the people (4:10). What does this mean? The emphasis on doom in Jeremiah's preaching is connected with his conviction that clarification cannot be achieved and the truth cannot be communicated to the people. The shalom prophets supported by the impeccable authority of the Jerusalem Temple assure the people that all is well, and Jeremiah urges that the people are not to be blamed for believing those who speak in the name of Yahweh. How in these circumstances can truth defeat the lie? It is this kind of prophetic imprisonment that frustrates Jeremiah's attempts to reach his community with a message he knows to be true. He is defeated by the authority of a religious institution with which Yahweh seems to have conspired to deny effectiveness to Jeremiah's witness. Jeremiah suffers pain because of his estrangement and rejection, in this regard serving as the forerunner of the One who came to his own and was rejected by them (John 1:11). It is understandable that he was identified by exegetes with the Suffering Servant of Isaiah 40–55.

5. *Feminist Literary Concerns.* Many scholars are reading Jeremiah with eyes for gender issues and have discovered a plenitude of female language and imagery, yet with ambiguities in the way these images have been employed (see K. O'Connor [1992]). For instance, the pain of Jerusalem is personified in the suffering of women, suggesting that the prophet was sensitive to the women's plight. Moreover, God is portrayed as a mother (31:20) and as one who laments and weeps over Israel (8:19–9:3), a traditionally female role in the ancient Near East. In contrast, female imagery is negatively coded in personified Israel, the adulterous woman, prostitute, and wicked daughter. Additionally, women in Judah are directly aligned with idolatry when they are accused of kneading dough to bake cakes for the queen of heaven (7:18) or, most likely, the goddess they worship alongside the God of Israel (see S. Ackerman [1989]).

Bibliography: S. Ackerman, "'And the Women Knead Dough': The Worship of the Queen of Heaven in the Sixth-century Judah," *Gender and Difference in Ancient Israel* (ed. P. L. Day, 1989) 75-94. **A. Bauer**, *Gender in the Book of Jeremiah* (Studies in Biblical Literature 5, 1999). **P. M. Bogaert**, *Le Livre de Jérémie: Le prophète et son milieu, les oracles et leur transmission* (BETL 54, 1981). **J. Bright**, *Jeremiah* (AB 21, 1965). **R. P. Carroll**, *From Chaos to Covenant: Uses of Prophecy in the Book of Jeremiah* (1981); *Jeremiah: A Commentary* (OTL, 1986); *Jeremiah* (OTG, 1989). **B. S. Childs**, *Introduction to the OT as Scripture* (1979) 339-541. **A. H. W. Curtis** and **T. Römer**, eds., *The Book of Jeremiah and Its Reception = le livre de Jérémie et sa réception* (BETL 138, 1997). **B. Duhm**, *Das Buch Jeremia* (KHC 11, 1901). **O. Eissfeldt**, *The OT: An Introduction* (1964; ET 1965) 346-65. **J. Ferry**, *Illusions et salut dans la prédication propheétique de Jérémie* (BZAW 269, 1999). **K.G. Friebel**, *Jeremiah's and Ezekiel's Sign-Acts* (JSOTSup 283, 1999). **W. Gross** (ed.), *Jeremia und die "deuteronomische Bewegung"* (BBB 98, 1995). **S. Herrmann**, *Jeremia: Der Prophet und das Buch* (Erträge der Forschung 271, 1990). *Jeremiah* (BKAT 12, 1986–). **J. Hill**, *Friend or Foe? The Figure of Babylon in the Book of Jeremiah MT* (BibInt 40, 1999). **W.L. Holladay**, *Jeremiah* (Hermeneia, 2 vols., 1986–89). **F. Horst**, "Die Anfänge des Propheten Jeremia," *ZAW* 41 (1923) 111-12. **B. Huwyler**, *Jeremia und die Völker* (FAT 20, 1997). **J. P. Hyatt**, "The Deuteronomic Edition of Jeremiah," *Vanderbilt Studies in the Humanities 1* (ed. R. C. Beatty et al., 1951) 77-95 Perdue-Kovacs, 247-67; "The Beginning of Jeremiah's Prophecy," *ZAW* 78 (1966) 204-14 Perdue-Kovacs, 63-87. **N. Ittmann**, *Die Konfessionen Jeremias* (WMANT 54, 1981). **M. Kessler,** *Battle of the Gods: The God of Israel Versus Marduk of Babylon: A Literary/Theological Interpretation of Jeremiah 50-51* (2003). **J. Kiss**, *Die Klage Gottes und des Propheten: ihre Rolle in der Komposition und Redaktion von Jer 11-12, 14-15 und 18* (WMANT 99, 2003). **H. Lalleman deWinkel,** *Jerimaih in Prophetic Tradition: An Examination of the Book of Jeremiah in the Light of Israel's Prophetic Traditions* (CBET 26, 2000). **C. Maier,** *Jeremia als Lehrer der Tora: Soziale Gebote des Deuteronomiums in Fortschreibungen des Jeremiabuches* (FRLANT 196, 2002). **J. Maier**, *Ägypten-Israels Herkunft und Geschick: Studie über einen theo-politischen Zentralbegriff im hebräischen Jeremiabuch* (ÖBS 21, 2002). **S. Manfredi**, *Geremia in* *dialogo: nessi con le tradizioni profeticche e originalità in Ger 4,5 – 6,30* (2002). **W. McKane**, *A Critical and Exegetical Commentary on Jeremiah* (ICC, 2 vols., 1986-96). **S. Mowinckel**, *Zur Komposition des Buches Jeremia* (SUVK 2, historisk-filosofisk Klasse 5, 1914). **E. W. Nicholson**, *Preaching to the Exiles: A Study of the Prose Tradition in the Book of Jeremiah* (1970). **K. M. O'Connor**, "Jeremiah," *Women's Bible Commentary* (eds. C. A. Newsom and S. H. Ringe, 1992). **G. H. Parke-Taylor**, *The Formation of the Book of Jeremiah: Doublets and Recurring Phrases* (SBLMS 51, 2000). **L. G. Perdue** and **B. W. Kovacs** (eds.), *A Prophet to the Nations: Essays in Jeremiah Studies* (1984). **R. F. Person**, *The Kings-Isaiah and Kings-Jeremiah Recensions* (BZAW 252, 1997). **H. G. Reventlow**, *Liturgie und prophetisches Ich bei Jeremia* (1963). **C. Rietzschel**, *Das Problem der Urrolle* (1966). **H. H. Rowley**, "The Prophet Jeremiah and the Book of Deuteronomy," *Studies in OT Prophecy Presented to Professor T. H. Robinson* (1950) 157-74 = his *From Moses to Qumran: Studies in the OT* (1963) 187-208; "The Early Prophecies of Jeremiah in Their Setting," *BJRL* 45 (1962–63) 198-234 = his *Men of God* (1963) 133-68 = Perdue-Kovacs, 13-61. **W. Rudolph**, *Jeremia* (HAT 1, 12, 1947, 1968). **C. J. Sharp**, *Prophecy and Ideology in Jeremiah: Struggles for Authority in Deutero-Jeremianic Prose* (2003). **A. G. Shead**, *The Open Book and the Sealed Book: Jeremiah 32 in its Hebrew and Greek Recensions* (JSOT 347, 2002). **J. Skinner**, *Prophecy and Religion: Studies in the Life of Jeremiah* (1992). **G. A. Smith**, *Jeremiah* (Baird Lectures, 1922). **J. Stiebert**, *The Constructions of Shame in the Hebrew Bible: the Prophetic Contribution* (JSOTSup 346, 2002). **L. Stulman**, *Order amid Chaos: Jeremiah as Symbolic Tapestry* (Biblical Seminar 57, 1998). **W. Thiel**, *Die deuteronomistische Redaktion von Jeremia 1–25* (WMANT 41, 1973); *Die deuteronomistische Redaktion von Jeremia 26–45* (WMANT 52, 1981). **J. D. Thompson**, *A Critical Concordance to the Septuagint Jeremiah* (The Computer Bible 74, 2000). **H. Weippert**, *Die Prosareden des Jeremiabuches* (BZAW 132, 1973). **A. Weiser**, *Das Buch Jeremia* (ATD 20-21, 1952, 1969). **A. C. Welch**, *Jeremiah: His Time and His Work* (1951). **C. F. Whitley**, "The Date of Jeremiah's Call," *VT 14* (1964) 467-83 = Perdue-Kovacs, 73-87; "Carchemish and Jeremiah," *ZAW 80* (1968) 38-49 = Perdue-Kovacs, 163-73.

W. McKane

Lamentations

One of the Five Scrolls (*Megilloth*) of the Kethubim section of the HB, Lamentations is recited in Jewish services for *Tishe ʿah be-Ab*, the ninth day of the month Ab, as a memorial to the destruction of Jerusalem and the Solomonic and Herodian temples. In the Leningrad and Aleppo codices the Five Scrolls are grouped together, with Lamentations appearing fourth, while in most printed HBs Lamentations appears third among the scrolls according to its place in the annual Jewish liturgical calendar.

The book, named *ʾêkâ* (How?) in the Hebraic tradition for the first word of the book, is also known as *qînôtt* (Laments) and *megillath ʾêkâ/qînôth* (*Scroll of How?/Laments*) in rabbinic writings (see Jerome's term *Cinoth* in his *Prologus Galeatus*). It is called *threnoi* (Dirges) or *threnoi ʾIeremíou* (Dirges of Jeremiah) in the Septuagint, *Lamentationes* in the Latin, and "The Book of Lamentations of Jeremiah the Prophet" in the Syriac Peshitta.

The five chapters of Lamentations are five alphabetic poems, the first four of which are alphabetic acrostics. (*ʿayin/pe* is reversed in poems 2–4.) The fifth poem is considered to be alphabetic because it contains twenty-two verses, the number of letters in the Hebrew alphabet, even though it appears not to be an acrostic. (See, however, S. Bergler, "Threni V—nur ein alphabetisierendes Lied? Versuch einer Deutung," *VT* 27 (1977) 304-20, for a not altogether convincing attempt to read the opening letter of each verse as an acrostic sentence.)

Judging from manuscript evidence and from the versions, the text of Lamentations has not suffered significant deterioration. Moreover, there are no indications of any great difficulty with canonizing the book, in contrast to Song of Songs, Ecclesiastes, and Esther. The problems of interpreting Lamentations have focused on issues of authorship and date, purpose and theology, literary analysis, and interpretation of the *dramatis personae*.

1. *Author and Date*. Although the book of Lamentations is anonymous in the HB, Jeremiah was viewed universally as its author before the era of historical and literary criticism. Its date of composition was placed either shortly after the destruction of Jerusalem by the Babylonians (c. 586 B.C.E.) or at the time of King Josiah's death (see 2 Chr 35:25). In addition to the Septuagint, the Targum also attributes Jeremiad authorship, as do *Lamentations Rabbah* (see, e.g., Petihtoth 12-14, 22, 26, 27, 31, 32, and *Parashah One* on Lam 1:1) and rabbinic tradition (see, e.g., *b. Babylonian Talmud, B. Bat.* 15a). In the Septuagint, the Peshitta, and the Vulgate, Lamentations is placed immediately following the book of Jeremiah; in the Septuagint and the Vulgate, Lamentations opens with a prologue or subtitle attributing it to the prophet Jeremiah. The church fathers consistently assumed Jeremiah to be the author. In the Middle Ages Rashi began his commentary by stating that Jeremiah wrote Lamentations and that it was the scroll that King Jehoiakim burned. Ibn Ezra accepted Jeremiah as author but denied on textual grounds that Lamentations was the scroll Jehoiakim burned. Calvin (see, e.g., comments on Lam 1:1; 2:20; 3:1), along with other reform scholars, continued in this tradition.

The first to question Jeremiad authorship seems to have been H. von der Hardt, who in 1712 proposed that the five poems were composed by Daniel, Shadrach, Meshach, Abednego, and King Jehoiachin respectively (G. Ricciotti [1924] 35). Most scholars of the nineteenth century (e.g., J. Augusti, C. Conz, H. Ewald, E. Schrader, T. Nöldeke, A. Kuenen, C. Nägelsbach, T. Cheyne) concluded, however, that Jeremiad authorship could not be maintained on the basis of either internal or external evidence. They tended to look to some student(s) of Jeremiah as author(s), although a few continued to support Jeremiah's authorship (see C. Keil [1872] and W. Hornblower [Nägelsbach, 1871]; O. Thenius [1855] held that only chaps. 2 and 4 were from Jeremiah). Most twentieth-century writers find the evidence insufficient to establish authorship or unity of authorship for the five poems. N. Gottwald, for example, judged that "the writer(s) could have been a prophet, a priest, or a governmental or private lay figure" (*The Hebrew Bible: A Socio-Literary Introduction* [1985] 546).

As for the date of composition, most late twentieth-century authorities find no strong reason to date Lamentations later than the sixth century B.C.E. In earlier times it was thought that Jeremiah composed these five laments as elegies for King Josiah as suggested by 2 Chr 35:25; however, internal evidence militates against this view since the subject matter of Lamentations clearly deals with Jerusalem's collapse, even though the Targum refers the statement in Lam 4:20 to the death of Josiah.

2. *Purpose and Theology.* The question of why these five poems were composed remains far from settled. Until modern times several verses from Lamentations were viewed as prophetic and messianic, although Lamentations is never cited or paraphrased in the NT. (Some have seen Lam 3:30 reflected in Matt 5:39.) Clement of Alexandria (*Paed.* 1:9) cited Lam 1:1-2, 8, while Lam 4:20, which mentions "the Lord's anointed," was applied to Jesus by such church fathers as Justin Martyr (*First Apology* 72), Irenaeus (*Demonstration of the Apostolic Preaching* 71), Tertullian (*Against Marcion* 3:6), and Clement of Alexandria (*Extracts from the Writings of Theodotus* 18:2). J. Daniélou (1966) concluded that Lam 4:20 was included from the earliest times among the *Testimonia* collections of HB texts bearing witness to Christ. Methodius quoted Lam 3:34 in several preserved references as having christological meaning, while Gregory the Great cited various Lamentation texts in his *Moralia* on Job as applying to the tribulations of Christ and the church. The Carolingian commentary of Rabanus Maurus took the book as a continuation of Jeremiah and saw it as a warning to all kings and kingdoms and to each Christian to wage spiritual war against sin by the power of Christ and the sacraments. In about 850, during a time of great disillusionment, Paschasius Radbertus, drawing heavily on Rabanus, chose to comment on Lamentations in order to encourage purification through suffering (E. Matter [1982]). Calvin, while seeking the meaning of specific statements in the text in historical settings known to him, saw the book as an extension of the predictive prophecy found in the book of Jeremiah.

Early Jewish interpretation also saw predictions of later events in some Lamentations statements. For example, Lam 1:19 ("my priests and elders perished in the city") was viewed in the Targum as a prediction of Jerusalem's destruction in 70 C.E. The Targum to Lam 4:22 looks into the future when the congregation of Zion will be freed from its punishment by the Messiah King and when the persecutors, "wicked Rome built up in Italy," will be afflicted by the Persians and their territory filled with Edomites. Likewise the Targum paraphrases Lam 5:11 ("Women were ravished in Zion.") as "Women who had married husbands in Zion were raped by Romans." By and large, the great Midrash on Lamentations focuses on the teachings of the Tanna'im and the Amora'im based on Lamentations; but it does not use the prophecy-fulfillment mode of interpretation evident in the Targum. It rather uses similar midrashic methodologies on Lamentations as employed on other Scripture by Midrash Rabbah, for example.

Modern interpreters have viewed the intention of the book from vastly different perspectives. One approach is to relate its purpose to its theology, which is usually seen to be hope in the face of tragedy (see especially Gottwald [1962]). A. Mintz ("The Rhetoric of Lamentations," *Prooftexts* 2 [1982] 1-17) argues that the theme of Lamentations is "an exploration of the traumatized relations between Israel and God in the immediate aftermath of the Destruction," in "dramatized speech and not theological statement" (4). He emphasizes the book's theological role as expressing the horror of war and its aftermath of human suffering and notes that there is no hint of an answer from God in the five poems. This marks the difference between lamentation and consolation; lamentation as a genre records the human struggle "to speak in the face of God's silence," while consolation records answers "from outside" in the form of God's word, which "breaks through" to mortals to end the silence.

Some scholars have interpreted Lamentations as a polemic against the pro-Babylonian party at the end of the Davidic monarchy (G. Brunet [1968]). A similar theological view suggests that Lamentations was developed as a paradigm for suffering in all kinds of catastrophes (M. Cohen [1988]). A slightly different theological direction was followed by those who explored the theme of hope in the face of disaster as it relates to deuteronomic theology (Gottwald [1962] and B. Albrektson [1963]).

In the 1980s various writers focused on applying literary analysis to understanding Lamentations' message. B. Johnson ("Form and Message in Lamentations," ZAW 97 [1985] 58-73) connected structure and message and found in the middle of the central chapter a theological answer to the question of whether Jerusalem's destruction and the accompanying human suffering had any meaning: "The distress is a punishment, but a punishment aimed at rehabilitation, not at definite rejection" (73). (See also the interpretation of W. Shea [1979], who draws attention to both the *qînâ* elegiac structure and the use of chiasmus.) Several writers with cuneiform background have examined Lamentations from the standpoint of Mesopotamian laments and have suggested that its purpose and theology were associated with liturgical use at the Temple site.

3. *Literary Analysis.* Numerous scholars of the past two hundred years (e.g., R. Lowth, W. de Wette, Keil, and K. Budde) have analyzed the language of Lamentations and associated it with the *qînâ* that is, the ancient funeral dirge. Budde, in his article "Das hebräische Klagelied" (*ZAW* 2 [1882] 1-52), delineated the metrical pattern of the elegy form in which the verse consists usually of two members divided into two parts, the first of usual length, the second shorter. Later analysts have followed Budde's lead (see especially H. Jahnow [1923]). M. Alexiou describes the similiarities between laments for the dead and laments over the fall of cities in Greek culture from ancient to modern times and calls attention to the prominent role of women in performing the laments while men performed ritual acts (*The Ritual Lament in Greek Tradition* [1974] chaps. 4–6). Shea proposes that the book in its overarching form fits the 3:2 *qînâ* pattern—that is, that the first three chapters form a unit followed by the last two chapters as the shortened unit.

H. Gunkel (1929) drew attention to Lamentations' similiarity to the communal lament *Gattung* in the psalms. Gottwald (1985, 542) and B. Johnson (1985) observed the mixed nature of the poetic forms appearing in Lamentations. Gottwald found elements of the individual lament, the communal lament, wisdom language, thanksgiving idiom, hymnic wording, and prophetic speech, but these patterns are not used in any consistent way. The picture is further complicated by the use of alphabetical acrostics in poems 1–4. Johnson, by reference to the *atbash* principle displayed in Jer 25:26 and 51:41, concluded that the use of the alphabetic acrostics was meant to suggest the editor's concern for chiasmus, so that the focal point of the message is to be found in the center of chapter 3.

S. Kramer (1959) made the claim that "it was the Sumerian poets who originated and developed the 'lamentation' genre." He later claimed that "there can be little doubt that the biblical Book of Lamentations owes no little of its form and content to its Mesopotamian forerunners." T. McDaniel (1968) raised the issue of possible connections between the Mesopotamian city lament genre and Lamentations, but he concluded that any connection is highly unlikely since the city laments were so far removed from Lamentations in spatial and temporal terms. W. Gwaltney (1983) has explored the broader range of Mesopotamian laments that cover the entire history of cuneiform literature. He concludes that, while the Mesopotamian city laments remained a part of the classical Sumerian literature largely restricted to the school curriculum, the liturgical laments were maintained as an ongoing religious pool of poetry sung both in special rituals and in daily rituals in the cults of most Mesopotamian deities.

The Mesopotamian lament genre, its history of development, and its place in religious practice are important for the study of Lamentations, since Mesopotamia is the only clear context in which we possess both lament poetry and the details of its liturgical use. A comparison of Mesopotamian practice with the biblical book suggests an alternative mode of interpretation through liturgical analysis.

Mesopotamian lament poetry may be traced over a period of about 2,000 years. The earliest stage of formal laments emerged as early as the twenty-fourth century B.C.E. as a cultic response to the looting of Lagash by Lugalzagessi. No laments remain from the ensuing Akkadian, Gutian, or Ur III eras, but the five extant Sumerian city laments were created about 2000 B.C.E. to memorialize the wholesale destruction brought upon Mesopotamia in this era. These city laments were preserved as canonized material to be copied by generations of student scribes but dropped out of scholastic use in the first millennium.

These classical laments were augmented by the *ershemma* and *balag* laments in the Old Babylonian era. Originating shortly after 2000 B.C.E. and composed in the Emesal (feminine) dialect of Sumerian to be performed by gala priests in a high-pitched wailing mode, *ershemma* and *balag* laments came to be combined for cultic use in the first millennium B.C.E. These *balag-ershemmas* were performed in at least four ritual circumstances, including rites of daily offerings and sacrifices and special ceremonies, like the ritual for covering the sacred kettle drum. They might also be chanted as a part of the *namburbi* ritual for warding off portended evil. They continued to be used in their original role—in rituals for the demolishing of damaged walls and sacred buildings—in which their main function was to appease the potentially destructive god so that the building activities could proceed without danger.

A comparison of Lamentations with first millennium Mesopotamian *balag-ershemma* laments in terms of their content and theology, poetic devices, *Sitz im Kultus*, and lament form suggests a liturgical origin for Lamentations. These poems continue to be used liturgically in Jewish tradition to mark the tragedies associated with Jerusalem's fall to the Babylonians and to the Romans and in Christian tradition to mark the tenebrae portion of Holy Week. Such an interpretation suggests that these five poems may have been composed by levitical poets/musicians for liturgical use.

4. Interpretation of dramatis personae. Commentators have noted the change in speaking voice throughout Lamentations and have debated who the characters speaking in the first person might be and what meaning is conveyed through this means. At times the "I" is feminine and at times masculine. Frequently the first-person speaker is Jerusalem personified. Reminiscent of Greek tragedy, such changes in speaker point to the dramatic quality of the poems (see Gottwald [1985] 543 and W. Lanahan [1974] 41-49). M. Biddle (1991) has explored the implications of the personification of Jerusalem by the Lamentations poets and concluded that the personification of the city as a lady with the ability to speak in the first person reflects common cultural thought patterns in which the city was viewed as the mother of its inhabitants and the central female mediary in divine/human relations.

Bibliography: B. Albrektson, *Studies in the Text and Theology of the Book of Lamentations with a Critical Edition of the Peshitta Text* (1963). **D. Bergant,** "The Challenge of Hermeneutics: Lamentations 1.1-11, a Test Case," *CBQ* 64 (2002) 1-16. **U. Berges,** tr., *Klagelieder* (Herders theologischer Kommentar zum Alten Testament, 2002). **A. Berlin,** *Lamentations: A Commentary* (OTL, 2002). **M. Biddle,** "The Figure of Lady Jerusalem: Identification, Deification, and Personification of Cities in the Ancient Near East," *The Biblical Canon in Comparative Perspective* (Scripture in Context 4, ed. W. Hallo, B. Batto, and K. Lawson Younger, Jr. 1983) 173-194. **W. C. Bouzard, Jr.,** *We Have Heard with Our Ears, O God: Sources of Communal Laments in the Psalms* (SBLDS 159, 1997). **C. M. M. Brady,** *The Rabbinic Targum of Lamentations: Vindicating God* (2003). **G. Brunet,** *Le lamentations contre Jérémie:*

Réinterpretation des quatre premières lamentations (1968). C. **Budde,** "Das hebräische Klagelied," *ZAW* 2 (1882) 1-52. **H. I. Caro,** *Beiträge zur ältesten Exegese des Buches Threni mit besonderer Berücksichtigung des Midrash und Targum* (1893). M. E. **Cohen,** *The Canonical Lamentations of Ancient Mesopotamia* (2 vols., 1988). A. **Cooper,** "The Message of Lamentations," *JANESCU* 28 (2001) 1-18. J. **Daniélou,** " 'Nous Vivons á son ombre' (Lam 4, 20)," *Études d' exégèse judéo-chrétienne (Les Testimonia)* (TH 5, 1966) 76-95. A. R. P. **Diamond,** K. M. O'**Connor,** and L. **Stulman (eds.),** *Troubling Jeremiah* (JSOTSup 260, 1999). F. W. **Dobbs-Allsopp,** *Weep, O Daughter of Zion: A Study of the City-lament Genre in the HB* (BibOr 44, 1993); "Tragedy, Tradition, and Theology in the Book of Lamentations," *JSOT* 74 (997) 29-60; "The Enjambing Line in Lamentation: A Taxonomy," *ZAW* 113 (2001) 219-39; "The Effects of the Enjambment of Lamentations," *ZAW* 113 (2001) 370-85. F. W. **Dobbs-Allsopp** and T. **Linafelt,** "The Rape of Zion in Thr 1,10," *ZAW* 113 (2001) 77-81. P. W. **Ferris,** Jr., *The Genre of Communal Lament in the Bible and the Ancient Near East* (SBLDS 127, 1992). R. **Gordis,** *The Song of Songs and Lamentations: A Modern Translation and Commentary* (1974). N. K. **Gottwald,** *Studies in the Book of Lamentations* (SBT 14, 1962). D. **Guest,** "Hiding Behind the Naked Women in Lamentations: A Recriminative Response," *BibInt* 7 (1999) 413-48. M. D. **Guinon,** "Lamentations," *NJBC* (1990). H. **Gunkel,** "Klagelieder Jeremiae" *RGG* 2 (1929) 3:1049-52. W. C. **Gwaltney,** "The Biblical Book of Lamentations in the Context of Near Eastern Lament Literature," *More Essays on the Comparative Method* (Scripture in Context 2, ed. W. W. Hallo, J. C. Moyer, and L. G. Perdue, 1983) 191-211. K. M. **Heim,** "The Personification of Jerusalem and the Drama of Her Bereavement in Lamentations," in *Zion, City of Our God* (ed. R.S. Hess and G.J. Wenham, 1999) 129-69. D. R. **Hillers,** *Lamentations* (AB 7A, 1972, 1992). J. **Hunter,** *Faces of a Lamenting City: The Development and Coherence of the Book of Lamentations* (BEATAJ 39, 1996). H. **Jahnow,** *Das hebräische Leichenlied im Rahmen der Völkerdichtung* (BZAW 36, 1923). B. **Johnson,** "Form and Message in Lamentations," *ZAW* 97 (1985) 58-73. C. F. **Keil,** *Biblischer Commentar uber den propheten Jeremia und die Klagelieder* (BCAT, 1872). S. N. **Kramer,** "Sumerian Literature and the Bible," AnBib 12 (1959) 196-97. R. **Kutscher,** *Oh Angry Sea (a-ab-ba hu-luh-ha): The History of a Sumerian Congregational Lament* (1975). A. **Labahn,** "Trauern als Bewältigung der Vergangenheit zur Gestaltung der Zukunft: Bemerkungen zur anthropologischen Theologie der Klagelieder," *VT* 52 (2002) 513-27. W. **Lanahan,** "The Speaking Voice in the Book of Lamentations," *JBL* 93 (1974) 41-49. E. **Levine,** *The Aramaic Version of Lamentations* (1976). T. **Linafelt,** *Surviving Lamentations: Catastrophe, Lament, and Protest in the Afterlife of a Biblical Book* (2000). T. F. **McDaniel,** "The Alleged Sumerian Influences upon Lamentations," *VT 18* (1968) 198-209. E. A. **Matter,** "The Lamentations Commentaries of Hrabanus Maurus and Paschasius Radbertus," *Traditio* 38 (1982) 137-63. C.W. **Miller,** "Reading Voices: Personification, Dialogism, and the Reader of Lamentations 1," *BibInt* 9 (2001) 393-408; "The Book of Lamentations in Recent Research," *Currents in Biblical Research* 1 (2002) 9-29. C. W. E. **Nägelsbach,** *The Lamentations of Jeremiah: Theologically and Homiletically Expounded* (tr., en., and ed. W. Hornblower, 1871). J. **Neusner,** *Lamentations Rabbah: An Analytical Translation* (1989); *Israel After Calamity: The Book of Lamentations* (1995). K. M. O'**Connor,** "Lamentations," *The Women's Bible Commentary* (ed. C. A. Newsom and S. H. Ringe, 1992) 178-82. I. W. **Provan,** *Lamentations; Based on the RSV* (NCBC, 1991). H. S. **Pyper,** "Reading Lamentations," *JSOT* 95 (2001) 55-69. D. J. **Reimer,** "Good Grief? A Psychological Reading of Lamentations," *ZAW* 114 (2002) 542-59. J. **Renkema,** "The Literary Structure of Lamentations," JSOTSup 74 (1988) 294-396. G. **Ricciotti,** *Le Lamentazioni de Geremia* (1924). Y. **Sabar,** "Lēel-Hūza: Story and History in a Cycle of Lamentations for the Ninth of Ab in the Jewish Neo-Aramaic Dialect of Zakho," *JSS* 21 (1976) 138-62. R. B. **Salters,** *Jonah and Lamentations* (OTGu, 1994); "Structure and Implications in Lamentations 1," *SJOT* 14 (2000)

293-300. **W. H. Shea,** "The Qinah Structure of the Book of Lamentations," *Bib* 60 (1979) 103-7. **J. M. Schonfelder,** *Die Klagelieder des Jeremias nach rabbinischer Auslegung* (1887). **O. Thenius,** *Die Klagelieder* (1855). **J.D. Thompson,** *A Critical Concordance to the Septuagint Lamentations* (The Computer Bible 75, 2000). **B. Weber,** "Zion's Cause: The Presentation of Pain in the Book of Lamentatins," in *Strange Fire* (ed. T. Linafelt, 2000) 267-79. **C. Westermann,** *Die Klagelieder: Forschungsgeschichte und Auslegung* (1990; ET, *Lamentations: Issues and Interpretation* [1994]). **H. Wiesmann,** "Der Kommentar des hl. Thomas von Aquin zu den Klageliedern des Jeremias," *Scholastik* 4 (1929) 78-91.

W. C. Gwaltney, Jr.

THE LATTER PROPHETS: MAJOR

Ezekiel

1. *Early Rabbinic Interpretation.* In early rabbinic interpretation controversy over Ezekiel centered on three topics: (1) The vision of chaps. 1, 8, and 10 is referred to already in Ben Sira 49:8 as a vision of the divine "chariot" (Heb., *merkābâ*, a term not used by Ezekiel himself). Some considered the study of chap. 1 a source of joyful enlightenment (*b. Hag.* 14b), but others held it to be extremely dangerous (cf. *b. Hag* 13a, in which fire devours a child who is studying chap. 1). (2) Ezekiel intensely condemned Israel and Jerusalem, especially in chap. 16. (3) The vision of chaps. 40–48 contains laws contradicting laws in the Torah (e.g., Ezek 44:22; Lev 21:14). Only after extensive argument was the book accepted as canonical (see *b. Šabb.* 13b), and some authorities continued to prohibit the public reading of chaps. 1 and 16 (*b. Meg.* 4:10). Chapter 1 is, however, the prescribed haftarah for the first day of Shavuot (cf. *t. Meg.* 4:34).

Already in the Tannaitic period speculation on the *merkābâ* had grown into a complex tradition of mystical practice and writing (see, e.g., *t. Hag.* 211-12), which included early *hekhalot* literature (reports of, and instructions for achieving, visions of the heavenly palaces) and various apocalypses that included visions of the *merkābâ*. The Qumran *Songs of the Sabbath Sacrifice* are part of this *hekhalot* tradition. The "living creatures" of Ezekiel's vision formed the basis for the development of angelology in this period, and angelic hymns were prominent in both hekhalot and apocalyptic literature. Ezekiel's vision of the dry bones in chap. 37 was interpreted as evidence for the resurrection of the body (see, e.g., the depictions of Ezekiel in the third-century B.C.E. frescoes from Dura-Europos, and *b. Meg.* 31a).

2. *Early Christian Interpretation.* a. *NT.* Although never quoted directly in the NT, Ezekiel is the source for the image of the Davidic Messiah as "the good shepherd" (Ezekiel 34; Matt 18:12-14; John 10:11-18, etc.; cf. Heb 13:20; Ezek 37:24), and the book of Revelation contains extensive reworking of Ezekiel's visions and prophecies in terms of the events of the Roman period. Like early Jewish apocalypses, Revelation includes a vision of the divine throne/chariot patterned after Ezekiel 1 and adds the hymns of angel choruses (Rev 4:1-8). Other images in Revelation derived from Ezekiel include the eating of the scroll (Ezek 2:8-9; Rev 5:1, 10:1-4, 8-11), condemnation of the "whore" (Ezekiel 16, 23; Rev 17:1-6, 15-18), the battle with Gog (Ezekiel 38–39; Revelation 19–20), and the vision of the new temple (Ezekiel 40–48; Revelation 11, 21–22).

b. *Early fathers.* Origen's twenty-five-book commentary on Ezekiel was the most influential of the early Christian commentaries but survives only in a few fragments. Fourteen of his homilies on Ezekiel are preserved in Jerome's translation. Major commentaries by both Jerome and Theodoret as well as several homilies by Gregory the Great are extant, together with comments on isolated passages by Justin, Cyprian, Clement of Rome, Ambrose, Tertullian, and others. The book figures in patristic writings primarily in typological readings of the HB. Origen, for example, depicts Ezekiel as a type of Christ, who in his thirtieth year saw the heavens opened while standing by a river; Ezekiel's struggles with false prophets represent the church's struggle against the heretics; and the corruption of the woman Jerusalem in chap. 16 represents the soul's corruption by sin.

Ezekiel 9:4-6 is read by various fathers as prefiguring the salvation of the Christians, whose foreheads are marked (in baptism) with the cross. Chapter 1 is interpreted in this period as a vision of Christ seated on the throne. The four living beings are the four Gospels (Irenaeus) or the evangelists themselves (Hippolytus), with the lion representing Matthew; the man, Mark; the ox, Luke; and the eagle, John. Interpretation of chap. 1 figures in patristic debate on the substance of God, with some fathers maintaining that Ezekiel saw only Christ and not God (since

God is invisible), others arguing that Christ and God were represented by the *hašmal* and fire (1:27) respectively (and are therefore two substances), and so on. Ezekiel 37 is widely cited as a prophecy of the resurrection of the body and Ezekiel 14 as proof that salvation depends on individual repentance.

3. *Medieval Interpretation*. a. *Jewish*. Within Jewish circles speculation on Ezekiel's chariot vision contributed to the flowering of the mystical tradition, including the development of Kabbalism and Hasidism in the twelfth century and following. The commentaries of Rashi, Eliezer of Beaugency, and D. Kimhi represent the range of approaches taken toward Ezekiel in Jewish biblical scholarship of the period. Rashi took a relatively traditionalist stance in his comments, deferring to the early rabbis as authoritative and refusing to comment on the "forbidden" verses (1:27; 8:2). He did, however, consistently temper midrashic tradition by his preference for the *pěšat*, the literal sense of the text, and frequently elucidated passages in terms of the historical events of the prophet's own time. Eliezer's interpretation is relatively independent of the rabbinic tradition and is primarily based on semantic and rhetorical rather than theological criteria.

Kimhi's work reflects this same relative freedom from rabbinic tradition but includes both literalist and speculative philosophical interpretation. A brilliant philologist, Kimhi was also a follower of Maimonides, whose *Guide of the Perplexed* used philosophical categories to expound the chariot for the already advanced (but still perplexed) student. Kimhi wrote a philological commentary for the lay reader, following it with an esoteric treatise interpreting the chariot as a revelation to human intelligence of the divine intelligence guiding the spheres.

b. *Christian*. Many medieval Christian works on Ezekiel, including a series of popular and controversial lectures by Abelard, have been lost. Although most of the extant commentaries expand on the allegorical interpretations of Gregory the Great, the Victorines represent the movement within Christian exegesis toward a literal reading. Hugh of St. Victor explicitly criticized Gregory's failure to address the literal meaning of Ezekiel's visions, and Rirchard of St. Victor, after paying due respect to Gregory, explicated the visions according to the "plain" sense, describing in detail the animals and chariot of chap. 1 and giving diagrams of Ezekiel's temple. Andrew of St. Victor, informed by the work of Jewish scholars, focused on the book's meaning for Ezekiel and his first audience. In his comments on 1:1, for example, he ignored the traditional debate over how Ezekiel could "see" God and read the verse simply as the book's introduction: Ezekiel "saw visions of God"—namely, God's intentions as expressed in the book.

4. *Reformation and Enlightenment Interpretation*. As typological interpretations declined two strands in the interpretation of Ezekiel predominated: the increasingly important historical study of the text and an almost independent tradition of mystical interpretation. The book was not especially important in the work of the Reformers. In the preface to his translation Luther commented briefly on Ezekiel's visions as prophecies of the reign of Christ but referred the reader to the work of Nicholas of Lyra for details. Calvin began a substantial commentary but died before its completion. In the dialogue with Jerome and Theodoret, Calvin rejected typological interpretations (the notion that the mark on the forehead in Ezek 9:4 is a cross, he considered a "figment") in favor of "the simple and genuine"—that is, historical and moral sense. The 1605 commentary of Prado and Villalpando ("The Champollion of the Temple") was acclaimed for both its philological excellence and its detailed (if anachronistic) illustrations of the temple. In the eighteenth century, analysis of the prophet's poetic style was added to historical concerns. Although written after the supposed golden age of Hebrew poetry, the book's style was praised by both J.G. Eichorn and R. Lowth (though J. D. Michaelis considered it inferior). The tradition of mystical speculation on Ezekiel spread to Christian circles during this

period, taking such diverse forms as J. Reuchlin's Christian Kabbalist exposition of the chariot (1517) and W. Blake's engravings of, and reported "conversation" with, the prophet (1790).

5. *Nineteenth- and Twentieth-century Interpretations.* In the early nineteenth century interpretators focused on refining text-critical and historical analysis of Ezekiel. Although a few eighteenth-century writers had already challenged the book's unity (most notably an anonymous critic who in 1798 claimed Daniel as the author of fourteen chapters of Ezekiel), these challenges had little initial impact (see the responses of E. Rosenmüller [1826] and H. Hävernick [1843]). Only gradually did doubts regarding Ezekiel's unity and authenticity take hold. H. Ewald in 1841 claimed several stages in the book's writing, all at the hand of Ezekiel. F. Hitzig (1847) contributed primarily to the book's textual criticism (favoring, as had Ewald, the text of the LXX over the MT) but also pronounced several verses to be glosses. As late as 1880 R. Smend, while sharing Ewald's view of Ezekiel's essential literary origins, believed the book to have been written as a unit and to be so finely structured that "it must be accepted or rejected as a whole." In 1886 C. Cornill systematically reconstructed a Hebrew text based largely on the LXX , a work that remained the standard for textual criticism of Ezekiel well into the twentieth century. Cornill, while radical in his textual criticism, considered Ezekiel the author (although writing in several stages) of the entire book. The studies of C. Keil (1868) and especially of A. Davidson (1892) are noteworthy in this period for their attention both to the book's historical background and to the distinctive features of its literary style. In addition to scholarly treatments Ezekiel figured prominently in African American spirituals and preaching, in which the prophet's message of hope to an exiled and dispersed people was reinterpreted in light of the African American experience.

By the turn of the century scholarly doubts regarding the book's unity were giving way to the assumption of disunity. In 1900 R. Kraetzschmar argued on the basis of the book's many repetitions that Ezekiel contained a combination of two parallel recensions of an original text. J. Herrmann (1908, 1924) claimed to find strata of both early and late work by Ezekiel plus material added by a redactor. Only in 1924, however, did the full impact of redaction criticism hit Ezekiel studies with the publication of G. Hölscher's argument that fewer than 144 of the book's 1,273 verses contained the actual words of the impassioned prophet. The rest was the work of a plodding and prosaic fifth-century redactor.

Ezekiel had long been criticized by such scholars as H. Gesenius, W. De Wette, and F. Hitzig for his "narrow" and "shallow" legalism and was considered a precursor of the "decline" toward rabbinic Judaism. Rather than decrying Ezekiel as "legalistic," Hölscher declared Ezekiel's legal material and most of the book's other prose material inauthentic. He could thus extol Ezekiel the free-spirited poet while condemning the author of the bulk of the book as "the stiff, priestly writer and pathfinder of a legalistic and ritualistic Judaism." Hölscher's radical conclusions gave new impetus to redaction criticism of the book, and for the next twenty years research focused on the "problem of Ezekiel"—namely, questions regarding the date, unity, and place of the book's composition. Numerous studies traced Ezekiel's (the prophet's and the book's) migrations through various countries and over several centuries.

In *Pseudo-Ezekiel* (1930) C. C. Torrey claimed the book to be a pseudepigraph from Jerusalem of the second or third century that originally purported to have been written under Manasseh but was subsequently rewritten in Judah with a Babylonian setting. V. Herntrich (1932) posited that Ezekiel wrote chaps. 1–24 in Jerusalem (and therefore had the knowledge of events in the city these chapters imply), but that a later exilic editor had added a Babylonian framework to the original prophecies.

A. Bertholet (1936) and W.A. Irwin (1943) each argued that Ezekiel had begun his career in Jerusalem but finished it in Babylonia, after which his collected prophecies had been further edited. In addition Irwin isolated a small core (parts of 251 verses) as containing Ezekiel's original prophecies, brief poetic utterances that had been interpreted and misinterpreted over several centuries of redaction.

In the early 1950s both C. Howie (1950) and G. Fohrer (1952) rejected attempts to reconstruct a date, place, and author other than those claimed within the book itself. Fohrer argued primarily on the basis of rhythmic analysis that Ezekiel wrote and edited most of the book. H. Rowley, in an excellent review of the state of the discipline (1953), also concluded with a relatively traditional assessment of the text. Nonetheless, in the same year Irwin claimed widespread agreement that the book is a composite construction and that Ezekiel delivered some or all of his oracles in Jerusalem.

W. Eichrodt's 1965 commentary illustrates the difficulties of finding a middle way between naive acceptance and radical reconstruction of the text. Purporting to trust what the book says about itself, Eichrodt envisioned Ezekiel as a writing prophet who did much "collecting" and arranging of his own writings. Eichrodt then isolated a series of authentic oracles saved and added, not by the prophet, but by his disciples, and finally posited a redactor who also contributed "extensive additions."

The work of W. Zimmerli moves toward reconciliation of redaction criticism with the compelling sense of the book's unity that had prevailed into the twentieth century. His massive commentary (1969) provides a definitive critical apparatus and a form-critical analysis and puts forth a new theory on the redaction history of the book, arguing that an original "core" of prophetic material underwent a process of *Nachinterpretation*, ongoing commentary within an Ezekielien school, each generation of which reread both the core and the earlier interpretations in light of its own situation. Zimmerli thus claimed that even the secondary and tertiary additions and revisions, which he saw throughout, "point back" to the prophet.

While Zimmerli's work represents a significant moderation of the redaction-critical extremes of the first half of the century, the commentary of M. Greenberg (1983, 1997) marks a decisive break with redaction criticism of Ezekiel. Rejecting attempts to judge an ancient text according to modern notions of unity and consistency, he proposes a "holistic" method for reading the book, combining the tools of textual criticism, historical reconstruction, observations of ancient and medieval commentators, and close literary analysis with the goal of explicating the inner logic and implications of the text on its own terms. Without denying the presence of glosses and later editorial work, his commentary reopens the synchronic study of Ezekiel in its full complexity, and along with a widespread interest in "final form" modes of criticism in the final decades of the twentieth century, has produced a profusion of studies that focus on the book's unity and explore its literary technique.

E. Davis's 1989 monograph, *Swallowing the Scroll*, explores the possibility that Ezekiel was the first writing prophet, claiming that many of the book's idiosyncrasies are consistent with the prophet's effort to forge a new literary idiom. Such commentators as R. Hals (1988) and D. Block (1997) as well as scholars undertaking more specialized research assume the book's substantial unity and the probability that much of the material and its compilation derive from a historical Ezekiel.

Feminist critics have published widely on the previously unexplored dynamics and implications of the sexual violence depicted in chaps. 16 and 23 (K. Darr [1992], J. Galambush [1992], F. Van Dijk-Hemmes [1993], J. W. Tarlin [1997], C. J. Dempsey [1998], M. E. Shields [1998], L. Day [2000]). D. Halperin's *Seeking Ezekiel* (1993) offers a psychoanalytic interpretation of the historical Ezekiel based on the bizarre persona depicted in the text. After several decades of intensive work isolating, dating, and analyzing the book's various layers, scholars have returned to the earlier consensus regarding Ezekiel's essential unity and set about to explicate its distinctive literary features.

Bibliography: M. **Aberbach**, "Ezekiel in the Aggadah," *EncJud* 6 (1971) 1095. **D. I. Abrabanel**, *Peruš 'al nevi'îm 'aharonim* (1957). **L. C. Allen**, *Ezekiel 20–48* (WBC 29, 1990); *Ezekiel 1–19* (WBC 28, 1994). **Andrew of St. Victor**, *Expositionem in Ezechielem* (CCCM 53E, ed. M. A. Signor, 1991). P. **Auvray**, "Ezéchiel," *DBSup* 8 (1972) 759-91. A. **Bertholet** and **K. Galling**, *Hesekiel* (HAT, 1936). **D. I. Block**, *The Book of Ezekiel: Chapters 1–24* (NICOT, 1997); *The Book of Ezekiel: Chapters 25–48* (NICOT, 1998). **L. Boadt**, "The Poetry of Prophetic Persuasion: Preserving the Prophet's Persona," *CBQ* 59 (1997) 1-21. A. **Böckler**, "Ist Gott Schuldig, wenn ein gerechter Stolpert? Zur Exegese von Ez iii 20," *VT* 48 (1998) 437-52. **E. A. de Boer**, *John Calvin on the Visions of Ezekiel : Historical and Hermeneutical Studies in John Calvin's "Sermons inédits," especially on Ezek. 36-48* (Kerkhistorische bijdragen 21, 2004). N.R. **Bowen**, "The Daughters of Your People: Female Prophets in Ezekiel 13:17-23," *JBL* 118 (1999) 417-33. G. **Braulik**, "Ezechiel und Deuteronomium: die 'Sippenhaftung' in Ezechiel 18,20 und Deuteronomium 24, 16, unter Berücksichtigung von Jeremia 31,29-30 und 2 Könige 14, 6," *BZ* 44 (2000) 206-232. **E. Broome**, "Ezekiel's Abnormal Personality," *JBL* 65 (1946) 277-92. J. **Calvin**, *Commentaries on the First Twenty Chapters of Ezekiel* (1565; see the ET of T. Meyers [1848] for a review of literature [2:403-7] and of then current research [1:v-xxxii]). J. G. **Carpzov**, *Introductio ad libros canonicos bibliorum Veteris Testamenti omnes* (1721) 3:225-27. **R. B. Chisholm, Jr.**, "Does God Deceive?" *BSac* 155 (1998) 11-28. **G. A. Cooke**, *A Critical and Exegetical Commentary on the Book of Ezekiel* (ICC, 1936). **C. H. Cornill**, *Das Buch des Propheten Ezechiel* (1886). **M. A. Corral**, *Ezekiel's Oracles Against Tyre: Historical Reality and Motivations* (BibOr 46, 2002). J. **Daniélou**, *Études d'exégèse judéo-chrétienne* (1966). J. **Darling**, *Cyclopaedia Bibliographica* 2 (1859) 670-82. **K. P. Darr**, "Ezekiel," *Women's Bible Commentary* (ed. C. A. Newsom and S. H. Ringe, 1992) 183-90. **E. Dassmann**, "Hesekiel," *RAC* 14 (1988) 1132-191. A. B. **Davidson**, *The Book of the Prophet Ezekiel* (CBSC, 1892). **E. F. Davis**, *Swallowing the Scroll: Textuality and the Dynamics of Discourse in Ezekiel's Prophecy* (JSOTSup 78, 1989). **L. Day**, "Adulterous Jerusalem's Imagined Demise: Death of a Metaphor in Ezekiel xvi," *VT* 50 (2000) 285-309; "The Bitch Had it Coming to Her: Rhetoric and Interpretation in Ezekiel 16," *BibInt* 8 (2000) 231-54; "Rhetoric and Domestic Violence in Ezekiel 16," *BibInt* 8 (2000) 205-30. **C. J. Dempsey**, "The 'Whore' of Ezekiel 16: the Impact and Ramifications of Gender-Specific Metaphors in Light of Biblical Law and Divine Judgment," in *Gender and Law in the Hebrew Bible and the Ancient Near East* (ed. V. H. Matthews, B. M. Levinson, T. Frymer-Kensky, JSOTSup 262, 1998) 57-78. **W. Eichrodt**, *Der Prophet Hesekiel* (ATD 22, 2 vols., 1959–66; ET, OTL [1970]). **Eliezer of Beaugency**, *Kommentar zu Ezechiel und den XII Kleinen Propheten* (ed. S. Poznanski, 1909). **L. M. Eslinger**, "Ezekiel 20 and the Metaphor of Historical Teleology : Concepts of Biblical History," *JSOT* 81 (1998) 93-125. **J. C. Exum**, "Abuse, Desire, and the Body : Ezekiel and the Song of Songs," *BibInt* 8 (2000) 205-23. **H. Ewald**, *Die Propheten des Alten Bundes erklärt* (1841). **F. Fechter**, "Priesthood in Exile according to the Book of Ezekiel," *SBLSP* 39 (2000) 673-99. **G. Fohrer**, *Die Hauptprobleme des Buches Ezechiel* (BZAW 72, 1952). **K. S. Freedy** and **D. B. Redford**, "The Dates in Ezekiel in Relation to Biblical, Babylonian, and Egyptian Sources," *JAOS* 90 (1970) 462-85. **J. Galambush**, *Jerusalem in the Book of Ezekiel: The City as Yahweh's Wife* (SBLDS 130, 1992). **H. Gese**, *Der Verfassungsentwurf des Ezechiel* (Kap. 40–48) *traditionsgeschichtlich untersucht* (BHT 25, 1957). **M. Greenburg**, *EncJud* 6 (1971) 1078-95; *Ezekiel 1-20* (AB 22, 1983); *Ezekiel 21–37* (AB 22A, 1997). **Gregory I, Pope**, *Sancti Gregorii Magni Homiliae in Hiezechihelem Prophetam* (CCSL 142, ed. M. Adriaen, 1971). **C. D. Gross**, "Whom am I? and Other Puzzles in Ezekiel 24," *BT* 54 (2003) 325-31. **N. Habel**, "The Silence of the Lands: the Ecojustice Implications of Ezekiel's Judgment Oracles," *SBLSP* 40 (2001) 305-20. **D. J. Halperin**, *The Faces of the Chariot* (1988); "Origen, Ezekiel's

Merkabah, and the Ascension of Moses," *CH* 50 (1981) 261-75. **R. Hals,** *Ezekiel* (FOTL, 1988); *Seeking Ezekiel: Text and Psychology* (1993). **J. B. Harford,** *Studies in the Book of Ezekiel* (1935). **P.J. Harland,** "A Land Full of Violence: the Value of Human Life in the Book of the Prophet Ezekiel," in *New Heaven and New Earth: Prophecy and the Millenium* (ed. P.J. Harland and C.T.R. Hayward, VTSup 77, 1999) 113-27. **V. Herntrich,** *Ezechielprobleme* (BZAW 61, 1932). **J. Herrmann,** *Ezechiel* (KAT 11, 1908, 1924). **F. Hitzig,** *Der Prophet Ezechiel* (1847). **G. Hölscher,** *Hesekiel: Der Dichter und das Buch* (BZAW 39, 1924). **C. G. Howie,** *The Date and Composition of Ezekiel* (JBLMS 4, 1950). **A. Hurvitz,** *A Linguistic Study of the Relationship Between the Priestly Source and the Book of Ezekiel: A New Approach to an Old Problem* (CRB 20, 1982). **W. A. Irwin,** *The Problem of Ezekiel: An Inductive Study* (1943); "Ezekiel Research Since 1943," *VT* 3 (1953) 54-66. **Jerome,** *Commentarii in Ezechielem* (CCSL 75, ed. M. Adriaen and F. Glorie, 1964). **S. T. Kamionkowski,** *Gender Reversal and Cosmic Chaos: A Study on the Book of Ezekiel* (JSOTSup 368, 2003). **R. Kasher,** "Anthropomorphism, Holiness, and Cult: A New Look at Ezekiel 40-48," *ZAW* 110 (1998) 192-208. **K. F. Keil,** *Biblischer Commentar über den Propheten Ezechiel* (1868; ET 1896); *Introduction* (1882) 1:353-63 (review of literature). **D. Kimhi,** commentary in *Mikra' ot Gedolot.* **R. L. Kohn,** *A New Heart and a New Soul: Ezekiel, the Exile and the Torah* (JSOTSup 2002); "Ezekiel at the Turn of the Century," *Currents in Biblical Research* 2 (2003) 9-31. **S. Kreuzer,** "Die Verwendung der Mächtigkeitsformel ausserhalb des Deuteronomiums: Literarische und Theologisische Linien zu Jer, Ez, DtrG, und P," *ZAW* 109 (1997) 369-84. **C. Kuhl,** "Zur Geschichte der Hesekiel-Forschung," *TRu NF* 5 (1933) 92-118; "Neuere Hesekiel-literatur," *TRu NF* 20 (1952) 1-26; "Zum Stand der Hesekiel-Forschung," *TRu NF* 24 (1956-57) 1-53. **E. Kutsch,** *Die chronologischen Daten des Ezechielbuches* (OBO 62, 1985). **J. F. Kutsko,** *Between Heaven and Earth: Divine Presence and Absence in the Book of Ezekiel* (Biblical and Judaic Studies 7, 2000). **B. Lang,** *Ezechiel, Der Prophet und das Buch* (Enträge der Forschung 153, 1981), esp. his review of recent research, 1-18. **J. E. Lapsley,** *Can These Bones Live? The Problem of the Moral Self in the Book of Ezekiel* (BZAW 301, 2000). **D. Launderville,** "Ezekiel's Cherub: A Promising Symbol or Dangerous Tool?" *CBQ* 65 (2003) 165-83. **J. D. Levenson,** *Theology of the Program of Restoration of Ezekiel 40–48* (HSM 10, 1976). **J. Lust** (ed.), *Ezekiel and His Book: Textual and Literary Criticism and Their Interrelation* (BETL 74, 1986); "The Spirit of the Lord, or the Wrath of the Lord? Ezekiel 39,29," *ETL* 78 (2002) 148-55. **C. MacKay,** "Ezekiel in the NT," *CQR* 162 (1961) 4-16. **A. Malamat,** "New Mari Documents and the Prophecy of Ezekiel," in *Tehillah le-Moshe : Biblical and Judaic Studies in Honor of Moshe Greenberg* (ed. M. Cogan, B.L. Eichler, J.H. Tigay., M. Fishbane, 1997) 71-76. **A. Mein,** "Ezekiel as a Priest in Exile," in *The Elusive Prophet: the Prophet as a Historical Person, Literary Character and Anonymous Artist,* ed. J. C. de Moor (2001) 199-213. **R. Nay,** *Jahwe im Dialog: Kommunikationsanalytische Untersuchung von Ez 14, 1-11 unter Berücksichtigung des dialogischen Rahmens in Ez 8-11 und Ez 20* (AnBib, 1999). **W. Neuss,** *Der Entwicklung der theologischen Auffassung des Buches Ezekiel zur Zeit der Frühscholastik* (1911); *Das Buch Ezechiel in Theologie und Kunst bis zum Ende des 12. Jahrhunderts* (1912). **M. S. Odell,** "You Are What You Eat: Ezekiel and the Scroll," *JBL* 117 (1998) 229-48; and J.T. Strong, eds., *The Book of Ezekiel: Theological and Anthropological Perspectives* (2000). **S. M. Olyan,** "We are Utterly Cut Off": Some Possible Nuances of *ngzrnw* in Ezek 37.11," *CBQ* 65 (2003) 43-51. **Origen,** *Homiliae in Ezechielem* (GCS 33, ed. W. A. Baehrens, 1925); *In Ezechielem Homiliae* (SC 352, ed. M. Borret, 1989). **C. L. Patton,** "Priest, Prophet, and Exile: Ezekiel as a Literary Construct," SBLSP 39 (2000) 700-27. **B. W. R. Pearson,** "Dry Bones in the Judean Desert: The Messiah of Ephraim, Ezekiel 37, and the Post-Revolutionary Followers of Bar Kokhba," *JSJ* 29 (1998) 192-201. **E. Philippe,** "Ezéchiel," *DB* 2 (1926) 2149-62. **H. Prado** and **J. B. Villalpando,** *In Ezechielem* (3 vols., 1596). **Rashi,**

Commentary in *Mikra'ot Gedolot*. **T. Renz**, *The Rhetorical Function of the Book of Ezekiel* (VTSup 76, 1999). **C. C. Rowland**, "The Influence of the First Chapter of Ezekiel on Jewish and Early Christian Literature" (diss., Cambridge University, 1974). **H. H. Rowley**, "The Book of Ezekiel in Modern Study," *BJRL* 36 (1953-54) 146-90 = *Men of God* (1963) 169-210. **T. A. Rudnig**, *Heilig and Profan: Redaktionskritische Studien zu Ez 40-48* (BZAW 287, 2000). **J. P. Ruiz**, *Ezekiel in the Apocalypse: The Transformation of Prophetic Language in Revelation* 16, 17-19, 10 (1989). **G. Scholem**, *Jewish Gnosticism, Mysticisim, and Talmudic Tradition* (1965). **M. E. Shields**, "Multiple Exposures: Body Rhetoric and Gender Characterization in Ezekiel 16," *JFSR* 14 (1998) 5-18; "Gender and Violence in Ezekiel 23," SBLSP 37 (1998) 86-105. **S. Spiegel**, "Ezekiel or Pseudo-Ezekiel?" *HTR* 24 (1931) 245-321; "Toward Certainty in Ezekiel," *JBL* 44 (1935) 145-71. **K. Stevenson**, 'Animal Rites: the Four Living Creatures in Patristic Exegesis and Liturgy,' *StPtr* 34 (2001) 470-92. **J. Stiebert**, "Shame and Prophecy: Approaches Past and Present," *BibInt* 8 (2000) 255-75; *The Construction of Shame in the Hebrew Bible: The Prophetic Contribution* (JSOTSup 346, 2002). **K. R. Stevenson**, *The Vision of Transformation: The Territorial Rhetoric of Ezekiel 40-48* (SBLDS 154, 1996). **M. A. Sweeney**, "Ezekiel: Zadokite Priest and Visionary Prophet of the Exile," SBLSP 39 (2000) 728-51. **S. Talmon**, "Fragments of an Ezekiel Scroll from Masada (Ezekiel 35:11-38:14): MasEzek, Masada 1043-2220," in *Tehillah le-Moshe : Biblical and Judaic Studies in Honor of Moshe Greenberg* (ed. M. Cogan, B.L. Eichler, J.H. Tigay., M. Fishbane, 1997) 53-69; "The Structuring of Biblical Books: Studies in the Book of Ezekiel," *ASTI* 10 (1976) 129-53. **E. Tamez**, "Dreaming from Exile: a Rereading of Ezekiel 47:1-12," in *Liberating Eschatology: Essays in Honor of Letty M. Russell* (ed. M.A. Farley and S. Jones, 1999) 68-74. **J. W. Tarlin**, "Utopia and Pornography in Ezekiel: Violence, Hope, and the Shattered Male Subject," in *Reading Bibles, Writing Bodies: Identity and the Book* (ed. T. K. Beal and D. M. Gunn, 1997) 175-83. **F. Van Dijk-Hemmes**, "The Metaphorization of Woman in Prophetic Speech: An Analysis of Ezekiel 23," *VT* 43 (1993) 162-70. **W. A. Van Gemeren**, "The Exegesis of Ezekiel's 'Chariot' Chapters in Twelfth-century Hebrew Commentaries" (diss., University of Wisconsin, 1974). **A. Vanhoye**, "L'utilisation du livre d'Ézéchiel dans l'Apocalypse," *Bib* 43 (1962) 436-76. **J. W. Wevers**, *Studies in the Text Histories of Deuteronomy and Ezekiel* (MSU 26, 2003). **R. Wischnitzer-Bernstein**, "The Conception of the Resurrection in the Ezekiel Panel of the Dura Synagogue," *JBL* 60 (1941) 43-55. **K. L. Wong**, *The Idea of Retribution in the Book of Ezekiel* (VTSup 86, 2001); "The Masoretic and Septuagint Texts of Ezekiel 39, 21-29," *ETL* 78 (2002) 130-47; Profanation/ Sanctification and the Past, Present, and Future of Israel in the Book of Ezekiel," *JSOT* 28 (2003) 210-39. **W. Zimmerli**, *Ezekiel 1, 2* (BKAT 13, 1969; ET, Hermeneia [2 vols., 1979-83]), with review of literature in 1:3-8; and update, 2:xi-xviii.

J. G. GALAMBUSH

THE LATTER PROPHETS: MAJOR

Daniel

Modern critical scholarship has reached a near-consensus that the book of Daniel essentially attained its canonical form in the years 167–164 B.C.E., during the reign of the Greco-Syrian king Antiochus IV Epiphanes (175–163 B.C.E.). This means that Daniel is the last composition to have been written that is now included in the collection of works known as the HB.

1. *Early Interpretation*. The impact of the book of Daniel on early Judaism was felt almost immediately and is well attested in the first century B.C.E. This history of interpretation developed partly in the Egyptian diaspora and partly at home in the sectarian milieu of the Judean community. In Egypt the process remains visible in the shape taken by the book of Daniel in the LXX . This Greek version of Daniel is thought to have been produced at Alexandria about 100 B.C.E. Although both Jews and early Christians eventually stopped making use of LXX-Dan in favor of a more literal Greek translation of the book attributed to Theodotion, which is possibly as old as the first century B.C.E., the presence in both of these versions of rather extensive additions to the canonical book (including the narratives of Susanna and of Bel and the Dragon and the two-part poem inserted between Dan 3:23 and 3:24 called The Prayer of Azariah and the Song of the Three Young Men) suggests that the cycle of legends about Daniel was larger and richer than the canonical version would admit.

The same can be said about the foreground of the book of Daniel in the milieu of Jewish sectarianism in Judea. At Qumran the book was essential to the self-understanding of the elect members of the sect who considered themselves to be "saints" (Dan 7:21-22; cf. the *War Scroll* [1QM] 3:5; 6:6). Fragments of the actual text of Daniel used there disclose only minor variations from the received MT and with a few exceptions support it and Theod-Dan against LXX-Dan. The Aramaic portion begins at 2:4b and ends at 7:28, exactly as in the Masoretic tradition. More significant for our purposes are the echoes of the book that ring throughout the literature of the sectarians at Qumran. The book of Daniel is reckoned by them among the prophets (cf. Matt 24:15), and is not considered a wisdom writing as it is in the HB. The hero, Daniel, is the inspiration for three Aramaic pseudo-Daniel stories found in Cave 4; further, chapter 4 is paralleled in significant ways by the important Aramaic *Prayer of Nabonidus* (4QPrNab), in which the last Babylonian king is cured of a serious disease by a Jewish exorcist, who then directs him to honor in writing the name of God Most High.

The evolution of the concept "son of man" from its origins in Daniel cannot be understood apart from its elaboration in the Jewish apocalypses 4 Ezra (= 2 Esdras 3-14 of our Apocrypha) and Enoch. Unlike his prototype in Dan 7:13, the cloud-riding son of man of 4 Ezra 13 is clearly a heavenly figure who was created at the beginning of time and whose epiphany in the world of human beings is associated with the Day of Judgment. The same is true of the son of man in the Parables of Enoch (chaps. 37-71). In 1 Enoch 46—which is a retelling or Midrash on the judgment scene of Daniel 7—and in chaps. 48 and 62, the son of man is himself the judge. From these extra-canonical sources it becomes easier to understand the picture drawn of the son of man in the so-called little apocalypses of the Synoptic Gospels (Matthew 24–25; Mark 13; Luke 21:5-36; cf. Luke 17:22-37). Whether Jesus ever intended to identify himself with a coming eschatological judge, or whether that link with the elaborated "son of man" imagery of contemporary Jewish apocalyptic was made by the early church are subjects discussed by H. Tödt (1965), using insights already developed by R. Bultmann, E. Lohmeyer, and others.

In addition to the uses to which the book of Daniel was put in the synoptic Gospels, a complete discussion of the earliest chapter in the history of Christian interpretation of the book—namely, the NT—would include extended examination of its many reutilizations and transformations in Revelation. In this brief treatment of the subject, suffice it to point out that the cloud-borne Son of man of Rev 1:7 is both Jesus and judge, whose clothing and appearance resemble those of God (Rev 1:12-16; cf. Rev. 14:14-16). The animal allegory of Revelation 13 builds on the prototype of Dan 7:1-8; the final judgment scene in Rev 20:11-15 (cf. Rev 4:2-11) is also a refraction of Dan 7:13-14.

2. *Patristic Interpretation.* The book of Daniel continued to have a lasting effect on the thought of Christian writers after the first century C.E. Although Irenaeus (c. 130-200), bishop of Lyons, did not leave a commentary on it, he did help to set the basic lines of interpretation that were followed in subsequent centuries. The "stone not made by human hands" (Dan 2:34) is Jesus Christ and so is the "one like a son of man" who comes in the clouds (Dan 7:13). However, the appearance of the Christ in the clouds is deferred until the second advent, at which time the consummation of history would also result in the awarding of dominion to "the saints of the most high" (Dan 7:27)—that is, Christian believers and martyrs (see Rev 20:4-6). Irenaeus helped to establish the tradition of millenarian eschatology by suggesting that the span of time from the completion of creation until the consummation is in fact an exact equivalent to the six-day period of creation, reckoned on the formula one day = 1,000 years (i.e., a millennium). The seventh millennium, corresponding to God's day of sabbath rest in the beginning of time, would separate the consummation of history from the day of the final judgment of cosmic evil.

Patristic commentators on the book of Daniel included Hippolytus of Rome (170–236), Origen, Chrysostom, Jerome, and Theodoret of Cyrrhus. Ephraem, one of the Syriac-speaking church fathers of Eastern Christianity, contributed a commentary in the fourth century C.E. Jerome's commentary is the most accessible to us through the reprint of the translation by G. Archer, Jr. (1958) and the excellent monograph on the work by J. Braverman (1978). As is well known, Jerome returned to the original Hebrew/Aramaic text of the HB for his work of translation into Latin, and a concern for accuracy and for thorough attention to Jewish interpretation characterizes his commentary as well.

Using his discussion of Daniel 7 as an example of Jerome's work, we find him paying exquisite attention to the textual and historical details of the beasts and horns of vv. 1-8. Although he had precedent even in the NT, Jerome argued vigorously that the sequence of world empires represented by the four beasts is Babylon, Persia (the Persians were so bear-like in their spartan manner of life that "they used to use salt and nasturtium-cress in their relish," 74), the Macedonians (the four wings and four heads of the third beast, the leopard, are taken to refer to the so-called Diadochi, the four successors of Alexander among whom his empire was divided), and Rome. If the fourth beast is Rome, then the ten little horns of Dan 7:7-8 are clearly Roman rulers. However, since they appear simultaneously and not seriatim, they must be leaders who divide the empire among themselves; and because this event had not in fact happened, the seer must now be looking forward to the end times. Such an understanding enabled Jerome to assimilate the balance of the judgment scene, and indeed the entire chapter, to NT apocalyptic texts. The little horn is the antichrist (see 2 Thessalonians 2); the throne is that spoken of in Rev 4:2-11; the one like the son of man is the triumphant Christ of the eschaton called by John the lion of the tribe of Judah (Rev 5:5), who, though equal with God, had humbled himself by taking on the form of a servant (Phil 2:6-8). The saints are, of course, those who belong to Christ; and the kingdom they are given (Dan 7:18) is not an earthly one but is the heavenly abode of the saints. Their kingdom thus stands in stark contrast to that of the four earthly kingdoms of the beasts. This established, Jerome cries, "Away, then, with the fable about a millennium!" The establishment of the kingdom of the saints is for him the final event of history and is not part of a 1,000-year transitional period as it was for Irenaeus and Hippolytus.

Throughout his discussion of chapter 7 and the rest of the commentary, Jerome is at pains to rebut the critical views of Porphyry, the Neoplatonist philosopher of Tyre. Although Porphyry's work is lost, by assembling the references to him in Jerome's commentary it is possible to show that Porphyry understood the four beasts to refer respectively to the Babylonian, Medo-Persian, Alexandrian, and Seleucid empires. In other words, Porphyry's views were identical with those of many modern critical commentators. Furthermore, the stone of Dan 2:34 and the "one like a son of man" in Dan 7:13 were symbols of human figures—the Jews in their triumph at the eschaton in the first instance, and perhaps the triumph of the Maccabees over the forces of Antiochus IV Epiphanes in 164 B.C.E. in the second. M. Casey (1976) has shown that Porphyry was not entirely original in this rather more realistic understanding of the book's historical scenario and that indeed much of the same position is taken in writers of the Eastern and Syriac-speaking church—Aphrahat (early 4th cent.), Ephraem, Polychronius (d. c. 430), and the glosses in the Syriac version of the HB.

3. *Medieval Jewish and Christian Interpretation.* The medieval scholastics Albertus Magnus (c. 1200–1280) and Nicholas of Lyra, a Franciscan professor at the University of Paris (d. c. 1340), each wrote important commentaries on the book of Daniel. Like other medieval writers, including the great Thomas Aquinas, these commentators' understanding of the book reflects their knowledge of Jewish interpretation. All the great Jewish commentators of the period interpreted the book, including Saadia Gaon, Rashi, and A. Ibn Ezra. The fullest and most accessible commentary is the sectarian exegesis of the Karaite Jephet Ibn Ali (c. 1000). Scattered comments elsewhere in the rabbinic corpus reveal the basic lines of Jewish interpretation, particularly of the crucial chapter 7. The ninth century C.E. *Pirqe de R. Eliezer*, perhaps drawing upon considerably older traditional material, uses the description of the divine court in Dan 7:10 to explicate the scene of the second day of creation (Gen 1:6-8): "The hayyoth [living ones, one of the four classes of ministering angels known in Jewish exegesis] stand in awe and dread, in fear and trembling, and from the perspiraton of their faces a river of fire arises and goes forth before him, as it is said, 'A fiery stream issued and came forth before him . . . ' (Dan 7:10)." In other words, the fiery stream that illuminates the heavenly firmament is proved from Dan 7:10 to be angels' sweat.

More significant for our purposes is the clear identification made earlier in the rabbinic tradition of the son of man in Dan 7:13 with the Messiah. In a long list of sayings beginning, "The son of David will not come until," found in the Babylonian Talmud, this tradition is preserved: "R. Alexandri said: 'R. Joshua opposed two verses: it is written, "And behold, one like the son of man came with the clouds of heaven" [Dan 7:13] whilst [elsewhere] it is written, "[Behold, thy king cometh unto thee . . .] lowly, and riding upon an ass!" [Zech 9:9]. If they are meritorious, [he will come] "with the clouds of heaven"; if not, "lowly and riding upon an ass" (*b. Sanh.* 98a). This understanding of the son of man sees him as a future figure, a metaphor of a yet-to-come Messiah whose mode of epiphany is linked with the obedience of Israel and whose glory is thus bound up with Israel's own merited honor.

4. *The Reformation.* Although Luther made considerable use of the book of Daniel, both in his polemic against papal authority and in pastoral settings, and wrote a lengthy preface to the book in his Bible translation of 1530, he did not publish a separate commentary on the work. The great commentary deriving from the Reformation is that of Calvin, whose work appeared in 1561, only a year before the devastating wars of religion began. In his interpretation of the key phrases "one like a son of man" (Dan 7:13) and the "saints of the Most High" (Dan 7:18), Calvin avoids "subtle allegories" and forced expositions in favor of what he believes to be the plain meaning of the text. Of the expression "son of man," he says, "Without doubt, this is to be understood of Christ" (40). However, Calvin takes the simile seriously: The figure appearing in the clouds is like the Son of man. Although Christ had not yet assumed his incarnate form, he would in time do so. (Calvin quotes Tertullian here: "Then the Son of God put on a

specimen of his humanity," and then adds, "This was a symbol, therefore, of Christ's future flesh, although that flesh did not yet exist" [41].) By referring to Christ both as Son of man and as one who "came to the Ancient of Days" (taken as a reference to Christ's ascension and the commencement of his heavenly reign), Daniel thus affirms both the humanity and the divinity of Christ and gives no comfort to those of Manichaean tendencies who would see in Dan 7:13-14 evidence that the human appearance of Christ was only an illusion.

If the son of man who receives the dominion from God in Dan 7:13-14 is the Christ, a burning question makes itself felt: To which of Christ's advents is the writer referring? Here Calvin takes a position that is, by his own admission, contrary to the consensus of previous Christian interpreters. This event is not the second advent of Christ and the last judgment but rather the first advent: "This vision ought not to be explained as the final advent of Christ, but of the intermediate state of the church. The saints began to reign under heaven, when Christ ushered in his kingdom by the proclamation of his gospel" (75). This position is reinforced not only by the equation of the "books" to the gospel but also by Calvin's acceptance of the by then commonplace idea that the fourth beast is Rome and is therefore contemporaneous with Jesus of the first century C.E. The ten horns signify the collective leadership of the Roman republic, and the little horn in a general way signifies the dictatorship of the Caesars, which plucks up the former democracy. In Calvin's view, the rule of Christ certainly supplants that of the fourth beast, both visibly and invisibly, and the prophecy of destruction of v. 11 was fulfilled "from the time when foreigners obtained mastery" in Rome.

Given the violent hostilities of the time in which Calvin wrote on Daniel, one might have expected him to identify the event of Dan 7:9-14 with the second advent of Christ and to link the fourth beast, not with Rome, but with the Roman Catholic Church. The text could then have functioned admirably as solace to the embattled and endangered communities of the French and Swiss Reformation. But Calvin is led by his understanding of the plain meaning of the text away from such an extravagant extension of the prophecy out of the chronological horizon demanded by the animal allegory. Nevertheless, the text as he understands it does offer a basis for profound hope to the forces of righteousness in his own day. That hope lies in his identification of the "saints of the lofty ones" of vv. 18, 22-23, and 27, as "sons of God, or his elect people, or the church."

But if the son of man and the saints are equated in the text of Daniel 7, how can Calvin separate them into Christ and the church? To do so amounts to separating the dream (7:2-14) from its interpretation (7:17-27). Calvin is not troubled by this problem, for the principle of pars pro toto comes to his rescue. The two terms can simply be assimilated to each other; where Christ is, there is the church. The power exercised by the saints in v. 27 depends utterly upon the dominion being exercised by Christ at the Father's right hand (vv. 13-14). The covenant of adoption that the saints enjoy is founded on Christ, and the identity of the two depends thus utterly on the sequence: first the incarnation and the exaltation of Christ, figuratively represented in 7:13; then the adoption of the saints and the dominion of the church in and through Christ, represented in vv. 18, 22, and 27.

This leads to a final observation about Calvin's interpretation of the most important chapter of Daniel. If the events referred to in chap. 7 center around the first advent of the Christ and if the exaltation of Christ is also the beginning of the dominion of his body the church, then we have in Calvin the basis for the high eschatological expectation that so often characterized Calvinists and the Reformed movement in later generations. Christ and the saints have dominion in the earth for a period of limited but unspecified duration, beginning with the first advent of Christ and the first proclamation of his gospel and ending with the Parousia. Daniel 7 is thus a vision "of the intermediate state of the church. The saints began to reign under heaven, when Christ ushered in his kingdom by the promulgation of his gospel" (75)—and the implications of this exalted if hidden status of the church for its proper authority in the earth are profound. These are given concrete shape not only in Calvin's Geneva but also in Cromwell's Holy Commonwealth and in the colony of Massachusetts Bay.

5. *Puritan Interpretations.* In fact, it was among English and American Puritans of the seventeenth century that the book of Daniel enjoyed what was perhaps its greatest interpretive vogue. In it as well as in other biblical texts the Reformers of church and state found warrant for the radical social changes they sought—the egalitarian rule of the saints and the rejection of hierarchy in all of its forms, civil and religious. They even found there a basis for regicide (in the execution of King Charles I on Jan. 30, 1649) and for the establishment of the modern world's first "republic," the British Commonwealth led by the Lord Protector O. Cromwell.

When the increasingly normative millennialist reading of the end-time scenarios of Daniel 7–12 among English-speaking Reformed Christians was combined with a typological approach to the text of the Bible, a powerful dynamic for social and political action was unleashed. It worked this way. The rule of the saints (for whom the "one like a son of man" is a cipher, according to Dan 7:18) is, according to the transformation of the Danielic picture found in Rev 20:1-6, to occur on earth under Christ's aegis during the millennium before the last judgment and the end of the world as we know it. The "saints" of biblical expectation were related by analogy to the Reform movement in Protestantism; and the binding of the "dragon, that ancient serpent, who is the Devil and Satan" (Rev 20:2), which marks the beginning of the 1,000-year transitional period between this age and the next was seen as the type of the Protestant Reformation. Thus did it become abundantly clear to the radical Puritans, the Diggers, Ranters, Levellers, and Fifth-Monarchy men (those who claimed to be the vanguard of that eternal kingdom that will succeed the four world empires—the stone not made with human hands of Dan 2:34, 44-45, and the saints of the Most High of Dan 7:18, 27) that they were in fact those saints whose destiny it was to introduce the new order of the age (*novus ordo seclorum,* a motto that not accidentally can still be seen on the obverse of the Great Seal of the United States).

The names of authors and titles of works that contributed to this ferment are legion: T. Parker wrote The Visions and Prophecies of Daniel Expounded in 1646; J. Archer's book, The Personal Reign of Christ upon Earth, etc., went through at least six editions down to 1661. M. Cary contributed The Little Horn's Doom and Downfall: Or a Scripture-Prophesie of King James, and King Charles, and of this present Parliament unfolded, etc. (1651). Perhaps the most interesting of the lot is the Fifth Monarchy man and sometime New Englander W. Aspinwall, who in 1654 urged the revolution on with his book, *An Explication and Application of the Seventh Chapter of Daniel . . . Wherein Is Briefly Shewed the State and Downfall of the Four Monarchies; But More Largely of the Roman Monarchy, and the Ten Horns or Kingdoms; and in Particular, the Beheading of Charles Stuart, Who Is Proved to Be the Little Horn by Many Characters, That Cannot be Applied to Any Before or After Him,* etc. The literature of the period has been helpfully surveyed in the studies of K. Firth (1979), B. Ball (1975), P. Rogers (1966), and P. Toon (1970). R. Bloch (1985) pushes farther into eighteenth-century American Puritan writing.

6. *Eighteenth-Century Interpretation.* With the restoration of the Stuart monarchy of Charles II in 1669 and the reestablishment of the Church of England, much of the apocalyptic fervor that had animated public life subsided, and with it much interest in the book of Daniel. Late in the seventeenth century H. More, one of the group of "Cambridge Platonists" who believed in the twin lights of human faith and human reason, wrote a relatively sober account of the book called A Plain and Continued Exposition of the Several Prophecies or Divine Visions of the Prophet Daniel, etc. (1681). Here was an effort to assess the significance of this book in a manner that backed away from the enthusiasm of millennialism and direct historical application.

Much of the interest in the ensuing decades turned to calendrical matters and to the book's relationship to the large sweep of human history rather than to its significance for understanding immediately contemporary history. I. Newton's 1733 work *Observations Upon the Prophecies of Daniel and the Apocalypse of St. John* is in this vein. For Newton, a great deal was at stake with the book of Daniel, for "to reject his prophecies, is to reject the Christian religion. For this religion is founded upon his prophecy concerning the Messiah" (155 in Whitla ed. [1922]). As scientist, astronomer, and mathematician, Newton was naturally inclined to calculate chronology. Beginning with the accepted notion that the legs that terminate in feet and toes composed of iron and clay represented Rome (Dan 2:33), he found it necessary to examine the many digits into which the Roman Empire broke in its latter days. By dint of close calculations Newton assigned the toes (and the ten horns of Dan 7:7) to kingdoms ranging from the Vandals in Spain and Africa at the beginning, through the Britons, the Huns, the Lombards, and the kingdom at Ravenna at the end. The eleventh horn of the fourth beast is the church of Rome, which in the eighth century uprooted the exarchate of Ravenna, the kingdom of the Lombards, and the senate and dukedom of Rome (= the three horns of Dan 7:8). The power of this eleventh horn to change the times and the laws is demonstrated through citations of papal decretals as well as of secular sources under the political power of the Roman see. Newton reckoned the dominion of that power (the time, two times, and half a time of Dan 7:25) to be 1,260 solar years, after which (v, 26) "the judgment is to sit, and they shall take away his dominion, not at once but by degrees" (215-16). This same Newton, who was confident that he could perceive in the book a true chronology of future history, was one of the early ones to raise a critical question about it. He made a distinction between the last six chapters, which he said "contained prophecies written at several times by Daniel himself" and the first six chapters, which are "a collection of historical papers written by other authors" (Whitla ed., 145).

7. *Modern Critical Interpreters and Their Opponents*. Since the flowering of historical criticism in the nineteenth century, controversial passages such as the seventy weeks of Dan 9:24-27 (a text J. Montgomery called "the dismal swamp of OT criticism" [1927, 400]) became the battlefields between those who expected to find the timetable for the culmination of world history cryptically hidden within them and those who sought, not historical and predictive values, but an overall theological appreciation of God's lordship over the future. Larger issues that have usually divided the more traditional commentators from the more critical ones have been these:

a. *The unity of the book*. Traditionalists generally contend that the narratives about Daniel in chaps. 1–6 are from the same hand or circle that gave us the vision accounts by Daniel in chaps. 7–12. Critical commentaries have often found the materials to differ too radically in both literary style and theological content to have come from the same hand, although one of the most eminent modern critical scholars, H. Rowley, argued that a single person wrote the entire book of Daniel. Other studies have said that it does not matter and that the two halves belong together because a program of "interim ethics" (chaps. 1–6) is appropriately coupled to the assurance of final victory and the vindication of the saints (chaps. 7–12).

b. *Language*. Nobody has yet explained to the general satisfaction why the book of Daniel, which begins in a clear late biblical Hebrew, suddenly in 2:4*b* switches to the lingua franca of the Middle East known as Official Aramaic and then reverts to Hebrew again in chaps. 8–12. Traditionalists and critical interpreters do not separate into their respective camps on this issue. H. Ginsberg's theory that the entire book, except for the "interpolated" prayer of 9:4b-19, was originally written in Aramaic and that parts of it were then translated into Hebrew in order to make it more accessible and perhaps more authoritative to its devout Jewish readers has often been favored.

c. *Author*. Traditional interpreters take at face value the claim of the book that Daniel wrote down the dreams and visions of chaps. 7–12 (see Dan 7:1) and that he or some contemporary recorded the tales of chaps. 1–6. Modern critical interpreters tend to view the entire book as a pseudepigraphon, attributed by the circles that actually wrote it to the ancient worthy and wise man Dan'el, known even in the fourteenth century B.C.E. Canaanite literature of Ugarit and mentioned twice in Ezekiel-once in the same breath with the ancient righteous Gentiles, Noah and Job (Ezek 14:14, 20), and once as a man of preeminent wisdom (28:3).

d. *Date*. Traditionalists take seriously the internal dates of the book, beginning with the conquest of Jerusalem by Nebuchadnezzar, king of Babylon (Dan 1:1), and ending with the third year of Cyrus, king of Persia (Dan 10:1). This span of years, sometimes reckoned as 597–536 B.C.E., suggests that Daniel worked for about sixty-one years entirely within the community of the Jewish exiles in Babylon. Adherence to the given dates renders the visions of four succeeding world empires in chaps. 2 and 7, only the first two or three of which could have existed during Daniel's own lifetime, impressively accurate predictions of the future; even more impressive is the detailed account of Near Eastern history contained in 11:2–12:3. It also builds confidence that the denouement of history, which forms part of the same prophetic sequence in such texts as Dan 2:34-35; 7:9-13; and 11:40–12:3, will also come about as foreseen. The problem of timing, involving the proper interpretation of such chronological references as the seventy weeks of Dan 9:24-27 and the "time, two times, and half a time" of Dan 7:25 (cf. 8:14; 9:27; 12:7, 11- 12) hinges for traditional interpreters, as we have already seen, on identifying the fourth part of the colossus in Daniel 2 and the fourth beast in Daniel 7 with Rome. Inasmuch as Rome lingered for a long time and may even be said to be with us to this day in modern European nations, the gap between the fulfilled and the unfulfilled prophecies ("the great parenthesis" elaborated by H. Ironside [1943]) can by this means be closed. Daniel, who foresaw the rise of Rome even before the end of the HB period, can be understood to be predictive for our own future.

Critical interpreters, in contrast, view the question of the book's date very much in the same way as did the pagan Porphyry of ancient times, without, however, scorning the book because much of its "prophecy" is after the fact. On the contrary, to argue, as this scholarly tradition does, that the book reached its present form during the three years of oppression and persecution of the Jews by Antiochus IV Epiphanes (167–164 B.C.E.) and that this Greco-Syrian tyrant is in fact the "little horn" of Dan 7:8, the "one who makes desolate" of 9:27, and the "king of the north" of 11:20-45 is to take the book seriously as an "incarnate Word of God." It shares the limitations all human beings have when it comes to predicting the events of the future; in fact, it erred in suggesting that the eschaton would occur "a time, two times, and half a time" (= three and a half years?) from the writing of the book. But it addressed the crucial issue that confronted the community of observant, faithful Jews who were determined to resist the onslaught of Hellenistic culture and religious opposition. It gave them the encouraging messages that tyranny cannot prevail because God loathes it; that God will vindicate all obedience and loyalty in God's kingdom, which is coming; and that the saints have work of courage and obedience to do in the interim.

It remains simply to identify some of the participants on either side of this debate from the end of the nineteenth through the twentieth centuries. At the extreme edge of the traditionalist stream of interpretation are the exponents of the ideology of "premillennial dispensationalism," who incorporate Daniel's chronology of the future into a unified synthetic scheme for calculating the rapid and near approach of the Day of Judgment. From the turn of the century work of R. Anderson (1895), the full-scale commentary of A. Gaebelein (1911), and the annotations in the C. Scofield *Reference Bible*, first published in 1909, through the writings of Ironside, J. Walvoord (1971), J. Pentecost (1958), and the pages of Dallas Theological Seminary's periodical *Bibliotheca Sacra,* this ideological use of the book of Daniel is seen today in the popular form given it by H. Lindsey (1970).

The sectarian readings of Daniel by W. Miller and E. White, the founder and prophetess of

Seventh-Day Adventism, have yielded to contemporary Adventist commentators whose work belongs more nearly in the mainstream of traditional conservative "messianic" interpretation— e.g., G. Price (1955) and G. Hasel (1976). They join the 150-year-old company of other commentators who have defended the book's "integrity" against critical approaches: C. Keil, E. Hengstenberg, and T. Kliefoth (1868) in Germany; E. B. Pusey and C. Boutflower (1903) in Britain; M. Stuart, R. Wilson (2 vols. 1917, 1938), and E. Young (1949) in the United States. (The entire traditionalist stream is discussed in detail by D. Beegle [1978].)

Even before Newton's time commentators occasionally had concluded that Daniel was written in the days of Antiochus IV Epiphanes and that the "prophecies" are *vaticinia ex eventu,* "prophecies after the fact." However, it remained for the nineteenth century to bring forth full-scale commentaries based on a historical-critical reading, including those of L. Bertholdt (1806), H. Ewald (1868), and G. Behrmann (1894) in Germany; and those of S. Driver (1900), F. Farrar (1895), and A. Bevan (1892) in England. Early in the twentieth century R. Charles (1929) interested himself in Daniel as he interested himself in the non-canonical Jewish apocalyptic books; however, perhaps the fullest expression of the critical approach was Montgomery's work in the ICC series. Since that 1927 benchmark the critical tradition has been enriched by other works, including K. Marti (1901), O. Plöger (1865), and A. Bentzen (1952) in Germany; M. Delcor (1971) and A. Lacocque (1979) in France; Ginsberg (1948), Rowley (1950-51), N. Porteous (1965), and L. Hartman and A. Di Lella (1978) in England and America. Daniel's theological and hermeneutical issues have been explored by W. Towner and J. Gammie; J. Collins has given special attention both to the mythological traditions and to the literary genres employed by the book's authors. Collins's magisterial commentary on Daniel in the Hermeneia series (1993) will define the state of the art in Daniel studies for years to come.

Bibliography: R. Anderson, *Daniel in the Critics' Den* (1895). **H. Avalos,** "Daniel 9:24-25 and Mesopotamian Temple Rededications," *JBL* 117 (1998) 507-11. **B. W. Ball,** *A Great Expectation: Eschatological Thought in English Protestantism to 1660* (1975). **G. K. Beale,** *The Use of Daniel in Jewish Apocalyptic Literature and in the Revelation of St. John* (1984). **A. Bedenbender,** *Der Gott der Welt tritt auf den Sinai: Entstehung, Entwicklung und Funktionsweise der frühjüdischen Apokalyptik* (Arbeiten zur neutestamentlichen Theologie und Zeitgeschichte 8, 2000). **D. M. Beegle,** *Prophecy and Prediction* (1978). **G. Behrmann,** Das Buch Daniel (HKAT 3, 2, 1894). **A. Bentzen,** Daniel (HAT 1, 19, 1937, 1952). **K Berger,** Die griechische Daniel-Diegese: Eine Altkirchliche Apokalypse. Text, Übersetzung, und Kommentar (SPB 27, 1976). **L. Bertholdt,** *Daniel* (1806). **A. A. Bevan,** *A Short Commentary on the Book of Daniel* (1892). **R. Bloch,** *Visionary Republic: Millennial Themes in American Thought, 1756-1800* (1985). **R. Bodenmann,** Naissance d'une exégèse: Daniel dans l' église ancienne des trois premiers siècles (BGBE, 1986). **C. Boutflower,** *In and Around the Book of Daniel* (1903). **J. Braverman,** *Jerome's Commentary on Daniel: A Study of Comparative Jewish and Christian Interpretations of the HB* (CBQMS 7, 1978). **A. Brenner,** ed., *Prophets and Daniel* (FCB, second series 8, 2001). **L.P. Bruce,** "Discourse Theme and the Narratives of Daniel," *BSac* 160 (2003) 174-86. **G.W. Buchanan,** *The Book of Daniel* (Mellen Biblical Commentary, OT 25, 1999). **J. Calvin,** *Commentaries on the Book of the Prophet Daniel* (2 vols., 1948). **M. Casey,** "Porphyry and the Origin of the Book of Daniel," *JTS* 27 (1976) 15-33; *Son of Man: The Interpretation and Influence of Daniel 7* (1979). **R. H. Charles,** *A Critical and Exegetical Commentary on the Book of Daniel* (1929). **J. J. Collins,** *The Apocalyptic Vision of the Book of Daniel* (HSM 16, 1977); *Daniel: With an Introduction to Apocalyptic Literature* (FOTL 20, 1984); *Daniel* (Hermeneia, 1993); *Seers, Sibyls, and Sages in Hellenistic-Roman Judaism* (1997, 2001); and **P. W. Flint,** eds., *The Book of Daniel: Composition and Reception* (VTSup 83, 2001). **T. Craven,** "Daniel and Its Additions," *The Women's Bible*

Commentary (ed. C. A. Newsom and S. H. Ringe, 1992) 191-94. **M. Delcor**, *Le livre de Daniel* (SB, 1971). **S. R. Driver**, *The Book of Daniel* (CBSC 23, 1900). **J. Eggler**, *Influences and Traditions Underlying the Vision of Daniel 7:2-14: The Research History from the End of the 19th Century to the Present* (OBO 177, 2000). **G. H. Ewald**, *Daniel* (1868). **F. W. Farrar**, *The Book of Daniel* (1895). **M. H. Farris**, "The Formative Interpretations of the Seventy Weeks of Daniel" (diss., University of Toronto, 1990). **D. N. Fewell**, *Circle of Sovereignty: Plotting Politics in the Book of Daniel* (1988). **K. R. Firth**, *The Apocalyptic Tradition in Reformation Britain, 1530–1645* (Oxford Historical Monographs, 1979). **C. H. T. Fletcher-Louis**, "The High Priest as Divine Mediator in the Hebrew Bible: Dan 7:13 as a Test Case," SBLSP 36 (1997) 161-93. **F. Fraidl**, *Die Exegese der siebzig Wochen Daniels in der alten und mittleren Zeit* (1883). **A. C. Gaebelein**, *The Prophet Daniel: A Key to the Visions and Prophecies of the Book of Daniel* (1911). **J. G. Gammie**, *Daniel* (Knox Preaching Guides, 1983); "A Journey Through Danielic Spaces: The Book of Daniel in the Theology and Piety of the Christian Community," *Int* 39 (1985) 144-56. **H. L. Ginsberg**, *Studies in Daniel* (TSJTSA 14, 1948); "The Oldest Interpretation of the Suffering Servant," *VT* 3 (1953). **J. Goldingay**, *Daniel* (WBC 30, 1988). **D. E. Gowan**, *Daniel* (Abingdon Old Testament Commentary, 2001). **D. J. Harrington**, "The Ideology of Rule in Daniel 7-12," SBLSP 38 (1999) 540-51. **L. Hartman** and **A. Di Lella**, *The Book of Daniel: A New Translation with Notes and Commentary on Chapters 1–9* (AB 23, 1978). **G. F. Hasel**, "The Seventy Weeks of Daniel 9:24-27," *The Ministry*, supp. (May 1976). **D. Hellholm**, ed., *Apocalypticism in the Mediterranean World and the Near East: Proceedings of the International Colloquium on Apocalypticism* (1983). E. **W. Hengstenberg**, *Die Authentie des Daniel und die Integrität des Sacharjah* (1831). **M. Henze**, *The Madness of King Nebuchadnezzar: the Ancient Near Eastern Origins and Early History of Interpretation of Daniel 4* (JSJSup 61, 199); "The Narrative Frame of Daniel: A Literary Assessment," *JSJ* 32 (2001) 5-24. **Hippolytus**, *Kommentar zu Daniel* (tr. G.N. Bonwetsch, GCS 7, 2000). **H. A. Ironside**, *The Great Parenthesis* (1943). **Jerome**, *Jerome's Commentary on Daniel* (tr. G.Archer, Jr., 1958). **O. Keel**, *Hellenismus und Judentum: vier Studien zu Daniel 7 und zur Religionsnot unter Antiochus IV* (OBO 178, 2000). **C. F. Keil**, *The Book of the Prophet Daniel* (1884). **H.G. Kippenberg**, *Religions und Klassenbildung im antiken Judaä* (1982). **T. Kliefoth**, *Das Buch Daniel* (1868). **K. Koch**, *Das Buch Daniel* (EdF 144, 1980). **H. S. Kvanvig**, *The Roots of Apocalyptic: The Mesopotamian Background of the Enoch Figure and of the Son of Man* (1988). **A. Lacocque**, *The Book of Daniel* (1979). **H. Lindsey**, *The Late Great Planet Earth* (1970). **E. C. Lucas**, "Daniel: Resolving the Enigma," *VT* 50 (2000) 66-80. **D. S. Margoliouth** (ed.), *Commentary on the Book of Daniel by Jephet Ibn Ali the Karaite* (1889). **K. Marti**, *Das Buch Daniel* (KHC, Anecdota Oxoniensia, 1901). **G. K. McKay**, "The Eastern Christian Exegetical Tradition of Daniel's Vision of the Ancient of Days," *JECS* 7 (1999) 139-61. **A. Mertens**, *Das Buch Daniel im Lichte der Texte vom Toten Meer* (SBM 12, 1971). **J. A. Montgomery**, *A Critical and Exegetical Commentary on the Book of Daniel* (ICC, 1927). **B. Naor**, "Joseph and Daniel: Court Jews and Dreamers," *JBQ* 30 (2002) 10-16. **I. Newton**, *Observations Upon the Prophecies of Daniel and the Apocalypse of St. John* (1733). **J. D. Pentecost**, *Things to Come* (1958). **O. Plöger**, *Das Buch Daniel* (KAT 18, 1965). **N. Porteous**, *Daniel* (OTL, 1965). **G. M. Price**, *The Greatest of the Prophets* (1955). **E. B. Pusey**, *Daniel the Prophet* (1868). **P. L. Redditt**, *Daniel* (NCB , 1999); "Daniel 9: Its Structure and Meaning," *CBQ* 62 (2000) 236-4. **P. G. Rogers**, *The Fifth Monarchy Men* (1966). **J. Roloff**, *Die Adaption der Tiervision (Daniel 7) in frühjüdischer und frühchristlicher Apokalyptik* (SBAW, 2002). **C. Rowland**, *The Open Heaven: A Study of Apocalyptic in Judaism and Early Christianity* (1982). **H. H. Rowley**, "The Unity of the Book of Daniel," *HUCA* 33 (1950-51) 233-73; *The Servant of the Lord and Other Essays on the OT* (1965) 249-80. **C. I. Scofield** (ed.), *Scofield Reference Bible* (1909; new ed., 1967). **C. L. Seow**, *Daniel* (Westminster Bible

Companion, 2003). **D. Smith**, *The Religion of the Landless: The Sociology of the Babylonian Exile* (1989). **D. L. Smith-Christopher**, "The Book of Daniel," *NIB* (1996) 7:17-152. **M. Stuart**, *A Commentary on the Book of Daniel* (1850). **M. A. Sweeney**, "The End of Eschatology in Daniel? Theological and Socio-Political Ramifications of the Changing Contexts of Interpretation," *BibInt* 9 (2001) 123-40. **J. P. Tanner**, "The Literary Structure of the Book of Daniel," *BSac* 160 (2003) 269-82. **J. D. Thompson**, *A Critical Concordance to the Septuagint: Daniel* (The Computer Bible 77, 2000). **H. E. Tödt,** *The Son of Man in the Synoptic Tradition* (NTL, 1965). **P. Toon** (ed.), *Puritans, the Millennium, and the Future of Israel* (1970). **W. S. Towner**, "Were the English Puritans `The Saints of the Most High'? Issues in the Pre-critical Interpretation of Daniel 7," *Int* 37 (1983) 46-63; *Daniel* (Interpretation, 1984). **J. C. VanderKam**, *Enoch and the Growth of Apocalyptic Tradition* (CBQMS 16, 1984). **P. M. Venter**, "Daniel and Enoch: Two Different Reactions," *HvTSt* 53 (1997), 68-91. **H. M. Wahl**, "Das Motiv des 'Aufstiegs' in der Hofgeschichte: Am Beispiel von Joseph, Esther und Daniel," *ZAW* 112 (2000) 59-74. **J. F. Walvoord,** *Daniel the Key to Prophetic Revelation* (1971). **J. Weinberg**, *The Citizen Temple Community* (1992). **W. Whitla**, *Sir I. Newton's Daniel and the Apocalypse* (1922). **R. D. Wilson**, *Studies in the Book of Daniel: A Discussion of the Historical Questions* (2 vols., 1917, 1938). **E. J. Young**, *The Prophecy of Daniel: A Commentary* (1949). **M. A. Zier**, "The Latin Interpretation of Daniel in the Middle Ages: An Historical Survey" (diss., Toronto, 1981); "The Medieval Latin Interpretation of Daniel: Antecedents to Andrew of St. Victor," *RTAM* 58 (1991) 43-78.

W. S. TOWNER

THE LATTER PROPHETS: MINOR

Hosea

1. *The Early Church.* Significant exegeses of the book of Hosea were composed by Jerome, Theodore of Mposuestia, Cyril of Alexandria, Julian of Aeclanum , and Theodoret of Cyrrhus. Of these, Jerome's was the most important in which he explored the literal sense of Hosea's words. He also mentions several no longer extant commentaries written before his time: the commentary of Apollinaris Laodicenus, Origen's small book (*peri tou pos onomasthe en to Osee Egraim*), and Pierius' *Tractatus longissimus.* Eusebius of Caesarea also wrote about Hosea in the eighteenth book of his *Euangelike apodeixis,* and Didymus the Blind composed three books on Hosea at Jerome's request.

Theodore of Mopsuestia's commentary—on the Minor Prophets remains the only one preserved entirely in the Greek—used both a historical-grammatical approach oriented to the literal sense of the biblical text and the typological interpretation (which established the connection of the Hebrew Bible to the New Testament). Cyril of Alexandria defended the historicity of the events portrayed in the book but interpreted the text allegorically. Theodoret of Cyrrhus used a historical-grammatical approach, frequently also used typological and allegorical exegesis.

2. *The Middle Ages.* Several important commentaries were written during this period. Theophylakt of Achrida understood his exegesis of Hosea as a compendium of earlier exegeses. Guibert of Nogent limited himself to a moral interpretation. Rupert of Deutz sought to trace out the mystery of the kingdom of God and to inquire after the meaning hidden in the letters. Andrew of St. Victor based his exegesis on Jerome and attempted to understand Hosea from the prophet's own time. S. Langton commented on Hosea according to the threefold sense of the text: literal, moral, and allegorical. Albertus Magnus also contributed an important commentary.

3. *Luther and Calvin.* Luther's principal concern in his exegesis of the book of Hosea was the "uncompromising assertion of the literal sense" (G. Krause [1962] 115). He saw Hosea primarily as a preacher, as he saw all the prophets; he stressed that Hosea was rooted in Israel's tradition of faith, and that individual parts of the book derived from different periods. Calvin concentrated on philological questions, occasionally making connections to the Christian church.

4. *The Sixteenth Through the Eighteenth Centuries.* Treatments written during the sixteenth century include J. Wigand, *In XII Prophetas Minores explicationes succinctae, ordinem rerum, textus sententiam, et doctrinas praecipuas strictissime indicantes* (1566); H. Mollerus, *Enarratio brevis et grammatica concionum Hoseae, excepta ex publicis praelectionibus...in schola Wittenbergensi* (Möller [1567]); and L. Osiander the Elder, *Biblia latina...,* vol. 5, *Ezechiel, Daniel, Osse...* (1579). Of particular note in the seventeenth century are the works of S. Gesner, *Commentarius in oseam Prophetam...* (1614); B. Krakevitz, *Commentarius in Hoseam...* (1619); B. Meisner, *Hoseas novo commentario per textus analysin, ejusdem exegesin, dubiorum solutionem, et locorum communium annotationem...* (1620); J. H. Ursinus, *Hoseas, commentario literali ex optimis interpretibus concinnato...Opus posthumum* (1677); and S. Schmidt, *In Prophetam Hoseam Commentarius...* (1687). But above all stands the great work of E. Pococke, *A Commentary on the Prophecy of Hosea* (1685). Exegesis during the eighteenth century includes the work of H. von der Hardt, *Hoseas historiae et antiquitati redditus libris XXIX pro nativa interpretandi virtute cum dissertationibus in Raschium* (1712); J. W. Petersen, *Die Erklärung der zwölf kleinen Propheten...* (1723); W. Lowth, *A Commentary upon the Larger and Lesser Prophets...* (1739); J. G. Schroeer, *Der Prophet Hosea...* (1782); J. C. Volborth, *Erklärung des Propheten Hosea* (1787); C. G. Kuinoel, *Hosea oracula hebraice et latine perpetua annotatione...* (1792); and E. G. Bockel, *Hoseas* (1807).

5. *Important Commentaries Since 1800.* The foundation for the modern historical-critical work on the book of Hosea was laid in the nineteenth century through a number of important commentaries, beginning with the interpretation of E. Rosenmüller, *Scholia in Vetus Testamentum im Compendium Redacta* (ed. J. C. S. Lechner, *Scholia in Prophetas Minores* 6 [1836] 4-70) and carried on through the work of F. Hitzig/H. Steiner (1838), H. Ewald (1867), A. Wünsche (1868), T. Cheyne (1884), C. Keil (1888), and C. von Orelli (1908). All of these are primarily philological in nature and are concerned with the text. Wünsche's commentary *Der Prophet Hosea* (1868) surveyed the medieval rabbinic exegetes as well as the book's targumic translation (see S. Coleman [1960]). Keil concentrated on the clarification of questions of biblical archaeology in addition to philology. With the appearance of J. Wellhausen's commentary (1898), intense literary-critical questions came into focus alongside philological ones. Noteworthy from the first half of the twentieth century are the commentaries of K. Marti, *Das Dodekapropheton* (KHC, 1904); W. R. Harper, *A Critical and Exegetical Commentary on Amos and Hosea* (ICC, 1905); A. Ehrlich, *Randglossen zur hebräischen Bibel: Textkritisches, sprachliches und sachliches*, vol. 5 (19121968); E. Sellin, *Das Zwölfprophetenbuch* (KAT XII, 1922); J. Lindblom, *Hosea, literarisch untersucht* (1927); S. Brown, *The Book of Hosea* (WC, 1932); T. Robinson and F. Horst (1964); J. Lippl and J. Theis, *Die zwölf kleinen Propheten, 1. Halfte, Osee, Joel, Amos, Abdias, Jonas, Michaas* (HSAT VIII 3 I, 1937); and F. Nötscher, *Zwölfprophetenbuch oder kleine Propheten* (1954). The most influential commentaries have been those of H. W. Wolff (1965); W. Rudolph (1966); J. Mays, *Hosea: A Commentary* (OTL, 1969); F. Andersen and D. N. Freedman, *Hosea: A New Translation with Introduction and Commentary* (AB 24, 1980); A. Deissler, *Zwölf Propheten: Hosea—Joel—Amos* (Die Neue Echter Bibel, 1981); and J. Jeremias, *Der Prophet Hosea* (ATD 24, 1, 1983).

6. *The Text.* The text of Hosea is in many verses so badly preserved that the original sense can scarcely be determined with certainty (e.g., 9:13, 11:7). Consequently, commentaries deal exhaustively with text-critical issues, and the relationship of the MT to the Septuagint takes on particular significance. H.S. Nyberg (1935, 113-17) assumes that the Septuagint can make no essential contribution to the solution of the text-critical problems in Hosea. Conversely, G. Patterson (1890/91, 190-121) views the value of the Septuagint positively in this respect, explaining most of the discrepancies through the thesis that the Septuagint translator consciously sought to tailor his work to his audience. Indeed, Patterson's position is to be preferred to that of Nyberg, since the interpretative *Tendenz* of the Septuagint is clear where it completes, improves, smooths over, and interprets the text on theological-contextual and syntactical-stylistic grounds without altering its fundamental sense. Where the Septuagint diverges from the essence of the MT, however, one must reckon with an unclear and corrupt *Vorlage*.

7. *The Transmission of Hosea's Words.* Since the beginning of the nineteenth century there has been agreement among scholars that the present book of Hosea was put together from two separate parts: chaps. 1–3 and chaps. 4–14 (Rosenmüller [1836] 8-9). H. Ginsberg (1971), however, following H. Graetz and Y. Kaufmann, has argued for two Hoseas. The first (chaps. 1–3) belonged to the period of the Omride dynasty in the ninth century, with the second belonging to the eighth-century prophet.

a. *Chapters 1–3.* The third-person report of Hosea's marriage in chap. 1 and the first-person report of his marriage in chap. 3 show that Hosea 1–3 itself stems from different literary connections. Perhaps these two chapters contain two different reports of a single marriage of Hosea from two different hands. Chapter 3 may also be seen as the autobiographical resumption of the biographical narrative of chap. 1 (Robinson [1964] 15-16). Perhaps a prophetic disciple who wanted to present the beginning of Hosea's life as a prophet stands behind chap. 1 (H. Wolff [1965] xxix-xxxii). L. Ruppert (1982) regards the history of the transmission of chaps. 1–3 as far more complicated since he assumes a total of four phases of transmission: the core unit A,

2:4-7, 10-15; composition B, 2:4-7, 8-9, 10-15, 16-17, 19; composition C, 2:4-7, 8-9, 10-15, 16-17ab, 18ab, 19, 21-22; composition D, 2:4-7, 8-9, 10-15, 16-17, 18ab, 19, 21-22, 23ab, 24.

Marriage of Hosea. (1) In the nineteenth century, Hosea's marriage was often interpreted as an allegory on Yahweh's relationship to Israel (Hitzig/Steiner [1838] 8; Wünsche [1868] 9), or (2) Hosea's marriage is an *imitatio* of the experience God has with Israel; Yahweh has commanded him to marry a wife inclined to adultery (Ewald [1867] 192; Wellhausen [1898] 105-8). (3) Chapters 1–3 describe Hosea's marriage, at Yahweh's command, to a sacral prostitute, (Robinson [1964] 17), who is described as a whore. Canaanite fertility cults (in which virgins were ritually sacrificed to the deity) had gained a hold in Israel (Wolff [1976] 14-16).

Feminist and Womanist biblical scholars wrestle with the marriage metaphor's usefulness for the church and synagogue as a desirable image for God. Why, they ask, is so much violence and pornography present in Hosea 1–3 (see D. Setel [1985]; G. Yee [1992]; R. Weems [1989, 1995])? This violence is a punishment for wayward Israel, who is embodied female. Feminists worry that this marriage metaphor, which can be interpreted as a powerful illustration of a loving and forgiving God, in reality becomes a model and justification for physically abusive relationships.

b. *Chapters 4–14.* These chapters consist of different units with diverse imagery. Wolff (1976, xxix-xxxii) believes that kerygmatic units can be recognized here, while Jeremias (1983) theorizes that disciples of Hosea composed, shortened, and assembled in chaps. 4–11 the words of Hosea. According to the investigation by Yee (1987), four redactional phases can be distinguished: Hosea (H), the collector (C), the first redactor (R^1), and a final redactor (R^2). What is clear about the formation process is that the final stage is to be ascribed to a Judean editor (Jeremias [1983] 18; G. Emmerson [1984] 156-64).

8. *The Spiritual Provenance of Hosea.* Commentaries question whether Hosea came from a priestly or a prophetic background (Wünsche [1868]; Rudolph [1966]). Wolff (1956) concluded on the basis of 6:4-6; 9:7-9; 12:8-11, 13-15 that Hosea stood in closest alliance to the prophets, in decided opposition to Israel's monarchy and priesthood. According to E. Zenger (1982), the book of Hosea documents Hosea's claim that he was the bearer of a particular prophetic office (*successio prophetica*, 11:4). This form of prophecy stood in fundamental political competition with the existing organs of state; therefore, the anti-Canaanite and anti-monarchical polemic of Hosea must be understood as criticism of state and cult.

9. *The Salvation Traditions of Israel.* Hosea relies extensively on the traditions of Israel. Allusions to the Jacob traditions are found in 5:1-2 and 12:4-5. It is heavily disputed whether Jacob is understood here as a positive or a negative figure (e.g., H. D. Neef [1987] 15-49). The majority of exegetes assume that 12:13-14 opposes Jacob, who serves a woman, to Moses, who stands in service to God. A sizable group of scholars deny that 12:13-14 come from Hosea at all.

Features of the desert election tradition appear in 2:16-17; 9:10-17; 10:1-2, 11-13a; 11:1-7; 12:10; 13:4-8. These are variously interpreted as a symbol of a nomadic ideal of Hosea; as part of the exodus and Sinai tradition; as an independent election tradition distinct from the exodus; or as an Ishmaelite tribal tradition. Texts ascribed to the desert election tradition share a description of the desert period as the time of intimate community between Yahweh and Israel (Neef, 58-119).

Highly controversial in the discussion is the covenant tradition in Hosea (2:20; 6:7; 8:1; 10:4; 12:2). Many scholars eliminate as non-Hoseanic passages that employ the term "covenant" (L. Perlitt [1969] 150-53; but see E. Nicholson [1986]). Other connections include the decalogue (4:2; 8:4-6; 12:10; 13:1-4), wisdom tradition (2:21; 4:1; 5:12; 8:7; 12:8), Gilgal (4:15; 9:15; 12:11), Gibeah (5:8; 9:9; 10:9), and Admah and Zeboim (11:8).

10. *The Portrayal of the Divine in Hosea and in Ugarit.* Excavations at Ugarit since 1929

have given new impetus to the study of Hosea's polemic against the Canaanite Baal cult (e.g., W. Kuhnig [1974]). D. Kinet (1977) contrasts Baalism and Yahwism: Baal follows the seasonal cycle of nature, while Yahweh is absolute lord over nature, life, and death; in contrast to Yahwism, Baalism lacks a historical dimension; in the Ugaritic texts no ethical order is bound up with the being or working of Baal, whereas the book of Hosea is completely caught up in Israel's moral failure as the people of God; the citizen of Ugarit knew that every death in the world of vegetation would be followed by rebirth, but Hosea struggled passionately against the religious complacency of his people; in Ugarit the numerous offerings find their justification in the certainty of the return of Baal, while in Hosea sacrifice can replace neither the obligations of Israel to Yahweh nor the ethical relationship as such; the Hoseanic understanding of Yahweh is determined by the intensive depiction of conflict between Yahweh and the people, while in the religion of Baal the only conflict is between the various gods (209-27).

11. *Hosea's Relationship to the Monarchy.* Hosea comments on the monarchy several times in his preaching (1:4; 3:4; 7:3-7; 8:4; 10:3-4, 7, 15; 13:9-11), and his pronouncements are frequently resolved through a succession of bloody revolutions and regicides. Hosea does not, however, reject the monarchy in and of itself; rather, he criticizes the complete contempt for divine justice among the kings, who are representatives of Yahweh's people. The deep entanglement of Israel in guilt and divine wrath is seen, according to Hosea, in the demise of the monarchy.

Recent commentaries on Hosea include Sweeney (2000) and Stone's commentary (2001), from a gay perspective. Braaten (2001) offers an environmental theology; Gisin (2002) studies the authenticity of Hosea as the book's author. Setel (1985), Sherwood (1996), Brenner (1995), Keefe (2001), and Törnkvist (1998) offer feminist critiques of Hosea; Nwaoru (1999) and Oestreich (1998) study Hosea's metaphors; and Premnath (2003) includes a social science analysis.

Bibliography: R. Abma, *Bonds of Love: Methodic Studies of Prophetic Texts with Marriage Imagery (Isaiah 50:1-3 and 54:1-10, Hosea 1–3, Jeremiah 2–3)* (Studia Semitica Neerlandica 40, 1999). **P. R. Ackroyd,** "Hosea and Jacob," *VT* 13 (1963) 245-59. **R. Bach,** "Die Erwählung Israels in der Wüste," (diss., Bonn, 1952). **C. Barth,** "Zur Bedeutung der Wüstentradition," *VTSup* 15 (1966) 137-51. **B. C. Birch,** *Hosea, Joel, Amos* (Westminster Bible Companion, 1997). **S. Bitter,** *Die Ehe des Propheten Hosea: Eine auslegungsgeschichtliche Studie* (GTA 3, 1975) 102-80. **P. G. Borbone,** "L'uccisione dei profeti (Osea 6:5)," *Hen* 6 (1984) 271-92; "Il terzo incomodo: L'interpretazione del testo masoretico di Osea 3:1," *Hen* 7 (1985) 151-60; "Riflessioni sulla critica del testo dell'antico testamento ebraico in riferimento al libro di Osea," *Hen* 8 (1986) 281-309. **G. Bouwman,** *Des Julian von Aeclanum Kommentar zu den Propheten Osee, Joel, und Amos* (AnBib 9, 1958). **L. J. Braaten,** "Earth community in Hosea 2," *The Earth story in the Psalms and the Prophets* (ed. N. C. Habel, Earth Bible 4, 2001). **A. Brenner,** ed., *A Feminist Companion to the Latter Propohets* (FCB 8, 1995). **K. Budde,** "The Nomadic Ideal in the OT," *The New World* (December, 1895) 1-20. **M. Buss,** *The Prophetic Word of Hosea: A Morphological Study* (BZAW 111, 1969). **J. Calvin,** *Hoseas* (CR 70, 198-514; ET Commentaries on the Twelve Minor Prophets [4 vols. 1846-49, repr. 1950]). **A. Caquot,** "Osee et la Royaute," *RHPR* 41 (1961) 123-46. **U. Cassuto,** "The Prophet Hosea and the Books of the Pentateuch," *Biblical and Oriental Studies, vol. 1, Bible* (1973) 79-100. **H. Cazelles,** "The Problem of the Kings in Osee 8:4," *CBQ* 11 (1949) 14-25. **T. K. Cheyne,** *Hosea* (CBSC, 1884). **S. Coleman,** *Hosea Concepts in Midrash and Talmud* (1960). **G. Cooper and J. Goldingay,** "Hosea and Gomer Visit the Marriage Counselor," *First Person: Essays in Biblical Autobiography* (ed. P. R. Davies, Biblical Seminar 81, 2002).**Cyril of Alexandria,** *Cyrilli Alexandriae Archiepiscopi in Oseam Prophetam Commentarius* (PG 71, 1-328). **D. R. Daniels,**

Hosea and Salvation History: The Early Traditions of Israel in the Prophecy of Hosea (BZAW 191, 1990). **F. Diedrich,** *Die Anspielungen auf die Jakob-Tradition in Hosea 12:1–13:3: Ein literaturwissenschaftlicher Beitrag zur Exegese früher Prophetentexte* (FzB 27, 1977). **G. I. Emmerson,** *Hosea: An Israelite Prophet in Judean Perspective* (JSOTSup 28, 1984). **H. Ewald,** *Die Propheten des Alten Bundes* (3 vols., 1867-1868). **B. Fuss,** *"Dies ist die Zeit, von der geschrieben ist-" : Die expliziten Zitate aus dem Buch Hosea in den Handschriften von Qumran und im Neuen Testament* (NTAbh n.f. 37, 2000). **K. Galling,** *Die Erwählungstraditionen Israels* (BZAW 48, 1928). **A. Gelston,** "Kingship in the Book of Hosea," *OTS 19* (1974) 71-85. **H. L. Ginsberg,** "Hosea, Book of," *EncJud* 8 (1971). **W. Gisin,** *Hosea: Ein literarisches Netzwerk beweist seine Authentizität* (BBB 139, 2002). **E. M. Good,** "The Composition of Hosea," *SEA* 31 (1966) 21-63; "Hosea and the Jacob Tradition," *VT* 16 (1966) 13-51. **S. Grätz,** *Der strafende Wettergott: Erwägungen zur Traditionsgeschichte des Adad-Fluchs im Alten Orient und im Alten Testament* (BBB 114, 1998). **Guibert von Nogent,** *Ad Tropologias in Prophetas Osee et Amos ac Lamentationes Jeremiae* (PL 156, 337-416). **K. M. Hayes,** *"The Earth Mourns": Prophetic Metaphor and Oral Aesthetic* (Academia Biblica 8, 2002). **Hieronymus (Jerome),** *Commentariorum in Osee Prophetam* (CCSL 76, 1-158). **F. Hitzig and H. Steiner,** *Die zwölf kleinen Propheten* (KEH, 1838 = 1881). **F. L. Hossfeld,** *Der Dekalog: Seine späten Fassungen, die originale Komposition, und seine Vorstufen* (OBO 45, 1982). **E. Jacob,** "Der Prophet Hosea und die Geschichte," *EvTh* 24 (1964) 281-90. **C. Jeremias,** "Die Erzväter in der Verkündigung der Propheten," *Beitrage zur alttestamentlichen Theologie: Festschrift W. Zimmerli zum 70 Geburtstag* (1977) 206-22. **A. A. Keefe,** *Woman's Body and the Social Body in Hosea* (JSOTSup 338, Gender, Culture, Theory 10, 2001). **C. F. Keil,** *Biblischer Commentar über die zwolf kleinen Propheten* (1888[3]). **A. Kerrigan, O.F.M.,** *St. Cyril of Alexandria, Interpreter of the OT* (AnBib 2, 1952). **D. Kinet,** *Ba'al und Jahwe: Ein Beitrag zur Theologie des Hoseabuches* (EHS.T 87, 1977). **M. Kockert,** "Prophetie und Geschichte im Hoseabuch," *ZTK* 85 (1988) 3-30. **G. Krause,** *Studien zu Luthers Auslegung der kleinen Propheten* (BHT 33, 1962). **W. Kuhnigk,** *Nordwestsemitische Studien zum Hoseabuch* (BibOr 27, 1974). **R. Kümpel,** "Die Berufung Israels: Ein Beitrag zur Theologie des Hosea," (diss., Bonn, 1973). **F. Landy,** "In the Wilderness of Speech: Problems of Metaphor in Hosea," *Beauty and the Enigma: And other Essays on the Hebrew Bible* (JSOTSup 312, 2001). **M. Luther,** *Hosea* (WA 13, 2-66; ET Lectures on the Minor Prophets [1975]). **M. Mulzer,** *Alarm für Benjamin: Text, Struktur und Bedeutung in Hos 5,8-8,14* (Arbeiten zu Text und Sprache im Alten Testament 74, 2003). **T. Naumann,** *Hoseas Erben: Strukturen der Nachinterpretation im Buch Hosea* (BWANT 131, 1991). **H. D. Neef,** "Der Septuaginta-Text und der Masoreten-Text des Hoseabuches im Vergleich," *Bib* 67 (1986) 195-220; *Die Heilstraditionen Israels in der Verkundigung des Propheten Hosea* (BZAW 169, 1987). **E. W. Nicholson,** *God and His People: Covenant and Theology in the OT* (1986). **M. Nissinen,** *Prophetie, Redaktion, und Fortschreibung im Hoseabuch: Studien zum Werdegang eines Prophetenbuches im Lichte von Hos 4 und 11* (AOAT 231, 1991). **E. O. Nwaoru,** *Imagery in the Prophecy of Hosea* (Ägypten und Altes Testament 41, 1999). **H. S. Nyberg,** *Studien zum Hoseabuche* (1935). **B. Oestreich,** *Metaphors and Similes for Yahweh in Hosea, 14:2-9 (1-8): A Study of Hoseanic Pictorial Language* (Friedensauer Schriftenreihe, Reihe A, Theologie 1, 1998). **C. von Orelli,** *Die zwölf kleinen Propheten* (KK, 1908[3]). **G. H. Patterson,** "The Septuagint Text of Hosea Compared with the MT," *Hebraica* 7 (1890/91) 190-221. **M. C. Pennacchio,** *Propheta insaniens: l'esegesi patristica di Osea tra profezia e storia* (Studie ephemeridis Augustinianum 81, 2002). **L. Perlitt,** *Bundestheologie im Alten Testment* (WMANT 36, 1969). **H. Pfeiffer,** *Das Heiligtum von Bethel im Spiegel des Hoseabuches* (FRLANT 183, 1999). **D. N. Premnath,** *Eighth Century Prophets: A Social Analysis* (2003). **T. H. Robinson and F. Horst,** *Die zwölf kleinen Propheten* (HAT 14, 1964). **E. F. C. Rosenmüller,** *Scholia* 6 (1836) 4-170. **L. Rowlett,** "Lovers and Raisin Cakes:

Food, Sex and Divine Insecurity in Hosea," *Queer Commentary and the Hebrew Bible* (ed. K. Stone, JSTOSup 334, 2001). **H. H. Rowley,** "The Marriage of Hosea," *Men of God* (1963) 66-97. **W. Rudolph,** *Hosea: A Commentary* (KAT XIII, 1, 1966). **Rufinus,** *Commentarius in Prophetas Minores Tres Osee, Joel et Amos, Rufino Aquileiensi Presbytero, Commentarius in Oseam* (PL 21, 959-1034). **Rupert von Deutz,** *Ruperti Abbatis Tuitiensis Commentariorum in Duodecim Prophetas Minores. Libri XXXI. Prologus Ruperti in Osee Prophetam—In Osee Prophetam* (PL 168, 11-204). **L. Ruppert,** "Herkunft und Bedeutung der Jakob-Tradition bei Hosea," *Bib* 52 (1971) 488-504; "Beobachtungen zur Literar- und Kompositionskritik von Hosea 1–3," *Künder des Wortes: Festschrift J. Schreiner zum 60. Geburtstag* (1982) 163-82. **T. D. Setel,** "Prophets and Pornography: Female Sexual Imagery in Hosea," *Feminist Interpretation of the Bible* (ed. L. Russell, 1985) 86-95. **Y. Sherwood,** *The Prostitute and the Prophet: Hosea's Marriage in Literary-Theoretical Perspective* (JSOTSup 212; Gender, Culture, Theory 2, 1996). **M. A. Sweeney,** *The Twelve Prophets* (Berit Olam, 2000). **Theodore of Mopsuestia,** *Theodori Mopsuesteni Commentarius in XII Prophetas: Einleitung und Ausgabe von H. N. Sprenger* (Göttinger Orientforschungen V, 1, 1977). **Theodoret of Cyrrhus,** *Beati Theodoreti Episcopi Cyrensis Enarratio in Oseam Prophetam* (PG 81, 1551-632). **Theophylact,** *Theophylacti Expositio in Prophetam Oseam, Commentaris in Oseam* (PG 126, 565-820). **W. Thiel,** "Die Rede vom 'Bund' in den Prophetenbüchern," *ThV IX* (1977) 11-36. **R. Törnkvist,** *The Use and Abuse of Female Sexual Imagery in the Book of Hosea: A Feminist Critical Approach to Hos 1–3* (Acta Universitatis Upsaliensis, Uppsala Women's Studies A, Women in Religion 7, 1998). **L. Treitel,** *Die alexandrinische Uebersetzung des Buches Hosea, Heft 1* (1887); "Die Septuaginta zu Hosea," *MGDJ* 41 (1897) 433-54. **J. M. Trotter,** *Reading Hosea in Achaemenid Yehud* (JSOTSup 328, 2001). **H. Utzschneider,** *Hosea: Prophet vor dem Ende* (OBO 31, 1980). **K. Vollers,** "Das Dodekapropheton der Alexandriner," *ZAW* 3 (1883) 219-72. **J. Vollmer,** *Geschichtliche Rückblicke und Motive in der Prophetie des Amos, Hosea, und Jesaja* (BZAW 119, 1971). **T. C. Vriezen,** "La Tradition de Jacob dans Osee XII," *OTS* 1 (1942) 64-78. **R. J. Weems,** "Gomer: Victim of Violence or Victim of Metaphor?" *Semeia* 47 (1989) 87-104; *Battered Love: Marriage, Sex, and Violence in the Hebrew Prophets* (OBT, 1995). **J. Wellhausen,** *Die kleinen Propheten* (1898, 1963). **I. Willi-Plein,** *Vorformen der Schriftexegese innerhalb des Alten Testaments: Untersuchungen zum literarischem Werden der auf Amos, Hosea, und Micha zurückgehenden Bücher im hebräischen Zwölfprophetenbuch* (BZAW 123, 1971). **H. W. Wolff,** "Hoseas geistige Heimat," *TLZ* 81 (1956) 83-94 = *Gesammelte Studien zum Alten Testament* (TBü 22, 1973) 232-50; *Hosea* (Hermeneia, 1965; ET 1974). **A. Wünsche,** *Der Prophet Hosea übersetzt und erklärt mit Benutzung der Targumin, der jüdischem Ausleger Raschi, Aben Ezra, und D. Kimchi* (1868). **G. A. Yee,** *Composition and Tradition in the Book of Hosea: A Redaction Critical Investigation* (SBLDS 102, 1987); "Hosea," *Women's Bible Commentary* (ed. C. A. Newsom and S. H. Ringe, 1992) 195-204; "The Book of Hosea," *NIB* (1996) 7:195-298. **E. Zenger,** " 'Durch Menschen zog ich sie . . . ' (Hos 11:4): Beobachtungen zum Verständnis des prophetischen Amtes im Hoseabuch," *Künder des Wortes: Festschrift J. Schreiner zum 60. Geburtstag* (1982) 183-201.

H.-D. Neef

Joel

This short book of seventy-three verses, the second of the Minor Prophets in the MT, presents several interpretive problems: namely, the "locust" passages in chaps. 1–2 and what they describe; the relationship between the disasters recounted in those chapters and their reversal in chaps. 3–4; and the nature of the "day of the LORD" in the book as a whole. Troublesome historical-critical issues include the book's compositional unity and the date of its composition.

In Hebrew bibles, the book of Joel has four chapters, a division used in rabbinical bibles from the sixteenth century C.E. Some English translations (e.g., the Jewish Publication Society Bible and the NAB) follow this convention. Other English translations follow the thirteenth-century tripartite division that S. Langton imposed on the Vulgate Joel and later used in the Greek Septuagint Joel. In these translations Joel 3:1-5 equals 2:28-32, and Joel 4:1-21 matches 3:1-21.

1. *Date of Composition.* Unlike most other prophetic books, neither the superscription (Joel 1:1; cf., e.g., Hos 1:1 and Amos 1:1) nor the text itself offers any historical information about the time of Joel's ministry. Nor is the book's position in the canon any help. Literary (cf., e.g., Joel 4:16a [3:16a] and Amos 1:2a; Joel 4:18a [3:18a] and Amos 9:13b) rather than chronological considerations may have won Joel its place between Hosea and Amos in the MT. Hypotheses about date, then, are based on internal allusion and linguistic data. The range of opinions (from the 9th cent. to the 3rd cent. B.C.E.) attests that neither of these sources yields a certain date. The majority of commentators, nevertheless, place the book in the postexilic period, probably in the era following Ezra and Nehemiah.

Among other elements, this time frame best accommodates the absence of any mention of a king, emphasis on leadership roles assumed by the priests, an established and favorably regarded temple cultus, and the availability of a recognized prophetic tradition as a source for material (e.g., 1:15 = Isa 13:6; 2:6 = Nah 2:11[10]; 2:14 = Jonah 3:9; 4:18 [3:18] = Amos 9:13). This period also accounts for the few late linguistic features found in the text: e.g., *sop* (Joel 2:20a); *sahanâ* (2:20b), elsewhere only in Sir 11:12; the participle *měšārēt* (Joel 1:9, 13; 2:17), used in apposition to priests and Levites only in late biblical Hebrew (2 Chr 29:11; Ezra 8:17).

2. *Unity of Composition.* Patristic, rabbinical, and Reformation interpreters regarded the book as a unity, the work of the prophet Joel. However, nineteenth-century scholars like M. Vernes (1845–1923) and J. Rothstein (1853–1926) questioned whether the entire book should be attributed to the prophet. Building on that suggestion, B. Duhm (1911) claimed that he had isolated Joel's original material from later additions. Duhm assigned 1:1–2:17 (with the exception of the *yôm* YHWH "day of the LORD" passages [1:15; 2:1b, 11b]) to Joel and described this material as an original poem describing devastation by locusts, an invading army, and a drought. The remainder of the book, according to Duhm, is the work of a Maccabean synagogue preacher preoccupied with eschatology and the day of the Lord. In order to link his own prose work (chaps. 3–4) to the original poem, this preacher added the *yôm* YHWH references, thus transforming the locust invasion into a sign of this future event. Independent of Duhm, J. Bewer (1911) also concluded that the day of the Lord passages were secondary, the work of a later apocalyptist who combined two pieces Joel had written on separate occasions.

Variations and modifications of Duhm's hypothesis dominated later study of the book. Some scholars, however, argued that cultic background and concerns unified the book; for the most part, they found that the book's structure mirrored the structure of a lament liturgy and supported their theory that Joel alone, as the prophet who presided at such a liturgy, was the book's author (A. Kapelrud [1948]; M. Bic [1960]; C. A. Keller [1965]; A. Deissler [1981]; Jorg

Jeremias [1987]; and, to a lesser extent, G. Ahlström 1972]). While acknowledging the text's cultic elements, L. Dennefeld (1924, 1925, 1926) and J. Bourke (1959) identify the *yôm* YHWH as the motif Joel used to unify the text.

H. W. Wolff's form-critical analysis (1977) has most persuasively demonstrated the book's compositional unity at the hand of the prophet Joel. Wolff pointed out several features that unite the book and suggest a single author: e.g., a near-perfect structural symmetry, along with interlocking catchwords and catchphrases. Wolff did, however, consider 2:3b; 3:2[2:29]; and 4:4-8[3:4-8] to be later additions (perhaps by Joel himself) and 2:26b to be a copying error from 2:27. Later commentators, e.g., W. Rudolph (1971), L. Allen (1976), and W. Prinsloo (1985), also acknowledge the book's unity.

More recently, O. Loretz (1986) has used colometric analysis to isolate eight separate strata of tradition in the book of Joel. The earliest and most important are the texts intended as rites of lamentation and fasting to persuade the Lord to send rain (1:8-10, 11-12, 13, 14-17, 18-20; 2:12-14, 15-19, 21-24; 4:18 [3:18]); the locust passages (1:4, 5-7; 2:3b-8a, 25) are only secondary, intended to emphasize the severity of the drought, which for Loretz is the occasion for Joel's writing. To this core material later editors added layer after layer of material. A final redactor added the day of the Lord passages (1:15b; 2:1b, 11b; 3:4b[2:31]; 4:14b[3:14b]).

Like Loretz, S. Bergler (1988) argues that the book uses earlier materials; however, for Bergler, Joel himself shaped these materials into a final unity. He suggests that the core of the book is a poem about the effects of drought on the natural and the human world (1:5, 9-13, 17-20); this poem Joel transforms into a prayer in order to link the drought with the day of the Lord. The locust passages are meant to remind Joel's audience about the locust plague of the exodus, the divine intervention that inaugurated Judah's eschatological age.

R. Simkins (1991) and J. Crenshaw (1995) take the book as a unity originating with Joel, including the troublesome 4:4-8[3:4-8]. At the same time they acknowledge Joel's reliance on the larger prophetic tradition.

3. *Structure*. Like its date and compositional unity, the book's structure has been viewed in a number of different ways. Prinsloo, e.g., finds no real turning point in the text; a progression of passages, interlocked by repetition, builds to a climax in 4:18-21. Others maintain that the text falls naturally into two parts. Rudolph and Deissler make the division on the basis of content at the end of chap. 2 (v. 27). Thus chaps. 1–2 describe contemporary events; chaps. 3–4, eschatological events. Ahlström, Wolff, Allen, Jeremias, and G. Ogden (1987), using literary form as a criterion, divide the book after 2:17. In this view, Joel 1:2–2:17 resembles a communal lament to which 2:19b–4:21[3:21] is the Lord's response.

Wolff suggests that the elements of 1:4–2:18 are almost symmetrically balanced by the elements of 2:19–4:3, 9-17[3:3, 9-17]. E. Henry (1985) identifies ten units in a quasi-chiastic structure whose two-part center is the penitential assembly (2:15-17); a new divine intervention as the Lord's response (2:18-27). Building on Wolff's analysis, D. Garrett (1985) also locates two turning points in the text (2:17 and 2:18); two interlocking chiasms (1:2–2:27; 2:2–4:21[3:21]) unite the book, each one moving from punishment to forgiveness.

Unlike other scholars, Simkins argues that the material in chaps. 3–4 neither continues the prophetic speech begun in 2:19b nor describes some future event. Rather, the entire book announces that a single day of the Lord is imminent.

4. *Interpretation of the Locust Passages*. The locust passages in chap. 1 and the reference of Joel 2:1-11 have generated varied interpretations. Most patristic and medieval interpreters read the locust invasion (Joel 1:4-7) as an allegory of a future historical military invasion, perhaps because the targum for 2:25 translated the Hebrew terms repeated from 1:4 as "peoples, tongues, governments, and kingdoms." A marginal gloss on the sixth-century Greek codex Q is even more specific: Egyptians, Babylonians, Assyrians and Greeks. Some contemporary interpreters, such

as Ogden and D. Stuart (1976), follow this view, asserting that the locusts of chap. 1 are metaphors for the 587 B.C.E. Babylonian assault on Jerusalem. Such medieval Jewish scholars as Rashi, A. Ibn Ezra, and D. Kimhi and the Christian interpreters Jerome, Luther, and Calvin took the passage at face value. Anticipating the work of K. Credner (1831), these commentators understood Joel 1:4-7 to describe an actual locust invasion. Today most interpreters agree that a real locust plague occasioned Joel's preaching. Notable exceptions are Loretz and Bergler (see discussion below).

Scholarly opinion is also divided on the reference of Joel 2:1-11. Most interpreters agree that the poem describes either another phase of the invasion of 1:4-7 or an invasion of a new swarm of locusts (e.g., Allen, Bewer, Deissler, J. Thompson, Rudolph, Simkins). Details like the shaking of heaven and earth, hardly the work of real locusts, are interpreted as elements borrowed from the day of the Lord tradition and used to identify the locusts as the day itself or as its forerunners. Along with earlier Jewish and Christian commentators, a few scholars think that the poem describes the attack of an eschatological army, either a military force in the tradition of the "enemy from the north" or grotesque insects like those of Rev 9:1-11 (e.g., Jeremias, Keller, Ogden, Wolff).

None of the interpretations of 2:1-11 suggest a disaster that would intensify Judah's plight in the immediate future. A second infestation of locusts in the following spring is feasible; however, such an infestation would have been a weak threat at the end of summer when Joel preaches. The Palestinian meteorological cycle offers a better candidate for an immediate danger. At the end of a normal summer Judah needs rain. Joel fears that the east wind, which usually precedes the arrival of the winter rains and eventually gives way to them, will last too long and prevent the rain's timely arrival. Joel's use of locust and military imagery identifies this windstorm as the Lord's own army, coming to destroy the Judahites because, like drunkards, they have not understood the significance of the present agricultural crisis.

5. *Interpretation of the Book as a Whole.* Commentators offer a variety of interpretations for the book as a whole. According to Kapelrud, Joel was a cult prophet who used a locust plague as an occasion to castigate his audience for its participation in mourning rites for the fertility god Baal during the dry summer. The locusts were a sign that the day of the Lord, Judah's punishment for worshiping the wrong god, was imminent. Once the people repented, Joel announced that in the future the day of the Lord would mean blessing for Judah and disaster for its enemy. Ahlström, on the other hand, makes Joel a Jerusalem Temple prophet who pleads with the people to turn away from Baal worship and return to the Lord. The locusts are punishment for violating the covenant. Once the people return to the covenant through right worship, they receive the covenant blessings of rain and agricultural plenty.

Wolff argued that Joel's postexilic religious community in Jerusalem viewed itself as the fulfillment of God's plan for Israel, having forgotten the still unfulfilled prophetic word about the day of the Lord; they saw no further need for the Lord's intervention. The locust plague and the drought are evidence that the Judahites are soon going to be punished for their self-sufficiency unless they repent. Once they do acknowledge that the Lord is still active in their history, the day of the Lord (2:1-11) is withheld. Wolff understands Joel 2:1-11 as a description of the Lord leading the army of nations, Ezekiel's eschatological "enemy from the north," to destroy Israel. In chaps. 3–4, Joel shows how the Lord will deliver a faithful Israel from this final onslaught of the nations when it does occur and how he will establish the people in security and prosperity.

For Rudolph, the book records Joel's evolution from a prophet of doom to a prophet of salvation. As a cult prophet and a contemporary of Jeremiah, Joel interpreted a locust infestation (1:4-7; 2:1-11) and an accompanying drought as signs of an approaching day of the Lord that would bring destruction to Judah and Jerusalem. Later, after the people had repented and the drought ended, Joel received a new word from the Lord in which he learned that the locusts and the drought had, in fact, nothing to do with the *yôm* YHWH. Thus, the "news never heard before" (1:1-3) refers to the Lord's announcement that any future day of the Lord would inaugurate an era of prosperity and security for Judah and would herald its enemies' destruction (chaps. 3–4). Rudolph thinks that Joel had in mind an imminent destruction of Babylon.

Like Rudolph, Crenshaw identified a unique locust infestation and a dry summer marked by the failure of all streams as the occasion for Joel's preaching. In 2:1-11, mixing military and natural imagery, Joel describes an onslaught of locusts as the divine army that God later promises to destroy, perhaps because they exceeded their charge. After a poem consoling people, land, and animals with the news that the coming rain will restore what had been lost, Joel 3[2:28-32] assures the faithful of continued divine protection when the *yôm* YHWH does finally arrive. Joel 4 (3) describes the destruction of Judah's enemies and Judah's own establishment as a secure autonomous nation.

Ogden has suggested that the book reflects conditions existing in the land of Judah that the exiles found on their return from Babylon in 537 B.C.E. Joel describes this situation with imagery drawn from the damage done by locusts, drought, and pillaging armies. Chapter 4 contains oracles against the nations that Joel delivered on different occasions when he presided at communal lament liturgies.

Loretz argues that the book's purpose was to interpret eschatologically a series of drought-fasting-rain passages that form the earliest literary tradition in the text. Under the influence of the later *yôm* YHWH passages, the revitalizing effect of rain in reversing the drought became a symbol for the permanent change the Lord would someday effect in Judah's fortunes (see discussion above). This interpretation, of course, takes the *yôm* YHWH as the manifestation of the deity in a rainstorm.

Like Loretz, Bergler makes a drought the book's central concern; however, he identifies Joel as a postexilic prophet trying to counter his audience's loss of religious enthusiasm. Joel uses traditional poems about drought and about the enemy from the north to demonstrate how the present drought is the beginning of the future *yôm* YHWH. He links the effects of the locust plague in the exodus narrative (Exodus 10) with the effects on the land of the invasion of the enemy from the north. Once the people participate in the penitential assembly, Joel answers their lament with an oracle of salvation. Bergler identifies the drought as the "teacher of righteousness," a sign of the day of the Lord. Judah, however, lives already in an eschatological era inaugurated by the Lord's activity in the exodus. Consequently, the people face no further danger; rather, the Phoenicians and the Philistines are the target of the coming calamity.

Simkins's important study emphasizes that in the book of Joel the day of the Lord is an event in the history of creation. Judah has already endured one locust infestation, resulting in crop loss and interruption of temple worship. More to the point, the neighboring peoples have shamed Judah by invading and pillaging the land and by selling some of the people into slavery. Now, as Joel is writing, a new locust invasion is beginning (2:1-11). His audience construes these events as evidence that the Lord is indifferent to them. Joel, however, views this invasion as fulfillment of the day of the Lord expectations. The locusts are the "enemy from the north," whose invasion as part of this event results in the Lord's judgment against the nations. The day of the Lord is simultaneously an event in human history, Judah's deliverance from its enemies' oppression, and an event in the history of nature, the renewal of the created order. Simkins argues that both events together mirror a conflict myth in which the Lord battles those forces that threaten the natural and historical orders.

All of these interpretations contain important insights that enrich one's appreciation of the book of Joel. However, they disregard important elements of the meteorological cycle that makes agriculture possible in Palestine. This cycle is an important exegetical key to the book of Joel, given its preoccupation with crops, rain, and pestilence. On this understanding, Joel's prophetic ministry is set during the fall interchange period, at the cusp of a new year. Chapter 1 recounts the recently concluded, failed agricultural season: an unusually large locust infestation in the spring, withering of the remaining grain in late spring, the normally dry summer (perhaps exacerbated by inadequate rains the previous winter). Chapter 2 opens with a description (2:1-11) of one of the two meteorological possibilities Judah could expect given the seasonal setting of Joel's preaching. One possibility is the revitalizing rain; the other is an east wind storm, which typically precedes the rain (for a description comparable to 2:1-11, see D. Grossman [1988] 75-76). Once the people heed Joel's call to repentance (implied by 2:18), he announces that the rain will arrive (1:19-27). Joel calls this abundant rain *hammôreh liṣedāqâ* (2:23), a phrase that identifies the rain as a teacher of truth and foreshadows the future outpouring of the Lord's knowledge on all Judahites (3:1-4[2:28-31]).

In chaps. 3–4 Joel focuses on that point in the distant future when the Lord will intervene once and for all. The imagery for both these chapters is drawn from the competing storms of the fall interchange period. First, the Lord promises the Judahites the capacity to understand what will happen so they do not lose hope. The divine army, under the figure of an east wind (3:3-4[2:30-31]; 4:14b-17[3:14b-17]), will attack the armies of the nations gathered in the Valley of Jehoshaphat when "YHWH executes punishment" (4:2, 12-14[3:2, 12-14]) at the foot of Mount Zion. It will then move on to destroy all of Judah's enemies, turning their lands into deserts and slaying their inhabitants. The faithful of Judah, on the other hand, will enjoy protection, political autonomy, economic security, and agricultural abundance because the Lord dwells among them permanently. In this interpretation, the *yôm* YHWH is a natural phenomenon, the east wind storm of the fall interchange period, which destroys Judah's enemies as the prelude to its revitalization (K. Nash [1989]).

Bibliography: E. Achtemeier, "The Book of Joel," *NIB* (1996) 7:299-336. **G. W. Ahlström,** *Joel and the Temple Cult of Jerusalem* (VTSup 21, 1972). **L. Allen,** *The Books of Joel, Obadiah, Jonah, and Micah* (NICOT, 1976). **J. Barton,** *Joel and Obadiah: A Commentary* (OTL, 2001). **S. Bergler,** *Joel als Schriftinterpret* (BEATAJ 16, 1988). **J. A. Bewer,** *A Critical and Exegetical Commentary on Micah, Zephaniah, Nahum, Habakkuk, Obadiah and Joel* (ICC, 1911). **M. Bic,** *Das Buch Joel* (1960). **B. C. Birch,** *Hosea, Joel, and Amos* (Westminster Bible Companion, 1997). **J. Bourke,** "Le jour de Yahvé dans Joël," *RB* 66 (1959) 5-31, 191-221. **R. J. Coggins,** *Joel and Amos* (NCB 2000); "Joel," *Currents in Biblical Research* 2 (2003) 85-103. **K. A. Credner,** *Der Prophet Joel übersetzt und erklärt* (1831). **J. L. Crenshaw,** *Joel* (AB 24C, 1995); "Freeing the Imagination: The Conclusion of the Book of Joel," in *Prophecy and the Prophets* (Y. Gitay, ed., SemieaSt, 1997) 129-47. **U. Dahmen,** *Die Bücher Joel und Amos* (Neuer Stuttgarter Kommentar, AT, 23, 2001). **A. Deissler,** *Zwölf Propheten: Hosea, Joel, Amos* (Die neue Echter Bibel, 1981). **L. Dennefeld,** "Les problèmes du livre de Joël," *RevScRel* 4 (1924) 555-75; 5 (1925) 35-37, 591-608; 6 (1926) 26-49. **B. Duhm,** "Anmerkungen zu den zwölf Propheten," *ZAW* 31 (1911) 184-88. **D. A. Garrett,** "The Structure of Joel," *JETS* 28 (1985) 289-97. **B. Glazier- McDonald,** "Joel," *The Women's Bible Commentary* (C. A. Newsom and S. H. Ringe, eds., 1992) 203-4. **D. Grossman,** *The Yellow Wind* (1988). **K. M. Hayes,** "The Earth Mourns": Prophetic Metaphor and Oral Aesthetic (Academia Biblica 8, 1997). **E. Henry,** *Le Livre prophétique de Joël: Étude stylistique et exégétique* (1985). **E. Jacob, C.-A. Keller,** and **S. Amsler,** *Osée, Joël, Amos, Abadias, Jonas* (CAT, 1965). **J. Jeremias,** "Joel/Joelbuch," *TRE* 17 (1987) 91-97. **A. S. Kapelrud,** *Joel Studies* (1948). **O. Loretz,** *Regenritual und Jahwetag im Joelbuch* (1986). **S. F. Mathews,** "The Power to Endure and Be Transformed: Sun and Moon Imagery in Joel and Revelation 6," in *Imagery and Imagination in Biblical Literature* (ed. L. Boadt and M. S. Smith; CBQMS 32, 2001) 35-49. **A. Meinhold,** "Zur Rolle des Tag-JHWHs-

Gedichte Joel 2,1-11 im XII-Propheten-Buch," in *Verbindungslinien* (A. Graupner, H. Delkurt, and A.B. Ernst, eds., 2000). **A. Merx,** *Die Prophetie des Joel und ihre Ausleger von den ältesten Zeiten bis zu den Reformatoren* (1879). **K. S. Nash,** "The Palestinian Agricultural Year and the Book of Joel" (diss., Catholic University, 1989). **J. D. Nogalski,** "Joel as 'Literary Anchor' for the Book of the Twelve," in *Reading and Hearing the Book of the Twelve* (ed. J.D. Nogalski and M. A. Sweeney, 2000) 91-109. **G. S. Ogden** and **R. R. Deutsch,** *A Promise of Hope, a Call to Obedience: A Commentary on the Books of Joel and Malachi* (ITC, 1987). **W. S. Prinsloo,** *The Theology of the Book of Joel* (BZAW 163, 1985). **P. L. Redditt** and **A. Schart** (eds.), *Thematic Threads in the Book of the Twelve* (BZAW 325, 2003). **W. Rudolph,** *Joel, Amos, Obadja, Jona* (KAT, 1971). **R. Simkins,** *Yahweh's Activity in History and Nature in the Book of Joel* (ANETS 10, 1991). **J. Stiebert,** "Shame and Prophecy: Approaches Past and Present," *BibInt* 8 (2000) 255-75. **D. Stuart,** "The Sovereign's Day of Conquest," *BASOR* 221 (1976) 159-64. **M. A. Sweeney,** "The Place and Function of Joel in the Book of the Twelve," *SBLSP* 38 (1999) 570-95. **J. A. Thompson,** "Joel's Locust in the Light of Near Eastern Parallels," *JNES* 14 (1955) 52-55; "The Book of Joel: Introduction and Exegesis," *IB* (1956) 6:729-60. M.-T. Wacker, "Gottes Groll, Gottes Güte und Gottes Gerechtigkeit nach dem Joel-Buch," in *Das Drama der Barmherzigkeit Gottes: Studien zur biblischen Gottesrede und ihrer Wirkungsgeschichte in Judentum und Christentum* (ed. R. Scoralick, SBS 183, 2000) 207-23. **G. Widmer,** *Die Kommentare von Raschi, Ibn Ezra, Radaq zu Joel: Text, Übersetzung, und Erläuterung mit einer Einführung in der rabbinische Biblexegese* (1945). **H. W. Wolff,** *Joel and Amos* (Hermeneia, 1977). **E. Zenger** (ed.), *"Wort Jhwhs, das geschah—" (Hos 1,1): Studien zum Zwölfprophetenbuch* (Herders biblische Studien 35, 2002).

K. S. Nash

THE LATTER PROPHETS: MINOR

Amos

R. Cripps (1929, 1955) calls Amos "perhaps the most important prophet in the OT." Although the book comes third in traditional orderings of the Minor Prophets, Amos ranks first in the heart of most readers. There are many reasons for this: the beauty of his language—especially apparent in the Hebrew; his impassioned plea for social justice; and the man's courage, not to say temerity, in attacking the powerful politico-religious establishment of the northern kingdom of Israel. Here, however, is where unity concerning the interpretation of Amos ends; his very popularity and importance have generated an enormous amount of secondary literature with, predictably, many conflicting opinions.

J. Hayes lays out three stages of modern (c. 1880 onward) critical study of Amos concerned with the prophet, his religion, and finally, the text. A fourth area of inquiry, which we might call the sociology of Amos, may, thanks to N. Gottwald and others, be the next step. In any case, we are beginning to witness a rather remarkable reevaluation of Amos and his book, including his origin, status in society, place in and sense of history, language, and the unity of the book ascribed to him.

The traditional Christian view of Amos as a simple Judean shepherd goes back to Augustine, who marveled that such words as Amos's could come from a rustic. This immensely popular view, conjuring up images of David versus Goliath or Jesus and the Temple elders, had no trouble surmounting occasional challenges until the nineteenth century. It was an image that the Judeo-Christian tradition could appreciate.

Luther, for example, shared God's apparent delight in choosing the meek to challenge the mighty; he began his Amos commentary by comparing Amos's situation in Israel with his own vis-à-vis the pope. Following his example, commentators who reflect the first stirrings of modern (Protestant) scholarship at the end of the nineteenth century concerned themselves mainly with the person of the prophet, although Luther also maintained that the person was less important than his message.

Regarding the person of Amos, we know that the earliest Talmudic commentators (see H. Routtenberg [1971]) who mention Amos lived, like Augustine, nearly 1,000 years after the prophet—but only shortly after one who said that the meek would inherit the earth. Seeing Amos as one of the latter was natural for Christians; however, the scanty Jewish sources (*Tg. Onq.*, *b. Ned.* 38a) suggest, rather, that Amos was a wealthy shepherd. This would have contradicted Augustine's most dearly held notions. Indeed, there is almost nothing about Amos that commentators, Jewish and Christian, ancient and modern, have not contested.

1. *Background.* There is general agreement that Amos's career was very brief; no scholar assigns him more than a year's public ministry, sometime between 765 and 740 B.C.E. (though few go as far as J. Morgenstern, who reduces it to a single day!). At least some of his remarks were delivered at the national shrine of Bethel, perhaps on the day of the fall festival.

The traditional view locates Amos's hometown in Judean Tekoa (1:1), where, according to Eusebius's *Onomasticon*, his tomb was still extant in the third century. Contrarily, medieval Jewish commentary (D. Kimhi; see S. Berkowitz [1939]) casually identifies him as hailing from Asher in the north. Cyril of Alexandria (5th cent.) reported a northern origin, but few have taken this or any other northern suggestion seriously. The book gives us little help: neither a patronymic nor a designated place of origin like the ninth-century northern hero/prophet Elijah the Gileadite. Positing a northern origin for Amos would solve many problems, but the more obvious questions concerning his period and his profession(s) should be addressed first.

2. *Chronology.* Dates for Amos's prophetic activities have ranged from c. 780 to c. 740.

Amos's placement in this forty-year period is significant because the signal event of that span—namely, the rise of Assyria under Tiglath-pileser III—can be pinpointed to 745 B.C.E. Was Amos knowledgeable of Assyria's new strength (R. Coote [1981])? Probably not. Consensus follows the book's superscription and places Amos between c. 767 and c. 753 B.C.E. But if Amos was not exactly contemporary to Tiglath-pileser, can it at least be suggested (with E. Hammerschaimb [1946]) that Assyria's rise was so imminent as to cast its shadow before it? (This presumes, for the moment, that the entire text of Amos was written before 745.) Here, too, the answer will probably be no.

Most scholars from 1880 onward accept the view that the northern kingdom, locus for Amos's activities, was enjoying almost unprecedented prosperity before the Assyrian invasion; but some (M. Haran [1968]; S. Cohen [1965]; J. Hayes [1989]) feel Israel was already in decline. Was Amos predicting ruin or merely describing in strong terms what others could already see?

Lost in this controversy concerning the international situation is any real sense of the sectional animosities in Israel. (Cf. the Judean reaction to help from the Samaritans in Ezra 4:1 or the reception of Philip's news by Nathaniel, John 1:46.) It is important to note that the fracture of Solomon's kingdom never mended. In fact, there had been a bloody encounter—scarcely noticed by Bible historians—won by the north in c. 792 B.C.E. (following the chronology of E. Thiele) only twenty-five years before Amos's time. Perhaps these events had little impact; but it is significant that the Judean king Amaziah, held hostage for a further ten years, returned home to find his son Uzziah king. Amaziah was murdered in c. 767, almost coincidental with the beginning of Amos's career.

3. *Occupation.* Amos's occupation is an area of great conjecture. Today he is enshrined "among the prophets," but there is a strong suspicion that this membership is posthumously conferred. For one thing, although he speaks prophetically, his words contain an explicit denial of having been a prophet (7:14). As H. Rowley (1947) pointed out, the crucial verse lacks a verb, leading E. Worthwein (1950) to posit that Amos underwent a sort of interruption or mid-career change in the nature of his prophecy from supporting the official cult to opposing it. But we do not really know whether he was a prophet at all. In 3:7 he seems to indicate that he is, indeed, one. And his capacity for predicting ruin is obvious from the oracles with which the book begins. J. Blenkinsopp (1983), however, states that 3:7 is the "most obvious Deuteronomistic interpolation" in the whole book; and the authenticity of many of the oracles is questioned.

Even if Amos were a prophet, he would likely have had another livelihood. In fact, he identifies himself as a "dresser" (?) of sycamore trees and a "herdsman" (7:14). Traditional identification sidesteps the fact that, although he says he was taken "from behind the flocks" (7:15), the usual word for "shepherd" is not used to describe his activities. Modern discoveries in cognate languages, especially Ugaritic, have convinced some scholars (A. Kapelrud [1956]; P. Craigie [1982]) that Amos was an influential sheep owner/dealer (as the Jewish tradition had long remembered) with perhaps some connection to the cult.

This makes sense. As much as we admire his outburst, an Israelite festival was no New England town meeting at which anyone could speak at will. Besides, who would listen to a simple shepherd and, on top of that, a Judean? How could anyone, much less an uneducated outsider, have commanded an Israelite audience? The answer to these questions may lie in an examination of Amos's other occupation, which had nothing to do with religion. Scholars assume that harvesting sycamore fruits (7:14) is proof of humble origin; who but a poor man would tend figs barely fit for human consumption? H. Oort (1836–1927) caused some consternation one hundred years ago by pointing out that sycamores do not grow at the altitude of Judean Tekoa (2,800 ft. above sea level). In addition, if Amos owned groves of trees, how can he be considered humble? G. A. Smith (1896–98), whose description of Judean Tekoa borders on the lyrical, responds that Amos must have been some sort of migrant worker; sycamores do grow in the Shephelah by Ein Gedi and in the north, the locus for Amos's preaching. But if he was a migrant worker, how did he also care for his sheep.

4. *Message.* The content of Amos's preaching has been subject to much attention: It is widely believed that he was simply anti-ritual. An economic connection with the cult would not preclude this, but it makes more sense to suggest that Amos's objections were along the line of "the letter killeth but the spirit giveth life." An empty and unfelt religiosity, especially when yoked with exploitation of the disadvantaged, makes mockery of the faith as we now know and practice it. In Amos's time, however, the notion prevailed in the northern kingdom that the poor were poor because they deserved it. In such a theology, helping the downtrodden could actually be viewed as countermanding God's will. But Amos's indictment bears special scrutiny, both for what it says and for what it omits.

His excoriation of various Israelite malpractices reads like the particulars in a court case. He seems to have an insider's knowledge of the various ways in which certain classes of impecunious people were taken advantage of by the wealthier, more powerful elements in Israelite society. F. Dijkema's wartime study calls Amos a critic of "second stage capitalism."

J. Greenfield (1974) showed that Amos was intimately acquainted with the marzea (a term found only in Amos 6:7 and Jer 16:5), a sort of upper-class country club and burial society in which sybaritic and perhaps orgiastic religious rites were performed. These rites, of course, were not part of later orthodox Israelite Judaism, but we know from recent discoveries that Judeans and Israelites were, at the least, syncretistic. What was a part of the northern kingdom's cult, and a big part to judge from Judean denunciations of it, was the golden calf.

Amos nowhere criticizes the northern kingdom for its use of the calves, golden or otherwise, that Jeroboam ben Nebat set up throughout the country (see 2 Kgs 12:25-33). This was noticed as early as 1884 by W. R. Smith, who said quietly that baals must not have been offensive to the northerners. But was not Amos a Judean? And in any case, why would the assumed Judean editors of Amos not have inserted this telling criticism of the northern kingdom, safely defunct after 720 B.C.E.? The text holds the answer to these questions.

5.*Text.* The book of Amos did not escape the documentary dissectionists who sought to distinguish the different strands of tradition compiled by different editors or authors in different eras of the text's production. For example, W. Irwin (1933) divided the text into groups of apothegms. J. Morgenstern (1941) identified seventy-seven original verses, twenty-nine more added later by Amos, and the rest added by disciples. A. Weiser proposed two books, like Isaiah's but integrated rather than juxtaposed. Most scholars favor some sort of partition, assuming that the original text has been puffed up by additions representing the concerns of later Jews. J. Wellhausen was particularly outraged by the ending of chapter 9, claiming that the prophet could not have made a 180-degree shift virtually in mid-verse (9:8; but cf. 5:15).

Other sections that have come in for more than their share of scrutiny are the five "visions," the eight "oracles," and Amos's confrontation with the priest Amaziah in 7:10-17. (J. Watts [1956], however, noted that 4:13; 5:8; and 9:5-6 seem to be parts of a hymn that he assumed were inserted into the text later. But they could also be hymnic material that Amos quotes.) If one subtracts all the verses that have been called into question, the remainder would be only a small fragment of what we have now.

Wellhausen, H. Gunkel, and A. Alt dominate much of twentieth-century writing on Amos. Following them, such scholars as H. W. Wolff (1969) and R. Coote (1981) seem to vie with each other in proposing ever more layers of accretions, a kind of moss gathered by the text as it rolls through history. Although pre-modern commentators would have been scandalized by redaction criticism (or by any of the modern schools), Jerome might have applauded M. Buber's (1949) suggestion that the Judah oracle was inserted at some relatively late date to ensure that readers/

listeners would know that the long oracle against Israel that follows it (2:9–3:2) was meant to criticize the northern kingdom exclusively.

Documentary or other reductionist hypotheses, however ingenious, are difficult to attach to a text that in its present state has only 146 verses. There is also some movement away from dissection and toward a more organic appreciation of Amos as a whole, e.g., S. Paul (1991). R. Smalley (1979) considers the book to be an organic whole pivoting on 5:9, but even so conservative a scholar as Y. Kaufmann (1960) did not attempt to defend the authenticity of the entire text.

Buried in the avalanche of modern criticism is B. Spinoza's suggestion that biblical texts ought to "wear down" through history, not grow. This may not hold, e.g., in the case of Isaiah; but certainly the smaller corpuses of the Minor Prophets, e.g., Obadiah, do not contain everything these men said.

Commentary is also interested in such broad subjects as the influences behind Amos. Wolff and his many disciples see a "wisdom" influence (depending in part on a certain vocabulary); others have seen "cultic" (G. Farr [1966]); "theophanic" (J. Crenshaw [1968]); "covenantal" (W. Brueggemann [1969]); "apodictic" (Würthwein [1950]); "psalmic" (A. Kapelrud [1956]); or "pre-Israelite prophetic" (N. Gottwald [1985]) influences. J. Mays (1969) compliments Amos on his versatility, and J. Barton (1980) cites his literary/intellectual merit.

6. *Language.* It might be that commentators are so concerned with the forest that they neglect its trees. There is a considerable number of strange or rare words and phrases in Amos; but since it is assumed that we do not have *ipsissima verba,* the exact words, there is relative neglect of those we do possess. Even if the words were not Amos's, are they the less carefully chosen? For example, in 1917 H. Schmidt noticed that Amos was not told to "return" to Judah but to "flee" there. Hayes correctly invokes J. Barr's *caveat* concerning over-reliance on etymologies of single words; but there are so many lexical anomalies—loan words and strange forms and spellings—that one wonders who is responsible for the present state of the text and why the fastidious rabbis of later Judaism did not clean it up. To cite the most outstanding example, Amos twice spells the name "Isaac" differently from almost any other biblical book (*sin* for *tsade*). W.R. Harper (1905) wrote that the "misspellings were all textual errors," but offered no clue as to how they were allowed to persist.

The prevailing view argues that Amos was a poor migratory shepherd from Judah who lived or worked in the north long enough to acquire detailed knowledge of its social and religious faults—and a local accent—and who, through a short public outburst at an important festival, manifested such charisma that he could command an audience of awestruck Israelites until the officiating priest could communicate with the king and secure some police (never mentioned or even alluded to in the text) to escort Amos politely off the premises. Furthermore, generations of admirers or disciples continually dredged up more of his words or, in some cases, invented words they felt their own times would like Amos to have said. This seems forced.

7. *New Perspectives.* The old view is currently being challenged from a number of perspectives. As early as 1915 Gunkel stated that copyists were not at liberty to change the texts that lay in front of them. If so, the presence of postexilic parts of Amos may be questioned. Furthermore, many modern writers now acknowledge that Amos was a person of some substance in his community, that his connection with Israelite flocks was on a high economic level, and that he may have even been an "inspector" of crown sycamores (S. Rosenbaum [1990]). If so, of which biblical kingdom was he a citizen?

In 1917 Schmidt mused that Amos's words would have a far different ring if spoken by an Israelite against his own king and country. It would appear that Amos's priestly adversary, Amaziah, thought so too, since he accused Amos of "treason" (*qeser*). A thorough study of this word in Scripture reveals it is always used to describe actions against one's own king or country. It is this suggestion that may finally point the way to a truer understanding of Amos. If Amos were a substantial and well-educated citizen of Israel (the northern kingdom), his book could show all the influences that Farr, Wolff, Brueggemann, et al. posit of it. The man himself might be assumed to have been influential enough to command an audience even during a national festival. Furthermore, his relatively mild treatment at the hands of the establishment, noticed by many scholars, would be better understood if Amos were not an indigent outsider, but a well-connected native; his intimate knowledge of the goings-on in a *marzeh* also points in this direction. As much emotional appeal as the traditional view has, it may be too much to ask the present text to support it. To borrow Voltaire's *bon mot* concerning the Holy Roman Empire, it would appear that Amos was not simple, was not a shepherd, and was not even a Judean.

If Amos was an employee of the northern kingdom, then we may presume he was not, initially, a prophet. What is more important, he would not have been considered a prophet until some time after his outburst, e.g., until the fall of the house of Jereboam or even until the destruction of the northern kingdom. If so, his words might have been cherished for decades by only a few people without suffering much editorial change—the more so if he were a northerner whose words remained unknown in Jerusalem, where the famous "deuteronomists" were so hard at work.

Relative obscurity would also help to explain why he follows Hosea and Joel in the canon, though perhaps he precedes both chronologically. If Amos's words came to light as late as the great Josianic reform (c. 625 B.C.E.), it might not be remembered exactly when he had lived; everyone, however, would know of his refuge and eventual death in Judean Tekoa.

8. *Importance*. Luther wrote, "Neither the man nor the place [of his residence] are important." He concluded correctly that what is important is Amos's message, pieces of which have achieved lives independent of their context: "Let justice roll down as the waters and righteousness as a mighty stream" (5:24); "Seek me and live" (5:14). Even here, however, there is dispute about the audience for whom these words were intended. Jewish and Christian traditions want to read in Amos the first universalist (largely on the basis of 9:7), but several moderns read him as more narrowly nationalist.

It is the genius of Amos and a reason for his enduring popularity that he, an anguished patriot aghast at the evils in his own country, would write words that speak to any country whose leaders pervert the commandments of the Sinaitic covenant. We learn from Amos's visions that God protects a country only so long as that country remains righteous. In that light, much of Western history from Amos's time to ours may be read as a series of footnotes.

Bibliography: P. A. Ackroyd, "A Judgement Narrative Between Kings and Chronicles? An Approach to Amos 7:9-17," *Canon and Authority: Essays in OT* (ed. G. W. Coats and B. O. Long, 1977) 71-87. **F. I. Andersen and D. N. Freedman**, *Amos* (AB 24A, 1989). **A. G. Auld**, *Amos* (1986). **J. Barton**, *Amos's Oracles Against the Nations: A Study of Amos 1:3–2:5* (1980). **A. Behrens**, *Prophetische Visionsschilderungen im Alten Testament: sprachliche Eigenarten, Funktion und Geschichte einer Gattung* (AOAT 292, 2002). **S. Berkowitz**, "Critical Edition of the Kimchi's Book of Amos" (diss., Cambridge, 1939). **B. C. Birch**, *Hosea, Joel, and Amos* (Westminster Bible Companion, 1997). **J. A. Blenkinsopp**, *A History of Prophecy in Israel* (1983) 86-96. **W. Brueggemann**, "Amos's Intercessory Formula," *VT 19* (1969) 385-99. **M. Buber**, *The Prophetic Faith* (1949). **M. D.Carroll**, *Amos: The Prophet and His Oracles* (2002). **R. J. Coggins**, *Joel and Amos* (NCB, 2000). **S. Cohen**, "The Political Background of the Words of Amos," *HUCA* 36 (1965) 153-60. **R. B. Coote**, *Amos Among the Prophets* (1981). **J. F. Craghan**, "The Prophet Amos in Recent Literature," *BTB* 2 (1972) 242-61. **P. C. Craigie**, "Amos the *qed* in the Light of Ugaritic," *SR* 11 (1982) 29-33. **J. L. Crenshaw**, "Amos and the Theophanic Tradition," *ZAW* 80 (1968) 203-15. **R. S. Cripps**, *A Critical and Exegetical Commentary on the Book of Amos* (1929, 1955). **U. Dahmen**, *Die Bücher Joel und Amos* (Neuer Stuttgarter Kommentar, AT, 23, 2001). **E. Dassmann**, "Amos," *RAC* 3 (1985) 333-50.

G. **Farr**, "The Language of Amos: Popular or Cultic?" *VT* 16 (1966) 312- 24. **Y. Gitay**, "A Study of Amos's Art of Speech: A Rhetorical Analysis of Amos 3:1-15," *CBQ* 42 (1980) 293-309. **N. K. Gottwald**, *The HB, A Socio-literary Introduction* (1985) 353-58. **D. E. Gowan**, "The Book of Amos," *NIB* (1996) 7:337-431. **J. C. Greenfield**, "The Mazea as a Social Institution," *Acta Antiqua* 22 (1974) 451-55. **E. Hammerschaimb**, *The Book of Amos: A Commentary* (1946, 1967, 1970). **M. Haran**, "Observations on the Historical Background of Amos 1:2–2:6," *IEJ* 18 (1968) 201-12. **W. R. Harper**, *A Critical and Exegetical Commentary on Amos and Hosea* (ICC 23, 1905). **G. F. Hasel**, *Understanding the Book of Amos: Basic Issues in Current Interpretations* (1991). **J. H. Hayes**, *Amos—the Eighth-century Prophet: His Times and His Preaching* (1989). **W. A. Irwin**, "The Thinking of Amos," *AJSL* 49 (1933) 102-14. **A. S. Kapelrud**, *Central Ideas in Amos* (1956). **Y. Kaufmann**, *The Religion of Israel: From Its Beginnings to the Babylonian Exile* (1960) 363-68. **P. H. Kelley**, "Contemporary Study of Amos and Prophetism," *RevExp* 63 (1966) 375-85. **K. Koch**, *Amos: Untersucht mit den Methoden einer strukturalen Formgeschichte* (3 vols., 1976). **L. Koehler**, "Amos-Forschungen von 1917 bis 1932," *TRu* 4 (1932) 195- 213. **M. Luther**, *Lectures on the Minor Prophets* (1975). **L. Markert**, "Amos/Amosbuch," *TRE* 2 (1978) 471-87. **J. L. Mays**, "Words About the Words of Amos: Recent Study of the Book of Amos," *Int* 13 (1959) 259-72; *Amos: A Commentary* (OTL, 1969). **L. Monloubou**, "Prophètes d'Israël: Amos," *DBSup* 8 (1969) 706-24. **K. Möller**, *A Prophet in Debate: the Rhetoric of Persuasion in the Book of Amos* (JSOTSup 372, 2003). **J. Morgenstern**, *Amos Studies I* (1941); "The Address of Amos: Text and Commentary," *HUCA* 32 (1961) 295-350. **H. Oort**, "De Profeet Amos," *ThT* 14 (1880) 114-59; "Het vanderland van Amos," *ThT* 25 (1891) 121-25. **A. W. Park**, *The Book of Amos as Composed and Read in Antiquity* (Studies in Biblical Literature 37, 2001). **S. M. Paul**, *Amos: A Commentary on the Book of Amos* (1991). **C. Peifer**, "Amos the Prophet: The Man and His Book," *TBT* 19 (1981) 295-300. **M. E. Polley**, *Amos and the Davidic Empire: A Socio-historical Approach* (1989). **D. N. Premnath**, *Eighth Century Prophets: A Social Analysis* (2003). **J. L. Rilett Wood**, *Amos in Song and Book Culture* (JSOTSup 337, 2002). **J. J. M. Roberts**, "Recent Trends in the Study of Amos," *ResQ* 13 (1970) 1-16. **S. N. Rosenbaum**, *Amos of Israel: A New Interpretation* (1990). **H. Routtenberg**, *Amos of Tekoa: A Study in Interpretation* (1971). **H. H. Rowley**, "Was Amos a *Nabi*?" *Festschrift für O. Eissfeldt* (ed. J. Fück, 1947) 191-98. **J. E. Sanderson**, "Amos," *Women's Bible Commentary* (ed. C. A. Newson and S. H. Ringe, 1992) 205-9. **H. Schmidt**, *Der Prophet Amos* (1917); "Die Herkunft des Propheten Amos," *K. Budde zum siebzigsten Geburtstag* (ed. K. Marti, BZAW 34, 1920) 158-71. **W. A. Smalley**, "Recursion Patterns and the Sectioning of Amos," *BiTr* 30 (1979) 118-27. **G. A. Smith**, *Book of the Twelve Prophets: Commonly Called the Minor* (2 vols., 1896–98). **W. R. Smith**, *The Prophets of Israel and Their Place in History to the Close of the Eighth Century BC* (1897). **H. R. Smythe**, "The Interpretation of Amos 4:13 in St. Athanasius and Didymus," *JTS* 1 (1950) 158-68. **J. A. Soggin**, *The Prophet Amos: A Translation and Commentary* (1987). **R. C. Steiner**, *Stockmen from Tekoa, Sycamores from Sheba: A Study of Amos' Occupations* (CBQMS 36, 2003). **S. Terrien**, "Amos and Wisdom," *Israel's Prophetic Heritage* (ed. B. W. Anderson and W. Harrelson, 1962) 108-15. **H. O. Thompson**, *The Book of Amos: An Annotated Bibliography* (1997). **A. Van der Wal**, *Amos: A Classified Biography* (1988). **J. D. W. Watts**, "An Old Hymn Preserved in the Book of Amos," *JNES* 15 (1956) 33-39; *Vision and Prophecy in Amos* (1958). **A. Weiser**, *Die Profetie des Amos* (BZAW 53, 1929). **J. Wellhausen**, *Die kleinen Propheten Übersetzt und erklärt* (1892). **H.W. Wolff**, *Joel and Amos: A Commentary on the Books of the Prophets Joel and Amos* (1969; ET Hermeneia, 1977). **E. Würthwein**, "Amos-Studien," *ZAW* 62 (1950) 10-52; *Wort und Existenz* (1970) 68-110.

S. N. ROSENBAUM

THE LATTER PROPHETS: MINOR

Obadiah

The shortest book in the Hebrew Bible (twenty-one verses), this prophecy concerning Edom has generated discussion primarily in four areas: identity of the prophet, date and historical setting, nature of composition, and message. During the earliest period discussion centered on the identity of Obadiah (worshiper of Yahweh). In rabbinic tradition the prophet was often linked with the Obadiah of Ahab's reign (1 Kgs 18:3-4) who was held to be an Edomite proselyte (*b. Sanh.* 39b) and descendant of Eliphaz (*Yal.* 2.549). He was thus a logical choice to deliver an oracle against Edom, since he remained faithful to Yahweh even while living with two such godless persons as Ahab and Jezebel. In contrast, Esau (Edom) had learned nothing of the life of good deeds, although living with pious Isaac and Rebekah. Obadiah received the gift of prophecy for having hidden one hundred prophets of Yahweh during Ahab's purge. Although rich, he exhausted his wealth in caring for these poor prophets until he was forced to borrow money at interest from Ahab's son Jehoram (*Exod. Rab.*, 31.3).

Whereas the identity of the prophet was a concern of the pre-critical era, the issue of date and historical setting has been a primary concern of the modern period. Central to this discussion has been the question of the historical referent for vv. 10-14. Three periods have been most frequently suggested: mid-ninth century B.C.E.; early to mid-sixth century B.C.E.; and mid- to late fifth century B.C.E. Numerous scholars (e.g., C. Keil 1868. E. Sellin 1929[3], J. Theis [937, F. Gaebelein 1946) have linked this prophecy to the period of Jehoram's difficulties with Edom (2 Kgs 8:20-22; 2 Chr 21:8-10). Reasons given in support for this position include (1) the canonical placement of the book within the Twelve (assuming the canonical arrangement reflects chronological reality); (2) the relation of Obadiah to Joel (Joel 2:32 quotes Obad 17; Joel is dated c. 830 B.C.E. by many of these scholars); (3) literary style (Obad is free of Aramaisms); and (4) the striking silence of Obadiah's prophecy regarding the destruction of Jerusalem and of the Temple (thus supposedly precluding the events of 586 B.C.E. from consideration).

Some scholars (e.g., E. Philippe 1912) have seen the initial fulfillment of Obadiah's prophecy in the Philistine and Arab raids against Judah (2 Chr 21:16-17); it is assumed that these marauders would also have sacked Edom at this time. Not surprisingly, the paucity of historical information regarding this period and the not infrequent speculative reconstruction of events have led most contemporary scholars to reject this early date. The era most frequently suggested in the modern period has been the time surrounding 586 B.C.E. Since the work of C. Caspari (1842), most scholars have dated the prophecy of Obadiah to the early years of the exile, a date proposed earlier by Calvin. Although solid historical information is lacking concerning Edom's role and posture during the Babylonian invasion of Judah, it has been assumed from such passages as Ps 137:7; Lam 4:18-22; Ezek 25:12-14; 35:1-15 that Edom at best refused to aid Judah in its struggle against Babylon and at worst exploited the situation. Thus, vv. 2-9 of Obad are read as prophetic threat rather than *vaticinia ex eventu* (so A. Edelkoort 1946–47, J. Smith 1905–6, A. Weiser 1967 [5]). Further, the relation of Obad to Jer 49:7-22 has been considered significant evidence for its placement in this period.

Not surprisingly, the book of Obad has been considered a most valuable source for reconstructing Edom's activity during this historical period. J. Wellhausen suggested a late date that often has been accepted (e.g., W. Nowack 1897, J. Bewer 1911). He dated the prophecy to the late fifth century, arguing that vv. 2-9 were not prophetic prediction but narrative description; thus the book reflected the Nabatean displacement of Edom during that period. These scholars also cited the eschatological character of vv. 16-21 and the supposed historical affinity with Mal 1:2-5 as further evidence for this late date. P. McCarter (1976) has suggested that vv. 6-7 provide the clue to the book's historical backdrop. He argues from archaeological data (Archaeology) that the Edomites were gradually displaced by the influx of Arabian tribes (Qedarites) during the Persian period and that Obadiah reflects this final expulsion of Edom.

In the modern era considerable energy has been focused on distinguishing between analysis of the present text and reconstruction of the events and sources underlying it. Consequently, determination of the book's date and historical setting is integrally related to the nature of its composition, a topic that has received much attention. Most frequently discussed have been the unity/integrity of the book, its relation to other Hebrew Bible materials (Jer 49:7-22; Joel), and its form and structure.

During the pre-critical era the unity of Obad was assumed. However, with the advent of the critical disciplines (especially source and form criticism), this unity was called into question. A simple reading of the text noted that in vv. 1-14 the nations were God's divine instrument of punishment, whereas in vv. 15-21 they were the object of punishment; in vv. 1-14 only Edom was threatened with punishment, whereas in vv. 15-21 all the nations were threatened (with Israel as the punishing agent); in vv. 1-14 Edom was addressed through the prophet's revelation, whereas in vv. 15-21 Israel was addressed. Although unity was argued principally on thematic and literary grounds, challenges arose from several quarters. J. G. Eichhorn was an early opponent to unity, arguing that vv. 17-21 constituted an appendix added during the time of Alexander Janneus (104–78 B.C.E.). Soon thereafter H. Ewald (1841) argued that the book derived from an exilic prophet (to whom he attributed vv. 11-14 and 19-21) who had made use of material from Obad 1-10 and material from another earlier prophet, Obad 15-18, both of whom he dated as contemporary with Isaiah. Noteworthy is the analysis of Wellhausen (1892), who attributed vv. 1-5, 7, 10-11, 13-14, and 15b to Obadiah, with the remaining verses being later additions and appendixes. Since the rise of source criticism numerous variations regarding the number of sources and the development of these materials into the present book have been proffered.

Although support for unity continues (e.g., A. Condamin 1900, O. Isopescul 1914, Theis, Edelkport, and G. Aalders 1958, M. Bic 1953, J. Scharbert 1967), most scholars of the modern period have considered Obadiah to be a compilation of units. Given the book's brevity, analysis often has been rather imaginative and speculative. Most frequently Obad is divided into two major sections: vv. 1-14 + v. 15b and v. 15a + vv. 16-21.

Central to this discussion has been the relation of Obad to Jer 49:7-22. Three positions have been argued: (1) Obad borrowed material from Jer; (2) Jer borrowed material from Obad; (3) both prophets borrowed from an earlier unknown source since the material in common appears in a different order and location in the two books. Scholars opting for the third position often have debated which prophet reflected more closely the original source, but such arguments are inconclusive. The literary relationship of Obad and Jere has clear ramifications for the dating of Obad, since priority or posteriority to Jeremiah could determine historical setting. However, the issue is further complicated by the realization that the Edom oracle in Jer 49 may itself be a late insertion.

With the rise of form criticism, the nature of the book's composition was analyzed from another perspective. H. W. Wolff (1977) has argued vigorously that Obad consists of an oracle of assurance delivered by a cult prophet in response to a prayer of lamentation by the worshiping people of Judah shortly after 586 B.C.E. For Wolff, vv. 1-14 and 15b comprise a single, unified discourse in which the prophet quotes earlier oracles, expanding and elaborating on them for his present situation. Conversely, vv. 15a, 16-21 are a collection of later additions skillfully linked through lexical and thematic ties. A liturgical setting for Obad was argued earlier by Bic, who considered it a liturgically expanded oracle for an annual royal enthronement festival.

In another direction, many form critics have seen in Obadiah's oracle various elements of a typical foreign nation oracle (i.e., identification of the enemy to be denounced; a warning to the enemy nation of its impending doom; a description of Yahweh's decisive intervention and punishment; a prediction of Israel's/Judah's future ascendancy over this enemy nation). G. Ogden (1982) has argued in a more balanced way that such passages as Obad and Jer 49 reflect prophetic responses to cultic laments (e.g., Ps 137).

A historical analysis of the meaning and message of Obad evidences the sociocultural horizons of the various interpreters. In the patristic period its signficance appears minimal (Obad is the only prophet with no citation in the index of the Ante-Nicene Fathers). Augustine cited Obad 17, 21 (*City of God* chap. 31), reading both references messianically: Mt. Esau represents the church of the Gentiles, which the apostles made safe through the preaching of the gospel. Conversely, Obadiah was apparently utilized in early Jewish anti-Christian polemic. In rabbinic interpretation the Edomites represented Christians and Edom the Roman Catholic Church. Such interpretation continued in D. Kimhi and in the commentary of Abravanel.

For a significant period of the modern era Obad, though largely neglected, was either cited by conservative scholars as an example of the fulfillment of prophecy or was considered an embarrassment by critical scholars, representing an inferior ethic of hate and punitive judgment. The former group focused on tracking the instances in which statements of Obad were realized negatively (e.g., Babylonian oppression; Nabatean expulsion; Maccabean punishment) and positively (e.g., the Christian church). For the latter group Obadiah reflected an ethic of vengeance and nationalism that was eclipsed and superseded in the ethic of J.

In the last decades of the twentieth century, more serious attention has been given to grappling with the theological significance of prophetic threats like Obadiah's. Contrary to earlier denigrations of the book's purely vindictive and punitive nature, newer assessments suggest the theological backdrop of Yahweh's sovereign rule and passion for justice as the controlling factors in this short prophetic oracle.

Recent commentaries on Obad include Barton (2001), Pagán (2003), and Sweeney (2000). Zvi (1999) in part analyzes possible Deuteronomistic redaction in the Minor Prophets by studying Obadiah.

Bibliography : **G. C. Aalders,** *Obadja en Jona* (1958). **M. Alomía,** "El Motivo del Remanente en Abdías," *Theologika* 11 (1996) 8-35. **J. Alexandre,** Abdias/Ovadia," *ETR* 54 (1979) 610-18. **L. C. Allen,** *Joel, Obadiah, Jonah, Micah* (1976). **M. A. Arroyo,** "El profeta Abdias," *CB* 11 (1954) 32-33. **K. Baltzer and H. Koester,** "Die Bezeichnung des Jakobus als Oblias = Obdias," *ZNW* 46 (1955) 141-42. **J. R. Bartlett,** "The Rise and Fall of the Kingdom of Edom," *PEQ* 104 (1972) 26-37. **G. A. Barton,** "Obadiah," *JE* 9 (1925²) 369-70. **J. Barton,** *Joel and Obadiah: A Commentary* (OTL, 2001). **H. Bekel,** "Ein vorexilisches Orakel über Edom in der Klagestrophe: Die gemeinsame Quelle von Obadja 1-9 und Jeremia 49:7-22,"*TSK* 80 (1907) 315-42. **E. Ben Zvi,** *A Historical-Critical Study of the Book of Obadiah* (BZAW 242, 1996). **J. A. Bewer,** *A Critical and Exegetical Commentary on Micah, Zephaniah, Nahum, Habakkuk, Obadiah, and Joel* (ICC, 1911). **M. Bic,** "Eine verkanntes Thronbesteigungfestorakel im Alten Testament," *ArOr* 19 (1951) 568-78; *Zur Problematik des Buches Obadja,* VTSup 1 (1953) 11-25. **L.F. Bliese,** "Chiastic and Homogeneous Metrical Structures Enhanced by Word Patterns in Obadiah," *JOTT* 6 (1993) 210-27. **E. Bonnard,** "Abdias," *DBSup* 8 (1969) 693-701. **A. J. Brawer,** "The Name Obadiah: Its Punctuation and Explanation," *BethMikra* 54 (1973) 418-27. **W. W. Cannon,** "Israel and Edom: The Oracle of Obadiah 1," *Theology* 14 (1927) 129-40, 191-200. **C.P. Caspari,** *Der Prophet Obadja* (1842). **D. J. Clark,** "Obadiah Reconsidered," *BT* 42 (1991) 326-336. **A. Condamin,** "L'unité d'Abdias," *RB* 9 (1900) 261-68. **B. C. Cresson,** "Israel and Edom: A Study of the Anti-Edom Bias in OT Religion" (diss., Duke University, 1963); "The Condemnation of Edom in Postexilic Judaism," *The Use of the OT in the New* (ed.

J. M. Efird, 1972) 125-48. **G. I. Davies,** "New Solution to a Crux in Obadiah 7," *VT* 27 (1977) 484-87. **F. Delitzsch,** "Wann weissagte Obadja?" *ZLThK* 12 (1851) 91-102. **M. B. Dick,** "A Syntactic Study of the Book of Obadiah," *Semitics* 9 (1984) 1-29. **B. Diebner and H. Schult,** "Edom in alttestamenlichen Texten der Makkabaerzeit," *DBAT* 8 (1975) 11-17. **J. Eaton,** *Obadiah, Nahum, Habakkuk, Zephaniah: Introduction and Commentary* (1961). **A. H. Edelkoort,** "De profetie van Obadja," *NTT* 1 (1946–47) 276-93. **J. G. Eichhorn,** *Introduction to the Study of the OT* (3 vols., 1780–83, 1803[3], 1823–24; ET 1888). **J. A. Emerton,** "Looking on One's Enemies," *VT* 51 (2001), 186-96. **G. H. A. Ewald,** *Commentary on the Prophets of the OT* (1841, 1867–68; ET 1875–81). **G. Fohrer,** "Die Spruche Obadjas," *Studia Biblica et Semitica Theodoro Christiano Vriezen qui munere professoris theologiae per XXV annos functus est, ab amicis, collegis, discipulis dedicata* (1966) 81-93. **A. J. Freeman,** "The Obadiah Problem" (diss., Southern Baptist Seminary, 1950). **H. Frey,** *Das Buch der Kirche in der Weltwende: Die kleinen nachexilischen Propheten* (BAT 24, 1948). **F. E. Gaebelein,** *The Servant and the Dove: Obadiah and Jonah, Their Messages and Their Work* (1946). **N. Glueck,** "The Boundaries of Edom," *HUCA* 11 (1936) 141-57. **J. Gray,** "The Diaspora of Israel and Judah in Obadiah v. 20," *ZAW* 65 (1953) 53-59. **J. Halevy,** "Le Livre d' Obadia," *Révue semitique d'épigraphie et d'histoire ancienne* 15 (1907) 165-83. **M. Haller,** "Edom im Urteil der Propheten," *Festschrift K. Marti* (BZAW 41, 1925) 109-17. **H. Halpern,** "Obadiah: The Smallest Book in the Bible," *JBQ* 26 (1998) 231-36. **O. Isopescul,** "Übersetzung und Auslegung des Buches Abdias," *Weiner Zeitschrift für die Kunde des Morgenlandes* (1914) 149-81. **C. Keil,** *Minor Prophets* (1868; ET 1977). **C. A. Keller,** *Abdias* (1965). **G. Krause,** *Studien zu Luthers Auslegung der Kleinen Propheten* (BHT 33, 1962). **T. Lescow,** "Die Koposition des Buches Obadja," *ZAW* 111 (1999) 380-98. **E. Lipinski,** "Obadiah," *EncJud* 12 (1971) 1304-6; "Obadiah 20," *VT* 23 (1973) 368-70. **S. Loewinger,** "Esau dans Abd. 6," *REJ* 110 (1951) 93-94. **F. Luciani,** "Il verbo bo' in Abd. 13," *RivB* 31 (1983) 209-11. **P. K. McCarter,** "Obadiah 7 and the Fall of Edom." *BASOR* 221 (1976) 87-91. **J. Maier,** "'Siehe, ich mach(t)e dich klein unter den Volkern...': Zum rabbinischen Assoziationshorizont von Obadja 2," *Kunden des Wortes: Beiträge zur Theologie der Propheten, Josef Schreiner zum 60* (1982) 203-16. **K. Marti,** *Der Prophet Obadja* (HSAT 2, 1923). **J. M. Myers,** "Edom and Judah in the Sixth Fifth Centuries BC," *Near Eastern Studies in Honor of W. F. Albright* (ed. H. Goedicke, 1971) 377-92. **K. Nash,** "Obadiah: Past Promises, Future Hope," *TBT* 2I5 (1987) 278-82. **D. Neiman,** "Sefarad: The Name of Spain," *JNES* 22 (1963) 128-32. **J. D. Nogalski,** "Obadiah 7: Textual Corruption or Politically Charged Metaphor?" *ZAW* 110 (1998) 67-71. **W. Nowack,** *Die kleinen Propheten* (KEH 3, 4, 1897, 1922). **G. S. Ogden,** "Prophetic Oracles Against Foreign Nations and Psalms of Communal Lament: The Relationship of Psalm 137 to Jeremiah 49:7-22 and Obadiah," *JSOT* 24 (1982) 89-97. **M. Ottoson,** "Sarafand/Sarepta and Its Phoenician Background," *Qadminot* 13 (1980) 122-26. **S. Pagán,** "The Book of Obadiah," *NIB* (1996) 7:433-459; "Obadiah," *NISB* (2003) 1293-95. **E. Philippe,** "Abdias," *DB* 1 (1912) 20-23. **A. T. Poé,** "The Book of Obadiah : a Study of Its Literary Artistry and Its Theological Message" (Ph.D. diss., Vanderbilt University, 1999). **P. R. Raabe,** *Obadiah* (AB 24D, 1996). **J. Renkema,** "The Literary Structure of Obadiah," in *Delimitation Criticism: A New Tool in Biblical Scholarship* (ed. M.C.A. Korpel and J.M. Oesch, 2000) 230-76. **J. M. Rinaldi,** "In librum Abdiae," *Verbum Domini* 19 (1939) 148-54, 147-79, 201-6. **R. B. Robertson,** "Levels of Naturalization in Obadiah," *JSOT* 40 (1988) 83-97. **T. H. Robinson,** "The Structure of the Book of Obadiah," *JTS* 17 (1916) 402-8; *Obadiah* (1964). **W. Rudolph,** "Joel, Amos, Obadja, Jona," *ZAW* 49 (1931) 222-31; *Obadja* (1971). **J. Scharbert,** *Die Propheten Israels um 600 v. Chr.* (1967). **E. Sellin,** *Joel, Amos, Obadja, Jona* (KAT, 13, 2, 1929). **J. M. P. Smith,** "The Structure of Obadiah," *AJSL* 22 (1905–6) 131-38. **S. D. Snyman,** "Yom (YHWH) in the Book of Obadiah," in *Goldene Äpfel in Silbernen Schalen* (ed. K.-D. Schunck, M. Augustin, BEAT-

AJ 20, 1992). **M. A. Sweeney,** *The Twelve Prophets* (Berit Olam, 2000). **J. Theis,**"Der Prophet Abdias," *Die zwölf kleinen Propheten* (*HSAT* 8.3, 1, ed. J. Lippl and J. Theis, 1937). **J. D. W. Watts,** *Obadiah: A Critical Exegetical Commentary* (1969). **J. Wehrle,** "Prophetie und Textanalyse: Die Komposition Obadja 1-21, interpretiert auf der Basis textlinguistischer und semiotischer Konzeptionen" (diss., Freiburg, 1981). **P. Weimar,** "Obadja: Eine redaktionskritische Analyse," *BN* 27 (1985) 35-99. **K. Weinberg,** "Biblische Motive in Stifters Abdias", *Horizonte Emuna* 7 (1972) 32-38. **A. Weiser,** *Das Buch der zwölf kleinen Propheten I: Die Propheten Hosea, Joel, Amos, Obadja, Jona, Micha* (1967). **J. Wellhausen,** *Die Kleinen Propheten übersetztund erklärt* (1892, 1898). **E. R. Wendland,** "Obadiah's Vision of 'The Day of the Lord': On the Importance of Rhetoric in the Biblical Text and in Bible Translations," *JOTT* 7 (1996) 54-86. **H. Winckler,** Obadja, *Altorientalische Forschungen* 2, 3 (1901) 425-32. **H. W. Wolff,** "Obadja: Ein Kultprophet als Interpret," *EvTh* 37 (1977) 372-84; *Obadiah and Jonah* (BKAT XIV, 3, 1977; ET 1986). **E. Ben Zvi,** *A Historical-Critical Study of the Book of Obadiah* (BZAW 242, 1996); "A Deuteronomistic Redaction in/among 'The Twelve'?: A Contribution from the Standpoint of the books of Micah, Zephaniah and Obadiah," *Those Elusive Deuteronomists: The Phenomenon of Pan-Deuteronomism* (ed. L. S. Schearing and S. L. McKenzie, JSOTSup 268, 1999) 232-61.

R.R. MARRS

THE LATTER PROPHETS: MINOR

Jonah

1. *Introduction.* The interpretation of the book of Jonah may begin within the HB itself. Many phrases and passages in the book either parallel directly or echo materials from other parts of the Bible (see A. Feuillet [1947]). To what extent these are conscious borrowings and to what extent Jonah or the other passage may be the primary source in any given case is debatable (see J. Magonet [1976, 1983] 65-84; L. Allen [1976] 177). Nevertheless, we are reminded that the process of reinterpretation within the HB is almost as old as the individual texts themselves and that the book of Jonah is a carefully wrought narrative composition within a long literary tradition. However, what might have been "story" to its initial hearers became "history" for subsequent generations up to the modern period.

2. *Jonah in Jewish Tradition.* a. *Midrash and Liturgy.* As elsewhere, rabbinic Midrash attempts to fill gaps in the narrative, explain seeming contradictions, and respond to polemical issues. For instance, Jonah was the son of the widow of Zarephath who offered Elijah hospitality (*Pirqe R. El.* 33), a tradition known to the church fathers. He fled to save Israel, risking death at the hands of heaven for suppressing his prophecy (*b. Sanh.* 11:5). If the Ninevites repented but Israel did not, God would punish the people, so Jonah was willing to sacrifice his own life to save them (Mek. Tractate Pisha, ed. J. Lauterbach, 7, 10). This vindication of Jonah's behavior may be an apologetic response to Matt 12:41 (see E. Urbach [1975] 558; E. Bickerman [1967] 16; for a fuller treatment, see L. Ginzberg [1954] 4:197, 239-53; 6:318 n. 9, 343-52, "Midrash Jonah"). The book of Jonah is the prophetic reading for the Day of Atonement, probably because of the theme of repentance (but see also *b. Ta'an* 2:1).

b. *Medieval Exegesis.* The major Jewish commentators of the medieval period (Rashi, A. Ibn Ezra, D. Kimhi, Abravanel, etc.) wrote complete commentaries on the book in their characteristic styles. They often anticipated the discussions about linguistic problems, sequence of events, anachronisms, and other issues of modern exegesis. Abraham bar Hayya (12th cent.) gives a philosophical interpretation on the theme of repentance. The *Zohar* contains an elaborate allegory in which "Jonah descending into the ship is symbolic of man's soul that descends into the world to enter the body" (Zohar Vayakhel 199a-200a; see U. Steffen, [1994] 11-56).

3. *Jonah in Christian Tradition.* Christian interpretations of the book follow the three direct references to Jonah in the Gospels. In Matt 12:41 and Luke 11:29-32 Jesus cites the conversion of the Ninevites as an example of repentance, whereas in Matt 12:40 Jonah's presence inside the fish is understood as prefiguring Christ's body in the tomb (see R. Edwards [1971] 1-24, 71-107; J. Motyer [1975] 350-52). These two applications of the book, as a source of moral examples and of types, continue into the patristic period. East Syrian Christianity emphasized the repentance of the Ninevites. In the Greek and Western fathers (surveyed by Y. Duval [1973]), one argument, following Matt 12:41, is to consider Jonah as the representative of Judaism; whereas Nineveh believed, Israel continues to refuse to acknowledge Jesus (Jerome— see Bickerman [1965] 241). By the end of the fourth century Jonah is portrayed as an envious person who begrudges the salvation of the Gentiles (Augustine). This view, however, is rejected by Jerome and Cyril of Alexandria because of the other tradition that envisions Jonah as prefiguring Christ (see Duval [1985] 105-6).

Jonah appears among the other biblical examples of deliverance from death in a type of early Christian prayer that closely follows a Jewish pattern (see *b. Ta'an* 2:4; a Jewish-Christian example is in Apostolic Constitutions 7, 37-38). This kind of exemplary prayer (see H. Leclercq, "Défunts") is a key to the sequences of biblical scenes in early Christian art in which Jonah figures twice, as thrown into the sea and as resting under the gourd, a symbol of repose after death (Leclercq, "Jonas"). Christian use of and comment on the book hardly went beyond the lines laid down in patristic times until the rise of modern critical discussion (see Steffen, 57-117).

4. *Jonah in Islamic Tradition*. Jonah (Yunus) appears four times in the Quran, and his story is told once more without naming him. *Sura* 10 is called the "*Sura* of Jonah" because of the prominent mention of his prophetic task, in fact, *Sura* 4:163 and 6:87 name him among other prophets of God. In 10:99 the people of Nineveh are held up as models of a community that profited from their belief and repented, yet the fullest version of the story (37:139-48) emphasizes Jonah's blameworthiness in refusing his mission. The remaining reference (68:48-50) does not mention him by name: "Wait for your Lord's decree, and do not be like him of the fish who cried out in despair." Amplifications of these stories, typical of Islamic tradition, can be found in "The Tales of the Prophets of al-Kisa'i" (see W. Thackston [1978]; Steffen, 119-40).

5. *Jonah in Modern Scholarship*. The major lines of scholarly inquiry were established by the end of the nineteenth century: (1) lower criticism (see P. Trible [1963] 1-51); (2) higher criticism, including the historicity of Jonah and hence the question of its genre; the sources of the book and the composition; the authenticity of the "psalm" in 2:3-10; the dating of the book; and its purpose.

a. *Historicity and Dating*. Before the modern period most commentators accepted the historicity of the book, although Gregory of Nazianzus in the fourth century and Theophylact in the eleventh gave allegorical interpretations (see E. Sutcliffe [1953] 669; Allen, 178). Among Jewish exegetes, R. Joseph ibn Caspi cited some unnamed commentators, perhaps influenced by Maimonides (*Guide of the Perplexed* 2.46), who understood the events of chaps. 1 and 2 as occurring in a prophetic vision (see Y. Kil [1973] 5-6; Bickerman [1965] 233, n. 7). With the rise of higher criticism the historicity of the narrative was questioned, and during the nineteenth century numerous defensive arguments were raised to support it (see Trible [1963] 127). Although still defended, the majority of scholars today no longer pursue this issue (see M. Burrows [1970] 80-85).

Decisive in the change of view have been issues like the "great fish" or rather the whole range of miraculous events within the book that suggest a parabolic rather than literal history. Archaeological evidence contradicts the assertion about the size of Nineveh, and there is no record of any such mass conversion of the city. Even the statement of Jesus about Jonah (Matt 12:39-41) need not assume Jesus' acceptance of the historicity of the event as it may merely reflect the conventional understanding or use of his Jewish audience (see Allen, 180).

Linked to the question of historicity is that of the dating of the book. Whereas traditional commentators (and conservative moderns) identify the Jonah ben Amittai of 2 Kgs 14:25 as the author of the narrative, most scholars accept a later dating for the book. Much of the evidence for dating can be argued in opposing ways, e.g., the statement in 3:3—"Nineveh was a great city"—may imply that at the time of composition it no longer existed or may merely reflect a particular Hebrew construction. The apparent relationship to other biblical passages, especially Jeremiah 18, would suggest a postexilic date, although the problem of whether such dependence exists at all, and if so in which direction, means that we are dealing only with probabilities, however persuasive. The presence of Aramaisms, which formerly was believed to indicate a late date, is now less certain proof; some of the maritime terminology may be of earlier Phoenician origin. However, the number of other words and linguistic constructions that reflect postexilic Hebrew is still highly suggestive of a late date (see H. W. Wolff [1977] 54-55; Allen, 187-88).

Another basis for dating is the assumption that (like the book of Ruth) Jonah reflects a "universalistic" opposition to the "particularistic" policies of Ezra and Nehemiah. The history of this view has been traced by Bickerman (1967, 16-28). Although some commentators have maintained it, others find no evidence within the book to support such a theory (see Allen, 188). Attempts to date the book through views of Israel's universalism are inconclusive (see Trible [1963] 111-12), as are those based on interpreting the "message" of the book-the latter often displaying circular reasoning (see Burrows, 104). The book was apparently known to Ben Sira (Sir 49:10) in the second century B.C.E., but the reference in Tobit 14:4, 8 (4th cent. B.C.E.) is problematic, as Codex B reads "Nahum" in place of "Jonah." The book's origin is probably best located in the fifth or fourth century B.C.E. (see Allen, 188).

b. *Genre*. Challenges to the historicity of the book led to the search for other ways of defining its nature. There is among scholars a tension between the religious concern to find an acceptable genre to validate the book if it is not really history (see B. Childs [1958] 53-61) and a purely scientific interest in correct definition. However, the various suggested genres all present problems, either because they are too generalized to be of much value in defining the book or so precise that the multiple dimensions of the book are no longer taken into account.

Allegorical interpretations have a long history based on linking the name Jonah ("dove") with passages like Hos 11:11—hence the fish symbolizes being "swallowed up" by Babylon (Jer 51:34, 44). However there is no way of controlling what tend to become purely arbitrary interpretations (see Burrows, 89-90). In addition, the genre of parable tends to be too loosely defined, and whereas other parables in the HB are briefer and make a single point, Jonah is more complex. Analogies with the narratives of Elijah and Elisha have suggested the terms "prophetic legend" or "prophetic history," however, the book tends to parody such stories rather than to belong to them, and the story has a broader compass than just the prophet himself (see Wolff [1965] 32).

Somewhat broader categories are suggested by Novelle, or wisdom story, in which the moral point is veiled within the overall narrative. Some scholars, recognizing the exaggeration and humor, have suggested parody or satire. Others look within Hebrew terminology for the appropriate category, e.g., *mashal* or *midrash*—but if it is a midrash in the rabbinic sense, on what verse is it a commentary (see Allen, 180)? Other studies offer a general description like "a didactic narrative, satirical in tone."

Literary approaches have brought new perspectives and reopened older questions. The "psalm" in 2:3-10 was long held to be inauthentic (inappropriate while Jonah was still not saved; poetry and not prose like the rest of the book, etc.). However, the recognition of narrative techniques within it that are common to the rest of the book (the irony of its use by Jonah, like other of his pious statements; its architectural counterpoint to chapter 3, etc.) suggest that it belongs to the original composition (see M. Landes [1967]; Magonet, 39-54; S. Ackerman [1981]).

c. *The Problem of Meaning*. Early attempts to discover "sources" on the model of pentateuchal cricism or to trace the mythological underpinning of the book (see Trible [1963] 131-43) have long since ceased. Recent studies of the history of interpretation examine some underlying presuppositions in evaluating the book. In his study of "antijudaism" in Jonah exegesis, W. Golka (1987; following Bickerman [1967]) traces the attitudes ascribed to Jonah in traditional Christian exegesis and modern scholarship. The view that Jonah represents an alleged Jewish nationalistic exclusiveness is still expressed in language of surprising vehemence (see W. Neil [1962] 964, 967). Such interpretations may be classified under the theme "Jews and Gentiles" and have evoked defensive responses classifiable as history of prophecy: (a) the question of the individual prophetic fate and (b) the meaning of the prophecy of judgment and hence questions about repentance and divine mercy. The book lends itself to many kinds of homiletic interpretation and to approaches from other disciplines, like psychoanalysis (see A. Lacocque and P.-E. Lacocque [1990]).

Literary studies in the late twentieth century have emphasized the multiple dimensions and ambiguities of the story by virtue of its being a narrative. The new emphasis is thus to indicate the complexity of interpretation. The reader is encouraged, not to take away a single message from the book, but rather, as its closing unanswered question implies, to enter into a personal dialogue with it.

Bibliography: J. S. Ackerman, "Satire and Symbolism in the Song of Jonah," *Traditions in Transformation: Turning Points in Biblical Faith (*ed. B. Halpern and J. D. Levenson, 1981) 213-46. **L. C. Allen**, *The Books of Joel, Obadiah, Jonah, and Micah* (NICOT, 1976) 173-235. **C. Bedini and A. Bigarelli** (eds.), *Il viaggio di Giona: Targum, Midrash, Commento di Rashi* (1999). **B. L. Berger**, "Picturing the Prophet: Focalization in the Book of Jonah," *SR* 29 (2000) 55-68. **E. J. Bickerman**, "Les deux erreurs du prophète Jonas," *RHPR* 45 (1965) 232-64; *Four Strange Books of the Bible* (1967) 1-49. **T. M. Bolin**, *Freedom Beyond Forgiveness: The Book of Jonah Re-examined* (JSOTSup 236, 1997). **R. H. Bowers**, *The Legend of Jonah: Fifty Odd Interpretations of Jonah from the NT Through the English Renaissance* (1971). **M. Burrows**, "The Literary Category of the Book of Jonah," *Translating and Understanding the OT* (ed. H. T. Frank and W. L. Reed, 1970) 80-107. **B. S. Childs**, "Jonah, a Study in OT Hermeneutics," *SJT 11* (1958) 53-61. **S. L. Cook and S. C. Winter** (eds.), *On the Way to Ninevah: Studies in Honor of George M. Landes* (ASOR Books 4, 1999). **K. M. Craig**, *A Poetics of Jonah: Art in the Service of Ideology* (1999); "Jonah in Recent Research," *Currents in Research* 7 (1999) 97-118. **Y. M. Duval**, *Le Livre de Jonas dans la littérature chrétienne grecque et latine* (2 vols., 1973); (ed.) *Jérôme: Commentaire sur Jonas* (SC 323, 1985). **R. A. Edwards**, *The Sign of Jonah in the Theology of the Evangelists and Q* (1971). **B. Ego**, "The Repentance of Ninevah in the Story of Jonah and Nahum's Prophecy of the City's Destruction: Aggadic Solutions for an Exegetical Problem in the Book of the Twelve" (SBLSP 39, 2000) 243-53. **A. Z. Ephros**, "The Book of Jonah as Allegory," *JBQ* 27 (1999) 141-51. **A. Feuillet**, "Les Sources du Livre de Jonas," *RB* 54 (1947) 161-86; "Le Livre de Jonas," *La Sainte Bible* (1966). **S. Frieling** (ed.), *Der Rebellische Prophet: Jona in der modernen Literatur* (1999). **S. Frolov**, "Returning the Ticket: God and His Prophet in the Book of Jonah," *JSOT* 86 (1999) 85-105. **J. H. Gaines**, *Forgiveness in a Wounded World: Jonah's Dilemma* (Studies in Biblical Literature 5, 2003). **L. Ginzberg**, *The Legends of the Jews* (7 vols., 1954). **F. W. Golka**, "Jonaexegese und Antijudaismus," *Zeitschrift für Kirche und Israel* (1987). **C. B. Houk**, "Linguistic Patterns in Jonah," *JSOT* 77 (1998) 81-102. **R. T. Hyman**, "Seeking Vindication, Especially in Jonah," *JBQ* 30 (2002) 17-25. **L. Jonker**, "Reading Jonah Multidimensionally: A Multidimensional Reading Strategy for Biblical Interpretation," *Scriptura* 64 (1998) 1-15. **P. Kahn**, "The Epilogue to Jonah," *JBQ* 28 (2000) 146-55. **Y. Kil**, "*sēfer yônâ*" (*d ʿat miqrāʾ: terê ʿāsār*, 1, 1973). **G. M. Landes**, "The Kerygma of the Book of Jonah," *Int* 21 (1967) 3-31. **A. Lacocque and P. E. Lacocque**, *Jonah: A Psycho-Religious Approach to the Prophet* (1990). **H. Leclercq**, "Défunts," *DACL* 4, 430-40; "Jonas," *DACL* 7, 2572-613. **J. Z. Lauterbach** (tr.), *Mekilta De-Rabbi Ishmael* (3 vols., 1933). **C. Lichtert**, "Récit et noms de Dieu dans le livre de Jonas," *Bib* 84 (2003) 247-51. **J. Magonet**, *Form and Meaning: Studies in Literary Techniques in the Book of Jonah* (1976, 1983). **B. H. Mehlman and D. F. Polish** (tr.), "Midrash Jonah" *CCARJ* 24, 1 (1977) 30-41. **J. A. Miles, Jr.**, "Laughing at the Bible: Jonah as Parody," *JQR* 6 (1975) 168-81. **R. W. L. Moberly**, "Preaching for a Response? Jonah's Message to the Ninevites Reconsidered," *VT* 53 (2003) 156-68. **J. A. Motyer**, "Jonah," *New International Dictionary of NT Theology* 2 (1975) 350-52. **M. Mulzer**, "Die Busse der Tiere in Jona 3,7f. und Jdt 4,10," *BN* 111 (2002) 76-89; "Satzgrenzen im Jonahbuch im Vergleich von hebräischer und griechischer Testtradition," *BN* 113 (2002) 61-68; "Die Länge der Stadtmauern und die Fläche des antiken Ninive: eine Präzisierung," *BN* 118 (2003) 124-35. **W. Neil**, "Jonah, Book of," *IDB* (1962) 2:964-67. **P.J. Nel**, "The Symbolism and Function of Epic Space in Jonah," *JNSL* 25

(1999) 215-24. **J.-V. Niclós**, "Comentario al profeta Jonás de Abraham ibn Ezra y la liturgia del perdón: Introduction, traduccioón, notas y texto hebreo," *Estudios bíbicos* 57 (1999) 483-515. **J. M. Sasson**, *Jonah* (AB 24B, 1990). **Y. Sherwood**, "Rocking the Boat: Jonah and the New Historicism," *BibInt* 5 (1997) 364-402; "Cross-Currents in the Book of Jonah: Some Jewish and Cultural Midrashim on a Traditonal Text," *BibInt* 6 (1998) 49-79; *A Biblical Text and Its Afterlives: The Survival of Jonah in Western Culture* (2000). **U. Simon**, *Jona: Ein Jüdischer Kommentar* (SBS 157, 1994); *Jonah: The Traditional Hebrew Text with the New JPS Translation* (tr. L.J. Schramm JPS Torah Commentary, 1999). **U. Steffen**, *Die Jona-Geschichte: Ihre Auslegung und Darstellung im Judentum, Christentum, und Islam* (1994). **E. F. Sutcliffe**, "Jonas (Jonah)," *A Catholic Commentary on Holy Scripture* (1953) 669-71. **W. M. Thackston, Jr.**, *The Tales of the Prophets of al-Kisa'i* (1978). **P. L. Trible**, "Studies in the Book of Jonah" (diss., Columbia University, 1963); *Rhetorical Criticism: Context, Method, and the Book of Jonah* (1994); "The Book of Jonah," *NIB* (1996) 7:461-530. **E. E. Urbach**, *The Sages: Their Concepts and Beliefs* (2 vols., 1975). **H. W. Wolff**, *Studien zum Jonabuch* (Biblischen Studien 47, 1965); *Obadiah and Jonah* (BKAT 14, 3, 1977; ET 1986). **B. M. Zapff**, "Die Völkerperspektive des Michabuches als 'Systematisierung' der divergierenden Sicht der Völker in den Büchern Joël, Jona und Nahum: Überlegungen zu einer buchübergreifenden Exegese im Doekapropheton," *BN* 98 (1999) 86-99. **E. Ben Zvi**, *Signs of Jonah: Reading and Rereading in Ancient Yehud* (JSOTSup 367, 2003).

J. MAGONET

THE LATTER PROPHETS: MINOR

Micah

Micah 3:12 is quoted in Jer 26:18; 5:1[2]; in Matt 2:6 (cf. John 7:42); 7:6; 10:35-36; and in Luke 12:53 (cf. Matt 10:21; Mark 13:12). Some scholars think there is a relationship between Mic 5:1[2] and Isa 7:14.

1. *Dead Sea Scrolls.* Two Hebrew fragments of the book of Micah were found in caves near Qumran dating from the second to the first centuries B.C.E.: from Cave 1, 1QpMi (1Q14), which cites 1:2-5 and has a sectarian commentary on 1:5-7, 1:8-9, and 6:14-16; and from Cave 4, 4QpMi (4Q168), which has a sectarian commentary on 4:8-12. A long scroll of the Minor Prophets in Hebrew was discovered at Wadi Murabbaᶜ at in the Bar Kokhba Caves (Mur 88) dating from the end of the first century C.E. and containing Mic 1:5-3:4. There is also a scroll of the Minor Prophets in Greek dating from the middle of the first century C.E. and containing Mic 1:1–5:6 (with lacunae). Jerome and Calvin both wrote commentaries on the Minor Prophets, including Micah, that do not deal with critical issues but are concerned with theological matters.

2. *Early Interpretation.* In 1782 J. D. Michaelis attempted to deal with the apparent anachronisms of Micah 4–5 by arguing that Micah 1–5 embodies a chronological sweep from Micah to Christ. Micah 3:12 announces Nebuchadnezzar's overthrow of Jerusalem in 587 B.C.E.; chap. 4 describes events after the fall of Babylon to Late Judaism; and chap. 5 announces the birth of Jesus at Bethlehem and the coming of the kingdom of Christ. A. Hartmann (1800) argued that Micah preached partly during the reign of Manasseh (contrary to 1:1), that the present book came into being during the exilic period, and that an editor added 4:9-14 and 7:7-17.

While several scholars rejected Hartmann's position, H. Ewald (1867) contended that whereas Micah 1–5 (except 1:1 and 2:12-13) were from Micah of Moresheth, chaps. 6–7 originated from someone living in the days of Manasseh, since the language and tone of these two sections are so different. T. Roorda (1801–74) proposed several textual emendations (1869), over fifteen of which also appear in the *BHS* apparatus(1968–). In 1871 H. Oort contended that Mic 4:1-10 and 5:1[2] originally announced the fall of the Davidic dynasty and the restoration of Saul's dynasty and that 4:11-13 is a later addition, a view he later renounced. In 1872 M. de Goeje (1872) suggested that Mic 4:1-5 was a quotation from an earlier prophet that Micah's opponents had used against him. J. Wellhausen (1878) declared that Mic 7:7-20 had originated a century after the time of Micah of Moresheth, because its language and thought are so similar to that of Deutero-Isaiah.

Beginning in 1881 B. Stade argued that only Mic 1:5b–2:11 and chap. 3 are authentic. Micah 1:1-5a; 2:12-13; and chaps. 4–7 are late because they refer to events much later than the eighth century B.C.E. (e.g., the nations coming to Jerusalem to learn of Yahweh in 4:1-5). Stade's view has had a great impact on Micah research. The denial of the genuineness of half or more of the book of Micah raised the question of how the book came to be. Within the next half-century at least five theories arose, each championed by several scholars.

a. *The Literary-Historical Solution.* Stade contended that as the genuine Mican oracles (1:5b–2:11; 3) were handed down, two epigones in different periods added the other material in chaps. 1–5. Jeremiah 26:16-19 shows that the original book ended with 3:12. The first epigone, then, lived after Jeremiah; he added 4:1-4; 4:11–5:3[4]; and 5:6-8, 9-14[7-9, 10-15] to correct the message of doom in chaps. 1–3. Later, a second epigone, assuming that Micah was responsible for the additions of the first epigone, added 4:5-10 and 5:4-5[5-6] to declare that Israel's enemies would be defeated. Stade did not deal with 6:1–7:6 but dated 7:7-20 to the Greek period.

b. *The Chronological Explanation.* A. van Hoonacker (1908) argued that the book contains three sets of oracles from Micah dating from different periods in his prophetic career and arranged in chronological order. Chapters 1–3 pertain to Shalmaneser V's invasion of Palestine in 725–722 B.C.E., thus explaining the announcement of the fall of Samaria in 1:5-7. Jeremiah 26:18 dates Mic 3:12 to the reign of Hezekiah, who became king of Judah in 727 B.C.E. (2 Kgs 18:9-10). Micah delivered the oracles in chaps. 4–5 to encourage Hezekiah's reform, (cf. Jer 26:19). Chapters 6–7 contain a dramatic fiction, couched in the present and future but referring to the past, that is directed at northern Israelites left in the land after the fall of Samaria. "I" is Samaria, who realizes that her punishment is due to her sins. But if she repents, Yahweh will bring her back.

c. *The Rearrangement Proposal.* Some scholars thought that the incoherence of the book is due to a disarrangement of the materials during transmission. In 1891 H. Elhorst (1861–1924) proposed that the original order was chaps. 1, 2–3, 6–7, 4–5. The first copyist arranged these chaps. in double columns in certain order. A second copyist misunderstood this order and so copied chaps. 2 and 3 incorrectly. Three other copyists made their own mistakes, resulting in the present form of the book. Elhorst claimed to have restored the "original order."

d. *The Compilation View.* Several critics explained the present form of the book as a compilation of originally independent collections of oracles. For example, W. R. Smith (1882) thought these collections were chaps. 1–5 and 6–7, while W. Baudissin (1901) regarded them as 1–3; 4–5; 6:1–7:6; and 7:7-20.

e. *The Anthological Analysis.* The most widespread view was that Micah is an anthology of prophetic pieces originating at various times with different authors. K. Budde (1927) described Zechariah 9–14 and Micah 4–7 as "catch-alls" for late eschatological oracles. An outspoken advocate of this view was J. Lindblom (1929), who insisted that each pericope within the book must be interpreted in isolation because the present arrangement of the book is accidental. Thus all attempts to find coherence are doomed to failure.

3. *From Lindblom (1929) to Lescow (1972).* During the next four decades these five explanations were reiterated. R. Wolfe (1935) contended that thirteen redactors inserted materials into the Book of the Twelve, seven of whom contributed to the book of Micah between 540 and 225 B.C.E. T. Robinson (1936) found no coherence in the book. He maintained that various redactors at different times changed the earlier text and that three collectors pieced together disconnected fragments of originally longer prophetic oracles to produce the final form of the book.

In contrast, S. Mowinckel (1944) reasoned that most of 1:2–2:11; 3; and possibly 6:1–7:7 are genuine. The present form of the book was purposefully arranged by combining two originally independent collections: chaps. 1–5 and 6–7, each with a section of doom followed by a section of hope. A. Weiser (1949) believed that most of the book of Micah is genuine and that it was arranged in an orderly fashion. Most of the later additions (1:1; 2:12-13; 4:1-8; 5:6-8, 14[7-9, 15]; 7:8-20) are liturgical the responses of the later community .

W. Beyerlin (1959) was concerned with the cultic traditions assumed by Micah and his audiences in the authentic material in the book. He isolated five traditions: (a) "Israel" as a term for the amphictyonic league; (b) the theophany; (c) the amphictyonic laws; (d) exodus-conquest; and (e) David-Jerusalem. Accordingly, Beyerlin thinks most of the material in the book is genuine. A. Kapelrud (1961) declared that virtually all the material in the book is genuine. The structure and terminology fit the cultic drama of Israelite religion in the eighth century B.C.E.

R. Vuilleumier (1971) attributed most of the material to Micah (except 1:1, 5, 12b, 13b; 2:12-13; 4:10, 13; 5:4b-5a, 8, 14[5b-6a, 9, 15]; 7:8-20) and saw a purposeful structure following a doom-hope pattern (doom in chaps. 1–3 and hope in 4–5; doom in 6:1–7:7 and hope in 7:8-20). He detected five steps in the book's formation: (a) the authentic material in chaps. 1–5 was collected; (b) a series of later Mican oracles (6:1–7:7) was added; (c) 2:12-13 was added during the exilic period; (d) 7:8-20 was added during the Persian age; (e) brief modifications and additions were made at various times.

T. Lescow (1972) found four stages in the book's growth. Genuine material is limited to chaps. 1–3 (omitting 1:1, 5b-7, 13b, 16; 2:12-13). During the exilic period interpolations were made in chaps. 1–3, and songs and other material were added (4:6-5:14[5:15]). Between 516 and the beginning of the fourth century B.C.E., 1:1 and 4:1-5 were added. Finally 1:6-7 and chaps. 6–7 were added as an anti-Samaritan polemic during the Samaritan schism in the fourth century B.C.E.

4. *From 1972 to Present.* W. Rudolfph (1975) maintains that most of the book is authentic (excepting 1:1; 4:1-4; 5:6-8[5:7-9]; and 7:8-20). Some of the authentic sections (2:12-13; 4:9, 11-13) were written by Micah's opponents. The book falls into chaps. 1–2; 3–5; 6–7. However, the redactor(s) had no purpose in mind (theological or otherwise) by this arrangement, except perhaps to temper Micah's harsh proclamations of judgment with words of hope. L. Allen (1976) accepts most of the book as genuine (excepting 4:6-8 and 7:8-20) and analyzes its structure as chaps. 1–2; 3–5; 6–7. The book was handed down and "re-actualized" until 7:8-20 was added during the time of Haggai and Zechariah to reapply Micah's message to a new historical situation.

J. L. Mays (1976) divides the book into two parts, chaps. 1–5 and 6–7, each of which contains judgment followed by salvation. This does not reflect a historical development but the redactor's theology that Yahweh is responsible for both destruction and restoration. Only 1:3-5a, 8-15; 2:1-11; and chap. 3 are authentic; preserved orally by Micah himself, they were handed down through his disciples. This collection was later expanded in connection with Josiah's reform. In the exilic period a collection of salvation oracles was added in two stages: Chapters 1–5 were completed after the rebuilding of the Second Temple in 515 B.C.E. From the late pre-exilic period onward, chaps. 6–7 grew until they reached their final form and were added to chaps. 1–5 in the early fifth century B.C.E.

A. van der Woude (1976) argues that the entire book comes from the eighth century B.C.E. but from two different prophets. Chapters 6–7 come from a contemporary of Hosea in northern Israel in the days of Jotham and Ahaz, "Deutero-Micah." Chapters 1–5 are from Micah of Moresheth, who delivered the first chapter before the fall of Samaria, c. 723 B.C.E., and chaps. 2–5 c. 714 B.C.E., when Hezekiah joined the Philistines in a rebellion against Sargon II of Assyria. Chapters 1–5 contain several words by Micah's opponents (2:12-13; 4:1-9, 11-13; 5:4-5, 7-14[5:6, 8-15]).

B. Renaud (1977) traces a complicated history of the evolution of the book's growth from genuine material in 1:3–2:11; 3; 6:9-15 in the eighth century to its final form in the second century B.C.E. The first stage shows that Micah was a prophet of judgment. The second stage occurred during the exilic period when a tradent added judgment material to produce 1:3–2:11; 3; 6:2–7:7 . The third stage took place in the Persian period (5th–4th cents. B.C.E.) as Jewish priests sought to encourage their suffering comrades with words of hope. They added 1:2; chaps. 4–5 (including 2:12-13); 6:1; and 7:8-20, giving the book a judgment-salvation structure: chaps. 1–3 and 4–5; 6:1–7:6 and 7:7-20. The fourth stage occurred in the second century B.C.E. when circles related to "Deutero-Zechariah" made some minor changes in 1:5; 3:12; and 6:16; and moved 2:12-13 to its present position. H. Wolff's approach (1980) is very similar. He sees three stages in the book's growth: The genuine material is 1:6, 7b-13a, 14-16; 2:1-4, 6-11; 3. Deuteronomists added a commentary consisting of 1:3-5, 7a, 13b. Then several prophets in the early postexilic period (6th cent. B.C.E.) added additional judgment oracles in 6:1–7:7, hope oracles in 2:12-13 and chaps. 4–5, the liturgical ending in 7:8-20, and the introduction in 1:1-2.

D. Hillers (1984) despairs of any attempt to reconstruct a history of the growth of the book and contends that no meaningful structure is to be ascertained. He thinks that almost all the material is genuine. In response to oppression, Micah and his associates launched a "movement of revitalization," condemning the existing order and envisioning a new age. R. L. Smith (1984) believes that most of the book is authentic, with some editing and supplementing in the time of Jeremiah and in the exilic or early postexilic period. The proper arrangement of the book is chaps. 1–2; 3–5; 6–7.

The unity, coherence, and authenticity of the material in Micah have been the subject of several dissertations in the last decades of the twentieth century. D. Hagstrom (1982, pub. 1988) argued that "the book of Micah displays an overall literary coherence which renders it capable of meaningful construal as a unit." The two main subunits, chaps. 1–5 and 6–7, correspond in structure, display similar terminology, interlock through common motifs and other linking correspondences, and cohere theologically. L. Luker's dissertation (1985), with an extensive history of research (pp. 8-88), focuses on the redactional unity expressed through three pervasive themes: Divine Warrior, lament, and the personification of city/nation as female. K. Cuffey's work (1987), also with a history of interpretation (4-124), stresses the coherence of the four units in the book (1–2; 3:1–4:8; 4:9–5:14; and 6–7), focusing on the oracles of doom followed by the promises of hope. C. Shaw (1990, pub. 1993) has argued that Micah was a pro-Davidic prophet whose six oracles (1:2-16; 2:1-13; 3:1–4:8; 4:9–5:14; 6:1–7:7; 7:8-20) are arranged chronologically and derive from various strategic periods in Judean-Israelite history which date from the years of Jotham's reign (759/58–744/43 B.C.E.) to the time immediately after the capture of Samaria by Shalmaneser V in 722/21 B.C.E.

Recent commentaries on Micah include Anderson and Freedman (2000), Kessler (1999), and ben Zvi (2000). Jacobs (2001) studies the linguistic and thematic coherence of the book. Premnath (2003) uses social science methods to study the teachings of the eighth century prophets (including Micah) on land tenure and accumulation. Runions (2001) uses H. K. Bhabha's insights on cultural studies, ideological interpretation, and literary criticism to analyze various aspects of Micah. Utzschneider (1999) uses drama criticism and theory to interpret the literary character of Micah. Wagenaar (2001) studies the redaction of Micah.

5. *The Task Ahead.* The research and evaluations of the book of Micah focus attention on five major areas of concern for future work. First, further work needs to be done on the text, especially on 1:10-15; 2:6-11; and 6:9-13, 16. Second, exegesis of specific passages calls for careful and extended attention. Third, the criteria used for determining the date and historical background of the various pericopes require reevaluation. Fourth, the tradition-historical question of how the book of Micah came to be and the redactional question of the structure and intention of the present form of the book need further examination. Finally, the theology of the prophet Micah and of the book of Micah deserve careful consideration, along with attempts to discover how these fit into the theological analysis of the entire HB.

Bibliography: L. C. Allen, *The Books of Joel, Obadiah, Jonah, and Micah* (NICOT, 1976) 239-404. **F. I. Andersen and D. N. Freedman,** *Micah: A New Translation with Introduction and Commentary* (AB 24E, 2000). **K. L. Barker,** "A Literary Analysis of the Book of Micah," *BSac* 155 (1998) 437-48. **W. W. F. Baudissin,** *Einleitung in die Bücher des Alten Testaments* (1901) 518-33. **W. Beyerlin,** *Die Kulttraditionen Israels in der Verkündigung des Propheten Micha* (FRLANT NF 54, 1959). **M. E. Biddle,** " 'Israel' and 'Jacob' in the Book of Micah: Micah in the Context of the Twelve," SBLSP 37 (1998) 850-71 and repr. in *Reading and Hearing the book of the Twelve* (ed. J. D. Nogalski and M. A. Sweeney, 2000) 146-65. **K. Budde,** "Verfasser und Stelle von Micha iv 1-4 (Jes. ii 2-4)," *ZDMG 81* (1927) 152-58. **J. H. Cha,** *Micha und Jeremia* (BBB 107, 1996). **S. L. Cook,** "Micah's Deuteronomic Redaction and the Deuteronomists' Identity," in *Those Elusive Deuteronomists: The Phenomenon of Pan-Deuteronomism* (ed. L. S. Schearing and S. L. McKenzie, JSOTSup 268, 1999) 216-31. **K. H. Cuffey,** "The Coherence of

Micah: A Review of the Proposals and a New Interpretation" (diss., Drew University, 1987); "Remnant, Redactor, and Biblical Theologian: A Comparative Study of Coherence in Micah and the Twelve," in *Reading and Hearing the book of the Twelve* (ed. J. D. Nogalski and M.A. Sweeney, 2000) 185-208. **C. J. Dempsey**, "Micah 2–3: Literary Artistry, Ethical Message, and Some Consideration about the Image of Yahweh and Micah," *JSOT* 85 (1999) 117-28. **H. J. Elhorst**, *De Prophetie van Micha* (1891). **G. H. A. Ewald**, *Commentary on the Prophets of the OT* (1867; ET 1876) 2:289-339. **M. A. García Rodríguez**, *Ethiopian Biblical Commentaries on the Prophet Micah* (Äthiopistische Forschungen 52, 1999). **M. J. de Goeje**, "Proeve van Verklaring van Micha 4, vs. 1-5, vs. 2," *ThT* 6 (1872) 279-84. **D. G. Hagstrom**, *The Coherence of the Book of Micah: A Literary Analysis* (SBLDS 89, 1988). **A. T. Hartmann**, *Micha neu übersetzt und erläutert* (1800). **D. R. Hillers**, *Micah* (Hermeneia, 1984). **A. van Hoonacker**, *Les douze petits prophètes* (1908) 339-411. **M. R. Jacobs,** *The Conceptual Coherence of the Book of Micah* (JSOTSup 322, 2001). **K. Jeppesen**, "New Aspects of Micah Research," *JSOT* 8 (1978) 3-32; "How the Book of Micah Lost Its Integrity: Outline of the History of the Criticism of the Book of Micah with Emphasis on the Nineteenth Century," *StTh* 33 (1979) 101-31. **J. Jeremias**, "Tradition and Redaktion in Micha 3," in *Verbindungslinien: Festschrift für Werner H. Schmidt zum 65. Geburtstag* (ed. A. Graupner, H. Delkurt, und AB. Ernst (2000) 137-51. **W. C. Kaiser**, *The Communicator's Commentary: Micah, Malachi* (CCSOT 21, 1992). **A. S. Kapelrud**, "Eschatology in the Book of Micah," *VT* 11 (1961) 392-405. **R. Kessler,** *Micha* (HTKAT, 1999); "Zwischen Tempel und Tora: Das Michabuch im Diskurs der Perserzeit," *BZ* 44 (2000) 21-36. **P. J. King**, *Amos, Hosea, Micah: An Archaeological Commentary* (1988). **T. Lescow**, "Redaktionsgeschichtliche Analyse von Micha 1–5," *ZAW* 84 (1972) 46-85; "Redaktionsgeschichtliche Analyse von Micha 6–7," *ZAW* 84 (1972) 182-212; *Worte und Wirkungen des Propheten Micha: Ein kompositionsgeschichtlicher Kommentar* (AT 84, 1997). **Y. Levin**, "The Search for Moresheth-gath: A New Proposal," *PEQ* 134 (2002) 28-36. **J. Lindblom**, *Micha literarisch untersucht* (1929). **L. M. Luker**, "Doom and Hope in Micah: The Redaction of the Oracles Attributed to an Eighth-century Prophet" (diss., Vanderbilt University, 1985). **J. Luque**, "Leyendo Isaías, Oseas y Miqueas: Estructuras literarias semejantes del Siglo VIII AC," *Theologika* 14 (1999), 154-70. **W. McKane**, *The Book of Micah: Introduction and Commentary* (1998). **R. Mason**, *Micah, Nahum, and Obadiah* (OTGu, 1991). **J. L. Mays**, *Micah: A Commentary* (OTL, 1976). **W. McKane**, *The Book of Micah: Introduction and Commentary* (1998). **J. D. Michaelis**, *OEB* 20 (1782) 169-84. **J. C. Moor**, "Micah 7:1-13: The Lament of a Disillusioned Prophet," in *Delimination Criticism: A New Tool in Biblical Scholarship* (ed. M.C.A. Korpel and J.M. Oesch, 2000) 149-96. **S. Mowinckle**, *Det Gamle Testamente 3* (1944) 666-94. **H. Oort**, "Het Beth-Efraat van Micha V:1," *ThT* 5 (1871) 501-11. **E. Otto**, *TRE* 22 (1992) 695-704. **D. N. Premnath** *Eighth Century Prophets: A Social Analysis* (2003). **B. Renaud**, *La Formation du Livre de Michée* (EB, 1977). **T. H. Robinson**, *Die zwölf kleinen Propheten* (HAT 14, 1, 1936) 127-52. **T. Roorda**, *Commentarius in vaticinium Michae* (1869). **W. Rudolph**, *Micha, Nahum, Habakuk, Zephanja* (KAT 13, 3, 1975) 21-140. **E. Runions,** *Changing Subjects: Gender, Nation, and Future in Micah* (Playing the Texts 7, 2001); "Playing it Again: Utopia, Contradiction, Hybrid Space and the Bright Future in Micah," in *The Labour of Reading* (ed. F. C. Black, R. Boer, E. Runions; SBL SemeiaSt, 1999) 285-300. **C. S. Shaw**, *The Speeches of Micah: A Rhetorical-historical Analysis* (JSOTSup 125, 1993). **D. J. Simundson**, "The Book of Micah," *NIB* (1996) 7:531-89. **R. L. Smith**, *Micah-Malachi* (WBC 32, 1984) 2-60. **W. R. Smith**, *The Prophets of Israel and Their Place in History to the Close of the Eighth Century BC* (1882). **B. Stade**, "Bemerkungen über das Buch Micha," *ZAW* 1 (1881) 161-72. **M.A. Sweeney**, "Micah's Debate with Isaiah," *JSOT* 93 (2001) 111-124. **H. Utzschneider,** *Michas Reise in die Zeit: Studien zum Drama als Genre der prophetischen Literatur des Alten Testaments* (SBS 180, 1999). **R. Vuilleumier** (with C. A. Keller), *Michée, Nahoum, Habacuc, Sophonie* (CAT 11b, 1971) 5-92. **J. A. Wagenaar**, "'From Edom He Went Up...': Some

Remarks on the Text and Interpretation of Micah 2:12-13," *VT* 50 (2000) 531-39; *Judgement and Salvation: The Composition and Redaction of Micah 2–5* (VTSup 85, 2001). **A. van der Wal**, *Micah: A Classified Bibliography* (Applicatio 8, 1990). **A. Weiser**, *Das Buch der zwölf kleinen Propheten* (ATD 24, 1949) 200-61. **J. Wellhausen** (ed.), *Einleitung in das Alte Testament* (F. Bleek, 1878). **W. J. Wessels**, "Cheating at the Market Place: Impressions from Micah 6:9-16," *Skrif en kerk* 21 (2000) 406-415. **J. T. Willis**, "The Structure of the Book of Micah," *SEÄ* 34 (1969) 5-42; "Thoughts on a Redactional Analysis of the Book of Micah," *SBLSP* (1978) 87-107. **R. E. Wolfe**, "The Editing of the Book of the Twelve," *ZAW* 53 (1935) 90-129. **H. W. Wolff**, *Micah the Prophet* (1978, ET 1981); *Micah: A Commentary* (BKAT 14, 4, 1982; ET 1990). **J. R. Wood**, "Speech and Action in Micah's Prophecy," *CBQ* 62 (2000) 645-62. **A. S. van der Woude**, *Micha* (De Prediking van het Oude Testament, 1976). **B. M. Zapff**, *Redaktionsgeschichtliche Studien zum Michabuch im Kontext des Dodekapropheten* (BZAW 256, 1997); "Die Völkerperspektive des Michabuchas als 'Systematisierung' der divergierenden Sicht der Völker in den Büchern Joël, Jona und Nahum: Überlegungen zu einer buchübergreifenden Exegese im Dodeka propheton," *BN* 98 (1999) 86-99. **E. ben Zvi**, *Micah* (FOTL 21B, 2000); "Wrongdoers, Wrongdoing, and Righting Wrongs in Micah 2," *BibInt* 7 (1999) 87-100; "A Deuteronomistic Redaction in/among 'The Twelve': A Contribution from the Standpoint of the Books of Micah, Zephaniah and Obadiah in *Those Elusive Deuteronomists: The Phenomenon of Pan-Deuteronomism* (ed. L. S. Schearing and S. L. McKenzie, JSOTSup 268, 1999), 232-61.

J. T. WILLIS

THE LATTER PROPHETS: MINORS

Nahum

Interpretation of the book of Nahum through the centuries has focused on the need to trust God in the presence of tyranny. Yahweh remains a dependable refuge for the people of Israel in the face of national injustice, whether at the hands of Assyria, Babylon, or Rome.

The opening verses of the book witness to the phenomenon of what N. Sarna has called "inner biblical exegesis" (M. Fishbane [1988] vii-viii). Original terms of compassion from the so-called attribute formula in Exod 34:6-7 are here transformed into terms of war: "who maintains *kindness* [*nōṣēr*]" becomes "*who rages* [*nôtēr*] against his *enemies*"; "*assuages* anger" becomes "*long* of anger"; and "great in *kindness*" becomes "mighty in *power*" (Fishbane [1977] 280-81). In short, the book of Nahum is a reinterpretation of a central text from the Torah in a moment of need concerning Israel's national security. Though Yahweh is merciful and slow to anger, this time patience toward those who flout Yahweh has run out.

The Qumran pesher 4QpNah (4Q169) interpreted the text of Nahum as a prophecy of impending disaster against the community's enemies, in which the foes of old are identified with contemporary nations (M. Horgan [1979] 158-59). One Greek tradition of Tob 14:4 (Codex Sinaiticus), which has its fictional setting in ancient Nineveh, cited the prediction of the fall of Nineveh by Nahum (elsewhere Jonah) that the writer saw fulfilled at the hands of Nebuchadnezzar and Ahasuerus (both names used anachronistically). This reading of Nahum as prophecy from an earlier time that was subsequently fulfilled appears also in Josephus (*A. J.* 9.11.3). The Aramaic targum of Nahum emphasizes God's faithfulness toward God's people while expecting the ultimate destruction of the nations who have devastated Israel and its Temple. Nahum is here presented as later than Jonah, which reflects the Hebrew ordering of the individual books within the Book of the Twelve (Minor Prophets).

The book of Nahum is quoted only once in the NT (Rom 10:15; cf. Nah 1:15, Isa 52:7). Among the church fathers the book is cited infrequently: Tertullian (twice), Clement of Alexandria (once), Origen (four times), Eusebius (eight times), Epiphanius (c. 315-403; five times), Cyrial of Alexandria (twice), Hippolytus Romanus (c. 170–c. 236; twice), Melito of Sardis (once), and Chrysostom (twice). Jerome presented a spiritual interpretation in which the book predicts the certain destruction of those who reject God and remain outside the church (see J. Kelly [1975] 163-66).

The book of Nahum received relatively little attention within Jewish interpretation as well: eight references in the Babylonian Talmud and thirty-one in *Midrash Rabbah*. The interpretation of the medieval exegetes Rashi, A. Ibn Ezra, and D. Kimhi focuses on the judgment of God on Israel's national enemies.

Like the mainstream of Jewish exegesis before him, Luther's *Lectures on Nahum* (1525) assume a historical approach. Nahum is taken as a contemporary of Isaiah who predicted Judah's suffering under Sennacherib, the preservation of a righteous remnant, and the coming destruction of Nineveh. Thus Nahum (meaning "consolation" or "comfort") brought comfort to God's people in time of need. Few interpreters have expressed the essential message of Nahum more clearly than Luther when he wrote: "The book teaches us to trust God and to believe, especially when we despair of all human help, human powers, and counsel, that the Lord stands by those who are His, shields His own against all attacks of the enemy, be they ever so powerful" (see W. Maier [1959] 86). Although Calvin's commentary is more detailed, it also is theological in orientation.

The book of Nahum was singled out by R. Lowth (*De sacra poesi Hebraeorum* [1763] 281) for its aesthetic brilliance. With the subsequent development of historical criticism in the nineteenth century, the question of the historical and geographic origin of the book began to be viewed as the key to its interpretation. Supposed reference to the invasion of Sennacherib and linguistic ties to Isaiah led some scholars to posit a date late in the reign of Hezekiah. But the discovery that Thebes fell to Assyria in 663 B.C.E. (Neh 3:8-10) led most critical scholars to argue for a date of composition closer to the actual fall of Nineveh in 612 B.C.E. The discovery of what appeared to be a partial acrostic poem in 1:3-7 by a German pastor, G. Frohnmeyer, subsequently attracted attention within the scholarly community, particularly when H. Gunkel (1893) argued that this "broken acrostic" was added to the book by a postexilic editor. Like many other texts in the HB, Nahum was now regarded as composite.

Although many interpreters continued to read the book as witnessing to God's just rule in history, others noted the non-religious character of the poetry in chaps. 2–3 and the prophet's failure to address the sins of Judah. Some scholars began to judge Nahum as a nationalistic prophet, perhaps even allied with the "false prophets" condemned by Jeremiah. Such views continue to be held in some circles.

In 1907 P. Haupt argued that the book was not prophecy at all but the festival liturgy composed for the celebration of the Day of Nikanor on the 13th of Adar, 161 B.C.E. Although the Maccabean date was subsequently rejected, the idea that the book was a festival liturgy had profound influence in academic circles. In 1926 P. Humbert argued that the book was a prophetic liturgy used at the new year festival in Jerusalem in 612 B.C.E. to celebrate the fall of Nineveh. In 1946 A. Haldar argued that it was the work of cultic prophets who used the language of ritual combat in the new year festival as a curse on Israel's political enemies, the Assyrians. Subsequent studies placed the book within the sphere of international politics in pre-monarchic Israel, as reflected in the larger tradition of oracles against foreign nations in the prophetic literature. Perhaps the most attractive hypothesis along these lines was made in 1975 by J. Watts, who suggested that the book of Nahum, along with Habakkuk and Obadiah, was a liturgical expression of foreign prophecies that was part of the "Day of Yahweh" section of the Royal Zion Festival in ancient Jerusalem. J. Eaton has shown that no simple distinction exists between what some have called "cultic" and other modes of prophecy in ancient Israel.

Although a date close to the actual fall of Nineveh in 612 B.C.E. is frequently assumed, an earlier date is certainly possible. If the revolt of Manasseh against Assyria cited in 2 Chronicles 33 is not to be dismissed as a figment of the author's imagination, the situation as it existed in Judah c. 652–648 B.C.E. fits the occasion rather well. The basis for such a revolt on Manasseh's part would have been the conviction that Assyria's days were numbered. The book of Nahum presents precisely that message and may have been used to persuade the Judean king to take part in such a revolt—the assurance that Assyria's fall was certain, in fact that it was ordained of God the Divine Warrior. The book would then have taken on deeper meaning as part of the theological basis for the subsequent resurgence of Judean independence under King Josiah, especially after the death of Asshurbanipal in c. 630 B.C.E. The final destruction of Nineveh in 612 would have been the ultimate fulfillment of this prophecy and would thus explain the book's inclusion in the canon.

The study of Nahum in relation to holy war in ancient Israel has raised new questions. K. Cathcart (1975) and D. Christensen (1975, 166-175) make a distinction between holy war as a military institution and the "war of Yahweh," which reflects a cultic event within the worship experience of the people of ancient Israel during the preexilic era (i.e., before the destruction of the Temple in Jerusalem in 587 B.C.E.). This distinction points the way toward an important new impulse in the study of Nahum—namely, the shift from attempts to recover the historical setting that produced the book to a focus on the received literary text itself within the canonical process that produced the Book of the Twelve as one of the four primary sections of the latter prophets (J. Nogalski [1993]).

The acrostic hymn in Nahum 1, which is based on at least the first half of the Hebrew alphabet, has apparently been adapted to a new purpose by the author of the book, perhaps to form a cipher (code) from the sequence of letters and/or other opening elements, as A. van der Woude has suggested (1977). This cipher contains a summary of the meaning of the book: "I am the exalted Yahweh; and [I am] in the presence of sin. In a flood [I am] bringing a full end completely" see Christensen [1988] 51-58).

Later studies suggest that Nahum is to be read in conjunction with the foreign nation oracles of Isaiah 13–23 in particular. The first heading *massah* (Nah 1:1a) may well be an invitation to associate the book with this Isaiah material. The book may also be interpreted in relation to the wider oral and literary traditions of HB prophecy (R. Coggins [1982] 79-85). Moreover, as B. Childs has argued, its final form testifies to God's ultimate triumph over all foes. Traditional critical assessments miss the authoritative hermeneutical role of this "canonical shaping" (Childs [1979] 440-46).

In its poetic form the book of Nahum has no superior within the prophetic literature of the Hebrew Bible. The vivid and rapid succession of images gives it a peculiar power. It delineates the swift and unerring execution of divine fury against the merciless foes of God and of God's people. At the same time it also points rather sharply to God as the sure refuge and security for those who obey and trust God. Careful analysis of the poetry in the book reveals an elegant literary structure. The best way to explain its remarkable structural symmetry is to posit musical influence (Christensen [1989] 159-69). The Hebrew text bears the mark of original musical composition and performance within an ancient Israelite liturgical setting; thus it is likely that Nahum was a central prophet functioning within the Temple cult in Jerusalem. The book belongs to the so-called oracles against foreign nations and as such was probably motivated by political aims. In its present canonical form it is closely related to the book of Habakkuk; in fact, the two books may be outlined as a single literary unit as follows:

A—Hymn of theophany (Nahum 1)
   B—Taunt song against Nineveh (Nahum 2–3)
      X—The problem of theodicy (Habakkuk 1)
   B´—Taunt song against the "wicked one" (Habakkuk 2)
A´—Hymn of theophany (Habakkuk 3)

Nahum is primarily a book about God's justice, not about human vengeance, hatred, and military conquest; it is best read as a complement to the book of Jonah. The book of Jonah may be read as a midrashic reflection on Exod 34:6 and God's steadfast love (*ḥesed*), whereas the book of Nahum reflects Exod 34:7 and God's wrath. In short, Nahum focuses on the "dark side" of God, while Jonah portrays God's mercy and compassion toward the same wicked city. Both aspects are essential for an understanding of the divine nature.

Bibliography: E. Ball, "'When the Towers Fall': Interpreting Nahum as Christian Scripture," *In Search of True Wisdom: Essays in Old Testament Interpretation in Honour of Ronald E. Clements* (ed. E. Ball, JSOTSup 292, 1999).**B. J. Bamberger**, "The Changing Image of the Prophet in Jewish Thought," *Interpreting the Prophetic Tradition* (ed. H. M. Orlinsky, 1969) 301-23. **J. Calvin**, *Commentaries on the Twelve Minor Prophets* (1950) 4:183-312. **K. Cathcart**, *Nahum in the Light of Northwest Semitic* (BibOr 26, 1973); "Treaty-curses and the Book of Nahum," *CBQ* 35 (1973) 179-87; "The Divine Warrior and the War of Yahweh in Nahum," *Biblical Studies in Contemporary Thought* (ed. M. W. Ward, 1975). **B. S. Childs**, *Introduction to the OT as Scripture* (1979) 440-46. **D. L. Christensen**, *Transformations of the War Oracle in OT Prophecy: Studies in the Oracles Against the Nations* (HDR 3, 1975) 166-75; "The Acrostic of Nahum Once Again: A Prosodic Analysis of Nahum 1, 1-10," *ZAW* 99 (1987) 409-15; "The Book of Nahum: The Question of Authorship Within the Canonical Process," *JETS* 31 (1988) 51-58; "Nahum," *HBC* (1988) 736-38; "The Book of Nahum as a Liturgical

Composition: A Prosodic Analysis," *JETS* 32 (1989) 159-69. **R. J. Coggins**, "An Alternative Prophetic Tradition?" *Israel's Prophetic Tradition: Essays in Honour of P. R. Ackroyd* (ed. R. J. Coggins et al., 1982) 77-94. **G. L. Doudna,** *4Q Pesher Nahum: A Critical Edition* (JSPSup 35, Copenhagen International Seminar 8, 2001). **J. H. Eaton**, *Vision in Worship: The Relation of Prophecy and Liturgy in the OT* (1981) 14-21. **B. Ego,** "The Repentance of Nineveh in the Story of Jonah and Nahum's Prophecy of the City's Destruction: A Coherent Reading of the Book of the Twelve as Reflected in the Aggada," SBLSP 39 (2000) 243-53, repr. in *Thematic Threads in the Book of the Twelve* (ed. P. L. Redditt and A. Schart, BZAW 325, 2003). **H.-J. Fabry**, "The Reception of Nahum and Habakkuk in the Septugint and Qumran," in *Emanuel: Studies in Hebrew Bible, Septuagint, and Dead Sea scrolls in Honor of Emanuel Tov* (ed. S.M. Paul; VTSup 94, 2003) 241-56. **M. Fishbane**, "Torah and Tradition," *Tradition and Theology in the OT* (ed. D. A. Knight, 1977) 275-300; *Biblical Interpretation in Ancient Israel* (1988). **M. H. Floyd,** *Minor Prophets. Part 2* (FOTL 22, 2000). **F. O. García-Treto**, "The Book of Nahum," *NIB* (1996) 7:591-619. **H. Gunkel**, "Nahum 1," *ZAW* 13 (1893) 223-44. **A. Haldar**, *Studies in the Book of Nahum* (1947). **P. Haupt**, "Eine alttestamentliche Festliturgie für den Nikanortag," *ZDMG* 61 (1907) 275-97. **S. Hieronymi** [Jerome], *Comentarii in Prophetas Minores* (CCSL, 1970). **M. P. Horgan**, *Pesharim: Qumran Interpretation of Biblical Books* (CBQMS 8, 1979). **P. Humbert**, "Le problème du livre de Nahoum," *RHPR* 12 (1932) 1-15. **G. H. Johnston**, "Nahum's Rhetorical Allusions to Neo-Assyrian Conquest Metaphors," *BSac* 159 (2002) 21-45; "Nahum's Rhetorical Allusions to the Neo-Assyrian Lion Motif," *BSac* 158 (2001) 287-307; "Nahum's Rhetorical Allusions to Neo-Assyrian Treat Curses," *BSac* 158 (2001) 415-36. **H. Kamsler**, "Nahum: The Little-Known Prophet," *JBQ* 28 (2000) 182-84. **J. N. D. Kelly**, *Jerome* (1975) 163-66. **M. Luther**, *Lectures on the Minor Prophets* (LW, vol. 18, 1975). **W. A. Maier**, *The Book of Nahum: A Commentary* (1959). **J. Mann**, *The Bible as Read and Preached in the Old Synagogue* (1966). **N. D. Nogalski**, "The Redactional Shaping of Nahum 1 for the Book of the Twelve," *Among the Prophets* (ed. P. Davies and D. Clines, JSOTSup 144, 1993) 193-202; *Literary Precursors to the Book of the Twelve* (BZAW 217, 1993); *Redactional Processes in the Book of the Twelve* (BZAW 218, 1993). **I. Nowell**, "Nahum," *NISB* (2003) 1315-1319. **J. M. O'Brien**, *Nahum* (Readings, 2002). **R. Patterson**, "A Literary Look at Nahum, Habakkuk, and Zephaniah," *Grace Theological Journal 11* (1990) 17-27. **A. Pinker**, "On the Meaning of *htkbd* in Nahum 3.15," VT 53 (2003) 558-61. **V. M. Premstaller**, "Prophecy Goes Hollywood: A Fresh Approach to Nah 2," *BN* 118 (2003) 46-50. **P. E. Pusey** (ed.), *Cyrilli Archiepiscopi Alexandrini, In XII Prophetas* (1868). **J. J. M. Roberts**, *Nahum, Habakkuk, and Zephaniah* (OTL, 1991). **W. Rudolph**, *Micha—Nahum—Habakkuk—Zephania* (KAT 13, 3, 1975). **H. W. F. Saggs**, "Nahum and the fall of Nineveh," *JTS* 20 (1969) 220-25. **K. Seybold**, *Profane Prophetie: Studien zum Buch Nahum* (SBS 135, 1989); *Nahum, Habakkuk, Zephanja* (Zürcher Bibelkommentare, 1991). **H. N. Sprenger**, *Theodori Mopsuesteni Commentarius in XII Prophetas* (1977). **K. Spronk**, "Acrostics in the Book of Nahum," *ZAW* 110 (1998) 209-222. **M. Sweeney**, "Concerning the Structure and Generic Character of the Book of Nahum," *ZAW* 104 (1992) 364-77; *The Twelve Prophets* (2 vols., Berit Olam, 2000). **A. Van der Wal**, *Nahum, Habakkuk: A Classified Bibliography* (1988). **J. D. W. Watts**, *The Books of Joel, Obadiah, Jonah, Nahum, Habakkuk, and Zephaniah* (CBC, 1975). **M. Weigl**, "Current Research on the Book of Nahum: Exegetical Methodologies in Turmoil?" *Currents in Research* 9 (2001) 81-130. **A. S. van der Woude**, "The Book of Nahum: A Letter Written in Exile," *OTS* 20 (1977) 108-26. **B. M. Zapff**, "The Perspective on the Nations in the Book of Micah as a 'Systematization' of the Nations' Role in Joel, Jonah, and Nahum? Reflections on the Context-Oriented Exegesis," *Thematic Threads in the Book of the Twelve* (ed. P. L. Redditt and A. Schart, BZAW 325, 2003).

D. L. CHRISTENSEN

THE LATTER PROPHETS: MINOR

Habakkuk

Habakkuk occupies the eighth place in the Book of the Twelve (Hebrew canon) or the Minor Prophets (Christian canon) and is comprised of three brief chapters, the first two of which consist of prophetic speeches and the last of a prayer. The prophet is not mentioned elsewhere in the HB, but in the story of *Bel and the Dragon* in the deuterocanonical *Additions to Daniel* he is reported to have been carried by an angel to Babylon, where he gave food to Daniel in the lion pit (Dan 14:33-39). Before the modern era Habakkuk was mined for its eschatological or christological value as well as for its teaching on faith and obedience to God. These interests continued into the Reformation period but with the additional concern for the book's historical background. In the nineteenth century, scholarly attention began to focus on the literary unity and arrangement of the book, the relation of the prophet and his book to the cult, the most appropriate form-critical categories to describe the work and its parts, the origin of chap. 3, and the historical setting and theological message of the book.

Evidence of early Jewish interpretation of Habakkuk may be found in the Greek versions, the *Targum of Jonathan*, and the Habakkuk pesher from the Dead Sea Scrolls found at Qumran (1QpHab lacks the final chapter). The pesher from Qumran interprets the text with reference to the Teacher of Righteousness, the Wicked Priest, the Prophet of Lies, and other matters of immediate concern to the author and the community at Qumran. Habakkuk 2:4b is understood to mean that God will deliver from "the house of judgment [= damnation?]" all in Judah who obey the law because of their patient suffering and their steadfast faith in the Teacher of Right" (i.e., their faith in the one who teaches the law correctly; W. Brownlee [1979] 125). In Jewish discussions of eschatology and the delay of the end, Hab 2:3-4 played a critical role, warning against unbridled expectations and assuring that the end was imminent.

While early Jewish interpreters regularly used Hab 2:3 for eschatological reflection, their Christian counterparts favored Hab 2:4. Paul, for example, cited the verse twice (Rom 1:17; Gal 3:11) as a prooftext for his doctrine of justification by faith, contrasting with typical Jewish use of the verse to exhort audiences to faithful obedience to God. Nevertheless, Heb 10:35-38 cites Hab 2:3-4 in the course of an exhortation to Christians to endure persecution and hardship for the sake of their hope, a point underscored by the memorable discourse on faith in Hebrews 11. Finally, Acts 13:41 reports that Paul concluded his sermon at the synagogue in Antioch of Pisidia with a citation of Hab 1:5, warning his Jewish audience not to repeat the example of their ancestors by refusing to accept God's most recent activity in Jesus. A. Strobel's 1961 historical and philological study examined the motifs and traditions at work in the idea of the delay of the parousia in light of the late Jewish and primitive Christian history of Hab 2:2ff.

Among later Christian writers the christological interpretation of Habakkuk was dominant: Hab 2:3 and chap. 3 were related to the parousia and eschaton, and Hab 2:4 to faith in Jesus Christ. Cyril of Alexandria's commentary on Habakkuk (PG 71.871-72), for example, finds the historical fulfillment of the promise that the prophet's vision would be accomplished (Hab 2:3) in Cyrus's victory over Babylon, but its spiritual fulfillment in Christ. Similarly, the condemnation of the arrogant man in Hab 2:5 should be related historically to Nebuchadnezzar but spiritually to Satan (PG 71.873-74). Augustine (*City of God* 18:32) also provides an example of christological interpretation of Habakkuk, suggesting that the prayer of Habakkuk 3 was the prophet's address to Christ and that the statement of the LXX text of Hab 3:2, "in the midst of two living ones, thou shalt be known," was a reference to the position of Christ between the OT and the NT, or his crucifixion between two robbers (Mark 15:27), or his place between Moses and Elijah in the transfiguration scene (Mark 9:2-8). Moreover, the deuterocanonical story (Dan

14:33-39) about an angel transporting Habakkuk with food to Daniel in the lions' den was accepted by Jerome (*Commentariorum in Abacuc prophetam* [CCSL 76A] 580) and others as evidence that the prophet was a contemporary of Daniel and finds expression in early Christian iconography, which typically depicts the prophet bearing a gift of food, usually loaves and/or fish.

In the Reformation period Luther rejected Jerome's use of "Daniel, Bel, and the Dragon" for the dating and interpretation of Habakkuk since the former was not in the Hebrew canon. Luther concluded that Habakkuk prophesied to Judah and Benjamin before the Babylonian captivity that God would punish them by the power of Babylon (Habakkuk 1), which would in turn be destroyed (Habakkuk 2); he interpreted Habakkuk 3 as a prayer for the godly who went into Babylonian exile. Since the destruction of Babylon was not completed until after the exile, Luther suggested that the prophet's activity extended from the preexilic to the postexilic period, although he allowed for the possibility that the prophet spoke of future events as though they were past or presently occurring ("described as past or as now present things that were still in the future," LW 19:119). Luther believed that Hab 2:4 meant that godly people were saved from destruction and lived because they waited on the Lord; in a more christological vein he maintained that Habakkuk intended to strengthen and comfort his people so that they would not despair of Christ's coming.

Calvin (*Commentaries on the Twelve Minor Prophets*, vol. 4) opposed the traditional christological interpretation of Habakkuk, proposing instead that the book be understood against the background of the prophet's own day. He claimed that, while certainty is impossible, the prophet probably prophesied under Manasseh or another king before Zedekiah, condemning the sin of Judah and warning of destruction by Babylon. Habakkuk 3 consists of a prayer that the prophet dictated for his people to use in their devotions in exile. In spite of his strictures against traditional christological interpretation of the book, however, Calvin approved of the use of Hab 1:5 in Acts 13:41 and that of Hab 2:4 by Paul.

Although E. Rosenmüller (1827) had suggested that Habakkuk 2 was from a time later than the prophet Habakkuk, it was with J. von Gumpach (1860) that the source-critical study of Habakkuk began in earnest in the nineteenth century. Noting the similarities between Hab 1:6-11 and Jeremiah 4–6, von Gumpach concluded that Hab 1:1-14 was a separate oracle that referred to the Scythian invasion. Most of the rest of the book was, he thought, a later oracle concerning Judah's deliverance. (Only M. de Goeje [1861] would follow closely this analysis of two separate oracles.) Almost thirty years passed, however, before further progress was made in solving the problems that von Gumpach had identified.

The most notable nineteenth-century source-critical study of the book was issued by B. Stade (1884), who argued that only Hab 1:2–2:8 derived from the prophet. He maintained that Hab 2:9-11 and 2:15-17 described a Palestinian enemy and not the Chaldean invader of 1:6; that Hab 2:12-14, 18-20 were also later additions to the book; and that Hab 3:2-19 was probably a postexilic psalm. Another influential contribution from this period was F. Giesebrecht's proposal (1890) that Hab 1:5-11, which mentions the Chaldeans, interrupts Habakkuk's complaint and so in its present context is apparently misplaced. He proposed that the verses be restored to their original place before Hab 1:1, where they had been set during the exile as an introduction to the book. In addition, Giesebrecht regarded Hab 2:12-17, 20, and chap. 3 as secondary expansions. Although J. Wellhausen (1892) and W. Nowack (1922) agreed with Giesebrecht's conclusions about Habakkuk 2–3, they dated the book as a whole to the preexilic period. Moreover, Wellhausen (1898) later argued that chap. 3 was the community's prayer for God to act again as at the exodus and that the proper close for the poem has been lost, since vv. 17-19 cannot be genuine.

In response to the fragmenting effects of source analysis on the interpretation of Habakkuk,

K. Budde (1893) maintained that Habakkuk 1–2 was a literary unity. Since Hab 1:5-11 interrupted the continuous complaint of 1:2-4, 12-17, however, the former should be read as God's answer to the prophet's complaint and relocated after 2:4, before the woe sayings that begin in 2:5. Therefore, the foreign oppressor, Assyria, would be conquered by another, Chaldea. This view was accepted by C. Cornill (*Einleitung in das AT* [1898]) and G. A. Smith (*The Book of the Twelve Prophets* [1896–98]), although Smith regarded the first oppressor as Egypt. O. Happel (1900) also viewed Habakkuk as a literary unity and believed that it portrayed the eschatological messianic age in terms of the Seleucid persecutions of the Jews. W. Betteridge (1903) followed Budde's suggestion that the Chaldeans were the punishers of Assyria but accepted the canonical ordering of the text and dated Habakkuk to c. 700 B.C.E.

In 1894 W. Rothstein proposed an interpretation that would find final acceptance in some form among a number of later scholars. He believed that the core of Habakkuk was an older prophecy referring to the godless in Judah that was reworked later to refer to Babylon. M. Lauterburg's proposal (1896) that the reference to "Chaldeans" in 1:6 was a scribal correction or insertion and that 1:5-11 originally referred to the Persians led him to assign an exilic or postexilic date to the book and signaled the importance that the reference to the Chaldeans in 1:6 would play for subsequent research. K. Marti (1904), instead of reckoning with later supplementations as Rothstein had, believed that the book was composed from various independent fragments of tradition from the preexilic, exilic, and postexilic periods. Only the "Chaldea-oracle" (1:5-10, 14-15) could be traced back with confidence to the prophet.

B. Duhm (1906) responded to the extreme views of Marti and other source critics by suggesting that "Chaldeans" (Hab 1:6) be emended to "Kittim" and that the latter be interpreted with reference to the Greeks and the book thus dated to the reign of Alexander the Great (333-331 B.C.E.). Independent of Duhm's influence, C. C. Torrey (1935) reached similar conclusions, adding that "wine" in 2:5 be emended to "Javan" (Gr.); he believed that the entire work was a "meditation" on the conquests of Alexander the Great. While Duhm and Torrey won few converts to their view, they demonstrated the critical role of Hab 1:6 for assessing the historical setting of the entire book.

In 1911 two other works appeared that produced distinctive source-critical interpretations. Continuing the work of his 1909 Oxford dissertation, G. Stonehouse dated Habakkuk to the time of the Chaldean invasion of Syria-Palestine in 604/3 but held that chap. 3 was the prophet's reworking of an earlier composition. P. Riessler, on the other hand, proposed that Habakkuk was little more than a collection of various pre- and postexilic prophecies.

Form-critical and cult-functional analyses of Habakkuk became dominant in the twentieth century. H. Gunkel (1895) had described the mythical function of the themes in Habakkuk 3, comparing the chapter with the Babylonian creation stories and associating it with religious ritual. Among the first to suggest that there was a liturgical redaction of Habakkuk was F. Kelly (1902); and in 1911, H. Thackeray, working from the Barberini Greek version of Habakkuk 3, found a liturgical function for this part of Habakkuk. On the basis of the late dating of Habakkuk and its literary unity, S. Mowinckel (1923), as well as E. Balla (1928), E. Sellin (1929, 1930), P. Humbert (1944), and others came to regard the book as a cult-prophetic liturgy. Mowinckel regarded it as the prophetical part of an actual Temple liturgy and eventually (1953) came to associate it with the autumnal new year's festival. W. Caspari (1914) suggested that the entire book was liturgical; F. Stephens (1924) pointed out parallels between Habakkuk 3 and the Babylonian creation stories; and U. Cassuto (1935–37) saw a Ugaritic origin for the mythical elements in chap. 3 (see also W. Irwin [1942]). P. Humbert (1944) concluded that the book was composed for a day of repentance and condemned the actions of Jehoiakim's supporters (1:2-4, 13; 2:4-5). Finally, J. Jeremias (1970) argued that Habakkuk was a cult prophet whose various sermons were edited in the late exilic period for an anti-Babylonian liturgy.

Scholars continue to debate the book's literary unity, historical setting, genre, and manner of origin as well as its and the prophet's relation to the cult and the nature of the commentary on the book found at Qumran. Many writers view the book as a literary unity (e.g., the rhetorical investigation of the book by D. Bratcher [1984]; an exploration of the form-critical aspects of the book by M. Sweeney [1991]; and commentaries by M. Roberts [1991] and R. Haak [1991]); and while they differ over the identification of its genre, they tend to agree that it has little direct connection with the cult. Sweeney calls the book a "prophetic affirmation of divine sovereignty and justice" and believes that it was intended to persuade Judah in the late seventh century that God's elevation of the Neo-Babylonian empire to power contradicts neither God's nature nor the divine promises to the people. Roberts also dates Habakkuk's speeches—which he sees as oral compositions—to this period, although he assigns Hab 1:11-17 and 2:6-19 to the period after 597 B.C.E. Either the prophet, whose relation to the cult is unclear, or a later editor arranged these oral compositions into a connected meditation about theodicy, in some instances redirecting them (e.g., woe speeches originally uttered against a Judean oppressor like Jehoiakim now address Babylon). Although Haak also doubts the cultic or legal setting of the book, he believes that it was from the first a written—rather than oral—composition. The prophet supported the deposed king Jehoahaz and was pro-Babylonian; but since his early declarations in Babylon's favor had not been fulfilled, he wrote these to confirm them. He did not survive Babylon's assault on Jerusalem; and his prophecies were carried to Babylon, where they were revised with an anti-Babylonian slant. The genre of the book is that of a complaint.

Finally, investigations of Habakkuk 3 typically seek its origin in an archaic hymn (T. Hiebert [1986]; Roberts [1991]). The most elaborate and imaginative expression of this view is in Hiebert's 1984 Harvard dissertation (1986), which concludes that the chapter was a single literary unit in the form of a victory song for Yahweh and was structured according to the mythological scheme found in the Baal cycle at Ugarit and the Accadian *Enuma Elish*. The chapter derived from the pre-monarchic period, had a cultic setting, and was associated with the southern sanctuary at Kuntillet 'Ajrud. In the postexilic period the chapter was attached to Habakkuk and was reinterpreted—perhaps by those who edited Isaiah and Zechariah—with reference to God's future actions as a cosmic divine warrior.

Bibliography: F. I. Andersen, *Habakkuk: A New Translation with Introduction and Commentary* (AB 25, 2001).**E. Balla**, "Habakuk," *RGG* (1928) 1556-557. **A. J. Baumgartner**, *Le prophète Habakuk: Introduction, critique et exégèse, avec examen sp,cial des commentaires rabbiniques du Talmud et de la tradition* (1885). **A. O. Bellis**, 'Habakkuk 2:4b: Intertextuality and Hermeneutics,' in *Jews, Christians, and the Theology of the Hebrew Scriptures* (ed. A.O. Bellis and J.S. Kaminsky; SBLSymS 8, 2000). **W. R. Betteridge**, "The Interpretation of the Prophecy of Habakkuk," *AJT* 7 (1903) 647-61. **L. F. Bliese**, "The Poetics of Habakkuk," *JOTT* 12 (1999) 47-75. **D. R. Bratcher**, "The Theological Message of Habakkuk: A Literary-Rhetorical Analysis" (diss., Union Theological Seminary, Richmond, 1984). **W. H. Brownlee**, *The Midrash Pesher of Habakkuk* (SBLMS 24, 1979). **K. Budde**, "Die Bücher Habakkuk und Sephanja," *TSK* 66 (1893) 383-93; "Habakkuk," *EncBib* (1901) 1921-28. **W. Caspari**, *Die israelitischen Propheten* (1914). **U. Cassuto**, "Il capitolo 3 di Habaquq e i testi di Ras Shamra," *AStE* (1935–37) 7-22. **S. Coleman**, "The Dialogue of Habakkuk in Rabbinic Doctrine," *Abr-nahrain* 5 (1964–65) 57-85. **E. Cothenet**, "Habacuc," *DBSup* 8 (1972) 791–811. **O. Dangl**, "Habakkuk in Recent Research," *Currents in Research* 9 (2001), 131-68. **B. Duhm**, *Das Buch Habakuk* (1906). **K. Elliger**, *Studien zum Habakuk-Kommentar vom Toten Meer* (BHT 15, 1953). **M. Eszenyei Széles**, *Wrath and Mercy: A Commentary on the Books of Habakkuk and Zephaniah* (1987). **H.-J. Fabry**, "The Reception of Nahum and Habakkuk in the Septugint and Qumran," in *Emanuel: Studies in Hebrew Bible, Septuagint, and Dead Sea scrolls in Honor of*

Emanuel Tov (ed. S.M. Paul; VTSup 94, 2003) 241-56. **J. A. Fitzmyer**, "Habakkuk 2:3-4 and the NT," *De la Tōrah au Messie* (ed. M. Carrez et al., 1981) 447-55 = his *To Advance the Gospel* (1981) 236-46. **F. Giesebrecht**, *Beiträge zur Jesaiakritik: Nebst einer Studie über prophetische Schriftstellerei* (1890). **M. J. de Goeje**, "Beoordeling van: Der Prophet Habakuk von J. de Gumpach," *Nieuwe Jaarboeken voor wetenshappelijke Theologie 4* (1861) 304-19. **D. E. Gowan**, "The Triumph of Faith," *Habakkuk* (1976). **J. von Gumpach**, *Der Prophet Habakuk* (1860). **H. Gunkel**, *Schöpfung und Chaos in Urzeit und Endzeit* (1895). **R. D. Haak**, *Habakkuk* (VTSup 44, 1991). **O. Happel**, *Das Buch des Propheten Habackuk* (1900). **W. Herrmann**, "Das unerledigte Problem des Buches Habakkuk," *VT* 51 (2001) 481-96. **T. Hiebert**, *God of My Victory: The Ancient Hymn in Habakkuk* (HSM 38, 1986); "Habakkuk," *NIB* (1996) 7:619-55. **W. L. Holladay**, "Plausible Circumstances for the Prophecy of Habakkuk," *JBL* 120 (2001) 123-30. **P. Humbert**, *Problèmes du livre d'Habacuc* (MUN 18, 1944). B. Huwyler, "Habakuk und seine Psalmen," in *Prophetie und Psalmen: Festschrift für Klaus Seybold zum 65. Geburtstag* (ed. B. Huwyler, H.-P. Mathys und B. Weber; AOAT 280, 2001) 231-59. **W. A. Irwin**, "The Psalm of Habakkuk," *JNES* 1 (1942) 10-40; "The Mythological Background of Habakkuk, Chapter 3," *JNES* 15 (1956) 47-50. **J. Jeremias**, *Kultprophetie und Gerichtsverkündigung in der späten Königszeit Israels* (WMANT 35, 1970). **P. Jöcken**, *Das Buch Habakuk: Darstellung der Geschichte seiner kritischen Erforschung mit einer eigenen Beurteilung* (BBB 48, 1977). **F. T. Kelly**, "The Strophic Structure of Habakkuk," *AJSL* 18 (1902) 94-119. **M. Lauterburg**, "Habakuk," *Theologische Zeitschrift aus der Schweiz* 13 (1896) 74-102. **T. H. Lim**, "The Wicked Priest or the Liar?" in *The Dead Sea Scrolls in Their Historical Context* (ed. T. H. Lim, 2000) 45-51. **K. Marti**, *Das Dodekapropheton* (KHC, 1904). **S. Mowinckel**, *Psalmenstudien III* (1923); "Zum Psalm des Habakuk," *TZ* 9 (1953) 1-23. **W. Nowack**, *Die kleinen Propheten* (HKAT, 1922). **G. T. M. Prinsloo**, "Life for the Righteous, Doom for the Wicked: Reading Habakkuk from a Wisdom Perspective," *Skrif en kerk* 21 (2000) 621-40. **P. Riessler**, *Die kleinen Propheten oder das Zwölfprophetenbuch* (1911). **J. J. M. Roberts**, *Nahum, Habakkuk, and Zephaniah: A Commentary* (OTL, 1991). **E. F. K. Rosenmüller**, *Scholia in VT, Pars VII* (1827). **J. W. Rothstein**, "Über Habakkuk Kap. 1 und 2," *TSK* 67 (1894) 51-85. **J. A. Sanders**, "Habakkuk in Qumran, Paul, and the OT," *JR* 38 (1959) 232-44. **J. E. Sanderson**, *The Woman's Bible Commentary* (ed. C. A. Newsom and S. H. Ringe, 1992) 222-24. **E. Sellin**, *Das Zwölfprophetenbuch* (KAT 12, 1929, 1930). **N. Shupak**, "The God from Teman and the Egyptian Sun God: A Reconsideration of Habakkuk 3.3-7," *JANES* 28 (2001) 97-116. **B. Stade**, "Miscellen. 3. Habakuk," *ZAW* 4 (1884) 154-59. **W. Staerk**, "Zu Habakuk 1,5-11: Geschichte oder Mythos?" *ZAW* 51 (1933) 1-29. **F. J. Stephens**, "The Babylonian Dragon Myth in Habakkuk 3," *JBL* 43 (1924) 290-93. **G. G. V. Stonehouse**, *The Book of Habakkuk* (1911). **A. Strobel**, *Untersuchungen zum eschatologischen Verzögerungsproblem auf Grund der spätjüdisch-urchristlichen Geschichte von Habakuk 2,2ff.* (SNT 2, 1961); "Habakkuk," *RAC* 13 (1986) 203-26. **M. A. Sweeney**, "Structure, Genre, and Intent in the Book of Habakkuk," *VT* 41 (1991) 63-83. **H. S. J. Thackeray**, "Primitive Lectionary Notes in the Psalm of Habakkuk," *JTS* 12 (1911) 191-213. **C. C. Torrey**, "The Prophecy of Habakkuk," *Jewish Studies in Memory of G. A. Kohut* (1935) 565-82. **A. Van der Wal**, *Nahum, Habakkuk: A Classified Bibliography* (Applicatio 6, 1988). **J. Wellhausen**, *Skizzen und Vorarbeiten 5* (1892); *Die kleinen Propheten* (1898). **M. Wood**, "Pesher Habakkuk and the Targum of Jonathan ben Uzziel," *JSP* 19 (1999) 129-46. **J. Ziegler**, "Ochs und Esel in der Krippe: Biblisch-patristische Erwägungen zu Jes 1, 3 und Hab 3, 2 (LXX)," *MThZ* 3 (1952) 385-402.

M. P. GRAHAM

THE LATTER PROPHETS: MINOR

Zephaniah

The first clearly attested interpretation of the message of the prophet Zephaniah is in Sir 49:10, which refers to Zephaniah as one of the twelve prophets who were a source of comfort and hope for Israel. This stress on comfort and hope is already suggested by the present form of these books, for they all conclude with a note pointing to either salvation or hope or both. A Qumran pesher on Zephaniah (4Q170) points to relatively early exegetical activity aimed at decoding a text's true meaning governed by the interpretative community's theological concerns and the assumption that the true meaning is not found in the "plain meaning" of the text. Most Jewish traditions about the prophet Zephaniah concern certain aspects of his life and preaching (*Pesiq. Rab.* 26, 129b and *Yalkut Shimoni, b. Meg. 15a*, and *Lives of the Prophets* [*OTP* 2:379-99]).

Certain circles during the late Second Temple period also considered Zephaniah an apocalyptic figure as seen in the so-called *Apocalypse of Zephaniah* (OTP 1:497-507) and in *b. Sukk.* 52b. Significantly, in one of the few times in which Clement of Alexandria cited Zephaniah, he actually quoted from *Apoc. Zeph.* (*Strom.* 5.77). The book of Zephaniah was not among the most popular prophetic books in the first centuries C.E. In fact, there are relatively few quotations of the book in Christian and Jewish literature of the time (B. Ben Zvi [1971] 25-28).

Early exegetical works on Zephaniah took three different forms: proof texts, translations and textual versions, and commentaries. The *Haftarah* (assigned reading from the prophets) to Gen 11:1 is Zeph 3:9-17, 20. This functions as a proof text to indicate an ultimate reversal of the Tower of Babel episode.

Ancient translations are also exegetical works; e.g., *Tg. Neb.*, by choice of words and paraphrastic interpretation, tends to stress the transcendence of God, ethical concerns, and the issue of alien cults in Zephaniah, while the Vulgate stresses eschatological understandings (Zeph 3:8). Hebrew texts may also reflect and communicate exegetical choices. Thus the division into paragraphs attested to by the Hebrew text of Zephaniah from Muraba'at suggests, for instance, that Zeph 2:1-3 and Zeph 3:1 are more closely related to the following verses than to the preceding ones. (See also the division markers in 8HevXIIgr.)

Jerome's Zephaniah commentary was perhaps the most influential early commentary. Jewish medieval commentaries on Zephaniah include those by Rashi, D. Kimhi, A. Ibn Ezra, J. Kara, and Abravanel. Two main features of these commentaries are their emphasis on grammatical and philological issues and the attempt to understand the historical circumstances referred to in the book.

The most influential Reformation commentaries are those by Luther and Calvin; these, especially the latter, may be considered direct precursors of the modern historical-critical commentaries. Although Luther wrote in his commentary that "among the minor prophets, he [Zephaniah] makes the clearest prophecies about the kingdom of Christ" (1975, 319), he did not often refer to Zephaniah in his sermons. Zephaniah was among the less studied prophets in the following centuries.

In modern research the tendency until recently was to give a low value to both Zephaniah and the book (e.g., "Zephaniah can hardly be considered great as a poet," J. Smith [1911] 176). Several scholars claimed that neither the book nor the prophet reflect any "new ideas," that the book echoes ideas found elsewhere in the prophetic literature. Against this background it is not surprising to find only a few references to Zephaniah in the now-classic twentieth-century Hebrew Bible theologies of this century.

Change is easily perceptible in more recent work. Theological tendencies, whose influence has been on the rise in recent years, generally find Zephaniah relevant for the development of a biblical theological stance concerning poverty (e.g., N. Lohfink [1987]). The supposed African origin of Zephaniah has also evoked special interest in the United States (e.g., G. Rice [1979]).

Several comprehensive studies on Zephaniah have been published in the last decades, and they point to keen interest in the "historical prophet" and/or in the book (e.g., I. Ball [1988]; Ben Zvi; A. Berlin [1994]; R. Edler [1984]; P. House [1988]; H. Irsigler [1977]; G. Krinetzki [1977]; J. Roberts [1991]). Although some recent works have focused on literary aspects (e.g., House) and this trend may grow, the main question in Zephanic studies in this century as a whole has concerned the message of the historical prophet. Accordingly, questions about the social location of the prophet and his audience, and especially about the historical circumstances of his time, have come to the forefront. These circumstances have also provided the background against which scholars have attempted to elucidate the book's message concerning such issues as the Day of Yahweh and the poor (ʿaniyyîm). Of course, since it has been assumed that Zephaniah's message can be abstracted only from the authentic words of the prophet, the starting point has most often been the delimitation of the original text.

Although there is general agreement about the existence of small glosses in the text (e.g., 1:4), there is no scholarly consensus over which parts of the book are authentic. An overall view of the literature shows that the discussion has been centered on three blocks of material: 1:2-3; 2:7-11; and 3:8[14]-20.

Zephaniah 1:2-3, or certain parts of it, has been considered late, mainly because of its eschatological, or universal, outlook. Most scholars, including the vast majority of those who consider most of 1:2-3 authentic, consider v. 3 ("make the wicked stumble") to be an explanatory gloss introducing an ethical reason for the punishment and/or a reflection of the glossator's misunderstanding of the text (Roberts).

The main arguments for the lateness of 2:8-11, or most of these verses, involve stylistic differences: the mention of "remainder" (šeʾērît) and "to remain" (yātar) pointing to the remnant; the eschatological contents of v. 11; and historical improbability, i.e., the described situation of Moab and Ammon scorning Judah and taking advantage of its disgrace does not fit the historical data concerning the days of Josiah but those of the first decades of the sixth century. Those who attribute most or all of these verses to the Josianic period (and to the historical prophet Zephaniah) answer these objections by pointing to rhetorical and literary devices that unify the text; by asserting that objections based on contents are unconvincing; and by arguing that the announcement of judgment against Moab and Ammon is not impossible in Josiah's days, or that they, along with the other oracles against the nations in this book correspond exactly to the political situation in the time of Josiah (c. 628–621).

Concerning v. 7, expressions like "restore their fortunes" and "remnant of the house of Judah" and the theme of restoration are considered clear signs of lateness by some scholars; but others deny that these expressions are necessarily exilic or postexilic or that the prophet Zephaniah was devoid of nationalistic feelings. If all these verses are assigned to the historical prophet, then his message included an announcement of territorial expansion beyond the Judahite limits for the future Judahite remnant (or, according to another position, for his contemporaneous Judahites) and an announcement that Yahweh will cause the other gods to shrivel and all the peoples will bow down to Yahweh. If none of these verses are assigned to the historical prophet, then the remaining text includes two main oracles against the nations— namely, those against Assyria and Philistia. These countries are considered by many scholars to be the main enemies of Judah in the Josianic era. Those who follow this approach tend, accordingly, to stress the relative weight of the political and earthly elements in the prophet's message. If vv. 8-9a are to be attributed to the prophet, however, then there may be grounds for understanding the message in terms less dependent on concrete political-historical circumstances.

Many scholars have considered the unit 3:8-20 to be a late text that cannot be attributed to the historical prophet Zephaniah nor dated to the Josianic period. The basic assumption underlying this position is that words of salvation or comfort, and especially the motif of universal salvation, occur mainly (or only?) in exilic and postexilic literature. If 3:8-20 is late, the message of the prophet would have no (or almost no) words of salvation or comfort. The issue concerns the basic character of the prophet's message. If these two verses are removed, then 2:3 would probably have the same fate; therefore, the social-ethical message of Zephaniah would be removed as well. Other scholars consider 3:9-13 "Zephanic," mainly on the basis of its relation to vv. 1-8, or because they consider the idea that the peoples will serve Yahweh to be preexilic, or both. If these verses do belong to the historical prophet, then his message would also have included the image of a universal salvation and the universalistic image of all the peoples serving one God, Yahweh. Finally, if 3:14-20 or most of this material is authentic, then these verses receive a totally different meaning from what the address in the second person may suggest. They would not be a call of joy for the prophet's audience (like many psalms) but a call of joy for the future Jerusalem envisaged by the prophet, a Jerusalem that will come only for the "poor and humble" and only after the awesome judgment of the Day of Yahweh. It is noteworthy that these analyses stand or fall on the assumption that any part of the book of Zephaniah is "Zephanic" unless the opposite is proved (for a critique and a different proposal, see Ben Zvi).

On the basis of 1:1 most modern scholars claim that Zephaniah prophesied in the days of Josiah. There is no agreement, however, on the exact time frame during this period: before the reform, at the time of the reform, or after it? The arguments brought on behalf of the idea that he prophesied before the reform are basically: (a) Since the king is not mentioned in 1:4-9, even in v. 8, where the officers and the sons of the king are mentioned, then one may infer that the king had no real influence and power, i.e., Josiah was a minor (2 Kgs 22:1). (b) The cultic notice in 1:5 reflects the situation before the reform but not after. (c) The harsh words of Zephaniah make sense if addressed to such a syncretistic community. If this picture is correct, the message of Zephaniah may have prepared the ground for Josiah's reform.

Arguments (b) and (c) may also be interpreted as pointing to the time of the reform, in which case Zephaniah's message reflects the ideas of the group that welcomed and advanced the deuteronomic reform in Josiah's days. However, it should be noted that the message of the prophet, if taken at face value, was not "mend your ways and reform the cult and live." Rather, it was "the day of judgment will come regardless of what you or the community do, and only those 'humble' people who seek Yahweh will perhaps live." This literal understanding seems difficult to reconcile with Deuteronomy or with a real policy of reform. Alternatively, if Zephaniah was active in the reform, then his sayings should not be understood in a literal sense.

The proposal that Zephaniah prophesied after the reform is based on understanding *šeʾār habaʿal* in 1:4 as "the remnant of Baal." If this is correct, one may assume that Zephaniah knew about the reform, and in spite of it (or because its success was only partial) prophesied the coming judgment. After the reform may also mean after Josiah. J. P. Hyatt (1948), for instance, proposed the days of Jehoiakim. A different position has been taken by G. Smith (1929) and E. Lacheman (1950). They found many expressions pointing to an exilic or postexilic date and on the basis of the contents of chapter 3 concluded that the book was written c. 200 B.C.E. Ben Zvi proposes a post-monarchic date and maintains that neither the original message of a historical, seventh-century Zephaniah nor even his actual sayings can be convincingly reconstructed on the basis of the book bearing his name. He advances an understanding in terms of a post-monarchic community.

Questions about the composition and dating of the book and its main sections, the search for the historical Zephaniah and his message, and the study of the book against its historical circumstances are all likely to continue to be a focal point of Zephanic studies in the future. Berlin's statement that "the time of Josiah is not necessarily the time that the book was written, but it is *the time in which the book is set*" (Berlin, 38; emphasis in the original) may well serve as a starting point for many of these new studies. Of course, one may also expect a flourishing interest in works dealing mainly with literary and theological (and ideological) aspects of the book of Zephaniah.

Bibliography: I. Abrabanel, *Prophets and Writings: Perush* (1960), Hebrew. **R. W. Anderson**, Jr., "Zephaniah Ben Cushi and Cush of Benjamin: Traces of Cushite Presence in Syria-Palestine," *The Pitcher Is Broken: Memorial Essays for G. W. Ahlström* (JSOTSup 190, ed. S. W. Holloway and L. K. Handy, 1995) 45-70. **I. J. Ball,** *A Rhetorical Study of Zephaniah* (1988). **R. A. Bennett**, "Africa and the Biblical Period," *HTR* 64 (1971) 483-500; "The Book of Zephaniah," *NIB* (1996) 7:657-704. **E. Ben Zvi**, *A Historical-critical Study of the Book of Zephaniah* (BZAW 242, 1991). **A. Berlin**, *Zephaniah* (AB 25A, 1994). **M. Bolle**, *Sefer Zephaniah* (1970), Hebrew. **J. Calvin**, *Commentaries on the Twelve Minor Prophets 4* (1950). **H. Cazelles**, "Sophonie, Jérémie et les Scythes en Palestine," *RB* 74 (1967) 22-44. **D. Christensen**, "Zephaniah 2:4-15: A Theological Basis for Josiah's Program of Political Expansion," *CBQ* 46 (1984) 669-82. **B. G. Curtis**, "The Zion-daughter Oracles: Evidence on the Identity and Ideology of the Late Redactors of the Book of the Twelve," in *Reading and Hearing the Book of the Twelve* (ed. J. D. Nogalski and M. A. Sweeney; SBLSymS 15, 2000) 166-84. **A. B. Davidson**, *The Books of Nahum, Habakkuk, and Zephaniah* (1905). **M. de Roche**, "Zephaniah 1:2-3: The 'Sweeping' of Creation," *VT* 30 (1980) 104-9. **A. Edens**, "A Study of the Book of Zephaniah as to the Date, Extent, and Significance of the Genuine Writings" (diss., Vanderbilt University, 1954). **R. Edler**, *Das Kerygma des Propheten Zefanja*, (FThSt 126, 1984). **K. Elliger**, *Das Buch der zwölf Kleinen Propheten* (ATD 25, 2, 1951). **M. Eszeneyei Széles**, *Wrath and Mercy: A Commentary on the Books of Habakkuk and Zephaniah* (1987). **M. H. Floyd**, *Minor Prophets. Part 2* (FOTL 22, 2000). **G. Gerleman**, *Zephanja: Text kritisch und literarisch Untersucht* (1942). **R. D. Haak**, "'Cush' in Zephaniah," *The Pitcher Is Broken: Memorial Essays for G. W. Ahlström* (JSOTSup 190, ed. S. W. Holloway and L. K. Handy, 1995) 238-51. **S. Hieronymi**, *Commentarii in Prophet as Minores* (CCSL 76a, 1970) 655-711. **W. L. Holladay**, "Reading Zephaniah with a Concordance: Suggestions for a Redaction History," *JBL* 120 (2001) 671-84. **P. R. House**, *Zephaniah: A Prophetic Drama* (JSOTSup 69, 1988). **J. P. Hyatt**, "The Date and Background of Zephaniah," *JNES* 7 (1948) 25-29. **A. Ibn Ezra**, in *Miqraot Gedolot*. **H. Irsigler**, *Gottesgericht und Jahwetag* (ATSAT 3, 1977); "Der Freudenaufruf an Zion in Israels Prophetie: Zef 3, 14-15 und seine Parallelen," in *Steht nicht geschrieben?: Studien zur Bibel und ihrer Wirkungsgeschichte: Festschrift für Georg Schmuttermayr* (ed. J. Frühwald-König, F.R. Prostmeier, R. Zwick, 2001); *Zefanja* (Herders theologischer Kommentar zum Alten Testament, 2002). **Y. Kara**, in *Miqraot Gedolot*. **A. S. Kapelrud**, *The Message of the Prophet Zephaniah: Morphology and Ideas* (1975). **C. A. Keller**, *Nahoum, Habacuc, Sophonie* (CAT 11, b, 1971). **G. Krinetzki**, *Zefanjastudien: Motiv- und Traditionskritik und Komposition und Redaktionskritik* (1977). **G. Langohr**, "Livre de Sophonie et la critique d'authenticit,," *ETL* 52 (1976) 1-27; "Rédaction and composition du livre Sophonie," *Le Muséon* 89 (1976) 51-73. **N. Lohfink**, "Zephanja und das Israel der Armen," *BK* 39 (1984) 100-108; *Option for the Poor: The Basic Principle of Liberation Theology in the Light of the Bible* (1987). **M. Luther**, *Lectures on the Minor Prophets* (Luther's Works 18, 1975). *Miqraot Gedolot* with Malbim's *Commentary* (1964), Hebrew. **J. Nogalski**, *Literary Precursors of the Book of the Twelve* (BZAW 217, 1993) esp. 171-215. **P. E. Pusey** (ed.), *Sancti patris nostri Cyrilli Archi episcopi Alexandrini, in XII Prophetas 2* (1965) 167-240. **Radak**, in *Miqraot Gedolot*. **Rashi**, in *Miqraot Gedolot*. **B. Renaud**, "Le livre de Sophonie: Lejourde YHWH thème structurant de la synthèse rédactionelle," *RevScRel* 60 (1986) 1-33. **J.**

Ribera Florit, "Laversion aramaica del profeta Sofonías," *EstBib 40* (1982) 127-58. **G. Rice**, "The African Roots of the Prophet Zephaniah," *JRT* 36 (1979) 21-31. **J.J.M. Roberts,** *Nahum, Habakkuk, and Zephaniah* (OTL, 1991). **W. Rudolph**, *Micha-Nahum-Habakuk-Zephanja* (KAT 13, 4, 1975). **L. Sabottka**, *Zephanja: Versuch einer Neuübersetzung mit philologischem Kommentar* (BibOr 25, 1972). **J. E. Sanderson**, "Zephaniah," *The Women's Bible Commentary* (ed. C. A. Newsom and S. H. Ringe, 1992) 225-27. **J. Scharbert**, "Zefanja und die Reform des Joschija," *Künder des Wortes: Beiträge zur Theologie der Propheten* (FS J. Schreiner, ed., L. Ruppert et al., 1982) 237-53. **K. Seybold**, *Satirische Prophetie: Studienzum Buch Zefanja* (SBS 120, 1985). **H. Shy**, *Tanhum HaYerushalmi's Commentary on the Minor Prophets* (1991). **G. A. Smith**, *The Book of Twelve Prophets 2* (1929). **J. M. P. Smith**, *A Critical and Exegetical Commentary on Micah, Zephaniah, Nahum, Habakkuk, Obadiah, and Joel* (ICC, 1911). **L. P. Smith and E. R. Lacheman**, "The Authorship of the Book of Zephaniah," *JNES* 9 (1950) 137-42. **R. L. Smith**, *Micah-Malachi* (WBC 32, 1984). **H. N. Sprenger** (ed. and tr.), *Theodori Mopsuesteni Commentarius in XII Prophetas* (1977) 280-301. **M. Striek**, *Das vordeuteronomistische Zephanjabuch* (BBET 29, 1999). **M. A. Sweeney**, "A Form-Critical Reassessment of the Book of Zephaniah," *CBQ* 53 (1991) 388-408; *The Twelve Prophets* (Berit Olam, 2000); *Zephaniah: A Commentary* (Hermeneia, 2003). **J. Vlaardingerbroek**, *Zephaniah* (Historical Commentary on the Old Testament, 1999). **J. D. W. Watts**, *The Books of Joel, Obadiah, Jonah, Nahum, Habakkuk, and Zephaniah* (CBC, 1975). **M. Weigl**, *Zefanja und das 'Israel der Armen': Eine Untersuchung zur Theologie des Buches Zefanja* (1994). **D. L. Williams**, "The Date of Zephaniah," *JBL* 82 (1963) 77-88. **E. Ben Zvi**, "A Deuteronomistic Redaction in/among 'The Twelve'?: A Contribution from the Standpoint of the Books of Micah, Zephaniah and Obadiah," *Those Elusive Deuteronomists: The Phenomenon of Pan-Deuteronomism* (ed. L. S. Schearing and S. L. McKenzie, JSOTSup 268, 1999).

E. Ben Zvi

THE LATTER PROPHETS: MINOR

Haggai

1. *Early Jewish and Christian Interpretation.* Haggai is the first of three postexilic books in the Book of the Twelve, or the Minor Prophets. Early interpreters of this book appear to focus on the person of Haggai rather than on the content of the book. Ancient traditions (Pseudepiphanus, Dorotheus, Epiphanus) portray him coming to Israel as a youth from Babylon and at his death being buried with priestly honors near the priests. Pseudepiphanus believed that Haggai saw the Solomonic Temple, and Hesychius added that the prophet was of the tribe of Levi. The LXX, Itala, Vulgate, and Peshitta support these traditions by carrying the name of Haggai in the superscription to several psalms. A few rabbis believed that Haggai and Malachi were the same person, the former called *ml' k yhwh* and the latter called *ml' ky*. Jerome, however, went the farthest by citing the tradition that Haggai, Malachi, and John the Baptist were not real people but angels appearing in human form.

2. *Medieval and Reformation Periods.* Medieval Jewish exegetes connected Haggai with the Great Synagogue, either as a member (Rashi, I. Abravanel; J. G. Carpzov held a similar view in the 18th cent.) or as the one who assisted in handing down the tradition to the members ('Abot 1:1, Krakau [1662]; A. Hallevi ben David; D. Gans). In the medieval-Reformation period there was also discussion of the specific Darius (I or II) during whose reign Haggai prophesied. J. Scaliger, J. Tarnovius (1586–1629), J. Piscator (1546–1625), and A. Strauchius (1632–82) argued for Darius II, while the majority proposed Darius I (Calvin, L. Cappel, D. Petavius; so too already Josephus, Jerome, Theodore of Mopsuestia, and Theodoret). This debate raged as late as the seventeenth century, when H. Witsius set out the grounds for both sides without coming to a firm decision.

3. *Enlightenment.* In accordance with their disdain for material dealing with cult and priestly matters, scholars of the Enlightenment were almost uniformly negative in their assessment of Haggai. J. G. Eichhorn, for example, held that the style was affected and that the writer made the kind of mistakes to be expected of someone playing with a dead language. L. Bertholdt (1774–1822), J. Jahn (1750–1816), W. DeWette, and C. Keil also spoke negatively of Haggai's style. In addition, Eichhorn believed that only summaries of Haggai's oracles are extant in the present book. Bertholdt disagreed, maintaining that the oracles are too well-rounded to be mere summaries. He proposed instead that there remains at least a historical kernel to the oracles, which were reworked when put in written form. It was de Wette, however, who made the strongest negative assessment, writing that Haggai—without enthusiasm—reprimanded, exhorted, and promised in accordance with vulgar conceptions of retaliation and chauvinism, and that he displayed an unprophetical zeal for the establishment of the ancient cult (see A. Khler [1860] 26).

During the Enlightenment scholars for the first time challenged the traditional view that Haggai came from Babylon. In contrast to Franz Delitzsch, who held to the traditional view, H. Ewald (1868) and Keil (1888) both maintained that Haggai was born in the land of Israel and thus was never one of the exiles.

4. *Critical Scholarship.* With the development of historical criticism there was a shift in the scholarly attitude toward Haggai. Köhler (1835–97), who wrote the first major commentary on Haggai (1860), rehabilitated the prophet, differentiating between the older prophets' poetical style and Haggai's rhetorical mode. He pointed out that very little can be known about the person of the prophet, although he believed that Haggai did not return from Babylon as a youth. In addition, he held a positive view of Haggai's work and argued against de Wette that the prophet's oracles must have had some spirit and power because they accomplished his goal: His hearers agreed with him.

Since Köhler's time, the major critical issues in Haggai studies have been literary and redactional in nature. Literary critical study has focused particularly on the problems of 2:10-19. Köhler was one of the first to note that vv. 15-19 do not seem logically to follow 2:10-14. Later E. Sellin (1900–1901) argued that 1:15a was the date formula for a lost oracle. J. Rothstein (1908) put the two ideas together, theorizing that 2:15-19 was the lost oracle. He has been followed with some adaptations by the majority of scholars (e.g., H. Mitchell [1912]; F. Horst [1938]; K. Elliger [1967]). It is only more recently that Rothstein's hypothesis has been questioned by K. Koch (1967). While Koch's proposal of a shared threefold structure between the oracles in 1:2-8; 2:3-7; and 2:10-19 is gaining ground (see B. Childs [1979], D. Petersen [1984]), many scholars still hold the older view (H. W. Wolff [1988]; R. Mason [1977b]; C. Stuhlmueller [1988]).

Redactional discussions have revolved around the narrated discourse in Haggai, with W. Beuken (1967; see also P. Ackroyd [1951, 1952a]) doing the definitive work. On the basis of style, vocabulary, and theological perspective, Beuken isolated a systematic chronistic redaction. However, Mason has challenged Beuken's view, positing instead a redaction closer to the time of the oracles themselves. O. Plöger (1968) and P. Hanson (1975) have dealt with this question differently, distinguishing between "theocratic" and "apocalyptic" groups at work in early postexilic times and maintaining that the theocratic group, which was concerned with reestablishing a priestly power base, edited Haggai. This view, which contrasts the theocratic group adversely with the apocalyptic group, returns to a more negative view of the book, albeit from a new perspective.

Another related issue in recent scholarship is the amount and character of the redaction the book received. Whereas Beuken and Wolff view the original text as a group of short oracles that were bound together by an editor, O. Steck (1971), A. van der Woude (1988), and H. G. Reventlow (1993) see the original text as a group of longer discourses from the hand of the prophet set within a narrative editorial framework. M. Floyd (1995) has taken the debate a step further, arguing that the narrative introductions to Haggai's speeches are not to be seen as the work of a redactor(s). Rather, he argues that the narrative framework is integral to the work as a whole, acting to blur the boundaries between the narrator's and the prophet's voices.

C. Meyers and E. Meyers (1987) argue that "Haggai and the first eight chapters of the canonical book of Zechariah belong together as a composite work" (xliv; see also Klostermann [1896]). D. Petersen (1984) offers a form-critical study using Lohfink's rubric historische Kurzgeschichte to classify the book as "brief apologetic historical narrative" (35). J. Tollington's study (1993) discusses the ways in which Haggai continues in and modifies the tradition of classical prophecy. Among her more provocative conclusions are that Haggai's use of Amos "suggests... that the practice of direct 'borrowing' or quoting was beginning to be developed" at the time of Haggai (215) and that previous works were beginning to be seen in much the same way that Scripture is viewed today (202). Finally, W. March's commentary in the NIB (1996) is a well-balanced and accessible scholarly and theological work, useful for those in academia and those in the parish alike. As these works reveal, the study of Haggai is branching out in different directions; there is a much more positive view of the prophet and his work than that held by pre-critical scholars.

Bibliography: P. R. Ackroyd, "Studies in the Book of Haggai," *JJS* 2 (1951) 163-76; "Studies in the Book of Haggai," *JJS* 3 (1952a) 1-13; "The Book of Haggai and Zechariah 1–8," *JJS* 3 (1952b) 151-56; "Some Interpretive Glosses in the Book of Haggai," *JJS* 7 (1956) 163-67; "Two OT Historical Problems of the Early Persian Period," *JNES* 17 (1958) 13-27; "Haggai," *PCB* (ed. M. Black, 1962) 643-45; *Exile and Restoration: A Study of Hebrew Thought of the Sixth Century BC* (OTL, 1968) 153-70. **R. Bach**, "Haggai, Haggaibuch," *RGG 3*, 24-26. **J. G. Baldwin**,

Haggai, Zechariah, Malachi (TOTC, 1972). **J. Begrich**, "Die Priesterliche Tora," *Werden und Wesen des Alten Testaments* (BZAW 66, 1936) 63-68. **L. Bertholdt**, *Historisch-kritische Einleitung in sammtliche kanonische und apokryphische Schriften des alten und neuen Testaments* (6 vols., 1812-19). **W. A. M. Beuken**, *Haggai–Sacharja 1–8* (SSNID, 1967). **K. M. Beyse,** *Serubbabel und die Königserwartungen der Propeten Haggai und Sacharja: Ein historische und traditionsgeschictliche Untersuchung* (AT 1, 48, 1972). **E.J. Bickerman**, "En Marge de L'Écriture," *RB* 88 (1981) 19-41. **J. Blenkinsopp**, *A History of Prophecy in Israel* (1983). **P.F. Bloomhardt**, "The Poems of Haggai," *HUCA* 5 (1928) 153-95. **M. J. Boda**, "Majoring in the Minors: Recent Research on Haggai and Zechariah," *Currents in Biblical Research* 2 (2003) 33-68; "Haggai: Master Rhetorician," *TynBul* 51 (2000) 295-304. **K. Budde**, "Zum Text der Drei Letzten Kleinen Propheten," *ZAW* 26 (1906) 1-28 (7-17). **T. Chary**, *Aggée— Zacharie—Malachie* (SB, 1969); "Le Culte Chez les Prophétes Aggée et Zacharie," *Les Prophétes et le Culte a Partir de l'exil* (BdT 3, 1955) 119-59. **B.S. Childs**, *Introduction to the OT as Scripture* (1979). **R. J. Coggins**, *Haggai, Zechariah, Malachi* (OTGu, 1987). **A. Deissler**, "Aggée," *DBS* 8, 701-6; *Zwölf Propheten III: Zefanjia, Haggai, Sacharja, Maleachi* (*Die Neue Echter Bibel* 21, 1988). **B. Duhm**, "Anmerkungen zu den zwölf Propheten," *ZAW* 31 (1911) 1-43, 81-110, 161-204. **J. G. Eichhorn**, *Die Hebraischen Prophten* (3 vols., 1816–19). **K. Elliger**, *Das Buch der zwölf kleinen Propheten, vol. 2, Die Propheten Nahum, Habakuk, Zephanja, Haggai, Sacharja, Maleachi* (ATD 25, 1967). **H. Ewald**, *Die Propheten des Alten Bundes* (1868). **M. H. Floyd**, "The Nature of the Narrative and the Evidence of Redaction in Haggai," *VT* 45 (1995) 470-90. **D. N. Freedman**, "The Chronicler's Purpose," *CBQ* 23 (1961) 436-42. **A. Gelston**, "The Foundations of the Second Temple," *VT* 16 (1966) 232-35. **P. D. Hanson**, *The Dawn of Apocalyptic* (1975) 140ff., 173-78, 240-62. **F. Hesse**, *Verbannung und Heimkehr* (FS W. Rudolph, 1961) 109-34. **D. R. Hildebrand**, "Temple Ritual: A Paradigm for Moral Holiness in Haggai II 10-19," *VT* 39 (1989) 154-68. **F. Horst**, *Die zwölf kleinen Propheten* (HAT 1, 4, 1938). **F. James**, "Thoughts on Haggai and Zechariah," *JBL* 53 (1934) 229-35. **D. R. Jones**, *Haggai, Zechariah, and Malachi: Introduction and Commentary* (TBC, 1962). **C. F. Keil**, *Biblischer Commentar über die zwölf kleinen Propheten* (BCAT 3, 4, 1888). **J. Kessler**, *The Book of Haggai: Prophecy and Society in Early Persian Yehud* (VTSup 91, 2002); "Building the Second Temple: Questions of Time, Text, and History in Haggai 1:1-15," JSOT 27 (2002) 243-56. **A. Klostermann**, *Geschichte des Volkes Israel bis zur Restauration unter Esra und Nehemiah* (1896). **K. Koch**, "Haggais unreines Volk," *ZAW* 79 (1967) 52-66. **A. Köhler**, "Die Weissagungen Haggai's," *Die nachexilischen Propheten* (1860). **W. E. March**, "Haggai," *NIB* (1996) 7:706-32. **R. A. Mason**, *The Books of Haggai, Zechariah, and Malachi* (CBC, 1977a); "The Purpose of the 'Editorial Framework' of the Book of Haggai," *VT* 27 (1977b) 413-21. **H. G. May**, " 'This People' and 'This Nation' in Haggai," *VT* 18 (1968) 190-97. **H. G. Mitchell**, *Haggai, Zechariah, Malachi, and Jonah* (ICC, 1912). **A. Moenikes**, "Messianismus im Alten Testament (vor-apokaliptische Zeit)," *ZRGG* 40 (1988) 289-306. **E. M. Meyers**, "The Use of Tora in Haggai 2:11 and the Role of the Prophet in the Restoration Community," *The Word of the Lord Shall Go Forth* (FS D. N. Freedman, 1983) 69-76. **F. S. North**, "Critical Analysis of the Book of Haggai," *ZAW* 68 (1956) 25-46. **D. L. Petersen**, "Zerubbabel and Jerusalem Temple Reconstruction," *CBQ* 36 (1974) 366-72; *Haggai and Zechariah 1–8* (OTL, 1984). **O. Plöger**, *Theocracy and Eschatology* (1968). **O. Procksch**, *Die kleinen prophetischen Schriften nach dem Exil* (EzAT 3, 1916). P. L. Redditt, *Haggai, Zechariah, Malachi* (NCBC, 1995). **H. G. Reventlow**, *Die Propheten Haggai, Sacharja, und Maleachi* (ATD, 1993). **W. H. Rose**, *Zemah and Zerubbabel: Messianic Expectations in the Early Postexilic Period* (JSOTSup 304, 2000). **J. W. Rothstein**, *Juden und Samaritaner: Die grundlegende Scheidung von Judentum und Heidentum. Eine kritische Studie zum Buche Haggai und zur jüdischen Geschichte im ersten nachexilischen Jahrhundert* (BWANT 3, 1908). **W. Rudolph**, *Haggai, Sacharja 1–8, Sacharja 9–14, Maleachi*

(KAT 13, 4, 1976). **G. Sauer**, "Serubbabel in der Sicht Haggais und Secharjas," *Das ferne und nahe Wort* (FS L. Rost, BZAW 105, 1967) 199-207. **K.-D. Schunk,** "Die Attribute des escha-tologischen Messias: Strukturlinien in der Ausprägung des alttestamentlichen Messiasbildes," *TLZ* 111 (1986) 642-51. **E. Sellin**, *Studien zur entstehungsgeschichte der jüdischen Gemeinde nach dem babylonischen Exil* (1900–1901). **K. Seybold**, "Die Königserwartung bei den Propheten Haggai und Sacharja," *Jud* 28 (1972) 69-78. **R. T. Siebeck**, "The Messianism of Aggaeus and Proto-Zacharias," *CBQ* 19 (1957) 312-28. **O. H. Steck**, "Zu Haggai 1:2-11," *ZAW* 83 (1971) 3:35-79. **C. Stuhlmueller**, "Haggai, Zechariah, Malachi," *JBC* (ed. J.A. Fitzmyer, R. E. Brown, and R. E. Murphy, 1968) 387-401; *Rebuilding with Hope: A Commentary on the Books of Haggai and Zechariah* (ITC, 1988). **S. Sykes**, "Time and Space in Haggai–Zechariah 1–8: A Bakhtinian Analysis of a Prophetic Chronicle," *JSOT* 76 (1997) 97-24; *Time and Space in Haggai–Zechariah 1–8: A Bakhtinian Analysis of a Prophetic Chronicle* (Studies in Biblical Literature 24, 2002). **J. E. Tollington**, *Tradition and Innovation in Haggai and Zechariah 1–8* (JSOTSup 150, 1993); "Readings in Haggai: From the Prophet to the Completed Book, a Changing Message in Changing Times," in *The Crisis of Israelite Religion: Transformation of Religious Tradition in Exilic and Post-Exilic Times* (ed. B. Becking and M. C. A. Korpel; OtSt 42, 1999) 194-208. **T. N. Townsend**, "Additional Comments on Haggai II, 10-19," *VT* 18 (1968) 559-60. **J. M. Trotter**, "Was the Second Jerusalem Temple a Primarily Persian Project?" *SJOT* 15 (2001) 276-94. **A. S. Van der Woude**, "Serubbabel und die Messianischen Erwartungen des Propheten Sacharja," *ZAW* 100 (Supp., 1988) 138-56. **A. Van Hoonacker**, *Les Douze Petits Prophètes* (ÉB, 1908). **J. Vlaardingerbroek**, Zephaniah (tr. J. Vriend, 1999). **J. Wellhausen**, *Die kleinen Propheten übersetzt und erklärt* (1898 = 1963). **J. W. Whedbee**, "A Question-Answer Schema in Haggai 1: The Form and Function of Haggai 1:9-11," *Biblical and Near Eastern Studies: Festschrift in Honor of W. S. LaSor* (ed. G. A. Tuttle, 1978) 184-94. **H. Witsius**, *Miscellanea Sacra 4* (1692). **H. W. Wolff**, *Haggai: A Commentary* (tr. M. Kohl, 1988).

M.E. SHIELDS

THE LATTER PROPHETS: MINOR

Zechariah

Jewish interpretations. There was greater continuity with HB messianic belief and expectation in Jewish interpretation than in Christian interpretation (K. Kuhn [1958]). Generally the Jewish messianic belief did not focus as much on the person of the messiah as on a broader eschatological hope for God's final renewal in the messianic era (Klausner, 1955). Therefore, no great distance existed in Jewish tradition between a messianic and a historical interpretation or even a haggadic exposition. Zech. 11:10, 12-13, and 13:7-9, for example, were interpreted in messianic terms in *Bereshit Rabba* on Gen 49:10 or in the *Tosephta* (*Ta 'an.* 3:1) and by leading commentators like Rashi, A. Ibn Ezra, or Abravanel. Others interpreted these and other texts —especially 11:12-13—as references to an historical situation or person. The Targum is in this respect ambiguous, but it has had a decisive influence, e.g., on Rashi (J. Bonsirven [1939] 72-74, 140-41, 174-76; G. Vermes, CHB 1:199-231).

Christian interpretations. References to Zechariah, including both quotations and allusions, in the preaching of the early church are more frequent than to any other book among the Minor Prophets, due to the book's alleged apocalyptic character (Dodd, 1952 [61-74]). There are some differences between the references to Zechariah 1–8 and 9–14 respectively. Only two quotations from Zechariah 1–8 occur in the NT (Jude v. 9 to Zech 3:2 and a longer one in Eph 4:25 to Zech 8:16). Among forty-one references to Zechariah 9–14, on the other hand, are twenty-five in the Gospels, ten in Revelation, four in Paul, and two in Hebrews.

Quotations in Matt 21:5 and John 12:15 of Zech 9:9 (Dodd, 48-49; Leske [2000]); in Matt 27:9 of Zech 11:13; in John 19:37 of Zech 12:10; and in Matt 26:31 and Mark 14:27 of Zech 13:7 have a clear christological interpretation. This generally eschatological (or apocalyptic) and especially christological focus became imperative for subsequent interpretations in the church (Dodd, 119, 124, 127-28; F. F. Bruce [1961]; L. Hartman [1966] 235-52; C. Evans [1999]; J. Menken [2002]).

Not only in the Christian interpretation of the church but also to a lesser degree in the Jewish interpretation of the synagogue, the messianic understanding of the book was a focal point: For the church, Jesus of Nazareth was the fulfillment of the OT's messianic expectations; for the synagogue, there still remained a living hope for fulfillment. These different foci have made the interpretation of Zechariah variegated and complex.

Christian interpreters mainly pursued the hermeneutical pattern of the NT, focusing first of all on Jesus' personal fulfillment of the messianic expectations. This perspective brought into focus specific passages in the HB, especially from the Prophets and Psalms. Included with passages of this kind were texts like Zech 2:10-15; 3:1-8; 6:12; 9:9; 11:4-17; 12:10-12; 13:7, which became important proof texts to demonstrate Jesus' legitimacy as the true Messiah and the fulfillment of the kingdom of God. To some extent these proof texts formed specific traditions of "testimonies" in the old church, as may be seen in the writings of church fathers like Justin (see esp. O. Skarsaune [1987]) or Cyprian (M. Fahey [1971] 254-55, 623-27). Theodore of Mopsuestia of the Antiochene School stressed the literal sense and historical aspects of a text and read into Zech 9:9 or 11:4-17, not Christ, but Zerubbabel, the governor of Judah (L. Diestel [1869] 133; G. Diettrich [1902] 74-101; B. Smalley [1984] 356-58, who parallels the Antiochenes of the 5th cent. with the Victorines of Paris around the 12th cent.). Luther's lectures on the Minor Prophets (1524-26) demonstrate a balanced focus on the literal and historical sense and on the christological interpretation of passages like Zech 3:8; 6:12-13; 9:9; 11:4-17; 13:7-9; 12:10.

In Christian (as well as in Jewish) interpretations of the book there was a permanent tension between a theological and an historical understanding of the text. A turning point to a more decisive historical understanding came in the seventeenth century when H. Grotius (*Annotata ad VT* 2 [1644]) revitalized the older historical approach (M. Saebø, *StTh* [1969] 119-221), but especially when J. Mede (c. 1630) maintained that Zechariah 9-11 could not have been written by the prophet Zechariah but originated with Jeremiah. The argument was premised, surprisingly enough, on the orthodox doctrine of the inspiration of the Bible: Matthew 27:9 ascribes to Jeremiah the quote that comes from Zech 11:12-13; thus the author of Zechariah 9-11 had to be Jeremiah since the Holy Spirit could not be in error. This was one solution to the many possible interpretations of Matt 27:9 that had been widely debated for centuries.

Historical-Critical interpretations. The effect of such discussions, however, was to open historical-critical observations that not only often ran contrary to the traditional doctrinal position but also led to different divisions and datings of the book. Such was the case among English scholars who succeeded Mede (H. Hammond [1653]; W. Whiston [1722]; R. Kidder [1699], who also extended Jeremiah's authorship to Zechariah 12–14; W. Newcome [1785], who dated 9–11 to the time of Hosea and 12–14 to after the death of Josiah but before the exile).

Among German scholars B. Flügge (1784) divided Zechariah 9–14 into nine parts of preexilic origin. L. Bertholdt (1814) argued successfully for a preexilic authorship and, like Newcome, dated Zechariah 9–11 to the time of the Syro-Ephraimitic War. Although he regarded chaps. 12–14, which are restricted to Judah and Jerusalem, as later preexilic fragments that had been added to earlier Zechariah texts, he also maintained that Zechariah 9–11 originated from Zechariah ben Jeberechiah (Isa 8:2), who had become confused with the later prophet Zechariah ben Berechiah (Zech 1:1). The majority of critical scholars followed him (e.g., A. Knoble [1837]; H. Ewald [1840]; F. Bleek [1852]; E. von Ortenberg [1859]; S. Davidson [1863]; B. Duhm [1875]); but some (like E. Rosenmüller [1816] and F. Hitzig [1930]) extended the preexilic dating to the whole of Zechariah 9–14, while still others supposed a late postexilic date. In this respect, J. G. Eichorn shifted from a preexilic to a postexilic view of the dating of Zechariah 9–14 from the first (1783) to the fourth (1823/24) edition of his *Einleitung in das AT*. In his first edition he suggested that Zech 9:1-8 referred to the time of Alexander the Great, based on his assumption that a prophet primarily addresses not future but contemporary events. He also implied that 13:1–14:21 might refer to Maccabean times.

Finally, some scholars consistently defended the traditional view of Zecharian authorship of 9–14 (e.g., M. Beckhaus [1796]; E. Hengstenberg [1831]; W. de Wette [1833]; J. Burger [1841]; and, most comprehensively, C. Wright [1879]). But as their defense mostly meant criticism of the preexilic position, they were later used by scholars who, maintaining a late postexilic dating, had to attack the preexilic view (see below).

Thus in modern critical study of the book of Zechariah up to 1880, three main theories were in contention, among which the preexilic view was most generally held. Many scholars were in favor of the traditional position ascribing the whole book to the early postexilic prophet Zechariah, and some argued for a late postexilic dating (for all references see B. Otzen [1964] 11–25; Saebø, [*StTh*, 1969] 118-23).

A second turning point came with B. Stade (1848–1906), who in 1881/82 published an article in which he argued successfully for a late postexilic dating of Zechariah 9–14. His position became the dominant one for generations, although among his successors there were many variations in dating other parts of the text. Yet the preexilic theory faded almost totally after 1920 (with the exception of M. Segal [1935] and Otzen), and the defenders of the traditional view held a much less favorable status than before (Otzen, 26-34; Saebø, 123-32).

Stade, who renewed the debate on the book of Zechariah, combined some of the concerns of the earlier rival positions: recognizing the necessity for finding the historical background of the text, he agreed that Zechariah 9–14 appeared to be dependent on earlier prophets. On the other hand, he sought to find a totality in which the details would most likely fit within the framework of the prophetical movement's development. He found behind Zechariah 9–14 one eschatological author, Deutero-Zechariah, who around 280 B.C.E. used older prophetical material to create "in free reproduction" an "eschatological compendium" in response to the spiritual needs of his own time.

Modern interpretations. After Stade, the dating of Deutero-Zechariah to the later postexilic period was well established, but scholars have differed to some degree regarding the book's unity as well as on the dating of a Deutero-Zechariah (generally including 9–11 and 13:7-9) and of a Trito-Zechariah (12:1–13:6; 14; cf. e.g., Duhm [1911]) or of even smaller fragments or collections. Often Zechariah 12–14, or parts of it, was placed in Maccabean times (Saebø, 125-32). Also the earlier assignment of Zech 9:1-8 to the time of Alexander the Great has been renewed (K. Elliger [1950] 63-115; M. Delcor [1951] 110-24). Although there seems to be a consensus on a postexilic dating, there is still great variety in the specific details. In recent research, however, the question of historical location is not seen as much in regard to political-historical conditions as in the living process of prophetical form history and tradition history (e.g., M. Haller [1914]; A. Jepsen [1939]; F. Horst [1954]; Saebø [1969]; H. Birkeland [1938] 90-93; R.D. Moseman [2000]; F.I. Andersen [2000]). Structural viewpoints. have also been brought to the table (P. Lamarche [1961]; Otzen, 213-29). The present situation of study on the book of Zechariah, especially 9–14, is complex.

In summary, there are some significant tendencies in the study of Zechariah: (a) In the traditional (messianic or christological) and in the modern historical-critical study on the book with its strong focus on dating texts, there has been much selective reading and research. Thus the material's complex totality has not come to the fore in a sufficient way.

(b) Theologically and historically Zechariah 1–8 has to a great extent been overshadowed by Zechariah 9–14; scholarly discussion has been primarily about the whether or not there exists a Deutero-Zechariah. Usually the two parts are discussed in more or less complete isolation; but recent research may indicate new possibilities for handling the delicate question of the relationship of the books' two parts in a new way, paying more attention to Tradition-historical aspects (R. Mason [1976]).

(c) In the case of Zechariah's unique "night visions" in 1:7–6:8 (see, e.g., H. May [1938]; C. Jeremias [1930]; L. Rignell [1950]) and of his different prophetic oracles (see A. Petitjean [1969]), recent tradition-historical and redactional work has shown a levitical interest by the author together with a style related to that of the chronicler (see W. Beuken [1967]).

(d) Regarding Zechariah 9–14, many questions are still open; but it seems that the strong literary-critical and historical interest in its dating has in some degree diminished and that a new tradition-historical interest in the specific forms and the theological (and partly apocalyptic) content of the chapters has increased (P. Hanson [1979]; H. Lutz [1968]; R. North [1972]; O. Plöger [1959]; Saebø; I. Willi-Plein [1974]; D. Krause [1997]; Bergler [1998]; Evans [1999]).

(e) Current study of the book of Zechariah pursues these issues, as well as the development of late prophecy and apocalyptic, not only with regard to the two main parts of the book respectively but also for the book as a whole (E.W. Conrad [1999]; W.H. Rose [2000]; C. Tuckett [2003]; J. Boda and M. Floyd [2003]). Newer scholarship includes literary critiques (M.C. Love [1999]; S. Sykes [2002]; A. Wolters [2000]).

Bibliography: F. I. Andersen, "Reading the Book of Zechariah: A Review Essay," *Ancient Near Eastern Studies* 37 (2000) 229-40. **A. Behrens**, *Prophetische Visionsschilderungen im Alten Testament: sprachliche Eigenarten, Funktion und Geschichte einer Gattung* (AOAT 292, 2002). **S. Bergler**, "Jesus, Bar Kochba und das messianische Laubhüttenfest," *JSJ* 29 (1998) 143-91. **W. A. M. Beuken**, *Haggai–Sacharja 1–8: Studien zur Überlieferungsgeschichte der* *frühnachexilischen Prophetie* (SSN 10, 1967). **H. Birkeland**, *Zum hebräischen raditionswesen* (1938). **S. H. Blank**, "The Death of Zechariah in Rabbinic Literature," *HUCA* 12, 13 (1937/38) 327-46. **M. J. Boda**, "Oil, Crowns and Thrones: Prophet, Priest and King in Zechariah 1:7-6:15," *Journal of Hebrew Scripture* 3 (2000–2001); "From Fasts to Feasts: the Literary Function of Zechariah 7–8," *CBQ* 65 (2003) 390-407. **M. J. Boda, M. H. Floyd, R. Mason** (eds.), *Bringing Out the Treasure: Inner Biblical Allusion in Zechariah 9–14* (JSOTSup 370, 2003); "Majoring in the Minors: Recent Research on Haggai and Zechariah," *Currents in Biblical Research* 2 (2003) 33-68. **J. Bonsirven**, *Exégèse rabbinique et exégèse paulinienne* (1939). **F. F. Bruce**, "The Book of Zechariah and the Passion Narrative," *BJRL* 43 (1961) 336-53. **M. Cimosa**, "Observations on the Greek Translation of the Book of Zechariah," in *IX Congress of the International Organization for Septuagint and Cognate Studies* (ed. B.A. Taylor, 1997) 91-108. **E.W. Conrad**, *Zechariah* (Readings: A New Bible Commentary, 1999). **M. Delcor**, "Les allusions à Alexandre le Grand dans Zach 9:1-8," *VT* 1 (1951) 110-24. **H. Delkurt**, "Sacharja und der Kult," in V*erbindungslinien: Festschrift für Werner H. Schmidt zum 65. Geburtstag* (ed. A. Graupner, H. Delkurt and A. B. Ernst , 2000). **W. M. L. De Wette**, *Lehrbuch der historisch-kritischen Einleitung in die Bibel Alten und Neuen Testaments* (1833). **G. Diettrich**, *Išoʿdadh's Stellung in der Auslegungsgeschichte des Alten Testaments an seinen Kommentaren zu . . . Sach 9–14 . . . veranschaulicht* (BZAW 6, 1902). **L. Diestel**, *Geschichte des Alten Testaments in der christlichen Kirche* (1869). **L. Doutreleau** (ed.), *Didyme l' Aveugle, sur Zacharie 1–3* (SC 83-85, 1962). **C. H. Dodd**, *According to the Scriptures: The Sub-structure of NT Theology* (1952). **B. Duhm**, *The Ever-coming Kingdom of God: A Discussion on Religious Progress* (1911). **K. Elliger,** "Ein Zeugnis aus der jüdischen Gemeinde im Alexanderjahr 332 v Chr: eine territoralgeschichtliche Studie," ZAW 62 (1950) 63-115. **C. A. Evans**, "Jesus and Zechariah's Messianic Hope," in Authenticating the Activities of Jesus (ed. B. Chilton and C. A. Evans; New Testament Tools and Studies 28, 1999) 373-88; " 'The Two Sons of Oil': Early Evidence of Messianic Interpretation of Zechariah 4:14 in 4Q254 4 2," *Provo International Conference on the Dead Sea Scrolls* (ed. D.W. Parry and E. Ulrich, 1999) 566-75. **M. A. Fahey**, *Cyprian and the Bible: A Study in Third-century Exegesis* (BGBH 9, 1971). **M. H. Floyd**, "Zechariah and Changing Views of Second Temple Judaism in Recent Commentaries," *RelStRev* 25 (1999) 257-63. **L. Hartman**, *Prophecy Interpreted: The Formation of Some Jewish Apocalyptic Texts and of the Eschatological Discourse Mark 13 Par.* (ConBNT 1, 1966). **K. Galling**, *Studien zur Geschichte Israels im persischen Zeitalter* (1964) 109-48. **P. D. Hanson**, *The Dawn of Apocalyptic* (1979). **Y. Hoffman**, "The Fasts in the Book of Zechariah and the Fashioning of National Remembrance," in *Judah and the Judeans in the Neo-Babylonian Perod* (ed. O. Lipschitz and J. Blenkinsopp, 2003) 169-218. **D. Instone-Brewer**, "The Two Asses of Zechariah 9:9 in Matthew 21," *TynBul* 54 (2003) 87-98. **C. Jeremias**, *Die Nachtgesichte des Sacaria: Unters zu ihrer Stellung im Zusammenhang der Visionsberichte im Alten Testament und zu ihrem Bildmaterial* (FRLANT 117, 1977). **J. Klausner**, *The Messianic Idea in Israel* (1955). **D. Krause**, "The One Who Comes Unbinding the Blessing of Judah: Mark 11:1-10 as a Midrash on Genesis 49:11, Zechariah 9:9, and Psalm 118:25-26," in *Early Christian Interpretation of the Scriptures of Israel* (ed. C. A. Evans and J. A. Sanders; JSNTSup 148, 1997) 141-53. **G. Krause**, *Studien zu Luthers Auslegung der Kleinen Propheten* (BHT 33, 1962). **J. Kremer**, *Die Hirtenallegorie im Buche Zacharias auf ihre Messianität hin untersucht: Zugleich ein Beitrag zur Geschichte der Exegese* (ATA 11, 2, 1930). **K. G. Kuhn**, "Die beiden Messias in den Qumrantexten und die Messiasvorstellung in der rabbinischen Literatur," *ZAW* 70 (1958) 200-208. **P. Lamarche**, *Zacharie IX-XIV: Structure litteraire et messianisme* (1961). **A. M. Leske**, "Context and Meaning of Zechariah 9:9," *CBQ* 62 (2000) 663-78. **M. C. Love**, *The Evasive Text: Zechariah 1–8 and the Frustrated Reader* (JSOTSup 296, 1999). **H. M. Lutz**, *Jahwe, Jerusalem, und die Völker: Zur Vorgeschichte von Sach 12,1-8 und 14,1-5* (WMANT

27, 1968). **R. A. Mason**, "The Relation of Zechariah 9–14 to Proto-Zechariah," *ZAW* 88 (1976) 227-39. **H. G. May**, "A Key to the Interpretation of Zachariah's Visions," *JBL* 57 (1938) 173-84. **A. M'Caul**, *Rabbi D. Kimchi's Commentary on the Prophecies of Zechariah* (1837). **M. J. J. Menken**, "The Old Testament Quotation in Matthew 27:9-10: Textual Form and Content," *Bib* 83 (2002) 305-28. **C. L. and E. M. Meyers**, *Haggai, Zechariah 1–8*, (AB 25B, 1, 1987). **R. D. Moseman**, "Reading the Two Zechariahs as One," *RevExp* 97 (2000) 487-98. **R. North**, "Prophecy to Apocalyptic via Zechariah," *VTSup* 22 (1972) 47-71. **B. C. Ollenburger**, "The Book of Zechariah," *NIB* (1996) 7:733-840. **B. Otzen**, *Studien über Deuterosacharja* (1964). **H. G. L. Peels**, "The Blood 'from Abel to Zechariah' (Matthew 23, 35; Luke 11.50f) and the Canon of the Old Testament," *ZAW* 113 (2001) 583-601. **D. L. Petersen**, *Zechariah 9–14 and Malachi: A Commentary* (OTL, 1995). **A. Petitjean**, *Les oracles du Proto-Zacharie: Un programme de restauration pour la communaut, juive après l'exil* (1969). **J. R. Phillips**, "Zechariah's Vision and Joseph in Egypt: An Ancient Dialogue About Jewish Identity," *Conservative Judaism* 53 (2000) 51-61. **O. Plöger**, *Theokratie und Eschatologie* (WMANT 2, 1959; ET 1968). **H. G. Reventlow**, *Die Propheten Haggai, Sacharja, und Maleachi* (ATD 25, 2, 1993). **L. G. Rignell**, *Die Nachtgesichte des Sacharja: Eine exegetische Studie* (1950). **G. L. Robinson**, "The Prophecies of Zechariah with Special Reference to the Origin and Date of Chapters 9–14," *AJSL* 12 (1895–96) 1-92. **W. H. Rose**, *Zemah and Zerubbabel: Messianic Expectations in the Early Postexilic Period* (JSOTSup 304, 2000). **J. W. Rothstein**, *Die Nachtgesichte des Sacharja* (BWANT 8, 1910). **D. Rudman**, "Zechariah and the Priestly Law, " *SJOT* 14 (2000) 194-206. **M. Saebø**, "Die deuterosacharjanische Frage: Eine forschungsgeschichtliche Studie," *StTh 23* (1969) 115-40; *Sacharja 9–14: Untersuchungen von Text und Form* (WMANT 34, 1969). **O. Skarsaune**, *The Proof from Prophecy: A Study in Justin Martyr's Proof-Text Tradition* (NovTSup 56, 1987). **B. Smalley**, *The Study of the Bible in the Middle Ages* (1984). **B. Stade**, "Deuterozacharja: Eine kritische Studie," *ZAW* 1 (1881) 1-96; 2 (1882) 151-72, 275-309. **S. Sykes**, *Time and Space in Haggai-Zechariah 1–8 : a Bakhtinian Analysis of a Prophetic Chronicle* (2002). **J. M. Trotter**, "Was the Second Temple a Primarily Persian Project?" *SJOT* 15 (2001) 276-94. **S. S. Tuell**, *Haggai-Zechariah: Prophecy After the Manner of Ezekiel* (SBLSP 39, 2000) 263-86. **C. Tuckett** (ed.), *The Book of Zechariah and Its Influence* (2003). **S. J. De Vries**, *From Old Revelation to New: A Tradition-historical and Redaction-critical Study of Temporal Transitions in Prophetic Prediction* (1995). **I. Willi-Plein**, *Prophetie am Ende: Untersuchungen zu Sacharja 9–14* (BBB 42, 1974). **A. Wolters**, "Word Play in Zechariah," in *Puns and Pundits: Word Play in the Hebrew Bible and Ancient Near Eastern Literature* (ed. S.B. Noegel, 2000) 223-30; *Confessional Criticism and the Night Visions of Zechariah* (2000). **C. H. H. Wright**, *Zechariah and His Prophecies Considered in Relation to Modern Criticism* (1879).

M. SAEBØ

Malachi

The short book of Malachi, which closes the prophetic canon, has received more attention in the last two decades of the twentieth century than in any other period of its existence. While rising interest in the Persian period and its prophecy has generated an increase in commentary on Malachi, for centuries only selected features of the book received significant attention.

1. *Earliest Evidence.* The earliest evidence for the book is its inclusion in the Septuagint and a fragmentary Minor Prophets scroll from Qumran dated c. 150 B.C.E. (4QXIIa). Short references appear in several early texts: Sirach 49:10 mentions (but does not identify) twelve prophets; the Cairo Damascus document 6:11-14 cites Mal 1:10; Mal 1:13-14 appears in 5QpMal (= 5Q10); 4QarP alludes to Mal 3:23; and 2 Esdras 3:16 draws upon Mal 1:2-3.

In terms of canonical placement, which may have influenced later assessments of dating, Malachi appears consistently at the end of the Book of the Twelve in early Jewish and Christian lists, including the Muraba 'at and Nahal Hever scrolls as well as later Spanish manuscripts. The Talmud differs in its ordering of the Major Prophets; but it concludes the Prophets with Malachi, as do all early Christian lists. Even Junilius, who arranges the prophetic books chronologically, places Malachi last. The fragment 4QXIIa may prove to be an exception, however, since preliminary studies suggest that in it Jonah may follow Malachi.

2. *Early Judaism.* Intrigued that Malachi is not a proper name but a title meaning "my messenger," early Jewish commentators on the book sought to identify its author. A gloss in the *Targum Jonathan* identifies this messenger with Ezra; according to *b. Megillah* 15a, Joshua b. Karha also equated Malachi with Ezra, while R. Nahman believed the messenger to be Mordecai. Further speculation is given in *The Lives of the Prophets,* which, though dated to the fourth century C.E., may be an earlier composition. Here, Malachi is said to have been born in Sopha after the exile. The Septuagint translates *malachi* as "his messenger," while leaving the word untranslated in the book's title. Although Malachi bears no chronological markers and refers to no datable event, ancient writers consistently assumed its postexilic origin. 2 *Esdras* 14:44-47 attributes the writing of the twenty-four books of the canon to Ezra, implying Malachi's completion by this time, as does *b. Baba Bathra* 14b, which credits the men of the Great Assembly with writing the Book of the Twelve. Similarly, Josephus (*Contra Apion* 1.37-43) indicates that prophecy ended in the time of King Artaxerxes; and Tosephta *Soṭah* explains that "when Haggai, Zechariah and Malachi died, the Holy Spirit left Israel." *B. Rosh Hashanah* 19b names Malachi as one of the three prophets on which the almanac is fixed.

Malachi 3:23-24 (Eng. 4:4-5), which tells of a coming messenger, engendered some messianic interest during this period. *M. Baba Mezia* 1:8, 2:8, 3:4-5; and *m. Sheqalim* 2:5 describe Elijah as a forerunner of the Messiah, perhaps drawing from Malachi. The Dead Sea Scrolls fragment 4QarP explicitly cites the book in discussing the Messiah.

3. *Early Christianity.* The NT quotes Malachi to defend messianic claims for Jesus and the character of emergent Christianity, setting precedents for centuries of Christian interpretation. Combining Mal 3:23-24 with Isa 40:3, the Gospels identify John the Baptist with Elijah in his role as messianic precursor. Mark 1:2 and 9:11 echo the tradition of Elijah coming first; Luke 1:17 also attributes to John the purification role described in Mal 3:24. Outside of the Gospels, Paul (Rom 9:13) finds proof of God's election of Gentiles in Mal 1:2's contrast of the cases of Jacob and Esau.

The church fathers followed the NT in quoting the book to defend Christian rejection of Jewish practices. Justin (*Dialogue* 117.28.41) quoted 1:11 as proof that Gentiles are also people of God; the *Didache* 14:3 went further, finding in this passage justification for the Eucharist.

Christian writers of the period seldom speculated on the prophet's identity, although Pseudo-Epiphanius (*De vitis proph.*) suggested that "Malachi is of the tribe of Zebulun, born after the captivity."

4. *The Medieval Period*. The interpretation of Malachi in the medieval period closely followed contemporary exegetical and doctrinal controversies. While generating little interest in its own right, the book was used to defend divergent positions on messianism and proper biblical interpretation.

a. *Jewish*. Medieval Jewish interpretation drew on all of Scripture, including Malachi, to counter christological readings of the Tanakh and Christian claims that the coming of Christ had abrogated Mosaic law. With this concern, D. Kimhi quoted Mal 3:22 to argue the eternal validity of Torah and to establish that the Messiah had not come. Maimonides employed the book to defend the logic of sacrificial requirements and, with A. Ibn Ezra, to argue the inadequacy of Christian interpretations.

Kimhi and Maimonides also found in Malachi support for their philosophical interpretation of Scripture. Kimhi (MS Bodl. Huntington Don. 24) identified the "fearers" of 3:16 as those who contemplate in the intellect; for Maimonides (*Guide of the Perplexed* 3.19), Mal 3:6 proved the changelessness of the deity, and 3:13-16 defended God's omni-science and omnipotence.

b. *Christian*. Judaism's scriptural interpretation responded to the fervor of medieval Christian interpretation. Stressing the predictive nature of OT prophecy and armed with inferences drawn from the four senses of Scripture, Christian scholars of the medieval period read Malachi as thoroughly christological (O'Keefe, 1996). Following the Gospels, Theodore of Mopsuestia explained Mal 3:1 as referring to John the Baptist and 4:4-6 as predicting Elijah's return before Christ's second coming.

In addition to christological readings, medieval writers offered some historical analysis. Although cognizant of traditional Jewish identifications of Malachi with Ezra, Jerome (*Prologue to the Vulgate*) placed the prophet in the time of Haggai and Zechariah, voicing a historical principle that greatly influenced subsequent assessments of the book's dating: A book that is not explicitly dated is to be dated according to the book that immediately precedes it in the canon. Cyril of Alexandria also advanced this principle of dating, which may be reflected in Theodore's description of Malachi as postexilic.

5. *Renaissance/Reformation*. Numerous forces shaped biblical study during this period. The rise of humanism and the value it granted to antiquity fostered the study of ancient languages to the extent that in 1311 the Council of Vienna called for the establishment of chairs of Greek and Hebrew. Christian scholars engaged Hebraic tutors and gained facility in Talmud and Jewish commentary, forging some ties between Jewish and Christian commentary. The continuation of anti-Jewish sentiment in Christian Europe and the zeal of the Protestant Reformers to undercut ecclesiastical authority, however, reinforced scriptural defenses of various doctrinal positions.

a. *Christian*. Luther and Calvin demonstrated this blending of the humanistic and the doctrinal. On the one hand, they extolled the value of historical study of Scripture. Denying the canonical approach to dating books employed by Jerome, Luther argued for the necessity of searching out the historical sense of Scripture. Calvin agreed with this assessment; but, like Luther and in keeping with confessional aims, he retained Scripture's christological import by arguing that a passage can have different meanings for the past, the present, and the future. Calvin claimed, e.g., that Malachi's "sons of Levi" refers to the time of Ezra and Nehemiah as well as to the coming of Christ and to the corrupt leadership of his own time. In the case of the book's future promises, however, the meaning can only apply to the coming of Christ (*Commentary on Malachi* 3:1).

312

As in earlier times, the book of Malachi provided the period's interpreters a repository of passages for defending their own understandings. The humanist Erasmus argued that the differing fates of Jacob and Esau in 1:2 refer, not to eternal salvation, but to temporal misfortunes, given the primacy of free will. In the late sixteenth century, as anti-Jewish sentiments grew, the Protestant interpreter Urbanus Rhegius sought to refute Ibn Ezra and D. Kimhi, maintaining that all prophets—including Malachi—foretold the coming of Christ.

b. *Jewish.* Much Jewish exegesis of the sixteenth and seventeenth centuries continued to challenge Christian dogmatic claims. This task grew more onerous as Christians increasingly used and denigrated Jewish tradition in their arguments. Guided by such concerns, Abravanel forcefully argued that the Messiah had not come. He also offered historical commentary, claiming that all prophets except Obadiah are in chronological order and, thus, that Malachi is the latest of the postexilic prophets.

6. *Enlightenment.* Placing ultimate value on reason and natural religion and eschewing special revelation and particularism, the age of the Enlightenment found little value in a book that demands pure ritual and ends with an admonition to preserve Mosaic law. Such Jewish writers of the Emancipation as M. Mendelssohn quoted little from Scripture, instead arguing the universality of Judaism. The first major commentary on Malachi written by a Christian, but without an excessive christological emphasis, was produced by E. Pococke in 1677. Messianic readings of the book persisted in confessional settings, however. C. Jennens's selection of scriptural passages for Handel's Messiah drew on long-standing messianic interpretation; by placement, the recitative-aria-chorus sequence on Mal 3:1-3 equates the coming messenger of the covenant with Jesus.

7. *Early Modern.* The rise of historical criticism in the nineteenth and early twentieth centuries directed interest in Malachi away from creedal formulations to a concern with the historical information it provided.

a. *Dating.* While a postexilic composition had long been assumed, turn-of-the-century interpreters offered concrete arguments for Malachi's dating. Few followed the lead of A. von Bulmerincq, who identified each oracle unit in the book by season through the years 485-445 B.C.E. (*Einleitung* [1921-26] i, 140); most interpreters were content with a more general postexilic date based on the understanding that the book describes the religious and social failures between the tenures of Haggai–Zechariah and Ezra–Nehemiah. Specific arguments used to defend this assessment included the book's reference to Edom as fallen, its supposed criticism of the mixed marriages later outlawed by Ezra and Nehemiah, and its literary style.

Beginning in the mid-nineteenth century the destruction of Edom mentioned in 1:2 was identified with a Nabatean invasion—an identification used to undergird postexilic dating. This interpretation, advanced by Grätz (1875) and adopted by J. Wellhausen (1878), was echoed in numerous twentieth-century commentaries.

Much nineteenth- and twentieth-century scholarship found further evidence for this dating by connecting Mal 2:11-14 with Ezra–Nehemiah's annulment of marriages between Judean men and their foreign wives. In this understanding, Judah's "marrying the daughter of a foreign god" in 2:11 refers to intermarriage, and 2:14 applies covenantal terminology to the marriage relationship. During the century, however, a small number of scholars challenged this view; according to C. C. Torrey (1898) and F. Hvidberg (1962), the passage concerns worship of a female deity in the Temple; J. Matthews (1931) further associated the "tears and weeping" of 2:13-16 with ritual mourning for Tammuz.

Only a few scholars in the early modern period denied postexilic dating completely. H. Spoer (1908) and O. Holtzmann (1931) placed Malachi in the Maccabean era; Holtzmann greatly advanced the date and identified the "fearers" of 3:16 with the Hasideans of 1 Maccabees 2.

b. *Literary.* The development of form criticism in the early twentieth century encouraged study of the book's literary style. Most interpreters followed H. Gunkel and later A. Graffy (1984) in labeling the genre of Malachi as "disputation speech." The essential unity of the book was generally assumed, although the authenticity of 1:11 and 4:4-6 was occasionally questioned.

c. *Value*. Negative evaluations of Malachi dominated most of the nineteenth and twentieth centuries. Even more so than the other postexilic prophets, Malachi was deemed morally and literarily inferior to giants such as Isaiah and Jeremiah. Wellhausen, for example, argued that Malachi derives from the inferior postexilic age, during which the average person grew estranged from ritual and "Israelite" religion atrophied into "Judaism." Fed both by German scholarship's interest in source criticism and contemporary anti-Judaism, Wellhausen's analyses further traced in the book evidence of development within the Israelite priesthood. Because Malachi follows Deuteronomy in calling priests "sons of Levi" while reflecting some priestly ritual, Wellhausen claimed that it reveals a transitional stage between deuteronomic and priestly legislation.

In the late nineteenth and early twentieth centuries, bolstered by rising confidence in the ideas of evolution and progressive revelation, such liberal Protestants as H. Fosdick and such evangelicals as W. R. Smith adapted Wellhausen's developmental views to confessional applications. They viewed the rituals in Malachi, not so much as a retreat from earlier authentic religion, but as a temporary stage in God's continuing revelation.

8. *Late Twentieth Century*. The developments of late twentieth-century scholarship have affected Malachi studies in several ways. First, as more has been learned of the Persian experience in the province of Yehud (Judea) after the exile and as more attention turns to the sociological dimensions of the postexilic community (Rogerson, 1999), Malachi has been embraced as precious evidence about the period. P. Hanson (1979), for example, draws heavily from the book to explain the sociological tensions in the postexilic community between theocratic and hierocratic elements; and studies of the social function of the Second Temple have drawn upon Malachi's description of the priesthood and sacrificial cult.

Concomitant with this surge in information has been growing awareness of how essential the exile and its aftermath were for the formation of biblical writings (J.M. O'Brien, 1995). Recognizing Malachi's ties to the Haggai–Zechariah corpus (including the recurrence of *maśśā'* in Zech 9:1; 12:1; and Mal 1:1), such commentators J. Blenkinsopp (1983) have utilized the book in discussions on canonization. Studies concerning later redactions of the Book of the Twelve (B. G. Curtis, 1998) and how the Book of the Twelve was fashioned into a single volume have directed much attention to Malachi's role as the conclusion to the collection (Berry, 1996; Watts, 2000).

Earlier debates about the "daughter of a foreign god" have resurfaced in current discussions. J. O'Brien (1990, 1995, 1996), for example, maintains that the marriage described in Malachi is a modification of the marriage metaphor used elsewhere in the Prophets, though G. Hugenberger (1994) devotes a monograph to arguing that the HB in general and Malachi in particular consistently portray human marriage as a covenant.

As in earlier generations, the scholarly interests of the late twentieth century have helped to shape current understandings of the book of Malachi. Carried along by the currents of modern scholarly interest in canon formation, the literary and sociological activity of the Second Temple period, and the rise of messianism, Malachi has moved significantly inward from the periphery of prophetic investigation.

Bibliography: D. K. Berry, "Malachi's Dual Design: The Close of the Canon and What Comes Afterward," in *Forming Prophetic Literature: Essays on Isaiah and the Twelve in Honor of John D. W. Watts* (ed. P. R. House, 1996) 269-302. **J. Blenkinsopp**, *A History of Prophecy in Israel* (1983). **A. von Bulmerincq**, *Einleitung in das Buch des Propheten Maleachi* (Acta et Commentationes Universitatis Dorpantensis b. Humaniora, i, pt. 2; iii, pt. 1; vii, pt. 1; 1921-26);

Kommentar (ibid., xv, pt. 1; xix, pt. 1; xxiii, pt. 2; xxvi, pt. 1; xxvii, pt. 2, 1929-32). **R. J. Coggins**, *Haggai, Zechariah, Malachi* (OTGu, 1987). **B. G. Curtis**, "The Daughter of Zion Oracles and the Appendices to Malachi: Evidence on the Latter Redactors and Redaction of the Book of the Twelve," SBLSP 37/2 (1998) 872-92. **R. E. Fuller**, "The Minor Prophets Manuscripts from Qumran, Cave IV" (diss., Harvard University, 1988). **B. Glazier-McDonald**, *Malachi, the Divine Messenger* (SBLDS 98, 1987). **A. Graffy**, *A Prophet Confronts His People: The Disputation Speech in the Prophets* (AnBib 104, 1984). **H. Grätz**, "Die Anfänge der Nabataërherrschaft," *Monatsschrift für Wissenschaft und Geschichte des Judentums* 24 (1875) 49-67. **P. Hanson**, *The Dawn of Apocalyptic* (1979). **E. A. Heath**, "Divorce and Violence: Synonymous Parallelism in Malachi 2:16," *Ashland Theological Journal* 28 (1996) 1-8. **A.E. Hill**, *Malachi* (AB 25D, 1998). **O. Holtzmann**, "Der Prophet Maleachi und der Ursprung des Pharisäerbundes," *ARW* 29 (1931) 1-21. **P. R. House**, *The Unity of the Twelve* (JSOTSup 97, 1991). **G. P. Hugenberger**, *Marriage as Covenant: A Study of Biblical Law and Ethics Governing Marriage, Developed from the Perspective of Malachi* (1994). **F. F. Hvidberg**, *Weeping and Laughter in the OT* (1962). **C. F. Mariottini**, "Malachi: A Prophet for His Time," *JBQ* 26 (1998) 149-57. **J. G. Matthews**, "Tammuz Worship in the Book of Malachi," *Palestine Oriental Society Journal* 11 (1931) 42-50. **A. Meinhold**, *Maleachi* (BKAT 14/8, 2000). **J. Nogalski**, *Redactional Processes in the Book of the Twelve* (BZAW 218, 1993). **J. M. O'Brien**, *Priest and Levite in Malachi* (SBLDS 121, 1990); "Malachi in Recent Research," *CurBS* 3 (1995) 81-94; "On Saying 'No' To a Prophet," *Semeia* 72 (1995) 111-24; "Historical Inquiry as Liberator and Master: Malachi as a Post-Exilic Document," in *Yahweh/Baal Confrontation and Other Studies in Biblical Literature and Archaeology* (ed. J. M. O'Brien and F. L. Horton; Studies in the Bible and Early Christianity 35, 1995) 57-79; "Judah as Wife and Husband: Deconstructing Gender in Malachi," *JBL* 115 (1996) 241-50. **J. J. O'Keefe**, "Christianizing Malachi: Fifth-Century Insights from Cyril of Alexandria," *VC* 50 (1996) 136-58. **D. L. Petersen**, *Zechariah 9–14 and Malachi* (OTL, 1995). **E. Pfeiffer**, "Die Disputationsworte im Buche Maleachi," *EvTh* 19 (1959) 546-68. **J. N. Pohlig**, *An Exegetical Summary of Malachi* (1998). **P. L. Redditt**, *Haggai, Zechariah, and Malachi* (New Century Bible, 1995); "The God Who Loves and Hates," in *Shall Not the Judge of All the Earth Do What Is Right?: Studies on the Nature of God in Tribute to James L. Crenshaw* (ed. D. Penchansky and P. L. Redditt, 2000). **J. W. Rogerson**, "The Social Background of the Book of Malachi," in *New Heaven and New Earth: Prophecy and the Millenium* (ed. P. J. Harland and C. T. R. Heyward; VTSup 77, 1999) 171-79. **A. Schart**, "Putting the Eschatological Visions of Zechariah in Their Place: Malachi as a Hermeneutical Guide for the Last Section of the Book of the Twelve," in *Bringing Out the Treasure* (ed. M. J. Boda, JSOTSup 370, 2003) 333-43. **M. A. Shields**, "Syncretism and Divorce in Malachi 2,10-16," *ZAW* 111 (1999) 68-86. **D. A. Schneider**, "The Unity of the Book of the Twelve" (diss., Yale University, 1979). **E. M. Schuller**, "The Book of Malachi," *NIB* (1996) 7:841-77. **H. Spoer**, "Some New Considerations Toward Dating the Book of Malachi," *JQR* 20 (1908) 167-86. **D. C. Steinmetz** (ed.), *The Bible in the Sixteenth Century* (1990). **C. C. Torrey**, "The Prophecy of 'Malachi,'" *JBL* 17 (1898) 1-15. **O. D. Vena**, "Paul's Understanding of the Eschatological Prophet of Malachi 4:5-6," *BR* 44 (1999) 35-54. **J. D. W. Watts**, "A Frame for the Book of the Twelve: Hosea 1–3 and Malachi," in *Reading and Hearing the Book of the Twelve* (ed. J. D. Nogalski and M. Sweeney; SBLSymS 15, 2000) 209-17. **J. Wellhausen**, *Prolegomena to the History of Israel* (1878; ET 1885). **K. W. Weyde**, *Prophecy and Teaching: Prophetic Authority, Form Problems, and the Use of Traditions in the Book of Malachi* (BZAW 288, 2000). **M. Zehnder**, "A Fresh Look at Malachi ii 13-16," *VT* 53 (2003) 224-59.

J. M. O'BRIEN

GENERAL ARTICLE

Decalogue

Although not the oldest known legal code, Yahweh's covenantal requirements of the Israelites, the Decalogue (from the Greek *deka logoi*, "ten words"), found in Exod 34:28 and Deut 10:4), has become the best known in human culture. Applications to the most varied circumstances appear in the HB prophets (see M. Weiss, "The Decalogue in Prophetic Literature," in B. Segal [1990] 67-81), in the sayings of Jesus, in the writings of Paul, and in other early Christian and rabbinic sources (see W. Rordorf [1984]; G. Stemberger [1989]; F. Vokes [1968]; and D. Flusser, "The Ten Commandments and the NT," in Segal, 219-46).

The Decalogue's tenfold pattern has become a cultural archetype. It has been vigorously expounded by Jewish, Catholic, and Protestant thinkers throughout the centuries; and there have been endless imitations, offered as substitutes or parallels, and numerous critiques.

Although the stones on which the Ten Commandments were said to have been written, perhaps on both sides, before being deposited in the ark of the covenant have disappeared along with the ark, manuscript copies like the Nash Papyrus at Cambridge are among the oldest surviving biblical fragments. Some pious Jews believed the Decalogue to be the earliest model of alphabetic writing (the "ten words" teaching writing as well as righteousness).

Variations exist between the wording of the commandments in Exod 20:2-17 (172 words) and Deut 5:6-21 (189 words) and between the MT and ancient versions (Samaritan and Greek). Even the order of some of the commandments vary: Where the MT has murder, adultery, and theft, some traditions have adultery, theft, murder (Greek Exodus; see Luke 18:20; Rom 13:9) or adultery, murder, theft (Nash Papyrus, Greek Deuteronomy, and Philo (see M. Greenberg).

Three main systems of numbering the commandments exist. (Even the MT has been pointed for two different cantillations and thus two different divisions of the commandments; see M. Breuer, "Dividing the Decalogue into Verses and Commandments," in Segal, 291-330.) In one system, now used by most Protestants and found in Philo (*On the Decalogue* 50-51) and Josephus (*A. J.* 3.91-92), the order is (1) no other gods, (2) prohibition of images, (3) taking God's name in vain, (4) sabbath, (5) honoring parents, (6) killing, (7) adultery, (8) theft, (9) false witness, and (10) covetousness. The second system, used by Roman Catholics and Lutherans and already found in Augustine, combines (1) and (2) above and divides (10) into two commandments. The third, the traditional Jewish system, considers Exod 20:2 (Deut 5:6) as the first commandment ("I am YHWH . . . out of the house of bondage") and Exod 20:3-6 (Deut 5:7-10) as the second commandment. Early rabbinical sources, however, suggest that there was no absolute system of dividing the commandments in antiquity.

The division of the commandments into two tablets, with 1 to 5 on the first and 6 to 10 on the second (see first and third enumerations above), was already present in early tradition. The first five, all of which contain a reference to God, were considered to be concerned with proper worship of God; and the second five, none of which refers to God, with proper social and interpersonal relations (see G. Sarfatti).

Roman Catholic tradition has generally divided the commandments into 1-3 and 4-10. This already appears in Augustine (*PL* 3.620, 644), who associated the first three commandments with loving God and the final seven with love of neighbor. He was followed by Rabanus (PL 108.95-97, 863-64), Peter Lombard (*Sentences* 3.33.1-2; PL 192.830-31), and many others.

In Judaism there is also a tradition that the five laws on one tablet parallel those on the other:

How were the Ten Commandments arranged? Five on one tablet and five on the other. On the one tablet was written: "I am the Lord thy God." And opposite it on the other tablet was written: "Thou

shalt not murder." On the one tablet was written: "Thou shalt have no other god." And opposite it
on the other tablet was written: "Thou shalt not commit adultery." On the one tablet was written:
"Thou shalt not take." And opposite it on the other tablet was written: "Thou shalt not steal." On the
one tablet was written: "Remember the sabbath day to keep it holy." And opposite it on the other
tablet was written: "Thou shalt not bear false witness." On the one tablet was written: "Honor thy
father," etc. And opposite it on the other tablet was written: "Thou shalt not covet thy neighbor's
wife" (*Mek. Qod.* 8).

The Decalogue was recited together with the Shema in the daily sacrificial service in the
Temple (*m. Tamid* 5:1) during the Second Temple period but was prohibited by the rabbis outside of the Temple and after its destruction for fear that this practice would give the impression
that only the Decalogue, and not the other laws, was given to Moses at Sinai (*b. Ber.* 12a; see
E. Urbach, "The Role of the Ten Commandments in Jewish Worship," in Segal, 161-89).

The Jewish philosopher-exegete Philo considered the Ten Commandments to represent the
essence of biblical law or its fundamental principles. For him the Decalogue embodied the
whole of the Torah, and the other laws in the HB represented various manifestations or detailed
elaborations. He expounded this position in his *On the Decalogue* (*De decalogo*), the first work
to present a detailed exposition of the Decalogue, and in his *About the Particular Laws* (*De specialibus legibus*). It appears that he alone in antiquity regarded the Decalogue as a unique summation of the Torah (see Y. Amir, "The Decalogue According to Philo," in Segal, 121-60).

The NT quotes Jesus as referring positively to the Decalogue's stipulations (Matt 19:16-30;
Mark 10:17-31; Luke 18:18-30). A Matthean saying of Jesus affirms the commandments and
condemns those who break them in act, in word, or even in thought (Matt 5:17-32). Jesus also
appears to have reduced them to two basic principles: love of God and love of neighbor (Matt
22:34-40; Mark 12:28-31; Luke 10:25-28, quoting Deut 6:5 and Lev 19:18, neither in the
Decalogue). Paul sums up the law in one principle: "Love your neighbor as yourself" (Rom
13:8-10; Gal 5:14), referring only to what would have been the second table of stipulations.

The author of the epistle of James speaks of fulfilling the "royal law," which is stated as "You
shall love your neighbor as yourself." What is meant by the "royal law" is uncertain, but the
text continues to speak of adultery and murder as if the author were stating a central principle
summarizing the second half of the Decalogue. The writer declares that "whoever keeps the
whole law but fails in one point has become guilty of all of it" (Jas 2:10). This text appears to
grant priority to a simple principle but then places all the laws on the same footing.

The idea that transgression of one commandment leads to or is equivalent to breaking all
commandments also occurs in rabbinic literature. The *Mek. Shim.* on Exod 20:14 declares:
"When a person breaks one of them, he will end up by breaking them all" (quoted by Flusser
in Segal, 225; see 4 Macc 5:19-21; Philo, *Legatio ad Gaium* 115-17).

The practice of summarizing the commandments in a single principle was also known among
the rabbis. R. Akiba declared "You shall love your neighbor as yourself" to be the "great general rule of the Torah" (*Sipra Qod.* 2). Hillel, in responding to a pagan's request for a summary of the law, declared: "What is hateful to you, do not do to anyone else—that is the whole
Torah, and all the rest is commentary—go and learn it" (*b. Šabb.* 31a). Hillel's statement presents the negative form of what is called Jesus' Golden Rule (Matt 7:12; Luke 6:31), which,
however, is not presented in the NT as a synopsis of the commandments.

Rabbinic tradition also holds the view that the biblical characters summarized or reduced the commandments of the HB: "David came and reduced them to ten [Psalm 15] . . . Isaiah came and
reduced them to six [Isa 33:15] . . . Micah came and reduced them to three [Mic 6:8] . . .
Habakkuk came and reduced them to one" [Hab 2:8] (b. Mak. 24a).

Although in general early Christians believed that the cultic and purity laws of the HB were
superseded in the Christian era, the Decalogue, with the exception of the sabbath law, was con-

sidered obligatory. Paul had written that "when Gentiles who have not the law do by nature what the law requires, they are a law to themselves" (Rom 2:14). Thus the Decalogue came to be viewed as a manifestation of this natural law.

The second-century Valentinian Gnostic Ptolemy, in his *Letter to Flora* (preserved in Epiphanias's *Panarion* 33), argued, on the basis of his exegesis of sayings of Jesus, that only the Decalogue was given by the absolute God: "God's law in its pure form, unentangled with the inferior, is the Decalogue . . . Although they present the legislation in a pure form they need completion by the Savior since they did not possess perfection" (33.5.3). The other laws were attributed to Moses and the elders and were abolished by Christ. Ptolemy considered laws that require vengeance and retribution to be unjust. Some Christians even allegorized the Ten Commandments. For example, Clement of Alexandria in his *Stromata* (6.133-48) considered the prohibition against murder to refer to the destruction of true knowledge. In his more elementary *Paedagogos* (3.89), however, he stated that they needed no allegorization.

In the early medieval period rabbinic authorities developed the theory that there were 613 commandments in the HB: "Three hundred and sixty-five of them are negative commandments, like the number of days of the solar year, and two hundred and forty-eight are positive commandments, corresponding to the parts of the human body" (*b. Mak.* 23b). Homiletically it was argued that each part of the body requested its use to keep the commandments and each day asked that it not be used to transgress a commandment. The 613 commandments were traced to the numerical value of the word Torah (TWRH = 400 + 6 + 200 + 5 = 611), given by Moses, plus the first two commandments in the Decalogue, spoken by God directly.

Saadia, apparently independently of Philo, developed in his liturgical poem *Azharot* the idea that all 613 commandments are embodied in the Decalogue. He assumed that the entire body of laws had been spun out of the Ten Commandments. Although earlier rabbis had hesitated to emphasize the laws of the Decalogue over the other commandments, later, more philosophically oriented medieval Jewish thinkers generally were less hesitant to follow this idea.

In the eleventh century, in the *Bereshit Rabbati*, produced by or in circles associated with R. Moses ha-Darshan, the number of commandments was associated with the number of consonantal letters in the Exodus pericope enumerating the Decalogue: "The Tablets encompassed the 613 commandments, corresponding to the 613 letters from the first word of the Decalogue to ʿeka [your neighbor; the last word of the Decalogue], no more, no less" (quoted by Sarfatti in Segal, 389). Although Maimonides expounded the 613 commandments, he clearly argued against any privileged status of one law over another—that is, against considering some laws, e.g., the Decalogue, as essential and others as peripheral.

Medieval Christian thinkers tended to expound the Ten Commandments as manifestations of natural law. Thomas Aquinas divided the "old law" into *moralia, ceremonialia,* and *judicialia,* identifying the Decalogue as the former—moral rules that reason could discover to be necessary and timeless. The remaining regulations are either ritual-ceremonial or civic, with the latter being local, specific to a particular culture, and belonging to specific circumstances of time. In his *Summa Theologiae* (Ia2ae, Question 100), Thomas formulated his position to refute arguments that the Decalogue merely represented a collection of taboos or tribal customs and was relative rather than absolute (see 29:56-111 in the Blackfriars ed.).

Most medieval Christian theologians discussed the Decalogue, frequently offering very spiritualized and broad applications. L. Smith has surveyed several treatments in her dissertation (1986; in addition, see the discussions by R. Rolle in R. Allen [1988] and by Gregory Palmas [1296–1359] in S. Mouselimas [1980]).

In the fourteenth and fifteenth centuries the Decalogue came to play an important role in lay handbooks of spiritual guidance and in confessional works. Examples of such handbooks are the Lay Folk's Catechism attributed to J. Thoresby (d. 1373), archbishop of York; *Les fleurs des commandments* (c. 1490); and J. Gerson's *ABC des simple sens.* The Reformers placed the Decalogue in most of their catechisms, and some popular booklets associated the commandments with particular biblical narratives, illustrating them with woodcuts.

In the sixteenth century diverse attitudes toward the Decalogue and the laws of the HB developed. Luther primarily saw the law as making sin manifest and driving the conscience toward grace. This emphasis can be seen in his commentary on Gal 3:19 and 4:3. In his *How Christians Should Regard Moses* (1525), he argued that the "law of Moses . . . is no longer binding of us because it was given only to the people of Israel . . . even The Ten Commandments do not pertain to us" (*Luther's Works* 35 [1960] 164-65). In his preface to the Pentateuch he wrote, "When Christ comes the law ceases . . . The Ten Commandments also cease, not in the sense that they are no longer to be kept or fulfilled, but in the sense that the office of Moses [to produce a sense of sin and to drive one to God's mercy] in them ceases" (ibid., 244).

Calvin was much more positive toward the laws of the HB and toward the Decalogue than Luther was. His classical discussion of the topic is found in his *Institutes of the Christian Religion* (bk. 2, chaps. 7–8). In chapter 7 he outlined what came to be designated the threefold use of the law, which was also expounded by P. Melanchthon in the 1535 edition of his Loci communes, by J. Bullinger in his Decades (ET 1577), and by numerous Anglican divines. This theory argues that the law has a civil use, applying to all, Christian and non-Christian alike; a pedagogical use, leading sinners to recognize their hopelessly sinful state and to throw themselves upon God's mercy; and a didactic use, teaching even those saved by Christ's sacrifice and forgiveness restraint from vice and from yielding to never-ending temptation. In Calvin the third was the principal use since through it even the Christian gains a surer knowledge of the Lord's will and is exhorted and aroused to obedience (*Institutes* 2.7.12).

The mainline Protestant Reformers found themselves combating radical elements at the periphery of their movement: libertines and segments of the Anabaptists who held that Hebrew law and even the Decalogue were no longer binding. For a time this antinomian movement's most articulate spokesperson was J. Agricola (1527–40). Antinomianism was taken up by many of the spiritualist groups within the radical Reformation.

Four additional factors should be noted about Calvin's important interpretation: (1) His lucid exposition of the Decalogue and of HB moral law as a specially granted restatement of natural law, or as the law engraved upon the heart, prepared the way for later humanists and for Deists to stress the priority of natural law and religion over any form of revelatory law and religion and even to deny the necessity of the latter. (2) He stressed that the first tablet of the Decalogue contained commandments one to four, expressing duties toward God; and the second tablet, commandments six to ten, duties toward other humans. Thus the command to honor parents belonged to the second tablet. (3) In his exposition of the laws in Exodus–Deuteronomy, he related all of them to one or the other of the Ten Commandments. His commentary on these books took the form of a Mosaic harmony (1563; ET, 4 vols., 1852-55; for a summary, see T. Parker [1986] 122-75). (4) He argued that a moral commandment always implied and required its opposite counterpart (*Institutes* 2.8.8-9). "The commandment, 'You shall not kill' . . . contains . . . the requirement that we give our neighbor's life all the help we can."

Even prior to the rise of historical criticism, a wide diversity in the interpretations of the individual commandments existed. The following represent some of the most disputed.

The prohibition against images was understood in Judaism as prohibiting any representation of God or of any god, but not artistic decoration in general. Protestants protested against artistic practices in Roman Catholic and Orthodox iconography, with Calvinism and the radical Reformation being more iconoclastic than Lutheranism. Discussing this commandment, Calvin wrote: "Whatever

320

visible forms of God man devises are diametrically opposed to his nature . . . as soon as idols appear, true religion is corrupted and adulterated" (*Institutes* 2.8.17; see 1.11.2, 12).

The prohibition against vain use of the divine name was generally understood in Judaism as referring to swearing falsely, frivolously, or superfluously (Philo *On the Decalogue* 84-91; b. *Ber.* 33a). Many Anabaptists, on the basis of Jesus' statement, "Do not swear at all" (Matt 5:34; see Jas 5:12), refused to swear oaths in any forms. G. Fox (1624–91) and others followed this practice.

The sabbath command with different motivational clauses (cf. Exod 20:11 with Deut 5:15) was understood in Judaism as commanding a day of rest (further elaborated in the Mishnaic tractate *Šabbat*) but also six days of work. The day is not declared a day of worship in the HB. Early Christians celebrated the first day of the week (Sunday) as the Lord's day and a time of assembly Acts 20:7; 1 Cor 16:2). Sunday as a day of rest was enjoined in 306 at the Council of Elvira, and in 321 it was promulgated by Constantine and subsequently regulated in the church. The sabbath commandment was understood by Augustine as an adumbration of spiritual and heavenly rest (see, e.g., his Letters 55.9.17 in FC 12.274). Calvin saw the sabbath as foreshadowing spiritual rest. Its ceremonial aspects were abolished: "To overthrow superstition, the day sacred to the Jews was set aside" (*Institutes* 2.8.33). A strict "sabbathianism" in observing Sunday was advocated by neither Calvin nor Luther but was primarily an English and American Puritan phenomenon (see N. Bound, *True Doctrine of the Sabbath* [1595] and James I, *Books of Sports* [1618]). S. McGee (1976) has argued that two opposed interpretations of the laws of the Decalogue, e.g., the sabbath commandment, marked the two sides of the English civil war.

The commandment enjoining honor to parents, considered part of the first tablet in Judaism, was related to parental creativity, which parallels that of the divine. R. Simeon ben Yohai noted: "The three of them—God, one's father and one's mother—are partners in every person" (quoted by Greenberg in Segal, 104). Philo wrote of parents standing between the mortal and the immortal: "Parents copy His nature by begetting particular persons" and "the act of generation assimilates them to God, the generator of the All" (*On the Decalogue* 51, 107). Christian tradition, which associated this command with the second tablet, tended to extend its coverage to all in authority, priest, bishop, and pope (Roman Catholic) as well as princely ruler (stressed by Lutherans), or magistrates (especially favorite authorities for Calvin and the Reformed). Anabaptist and other radical Reformers, like Paracelsus, took the narrowest meaning in the interest of generally rejecting civil and ecclesiastical government and expressing a hope for the emergence of a kingdom of God on the moral basis of Christ's teachings in the Sermon on the Mount.

The commandment against killing has historically been related to the category of premeditated murder, excluding execution of criminals condemned by trial in courts of law, killing in self-defense or by accident, and killing by soldiers in times of war. Calvin read into it the positive—"concern oneself with the safety of all"—and extended it—"all violence, injury, and any harmful thing at all that may injure our neighbor's body are forbidden to us" (*Institutes* 2.8.39). Pacifists, like Paracelsus, have argued for as broad an application of the prohibition as possible, including opposition to capital punishment.

The prohibition of adultery was generally understood in antiquity as prohibiting sex with a married or betrothed female. Philo devoted a long discussion to the damage done to society from the violation of this commandment (*On the Decalogue* 121-31). Although Rashi, commenting on this text, declared that "adultery is only with another man's wife," other Jewish interpreters, like A. Ibn Ezra, extended the prohibition to include other forms of sexual activity. The medieval church interpreted the command to include all forms of *luxuria* (see Matt 5:27-28). Calvin concluded that "any union apart from marriage is accursed in his sight" (*Institute*

2.8.41). The Reformers generally argued that each man ought to take one wife and that none are to remain virgins as a vocation, the latter in contrast to Roman Catholicism.

The prohibition against stealing was understood by early Jewish rabbis as prohibiting kidnapping, the theft of persons, a conclusion arrived at on the basis of context: "And what is the context here? It is persons. Consequently, this commandment, too, deals with persons" (*b. Sanh.* 86a). This view has been adopted by some modern scholars (A. Alt, KS 1 [1953] 330-40; A. Phillips [1970] 130). The more general interpretation sees this command as prohibiting taking property by stealth and thus as defending the right of private property.

Although the commandment against false witness originally applied to preserving the integrity of the judicial process, it was quickly applied to lying in general.

Perhaps the most controversial of all the commandments is the one concerning covetousness (Exod 20:17 and Deut 5:21 are divided into two commandments in the Roman Catholic and Lutheran traditions, perhaps because of the "and" at the beginning of Deut. 5:22 and the introduction of a new verb, "desire/crave"). The main issue concerns whether the commandment forbids internal envious desire or whether it prohibits calculation and taking steps to acquire the object of one's desire—"anything that is your neighbor's" (for the issues see A. Rofé, "The Tenth Commandment in the Light of Four Deuteronomic Laws," in Segal, 45-65). Numerous rabbinical statements as well as Maimonides reflect the latter position. In discussing prohibitions 265 and 266 he wrote that "developing stratagems" and "devising a scheme" were prohibited. Levi ben Gershon concluded that "one does not violate the prohibition if one does not actually do something in order to obtain the coveted object" (quoted by Greenberg in Segal, 107). Philo (*On the Decalogue* 142-53) understood the prohibition as forbidding appetite and desire in general, seeing the idea as one of the issues behind the dietary laws. Christian tradition, relying on Jesus' teaching in the Sermon on the Mount, has applied this commandment to internal dispositions. Following Augustine, Calvin argued that "God commands us to keep the possessions of others untouched and safe, not only from injury or the wish to defraud, but even from the slightest covetousness that may trouble our hearts" (*Institutes* 2.8.50). In the eighteenth and nineteenth centuries some Jewish and Christian interpreters advocated the older rabbinic position (see A. Rofé, in Segal, 46-50), but many continued to argue that it concerns "a state of mind" (M. Weinfeld [1995] 9) and "aims to prevent the flagrantly evil acts enumerated in the preceding Commandments, by mastering those impulses which drive people to commit such acts" (Greenberg in Segal, 109; see B. Jackson [1971]).

The rise of the historical-critical approach to the Bible produced far-ranging changes in the treatment of the Decalogue. In 1772 the young J. Goethe (1749–1832) proposed that the original Decalogue was not to be found in Exod 20:2-17 or in Deut 5:6-21 but rather in Exod 34:14-26. His arguments were based on the fact that reference to the ten words occurs in Exod 34:28 but not in Exodus 20 and that the cultic interests of Exod 34:14-26 probably more correctly indicate the concerns of the early Israelites than do the other two texts. A similar view was advanced independently by F. Hitzig in 1838 and since then has been advocated by many scholars, especially under the influence of J. Wellhausen. Those supporting the latter position also argued that the traditional Decalogue presupposes a settled, agricultural life-style, not the nomadic desert conditions of Mosaic times, and that its high ethical ideals were probably produced under the influence of the prophets.

Historical-critical scholarship has given primary attention to three interrelated issues: the date and origin of the Decalogue, its original form and content, and its use and influence in ancient Israel. Four arguments were addressed that supposedly indicated that the MT form of the Decalogue was not original: (1) the mixture of positive and negative commands; (2) the presence of motive clauses in some commandments but not in others; (3) the different motivations for observing the sabbath (cf. Exod 20:11, with its cosmic, creation rationale, with Deut

5:14-15 and its humanitarian and salvation-history rationales); and (4) the shift from direct divine speech in the first two commands to indirect speech in the remainder. Assuming a uniformity in style and brevity in expression (the Decalogue is called "ten words" not "ten commandments"), scholars have made various attempts to reconstruct an original form generally containing all negative statements (see H. Rowley [1952]; E. Nielsen [1968]; W. Harrelson [1980, rev. ed. 1997]). Most of these reconstructions are highly similar (see Weinfeld, 5-7, for a combination of negative and positive commands).

Proposed datings for the reconstructed Decalogue range from the Mosaic period to very late in First Temple times or even in the Second Temple period. In his *History of Israel* (1938) T. Robinson, arguing for an early date, wrote: "The moral code in Exodus xx is timeless, and its provisions are valid for any condition of organized human society. There is, then, nothing in the code itself to prevent its having been promulgated by Moses, especially if the first few commandments are reduced to a simpler form" (96). Interpreters who assign an early date generally argue that the other laws were influenced by those in the Decalogue. Those advocating a late date tend to view the Decalogue as the summation rather than as the source of other biblical laws. Most scholars today view both versions of the Decalogue as late, probably postexilic, and as having been placed in their present position during the editing process. Some interpreters have argued that the laws of Deuteronomy 12-26 are structured to follow and elaborate on the stipulations of the Decalogue.

New impetus to the study of the Decalogue's origin was made by S. Mowinckel, who argued in his 1927 work that it originated and was used in worship services. Drawing on the so-called entry liturgies in Psalms 15 and 24 and on allusions to the Decalogue in Psalms 50 and 81, he suggested that it was used as part of a covenant renewal service in the annual fall festival of *Sukkot* (Tabernacles). Other scholars have also associated the Decalogue with worship; e.g., Weinfeld associates it with the spring festival of *Shavuot* (Weeks/Pentecost; see Weinfeld, 34-44 and J. Stamm and M. Andrews [1967] 22-75).

The form of the commandments in the Decalogue, apodictic without any accompanying consequence stipulation, was explored by A. Alt in a 1934 article (79-132). He distinguished this form of law from casuistic law, the latter characterized by its conditional style and accompanying stipulation of consequence ("if . . . then . . . "). Alt argued that the apodictic laws, and thus the Decalogue, were genuine Israelite law, not adopted from the Canaanites, and were primarily at home in the sphere of worship rather than in the judicial arena.

The study of ancient Near Eastern treaties, especially Hittite treaties, first widely developed in the 1950s by G. Mendenhall, led to new arguments about the Decalogue. These treaties (see M. Barré) contained preambles, stipulations, references to divine witnesses, and curses (sometimes blessings also) pronounced on the violator. Mendenhall argued that the Decalogue represents the stipulations of the treaty/covenant between God and Israel. And since the Hittite treaties dated from the fifteenth to the fourteenth centuries, then the biblical treaty form and the Decalogue could date from the era of Moses. More recent investigations have raised questions about the comparison of the Decalogue to treaty stipulations and have concluded that ancient Near Eastern treaty material influenced biblical texts the most in the eighth and seventh centuries B.C.E.

The distinctive nature and simplistic character of apodictic law advocated by Alt and the connection of the Decalogue with treaty stipulations and/or worship was challenged by Gerstenberger, who connected "the prohibitive form" with the life of the clan and the family. Today no single position about the Decalogue has complete support. C. Carmichael (1985) has even argued that laws in the HB, including those in the Decalogue, are primarily the product of deductions drawn from biblical narratives.

Several characteristics of the Ten Commandments have given them an appeal beyond the confines of synagogue and church: "'categorical imperatives' universally applicable, timeless, not dependent on any circumstances whatever . . . couched in the second person singular . . . addressed personally to each individual . . . " (Weinfeld, 8, 10).

Commandments five to ten resonate with universally recognized virtues. The Enlightenment rationalist I. Kant developed his own categorical imperative, one form of which was "so act that the rule of your act can be law universal." The utilitarians J. Bentham (1748–1832) and J. S. Mill (1806–73) hypothesized that the right act is that done for the greatest pleasure and the least pain. Harrelson has shown that the Decalogue can be related to the issue of human rights. G. Anscombe (1958) has explored the fact that secular thought has inherited in its deontology a sense of the "ought" ("thou shalt . . . thou shalt not") in its statement of duties but has rejected the theological context of revelation and tradition presupposed by the Decalogue. She questions whether methods of modern ethics can derive the "ought" from other than a divine command. If not, something like the Decalogue seems irreplaceable.

Bibliography: R. S. Allen (ed. and tr.*), R. Rolle: The English Writings* (ClWS, 1988) 86-89, 143-51. **A. Alt**, *Essays on OT History and Religion* (1966). **G. A. Anderson**, "Torah Before Sinai: The Do's and Don'ts Before the Ten Commandments," *BRev* 12 (1996) 38-44. **G. E. M. Anscombe**, "Modern Moral Philosophy," *Philosophy 33* (1958) 1-19. **M. Barré**, *ABD* 6:653-56. **J. Blenkinsopp**, *Wisdom and Law in the OT: The Ordering of Life in Israel and Early Judaism* (Oxford Bible Series, 1983). **G. Bourgeault**, Décalogue et morale chrétienne (Recherches 2, 1971). **A. Brenner**, "An Afterword: The Decalogue—Am I an Addressee?" in *A Feminist Companion to Exodus and Deuteronomy* (ed. A. Brenner, 1994) 255-58. **M. Breuer**, "Dividing the Decalogue into Verses and Commandments," in Segal, 291-330. **R. Brooks**, *The Spirit of the Ten Commandments: Shattering the Myth of Rabbinic Legalism* (1990). **E. Brunner**, *The Divine Imperative: A Study in Christian Ethics* (1937). **M. Buber**, *Moses* (1946). **C. M. Carmichael**, *Law and Narrative in the Bible: The Evidence of the Deuteronomic Laws and the Decalogue* (1985). **D. J. A. Clines**, "The Ten Commandments, Reading from Left to Right," in *Words Remembered, Texts Renewed : Essays in Honour of John F. A. Sawyer* (ed. J. Davies, G. Harvey and W. G. E. Watson; JSOTSup 195, 1995) 97-112. **P. Delhaye**, *Le Décalogue et sa place dans la morale chrétienne* (1963). **C. Dohmen**, "Der Dekaloganfang und sein Ursprung," *Bib* 74 (1993) 175-95 ; "Gottes Spuren nachgehen: Offenbarung in der Wirkungs geschichte," in *Gottes Offenbarung in der Welt: Horst Georg Pöhlmann zum 65. Geburtstag* (ed. F. Krüger, 1998) 260-74. **E. Dublanchy**, "Decalogue," *DTC* 4 (1911) 161-76. **T. R. Elssner**, "Das dekalogische Namensmissbrauch-Verbot (Ex 20, 7/Dtn 5,11)," *BN* 114-115 (2002), 61-70. **D. N. Freedman, J. C. Geoghegan, and M. M. Homan**, *The Nine Commandments : Uncovering a Hidden Pattern of Crime and Punishment in the Hebrew Bible* (ed. A.B. Beck, 2000). **S. Goldman**, *The Ten Commandments* (1963). **R. M. Grant**, "The Decalogue in Early Christianity," *HTR* 40 (1967) 1-17. **M. Greenberg**, "The Decalogue Tradition Critically Examined," in Segal, 83-119. **T. Haraguchi**, "A Rhetorical Study of the Deuteronomic Decalogue," *AJT* 16 (2002) 276-85. **W. Harrelson**, *The Ten Commandments and Human Rights* (1980, rev. ed., 1997). **D. Hartman**, *A Living Covenant: The Innovative Spirit in Traditional Judaism* (1985). **S. Hauerwas**, *The Truth About God: The Ten Commandments in Christian Life* (1999). **F.-L. Hossfeld**, "Der Dekalog als Grundgesetz: eine Problemanzeige," in *Liebe und Gebot: Studien zum Deuteronomium* (ed. L. Perlitt; FRLANT 190, 2000) 46-59. **B. Jackson**, "Liability for Mere Intention in Early Jewish Law," *HUCA 42* (1971) 197-225. **F. Kabasele Lumbala**, "Exodus 20:1-17: An African Perspective," in Pope-Levison (1999) 43-48. **M. M. Kaplan**, *The Ten Commandments Today* (n.d.). **R. G. Kratz**, "Der Dekalog im Exodusbuch," *VT* 44 (1994) 205-38. **D. Lioy**, *The Decalogue and the Sermon on the Mount* (Studies in Biblical Literature 66, 2004). **M. Lluch-Baixauli**, "El Tratado de Filón sobre el

Decálogo," *ScrTh* 29 (1997) 415-41; "La Interpretatción de Orígenes al Decálogo," *ScrTh* 30 (1998) 87-109. **M. van Loopik**, *Die Zehn Worte in der Mechilta* (Israelitisch denken lernen 4, 2000). **S. McGee**, *The Godly Man in Stuart England: Anglicans, Puritans, and the Two Tablets, 1620–70* (1976). **M. Maimonides**, *The Commandments: "Sefer Ha-Mitvoth" of Maimonides* (1967). **M. D. Matlock**, "Disobeying or Obeying the First Part of the Tenth Commandment: Alternative Meanings from Deuteronomy 25:5-10," *Proceedings—Eastern Great Lakes and Midwest Biblical Societies* 21 (2001) 91-103. **C. H. Moehlman**, *The Story of the Ten Commandments: A Study of the Hebrew Decalogue in Its Ancient and Modern Application* (1928). **S. Mouselimas**, "Saint Gregory Palamas' The Decalogue of the Law According to Christ, That Is, the New Covenant," *GOTR* 25 (1980) 297-305. **S. Mowinckel**, *Le Décalogue* (EHPhR 16, 1927). **J. Neusner** (ed.), *How Judaism Reads the Torah* (Judentum und Umwelt 41-42, 1993). **E. Nielsen**, *The Ten Commandments in New Perspective: A Traditio-historical Approach* (SBT 2, 7, 1968). **T. H. L. Parker**, *Calvin's OT Commentaries* (1986). **D. Patrick**, "The First Commandment in the Structure of the Pentateuch," *VT* 45 (1995) 107-18. **J. Pelikan**, *Spirit Versus Structure: Luther and the Institutions of the Church* (1968). **L. Perlitt** et al., *TRE* 8 (1981) 408-30. **A. C. J. Phillips**, *Ancient Israel's Criminal Law: A New Approach to the Decalogue* (1970). **A. Pinker**, "Decalogue or Dodecalogue?" *JBQ* 28 (2000) 233-44. **J. V. Pixley**, "Exodus 20:1-17: A Latin American Perspective," in Pope-Levison (1999), 37-41. **J. Plaskow**, *Standing Again at Sinai: Judaism from a Feminist Perspective* (1990). **P. Pope-Levison and J. R. Levison** (eds.), *Return to Babel: Global Perspectives on the Bible* (1999). **E. M. Poteat**, *Mandate to Humanity: An Inquiry into the History and Meaning of the Ten Commandments and Their Relation to Contemporary Culture* (1953). **H. Ro**, "The Exodus Decalogue in Deuteronomistic Redaction," *AJT* 16 (2002) 315-26. **H. A. Roetlisberger**, "The Decalogue in Catechetical Teaching of the Church" (diss., University of Edinburgh, 1962). **W. Rordorf**, "Beobachtungen zum Gebrauch des Dekalogs in der vorkonstatinisches Kirche," *The NT Age: Essays in Honor of B. Reicke* (1984) 437-92. **H. H. Rowley**, "Moses and the Decalogue," *BJRL* 32 (1952) 81-118=his *Men of God: Studies in OT History and Prophecy* (1963) 1-36. **R. J. Rushdoony**, *The Institutes of Biblical Law: A Chalcedon Study* (1973). **G. Sarfatti**, "The Tablets of the Law as a Symbol of Judaism," in Segal, 383-418. **W. H. Schmidt**, *Die Zehn Gebote im Rahmen alttestamentlicher Ethik* (EdF 281, 1993). **K. Schwarzwäller**, "Verantwortung des Glaubens: Freiheit und Liebe nach der Dekalogauslegung Martin Luthers," in *Freiheit als Leibe bei Martin Luther* (ET *Freedom as Love in Martin Luther*, ed. D.D. Bielfeldt, K. Schwarzwäller, 1995) 133-58. **M. S. Seale**, *Qur'an and Bible: Studies in Interpretation and Dialogue* (1978). **B. Z. Segal** (ed.), *The Ten Commandments in History and Tradition* (ET 1990). **L. J. Smith**, "Academic Commentaries on the Ten Commandments (c. 1150–c. 1279)" (diss., Oxford University, 1986). **G. M. Soares-Prabhu**, "Exodus 20:1-17: An Asian Perspective," in Pope-Levison (1999) 49-54. **J. J. Stamm and M. E. Andrews**, *The Ten Commandments in Recent Research* (SBT 2, 2, 1967). **D. C. Steinmetz**, "The Reformation and the Ten Commandments," *Int* 43 (1989) 256-66. **G. Stemberger**, "Der Dekalog im frühen Judentum," *JBTh* 4 (1989) 91-103. **T. Veijola**, *Moses Erben: Studien zum Dekalog, zum Deuteronomismus und zum Schriftgelehrtentum* (BWANT 8/9, 2000). **A. R. Vidler**, *Christ's Strange Work* (1944). **F. E. Vokes**, "The Ten Commandments in the NT and in First-century Judaism," *StEv* 5 (TU 103, ed. F. L. Cross, 1968) 146-54. **M. Weinfeld**, *Social Justice in Ancient Israel and in the Ancient Near East* (1995). **I. Wise**, "The Law," *The Hebrew Review 1* (1886) 12-31. **J. Witte, Jr. and T. C. Arthur**, "The Three Uses of the Law: A Protestant Source of the Purposes of Criminal Punishment?" *JLR* 19 (1993–94) 433-65. **D. Wright**, "The Ethical Use of the OT in Luther and Calvin: A Comparison," *SJT* 36 (1983) 463-85.

P. G. KUNTZ

GENERAL ARTICLES

Deuteronomistic History

The deuteronomistic history (DH), comprising Deuteronomy, Joshua, Judges, 1–2 Samuel, and 1–2 Kings, as a literary entity is hypothesized on the basis of the methods of literary and historical criticism. The classic theory of its delineation is credited to M. Noth, although he was anticipated by A. Kuenen, J. Wellhausen, and others who had recognized deuteronomistic influence in the composition of these books. Noth's work, however, separated these books from Genesis–Numbers, showing them to be an independent composition unconnected with the older Pentateuchal documents. Composed during the exile, according to Noth, the DH provided the first continuous history of Israel from the eve of its entry into the land until its exile from it, using a variety of older independent traditions.

1. *The Unity of the DH.* The unity of the work was clear to Noth (*Deuteronomistic History* [1943, ET 1981]) on four grounds. First, he considered the language (though not described with the detail later provided by M. Weinfeld [1972] and H.-D Hoffmann [1980]) to be easily recognizable and consistent. Second, Noth noted that speeches or narratives in deuteronomistic style appear at critical points in the history (Joshua 1; 12; 23; Judg 2:11-23; 1 Samuel 12; 1 Kgs 8:14-64; 2 Kgs 17:7-41), where they functioned to review the history, drawing from it the consequences of the people's obedience or disobedience to the divine demands. Third, a consistent chronology creates a unifying framework: for the monarchic period the chronologies of the kings of the two states of Israel and Judah interlink to provide a total single chronology of the period; for the pre-monarchic and early monarchic periods, the summary statement that 480 years separate the exodus from Egypt and the fourth year of the reign of Solomon (1 Kgs 6:1) could be reconciled with the detailed chronological information provided earlier, mainly through the omission of the concluding statement of 1 Sam 4:18 as a post-deuteronomistic addition. Fourth, Noth saw the work as having a theological consistency: there is a marked lack of positive interest in the cult: the relationship between Yahweh and Israel depend on obedience to covenant law rather than on sacrifice and other cultic practice.

The last point is related to Noth's description of the purpose of the work: to account for the course of the history of Israel and the definite end to which it came with the destruction of Jerusalem. Even when the opportunity presented itself (as in the reflections on the destruction of Israel [2 Kings 17] and Judah [2 Kings 24]), the deuteronomist did not make use of it to sketch out a future for the people beyond the disaster that had overtaken them. The history of Israel had come to an end in conformity with the curse attached to the covenant law.

a. Jepsen (1953) considered his independent study of the books of Kings generally to conform with Noth's results. Arguing that these books were based on two sources that were combined and supplemented by a priestly redactor after the destruction of Jerusalem, Jepsen held that a further prophetic (*nebiistic*) stage of redaction, which took place during the exile, represented the work of Noth's deuteronomistic historian. At this stage the quantity of the work was almost doubled through the inclusion of the Isaiah legends, oral traditions about the prophets, and other materials relating to the pre-monarchic and early monarchic periods, together with the familiar deuteronomistic themes of election, divine law, and apostasy.

Noth's work found wide agreement, but difficulties were perceived in relation to inconsistencies in the history. A major problem was the deuteronomistic attitude to the monarchy, for Noth's explanation of the conflicts apparent in 1 Samuel 8–12 (the deuteronomist, though antimonarchic, was faithful to his sources and was satisfied simply to "correct" their pro-monarchic expression by adding his own views) did not fit with other evidence, especially from Kings, that the historian was not bound in this way to his source material. In order to resolve this problem and so to preserve Noth's view of the unity of the history, H. Boecker (1969) argued for a different evaluation of the deuteronomistic attitude toward the monarchy. Accepting as deuteronomistic those parts of 1 Samuel 8–12 proposed as such by Noth, Boecker held that they cannot be classified as anti-monarchic: criticisms exist, but they are leveled not against the monarchy as such, but rather against particular aspects of it. So the problem inherent in Noth's study was resolved by the argument that Noth was right in assigning certain texts to the deuteronomist but wrong in his assessment of what those texts said about the monarchy. This revision, moreover, eased the tension in Noth's presentation between the deuteronomist's apparent anti-monarchism in 1 Samuel 8–12 and his approval of David in Kings.

Hoffmann's comprehensive study considers the main problem to lie in the view that the deuteronomist used written sources: This suggests that the work is the outcome of a redactional history, and that in turn weakens the case for its unity. Hoffmann, therefore, has adopted a traditio-historical view, which he understands to mean that the deuteronomist had little to do with written sources but was an original, creative author, making use of mainly oral tradition. Arguing that the intention of the deuteronomist was to write a history of Israel as a history of cultic reforms and reformers, Hoffmann proposes that for the monarchic period the deuteronomist has provided what is effectively a cult history: The many detailed accounts of cultic reforms carried out by both Israelite and Judean kings culminate in the account of Josiah's reform, in which the deuteronomist's exilic and early postexilic contemporaries are given a model of faithfulness to the law. Cultic reform is also the principle of organization for the premonarchic time: The accounts here are fewer, however, being found only for Saul, Gideon, Joshua, and Moses. The reform of Moses (Deut 9:7-29) presents an ideal program and model for all future cult reformers in the DH and prefigures the reform of Josiah.

The deuteronomist is understood by Hoffmann to be the author of the descriptions of these cultic reforms: the vocabulary, both general cultic terminology long recognized as deuteronomistic and also specific cultic terminology in the detailed accounts of reforms, does not reflect historically verifiable events but is part of the literary presentation, its detail being the deuteronomistic way of giving historical verisimilitude to his account.

Neither these proposals to maintain the unity of the DH nor those that attempt to apply modern literary criticism with the same purpose (R. Polzin [1980]; J. Van Seters [1983]) can be regarded as successful. The DH has been marked out in the first instance by the methods of historical-critical analysis, and it is appropriate that those methods should be followed through consistently in order to comprehend the origin of that work. Thus the internal breaks and points of unevenness remain significant indicators of the work's origin and history of construction. Boecker's proposals undervalue the strong anti-monarchism of some deuteronomistic passages in 1 Samuel 8–12, especially chap. 12. Hoffmann's view of cult reform as the deuteronomist's principal theme leaves too many gaps and inconsistencies: cult reforms are ascribed to Jehoshaphat (1 Kgs 22:46) that are already credited to his predecessor (1 Kgs 15:12); there is a lack of symmetry in the reform stories, and it is particularly striking that none is provided for David. In addition to this lack of balance, the point and purpose of the work in this description remain difficult to comprehend: It is inconceivable that an exilic or early postexilic deuteronomist would write for his contemporaries a work that insisted that no matter how good the individual might be (Josiah), the end of the nation could only be destruction.

2. *Editions of the DH.* That the deuteronomistic historian had a wholly negative view of Israel's history, regarding it as finally closed, has been a point of major contention in Noth's thesis, in reaction to which two divergent views of the work have been developed (see H. Weippert [1985]). The first may be traced to H. W. Wolff (1982) and the second to G. von Rad. Wolff argued that it was unlikely that the deuteronomist would have composed such an extensive history only to show Israel's guilt. Moreover, he preferred to think in terms of a deuteronomistic circle as the setting for

deuteronomistic redaction; and to a second deuteronomistic hand in this circle he assigned such passages as Deut 4:29-31 and 30:1-10, where the theme of return after judgment is prominent.

The shift of responsibility for the DH away from an individual author to a school or circle provided the possibility of distinguishing between layers of deuteronomistic editorial work, within which context it would then be possible to understand its having both negative and positive purposes. The most significant contributions to this development have come from R. Smend, W. Dietrich (1972), and T. Veijola.

Smend (1971) has argued that deuteronomistic texts in Joshua 1, 13, and 23 and Judges 2 are not unified compositions but incorporate later supplements to a basic deuteronomistic text. These supplements, forming a single, secondary layer, are concerned with obedience to the law and make Israel's success in its conquest of the land conditional on such obedience. Thus a distinction is drawn between the deuteronomistic historian (Dtr), for whom Israel's conquest of the land was complete and successful, and a later "nomistic" deuteronomistic editor (DtrN), for whom that conquest has been successful only "to this day" (Josh 23:9b).

Dietrich's detailed study of Kings attempted to distinguish a prophetic stage of redaction of the DH preceding the work of DtrN. Noting the regular formal pattern of prophecy and fulfillment, he argued that such prophetic passages are all additions to their contexts, that their form is found with the classical prophets, especially Jeremiah, and that their language has been influenced by both the prophets and the DH. The general intention of the redactor responsible for them (DtrP) is to unite prophecy with the deuteronomistic movement, showing history as the arena in which the prophetic word works itself out. The work of the deuteronomistic historian (Dtr), which reaches its conclusion in 2 Kgs 25:21, was carried out shortly after the fall of Jerusalem; DtrN added the conclusion in 2 Kgs 25:22-30, shortly after the release of King Jehoiachin; DtrP precedes DtrN and should be dated to the early part of the exilic period. Veijola (1975) traced all three layers back into the books of Samuel: DtrH is favorably disposed toward the monarchy and has a positive view of David as the servant of Yahweh; DtrP has subordinated the king to the prophet and presented the king as a source of guilt; DtrN holds up David as an ideal but only on the basis of his obedience to the commandments, while seeing the monarchy in general as an evil institution (1977).

Smend later (1978) brought these studies together into a modified synthesis that, although unable to assign every verse to its appropriate layer, attempted a full account of the development of the DH: Dtr offered a continuous account, based on different sources, beginning in Deut 1:1 and ending with 2 Kgs 25:30; DtrP introduced prophetic stories into the presentation of the monarchic period, the history of which ran its course according to the scheme prophecy-fulfillment; DtrN introduced an emphasis on the law throughout the work. All three belong closely together, the additions of the later redactors making use of the language of the work being edited; the task of distinguishing them is, therefore, difficult. In time, also, they are not far separated: Dtr, whose account ends with the release of Jehoiachin, cannot be dated before 560 B.C.E.; and the two stages of redaction were completed by the early postexilic period.

The approach initiated by von Rad involved understanding more radical change in the course of the development of the DH. Von Rad acknowledged that the deuteronomist wished to explain why the saving history had ended in catastrophe but argued that for the deuteronomist the judgment of the law was not the only power active in history; equally effectual was the promise of salvation in the Nathan prophecy (see also D. McCarthy [1965]). The work contains a messianic motif: The description of David and the measuring of his successors by means of his standard show that the deuteronomist "had a picture of the perfect anointed unremittingly present to his mind" (von Rad [1962] 345).

This tension between judgment and promise has been exploited by F. M. Cross [1973], who has argued that there are two themes in the DH. The first is the sin of Jeroboam and his successors, which reaches its climax in the account of the fall of the northern kingdom and in the meditation on that event in 2 Kgs 17:1-23. The second is the promise of grace to David and his house, which reaches its climax in the account of Josiah's reform in 2 Kings 22–23, where Josiah is said to have extirpated the cult of Jeroboam and attempted to restore the kingdom of David. By contrasting these two themes the deuteronomist created a work that functioned to propagate Josiah's reform: Josiah is the new David, and in him is to be found true faithfulness to Yahweh, as a result of which the restoration of the Davidic kingdom is taking place. The DH ended with the account of Josiah's reform and so was a preexilic composition. Its extension to bring the work up to the destruction of Jerusalem and the exile is the work of a second deuteronomistic editor, who has turned the history as a whole into an explanation of that catastrophe; this later editor's work can be found in Deuteronomy, Joshua, 1–2 Samuel, and 1–2 Kings.

Cross's thematic argument was given literary-critical support by D. Nelson (1981) in his study of the regnal formulas that frame the references to each king in Israel and Judah. The formulas normally display considerable variety, but in the case of the last four kings of Judah they are terse and fixed. Here they are the work of a later hand extending the work at a secondary stage. Nelson also marked out those parts of Kings that are with all probability to be assigned to the later editor: 1 Kgs 8:44-51; 9:6-9; 2 Kgs 17:7-20, 34b-40; 21:3b-15, all of which prepare for the destruction of Jerusalem and the exile.

Although there are points of contact between this approach and that of Smend, particularly in the anti-monarchic characterization of the later editor and in the passages assigned to him, Cross's approach is distinct in its conception of the significance of the change introduced by editorial work on the original DH. While according to Smend the editors introduced new emphases into a work whose basic nature remained relatively stable, Cross maintained that the original DH was fundamentally transformed by the later editor: The original work was designed as a paean of praise in support of the reforms of Josiah; the edited version is intended to explain the failure of the Davidic dynasty and the destruction of Jerusalem.

3. *Further Study of the DH*. Any attempt to synthesize the approaches of Cross and Smend (see A. Mayes [1983]) will not only yield a complex picture of the DH very different from that of Noth but will also inevitably raise fundamental questions about the DH. There is considerable uncertainty about the criteria by which redactional layers might be distinguished and so also about the functions of any of these redactions. Moreover, it is now clear that it cannot be assumed that a given stage of redaction is to be found through the whole or the majority of the DH. Those books that have traditionally been seen as parts of the DH have undergone processes of redactional development that cannot easily be traced through more than limited parts of that history, thus raising the question of the validity of referring to any such single literary entity as the DH (E. Knauf [1996]).

Major contributions to uncovering the redactional history of limited parts of the DH have come from a number of directions. First, Weippert (1972) has sought to achieve results for the books of Kings through a study of the judgment formulas. Three groups of these formulae are distinguished, relating to progressively more extensive or later sections of Kings, thus providing an outline of the history of the development of these books. This account of the history of Kings has been critically examined by A. Lemaire (1986) and I. Provan (1988). The latter in particular has pointed to different understandings in Kings of what is meant by worship at the high places as a means of distinguishing a preexilic edition, culminating in the account of the reign of Hezekiah from an exilic editing, to which only isolated additions were subsequently made. Similarly, W. Richter (1964) has sought to determine the history of the book of Judges by a study of the frameworks that brought the independent stories into a collection, and of introductory passages that brought deliverers and judges together into a comprehensive account of the period of the judges. G. Seitz (1971) has argued for two significant stages in the growth of

Deuteronomy marked by two series of superscriptions, the latter of which belongs to the stage that incorporated the work into the DH (see also Mayes [1979]).

Second, N. Lohfink's study (1981) of the kerygmata of the DH has isolated a distinctive form of expression in Deuteronomy 1–Joshua 22, through which the deuteronomist describes the conquest as Yahweh's dispossession of the older inhabitants of the land in favor of Israel. It suggests that Deuteronomy 1–Joshua 22 existed independently, perhaps in the historical context of Josiah's military intervention in the north and his taking of the land from the Assyrians. A deuteronomistic edition of Kings probably belonged to the same time, but only in the exile was any combination effected to yield the whole work extending from Deuteronomy to 2 Kings. Smend's DtrN is found by Lohfink also in Deuteronomy, but it is only a partial commentary since it does not appear in 1–2 Samuel and 1–2 Kings.

Third, a conjunction of literary-critical approaches with developing interest in the social, political, and religious milieu of the deuteronomist and in the question of the ideological function of the material in that milieu (P. Dutcher-Walls [1991]; R. Albertz [1996]) has led to a better-founded appreciation of certain stages in the development of the DH. Thus the analysis of the deuteronomic law by G. Braulik (1993) and Lohfink (1993) has shown that Deuteronomy 12–16 is the first major section of the law to which Deut 16:18–18:22 has been abruptly related at a secondary stage, while the social laws of Deuteronomy 19–25 differ from both in showing the least evidence of deuteronomic language and no concern with centralization. These sections reflect stages of growth that are integrally related to changing functions in a society in a process of rapid and fundamental transformation. The emphasis of the first section, the older cultic law of the lawbook, on cultic unity and purity has been expanded in the later sections to include a concern for the constitution and everyday life of the people in its relationship with Yahweh. The cultic law functioned to legitimate the reform of Josiah, but the more comprehensive law code, with its concern for the whole life of the people, relates to the needs of the exilic and early postexilic community. This development is open to being related to the history of the DH. Insofar as older stages of the DH may be related to Josiah's reform, they reflect its concern with the monarchy and with cultic unity and purity; later exilic stages, however, introduced such theological commentary as 2 Kgs 17:7-23, 34b-41, in which the welfare of Israel rests on the people as a whole and not solely on the king (see Mayes [1996]).

The relationship of the DH to the Tetrateuch also remains problematic. The issues here are exacerbated by the turmoil in pentateuchal criticism (see R. Whybray [1987, 1995]). Wellhausen and Noth (*Pentateuchal Traditions*) distinguished between the continuous strands J and E, which were later combined by a redactor and set within the framework of an originally independent P document. P extended only to the death of Moses; so the original conclusion of the J and E sources, relating the conquest of the land, was dropped in favor of the P framework. This work was then connected with the DH by transferring the priestly account of the death of Moses to the end of Deuteronomy.

Questions have been raised especially by H. Schmid (1976), R. Rendtorff (1977), M. Rose (1981), and Van Seters in relation to the existence of continuous J and E sources, the date of the J and E material, and its relationship to the DH. Rendtorff in particular finds that the links between the larger units of the Pentateuch go back to no earlier than an editorial layer to be identified as deuteronomic (see also Mayes [1983]). This may be taken to suggest that it was only at some stage(s) in the development of the DH that the Tetrateuch received a deuteronomistic editing (Smend [1978]), if not indeed its formative organization based on older independent traditions (Rendtorff, Rose).

Bibliography: **R. Albertz**, "Le milieu des Deutéronomistes," *Israel construit son histoire: L'historiographie deutéronomiste . . . la lumière des récherches recentes* (Le Monde de la Bible

34, ed. A. de Pury, T. Romer, J.-D. Macchi, 1996) 377-407. **A. G. Auld**, *Understanding Poets and Prophets: Essays in Honor of G.W. Anderson* (JSOTSup 152, 1993). **H. J. Boecker**, *Die Beurteilung der Anfänge des Königtums in den deuteronomistischen Abschnitten des 1. Samuelbuches: Ein Beitrag zum Problem des "Deuteronomistischen Geschichtswerks"* (WMANT 31, 1969). **G. Braulik**, "The Sequence of the Laws in Deuteronomy 12–26 and in the Decalogue," *A Song of Power and the Power of Song: Essays on the Book of Deuteronomy* (Sources for Biblical and Theological Study 3, ed. D. L. Christensen, 1993) 313-35. **A. F. Campbell**, "M. Noth and the Deuteronomistic History," *The History of Israel's Traditions: The Heritage of M. Noth* (ed. S. L. McKenzie, M. P. Graham, JSOTSup 182, 1994) 31-62; *Unfolding the Deuteronomistic History: Origins, Upgrades, Present Text* (2000). **F. M. Cross**, *Canaanite Myth and Hebrew Epic: Essays in the History of the Religion of Israel* (1973). **F. H. Cryer**, "On the Relationship Between the Yahwistic and the Deuteronomistic Histories," *BN* 29 (1985) 58-74. **J. C. deMoor** and **H. F. van Rooy** (eds.), *Past, Present, Future: The Deuteronomistic History and the Prophets* (*OtSt* 44, 2000). **W. Dietrich**, *Prophetie und Geschichte: Eine redaktionsgeschichtliche Untersuchung zum deuteronomistischen Geschichtswerk* (FRLANT 108, 1972); *Von David zu den Deuteronomisten: Studien zu den Geschichtsüberlieferungen des Alten Testaments* (BWANT 8.16, 2002). **W. J. Doorly**, *Obsession with Justice: The Story of the Deuteronomists* (1994). **P. Dutcher-Walls**, "The Social Location of the Deuteronomists: A Sociological Study of Factional Politics in Late Pre-Exilic Judah," *JSOT* 52 (1991) 77-94. **E. Eynikel**, *The Reform of King Josiah and the Composition of the Deuteronomistic History* (OtSt 33, 1996). **G.E. Gerbrandt**, *Kingship According to Deuteronomistic History* (SBLDS 87, 1986). **B. Green**, *How Are the Mighty Fallen? A Dialogical Study of King Saul in 1 Samuel* (JSOTSup 365, 2003). **G. Hens-Piazza**, *Of Methods, Monarchs, and Meanings: A Sociorhetorical Approach to Exegesis* (Studies in Old Testament Interpretation 3, 1996). **H. D. Hoffmann**, *Reform und Reformen: Untersuchungen zu einem Grundthema der deuteronomistischen eschichtsschreibung* (ATANT 66, 1980). **A. Jepsen**, *Die Quellen des Königbuches* (1953). **E. A. Knauf**, "L'Historiographie Deutéronomiste (DtrG) existet'elle?" *Israel construit son histoire* (1996) 409-18. **G. Knoppers**, *Two Nations Under God: The Deuteronomistic History of Solomon and the Dual Monarchies* (HSM 52, 53, 1993); and J. G. McConville (eds.), *Reconsidering Israel and Judah: Recent Studies on the Deuteronomistic History* (Sources for Biblical and Theological Study 8, 2000). **K. Latvus**, *God, Anger, and Ideology: The Anger of God in Joshua and Judges in Relation to Deuteronomy and the Priestly Writings* (1998). **A. Lemaire**, "Vers l'histoire de la rédaction des livres des Rois," *ZAW* 98 (1986) 221-36. **N. Lohfink**, "Kerygmata des deuteronomistischen Geschichtswerks," *Die Botschaft und die Boten* (FS H. W. Wolff. ed. J. Jeremias and L. Perlitt, 1981) 87-100; "Distribution of the Functions of Power: The Laws Concerning Public Offices in Deuteronomy 16:18–18:22," *A Song of Power and the Power of Song* (ed. D. L. Christensen, 1993) 336-52. **D. J. McCarthy**, "II Samuel 7 and the Structure of the Deuteronomistic History," *JBL* 84 (1965) 131-38. **S. L. McKenzie**, *The Chronicler's Use of the Deuteronomistic History* (Harvard Semitic Monographs 33, 1984); *The Trouble with Kings: The Composition of the Book of Kings in the Deuteronomistic History* (VTSup 42, 1991); (ed.), *The History of Israel's Traditions: The Heritage of Martin Noth* (JSOTSup 182, 1994); *Covenant* (Understanding Biblical Themes, 2000). **A. D. H. Mayes**, *Deuteronomy* (NCBC, 1979); *The Story of Israel Between Settlement and Exile: A Redactional Study of the Deuteronomistic History* (1983); "De l'ideologie deutéronomiste á la Theologie de l'Ancien Testament," *Israel construit son histoire* (1996) 477-508. **E. T. Mullen**, *Narrative History and Ethnic Boundaries: The Deuteronomistic Historian and the Creation of Israelite National Identity* (SBL Semeia Studies, 1993). **R. D. Nelson**, *The Double Redaction of the Deuteronomistic History* (JSOTSup 18, 1981). **F. A. J. Nielsen**, *The Tragedy in History: Herodotus and the Deuteronomistic History* (JSOTSup 251, 1997).

M. Noth, *Überlieferungsgeschichtliche Studien* (1943; ET, The Deuteronomistic History, 15, 1981, 1986); *Überlieferungsgeschichte des Pentateuch* (1948; ET, A History of Pentateuchal Traditions [1972]). **M. A. O'Brien**, *The Deuteronomistic History Hypothesis: A Reassessment* (OBO 92, 1989). **E. Otto**, *Das Deuteronomium im Pentateuch und Hexateuch: Studien zur Literaturgeschichte von Pentateuch und Hexateuch im Lichte des Deuteronomimrahmens* (FAT 30, 2000). **B. Peckham**, *The Composition of the Deuteronomistic History* (Harvard Semitic Monographs 35, 1985). **R. F. Person**, *The Deuteronomistic School: History, Social Setting, and Literature* (SBL Studies in Biblical Litertature 2, 2002). **R. Polzin**, *Moses and the Deuteronomist: Deuteronomy, Joshua, Judges* (A Literary Study of the DH, pt. 1, 1980). **I. W. Provan**, *Hezekiah and the Books of Kings: A Contribution to the Debate About the Composition of the Deuteronomistic History* (BZAW 172, 1988). **G. von Rad**, *Theologie des Alten Testaments* (vol. 1, 1957; vol. 2, 1960; ET, OT Theology [vol. 1, 1962; vol. 2, 1965]). **A. N. Radjawane**, "Das deuteronomistische Geschichtswerk," *TRu* 38 (1973–74) 177-216. **D. C. Raney**, *History as Narrative in the Deuteronomistic History and Chronicles* (Studies in the Bible and Early Christianity 56, 2003). **R. Rendtorff**, *Das überlieferungsgeschichtliche Problem des Pentateuch* (BZAW 147, 1977). **H. G. Reventlow, Y. Hoffman, B. Uffenheimer** (eds.), *Politics and Theopolitics in the Bible and Postbiblical Literature* (JSOTSup 171, 1994). **S. L. Richter**, *The Deuteronomistic History and the Name Theology* (BZAW 318, 2002). **W. Richter**, *Die Bearbeitungen des 'Retterbuches' in der deuteronomischen Epoche* (BBB 21, 1964). **T. Römer**, *The Future of the Deuteronomistic History* (BETL 147, 2000). **M. Rose**, *Deuteronomist und Jahwist: Untersuchungen zu den Berührungspunkten beider Literaturwerke* (ATANT 67, 1981). **H. N. Rösel**, *Von Josua bis Jojachin: Untersuchungen zu den deuteronomistischen Geschichtsbüchern des Alten Testaments* (VTSup 75, 1999). **L. S. Schearing** and **S. L. McKenzie** (eds.), *Those Elusive Deuteronomists: The Phenomenon of Pan-Deuteronomism* (JSOTSup 268, 1999). **H. H. Schmid**, *Der sogenannte Jahwist: Beobachtungen und Fragen zur Pentateuchforschung* (1976). **G. Seitz**, *Redaktionsgeschichtliche Studien zum Deuteronomium* (BWANT 5, 93, 1971). **R. Smend**, "Das Gesetz und die Völker: Ein Beitrag zur deuteronomistischen Redaktionsgeschichte," *Probleme biblischer Theologie* (G. von Rad zum 70. Geburtstag, ed. H. W. Wolff, 1971) 494-509; *Die Entstehung des Alten Testaments* (1978). **K. A. Stone**, *Sex, Honor, and Power in the Deuteronomistic History* (JSOTSup 234, 1996). **K. A. Swanson**, "Hezekiah's Reform and the Bronze Serpent," (diss., Vanderbilt University, 1999). **M. A. Sweeney**, *King Josiah of Judah: The Lost Messiah of Israel* (2001). **J. Van Seters**, *Abraham in History and Tradition* (1975); *In Search of History* (1983). **G. Vanoni**, "Beobachtungen zur deuteronomistischen Terminologie in 2 Kon 23, 25-25, 30, "*Das Deuteronomium: Entstehung, Gestalt und Botschaft* (BETL 68, ed. N. Lohfink, 1985) 357-62. **T. Veijola**, *Die ewige Dynastie: David und die Entstehung seiner Dynastie nach der deuteronomistischen Darstellung* (1975); *Das Königtum in der Beurteilung der deuteronomistischen Historiographie: Eine redaktionsgeschichtliche Untersuchung* (1977); *Moses Erben: Studien zum Dekalog, zum Deuteronomismus und zum Schriftgelehrtentum* (BWANT 8, 2000). **M. Weinfeld**, *Deuteronomy and the Deuteronomic School* (1972). **H. Weippert**, "Die 'deuteronomistischen' Beurteilungen der Könige von Israel und Juda und das Problem der Redaktion der Königsbücher," *Bib* 53 (1972) 301-39; "Das deuteronomistische Geschichtswerk," *TRu* 50 (1985) 213-49. **J. Wellhausen**, *Die Composition des Hexateuchs und der historischen Bücher des Alten Testaments* (1889, 1899). **R. N. Whybray**, The Making of the Pentateuch: A Methodological Study (JSOTSup 53, 1987); *Introduction to the Pentateuch* (1995). **H. W. Wolff**, "The Kerygma of the Deuteronomistic Historical Work," *The Vitality of OT Traditions* (ed. W. Brueggemann and H. W. Wolff, 1982) 83-100. **E. Würthwein**, *Studien zum Deuteronomistischen Geschichtswerk* (BZAW 227, 1994).

A.D.H. Mayes

GENERAL ARTICLES

Pentateuchal Criticism

1. *Moses Is the Author of the Pentateuch*. For centuries the leading belief in Judaism and Christianity, Mosaic authorship was not based on historical and literary investigation of how the Pentateuch arose. Instead, its object was to emphasize the Pentateuch's divine origin and authority. During the first centuries C.E. and the Middle Ages this authority was disputed. In Jewish (see Hiwi Al-Balkhi, 9th cent.) and Christian (e.g., Ptolemaeus *Letter to Flora*; *Pseudo-Clementine Homilies*) heretical circles and among adversaries of Judaism and Christianity (e.g., Ibn Hazm, 11th cent.) dogmatic and ethical objections to the content of the Pentateuch were formulated, sometimes with the conclusion that it could not be (entirely and throughout) the work of Moses. Partially to answer the question of how the Pentateuch could be dependable despite its long and tumultuous history, the idea that Ezra had taken responsibility for an inspired "new edition" of the Pentateuch (see Photius *Amphilochia* 101, 816), based on 2 Esdr 14:19-48, found adherents among the church fathers. Already in ancient times the authorship of certain passages was considered to be problematical, for instance Deut 34:5-12 (in *Pseudo-Clementine Homilies*), a passage that throughout the ages has played a part in this discussion. In the Middle Ages and thereafter others (e.g., Isaac ibn Jasos; A. Ibn Ezra) added additional passages (post- and amosaica; Gen 12:6; 36:31-39; Exod 16:35; Num 12:3; Deut 1:1; 2:12; 3:11, 14; etc.), although these initially did not lead to doubts about Mosaic authorship. Until the eighteenth century some scholars pointed out Moses' prophetic gifts (e.g., Philo of Alexandria [*Mos.* 2.291] and Flavius Josephus [*A.J.* 4.326]) regarding Deut 34:5-12 (*b. Baba Bathra* otherwise: Joshua is the author of this passage). Others meddled just as little with Mosaic authorship but were of the opinion that Ezra, whose name continues throughout the centuries to play a part in theories about how the Pentateuch arose (see C. Houtman [1981] 91-115), and/or Joshua and Eleazar or others were responsible for a number of additions.

2. *Moses Is Not the Author of the Pentateuch: The Emergence of Historical and Literary Criticism*. During the seventeenth century, under the influence of powerful currents of rationalism, several great intellects (e.g., T. Hobbes, I. de la Peyrère, B. Spinoza, R. Simon, J. Le Clerc) placed question marks next to the traditional representation of Mosaic authorship. They not only pointed out items that could not have stemmed from Moses (see sec. 1) but also drew attention to historical errors, inconsistencies, the presence of remarkable repetitions, differences in style, and deficiencies in the arrangement of material. In answering the question of the age and authorship of the Pentateuch, they wanted to rely on the facts of the writings themselves without prejudice. This path did not lead them to a denial of all Mosaic contribution to the Pentateuch—they attached much value to such texts as Exod 17:14; 24:4; Num 33:2; Deut 31:9— but to the position that the Pentateuch arose in a much more complex manner than tradition represented. This position evoked vehement opposition in the seventeenth and eighteenth centuries and had little influence as far as the more official literature is concerned. It did, however, exert influence among French (e.g., J. Meslier [1664–1729]) and English (e.g., T. Morgan [d. 1743]) free thinkers, whose criticism of the HB was much more far-reaching than simply the Mosaic authorship of the Pentateuch. Under such influence H. S. Reimarus formulated his criticism of the Bible in the second half of the eighteenth century in Germany, including the issue of Mosaic authorship, while in France Voltaire expressed critical sentiments about this matter. From this time onward, within biblical scholarship itself more detailed and initially more conservative theories than those of the seventeenth century were developed with respect to how the Pentateuch arose.

3. *The Older Documentary Hypothesis, the Fragmentary Hypothesis, the Supplementary*

Hypothesis, and the Newer Documentary Hypothesis. How could Moses have written what is recounted in Genesis? Among other possibilities, opponents and proponents of Mosaic authorship, e.g., J. Astruc (1753), have taken the position that Moses utilized written documents. Astruc set himself the objective of refuting the criticism of Hobbes and others (see sec. 2), maintaining that the unevenness ascertained in Genesis need not lead to a denial of Mosaic authorship. An acceptable explanation could be that Moses had written the history from before his time in a kind of tetrapla; later transcribers made this into a continuous story and are responsible for the chaos of the current version. Astruc made it his goal to provide a reconstruction of Moses' work, basing his theory on repetitions and alterations of the divine names YHWH and Elohim in Genesis and Exodus 1–2; from Exodus 3 onward Moses drew on his own experience. Known as the older documentary hypothesis, this theory gained adherents because of J. G. Eichhorn's refinements (1780–83). While also giving attention to the terminology used, Eichhorn demanded as criteria for distinguishing the documents variations in style and characteristic elements in the content, and he had little difficulty in ascribing important portions of the Pentateuch to Moses.

In the first half of the nineteenth century the theory known as the fragmentary hypothesis (the Pentateuch was compiled from larger and smaller fragments that are not interdependent and are often irreconcilable), presented by A. Geddes (1792, 1800) and developed and expanded by J. Vater (1802–5), captured great interest. With the appearance of Vater's work, a period of intensive reflection on the origins of the Pentateuch began in Germany and resulted in a diversity of positions. Characteristic of this period is that there is no easy way to label individual scholars as adherents of a particular theory with respect to their views on the origin of the Pentateuch. Furthermore, besides defenders of Mosaic authorship (F. Ranke, E. Hengstenberg, C. Keil, H. Hävernick) and scholars who accept the presence of extended Mosaic sections in the Pentateuch (e.g., F. Delitzsch), a number of writers whose reflections are characterized by radical historical criticism drew attention to themselves (W. de Wette, C. Gramberg, A. Hartmann, P. von Bohlen, J. Vatke, J. George). De Wett (1806–7) disputed, among other things, that Moses was the author of the laws in the Pentateuch. Other scholars denied Moses the ability to write and posited that the Pentateuch received its present form only after the exile.

Also characteristic of the first half of the nineteenth century is that a number of scholars (e.g., H. Ewald) considerably modified their positions. De Wette, for instance, who initially defended a form of the fragmentary theory, later accepted the supplementary theory developed by J. Stählin and H. Ewald and advanced by F. Bleek and J. Tuch. According to this theory, an elohistic *Grundschrift* runs from Genesis to Joshua, supplemented by a Jehovist (who utilized not only YHWH, but also Elohim). To a large extent, letting go of the conception that the Pentateuch is the work of Moses and/or contemporaries opened up the possibility of posing questions about whether the literary sources of Genesis reach farther into the Pentateuch. Critical scrutiny of the presumed coherence of Genesis and the following books on the part of adherents of the supplementary hypothesis led H. Hupfeld (1853) to the theory, later known as the newer documentary hypothesis, that the Hexateuch was constructed from a later priestly (P) and an earlier elohistic (E) document, which an editor combined with an even later Jehovistic (J) document; and in this work Deuteronomy was given a place. The theory that the Pentateuch was compiled from four sources had now taken shape.

4. *The Newer Documentary Hypothesis Defended in a New Form.* In the second half of the nineteenth century a growing number of biblical scholars in Germany and beyond (e.g., A. Kuenen and J. Wellhausen) accepted the theory that the Pentateuch was constructed from four documents/sources. They were able to combine and forge into an imposing conception the insights achieved during the nineteenth century in divergent areas of history and historical criticism and in the history of the religion of Israel by such scholars as de Wette, George, Vatke,

Ewald, Hupfeld, J. Colenso, E. Reuss, and K. Graf. According to this conception the esteemed ideas of how the HB arose furnished a convincing literary basis for an impressive picture of the religion of Israel, which was described by Wellhausen (1878): The history of Israel was the result of a process characterized by centralization, ritualization, and denaturalization/historicization of the cult; the nomadic and agricultural religion of early Israel developed via the emergence of the law in Josiah's time, in which the religion of the prophets exerted great influence, into the priestly legal religion of Judaism. This picture was based on the newer documentary hypothesis in a new guise: P is not the oldest, but the latest source of the Hexateuch, and the literary sources arose in the sequence J, E, D, P. This theory offered a good basis for the idea, voiced previously, that the legal portion of the Pentateuch (P) was vastly later than the prophets and had only been formed during the exile and thereafter. The Archimedian point of the picture sketched of Israel's religion is the idea, advanced by de Wette (1805), who himself shared the conception, that Deuteronomy was not only the law book of Josiah found in 622/621 B.C.E but was also conceived in order to initiate Josiah's reformation (2 Kings 22–23).

5. *Developments After Kuenen/Wellhausen, Ongoing Reflection on the Origins of the Pentateuch, and Divergent Ideas.* After 1900 acquaintance with ancient Near Eastern literature uncovered by archaeologists made its impact on Pentateuchal research. Under this influence and that of Germanic studies, H. Gunkel, and following in his footsteps H. Gressmann, intensely examined the pre-literary transmission of especially the narrative material in the Pentateuch. The result was that J and E were no longer regarded as authors but as schools that gathered orally transmitted folk narratives. The documentary theory obtained features of a fragmentary theory. More generally, acquaintance with the literature of the ancient Near East led to the recognition that later literary texts (P) could contain ancient material. It has even been asserted that archaeological results demonstrate the unsoundness of the documentary theory (e.g., K. Kitchen [1966]).

The new version of the documentary hypothesis was regarded in conservative Protestant circles as undermining the reliability of the Bible (e.g., the W. R. Smith case). Either Mosaic authorship (e.g., W. Green, E. Young, W. Möller) or the thesis that the Pentateuch is a compilation of Mosaic material (e.g., G. Aalders, R. Harrison) was clung to resolutely. This was especially true in Roman Catholic circles until a more liberal climate was created by the encyclical *Divino Afflante Spiritu* (1943) and the letter of the Pontifical Biblical Commission to Cardinal Suhard (1948). Before that time there was no room for moderate critical positions (M. Lagrante, F. von Hügel, A. van Hoonacker, H. Poels) because of the decree *De Mosaica Authentica Pentateuchi* (1906). Although Jewish circles showed some sympathy (e.g., E. Auerbach) for the documentary theory (Wellhausen was preceded by Jewish pioneers L. Zunz and A. Geiger), most Jewish scholars continued to defend Mosaic authorship (e.g., H. Wiener, M. Segal) or accent the unity of the present text while recognizing the diversity of the material contained therein (e.g., B. Jacob, M. Buber, U. Cassuto) and presented a modified version of the documentary theory: P is earlier than D; the Pentateuch is preexilic (Y. Kaufmann; cf. M. Weinfeld, M. Haran).

Certain scholars defended a completely new theory in combating the documentary hypothesis. B. Eerdman, for example, while fully recognizing the necessity of literary criticism, in conjunction with his concept that Israel's religion had been polytheistic until late times, advocated a kind of crystallization hypothesis. E. Robertson and R. Brinker defended the antiquity of the material in the Pentateuch: It was passed on in the various sanctuaries of ancient Israel after the entry into Canaan; Deuteronomy is the work of Samuel, etc. The new theories obtained little assent, however.

In the school of Kuenen/Wellhausen, the documentary theory was modified on the basis of continuing literary-critical investigation. Taking their cue from remarks in the work of the masters, they investigated the composition of the literary sources in minute detail, resulting in an atomistic analysis reminiscent of the fragmentary hypothesis and undermining the classical picture of the Pentateuch as the work of a limited number of authors, and with it the documentary hypothesis itself. This development evoked different reactions, including the development of a streamlined form of the documentary theory known as the newest documentary hypothesis, in which a fifth ancient source was reconstructed in addition to J, E, D, and P (R. Smend [son], O. Eissfeldt, G. Fohrer; cf. also J. Morgenstern, R. Pfeiffer, C. Simpson; different again J. Hempel); the tendency to limit the number of sources; the characterization of E as revising and supplementing (P. Volz, W. Rudolph, T. Vriezen, S. Mowinckel); and even the allotment to P. of such a status (Volz, Vriezen, I. Engnell; cf. M. Löhr). In this way the supplementary hypothesis was given a new lease on life after a fashion. The presence of the older strata outside the Hexateuch was defended by some authors (O. Eissfeldt, G. Hölscher, H. Schulte).

Gunkel and Gressmann directed their attention especially to the earliest stages of transmission. Inspired by them and by A. Alt, both G. von Rad and M. Noth have, each with his own emphasis, directed attention to the various stages of the process by which the Pentateuch came into being (*Überlieferungsgeschichte* [tradition history]). They held to the literary sources theory but gave this new content. Von Rad (1938) assigned J an important place in the Hexateuch's origin: Living at the time of David/Solomon, J expanded the canonical scheme of salvation history (which is rooted in the archaic cultic creed of Deut 25:5-9, itself a Hexateuch in a nutshell) with material from a very different provenance and is responsible for the *Einbau* of the initially independent Sinai tradition, for the *Ausbau* of the history of the patriarchs, and for the *Vorbau* of the pre-history. He made the variety of material serviceable to the theme dominating the scheme of salvation history, that of Landnahme. The addition of the E and P sources has not altered the picture drawn by J. In this fashion von Rad gave the supplementary hypothesis a new form.

Noth (1943; ET 1981) labeled Deuteronomy–Kings as a connected work and limited the presence of J, E, and P to the Tetrateuch. He postulated (1948; ET 1972) a communal substratum (*gemeinsame Grundlage* [G]) for J and E comprising the five main themes of the Pentateuch that had arisen in his proposed amphictony (1930) as a result of a growing mutual entanglement of the material transmitted by the unified tribes with the crystallization of the exodus tradition. These themes attracted much material from divergent provenance and probably received a settled form in the pre-literary phase of the transmission. J, E, and P were individual authors who each rendered the material with his own emphasis. Their work underlies the Pentateuch, which thus takes on the character of a collection.

Scandinavian scholars (J. Pedersen, I. Engnell) have also emphasized that the Pentateuch is the result of a complicated process of transmission. However, they opposed sharply the *interpretatio europeica moderna* of literary criticism, asserting that the material in the Pentateuch was transmitted between simultaneously coexisting circles and that in the transmission process archaic and later material congealed together. In connection with this they criticized Wellhausen's evolutionistic concept of Israel's religion. Pedersen initially regarded JE, D, and P as collections that obtained their present form in postexilic times but that are of pre- and postexilic date in terms of content. Engnell shared H. S. Nyberg's theory that the written HB was the creation of the postexilic Jewish community and that previously the oral transmission had been normative. His tradition-historical approach resulted in a new sources theory incorporating elements of the supplementary hypothesis: Genesis–Kings is composed of (a) a P work, the Tetrateuch, which has adopted JE material among other things, and (b) a D work, Deuteronomy–Kings, each of which received its definitive form in postexilic times. His views led some people to take into account not only written transmission in the origins of the Pentateuch but oral transmission as well (e.g., S. Mowinckel), and induced others to characterize the sources of the documentary hypothesis as streams of tradition (e.g., A. Bentzen, R. de Vaux).

In view of the fundamental place of Deuteronomy in Wellhausen's conception, it is understandable that much study has been made of this book. Points of investigation have been the problem of the extent of *Urdeuteronomium* and the relation of Deuteronomy to the Book of the Covenant, the Holiness Code, and the prophetic books (e.g., Jeremiah). The rejection of the identification of Deuteronomy with Josiah's law book already before Wellhausen (e.g., Reimarus, Gramberg, Vatke) was again brought up for discussion. A postexilic origin was defended (e.g., G. Berry, G. Hölscher, S. Mowinckel; O. Kaiser); and the idea that Deuteronomy imposed the centralization of the cult, an all-important point in Wellhausen's conception (T. Oestreicher, A. Welch, W. Stärk), was disputed. De Wette's notion regarding how Deuteronomy came into existence was mitigated before as well as after Wellhausen by the thesis that Deuteronomy had been assuming form since the time of Hezekiah or Manasseh. Ongoing literary-critical examination led to the explanation of Deuteronomy's origin by means of documentary and supplementary hypotheses, while form criticism and tradition criticism led to the conclusion that the book contains archaic material and is the result of a complicated process of transmission. Thus von Rad (1947) asserted that Deuteronomy is the product of a north Israelite restoration movement on the part of Levites, harking back to the traditions of the amphictyony. Other scholars as well abandoned the "classic" position that the book was the work of Jerusalemite priests and prophets in favor of a north Israelite origin. This theory has receded into the background, and M. Weinfeld's (1972) defense of authorship by scribes and wise men from Jerusalem court circles has received support from various quarters.

6. *Continuing Developments: Increasing Diversity of Opinion; Established Positions Subjected to Criticism.* Many scholars are now distancing themselves from representations initially accepted by those following in the footsteps of Noth and von Rad–e.g., the antiquity of the cultic creed, the institution of the amphictyony, and the independence of the Sinai tradition. Old problems like the character of E and P continue to be points of discussion, with the existence of E sometimes being doubted or denied (J. Van Seters; H. Schmid [1976]; M. Rose [1981]). The conception of P as a Bearbeitungsschicht (redactional layer; see sec. 5) has met with approval from various quarters, but it is also criticized (e.g., by J. Emerton [1988] and K. Koch [1987]); it even has been claimed that P continues as a source right into Kings (W. Resenhöfft [1977]).

The documentary theory is being presented again in new forms. P. Weimar and E. Zenger assign the Jehovist (JE) a prominent place in otherwise divergent conceptions. The suggestion (F. Winnett; cf. D. Redford, N. Wagner) that with regard to the Pentateuch's origin one should consider not merely the possible redactional combination of various sources but also the possibility of consecutive expansions/revisions of the material has found some approval (Van Seters, H. Schmitt, Kaiser). The existence of archaic layers is being denied. Even though there was never a full consensus on the dating of J and E, unanimity existed at least in the twentieth century as to their preexilic origin. This opinion is being surrendered. Van Seters (1975) and H. Schmid (1976), traveling different routes, have come to the conclusion that J ought to be dated in the exilic period. According to Van Seters (1992, 1994), the Deuteronomistic history (DtrH) is prior to J, who wrote his work in reaction to DtrH. (In comparison M. Rose [1981] maintains that the deuteronomistic history in older form is earlier than J, while C. Levin [1993] argues that Deuteronomy is prior to J and that J is earlier than or contemporary with the deuteronomistic history; Levin's J, however, differs from Van Seter's J in many respects). H. Vorländer (1978) advocates a dating in the exilic or postexilic period for the origin of JE.

These positions do not imply a radical break with the documentary theory, however. This is championed by R. Rendtorff (1977), who is of the opinion that consistent application of tradition criticism leads to the conclusion that there are no continuous layers in the Pentateuch and that the material is joined by priestly and deuteronomistic redactional notes (cf. E. Blum

[1984]), thereby returning, in fact, to the fragmentary theory. S. Tengström (1976, 1982), in contrast, maintains that a coherent epic underlies the Hexateuch. In his case the supplementary theory returns in a new form: A *Grunderzählung* (original narrative) from the eleventh century B.C.E. has been supplemented by deuteronomistic and priestly authors (L. Brisman [1990]; B. Renaud [1991]).

The documentary theory is being criticized, often in a fragmentary way. The argumentation on which the source theory rests is often dealt with to a limited degree or only partially, and questions are being left open. The newer positions have not yet crystallized; e.g., the consequences for the picture of Israel's religion are hardly dealt with. A comprehensive new conception has not been presented or has merely been given vague contours. Many elements in the approach and in the conclusions of the new studies are not new; instead, old ideas that were unable to achieve much recognition earlier are being defended in a new context and in sometimes varied forms. It is thus understandable that the documentary theory in its classic form continues to enjoy support as well, at least as far as the main issues are concerned (e.g., A. Gunneweg [1983, 1985]; E. Nicholson [1991]; L. Schmidt; W. Schmidt), since it continues to provide the most satisfactory answer to questions about the manner in which the Pentateuch came to be. Modified versions like the Jewish variant (see sec. 5) also still have their supporters (e.g., A. Hurvitz [1982]; J. Milgrom [1991]).

Next to the methods of textual investigation elicited by questioning the process of how the Pentateuch came into being (diachronic approach), there is a growing interest in new forms of textual analysis in reaction to the atomistic approach, which has played the leading role in HB studies. This shift has taken place under the influence of Jewish biblical interpretation (see sec. 5), literature studies, and linguistics, and as a result of the focus on scripture as canon. An important common feature of these new forms of textual analysis, whose great diversity is indicated by the names under which they are presented (rhetorical criticism, canonical criticism, stylistic and structural analysis, the logotechnical method [C. Schedl; C. J. Labuschagne, 1985], etc.), is the extensive consideration of problems of textual form and function in the present form of the Pentateuch, especially in its narrative sections. Sometimes this focus on the Pentateuch in its present form is accompanied by criticism of traditional methods and/or deliberately leaving the results of traditional methods outside of consideration (e.g., K. Deurloo and other members of the Amsterdam School; J. Fokkelman [1975]; R. Alter [1981]; R. Alter and F. Kermode [1988]). Sometimes the intention is to do justice to a neglected aspect of Pentateuch studies, and the idea is (formulated in terms of literary criticism) to draw attention to the redactional activity to which the Pentateuch owes its definitive form (e.g., B. Anderson [1978]; D. Clines [1978]; B. Childs [1974]; G. Coats; I. Kikawada and A. Quinn [1985]; R. Moberly [1983]; G. Rendsburg [1986]). Not only the narrative sections but also Pentateuchal law is made the object of stylistic, structural, and redactional analysis (e.g., by E. Otto [1989]; Y. Osumi; L. Schwienhorst-Schönberger [1990]), in combination with a renewed interest in the relation of the Pentateuchal legal collections to each other and to the ancient Near Eastern law traditions (e.g., R. Westbrook [1988]) and with special attention to OT law history (e.g., F. Crüsemann [1992]).

Bibliography: D. Ackermann, *August Klostermann und der Pentateuch: ein forschungs-geschichtlicher Beitrag zum Pentateuchproblem* (1997). **R. Alter**, *The Art of Biblical Narrative* (1981). **B. W. Anderson**, "From Analysis to Synthesis: The Interpretation of Genesis 1–11," *JBL* 97 (1978) 23-39. **J. Astruc**, *Conjectures sur les mémoires originaux dont il parait que Moise s'est servi pour composer la Genèse, avec des remarques qui appuient ou éclaireissent ces conjectures* (1753). **A. G. Auld**, "Keeping Up with Recent Studies VI: The Pentateuch," *ExpTim* 91 (1979–80) 297-302. **J. Blenkinsopp**, The Pentateuch: An Introduction to the First Five

Books of the Bible (1992); "Introduction to the Pentateuch," *NIB* (1994) 1:305-18. **E. Blum**, *Die Komposition der Vätergeschichte* (WMANT 57, 1984); *Studien zur Komposition des Pentateuch* (BZAW 189, 1990). **L. Brisman**, *The Voice of Jacob: On the Composition of Genesis* (1990). **F. Campbell** and **M. A. O'Brien**, *Sources of the Pentateuch: Texts, Introductions, Annotations* (1993). **H. Cazalles**, "Pentateuque," *DBSup* 7, 709-858. **B. S. Childs**, *The Book of Exodus: A Critical, Theological Commentary* (OTL, 1974); *Introduction to the OT as Scripture* (1979). **D. J. A. Clines**, *The Theme of the Pentateuch* (JSOTSup 10, 1978). **G. W. Coats**, *From Canaan to Egypt: Structural and Theological Context for the Joseph Story* (CBQMS 4, 1976); *Moses: Heroic Man, Man of God* (JSOTSup 57, 1988). **F. Crüsemann**, *Das Deuteronomium: Entstehung, Gestalt, und Botschaft* (ed. N. Lohfink, BETL 68, 1985); *Die Tora: Theologie und Sozialgeschichte des alttestamentlichen Gesetzes* (1992). **F. H. Cryer**, "On the Relationship Between the Yahwistic and the Deuteronomistic Histories," *BN* 29 (1985) 58-74. **S. J. De Vries**, "Kuenen's Pentateuchal Research in Comparison with Recent Pentateuchal Studies in North America," *Abraham Kuenen* (1828–91) (OTS 29, ed. P. Dirksen and A. Kooij, 1993) 128-47. **W. De Wette**, *Beiträge zur Einleitung in das AT* (2 vols., 1806–7). **L. Diestel**, *Geschichte des Alten Testaments in der christlichen Kirche* (1869). **T. B. Dozeman**, *God on the Mountain: A Study of Redaction, Theology, and Canon in Exodus 19–24* (1989). **J. G. Eichhorn**, *Introduction to the Study of the OT* (3 vols., 1780–83; ET 1888). **J. A. Emerton**, "An Examination of Some Attempts to Defend the Unity of the Flood Narrative in Genesis," *VT* 37 (1987) 401-20; "The Priestly Writer in Genesis," *JTS* 39 (1988) 381-400. **J. P. Fokkelman**, *Narrative Art in Genesis: Specimens of Stylistic and Structural Analysis* (1975). **T. E. Fretheim**, *The Pentateuch* (IBT, 1996). **R. E. Friedman**, "Torah (Pentateuch)," *ABD* (1992) 6:605-22. G. Garbini, "Torah e Mosè," *Pentateucho come Torah* (ed. B. G. Boschi, 1991) 83-96. **A.-A. García Santos**, *El Pentateuco: Historia y Sentido* (Horizonte Dos Mil: Textos y Monografías 12, 1998). **A. Geddes**, *Genesis–Joshua* (1792); *Critical Remarks on the Hebrew Scriptures: Corresponding with a New Translation of the Bible* (1800). **P. Gooder**, *The Pentateuch: A Story of Beginnings* (Continuum Bible Studies, 2000). **F. V. Greifenhagen**, *Egypt on the Pentateuch's Ideological Map: Constructing Biblical Israel's Identity* (JSOTSup 361, 2002). **A. H. J. Gunneweg**, "Ammerkungen und Anfragen zur neueren Pentateuchforschung," *TRu* 48 (1983) 227-53; *50* (1985) 107-31. **C. Houtman**, *Der Pentateuch: Die Geschichte seiner Erforschung neben einer Auswertung* (CBET 9, 1994); *Das Bundesbuch: Ein Kommentar* (DMOA 24, 1997) 7-48. **H. C. K. F. Hupfeld**, *Die Quellen der Genesis und die Art ihrer Zusammensetzung* (1853). **A. Hurvitz**, *A Linguistic Study of the Relationship Between the Priestly Source and the Book of Ezekiel: A New Approach to an Old Problem* (1982). **I. M. Kikawada** and **A. Quinn**, *Before Abraham Was: The Unity of Genesis 1–11* (1985). **D. A. Knight**, "The Pentateuch," *The HB and Its Modern Interpreters* (ed. D. A. Knight and G. M. Tucker, 1985) 263-96. **K. Koch**, "P—kein Redaktor! Erinnerung an zwei Eckdaten der Quellenscheidung," *VT* 37 (1987) 446-67. **H. J. Kraus**, *Geschichte der historisch-kritischen Erforschung des Alten Testaments* (1982). **C. J. Labuschagne**, "The Literary and Theological Function of Divine Speech in the Pentateuch" (VTSup 36, 1985) 154-72; "Neue Wege und Perspektiven in der Pentateuchforschung," *VT* 36 (1986) 146-62. **C. Levin**, *Der Jahwist* (FRLANT 157, 1993). **J. J. McDermott**, *Reading the Pentateuch: A Historical Introduction* (2002). **E. McQueen Gray**, *OT Criticism: Its Rise and Progress* (1923). **J. Milgrom**, *Leviticus 1–16* (AB, 1991) 3-51. **R. W. L. Moberly**, *At the Mountain of God: Story and Theology in Exodus 32–34* (JSOTSup 22, 1983). **A. R. Möller**, "Der Text als russische Puppe?" *BN* 17 [1982] 56-72); *Die Meerwundererzählung: Eine Redaktionskritische Analyse von Exod 13,17-14,31* (1985). **H. Najman**, *Seconding Sinai: The Development of Mosaic Discourse in Second Temple Judaism* (JSJSup 77, 2002). **E. W. Nicholson**, "The Pentateuch in Recent Research: A Time for Caution," VTSup 43 (1991) 10-21; *The Pentateuch in the Twentieth Century: The Legacy of J. Wellhausen* (1998). **M. Noth**, *Das System der zwölf*

Stämme Israels (BWANT 4,1, 1930); *The Deuteronomistic History* (1943; JSOTSup 15, 1981, 1991; *A History of the Pentateuchal Traditions* (1948; ET 1972). **Y. Osumi**, *Die Kompositionsgeschichte des Bundesbuches Exodus 20,22b–23,33* (OBO 105, 1991); *Le Pentateuque en question: Les origines et la composition des cinq premiers livres de la Bible á la lumière des recherches récentes* (ed. A. de Pury, 1991); *Le Pentateuque: Débats et recherches* (ed. P. Haudebert, 1992). **E. Otto**, *Wandel der Rechtsbegründungen in der Gesellschaftsgeschichte des Antiken Israel: Eine Rechtsgeschichte des "Bundesbuches" Exod 20:22–23:13* (1988); *Rechtsgeschichte der Redaktionen im Kodex Ešnunna und im "Bundesbuch": Eine redaktionsgeschichtliche und rechstvergleichende Studie zu altbabylonischen und altisraelitischen Rechtsüberlieferungen* (OBO 85, 1989); *Körperverletzungen in den Keilschriftrechten und im Alten Testament: Studien zum Rechtstransfer im Alten Testament* (1991); "Vom Bundesbuch zum Deuteronomium: Die deuteronomische Redaktion in Deut 12–26," *Biblische Theologie und gesellschaftlicher Wandel: für N. Lohfink S.J.* (ed. G. Braulik et al., 1993); "Gesetzesfortschreibung und Pentateuchredaktion," *ZAW* 107 (1995) 373-92; "Kritik der Pentateuchkomposition," *TRu* 60 (1995) 163-91; *Das Deuteronomium im Pentateuch und Hexateuch: Studien zur Literaturgeschichte von Pentateuch und Hexateuch im Lichte des Deuteronomimrahmens* (FAT 30, 2000); *Die Tora des Mose: die Geschichte der literarischen Vermittlung von Recht, Religon und Poltik durch die Mosegestalt* (2001). **I. Pardes**, *The Biography of Ancient Israel: National Narratives in the Bible* (Contraversions 14, 2000). **G. von Rad**, *Das formgeschichtliche Problem des Hexateuch* (BWANT 78, 1938; ET 1965). **B. Renaud**, *La théophanie du Sinai: Exod 19–24, exégèse et théologie* (1991). **G. A. Rendsburg**, *The Redaction of Genesis* (1986). **R. Rendtorff**, *The Problem of the Process of Transmission in the Pentateuch* (BZAW 147, 1977; ET, JSOTSup 89, 1990); "The Future of Pentateuchal Criticism," *Henoch* 6 (1984) 1-15; *Leviticus* (BKAT 3, 1, 1985) 1-12. **W. Resenhöfft**, *Die Genesis im Wortlaut ihrer drei Quellenschriften: Studien zur Integral-Analyse des Enneateuchs* (1974); *Die Geschichte Alt-Israels: Die Quellenschriften der Bücher Genesis bis Könige im deutschen Wortlaut isoliert 1-4* (1977); *Nachträge zur Textgestaltung der Geschichte Alt-Israels* (1979); *Die Quellenberichte im Joseph-Sinai-Komplex (Gen 37 bis Exod 24, mit 32-34)* (1983). **A. Rofé**, *Introduction to the Composition of the Pentateuch* (Biblical Seminar 58, 1999). **J. W. Rogerson**, *OT Criticism in the Nineteenth Century: England and Germany* (1984); *The Pentateuch* (BiSe 39, 1996). **T. Römer**, *Israels Väter: Untersuchungen zur Väterthematik im Deuteronomium und in der deuteronomistischen Tradition* (OBO 99, 1990). **M. Rose**, *Deuteronomist and Jahwist: Untersuchungen zu den Berührungspunkten beider Literaturwerke* (ATANT 67, 1981). **H. Rouillard**, *La péricope de Balaam (Nombres 22–24)* (1985). **L. Ruppert**, "Die Aporie der gegenwärtigen Pentateuch-diskussion und die Josepherzälung der Genesis," *BZ* 29 (1985) 31-48; "Zur neueren Diskussion um die Josefsgeschichte der Genesis," *BZ* 33 (1989) 92-97. **H. Schmid**, *Die Gestalt des Mose: Probleme alttestamentlicher Forschung unter Berücksichtigung der Pentateuchkrise* (1986). **H. H. Schmid**, *Der sogenannte Jahwist: Beobachtungen und Fragen zur Pentateuchforschung* (1976); "Auf der Suche nach neuen Perspektiven für die Pentateuchforschung" in *Volume du congrès* (ed. International Organization for the Study of Old Testament; VTSup 32, 1981) 375-94. **L. Schmidt**, *Literarische Studien zur Josephsgeschichte* (BZAW 167, 1986); "Jakob erschleicht sich den väterlichen Segen: Literarkritik und Redaktion von Genesis 27,1-45," *ZAW* 100 (1988) 159-83; *Beobachtungen zu der Plagenerzählung in Exodus VII 14–XI 10* (1990). **W. H. Schmidt**, "Ein Theologe in salomonischer Zeit? Plädoyer für den Jahwisten," *BZ* 25 (1981) 82-102; "Plädoyer für die Quellenscheidung," *BZ* 32 (1988) 1-14; "Elementare Erwägungen zur Quellenscheidung im Pentateuch," VTSup 43 (1991) 22-45. **H. C. Schmitt**, *Die nichtpriesterliche Josephsgeschichte: Ein Beitrag zur neuesten Pentateuchkritik* (BZAW 154, 1980); "Die Hintergründe der 'neuesten Pentateuchkritik' und der literarische Befund der Josefsgeschichte,

Gen 37–50," *ZAW* 97 (1985) 161-79; "Die Erzählung von der Versuchung Abrahams, Gen 22,1-19 und das Problem einer Theologie der elohistischen Pentateuchtexte," *BN* 34 (1986) 82-109. **B. J. Schwartz**, "The Priestly Account of the Theophany and Lawgiving at Sinai," *Texts, Temples, and Traditions: A Tribute to M. Haran* (ed. M. V. Fox et al., 1996) 103-34. **L. Schwienhorst-Schönberger**, *Das Bundesbuch (Exod 20,22–23,33): Studien zu seiner Entstehung und Theologie* (BZAW 188, 1990). **R. Smend**, "Ein halbes Jahrhundert alttestamentliche Einleitungswissenschaft," *TRu* 49 (1984) 3-30; *Deutsche Alttestamentler in drei Jahrhunderten: Mit 18 Abbildungen* (1989); *Epochen der Bibelkritik* (1991). **K. L. Sparks**, *The Pentateuch: An Annotated Bibliography* (2002). **S. O. Steingrimsson**, *Vom Zeichen zur Geschichte: Ein literar- und formkritische Untersuchung* (1979), on Exod 6:28–11:10; *Studies in the Book of Exodus: Redaction, Reception, Interpretation* (ed. M. Vervenne, BETL 126, 1996). **S. Tengström**, *Die Hexateucherzählung: Eine literaturgeschichtliche Studie* (1976); *Die Toledotformel und die literarische Struktur der priesterlichen Erweiterungsschicht im Pentateuch* (1981). **R. J. Thompson**, *Moses and the Law in a Century of Criticism Since Graf* (VTSup 19, 1970). **T. L. Thompson**, *The Origin of Ancient Israel, vol. 1, The Literary Formation of Genesis and Exodus 1–23* (JSOTSup 55, 1987). **J. Van Seters**, *Abraham in History and Tradition* (1975); *Prologue to History: The Yahwist as Historian in Genesis* (1992); *The Life of Moses: The Yahwist as Historian in Exodus–Numbers* (1994). **J. S. Vater**, *Commentar über den Pentateuch* (1802–05). **J. Vermeylen**, "La Formation du Pentateuque á la lumière de l'exégèse historico-critique," *RTL* 12 (1981) 324-46; *Voices from Amsterdam: A Modern Tradition of Reading Biblical Narrative* (ed. M. Kessler, 1994). **H. Vorländer**, *Die Entstehungszeit des jehowistischen Geschichtswerkes* (1978). **J. W. Watts**, Reading Law: The Rhetorical Shaping to the Pentateuch (Biblical Seminar 59, 1999); (ed.), *Persia and Torah: the Theory of Imperial Authorization of the Pentateuch* (SBLSymS 17, 2001). **P. Weimar**, *Untersuchungen zur Redaktionsgeschichte des Pentateuch* (BZAW 146, 1977); *Die Berufung des Mose: Literaturwissenschaftliche Analyse von Exodus 2,23–5,5* (OBO 32, 1980; cf. **J. Wellhausen**, *Prolegomena to the History of Israel* (1878; ET 1885). **G. J. Wenham**, "Method in Pentateuchal Criticism," *VT* 41 (1991) 84-109. **J. W. Wesselius**, *The Origin of the History of Israel: Herodotus's Histories as the Blueprint for the First Books of the Bible* (JSOTSup 345, 2002). **R. Westbrook**, *Studies in Biblical and Cuneiform Law* (1988). **R. N. Whybray**, *The Making of the Pentateuch: A Methodological Study* (JSOTSup 53, 1987); *Introduction to the Pentateuch* (1995). **E. Zenger**, "Wo steht die Pentateuch forschung heute?" *BZ* 24 (1980) 101-16; "Auf der Suche nach einem Weg aus der Pentateuchkrise," *TRev* 78 (1982) 353-62; *Israel am Sinai: Analysen und Interpretationen zu Exodus 17–34* (1985).

C. HOUTMAN

Poetry in the Hebrew Bible

Poetry is notoriously difficult to define; and so it is not surprising that it has not always been clear—nor is it now—what constitutes biblical poetry. The Bible sometimes employs terms like *šîr*, *mizmôr*, and *qînâ* in reference to songs, hymns, and laments, respectively; but these terms are lacking in many passages that have been deemed poetry by later interpreters. That is to say, the Bible seems to recognize some forms of poetry, but its terminology, and therefore presumably its literary concepts, does not correlate exactly with the modern literary genre of poetry. This article will offer a sketch of the major trends in the identification and analysis of biblical poetry from the post-biblical period to the present.

1. *The Graphic Presentation of Poems*. There is a scribal tradition, witnessed in manuscripts from Qumran, in medieval Masoretic manuscripts, and in Talmudic references, of setting off certain poems from the discourse surrounding them. Two visual patterns were used. One is, in rabbinic terminology, "small brick over large brick, large brick over small"—that is, an interlocking construction diagrammed either as:

or as:

The other is "small brick over small, large over large," producing two columns with space between them:

The poems most often presented in one or the other of these graphic forms are Exod 15:1-18; Deuteronomy 32; Judges 5; and 2 Samuel 22. In some manuscripts many more texts are written stichographically (arranged in rows or alternating verses), including the books of Psalms, Proverbs, Job, and occasionally Lamentations. Although the writing appears to be stichometric, a line of writing does not always correspond to a poetic line, so that while this scribal tradition may be helpful in adducing what the ancients considered to be poetry, it does not necessarily preserve structural or metrical features of the poems. It is even questionable whether the scribes intended to indicate poetry per se by the use of these patterns, for they also used the second pattern for lists like the kings of Canaan (Josh 12:9-24) and the sons of Haman (Esth 9:7-9). Perhaps these patterns were intended to set off, through visual means, texts that were in some way felt to be different from what surrounded them, but it is not clear why only certain poems and lists were marked in this manner.

With the advent of printing, the convention changed. Most printed Masoretic Bibles abandoned the stichographic presentation of Psalms, Proverbs, and Job and preserved only those passages the Talmud required to be written stichographically: the Song of the Sea (Exod 15:1-18), the Song of Deborah (Judges 5), and the lists in Joshua 12 and Esther 9.

Modern scholarly editions of the Bible have reversed this trend. In *Biblia Hebraica* and *Biblia Hebraica Stuttgartensia*, not only are the traditionally stichographic sections so printed, but in addition everything considered poetic by modern standards, including the speeches of the classical prophets and small "poems" within narratives, like 1 Sam 15:22-23, is printed stichographically.

2. *The Masoretic Accents.* In the Tiberian Masorah the books of Psalms, Proverbs, and Job are accented differently from the other twenty-one books of the HB. It is not clear whether this is a generic distinction or whether the accents have to do only with cantillation. Some scholars feel that some information about poetic meter may be recoverable from the accentual system.

The evidence from ancient times, as preserved in manuscripts and in the Masorah, is inconsistent and inconclusive regarding the recognition of poetry. Yet there arose early in the history of biblical interpretation the notion that the Bible contains poetry. Its definition and description varied from time to time and place to place depending on the investigator's own cultural milieu and stance vis-à-vis the Bible.

3. *The Influence of Classical Poetry and Rhetoric.* The spread of Greek culture into the Jewish world (and the spread of Jews into the Greek world) inevitably brought readers of the Bible into contact with the Greek idea of *poiesis*, which was then superimposed onto the Bible. Themes and subjects considered proper to Greek poetry were found to be poetic in the Bible as well; and meter, well defined and developed by the Greeks, was ascribed to biblical poems. The leading exponents of this approach were Philo and Josephus, who sought to interpret the Bible as a whole in a way meaningful to a Hellenistic audience.

The early church, which adopted the allegorical method of interpretation prevalent in the Greek period, also adopted much of the appreciation of Greek poetic forms. Church fathers (Origen, Eusebius, and others) spoke of poetic meter and tropes in connection with the psalms and with pericopes like Deuteronomy 32. Jerome, who was schooled in and admired Latin poetry, found its features, especially meter, to be present in, indeed surpassed by, the poetry of the Bible. Theodore of Mopsuestia noted the rhetorical use of certain types of repetition or parallelism, and Augustine spoke of meter and poetic figures in the Bible. To be sure, much of the church fathers' discussions of biblical poetry was designed to neutralize the tension between the attraction to and the rejection of secular (i.e., pagan) literature and to overcome the perceived lack of aesthetic appeal of the Bible (as judged by classical standards). Nevertheless, this early focus on meter and certain tropes that were later subsumed under parallelism represents a sustained effort at poetic analysis.

4. *Medieval Jewish Commentaries.* Although early Christian interpreters had no difficulty in seeing rhetorical tropes and figures in the Bible, their rabbinic contemporaries largely ignored these stylistic aspects. This silence regarding biblical poetry continued, for the most part, in the medieval Jewish commentaries, not so much due to literary ignorance as to different hermeneutic principles. For Jewish exegetes every word of scripture had its own significance; words and phrases were never just "decorative" stylistic devices but always bore some specific meaning. This interpretive approach had the effect of limiting the recognition and analysis of poetry. Medieval Jewish commentators did not seek to distinguish literary genres, let alone to define

346

the essential features of poetry. Nevertheless, one does find among some commentators, especially those from the Sephardic communities, an awareness of stylistic and poetic matters. A. Ibn Ezra and Rashbam, the grandson of Rashi and a leading Ashkenazic authority, noted that a certain amount of repetition and/or parallelism was stylistic and did not necessarily add new information. Abravanel, in his commentary on Exodus 15 and Isaiah 5, discussed at some length the types of biblical poems.

5. *The Influence of Arabic and Medieval Hebrew Poetry.* It is not so much in exegetical works as in separate philosophical and rhetorical treatises that one finds the medieval and Renaissance Jewish perceptions of biblical poetry. These treatises, written by Jews living in the Arab world, reflect the influence of the flourishing tradition of Arabic and medieval Hebrew poetry. Among them are the works of Saadia Gaon, Judah Halevi, and Moses ibn Habib. The only major work devoted entirely to Hebrew poetics is Moses ibn Ezra's *Kitab al-Muḥādarâ wa al-Mudhākarâ*, which is concerned mostly with the poetry of his day; but it was only natural that the features valued in Arabic rhetoric and also in medieval Hebrew poetry should be sought in the Bible. They were not always found, however. Ibn Ezra stated that the only poetry in the Bible is Psalms, Job, and Proverbs (the books with a special system of Masoretic accents) and that even these lack meter and rhyme, the two basic characteristics of Arabic poetry. As for stylistic repetition in the Bible, he apologetically noted that it is not bad style in the Bible, even though it was not acceptable in Arabic rhetoric. Jewish writers like ibn Ezra did not feel the same conflict between secular poetry and holy scripture as the church fathers did, but they strove to prove the superiority of Hebrew poetry to Arabic poetry and of biblical style to the style of the Quran.

It was not only the existence of vibrant contemporary poetic activity that impelled the search for poetry in the Bible. There was also the existence of the biblical term *šîr*, "song," which was equated with Arabic *shi'r*, "poetry"; the stichographic writing of certain biblical passages; and the Talmudic references to ten biblical songs. This meant that there must be poetry in the Bible. The problem was to identify it and to explain what made it poetic. Several types of answers were given: Poetry consisted of figurative language; biblical poetry originally had meter, but it was lost; *šîr* means something sung and does not imply meter; biblical poems do have meter in the sense that the lines are divided into two parts (like Arabic poems), even though the parts do not correspond in terms of long and short syllables (see J. Kugel [1981] 187-200).

These conclusions sound remarkably modern; indeed, they are still being put forth by some contemporary scholars. However, an important part of the modern definition of biblical poetry was yet to come. It was heralded by the work of Azariah dei Rossi.

6.*Azariah dei Rossi.* An Italian rabbi, dei Rossi exemplifies Renaissance scholarship. The citations in his Meor Ena yim (1573) reflect his wide-ranging knowledge of religious and secular literature, including classical and early Christian authors as well as rabbinic texts and the works of the Jewish scholars of medieval Spain. He agreed that the Bible contained poetry and that the poetry was *metrical*; according to his innovative definition of metrical, however, the meter of biblical poems was not based on the number of syllabic feet, but rather on the number of "ideas" or thought-units in each sentence or clause. Exempting certain words (like the introductory "he said" in Deut 32:20) from the metrical count, he found a general regularity in the number of ideas in the two halves of a verse and also saw that this number could change throughout the poem. Although he did not make extraordinary claims for his system—he admitted that it failed to fit numerous verses—it became one of the forerunners to studies of parallelism (it was known to R. Lowth through J. Buxtorf's translation, appended to his *Liber Cosri*) and also anticipated systems of thought-unit meter.

7. *Christian Schoettgen.* Another of Lowth's precursors was Schoettgen, who in his *Horae Hebraicae et Talmudicae* (1733) laid down a series of rules relating to exergasia, the trope in

which sentences with the same meaning are joined together (later known as parallelism). The prominence given to parallelism as opposed to meter and the categories corresponding to "synonymous" and "antithetic" are harbingers of Lowth, while the analysis of forms with ellipses and/or additions anticipates G. Gray's "complete," "incomplete," and "with/without compensation" forms of parallelism (1915, repr. 1972). But although Schoettgen's view of parallelism was extremely sophisticated, he considered parallelism to be a trope of Hebrew rhetoric, not a basic structural feature of poetry.

8. *Robert Lowth.* The work of Lowth is generally taken as the starting point in the modern study of biblical poetry. His main contribution was his definition and analysis of parallelismus membrorum in his *De sacra poesi hebraeorum* (*Lectures on the Sacred Poetry of the Hebrews* [1753]) and *Isaiah: A New Translation with a Preliminary Dissertation and Notes, Critical, Philological, and Exegetical* (1778). The introductory chapter of the latter work contains his definition of parallelism, which has become classic: "The correspondence of one Verse, or Line, with another I call Parallelism. When a proposition is delivered, and a second is subjoined to it, or drawn under it, equivalent, or contrasted with it in Sense; or similar to it in the form of Grammatical Construction; these I call Parallel Lines; and the words or phrases answering one to another in the corresponding Lines Parallel Terms" (see Lecture 19 of Lectures).

Lowth subdivided parallelism into three types: synonymous, antithetic, and synthetic. In synonymous parallelism the same sense is expressed in different, but equivalent, terms as in Ps 114:1:

When Israel went out from Egypt,
the house of Jacob from a strange people.

In antithetic parallelism "a thing is illustrated by its contrary being opposed to it" as in Prov 27:6:

The blows of a friend are faithful;
But the kisses of an enemy are treacherous.

Synthetic parallelism consists of similar constructions or a general correspondence of the lines but not a correspondence between all of the terms. Ecclesiastes 11:2 illustrates:

Give a portion to seven, and also to eight;
For you do not know what evil shall be upon the earth.

As a result of Lowth's lectures, the study of poetry shifted from the search for meter to the analysis of parallelism. This is not to say that meter was forgotten (Lowth thought that Hebrew poetry had meter but that it was irretrievable), but just that the analysis of parallelism proved more rewarding. Another important contribution by Lowth, which grew out of his concentration on parallelistic expression, was his inclusion of prophetic speech in the genre of poetry.

9. *Modern Influences on the Study of Poetry.* The study of biblical poetry has usually meant the study of its formal features. But first should be mentioned, however briefly, some of the trends in biblical studies and in literary criticism that have shaped the general stance on poetry and determined which of its aspects were to be examined.

Lowth is included among the Romantics—those whose historical research and critical examination did not prevent them from elevating the imaginative and emotional side of literary expression. For them Hebrew poetry was "sublime"—a term Lowth used repeatedly and defined as "that force of composition ... which strikes and overpowers the mind, which excites

348

the passions and which expresses ideas at once with perspicuity and elevation" (Lecture 14). The authors of this poetry led a simple pastoral life unencumbered by the "studies and pursuits" of later civilizations (Lecture 7) and thus epitomized the "natural man" idealized in the Romantic period.

As for the place of biblical poetry in the study of the history of literature, "the sacred Poetry is undoubtedly entitled to the first rank in this school since from it we are to learn both the origin of the art and how to estimate its excellence" (Lecture 2). Similar thoughts were expressed by Lowth's more influential German contemporary J. G. Herder in his *Vom Geist der ebraischen Poesie* (1782). Lowth's lectures, which had inspired Herder, were published in a German translation together with Herder's book in 1793. This attitude toward Hebrew poetry continued in the work of early nineteenth-century scholars and is witnessed in numerous commentaries on Psalms produced during this period.

Toward the end of the nineteenth century and the beginning of the twentieth, a new emphasis can be discerned. The interest in evolutionary development quickened in this post-Darwinian age, and earlier stages were viewed as more "primitive" than later ones. Since most biblicists were also orientalists—i.e., knowledgeable in Arabic and often travelers to the Middle East—and, in addition, were influenced by the newly emerging disciplines of linguistics and folklore, they could not resist comparisons between "primitive Hebrews" and the Arab culture they witnessed. The comparisons pertained to philology as well as to what T. Cheyne called "comparative ethnic-psychology." As J. Wellhausen put it: "I have no doubt that the original gifts and ideas of the Primitive Hebrews can most readily be understood by comparing Arabian antiquity" (quoted in Cheyne [1893] 73).

The late Victorian view of Hebrew poetry is perhaps best summed up by G. A. Smith in the 1910 Schweich lectures (pub. 1912): "All these facts of the language and syntax warn us not to expect in Hebrew poetry the regular, intricate and delicate metres of the Aryan styles. We are dealing with a people originally nomadic and to the end unskilled in architecture or any elaborate art. The essential looseness of their life, visible in their language, was bound to affect the highest achievements of their literature. When they did concentrate their minds on utterance, their earnestness would appear less in a passion for beauty than in a sense of urgency and responsibility. Israel was a people of prophets rather than poets" (10). Gone here is the celebration of the simple life and the Hebrew poetic genius.

One cannot discuss the history of the study of biblical poetry without mentioning the work of H. Gunkel on Psalms (1926, 1933). Gunkel, the father of form criticism, was sensitive to the Bible's literary aspects. He proposed a new classification system for the psalms that was to replace the Greek types (lyric, didactic, elegiac, etc.) widely used until then. Based on their content and to some extent on formulaic phrases, five main types of psalms plus a number of subtypes and mixed types were isolated. The main types were hymn, community lament, individual lament, individual thanksgiving song, and royal psalm. Form criticism aims to understand a work in relation to its original life setting, and so this approach stimulated studies of the place of the psalms in Israel's worship, along with a continued interest in the dating of the psalms and other poetry. In addition, because it was intent on finding generic patterns and formulas, it promoted the discovery of recurring phrases and usages and the analysis of the structure of poems.

While form criticism sought the common elements in various poems, rhetorical criticism shifted the emphasis to the distinctive usages in each poem. In a separate but similar move, those more familiar with literary criticism applied the approaches of New Criticism and *Werkinterpretation*, especially the technique of close reading. This produced a number of significant studies of biblical poetry and literary analyses of poetic texts. Notable are those by M. Weiss (1962), L. Alonso-Schökel (1963), and R. Alter (1985). These works not only advanced the interpretation of biblical poetry but also were important landmarks in the rise of literary approaches to the entire Bible. Concurrently, the following theories of oral composition and structural linguistics influenced the study of biblical poetry.

10. *Post-Lowthian Descriptions of the Formal Features of Biblical Poetry*. The recognition of poetry implies distinguishing it from other forms of literary discourse on the basis of formal criteria. Biblical poetry, at least since the time of Lowth, has been perceived as consisting of two formal features: meter and parallelism. Various descriptions give prominence to one or the other, but both are usually present to some degree. Both require the identification of the poetic line or set of lines (cola). Meter measures units within a line; parallelism describes the relationship between lines.

a. *Meter*. It has been difficult, if not impossible, for many scholars to conceive of poetry (or, more properly, verse) without meter; but what exactly was to be metered, or measured, in biblical poetry has rarely met with scholarly consensus. Numerous systems have been proposed, each differing from the others in some manner; in general they fall into one of three groups: accentual meter, syllabic meter, or word/thought-unit meter.

Accentual meter is the system advocated by J. Ley, E. Sievers (1901), and K. Budde (1882). This system counts only accented syllables, ignoring unaccented ones. Budde's contribution was the identification of *qînâ* meter, a line of three accented syllables followed by a line of two accented syllables, which is characteristic of laments.

The system in which all syllables are counted regardless of their length is syllabic meter. Associated with W. F. Albright and his students F. M. Cross and D. N. Freedman (1975), this system often involves the reconstruction of the original (pre-Masoretic) pronunciation. A combination of accentual and syllabic meter is alternating meter, proposed by S. Segert (1953, 1957), in which all syllables are counted and the stress is placed on the primary and secondary natural tones. The meter is then found to be one of alternating off/on stresses. None of these metric systems produced a scansion that was consistent throughout a poem or body of poems.

Another group of scholars subordinated meter to parallelism. They found that such meter as existed was really the rhythmic effect created by virtue of the fact that each set of lines (usually forming a parallelism) contained roughly the same number of thought-units or word-units. Thus a system of phonologic regularities, i.e., meter, was seen as deriving from semantic factors rather than from purely phonological ones. This is reminiscent of dei Rossi.

Two newer approaches to the question of meter deserve mention. Both introduce syntax into the search for meter and are thereby witnesses to the growing influence of linguistics on the study of biblical poetry. J. Kurylowicz has suggested that each word-complex, as defined by grammatical criteria, has one metrically significant accent. This is called the *accentus dominus*. Other accented syllables, called *accenti servi*, are subordinate. Kurylowicz's system replaces the semantic criteria of thought-unit meter with grammatical criteria. It also differentiates between accented syllables that are metrically significant and those that are not, thereby distinguishing meter, which constitutes a special use of phonology, from the general phonological workings of Hebrew.

In a step even farther removed from the measuring of phonological features, M. O'Connor (1980) has replaced the notion of meter with a system of syntactic constraints by which he defines a line of poetry. He finds that no line contains more than three clause predicators; no line contains fewer than one or more than four constituents (verb or nominal phrase plus dependent particles); and no line contains fewer than two or more than five units (individual verb or noun plus dependent particles). This description views syntactic regularity as primary and phonologic regularity as secondary. If Kurylowicz can be said to have replaced thought-units with grammatical units, O'Connor can be said to have replaced phonologic measurement with syntactic measurement.

b. *Parallelism*. Parallelism is often drawn into the search for meter, but it can and should be divorced from it, although not from the description of poetry as a whole. Since Lowth, it has been recognized as the dominant characteristic of biblical poetry; and the analysis of it, until the last decades of the twentieth century, derived directly from Lowth's definition and typology. The correspondence of line with line and word with word of which Lowth spoke was generally understood as sameness or identity by most of Lowth's successors, so the emphasis was put on the synonymity or redundancy in parallelism. At the same time closer inspection showed that within, or in addition to, Lowth's three major categories other categories could be found. Gray introduced the terms "complete" and "incomplete" parallelism "with or without compensation" to describe the lack of exact identity in some parallel terms. Others noted various structural types, e.g., chiastic parallelism, staircase parallelism, emblematic parallelism, janus parallelism. The typologies describing the relationship between parallel lines became more and more refined.

Emphasis turned from the lines to the terms in the wake of the discovery of Ugaritic poetry and the ascendency of the Parry-Lord theory of oral composition. It was noticed that Ugaritic poetry used many of the same sets of parallel terms that were found in the Bible, e.g., day/night, gold/silver, heaven/earth. Those sets of recurring words came to be known as "fixed word pairs" and were thought to be the functional equivalents of the formulas in Homeric and Yugoslavian poetry as discovered by Parry and Lord, i.e., the device that made oral composition possible. Lists of these pairs were collected, their frequency and the order of their members tabulated, and the semantic relationships between them analyzed. (Noteworthy is the "break-up of stereotyped phrases," first identified by E. Melamed [1961], in which a conventional phrase is divided over two parallel lines.) The bibliography on word pairs is extensive, with the names of M. Dahood and several Israeli scholars prominent (see Dahood's lists in *Ras Shamra Parallels* [1972–81] and Y. Avishur [1984]). In fact, most standard descriptions of biblical poetry from 1950 to 1980 include some discussion of word pairs.

The analyses of parallel lines and parallel word pairs represent increasingly complex typologies to categorize surface variations of underlying synonymity. A shift in perception began to be noticeable around 1980: Emphasis was put on the difference in parallel lines rather than on their sameness. J. Kugel (1981) rejected the notion of the synonymity of parallel lines, replacing it with the notion of continuity, which he expressed as "A, what's more, B." Alter, in a similar vein, spoke of the "consequentiality" of parallel lines. Parallel lines now came to be seen as adding new information containing an intensification or a progression rather than just repeating the same thought in different words. To be sure, the idea of difference or lack of redundancy in parallelism has ancient (especially Jewish) antecedents and is not altogether absent from Lowth's and Gray's discussions; but scholars had by and large lost sight of it.

Contemporaneous with but independent of the shift away from Lowthian approaches by Kugel and Alter came the introduction of linguistic models for the study of biblical parallelism (analogous to those of Kurylowicz and O'Connor for meter). A number of scholars offered grammatical analyses of parallelism (A. Berlin [1985]; T. Collins [1978]; S. Geller [1979]; E. Greenstein [1982]; M. O'Connor, D. Pardee [1988]; W. Watson) in which the relationship between parallel lines is described in terms of syntax instead of semantics. The influence of structural linguistics and especially of R. Jakobson is evident.

The most comprehensive of these studies is Berlin's since it involves not only grammar but also other linguistic aspects. Berlin views parallelism as a linguistic phenomenon involving equivalences and/or contrasts on the level of the word and/or the line. The linguistic aspects that are activated are the grammatical, the lexical, the semantic, and the phonological. In the grammatical aspect the syntax of the lines is equivalent (but not necessarily identical), i.e., the deep structures are the same. On the level of the word the grammatical aspect involves the use of terms that are from different morphological classes but fill the same syntactic function, or terms from the same morphological class that may manifest a contrast in gender, number, verbal form, etc. The lexical aspect is concerned with word pairs, which are seen here as the products of normal word association and are analyzable according to linguistic rules derived from word association games and experiments. The semantic aspect relates to the relationship between the meaning of the parallel lines, which Berlin analyzes as being either paradigmatic or syntagmatic. She finds tension or balance between the synonymity and the difference in the meaning of the lines—both being present to some degree. (This mediates between the position of the Lowth school on the one hand, and Kugel and Alter, on the other hand.) The phonologic aspect is activated in cases where terms with similar sounds or consonants are paired. Berlin's study is an attempt to present a unified linguistic explanation for all the phenomena subsumed under parallelism.

c. *The absence of "prose particles."* Although parallelism is an important dimension of biblical poetry, it cannot in and of itself serve to identify a poem since non-poetic discourse also contains parallelism. In addition, the existence of a metrical system or systems, sought for centuries, has proved to be a will-o'-the-wisp. In other words, the two generally acknowledged formal features of biblical poetry have not yielded sufficiently objective criteria for the identification of poetry. For this reason a few scholars have tried a different approach. It has been known at least since 1910 (see G. A. Smith, 11) that certain words and particles (the definite article, the relative pronoun *ʾašer*, the particle *ʾēt*) appear less frequently in poetry. Modern computer technology now makes the actual counting of these particles relatively easy, and their occurrence in the Bible has been tabulated (see F. Andersen and A. Forbes [1983]). This tabulation often confirms our intuition about what is to be labeled a poem and may indeed provide an objective basis for defining poetry. Unfortunately, it has as yet little to say about the nature of poetry or how it is to be analyzed.

d. *Other rhetorical features.* Much of the world's poetry utilizes an array of tropes and figures, and the Bible is no exception. Biblical poetry employs imagery, repetition, chiasm, inclusio, assonance, and so forth. Some of these, like chiasm, have been studied extensively; others, like metaphor, could benefit from more sophisticated treatment. There have also been efforts to analyze poetic structures and patterning above the level of the line or bicolon. A summary of poetic structures and figures, including an extensive bibliography, is found in Watson (1983).

In large measure, the study of biblical poetry is conditioned by the time and place of those who study it; yet certain observations seem to recur in almost every period, albeit couched in different frames of reference. The long-standing interest in biblical poetry has produced a fascinating chapter in the history of biblical interpretation.

Bibliography: L. Alonso-Schökel, *Estudios de poética hebrea* (1963); *A Manual of Hebrew Poetics* (1988). **R. Alter**, *The Art of Biblical Poetry* (1985). **F. I. Andersen** and **A. D. Forbes**, " 'Prose Particle' Counts of the HB," *The Word of the Lord Shall Go Forth* (ed. C. L. Meyers and M. O'Connor, 1983) 165-83. **Y. Avishur**, *Stylistic Studies of Word-pairs in Biblical and Ancient Semitic Literatures* (1984). **A. Baker**, "Parallelism: England's Contribution to Biblical Studies," *CBQ* 35 (1973) 429-40. **A. Berlin**, *The Dynamics of Biblical Parallelism* (1985); *Biblical Poetry Through Medieval Jewish Eyes* (1991); "Introduction to Hebrew Poetry," *NIB* (1996) 4:301-15. **D. Broadribb**, "A Historical Review of Studies of Hebrew Poetry," *Abr-Nahrain* 13 (1972–73) 66-87. **K. Budde**, "Das hebräische Klagelied," *ZAW* 2 (1882) 1-51; *Die Segen Moses* (1922). **G. B. Caird**, *The Language and Imagery of the Bible* (1980). **U. Cassuto**, *Biblical and Oriental Studies* (2 vols., 1973–75). **J. H. Charlesworth**, *Critical Reflections on the Odes of Solomon* (JSPSup 22, 1998). **T. K. Cheyne**, *Founders of OT Criticism: Biographical, Descriptive, and Critical Studies* (1893). **T. Collins**, *Line-forms in Hebrew Poetry: A Grammatical Approach to the Stylistic Study of the Hebrew Prophets* (1978). **A. M. Cooper**, "Biblical Poetics: A Linguistic

Approach" (diss., Yale Theological Seminary, 1976). **F. M. Cross** and **D. N. Freedman**, *Studies in Ancient Yahwistic Poetry* (1975). **R. C. Culley**, *Oral Formulaic Language in the Biblical Psalms* (1967). **M. Dahood**, *Psalms* (3 vols., AB 16, 17, 17A, 1965–70); "Ugaritic-Hebrew Parallel Pairs," *Ras Shamra Parallels 1* (ed. L. Fisher, 1972) 71-382; *2* (1975) 1-39; *3* (ed. S. Rummel, 1981) 1-206. **H. Fisch**, *Poetry with a Purpose* (1988). **J. P. Fokkelman**, *Major Poems of the Hebrew Bible: at the Interface of Hermeneutics and Structural Analysis* (3 vols.; Studia Semitica Neerlandica 37, 41, 43, 1998–); *Reading Biblical Poetry: an Introductory Guide* (2001). **D. N. Freedman**, *Pottery, Poetry, and Prophecy: Studies in Early Hebrew Poetry* (1980). **W. R. Garr**, "The *qinah*: A Study of Poetic Meter, Syntax, and Style," *ZAW* 95 (1983) 54-75. **S. Geller**, *Parallelism in Early Biblical Poetry* (1979). **E. S. Gerstenberger**, "The Lyrical Literature," *The HB and Its Modern Interpreters* (ed. D. A. Knight and G. M. Tucker, 1985) 409-44. **S. Gevirtz**, *Patterns in the Early Poetry of Israel* (1963). **J. Gluck**, "Assonance in Ancient Hebrew Poetry: Sound Patterns as a Literary Device," *De Fructu Oris Sui: Essays in Honour of A. van Selms* (ed. I. H. Eybers et al., 1971) 69-84. **R. Gordis**, "The Structure of Biblical Poetry," *Poets, Prophets, and Sages: Essays in Biblical Interpretation* (1971) 61-94. **G. B. Gray**, *The Forms of Hebrew Poetry Considered with Special Reference to the Criticism and Interpretation of the OT* (1915, repr. 1972). **E. L. Greenstein**, "How Does Parallelism Mean?" *A Sense of Text* (JQRS, 1982) 41-70. **D. Grossberg**, *Centripetal and Centrifugal Structures in Biblical Poetry* (1989). **H. Gunkel**, *Die Psalmen* (1926); *Introduction to Psalms: The Genres of the Religious Lyric of Israel* (1933; ET 1998). **J. G. Herder**, *Vom Geist der ebräischen Poesie: Eine Anleitung für die Liebhaber derselben und der ältesten Geschichte des menschlichen Geistes* (1782). **B. Hrushovski**, "Prosody, Hebrew," *EncJud* 13 (1971) 1195-203. **M. C. A. Korpel**, *The Structure of Classical Hebrew Poetry: Isaiah 40–55* (OtSt 41, 1998). **H. Kosmala**, "Form and Structure in Ancient Hebrew Poetry," *VT* 14 (1964) 423-45; 16 (1966) 152-80. **J. Krasovec**, *Antithetic Structure in Biblical Hebrew Poetry* (VTSup 35, 1984). **J. L. Kugel**, *The Idea of Biblical Poetry: Parallelism and Its History* (1981). **J. Kurylowicz**, *Studies in Semitic Grammar and Metrics* (1972); *Metrick und Sprachgeschichte* (1975). **F. Landy**, *Beauty and the Enigma: and Other Essays on the Hebrew Bible* (JSOTSup 312, 2001). **J. Ley**, *Grundzuge des Rhythmus des Vers- und Strophenbaues in der hebräischen Poesie* (1875); *Die metrischen Formen der hebräischen Poesie* (1886); *Leitfaden der Metrik der hebräischen Poesie nebst dem ersten buche der Psalmen nach rhythmischer Vers- und Strophenabteilung mit metrischer Analyse* (1887). **T. Longman**, "A Critique of Two Recent Metrical Systems," *Bib* 63 (1982) 230-54. **J. R. Lundbom**, *Jeremiah: A Study in Ancient Hebrew Rhetoric* (1975). **E. Z. Melamed**, "Break-up of Stereotype Phrases," *ScrHier* 8 (1961) 115-53. **A. di Marco**, "Der Chiasmus in der Bibel," *LB* 36 (1975) 21-79; *37* (1976) 49-68. **J. C. de Moor**, "The Art of Versification in Ugarit and Israel," *Studies in Bible and the Ancient Near East Presented to S. Loewenstamm on His Seventieth Birthday* (ed. Y. Avishur and J. Blau, 1978) 119-39; "II: The Formal Structure," *UF* 10 (1978) 187-217; "III: Further Illustrations of the Principle of Expansion," *UF* 12 (1980) 311-15. **J. Muilenburg**, "A Study in Hebrew Rhetoric: Repetition and Style" (VTSup 1, 1953) 97-111; "Poetry," *EncJud* 13 (1971) 670-81. **M. O'Connor**, *Hebrew Verse Structure* (1980). **D. Pardee**, "Ugaritic and Hebrew Metrics," *Ugaritic in Retrospect: Fifty Years of Ugarit and Ugaritic* (ed. G. D. Young, 1981) 113-30; *Ugaritic and Hebrew Poetic Parallelism: A Trial Cut* (1988). **S. Parker**, "Parallelism and Prosody in Ugaritic Narrative Verse," *UF* 6 (1974) 283-94. **P. D. Quinn-Miscall**, *Reading Isaiah: Poetry and Vision* (2001). **T. H. Robinson**, *The Poetry of the OT* (1947); "Hebrew Poetic Form: The English Tradition" (VTSup 1, 1953) 128-49. **R. Sappan**, *The Typical Features of the Syntax of Biblical Poetry in Its Classical Period* (1981), Hebrew. **G. M. Schramm**, "Poetic Patterning in Biblical Hebrew," *Michigan Oriental Studies in Honor of G. G. Cameron* (ed. L. Orlin, 1976) 167-91. **S. Segert**, "Vorarbeiten zur hebräischen Metrik," *ArOr* 21 (1953) 481-542; 25 (1957)

190-200. **E. Sievers**, *Metrische Studien, vol. 1, Studien zur hebr" ischen Metrik* (1901); *vol. 2, Die Hebräischen Genesis* (1904). **G. A. Smith**, *The Early Poetry of Israel in Its Physical and Social Origins* (1910); *1910 Schweich Lectures* (1912). **D. Stuart,** *Studies in Early Hebrew Meter* (1976). **S. L. Terrien**, *The Psalms: Strophic Structure and Theological Commentary* (2003). **D. R. Vance,** *The Question of Meter in Biblical Hebrew Poetry* (Studies in the Bible and Early Christianity 46, 2001). **W. G. E. Watson**, "Trends in the Development of Classical Hebrew Poetry: A Comparative Study," *UF* 14 (1982) 265-77; *Classical Hebrew Poetry: A Guide to Its Techniques* (1983). **W. R. Watters**, *Formula Criticism and Poetry of the OT* (BZAW 138, 1976). **M. Weiss**, *The Bible from Within* (1962; ET 1984). **P. Yoder**, "A–B Pairs and Oral Composition in Hebrew Poetry," *VT* 21 (1971) 470-89.

A. BERLIN

GENERAL ARTICLES

Prophecy and Prophets

No general statements or discussions of the nature and function of prophecy appear in the HB. Nonetheless, there do appear some hints regarding how prophecy was understood. (1) The prophets were viewed as "warners" to alert the people to their infidelity, to make them aware of coming judgment, and to call them back to their traditional religion (2 Kgs 17:13-14). (2) The prophets were conceived of as preachers of repentance calling for a return to God (Zech 1:4). (3) The prophets were predictors of the future, and the authenticity of their office and message was to be judged by the fulfillment of their predictions (Deut 18:20-22). (4) The prophets were authors of historiographical works (2 Chr 12:15; 13:22). (5) The prophets were proclaimers of mysteries and messages that they themselves perhaps did not completely understand (see the interpretation in Daniel 9 of the seventy years in Jer 25:1-14; 29:10 as seventy sabbatical, or 490, years).

In Num 12:6-8 and Deut 34:10-12, Moses is declared to be the archetypal prophet, exceeding all others, in spite of Deut 18:18 with its promise of a prophet like him. Thus he is depicted as the prophet by whom all other prophets must be judged; and, with all other prophets in a subordinate position to Moses, the prophetic canon (Joshua–Malachi) is placed in a secondary position to the Torah. (Note how the conclusions of two divisions of the canon subordinate other prophecy to Mosaic prophecy and Torah: Deut 34:10-12; Mal 4:4.)

In early Judaism and Christianity new directions and additional emphases may be seen in the understanding and interpretation of the prophets. Philo emphasized the origin, nature, and mode of prophetic revelation and knowledge (an issue already noted in Jer 23:18-22; for the main Philonic texts, see D. Winston, Philo of Alexandria [1981] 153-56). H. Wolfson ([1947], 2:3-72) summarized Philo's teaching on the four functions of prophecy as "prediction, propitiation, legislation, vision of things incorporeal" and the three types of prophecy (or revelation) as "prophecy through the Divine Spirit, by the Divine Voice, and through angels." Philo's employment of Plato's conception of inspiration, ecstasy, or frenzy is significant. In the *Timaeus*, Plato had associated the mantic faculty with that part of the soul located in the liver and concluded that true divination occurs only when the power of thought is shackled by sleep or illness or some paroxysm of frenzy. In a similar vein Philo declared: "The prophet utters nothing that is his own, but all his utterances are of alien derivation, the prompting of another." The prompter is God, by whom the prophet's "chords are invisibly plucked and smitten" (*Who Is the Heir?* 259; Winston's tr. 153). Philo confined such experiences to the just and upright, to those of moral perfection. In his Life of Moses he explored the prophetic role of Moses in detail (2.187-291).

In the Hebrew canon the designation *nebiim* (prophets) for the books Joshua–Malachi (excluding Daniel) indicates that prophetical works were conceived more broadly than in the Christian (Greek) canon, where only the books Isaiah–Malachi (including Daniel) were designated prophetic. This would suggest that a prophetic book was one written by an inspired person and combined narrative, prediction, moral teaching, and denunciation of sin. This view of prophets and of prophetical books is also suggested by Josephus, who, in discussing the twenty-two works he called "our books" or "our scriptures," wrote: "Five are the books of Moses, comprising the laws and the traditional history...From the death of Moses until Artaxerxes, who succeeded Xerxes as king of Persia, the prophets subsequent to Moses wrote the history of the events of their own times in thirteen books. The remaining four books contain hymns to God and precepts for the conduct of human life" (*C. Ap.* 1.39-41). For Josephus, who emphasized the role of prophets in his history, the exact succession of prophets had failed following

Artaxerxes; but prophecy per se had not totally ceased since Josephus even understood himself as performing an aspect of the prophetic role—namely, prediction of the future (see L. Feldman [1990]).

In the early church and at Qumran, the Prophets and other prophetic literature—in fact, practically all the literature that became the HB—were read through two perspectives: (1) as if it were apocalyptic literature—that is, as if it were all written as prediction of the last days whose true meaning would be disclosed in the final events of the end time (note Daniel's reading of Jeremiah, already mentioned); and (2) as if the life, history, and destiny of the two respective communities were the objects of the prophetic predictions and descriptions. Such a reading presupposed (1) that the biblical materials or prophecies contain hidden or secondary meanings and frames of reference (something like what has come to be called the *sensus plenior* in Roman Catholic interpretation) that transcend the simple and commonsense reading, and (2) that this secondary dimension of the text had become evident through its subsequent fulfillment or manifestation. NT and Qumran authors did not discuss whether the original hearers/readers understood this secondary or true referent.

In Mishnaic and Talmudic Judaism one finds the following emphases and perspectives on the prophets (see N. Glatzer [1946] and the collection of texts in H. Bialik and Y. Rannitzky [1992]).

(1) The prophets are subordinate to Moses, and thus prophetic preaching is subordinate to the law (*b. Šabb.* 104a).

(2) The prophets were a link in the chain of tradition from Moses to later generations: "Moses received the law from Sinai and committed it to Joshua, and Joshua to the elders, and the elders to the prophets, and the prophets committed it to the men of the Great Synagogue [a legendary group of 120 exiles who returned with Ezra]" (*m. ʾAbot* 1:1).

(3) The prophets made no innovations not covered in the law: "They neither took away from nor added aught to what is written in the Torah save only the reading of the Megillah" (*m. Meg.* 14a). This perspective is somewhat modified in other traditions, where the prophet is viewed as a rabbi who brings new insights out of old treasures (Glatzer, 129). These first three features mean that prophets were considered more as witnesses to previous revelation than as sources of new revelation; they were fundamentally proclaimers and interpreters of the law.

(4) The age of prophecy ended with the fall of the first Temple, or with the age of Haggai, Zechariah, and Malachi, although revelation continued through the Bath Qol, with the wise men being replacements for the prophets (*b. B. Bat.* 12a; *b. Sanh.* 11a).

(5) Worthiness and moral uprightness were required of the prophet: "The Holy One, blessed be He, causes His Divine presence to rest only on him who is strong, wealthy, wise, and meek" (*b. Ned.* 38a).

(6) Many prophets arose in Israel; according to one tradition, twice the number of people leaving Egypt. More specifically, it was argued that there were forty-eight prophets (including seven female prophets—Sarah, Miriam, Deborah, Hannah, Abigail, Huldah, and Esther) representing all the tribes (*b. Meg.* 14a; *b. Sukk.* 27b). (7) The notion of the prophets as representatives of the "merit of Israel" before God appears in many early medieval Jewish writers as an apologetic against the view that the prophets had proclaimed the end of Israel (see Glatzer, 130-36).

An anonymous work, probably Palestinian in origin (1st cent. C.E.?), the so-called *Lives of the Prophets* (for an ET see OTP 2:379-99; for a major study, see A. Schwemer [1995]) contains material about the prophets that supplements the biblical text: "The names of the prophets, and where they are from, and where they died and how, and where they lie." Surviving in Armenian, Ethiopic, Greek, Latin, and Syriac versions, the work treats the Major and Minor prophets, Daniel, and the seven non-literary prophets noted in the HB, giving evidence of an interest in filling out the biographies of the prophets. Hebrews 11:37 may indicate some knowledge of this material.

Within the developing church the ideas of a progressive revelation of the divine will through history, of Jesus and the church as the culmination of OT law and prophecy, and of the fulfillment of prophecy as proof of the authenticity and correctness of the Christian faith became staples in the church's exposition of its theology. The tendencies present in inner-biblical interpretation in the NT became more overt during the patristic period. The entire HB was widely read as prophecy, in the sense of promise and fulfillment, type and anti-type. The author of the Epistle of Barnabas interpreted ceremonial and cultic regulations and actions as hidden prefigurations and predictions of Christ and the church. Justin Martyr, especially in his *Dialogue with Trypho*, argued that the fulfillment of OT prophecies by Jesus and the church proved the truthfulness of Christianity, the transitory nature of the old covenant, and the church's replacement of Israel. In his On First Principles, especially in 4.1, Origen argued that the fulfillment of prophecy confirmed the divinity of Christ and the inspiration of scripture. The church fathers, like the NT authors, found Psalms to be a storehouse of predictions.

In their debates with Judaism many of the church fathers tended to read texts understood by both Jews and Christians as messianic in a metaphorical sense to make them more applicable to new claims. The debate between church and synagogue over prophecies and their fulfillment often centered around whether the events that gave rise to the church really fulfilled OT prophecies, Jews arguing negatively and Christians arguing affirmatively (see R. Wilken [1993]). The main issue was primarily the question of the reference of the texts—that is, whether the messianic age had begun with Jesus or whether it still lay in the future.

Members of the Antiochene School, especially Theodore of Mopsuestia, were more cautious in their finding of prophecies in the HB than were most of the fathers. Theodore tended to limit the texts to those so read in the NT. Thus he considered only a handful of psalms to be predictions about Christ, whereas Augustine read practically all the psalms prophetically and typologically. (For Augustine's theory of revelation and prophecy, see his *The Literal Interpretation of Genesis* bk. 12.)

A paradigm shift in the approach to prophecy can be seen among medieval Jewish philosophers, who sought to combine Torah and rational philosophy along the lines of the Muslims who studied Plato and Aristotle (the falasifa). Foremost in this regard were Saadia, Judah Halevi, and Maimonides (see Wolfson; A. Reines [1969–70, 1970]; A. Altmann [1978]; J. Macy [1986]).

Islamic philosophers had made several deductions about prophecy: (1) Prophecy (revelation) was a natural process; (2) prophecy was effected by God indirectly through an intermediary, the Active Intellect; and (3) certain qualifications were required of the recipient of prophetic revelation, including natural endowments, training in moral and practical virtues, and intellectual virtues and knowledge acquired through instruction in the arts and sciences. Prophetic revelation took place when the soul developed to a state of independence from the body and could reunite with the Active Intellect (sometimes referred to as the Holy Spirit or Gabriel).

Jewish philosophers objected to the principle that prophecy was the result of natural causation consequent on one's congenital, moral, and intellectual perfection. For them, God's will was involved, although for Maimonides only indirectly (see Altmann). Maimonides wrote: "The quiddity of prophecy, in truth, is an emanation that flows forth from God through the medium of the Active Intellect, first upon the rational faculty, and then upon the imaginative faculty" (tr. from Reines [1969–70] 327). As in the Bible, Jewish tradition and philosophy assigned Moses a superior status as prophet. Reines has described the differences Maimonides perceived between Mosaic and usual prophecy as follows: "In a well-known passage, Maimonides enumerates four differences between ordinary and Mosaic prophecy. Ordinary prophecy is apprehended in dreams or visions; Mosaic prophecy in full consciousness. Ordinary prophecy comes by means of an angel; Mosaic prophecy without an angel. The apprehension of ordinary prophecy is accompanied by fear and terror; Mosaic prophecy comes peacefully. Ordinary prophecy arrives involuntarily and unexpectedly; Moses' prophecy comes at will. These four differences are derivative, however, and they do not in themselves constitute the fundamental distinction between ordinary prophets and Moses. This distinction is that the ordinary prophets prophesied through the medium of imagination and Moses did not" (1969–70, 328-29). Although Moses received the law through non-imaginative means, he wrote the law in a subprophetic form—that is, as imaginative literature.

The goals of prophecy for Maimonides were the promulgation of divine law, the popular instruction in the law, and the urging of persons to adhere to the law. Like Philo, Maimonides read two senses into scriptural texts: an exoteric sense for the common populace, which could actually be deceptive if interpreted consistently in a literal reading, and an esoteric sense for the learned. For him, some of the "events" associated with the prophets, e.g., Hosea's marriage, were not historical.

Maimonides' synthesis, attempting a harmony between faith and reason, scripture and philosophy, tradition and Aristotelian thought, had a counterpart in the work of Thomas Aquinas, who was familiar with Maimonides' *Guide of the Perplexed* in Latin translation. However, since Thomas freed "the cognitive act from any link with the transcendent," he argued that prophecy was a divine gift, a supernatural experience (Altmann, 9; his article provides references to the main passages in the writings of Maimonides and Thomas).

Major discussions of the nature of prophecy and how prophetic knowledge and revelation were received and related to the divine and to the philosophy of knowledge appear in the writings of many medieval Christian theologians. J. P. Torrell (1977, 1992) has collected and commented on much of this material. For example, in the prologue to his commentary on Psalms (PL 191.55-62; ET in A. Minnis and A. Scott, Medieval Literary Theory and Criticism c. 1100–c. 1375: The Commentary Tradition [1988, 1991] 105-12), Peter Lombard described the various forms in which prophecy occurred: "Prophecy, then, is divine inspiration or revelation which proclaims the future outcome of events with immutable truth. Hence, a prophecy is called 'a vision' [*visio*] and the prophet is 'a seer' [*videns*]. Prophecy happens in four ways: through actual events or words, and through that which only seems to be said or to happen, that is, through dreams [*sommia*] and visions [*visiones*] . . . There is yet another kind of prophecy over and above these, which has a more honorable status than they have. This happens when prophecy takes place as a result of the pure, unaided inspiration of the Holy Spirit, without any outside help in the form of an event, words, vision, or dream. This was how David prophesied, solely through the inspiration of the Holy Spirit" (108-9).

Jewish rabbis, who were more exegetes than philosophers, e.g., Rashi and A. Ibm Ezra, carried out more traditional interpretation. Although Rashi read some of the HB prophecies as being related to the yet unrealized messianic age, he associated many of these with events in the course of Israelite history. The child spoken of in Isa 7:14 was thus interpreted as Isaiah's or as King Ahaz's son (Hezekiah) but was not understood messianically. In this Rashi was followed by Andrew of St. Victor.

Later biblical interpreters like Nicholas of Lyra argued that prophetical promises could have a double literal sense, one fulfilled in ancient times and another fulfilled in Jesus or to be realized in the end time. Sometimes HB (and NT) promises/prophecies were combined with nonbiblical "prophetic" material like the Hermetic literature and the Sibylline Oracles, e.g., by Joachim of Fiore (see R. Southern [1972]). HB prophecies were occasionally read by Jews as indicating a very near dawning of the final age, as in some of the writings of Abravanel, who was more philosopher than exegete (see J. Malherbe [1993]).

358

The Protestant Reformation witnessed radical readjustments in the overall interpretation of Scripture and in Scripture's role in theology. There was little break, however, in the understanding of the HB prophets. Luther's refusal to return to the ordering of the Hebrew canon even when adopting the contents of that canon typifies Christianity's veneration of the Prophets over other portions of the HB. In the Christian canon the ordering of the books ("the canonical intentionality") highlighted the prophetic division so that it became the key for reading the whole. In spite of Luther's emphasis on a literal reading of the text and his break with the use of the Quadigra, Christian and christological interest dominated his reading of the HB and especially of the prophetical books. Nonetheless, Luther often made suggestions about interpretation that sound quite modern. In his preface to the book of Isaiah, he wrote: "Two things are necessary to explain the prophet. The first is a knowledge of grammar, and this may be regarded as having the greatest weight. The second is more necessary, namely, a knowledge of the historical background, not only as an understanding of the events themselves as expressed in letters and syllables but as at the same time embracing rhetoric and dialectic, so that the figures of speech and the circumstances may be carefully heeded."

Commenting on Zech 1:7 in his 1526 commentary, Luther declared that "the books of the prophets are . . . to be divided into many discourses"; but he offered no detailed discourse analysis. In his Habakkuk commentary (1525), he stressed the role of the prophet as a preacher of judgment, which is intended to bring some to conversion. In the preface to the same book, Luther noted that the prophets pronounced "many prophecies that pertained only to their own time and served only their time." The futuristic and traditional messianic orientation, however, received the basic emphasis in Luther, as illustrated in his introduction to Joel: "All the prophets have one and the same message, for this is their one aim: they are all looking toward the coming of Christ or to the coming Kingdom of Christ."

Calvin's view of the prophets and his exposition of their works (see T. Parker [1986] 176-223) was not radically different from Luther's but did focus more on the prophets as preachers of the law. In the preface to his Isaiah commentary, Calvin wrote: "On the office of the Prophets it is usual for commentators to write long essays. But I prefer to summarize and say that we should relate the Prophets to the Law, from which they drew their teaching like streams from a spring. They made it their rule and so may justly be called and declared its interpreters; in nothing were they independent." Calvin's exposition of the prophetical books incorporated detailed analysis of the historical background to the prophets' activity; and he was less prone than other reformers to find predictions of Jesus in some texts, instead seeing many prophecies related to the course of ancient Israelite history.

Many second-generation Protestants compared the great Reformers to the Hebrew prophets and saw them, like Elijah against the Baal worshipers, as fighting the infidelity of the day (for them, the Roman Catholic Church). This drawing of analogies also resulted in the HB prophet's being viewed as if they were ancient Luthers and Calvins.

In his succinct but highly influential *Annotationes on the OT,* H. Grotius related prophetic texts usually understood as christological predictions to events in the normal course of ancient Israelite history. He did acknowledge that these could be applied to NT events and beliefs if given a spiritual or secondary meaning.

While Grotius was providing a detached interpretation of the Bible, other scholars were involved in an impassioned exposition of the prophetical material (especially the books of Daniel and Revelation) to locate the keys and clues to the course and culmination of history (see R. Popkin [1984]). Numerous persons claimed to be modern-day prophets. (M. Nostradamus [1503–66] was already a legend in his own day.) C. Hill (1993) has chronicled the diversity of popular biblical interpretation during the tumultuous period of the English Civil War, which overlapped the Thirty Years War (1618–48). For the first time in history biblical interpretation became truly democratic, and the temporary freedom of publication allowed for a free flow of ideas.

The Cambridge Platonist J. Smith (1618–52), combating the enthusiasts of his day, produced a major work entitled *Of Prophesie* (published in his *Select Discourses* [1660]), which drew on a host of medieval Jewish interpreters. He emphasized the rational dimension of the prophetic experience, although recognizing a mantic or ecstatic element, and argued that prophecy ceased in the days of the early church. His work was later translated into Latin and widely circulated by J. Le Clerc.

B. Spinoza, who along with T. Hobbes was considered one of the main arch-heretics of the seventeenth century, provided extensive discussion of prophecy in his *Tractatus Theologico-politicus* (1670; ET, R. Elwes [1883]). Spinoza set out to argue against the association of philosophy and theology/religion and for the independence of the two. In the process he, like E. Herbert, reduced religion and the fundamental dogmas of Scripture to a set of simple doctrines accessible to all, which he summarized as follows: "There exists a God, that is, a Supreme Being, who loves justice and charity, and who must be obeyed by whosoever would be saved; that the worship of this being consists in the practice of justice and love towards one's neighbour" (186-87). In turn, he reduced the prophets and the Bible to the level of the human, concluding that: (a) "The prophets only perceived God's revelation by the aid of imagination . . . by words and figures either real or imaginary" (24-25). "The power of prophecy implies not a peculiarly perfect mind, but a peculiarly vivid imagination" (19). Here he set himself against the view developed by Maimonides and others that prophetic knowledge came through the rational faculty. (b) "Prophecies varied, not only according to the imagination and physical temperament of the prophet, but also according to his particular opinions; and further, that prophecy never rendered the prophet wiser than he was before" (27). A cheerful prophet's words were cheerful; one who was melancholy spoke of wars and massacres. The educated and cultivated prophets perceived the mind of God in a cultivated way, and so forth. (c) "The prophets could be, and in fact were, ignorant" (39). (d) Prophets frequently "held conflicting opinions" (39). (e) The goal of prophetic activity was not knowledge but piety and obedience. (f) Since Spinoza did not believe in miracles—those in the Bible were events whose causes were not known at the time—predictions of the future were not based on supernatural revelation. (For a defense of the rationality of prophecy against Spinoza by E. Stillingfleet [1635–99], see G. Reedy, *The Bible and Reason* [1985] 145-55.) Spinoza emphasized the necessity of understanding the original context in which Scripture was produced and prophecies were delivered: "who was the speaker, what was the occasion, and to whom were the words addressed" (105).

Throughout the seventeenth and much of the eighteenth century, many British scientists and mathematicians—some associated with the Royal Society (founded in 1662) and most millenarians—worked to produce an analysis of biblical prophecy that would place the subject on a firm scientific basis (see Popkin [1984]). Foremost among this group were J. Napier (1550–1617), H. More, R. Boyle, I. Newton, and W. Whiston. A major catalyst for this approach was J. Mede's *Clavis Apocalyptica* (1627); primarily concerned with the interpretation of the book of Revelation, the work had widespread influence. Newton worked on biblical prophecy and chronology throughout much of his adult life and left many unpublished manuscripts on the topic. His successor at Cambridge, Whiston, delivered the 1707 Boyle lectures (established under Newton's influence for the purpose of defending Christianity) on *The Accomplishment of Scripture Prophecies* (1708), which represents a classical, if somewhat overdrawn, statement of this approach.

In opposition, Deists called into question the two foundational blocks of traditional Christian apologetics—namely, NT fulfillment of HB prophecies, and miracles as authenticating the truthfulness of the Bible and Christian origins. In *A Discourse on the Grounds and Reasons of the Christian Religion* (1724) and *The Scheme of Literal Prophecy Considered* (1726), A. Collins challenged Whiston and the argument from prophecy and denied the possibility of predicting future events. Collins's basic arguments were twofold: (a) The parallels between HB prophecies (predictions) and their supposed fulfillment in Christ and in the early church are arrived at only when the HB texts are understood and applied in secondary, typical, mystical, allegorical, or enigmatic ways—that is, in a sense different from the obvious and literal sense they bear in the HB. (b) Prophecies should be understood in terms that would have made sense in the context of their original employment. Isaiah 7:14, for example, must be understood in terms that would have been comprehensible to King Ahaz, the Judean ruler at the time.

At the same time that Deists and others were attacking traditional Christian apologetic, biblical scholars began focusing more on the ancient referents of the prophecies and playing down the idea that the prophets predicted events far into the future. This new emphasis can be seen in P. Pezron's (1639–1706) *Essai d'un commentaire litéral et historique sur les prophétes* (1693) and in S. White's (1677/8–1716) *Commentary on the Prophet Isaiah* (1709).

A further development in the early eighteenth century concerns the order and arrangement of material in the prophetical books. Near the end of the seventeenth century, scholars began to treat the sixth chapter of Isaiah as an account of the prophet's inaugural call, a rather novel idea at the time. This reading meant that the opening chapters (1–5) must belong to some period after the call; thus the order of the materials in the book could not be chronological. There followed attempts at determining the placement of these chapters and the principles around which the books were structured, what today is known as redaction criticism. These issues were especially explored by J. Koppe in his notes to the German edition of R. Lowth's translation of Isaiah (1780–81), which laid the foundations for the theory of a Deutero-Isaiah and for the division of the book of Isaiah into a multiplicity of independent oracles. The issues were also explored by T. Howes (1783), who was the first to examine how the prophetical books may have been redacted. Howes explored various options: The speeches were ordered chronologically in terms of their original delivery, in terms of when they were fulfilled, or poetically/rhetorically in an order "best suited to the purpose of persuasion and argumentation" (139).

The eighteenth century also witnessed the development of the theory that the prophets were poets and that the prophetical books are generally poetic in form. Lowth gave widespread popularity to this view in his *Lectures on the Sacred Poetry of the Hebrews* (1753; ET 1787), especially in lectures 18-21, and in his translation of Isaiah (1778). He translated most of Isaiah in poetic form and was followed by others who applied his approach to different prophetical books. Nonetheless, the idea of prophetic speech as primarily poetic was not generally accepted by translators until the second half of the twentieth century. The translators of the RV (1885) considered but declined to accept the idea.

Four factors dominated nineteenth-century research on the prophets and led to the development of approaches and methods already present in earlier discussions. In many respects these developments were a modified form of Spinoza's view of the biblical writings as reflections on poetics, morals, and religion produced by particular people, under particular circumstances, to meet particular needs.

First, source or historical-literary criticism of the prophetic books paralleled that of pentateuchal criticism, seeking to divide authentic from inauthentic material—that is, material deriving from the prophet whose name the book bore from material deriving from secondary additions, accretions, and editorial activity. Efforts were made to place the various components making up a prophetic book within particular historical and theological contexts. Typical and exemplary of this effort was B. Duhm's Isaiah commentary (1892).

A second factor was a consequence of Pentatuchal research. The theories of K. Graf, A. Kuenen, and J. Wellhausen led to the conclusion that the prophets preceded the law in the course of Israelite history. The prophets were, therefore, more likely to have been catalysts for the production of law rather than interpreters of preexisting codes. This view was expounded by Duhm (1875), Kuenen (1877), and Wellhausen (1878, 1883; ET 1885).

Third, nineteenth-century studies tended to reduce the essence of religion to morality. The prophets thus came to be viewed as the founders and advocates of ethical religion as opposed to cult and priesthood, which propounded a ritualized religion. Kuenen expressed this widely held view when he wrote: "Ethical monotheism is their [the prophets'] creation. They... ascended to the belief in one only, holy, and righteous God, who realizes his will, or moral good, in the world, and they have, by preaching and writing, made that belief the inalienable property of our race" (1877, 585).

A fourth and perhaps overarching factor was an emphasis on the prophets as spokespersons to their own times and thus not as predictors of events to come in some indeterminate future. Although the expression became common later, nineteenth-century scholars stressed the prophets as "forthtellers not foretellers." This demanded that the prophet and the prophetic materials must be understood in light of their historical contexts since their messages were intended for a contemporary audience and not for readers centuries later.

In the twentieth century issues in prophetical research have become more variegated and complex. Good surveys of this research, however, have been provided by H. Rowley (1945), O. Eissfeldt (1951), and G. Tucker (1985) and with selected readings, by P. Neumann (1979), D. Petersen (1986), R. Gordon (1995), and Y. Gitay (1997). Seven primary areas have received the greatest amount of attention.

The issue of prophetic speech forms was raised in a significant way by H. Gunkel in his form-critical studies (see J. Hayes [1973]). He argued that prophets delivered their messages orally and that the original oracles were short, metrical, and sometimes enigmatic and that they were presented in passionate, ecstatic speech. Such speech might be either a promise or a threat. Gunkel also argued that the prophets borrowed speech forms from various areas of Israelite life—the cult, warfare, law courts, popular wisdom, and so forth. C. Westermann (1960; ET 1967) and others have sought to further Gunkel's work in this area but without arriving at any specific and absolute criteria to determine an original prophetic genre. A survey of the variety of prophetic speech materials has been given by M. Sweeney (1996, 1-30).

A second major area of investigation has focused on the psychology of prophetic experience or what earlier researchers referred to as ecstatic experience. Although this matter had been a long-standing concern, G. Hölscher's 1914 work took transnormal experiences as characteristic of prophetic behavior and activity. For several decades scholars pursued this dimension of prophecy vigorously, but subsequent investigations and studies have tended to minimize this area as a helpful key to understanding the prophets (see Gordon [1995] 5-9, 21).

A third field of investigation has been the relationship of prophets to the cult or to general worship in ancient Israel. Although earlier scholars like W. R. Smith and Hölscher had given consideration to this area of research (see W. Bellinger [1984]), it was S. Mowinckel (1923) who presented a case for placing prophets into the worship life of ancient Israel. A. Johnson (1979) was a most consistent defender of a close relationship between the prophets, cult, and psalmody. For a time in the 1960s and 1970s, prophets were understood as mediators in covenant renewal services and/or as guardians of the covenant relationship (see W. Zimmerli [1965]). This position reasserted the old idea that the prophets were preachers of the law.

Fourth, G. von Rad and many of his students drew on the perspectives of tradition history to enlighten prophetic preaching. In the second volume of his OT Theology (1960; ET 1965), von Rad interpreted the prophets in terms of which ancient historical traditions (exodus, wilderness, David, Zion, etc.) they used in their preaching and how they employed these in speaking about both the past and the future.

Fifth, discovery and use of numerous ancient Near Eastern texts have produced what many scholars consider to be numerous parallels to the HB prophets and prophecy. These texts are in Egyptian, Akkadian, and Aramaic; they indicate that biblical prophecy should be studied in light of the ancient Near Eastern background. Assessment of the relevance and content of this material is offered by M. Ellis (1989) and N. Shupak (1989–90; see also the discussions in Gordon [1995] 29-73 and in H. Huffmon, *ABD*, 5:477-82).

Sixth, one of the blossoming fields of prophetic research has to do with sociocultural and anthropological aspects of prophecy (see J. Kselman [1985]; M. Buss [1980, 1981]; R. Wilson [1980]; R. Culley and T. Overholt [1982]; Gordon [1995] 275-412). Issues in this area focus on the social role of the prophets, their relationships to the contemporary culture and institutions, conflicts with other prophets, and the function of prophetic literature in a culture.

Finally, the origin and editing of the prophetical books has long been a concern of scholarship. In the last decades of the twentieth century, redaction criticism and an interest in the final form of the texts have produced an explosion of study in this area (see T. Collins [1993]; Gordon [1995] 415-522).

Bibliography: A. Altmann, "Maimonides and Thomas Aquinas: Natural or Divine Prophecy?" *AJS Review* 3 (1978) 1-19. **D. Arthur**, *A Smooth Stone: Biblical Prophecy in Historical Perspective* (2001). **J. Barton**, *Oracles of God: Perceptions of Ancient Prophecy in Israel After the Exile* (1986); "History and Rhetoric in the Prophets," *The Bible as Rhetoric: Studies in Biblical Persuasion and Credibility* (Warwick Studies in Philosophy and Literature, ed. M. Warner, 1990) 51-64. **T. K. Beal**, "Specters of Moses: Overtures to Biblical Hauntology," in *"Imagining" Biblical Worlds: Studies in Spatial, Social and Historical Constructs in Honor of James W. Flanagan* (ed. D. M. Gunn and P. M. McNutt; JSOTSup 359, 2002) 171-87. **P. M. Beaude**, "L'Accomplissement des proph,ties chez R. Simon," *RSPT* 60 (1976) 3-35. **A. Behrens**, *Prophetische Visionsschilderungen im Alten Testament: sprachliche Eigenarten, Funktion und Geschichte einer Gattung* (AOAT 292, 2002). **W. H. Bellinger,** *Psalmody and Prophecy* (JSOTSup 27, 1984). **R. M. Berchman** (ed.), *Mediators of the Divine: Horizons of Prophecy, Divination, Dreams, and Theurgy in Mediterranean Antiquity* (SFSHJ 163, 1998). **W. J. Bergen**, *Elisha and the End of Prophetism* (JSOTSup 286, 1999). **H. N. Bialik** and **Y. H. Rannitzky**, *The Book of Legends Sefer ha-aggadah: Legends from the Talmud and Midrash* (1992) 472-81. J. **Blenkinsopp**, *A History of Prophecy in Israel* (1983, 1996). **B. Britt**, Prophetic Concealment in a Biblical Type Scene," *CBQ* 64 (2002) 37-58. **L. L. Bronner**, "Biblical Prophetesses Through Rabbinic Lenses," *Judaism* 40 (1991) 171-83. **M. J. Buss**, "The Social Psychology of Prophecy," *Prophecy* (BZAW 150, ed. J. A. Emerton, 1980) 1-11; "An Anthropological Perspective upon Prophetic Call Narratives," *Semeia* 21 (1981) 9-30. **R. P. Carroll**, *When Prophecy Failed: Cognitive Dissonance in the Prophetic Traditions of the OT* (1979). **R. B. Chisholm**, *Handbook on the Prophets* (2002). **R. Coggins** et al., *Israel's Prophetic Tradition* (FS P. R. Ackroyd, 1982). **T. Collins**, *The Mantle of Elijah: The Redaction Criticism of the Prophetical Books* (Biblical Seminar 20, 1993). **E. W. Conrad**, *Reading the Later Prophets: Toward a New Canonical Criticism* (JSOTSup 376). **R. C. Culley** and **T. W. Overholt** (eds.), *Anthropological Perspectives on OT Prophecy* (Semeia 21, 1982). **J.C. DeMoor** (ed.), The Elusive Prophet: The Prophet as a Historical Person, Literary Character and Anonymous Artist (*OtSt* 45, 2001). **C. J. Dempsey**, *The Prophets: A Liberation-Critical Reading* (2000). **B. Duhm**, *Die Theologie des Propheten als Grundlage für die innere Entwicklungsgeschichte des israelitschen Religion* (1875); *Das Buch Jesaia* (1892, 1968). **O. Eissfeldt**, "The Prophetic Literature," *The OT and Modern Study: A Generation of Discovery and Research* (ed. H. H. Rowley, 1951) 115-61. **M. deJong Ellis**, "Observations on Mesopotamian Oracles and Prophetic Texts: Literary and Historiographic Considerations," *JCS*

41 (1989) 127-86. **L. H. Feldman**, "Prophets and Prophecy in Josephus," *JTS n.s. 41* (1990) 386-422. **L. E. Froom**, *The Prophetic Faith of Our Fathers: The Historical Development of Prophetic Interpretations* (4 vols., 1945–54). **Y. Gitay** (ed.), *Prophecy and Prophets: The Diversity of Contemporary Issues in Scholarship* (SemeiaSt, 1997). **N. N. Glatzer**, "A Study of the Talmudic Interpretation of Prophecy," *Review of Religion* 10 (1946) 115-37. **G. Glazov**, *The Bridling of the Tongue and the Opening of the Mouth in Biblical Prophecy* (2001). **R. P. Gordon** (ed.), *"The Place Is Too Small for Us" : The Israelite Prophets in Recent Scholarship* (Sources for Biblical and Theological Study 5, 1995). **D. E. Gowan**, *Theology of the Prophetic Books: The Death and Resurrection of Israel* (1998). **L. L. Grabbe** and **R. D. Haak** (eds.), *"Every City Shall Be Forsaken" : Urbanisim and Prophecy in Ancient Israel and the Near East* (JSOTSup 330, 2001). **R. Gray**, *Prophetic Figures in Late Second Temple Jewish Palestine: The Evidence from Josephus* (1993). **F. E. Greenspahn**, "Why Prophecy Ceased," *JBL* 108 (1989) 37-49. **W. P. Griffin**, *The God of the Prophets: An Analysis of Divine Action* (JSOTSup 249, 1997). **C. Grottanelli**, *Kings and Prophets: Monarchic Power, Inspired Leadership, and Sacred Text in Biblical Narrative* (1999). **J. H. Hayes**, "The History of the Form-critical Study of Prophecy," *SBLSP* (ed. G. McRae, 1973) 1:60-99. **K. M. Hayes**, *"The Earth Mourns" : Prophetic Metaphor and Oral Aesthetic* (SBL Academia Biblica 8, 2002). **R. Hayward** and **P. J. Harland** (eds.), *New Heaven and New Earth: Prophecy and the Millenium* (1999). **S. Hermann**, *Geschichte und Prophetie: Kleine Schriften zum Alten Testament* (BWANT 157, 2002). **A. J. Heschel**, *The Prophets* (1962). **C. Hill**, *The English Bible and the Seventeenth-century Revolution* (1993). **G. Hölscher**, *Die Propheten: Untersuchungen zur Religionensgeschichte Israels* (1914). **T. Howes,** *Doubts Concerning the Translation and Notes of the Bishop of London to Isaiah, Vindicating Ezekiel, Isaiah, and Other Jewish Prophets from Disorder in Arrangement* (1783). **R. R. Hutton**, *Charisma and Authority in Israelite Society* (1994) 105-37. **A. R. Johnson**, *The Cultic Prophet in Ancient Israel* (1944, 1962); *The Cultic Prophet and Israel's Psalmody* (1979). **N. Klaus**, *Pivot Patterns in the Former Prophets* (JSOTSup 247, 1999). **M. Köckert** and **M. Nissinen** (eds.), *Propheten in Mari, Assyrien und Israel* (FRLANT 201, 2003). **R. L. Kohn**, "A Prophet Like Moses? Rethinking Ezekiel's Relationship to the Torah," *ZAW* 114 (2002) 236-54. **E. König**, "Prophecy," *ERE* 10 (1919) 384-93. **H. T. Kreisel**, *Prophecy: The History of an Idea in Medieval Jewish Philosophy* (2001). **J. S. Kselman**, "The Social World of the Israelite Prophets: A Review Article," *RStR* 11 (1985) 120-29. **A. Kuenen**, *The Prophets and Prophecy in Israel* (2 vols., 1875; ET, 1 vol., 1877). **A. Lange**, *Vom prophetischen Wort zur prophetischen Tradition: Studien zur Traditions- und Reaktionsgeschichte innerprophetischer Konflikte in der Hebräischen Bibel* (FAT 34, 2002). **B. Lehnart**, *Prophet und König im Nordreich Israel: Studien zur sogenannten vorklassischen Prophetie im Nordreich Israel anhand der Saumel-, Elija- und Elischa-Überlieferungen* (VTSup 96, 2003). **J. Lindblom**, *Prophecy in Ancient Israel* (1962). **R. Lowth**, *Isaiah: A New Translation; With a Preliminary Dissertation, and Notes Critical, Philological, and Explanatory* (1778). **J. Macy**, "Prophecy in al-Farabi and Maimonides: The Imaginative and Rational Faculties," *Maimonides and Philosophy* (ed. S. Pines and Y. Yovel, 1986) 185-201. **J. S. Malherbe**, "Abravanel's Theory of Prophecy with Special Reference to His Commentary on Deuteronomy 18:9-22" (diss., University of Stellenbosch, 1993). **V. H. Matthews**, *Social World of the Hebrew Prophets* (2001). **J. L. Mays** and **P. J. Achtemeier** (eds.), *Interpreting the Prophets* (1987). **R. W. L. Moberly**, "Does God Lie to His Prophets? The Story of Micaiah ben Imlah as a Test Case," *HTR* 96 (2003) 1-23. **J.C. de Moor** (ed.), *The Elusive Prophet: The Prophet as a Historical Person, Literary Character and Anonymous Artist* (2001). **S. Mowinckel**, *Psalmenstudien III: Kultprophetie und prophetische Psalmen* (1923); *Prophecy and Tradition: The Prophetic Books in the Light of the Study of the Growth and History of the Tradition* (1946). **Y. Muffs**, "Agents of the Lord, Warrior for the People: The Prophet's

Paradox," *BRev* 18 (2002), 20-27, 56. **P. H. A. Neumann** (ed.), *Das Prophetenverständnis in der deutschsprachigen Forschung seit H. Ewald* (Wege der Forschung 307, 1979). **M. Nissinen** (ed.), *Prophecy in Its Ancient Near Eastern Context: Mesopotamian, Biblical, and Arabian Perspectives* (SLBSymS 13, 2000). **D. E. Orton** (ed.), *Prophecy in the Hebrew Bible: Selected Studies from Vetus Testamentum* (2000). **T. W. Overholt**, *Prophecy in Cross-cultural Perspective: A Sourcebook for Biblical Researchers* (Sources for Biblical Study 17, 1986). **T. H. L. Parker**, *Calvin's OT Commentaries* (1986). **D. L. Petersen**, *The Roles of Israel's Prophets* (JSOTSup 17, 1981); (ed.) *Prophecy in Israel* (IRT 10, 1986); *The Prophetic Literature: An Introduction* (2002). **E. A. Phillips**, "The Singular Prophet and Ideals of Torah: Miriam, Aaron, and Moses in Early Rabbinic Texts," in *The Function of Scripture in Early Jewish and Christian Tradition* (ed. C. A. Evans and J. A. Sanders; JSNTSup 154, 1998) 78-88. **R. H. Popkin**, "Predicting, Prophesying, Divining, and Foretelling from Nostradamus to Hume," *History of European Ideas 5* (1984) 117-35. **F. Postma, K. Spronk, E. Talstra** (eds.), *The New Things: Eschatology in Old Testament Prophecy* (ACEBTSup 3, 2002). **D. N. Premnath**, *Eighth Century Prophets: A Social Analysis* (2003). **J. P. Prévost**, *How to Read the Prophets* (1997). **L. Ramlot**, "Prophétisme," *DBSup* 8 (1972) 811-1222. **A. J. Reines**, "Maimonides' Concept of Mosaic Prophecy," *HUCA* 40-41 (1969–70) 325-61; *Maimonides and Abrabanel on Prophecy* (1970). **H. G. Reventlow**, "Die Prophetie im Urteil B. Duhms," *ZTK* 85 (1988) 259-74. **T. H. Robinson**, *Prophecy and the Prophets in Ancient Israel* (1923, 1953). **A. Rofé**, *The Prophetical Stories* (1982; ET 1988); *Mavo le-sifrut ha-nevu'ah* (ET = Introduction to the Prophetic Literature; Biblical Seminar 21, 1997). **H. H. Rowley**, "The Nature of OT Prophecy in the Light of Recent Study," *HTR* 38 (1945) 1-38 = his *The Servant of the Lord and Other Essays* (1965) 95-134. **W. H. Schmidt**, *Zukunftsgewissheit und Gegenwartskritik: Studien zur Eigenart der Prophetie* (Biblisch-theologische Studien 51, 2002). **A. M. Schwemer,** *Studien zu Frühjüdischen Prophetenlegenden Vitae Prophetarum* (3 vols., TSAJ 49-50, 1995). **Y. Sherwood**, " 'Darke Texts Needs Notes': On Prophetic Prophecy, John Donne, and the Baroque," JSOT 27 (2002) 47-74. **N. Shupak**, "Egyptian 'Prophecy' and Biblical Prophecy: Did the Phenomenon of Prophecy, in the Biblical Sense, Exist in Ancient Egypt?" *JEOL 31* (1989–90) 5-40. **U. Simon**, *Keri'ah sifrutit ba-Mikra, sipure Nevi'im* (ET = Reading Prophetic Narratives, trans. L. J. Schramm; Indiana Studies in Biblical Literature, 1997). **W. R. Smith**, *The Prophets of Israel and Their Place in History to the Close of the Eighth Century BC* (1882, 1895, repr. 2002). **R. W. Southern**, "Aspects of the European Tradition of History Writing: 3. History as Prophecy," *Transactions of the Royal Historical Society 5, 22* (1972) 159-80. **O. H. Steck**, *Prophetenbücher und ihr theologisches Zeugnis* (ET = The Prophetic Books and Their Theological Witness (trans. J. D. Nogalski, 2000). **M. Sweeney,** *Isaiah 1–39 with an Introduction to Prophetic Literature* (FOTL 16 [1996] 1-30). **J. P. Torrell**, *Théorie de la prophétie et philosophie de la connaissance aux environs de 1230* (SSL 40, 1977); *Recherches sur la théorie de la prophétie au moyen âge XIIe-XIVe siècles: Études et textes* (Dokimion 13, 1992). **G. M. Tucker**, "Prophecy and Prophetic Literature," *The HB and Its Modern Interpreters* (ed. D. A. Knight and G. M. Tucker, 1985) 325-68. **B. Uffenheimer**, *Nevu'ah ha-kedumah be-Yisra'el* (ET Early Prophecy in Israel, trans. D. Louvish; 1999). **C. Vitringa**, "On the Interpretation of Prophecy," *The Investigator 3, 4* (1834–35) 153-76. **R. J. Weems**, "Huldah, the Prophet: Reading a (Deuteronomistic) Woman's Identity," in *God So Near: Essays in Old Testament Theology in Honor of Patrick D. Miller* (ed. B.A. Strawn and N. R. Bowen, 2003) 321-39. **J. Wellhausen**, *Prolegomena to the History of Israel* (1878, 1883; ET 1885). **C. Westermann**, *Basic Forms of Prophetic Speech* (1960, 1964; ET 1967). **G. Widengren**, *Literary and Psychological Aspects of the Hebrew Prophets* (UUÅ 10, 1948). **R. L. Wilken**, "In novissimis diebus: Biblical Promises, Jewish Hopes, and Early Christian Exegesis," *JECS* 1 (1993) 1-19. **R. R. Wilson**, *Prophecy and Society in Ancient Israel* (1980).

H. A. Wolfson, "Hallevi and Maimonides on Prophecy," *JQR* 32 (1941–42) 345-70; *33* (1942-43) 49-82 = *Studies in the History of Philosophy and Religion* (2 vols., 1977) 2:60-119; *Philo: Foundations of Religious Philosophy in Judaism, Christianity, and Islam* (2 vols., 1947). **W. Zimmerli**, *The Law and the Prophets: A Study of the Meaning of the OT* (1965). **E. ben Zvi** and **M. H. Floyd** (eds.), *Writings and Speech in Israelite and Ancient Near Eastern Prophecy* (SBLSymS 10, 2000).

J. H. HAYES